COVID-19

COVID-19

Origin, Detection and Impact Analysis Using Artificial Intelligence Computational Techniques

Parag Verma
Ankur Dumka
Alaknanda Ashok
Amit Dumka
Anuj Bhardwaj

CRC Press
Taylor & Francis Group
Boca Raton London New York

CRC Press is an imprint of the
Taylor & Francis Group, an **informa** business

First Edition published 2022
by CRC Press
6000 Broken Sound Parkway NW, Suite 300, Boca Raton, FL 33487-2742

and by CRC Press
2 Park Square, Milton Park, Abingdon, Oxon, OX14 4RN

© 2022 Taylor & Francis Group, LLC
CRC Press is an imprint of Taylor & Francis Group, LLC

ISBN: 978-0-367-67466-3 (hbk)
ISBN: 978-0-367-67468-7 (pbk)
ISBN: 978-1-003-13141-0 (ebk)

Typeset in Times LT Std
by KnowledgeWorks Global Ltd.

This work is specially dedicated to our mentor Late Shri. Girdhari Lal Kak (Former, USF Convener-Dehradun Chapter) who had always encouraged us to move forward with a positive mindset. He is not with us today due to the COVID-19 pandemic, but his blessings and his guidance always inspire us to move forward. You (Kak Sir) will always live with us in our golden memories.

We would like to thank Monica Dumka, Mudita Bharadwaj, Naina, Siddhi, and our parents for all the support and time they have given to complete this project.

Contents

PART III   COVID-19 Detection: Advanced Image Processing with Artificial Intelligence Techniques

PART IV   Analysis of the Pre- and Post-Impact
of the COVID-19 Pandemic Crisis

Authors

Dr. Parag Verma is working as an Assistant Professor at Uttaranchal University, Dehradun. He has 8+ years of experience in the field of industry and academics. He has published 15+ international papers in reputed conferences and journals. He has contributed two books with publishers like Nerosa and Alpha, and is currently working on two more accepted books. He has also contributed four chapters for reputed publishers. He serves as an editorial board member of many reputed conferences and journals including Scopus. He is also a guest editor of International Journal of Society Systems Science (IJSSS) and many more. He is associated with many societies and organizations for the welfare of educationalist societies.

Dr. Ankur Dumka is working as Associate Professor in Women Institute of Technology, Dehradun. He has more than 12 years of experience from academic and industry. He is associated with Smart City, Dehradun, as an academic expert committee member and co-ordinator in terms of drafting of smart city proposal for Dehradun city. He has published 75 + international papers in reputed conferences and journals. He has contributed five books with publishers like Taylor and Francis Group, IGI global, etc., . He has also contributed 12 book chapters for reputed publishers and is also an editorial board member and/or guest editor of many reputed journals of repute.

Dr. Alaknanda Ashok is a dean and professor at the College of Technology, G. B. Pant University of Agriculture and Technology, Pantnagar. She has a large administrative experience as director of the Women Institute of Technology and controller of examiner of Uttarakhand Technical University. She has published more than 50 research papers in reputed journals and conferences. She is having 11 patents (4 international patent granted and 7 national patent published). She has had many research projects working under her supervision as project in charge. She has also contributed many book chapters and is currently working on proposed books with Taylor and Francis Group. She is also associated with many journals and conferences in the capacity of editor, editorial board member and convener.

Amit Dumka works as the Deputy Manager in Government Medical College, Haldwani, India. He has more than 17 years of experience with administrative and industry exposure. He has published many research papers in reputed journals and conferences. He is also associated with journals in the capacity of editorial board members and guest editor.

Dr. Anuj Bhardwaj has earned M. Tech. & PhD degrees in Computer Science. He is currently a Professor of Computer Science & Engineering with Chandigarh University, Mohali, Punjab. He has 12+ years of experience in the field of industry and academics. He has published 27+ international papers in reputed conferences and journals. He has contributed two books with publishers like Nerosa and Alpha, and is currently working on two more accepted books. He has also contributed six chapters for reputed publishers. His current research interests include pattern & character recognition, graphics & vision, artificial intelligence & neural networks and machine learning.

Part I

Origin and Background of COVID-19

1 Introduction to Emerging Respiratory Viruses with Coronavirus Disease (COVID-19)

KEY POINTS

- Outbreaks of previously unknown diseases.
- Known diseases that are rapidly increasing in incidence or geographic range in the last two decades.
- Persistence of infectious diseases that cannot be controlled.
- Non-influenza viral respiratory tract infections are a significant cause of morbidity and mortality worldwide.
- Early detection and characterization of novel and emerging viruses is important in limiting further transmission.
- Adenovirus 14 is associated with outbreaks of acute respiratory disease in military camps and the general population.
- Rhinovirus C and human bocavirus type 1 are commonly detected in infants and young children with respiratory tract illness, and are often associated with severe disease requiring hospitalization.

INTRODUCTION

We live in a universe of viruses. It is estimated that there are billions of types of viruses on earth, and ~320,000 types that infect mammals alone. Many viral species exist in our surrounding environment. As we live, breathe, eat, talk, and go about our daily activities, the number of viruses that we come into contact with is virtually infinite. Fortunately, only a relatively small number of viruses are known to infect humans.

The list of human viruses, however, is ever-growing, with three to four new species adding annually. The vast and diverse pool of animal viruses constitutes the major source from which novel human viral diseases emerge, posing an ever-looming threat to public health. SARS-CoV-2, or the "novel coronavirus," has announced itself as a new member of the family by causing the COVID-19 pandemic that is now wreaking havoc around the world.

The chain of transmission, both animal-to-human and human-to-human, is front and center to all novel animal-to-human infections. The aim of this chapter is to understand how viruses adapt and change through this chain of transmission, which might be relevant as we seek to better understand and control the current pandemic, as well as prepare for future outbreaks of animal-to-human viruses.

Together with influenza, the non-influenza Ribonucleic Acid (RNA) respiratory viruses (NIRVs), which include a respiratory syncytial virus, parainfluenza viruses, coronavirus, rhinovirus, and human metapneumovirus, represent a considerable global health burden, as recognized by WHO's Battle against Respiratory Viruses initiative. Viral respiratory tract infections (VRTIs) are some of the most common infections worldwide and represent a major public health concern. These infections are the fourth most common cause of death, globally, after ischemic heart disease, chronic obstructive pulmonary disease, and stroke, all of which are non-infectious chronic conditions (World Health Organization, 2018). In patients with these non-infective diseases, respiratory infections often trigger life-threatening exacerbations. Therefore, respiratory infections are the leading cause of death due to infection, worldwide. The infectious diseases that increase in incidence and tend to spread geographically within decades can be defined as emerging infections. Pathogens of these infections appear for the first time or they have existed previously and spread rapidly among the population and new geographical areas. Noninfluenza respiratory viruses cause infections in all age groups and are a major contributing factor to morbidity and mortality. Disease severity can range from mild, common cold-like illness to severe, life-threatening respiratory tract infection. The burden of non-influenza VRTIs is often more pronounced in individuals with chronic comorbidities or clinical risk factors. Moreover, it is estimated that 500 million non-influenza VRTIs occur annually in the United States, resulting in combined direct and indirect costs of $40 billion (Fendrick et al., 2003).

NEW AND NEWLY RECOGNIZED RESPIRATORY VIRUSES

Unlike seasonal influenza, pandemic influenza virus is a new virus that has not circulated in humans before, and to which humans have little or no immunity. Hence, the virus can cause significant illness or death and, when it acquires the ability of human-to-human transmission, could easily spread globally.

Four pandemics (Spanish flu in 1918, Asian flu in 1957, Hong Kong flu in 1968, and pandemic influenza A(H1N1) in 2009) have occurred since the early 20th century. Although the most recent pandemic due to A(H1N1)pdm09 was not as severe as the Spanish flu, the rate of patients requiring intensive care unit (ICU) admission was much higher than that due to seasonal influenza (Kotsimbos et al., 2010). However, the disease severity and impact on public health of an influenza strain can be determined by various factors, including the characteristics of circulating viruses (e.g., transmissibility), the time in the season, vaccine strains being used and the vaccination rate of the population. The World Health Organization (WHO) reported that the predominant influenza viruses in Asia, Europe, America, and Africa were A(H1N1)pdm09 and influenza B during the 2015–2016 season.[1] In East Asia, the predominant circulating virus was A(H1N1)pdm09 in the first half of the season, followed by influenza B virus in the second half of the season.

Although vaccination is the most effective way to prevent influenza infections, the current vaccination rates vary and are suboptimal in many countries (21–78% in the elderly) (Yoo, 2011). Furthermore, considering the variable and moderate effectiveness of current vaccines, rapid development of efficacious vaccines with long-lasting and cross-protective immunity or broad-spectrum neutralizing antibody will be needed (Elbahesh et al., 2019).

INFLUENZA VIRUSES

The influenza viruses are the world's most critical epidemic viruses. Influenza pandemics occurred earlier in 1918 (swine flu), 1957 (Asian flu), 1968 (Hong Kong flu), 1977 (Russian flu), and the most recent pandemic in 2009 (pandemic influenza A H1N1). It belongs to the Orthomyxoviridae family. Influenza is an enveloped virus with negative-stranded RNA consists of eight segments. There are four different types; A, B, C, and D (Jaijyan et al., 2018; Moesker et al., 2013). Influenza A virions possess two surface glycoproteins—the hemagglutinin (HA) and neuraminidase (NA)-which exert different functions. A total of 18 hemagglutinin and 11 neuraminidase subtypes are known to exist in nature (Moesker et al., 2013). They can infect birds and mammals, including man. Influenza B is restricted to human horde. Influenza C is isolated from humans, pigs, and dogs (Moesker et al., 2013). Influenza D viruses primarily affect cattle and human population in all age groups (Asha & Kumar, 2019). Seasonal influenza viruses kill 250,000–500,000, mostly older people each year around the world (World Health Organization, 2018).

H1N1 INFLUENZA

Influenza virus type A is very variable and shows a continuous antigen variation. It is a significant cause of epidemics and pandemics. The surface antigenic glycoproteins are subject to two main types of antigenic variation, namely: antigenic shift and antigenic drift. The antigen shift is an abrupt, significant change in an influenza A virus that leads to new HA and/or new HA and NA proteins in influenza viruses that infect man. The interruption can lead to a novel influenza A subtype in humans. These are small changes (or mutations) in the genes of influenza viruses that can guide to alterations in the surface proteins of the virus: HA (hemagglutinin) and NA (neuraminidase). The HA and NA surface proteins of influenza viruses are "antigens," which implies that they are seen by the immune system and can activate an immune response, including the production of antibodies that can halt the contagion. The changes associated with antigen drift occur continuously over time as the virus replicates. Most flu shots target the HA surface proteins/antigens of an influenza virus.

The most fatal and unforgettable outbreak "mother of the pandemic" virus occurred in 1918 named as Spanish influenza. In this eruption, approximately 50 million people were dead (Kilbourne, 2006; Honigsbaum, 2018). H1N1 was occurred in different years (1928, 1932, 1936, 1943, 1947) during this century (Jaijyan et al., 2018).

In 1977, H1N1 was reemerged and named as Russian flu, which mostly affected young people. In 2009, H1N1 was the reason of a new pandemic. It was first detected in the USA. This one delivered an unparalleled combination of influenza genes with a triple reassortment (Jaijyan et al., 2018).

H2N2 INFLUENZA

In 1957, a new strain appeared in the world named H2N2, emerged in humans in Southeast Asia and rapidly spread worldwide. The virus persists in wild and domestic birds. The reemergence of H2N2 in humans is a significant threat due to the absence of humoral immunity, and it was the case of the second pandemic of the 20th century (Jones et al., 2014).

AVIAN INFLUENZA (AI)

Humans are susceptible to avian influenza virus subtypes-A (H5N1), A (H7N9) and A (H9N2). Exposure to infected birds or contaminated environment is thought to underlie human infection with these viruses. There have been sporadic cases of human infections with AI and other zoonotic influenza viruses, but sustained humanto-human infection and transmission have been lacking. Although the public health risk from the currently known influenza viruses at the human-animal interface remains the same, the sustained human-to-human transmission of this virus is low. Avian influenza A viruses (AIVs) are among a terrifying emerging and reemerging pathogen because of their possible risk of causing an influenza pandemic. The growth in domestic animals and poultry worldwide is followed by the ascent of human AIV outbreaks.

A(H7N9) Virus

A human case of A(H7N9) infection was first reported in March 2013 in China. There have been five epidemics of A(H7N9) since the virus was first discovered; China is currently experiencing the fifth (Hui et al., 2017). As of 25 July 2018, a total of 1625 human infections have been reported since 2013 and the mortality rate is 38.3% (Table 1.1) (Hui et al., 2017). To date, although no human or animal infections by A(H7N9) have been detected at a poultry farm, the majority of infected patients had a link to infected live poultry or contaminated environments such as live poultry markets.

Li et al. reported that 81.6% of patients had a history of exposure to live animals, including chickens and ducks (hospitalization rate: 98.6%, pneumonia or respiratory failure rate: 91.2%) (Li et al., 2014). In particular, they found four family clusters and suggested the possibility of human-to-human transmission. However, while most human cases were caused by the low pathogenic AI A(H7N9), new cases of highly pathogenic A(H7N9) virus infection have also been confirmed since 2017 (Zhou et al., 2017).

A(H5N1) Virus

Influenza A(H5N1) viruses are endemic among poultry in parts of Asia, Africa, and the Middle East. Human cases of A(H5N1) were first detected in Hong Kong in 1997 (Yuen et al., 1998). After a six-year absence, human cases with confirmed influenza A(H5N1) virus infection re-emerged in 2003 in Southeast Asia. Since then, the highly pathogenic influenza haemagglutinin (H5) has evolved into many phylogenetically distinct clades and subclades (Abdel-Ghafar et al., 2008), and the infection has spread from East Asia to West Asia and Africa, with a high incidence in Egypt since November 2014 (Yuen et al., 1998). Vietnam has seen a total of 123 cases and 61 deaths since 2004, when the strain was first found there, through to 2012.

Overall, 903 cases of A(H5N1) virus were reported between 1997 and 2015, and most cases occurred between December and April (Lai et al., 2016). The rate of hospitalization was 90.3% and the case fatality rate was 53.5%. Upper respiratory tract symptoms were less prominent in human H5N1 cases under 30 years of age as compared to seasonal influenza, which is about 80% of the total number of cases. (Abdel-Ghafar et al., 2008). Compared to influenza A(H1N1)pdm09 virus, few clustering cases were reported and evidence for human-to-human transmission is still insufficient for A(H5N1) viruses (Wang et al., 2008, 2012).

Other AI Viruses

The first reported human case of A(H6N1) infection was a young woman with influenza-like illness in Taiwan in 2013 (Wei et al., 2013). The virus had a characteristic G228S substitution in the haemagglutinin protein, which might increase its affinity for the human

TABLE 1.1

Comparisons of Clinical and Epidemiological Features among AI Infections in Humans

Features	A(H5N1)	A(H7N9)	A(H5N6)	A(H9N2)	A(H10N8)	A(H3N2)v
Pathogenicity	HPAI	LPAI/HPAI	HPAI	LPAI	LPAI	N/A
First human case	Hong Kong in 1997	China in 2013	China in 2014	Hong Kong in 1999	China in 2013	United States in 2011
Regions with human cases	China, Laos, Cambodia, Thailand, Vietnam, Indonesia, Pakistan, Azerbaijan, Bangladesh, Turkey, Nigeria and Egypt	China, Taiwan, Malaysia and Hong Kong	China	Hong Kong, China, Bangladesh, serological evidence in Asia, Africa and Middle East	China	United States
Total number of human cases (years)	903 cases (1997–2015)	1625 cases (2013–2018)	17 cases (2014–2016)	28 cases (1999–2016)	3 cases (2013–2014)	405 cases (2011–2017)
Median ages (years)	19 (5–32)	61 (46–73)	35 (26–45) in recent nine cases reported by WHO	Mostly children	73, 56, 75	7 (range, 3 months–74 years) <18 years in 92%
Onset of illness to hospitalization (days)	4 (2–6)	4 (3–6)	3 (1–7) in recent nine cases	N/A	3, 7, 2	4 (1–16) in illness duration
Clinical characteristics	Less URT symptoms Admission rate: 90.3% Advanced life supports: 63%	ARDS: 57.8% MV: 61.5%	Usually severe infections	Mild or asymptomatic illness	Bilateral severe pneumonia in all cases	Mild illness
Mortality rate	53.30%	38.30%	58.80%	0%	66.60%	1/405
Epidemiological features	67.2% between December and April Recent epidemic in Egypt (2014)	Five epidemics Currently the largest epidemic	Sporadic infections	Sporadic infections	Sporadic infections	Sporadic infections A large epidemic in 2012 (n = 306)
Risk factors	Exposure to sick and dead poultry, and live poultry market	Exposure to live poultry (81.6%)	Exposure to dead poultry and live poultry	Exposure to live poultry and poultry farm	Exposure to live poultry market	Exposure to pigs

α2-6 linked sialic acid receptor and, therefore, increase the potential for human-to-human transmission (Wei et al., 2013).

The A(H5N6) virus is a new reassortant strain that contains gene segments from A(H5N1) and A(H5N2). The first human A(H5N6) infection was reported in a five-year-old girl who had visited a live poultry market in China in 2014 (Zhang et al., 2016). Influenza A(H5N6) outbreaks in birds and poultry have been reported in Vietnam and mainland China since 2014. To date, 16 human infections and six deaths due to A(H5N6) have occurred in mainland China.[2]

Regarding A(H10N8) infection, three human cases have been confirmed in Jiangxi Province in China since December 2013 (Liu et al., 2015; Xu et al., 2015). All three cases had severe bilateral pneumonia and two died. Surveillance at the suspected live poultry markets showed an increased prevalence of A(H10N8) viruses. Notably, this virus contains genes from A(H9N2) and was frequently co-infected with A(H9N2). This implies that novel reassortants could emerge.

Since 1990, influenza A(H9N2) has circulated among domestic poultry in Asian countries and has now globally expanded. So far, human infections have mainly been reported in Hong Kong and mainland China (Gu et al., 2017; Khan et al., 2015). Although A(H9N2) infection results in mild disease or asymptomatic illness, the emergence of this virus is worrisome because it could potentially transfer its genes to another strain. Recent analyses of A(H7N9) and A(H10N8) viruses suggest that they have acquired gene segments from influenza A(H9N2) virus (Guan et al., 2020; Liu et al., 2013).

AI is a notifiable disease listed by the OIE (World Organization for Animal Health). The early detection of outbreaks, followed by a prompt response, is the first step. Monitoring and controlling AI virus at its poultry source is also crucial.

The risk of death is highest among reported cases infected with H5N1, H5N6, H7N9, and H10N8 infections. Senior people and males tended to take in a lower hazard of infection with most AIV subtypes, except for H7N9. Visiting live poultry markets were generally reported by H7N9, H5N6, and H10N8 cases, while exposure to sick or dead bird mostly reported by H5N1, H7N2, H7N3, H7N4, H7N7, and H10N7 cases (Philippon et al., 2020).

HANTAVIRUS

Hantavirus pulmonary syndrome (HPS) has emerged from the infection with Sin Nombre virus (SNV). It is a negative-sensed, single-stranded RNA virus. The virus was first identified in the United States in 1995. Since then, 71 people were diagnosed as HPS, and all patients were California residents. Persons were usually exposed to SNV through inhalation of aerosolized excreta (e.g., saliva, urine, and faeces) from infected wild animals (rodents, typically deer mice). HPS has demonstrated a severe disease characterized by pulmonary edema, followed by respiratory failure than cardiogenic shock (Kjemtrup et al., 2019; MacNeil et al., 2011).

HUMAN METAPNEUMOVIRUS (HMPV)

HMPV is a negative-sense, single-stranded RNA virus of the family Pneumoviridae, cause of acute respiratory infection, particularly in children, immunocompromised patients, and the aged. HPMV genome was mostly similar to avian metapneumovirus serotype C. In 2001, researchers in the Netherlands identified HMPV from nasopharyngeal samples from 28 children. The virus is a leading cause of acute respiratory infection, particularly in children, immunocompromised patients, and the elderly. Almost every child is infected with HMPV by the age of five (Philippon et al., 2020).

Bocavirus

Human bocavirus (HBoV) is a member of the Parvovirus (DNA) family, detected in 2005. It is distributed worldwide, and evidence indicates that HBoV is the cause of the respiratory tract infections. Numerous studies demonstrate HBoV as a co-pathogen. Studies prove that its prevalence in asymptomatic patients is high (Körner et al., 2011).

Coronavirus

The Coronaviridae family includes a broad spectrum of animal and human viruses, with typical morphology. Before 2003, the virus family was known as the cause of only mild respiratory illness in humans. However, the emergence of severe acute respiratory virus (SARS-CoV) and MERS-CoV shows the zoonotic potential of causing severe disease outbreaks in humans (Burrell et al., 2016).

SARS-coronavirus (CoV) caused an outbreak that began in China in 2002 and eventually led to 8422 infections and 916 deaths in 37 countries (World Health Organization, 2004). No SARS cases have been reported since 2004 (World Health Organization, 2004). However, in September 2012, a novel CoV infection (i.e., MERSCoV) was reported in Saudi Arabia and a large number of people died from severe respiratory illness and acute kidney injury (i.e., 40–60%) (Zumla et al., 2015). In 2015, a large outbreak began in South Korea with a single case and eventually reached 186 cases through household and nosocomial transmission (Choi et al., 2016). As of September 2017, the WHO has reported 2103 cases of MERS-CoV and 733 deaths (World Health Organization, 2017).

Importantly, the SARS-CoV and MERS-CoV human outbreaks were epidemiologically similar in terms of healthcare-associated infections (Table 1.2) (Assiri et al., 2013; Kang et al., 2017). In China, 966 (18%) out of 5323 SARS cases were healthcare providers, and in the early days of the outbreak almost 90% of SARS patients were frontline healthcare providers (Chen et al., 2009). In the Korean MERS-CoV outbreak, five "superspreaders" spread MERS-CoV to a large number of people in hospitals (Kang et al., 2017). About 20% of patients with SARS progressed to hypoxia and required mechanical ventilation, with a case fatality rate of 9.6% (Christian et al., 2004; World Health Organization, 2003b). However, during the Korean MERS outbreak, pneumonia was detected in 80.8% (mechanical ventilation: 24.5%, extracorporeal membrane oxygenation: 7.1%) (World Health Organization, 2017).

MERS virus is stable in aerosol form, thus exacerbating the nosocomial spread of the virus during aerosolgenerating procedures. Hence, employment of strict infection control measures is needed to prevent nosocomial outbreaks (Hui et al., 2018).

Coronaviruses also have the largest positive-sense RNA genome, which is expressed by a complicated procedure.

This genomic type allows the formation of encrypting RNA transcripts in a genome. Somehow, encrypted sequences are progressing during the replication cycle and produce new types of coronavirus. Coronaviruses are classified into three groups, grounded on the antigenic properties of virus proteins: the spike (S), membrane (M), and nucleocapsid (N) proteins (Burrell et al., 2016).

TABLE 1.2

Outbreaks of Emerging and Reemerging Respiratory Viral Infections

Virus	Year	Region
Spanish Flu H1N1	1918	Spain (Donnelly et al., 2003)
Asian flu H2N2	1956	East Asia (Francis et al., 2019)
HCoV-229E HCoV-OC43	1960	The different part of the World (Graham et al., 2013)
Hong Kong Flu H3N2	1968	Hong Kong(Francis et al., 2019)
Hantavirus pulmonary syndrome	1993	USA (Cheng et al., 2020)
Influenza A H5N1	1997	Hong Kong (Francis et al., 2019)
Influenza A H9N2	1999	Hong Kong (Francis et al., 2019)
Human metapneumovirus	2001	Netherlands (Chowell et al., 2003)
SARS CoV	2002–2003	Guangdong, China (Cui et al., 2019)
Human CoV NL63	2004	Netherlands (Coutard et al., 2020)
Influenza A H7N7	2004	Netherlands (Francis et al., 2019)
Human CoV HKU1	2005	China (Coutard et al., 2020)
Triple reassortant H3N2 Influenza A	2005	Canada (Francis et al., 2019)
Bocavirus	2005	Sweden (Christian et al., 2004)
Influenza A H1N1 pmd09	2009	Mexico (Francis et al., 2019)
Adenovirus 14	2010	USA (Gralinski & Menachery, 2020)
Influenza (H3N2)v	2011	USA (Benvenuto et al., 2020)
MERS-CoV	2012	Saudi Arabia (Dikid et al., 2013)
Influenza A H7N9	2013	China (Francis et al., 2019)
Influenza A H10N7	2014	China (Francis et al., 2019)
SARS-CoV-2	2019	China (Elbahesh et al., 2019)

HCoV-229E and HCoV-OC43

Human virus HCoV-229E is one of the species in genus alphacoronavirus, and it is the first group. It is the first coronavirus, isolated from patients with upper respiratory tract infections in the 1965. Until late 2002, only two human coronaviruses were very well known– HCoV-229E and HCoV-OC43. HCoV-OC43 is from the genus betacoronavirus, and it is in the second group of coronaviruses. HCoV-OC43 also isolates from patients with upper respiratory tract infections. HCoV 229E and OC43 are the known causes of the common cold within the last 200 years. They are now globally endemic in humans, crossed species from their animal reservoirs (bats and cattle, respectively) to humans (Burrell et al., 2016).

Severe Acute Respiratory Syndrome Coronavirus (SARS-CoV)

Severe acute respiratory syndrome (SARS) has emerged initially from ancestral bat viruses. SARS-CoV was the first known major pandemic coronavirus. The disease occurred in late 2002 when an outbreak of acute community-acquired atypical pneumonia syndrome was first diagnosed in Guangdong Province, China. Over 8000 people were affected, with a crude fatality rate of 10% in more than 12 countries (Francis et al., 2019).

The WHO issued a worldwide warning about the disease on March 13, 2003. Although the cases generally remained confined to China, a few cases were reported from North and

South America, Europe, and Asia. Luckily, new cases with SARS has not been described since 2004.

Middle East Respiratory Syndrome Coronavirus (MERS-CoV)

MERS-CoV is a zoonotic viral disease that causes respiratory infection. It was first reported in Saudi Arabia in 2012 and has expanded to 26 different countries. Since 2012, over 2207 laboratory-confirmed cases and 787 deaths from MERS-CoV infection have occurred worldwide. The clinical spectrum of illness associated with MERSCoV ranges from asymptomatic infections to acute respiratory distress syndrome, resulting in multi-organ failure and mortality. The case-fatality rates have stayed high at three to four per ten cases (Cowling et al., 2015).

Francis et al. (2019) were mentioned around the emergency of newly reemerging corona-viruses. Due to coronaviruses genetic recombination, newly emerged ones may go to new genotypes and outbreaks.

They specially indicated the reservoir (horseshoe bats) of SARS-CoV-like viruses as a source of novel types of coronaviruses, because of the culture of eating exotic mammals in southern China. They said that it is a time bomb of the possibility of the reemergence of SARS (Burrell et al., 2016).

SARS-CoV-2

In December 2019, a novel coronavirus (SARS-CoV-2) was observed in three patients with pneumonia connected to the cluster of acute respiratory illness cases from Wuhan, China. By the end of March 2020, the virus spread all over the globe and caused a large global out-break. (Lai et al., 2020). On January 30 2020, the WHO declared the COVID-19 outbreak as the sixth public health emergency of international concern, following H1N1 (2009), polio (2014), Ebola in West Africa (2014), Zika (2016), and Ebola in the Democratic Republic of Congo (2019) (Peeri et al., 2020; Taubenberger & Morens, 2006). WHO announced a COVID-19 outbreak as pandemic on Mar 12, 2020.

SARS- CoV-2 was found to be a positive-sense, single-stranded RNA virus belonging to the genus Beta coronavirus, closely related to two bats-derived severe acute respiratory syndrome-like coronaviruses, bat-SLCoVZC45, and bat-SL-CoVZXC21 (Lai et al., 2020; Li et al., 2020).

Although early studies reported a possible link between animal-to-human transmission, later studies demonstrated human-to-human transmission of SARS-CoV-2 through droplets or direct contact. Besides symptomatic patient transmission, there are shreds of evidence of the possibility of transmission by asymptomatic carriers (Peeri et al., 2020).

TIMELINE OF THE EMERGING VIRUSES

In the past, a significant proportion of respiratory tract disease could not be attributed to a specific pathogen. With the advent of molecular detection and genotyping techniques, there has been a substantial increase in the recognition of several newly identified non-influenza respiratory viruses involved in disease. These potential pathogens have included severe acute respiratory syndrome coronavirus (SARS-CoV) and Middle East respiratory syndrome coronavirus (MERS-CoV), adenovirus type 14 (Ad14), human rhinovirus species C (RV-C), and human ebolaviruses. Diagnostic testing for these and other viruses is important because many of the signs and symptoms of infection overlap those of other viruses such as influenza, and would otherwise be ascribed to cases of influenza-like illness without an etiologic assessment.

The emergence of novel human pathogens and reemergence of several diseases is of particular concern in the current century (Dikid et al., 2013). Coronaviruses are one of the categories of the novel human pathogens. These coronaviruses are ubiquitous worldwide (Table 1.1) and were associated with relatively mild respiratory disease (e.g., the common cold) up to the emergence of the SARS-CoV in China in 2002. The SARS epidemic spread to 29 countries and infected more than 8000 people, with a case-fatality rate of approximately 10%. However, additional cases have not been documented since 2004. Nearly ten years later, another virulent coronavirus, MERS-CoV, emerged. The index case of MERS-CoV occurred in Saudi Arabia in June 2012 (Zaki et al., 2012).

There is a dominance of zoonotic infections, mostly originating in wildlife, among emerging health threats with a rate of 70%. Pathogens first emerge in themselves and rapidly mutate, which results in a transmission in humans with subsequent dissemination. According to the extent of the transmission, epidemic outbreaks may occur and progress to a pandemic.

Diseases that reappear after a significant decline are called as reemerging diseases. Reemergence may occur due to a breakdown in public health measures or the appearance of new strains of organisms. Respiratory infections with epidemic and pandemic potential that cause a global burden have plagued people since the beginning of human history. Outbreaks of such diseases have a significant impact on health and economic development in the Region.

Most emerging viruses come from animals and are zoonotic or vector-borne diseases belonging to the families Orthomyxoviridae, Paramyxoviridae, Picornaviridae, Coronaviridae, Adenoviridae, and Herpesviridae. Community-acquired respiratory viruses are critical pathogens such as influenza, respiratory syncytial virus, adenovirus, parainfluenza virus, human coronavirus, human metapneumovirus, rhinovirus, enterovirus, cause millions of deaths and hospitalizations around all over the world every year (Karron & Black, 2017; World Health Organization, 2018).

In the last century as Figure 1.1, influenza originated avian, and swine, severe acute respiratory syndrome-coronavirus (SARS-CoV) and the Middle East respiratory syndrome coronavirus (MERS-CoV) were the most damaging respiratory infections for human being all over the world (Zumla et al., 2014). These emerging viral respiratory infections derived from the animal world (Park et al., 2019). Mutations in the genetic material of RNA viruses accumulate in years and produce new strains of the viruses with new antigenic properties resulting in a transmission in humans (Jaijyan et al., 2018). The probability of pandemics with new viruses would be high in the future, as this type of mutations will reoccur.

The other mechanism of a virus is reassortment, which means that the host is infected with two different strains of viruses (animal and human viruses) than a new generation of a new virus with mixed genetic materials is developed and causes new pandemics (Jaijyan et al., 2018). Bird and swine influenza viruses obtain new gene segments through a reassortment with human strains.

The mutation in the genetic material of RNA-virus also sometimes drifts in time and builds a chimeric virus, containing nucleic acid fragments or proteins from two or more different viruses. This novel hybrid virus is different from parental viruses (Menachery et al., 2015).

Currently, COVID-19 caused by a zoonotic virus severe acute respiratory syndrome coronavirus 2 (SARS-CoV-2) was first determined in 2019 in Wuhan, the capital of China's Hubei province. Epidemiologic data show exposures of some initial cases in Huanan seafood and live animal market and early phylogenetic results suggest initial human infection in November

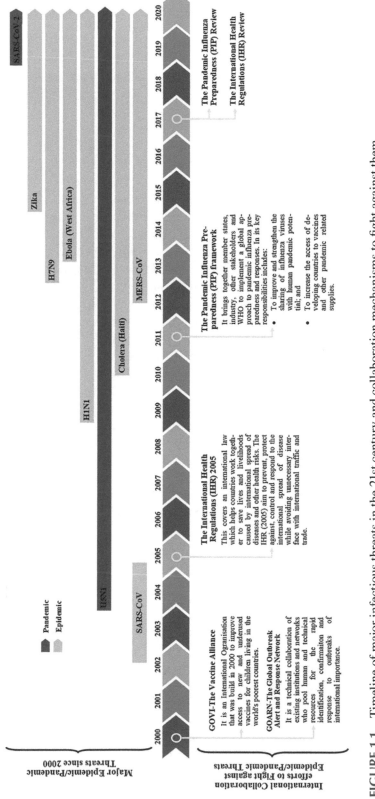

FIGURE 1.1 Timeline of major infectious threats in the 21st century and collaboration mechanisms to fight against them.

2019 followed by ongoing human-to-human transmission. Animal source has not been identified yet; and COVID-19 has since spread globally, resulting in the current 2019–2020 coronavirus pandemic. The majority of cases (approximately 96%) occur with mild respiratory symptoms, some progress to pneumonia, acute respiratory distress syndrome, respiratory insufficiency, and multi-organ failure. The overall rate of deaths per number of diagnosed cases is 4.6%; ranging from 0.2% to 15% according to age group and other health problems.

SARS-CoV-2

Coronavirus Disease 2019 (COVID-19) is a novel illness caused by infection with severe acute respiratory syndrome coronavirus 2 (SARS-CoV-2) (Zhou et al., 2020a; Zhu et al., 2020) Severe acute respiratory syndrome coronavirus 2 (SARS-CoV-2) is the third zoonotic coronavirus to cross the species barrier, infect humans and become transmitted between humans (Wu et al., 2020). Whereas the two other zoonotic coronaviruses, SARS-CoV and Middle East respiratory syndrome coronavirus (MERS-CoV), could be contained at the regional level, SARS-CoV-2 has led to a global pandemic. Although COVID-19 usually presents as a mild respiratory disease, like infections caused by the four endemic human coronavirus (HCoV-229E, HCoV-NL63, HCoV-OC43, and HCoV-HKU1), it can occasionally lead to severe alveolar inflammation. In a large study from China, ~15% of SARS-CoV-2-infected patients developed shortness of breath, radiological infiltrates in the lung and a drop in blood oxygen saturation (<93%), and 5% had critical illness requiring ventilation (Wu & McGoogan, 2020). Although such data might slightly overestimate the frequency of severe lung involvement, because testing for SARS-CoV-2 infection is not performed in milder cases and is therefore underestimated, COVID-19 undoubtedly constitutes a substantial risk factor for pulmonary failure. Histopathological findings of the lungs of deceased patients with COVID-19 showed extensive alveolar damage, fibrin deposits, widespread infiltration with immune cells and thrombosis of small and large pulmonary vessels (Wichmann et al., 2020). Even though the clinical picture of severe COVID-19 resembles that of acute respiratory distress syndrome (ARDS), these lung histopathological findings suggest that COVID-19 creates a specific form of alveolar disease that is different from other forms of ARDS. The risk of severe lung disease in the context of COVID-19 depends on certain, yet to be determined, susceptibility factors of the host. Higher age is one of the known risk factors and, as with the other zoonotic coronaviruses, the clinical course of COVID-19 is more severe in older individuals, whereas children and adolescents, who typically develop flu-like symptoms owing to the four endemic coronaviruses, are virtually spared from SARS and MERS (Hon et al., 2003).

Current Worldwide Scenario Of SARS-CoV-2

Coronaviruses (CoVs) constitute a large family of viruses found in nature. This novel virus, SARS-CoV-2, comes under the subgenus Sarbecovirus of the Orthocoronavirinae subfamily and is entirely different from the viruses responsible for MERSCoV and SARS-CoV (Zhu et al., 2020). The newly emerged SARS-CoV-2 is a group 2B coronavirus (Gralinski & Menachery, 2020). The genome sequences of SARS-CoV-2 obtained from patients share 79.5% sequence similarity to the sequence of SARS-CoV (Zhou et al., 2020b).

As on July 11, 2020, China has confirmed 85,487 cases with 4648 death cases of 2019-nCoV. In addition to China, more than 215 different countries from Europe, Northern

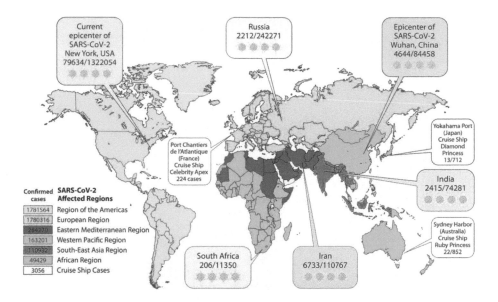

FIGURE 1.2 World map depicting the current scenario of COVID-19. Shown are countries, territories, or regions with reported confirmed cases of SARS-CoV-2 as of May 13, 2020. Different colors indicate different WHO-designated geographical regions with the number of confirmed cases. The WHO region-wise total number of confirmed cases is depicted in different color strips. The leading information on the confirmed cases and deaths from all six WHO-designated regions are depicted in circled balloons. The numbers of COVID-19 cases and fatalities on three major cruise ships are also depicted. (Based on data from the WHO at https://www.who.int/docs/default-source/coronaviruse/situation-reports/20200711-covid-19-sitrep-173.pdf?sfvrsn=949920b4_2)

America, Southeast Asia, Eastern Mediterranean, and Western Pacific Asia have reported the confirmed cases of this disease making the total tally of confirmed cases to 12,236,908 with death cases 551,687 worldwide (WHO Situation Report 173) (Figure 1.2).

Initially, the epicenter of the SARS-CoV-2 pandemic was China, which reported a significant number of deaths associated with COVID-19, with 84,458 laboratory confirmed cases and 4644 deaths as of May 13, 2020 (Figure 1.3). As of May 13, 2020, SARS-CoV-2 confirmed cases have been reported in more than 210 countries apart from China (Figures 1.2, 1.3 and 1.4) (WHO Situation Report 114) (Bastola et al., 2020).[3] COVID-19 has been reported on all continents except Antarctica. For many weeks, Italy was the focus of concerns regarding the large number of cases, with 221,216 cases and 30,911 deaths, but now, the United States is the country with the largest number of cases, 1,322,054, and 79,634 deaths. Now, the United Kingdom has even more cases (226,4671) and deaths (32,692) than Italy. A John Hopkins University web platform has provided daily updates on the basic epidemiology of the COVID-19 outbreak (https://gisanddata.maps.arcgis.com/ apps/ops-dashboard/index.html#/bda7594740fd40299423467b48e9ecf6) (Dong et al., 2020).

COVID-19 has also been confirmed on a cruise ship, named Diamond Princess, quarantined in Japanese waters (Port of Yokohama), as well as on other cruise ships around the world (239) (Figure 1.3). The significant events of the SARS-CoV-2/COVID-19 virus outbreak occurring since December 8, 2019 are presented as a timeline in Figure 1.5.

At the beginning, China experienced the majority of the burden associated with COVID-19 in the form of disease morbidity and mortality (Velavan & Meyer, 2020), but over time the COVID-19 menace moved to Europe, particularly Italy and Spain, and now the United

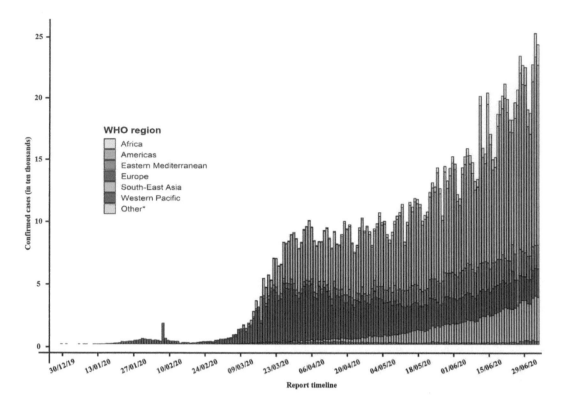

FIGURE 1.3   Bar chart of number of confirmed SARS-CoV-2 cases, by date of report and WHO region, December 30, 2019 through July 11, 2020.

States has the highest number of confirmed cases and deaths. The COVID-19 outbreak has also been associated with severe economic impacts globally due to the sudden interruption of global trade and supply chains that forced multinational companies to make decisions that led to significant economic losses (Ayittey et al., 2020). The recent increase in the number of confirmed critically ill patients with COVID-19 has already surpassed the intensive care supplies, limiting intensive care services to only a small portion of critically ill patients (Qiu et al., 2020). This might also have contributed to the increased case fatality rate observed in the COVID-19 outbreak.

TIME LINE OF THE OUTBREAK

During the first week of December 2019, a few cases of pneumonia appeared in the city of Wuhan, Hubei province of China. The patients exhibited a history of visiting the local nearby Huanan seafood market which deals in the sale of different live animals, where zoonotic (animal-to-human) transmission suspected as the main route of disease origin (Hui et al., 2020). First, the affected patients presented with pneumonia-like symptoms, followed by a severe acute respiratory infection. Some cases showed rapid development of ARDS followed by serious complications in the respiratory tract. On January 7, 2020, it was confirmed by the Chinese Center for Disease Control and Prevention (CDC) that a new coronavirus has emerged and was named 2019-nCoV. From the beginning of the pandemic to July 11, 2020, the WHO has been trying to control the pandemic in collaboration with

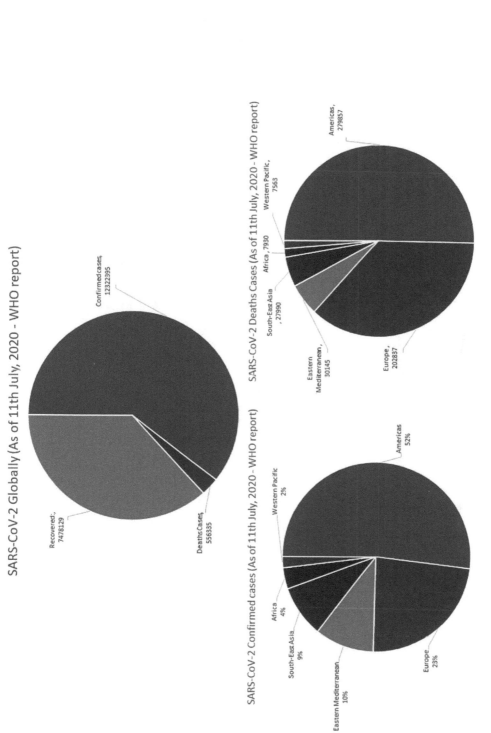

SARS-CoV-2 Globally (As of 11th July, 2020 - WHO report)

Confirmed cases,
12322395

Recovered;
7478129

Deaths Cases;
556335

SARS-CoV-2 Confirmed cases (As of 11th July, 2020 - WHO report)

Americas
52%

Europe
23%

Eastern Mediterranean
10%

South-East Asia
9%

Africa
4%

Western Pacific
2%

SARS-CoV-2 Deaths Cases (As of 11th July, 2020 - WHO report)

Americas,
279857

Western Pacific,
7563

Africa , 7930

South-East Asia
, 27990

Eastern
Mediterranean,
30145

Europe ,
202837

FIGURE 1.4 Pie chart for SARS-CoV-2 confirmed cases and deaths. Shown are laboratory-confirmed cases and deaths in China and the rest of the world. (top) Total number of cases worldwide by region. (bottom left) and (bottom right) SARS-CoV-2 confirmed cases and Deaths, respectively, in the top five affected countries from each WHO designated region, where maximum casualties were reported to WHO until July 11, 2020.

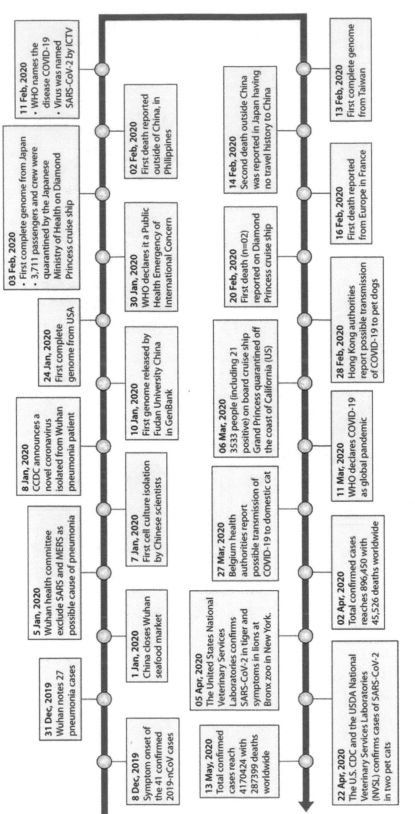

FIGURE 1.5 Timeline depicting the significant events that occurred during the SARS-CoV-2/COVID-19 virus outbreak. The timeline describes the significant events during the current SARS-CoV-2 outbreak, from December 8, 2019 to July 11, 2020. https://www.pharmaceutical-technology.com/news/coronavirus-a-timeline-of-how-the-deadly-outbreak-evolved/

the governments of all the countries of the world, with reference to the important steps taken by the WHO highlighted in the below timeline as follows. From the beginning of the pandemic to July 11, 2020, the WHO has been trying to control the pandemic in collaboration with the governments of all the countries of the world, with reference to the important steps taken by the WHO major events highlighted in the below timeline as follows.

Although the mortality rate due to 2019-nCoV is comparatively lesser than the earlier outbreaks of SARS and MERS-CoVs, as well as this virus presents relatively mild manifestations, the total number of cases are increasing speedily and are crossing the old census. There is a high risk of human-to-human transmission, which has also been reported in family clusters and medical workers. The infected patients with nCoV exhibit high fever and dyspnea with chest radiographs showing acute invasive lesions in both lungs.

EMERGENCE OF CORONAVIRUS (SARS-CoV-2)

The novel coronavirus was identified within one month (28 days) of the outbreak. This is impressively fast compared to the time taken to identify SARS-CoV reported in Foshan, Guangdong Province, China (125 days) (Cheng et al., 2020). Immediately after the confirmation of viral etiology, the Chinese virologists rapidly released the genomic sequence of SARS-CoV-2, which played a crucial role in controlling the spread of this newly emerged novel coronavirus to other parts of the world (Liu & Saif, 2020). The possible origin of SARS-CoV-2 and the first mode of disease transmission are not yet identified (Mahase, 2020a). Analysis of the initial cluster of infections suggests that the infected individuals had a common exposure point, a seafood market in Wuhan, Hubei Province, China (Figure 1.6). The restaurants of this market are well-known for providing different types of wild animals for human consumption (Hui et al., 2020). The Huanan South China Seafood Market also sells live animals, such as poultry, bats, snakes, and marmots (Lu et al., 2020). This might be the point where zoonotic (animal-to-human) transmission occurred (Hui et al., 2020). Although SARS-CoV-2 is alleged to have originated from an animal host (zoonotic origin) with further human-to-human transmission (Figure 1.6), the likelihood of foodborne transmission should be ruled out with further investigations, since it is a latent possibility (Rodriguez-Morales et al., 2020). Additionally, other potential and expected routes would be associated with transmission, as in other respiratory viruses, by direct contact, such as

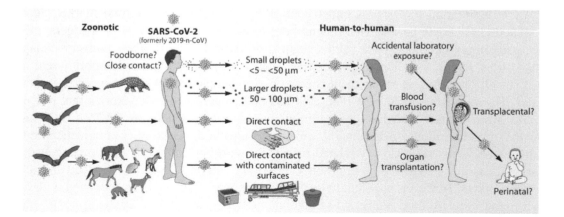

FIGURE 1.6 Potential transmission route of SARS-CoV-2.

shaking contaminated hands, or by direct contact with contaminated surfaces (Figure 1.6). Still, whether blood transfusion and organ transplantation (Ison & Hirsch, 2019), as well as transplacental and perinatal routes, are possible routes for SARS-CoV-2 transmission needs to be determined (Figure 1.6).

From experience with several outbreaks associated with known emerging viruses, higher pathogenicity of a virus is often associated with lower transmissibility. Compared to emerging viruses like Ebola virus, avian H7N9, SARS-CoV, and MERS-CoV, SARS-CoV-2 has relatively lower pathogenicity and moderate transmissibility (Chen, 2020). The risk of death among individuals infected with COVID-19 was calculated using the infection fatality risk (IFR). The IFR was found to be in the range of 0.3–0.6%, which is comparable to that of a previous Asian influenza pandemic (1957–1958) (Nishiura et al., 2020; Sanchez et al., 2015).

Notably, the reanalysis of the COVID-19 pandemic curve from the initial cluster of cases pointed to considerable human-to-human transmission. It is opined that the exposure history of SARS-CoV-2 at the Wuhan seafood market originated from human-to-human transmission rather than animal-to-human transmission (Nishiura et al., 2020); however, in light of the zoonotic spillover in COVID-19, is too early to fully endorse this idea (Rodriguez-Morales et al., 2020). Following the initial infection, human-to-human transmission has been observed with a preliminary reproduction number (R0) estimate of 1.4–2.5 (Mahase, 2020a; Parry, 2020), and recently it is estimated to be 2.24–3.58 (Zhao et al., 2020). In another study, the average reproductive number of COVID-19 was found to be 3.28, which is significantly higher than the initial WHO estimate of 1.4–2.5 (Liu et al., 2020). It is too early to obtain the exact R0 value, since there is a possibility of bias due to insufficient data. The higher R0 value is indicative of the more significant potential of SARS-CoV-2 transmission in a susceptible population. This is not the first time where the culinary practices of China have been blamed for the origin of novel coronavirus infection in humans. Previously, the animals present in the liveanimal market were identified to be the intermediate hosts of the SARS outbreak in China (Guan et al., 2003). Several wildlife species were found to harbor potentially evolving coronavirus strains that can overcome the species barrier (Monchatre-Leroy et al., 2017). One of the main principles of Chinese food culture is that live-slaughtered animals are considered more nutritious (Munster et al., 2020).

After four months of struggle that lasted from December 2019 to March 2020, the COVID-19 situation now seems under control in China. The wet animal markets have reopened, and people have started buying bats, dogs, cats, birds, scorpions, badgers, rabbits, pangolins (scaly anteaters), minks, soup from palm civet, ostriches, hamsters, snapping turtles, ducks, fish, Siamese crocodiles, and other animal meats without any fear of COVID-19. The Chinese government is encouraging people to feel they can return to normalcy. However, this could be a risk, as it has been mentioned in advisories that people should avoid contact with live-dead animals as much as possible, as SARS-CoV-2 has shown zoonotic spillover. Additionally, we cannot rule out the possibility of new mutations in the same virus being closely related to contact with both animals and humans at the market. In January 2020, China imposed a temporary ban on the sale of live-dead animals in wet markets. However, now hundreds of such wet markets have been reopened without optimizing standard food safety and sanitation practices (Knowles, 2020).

With China being the most populated country in the world and due to its domestic and international food exportation policies, the whole world is now facing the menace of

COVID-19, including China itself. Wet markets of live-dead animals do not maintain strict food hygienic practices. Fresh blood splashes are present everywhere, on the floor and tabletops, and such food customs could encourage many pathogens to adapt, mutate, and jump the species barrier. As a result, the whole world is suffering from novel SARS-CoV-2, with more than 4,170,424 cases and 287,399 deaths across the globe. There is an urgent need for a rational international campaign against the unhealthy food practices of China to encourage the sellers to increase hygienic food practices or close the crude live-dead animal wet markets. There is a need to modify food policies at national and international levels to avoid further life threats and economic consequences from any emerging or reemerging pandemic due to close animal-human interaction (Blakeman, 2020).

Even though individuals of all ages and sexes are susceptible to COVID-19, older people with an underlying chronic disease are more likely to become severely infected (Shen et al., 2020). Recently, individuals with asymptomatic infection were also found to act as a source of infection to susceptible individuals (Lin & Li, 2020). Both the asymptomatic and symptomatic patients secrete similar viral loads, which indicates that the transmission capacity of asymptomatic or minimally symptomatic patients is very high. Thus, SARSCoV-2 transmission can happen early in the course of infection (Zou et al., 2020). Atypical clinical manifestations have also been reported in COVID-19 in which the only reporting symptom was fatigue. Such patients may lack respiratory signs, such as fever, cough, and sputum (83). Hence, the clinicians must be on the look-out for the possible occurrence of atypical clinical manifestations to avoid the possibility of missed diagnosis. The early transmission ability of SARS-CoV-2 was found to be similar to or slightly higher than that of SARS-CoV, reflecting that it could be controlled despite moderate to high transmissibility (Hao et al., 2020).

Increasing reports of SARS-CoV-2 in sewage and wastewater warrants the need for further investigation due to the possibility of fecal-oral transmission. SARS-CoV-2 present in environmental compartments such as soil and water will finally end up in the wastewater and sewage sludge of treatment plants (Núñez-Delgado, 2020). Therefore, we have to reevaluate the current wastewater and sewage sludge treatment procedures and introduce advanced techniques that are specific and effective against SARS-CoV-2. Since there is active shedding of SARS-CoV-2 in the stool, the prevalence of infections in a large population can be studied using wastewater-based epidemiology. Recently, reverse transcription-quantitative PCR (RT-qPCR) was used to enumerate the copies of SARS-CoV-2 RNA concentrated from wastewater collected from a wastewater treatment plant (Ahmed et al., 2020). The calculated viral RNA copy numbers determine the number of infected individuals. The increasing reports of virus shedding via the fecal route warrants the introduction of negative fecal viral nucleic acid test results as one of the additional discharge criteria in laboratory-confirmed cases of COVID-19 (Ali et al., 2020).

The COVID-19 pandemic does not have any novel factors, other than the genetically unique pathogen and a further possible reservoir. The cause and the likely future outcome are just repetitions of our previous interactions with fatal coronaviruses. The only difference is the time of occurrence and the genetic distinctness of the pathogen involved. Mutations on the RNA-binding domain (RBD) of CoVs facilitated their capability of infecting newer hosts, thereby expanding their reach to all corners of the world (Wang et al., 2018). This is a potential threat to the health of both animals and humans. Advanced studies using Bayesian phylogeographic reconstruction identified the most probable origin of SARS-CoV-2 as the bat SARS-like (Peiris et al., 2005) coronavirus, circulating in the Rhinolophus bat family (Benvenuto et al., 2020).

Phylogenetic analysis of ten whole-genome sequences of SARS-CoV-2 showed that they are related to two CoVs of bat origin, namely, bat-SL-CoVZC45 and bat-SLCoVZXC21, which were reported during 2018 in China (Lu et al., 2020). It was reported that SARS-CoV-2 had been confirmed to use ACE2 as an entry receptor while exhibiting an RBD similar to that of SARS-CoV (17, 87, 254, 255). Several countries have provided recommendations to their people traveling to China (Biscayart et al., 2020). Compared to the previous coronavirus outbreaks caused by SARS-CoV and MERS-CoV, the efficiency of SARSCoV-2 human-to-human transmission was thought to be less. This assumption was based on the finding that health workers were affected less than they were in previous outbreaks of fatal coronaviruses (Gralinski & Menachery, 2020). Superspreading events are considered the main culprit for the extensive transmission of SARS and MERS (Hui et al., 2018; Peiris et al., 2005). Almost half of the MERS-CoV cases reported in Saudi Arabia are of secondary origin that occurred through contact with infected asymptomatic or symptomatic individuals through human-to-human transmission (Kritas et al., 2020). The occurrence of superspreading events in the COVID-19 outbreak cannot be ruled out until its possibility is evaluated. Like SARS and MERS, COVID-19 can also infect the lower respiratory tract, with milder symptoms. The basic reproduction number of COVID-19 has been found to be in the range of 2.8–3.3 based on real-time reports and 3.2–3.9 based on predicted infected cases (Zhou et al., 2020c).

COMPRESSION OF CORONAVIRUSES IN HUMANS—SARS-CoV, MERS-CoV, AND COVID-19

Coronavirus infection in humans is commonly associated with mild to severe respiratory diseases, with high fever, severe inflammation, cough, and internal organ dysfunction that can even lead to death. Most of the identified coronaviruses cause the common cold in humans. However, this changed when SARS-CoV was identified, paving the way for severe forms of the disease in humans. Our previous experience with the outbreaks of other coronaviruses, like SARS and MERS, suggests that the mode of transmission in COVID-19 as mainly human-to-human transmission via direct contact, droplets, and fomites. Recent studies have demonstrated that the virus could remain viable for hours in aerosols and up to days on surfaces; thus, aerosol and fomite contamination could play potent roles in the transmission of SARS-CoV-2 (Van Doremalen et al., 2020).

The immune response against coronavirus is vital to control and get rid of the infection. However, maladjusted immune responses may contribute to the immunopathology of the disease, resulting in impairment of pulmonary gas exchange. Understanding the interaction between CoVs and host innate immune systems could enlighten our understanding of the lung inflammation associated with this infection (Li et al., 2020).

SARS is a viral respiratory disease caused by a formerly unrecognized animal CoV that originated from the wet markets in southern China after adapting to the human host, thereby enabling transmission between humans (Peiris et al., 2005). The SARS outbreak reported in 2002 to 2003 had 8098 confirmed cases with 774 total deaths (9.6%) (World Health Organization, 2003a). The outbreak severely affected the Asia Pacific region, especially mainland China (Donnelly et al., 2003). Even though the case fatality rate (CFR) of SARS-CoV-2 (COVID-19) is lower than that of SARS-CoV, there exists a severe concern linked to this outbreak due to its epidemiological similarity to influenza viruses. This can fail the public health system, resulting in a pandemic (Wilder-Smith & Freedman, 2020).

MERS is another respiratory disease that was first reported in Saudi Arabia during the year 2012. The disease was found to have a CFR of around 35%. The analysis of available data sets suggests that the incubation period of SARS-CoV-2, SARS-CoV, and MERS-CoV is in almost the same range. The longest predicted incubation time of SARS-CoV-2 is 14 days. Hence, suspected individuals are isolated for 14 days to avoid the risk of further spread (Jiang et al., 2020). Even though a high similarity has been reported between the genome sequence of the new coronavirus (SARS-CoV-2) and SARS-like CoVs, the comparative analysis recognized a furin-like cleavage site in the SARS-CoV-2 S protein that is missing from other SARS-like CoVs (Coutard et al., 2020). The furin-like cleavage site is expected to play a role in the life cycle of the virus and disease pathogenicity and might even act as a therapeutic target for furin inhibitors. The highly contagious nature of SARS-CoV-2 compared to that of its predecessors might be the result of a stabilizing mutation that occurred in the endosome-associated-protein-like domain of nsp2 protein.

Similarly, the destabilizing mutation near the phosphatase domain of nsp3 proteins in SARS-CoV-2 could indicate a potential mechanism that differentiates it from other CoVs. Even though the CFR reported for COVID-19 is meager compared to those of the previous SARS and MERS outbreaks, it has caused more deaths than SARS and MERS combined (Mahase, 2020b). Possibly related to the viral pathogenesis is the recent finding of an 832-nucleotide (nt) deletion in ORF8, which appears to reduce the replicative fitness of the virus and leads to attenuated phenotypes of SARS-CoV-2 (Su et al., 2020). Importantly, the SARS-CoV, MERS-CoV and SARS-CoV-2 human outbreaks were epidemiologically similar in terms of healthcare-associated infections (Table 1.3).[4]

Coronavirus is the most prominent example of a virus that has crossed the species barrier twice from wild animals to humans during SARS and MERS outbreaks (Monchatre-Leroy et al., 2017; Song et al., 2019). The possibility of crossing the species barrier for the third time has also been suspected in the case of SARS-CoV-2 (COVID-19). Bats are recognized as a possible natural reservoir host of both SARS-CoV and MERS-CoV infection. In contrast, the possible intermediary host is the palm civet for SARS-CoV and the dromedary camel for MERS-CoV infection (Song et al., 2019). Bats are considered the ancestral hosts for both SARS and MERS. Bats are also considered the reservoir host of human coronaviruses like.

HCoV-229E and HCoV-NL63 (Graham et al., 2013). In the case of COVID-19, there are two possibilities for primary transmission: it can be transmitted either through intermediate hosts, similar to that of SARS and MERS, or directly from bats (Graham et al., 2013). The emergence paradigm put forward in the SARS outbreak suggests that SARS-CoV originated from bats (reservoir host) and later jumped to civets (intermediate host) and incorporated changes within the receptor-binding domain (RBD) to improve binding to civet ACE2. This civetadapted virus, during their subsequent exposure to humans at live markets, promoted further adaptations that resulted in the epidemic strain (Graham et al., 2013). Transmission can also occur directly from the reservoir host to humans without RBD adaptations. The bat coronavirus that is currently in circulation maintains specific "poised" spike proteins that facilitate human infection without the requirement of any mutations or adaptations (Menachery et al., 2015). Altogether, different species of bats carry a massive number of coronaviruses around the world (Cui et al., 2019).

The high plasticity in receptor usage, along with the feasibility of adaptive mutation and recombination, may result in frequent interspecies transmission of coronavirus from bats to animals and humans (Cui et al., 2019). The pathogenesis of most bat coronaviruses

TABLE 1.3

Comparisons of Clinical and Epidemiological Features between SARS-CoV and MERS-CoV Infections in Human

	SARS-CoV	MERS-CoV	SARS-CoV-2 (COVID-19)
Genus	Beta-CoV lineage B	Beta-CoV lineage C	Beta-CoV
First human case	China in 2002	Saudi Arabia in 2012	China in December, 2019
Regions with human cases	China, Hong Kong, Singapore, Vietnam, United States and Canada	Saudi Arabia, United Kingdom, South Korea Arab Emirates, Qatar, Oman and Iran	China, United States of America, European Countries, worldwide (more than 215 countries)
Total number of human cases (years)	8422 cases (November 2002–July 2003) But, the last case was reported in May 2004	2182 (September 2012–February 2018)46 One recent case in Oman in November 2017	12,322,395 (December 2019 to July 11, 2019) and soon
Median ages (years)	Less than or equal to 45 years	56 (14–94)	All age groups but high risk for <15and ≥ 45
Incubation period (days)	4.6 (3.8–5.8)	5.2 (1.9–14.7)	7 (5.5–15.5)
Clinical characteristics	Invasive mechanical ventilation in 17%	Invasive mechanical ventilation in 37% (70% in another case series) Frequent acute kidney injury (~43%) Frequent vasopressor use Pneumonia in 80.8% (Korea)39	Fever, Dry cough, Tiredness, Shortness of breath: >/= 60 for children younger than two months old, >50 per minute for 2–12 months old children, >40 per minute for 1–5 years old children, >30 per minute for children younger than five years old (regardless of crying or fever episode), Decreased saturation </=92%, Fever over 3–5 days
Mortality rate	9.6% (774/8098 cases)37 11.0% (916/8422 cases)44	39.0% in Saudi Arabia 20.4% in Korea39	3.4% Worldwide as of WHO
Epidemiological features	Female predominance Nosocomial transmission Healthcare worker: 22% in China or >40% in Canada Mostly young people	Most cases from Arabian Peninsula Underlying co-morbidities (96%) Human-to-human transmission (~50%) in Saudi Arabia Nosocomial transmission Healthcare worker: 21% in Korea A large outbreak in Korea (2015)	Human who have travelled or lived in the epicentrum of the coronavirus infection for 14 days prior to the onset of the disease; Human who were in contact with people from the epicentrum of infection with high fever or respiratory symptoms; Human from families or other cluster foci of the new viral disease; new-borns who were born to mothers infected with the new coronavirus infection
Risk factors	Employment in an occupation associated with an increased SARS-CoV exposure Close contract of a person under investigation for SARS Travelling to areas experiencing an outbreak	Direct contact to dromedaries Travel to Middle East and North Africa	Direct contact to dromedaries Travel to infected areas

is unknown, as most of these viruses are not isolated and studied. Hedgehog coronavirus HKU31, a Betacoronavirus, has been identified from amur hedgehogs in China. Studies show that hedgehogs are the reservoir of Betacoronavirus, and there is evidence of recombination.

The current scientific evidence available on MERS infection suggests that the significant reservoir host, as well as the animal source of MERS infection in humans, is the dromedary camels. The infected dromedary camels may not show any visible signs of infection, making it challenging to identify animals actively excreting MERSCoV that has the potential to infect humans. However, they may shed MERS-CoV through milk, urine, feces, and nasal and eye discharge and can also be found in the raw organs (World Health Organization, 2017). In a study conducted to evaluate the susceptibility of animal species to MERS-CoV infection, llamas and pigs were found to be susceptible, indicating the possibility of MERS-CoV circulation in animal species other than dromedary camels (Vergara-Alert et al., 2017).

Following the outbreak of SARS in China, SARS-CoV-like viruses were isolated from Himalayan palm civets (Paguma larvata) and raccoon dogs (Nyctereutes procyonoides) found in a live-animal market in Guangdong, China. The animal isolates obtained from the live-animal market retained a 29-nucleotide sequence that was not present in most of the human isolates (Guan et al., 2003). These findings were critical in identifying the possibility of interspecies transmission in SARS-CoV. The higher diversity and prevalence of bat coronaviruses in this region compared to those in previous reports indicate a host/pathogen coevolution. SARS-like coronaviruses also have been found circulating in the Chinese horseshoe bat (Rhinolophus sinicus) populations. The in vitro and in vivo studies carried out on the isolated virus confirmed that there is a potential risk for the reemergence of SARS-CoV infection from the viruses that are currently circulating in the bat population (Menachery et al., 2015).

PREVENTION, CONTROL, AND MANAGEMENT STRATEGIES FROM SARS-CoV-2

The prevention and management are very important issues to control the spreading nature of SARs-CoV-2 infection. Therefore, there is a great need for the collective efforts of the public and the government. The regular and the proper care of the homes and hospitals are very important to control this calamity. The regular recommendations to minimize the infection are cleaning of the area.

While a dedicated, collaborative international effort has resulted in substantial understanding of this disease with remarkable speed, critical information is still lacking. We detail a variety of knowledge gaps that should be addressed through a set of activities to optimize prevention and control of SARS-CoV-2.

Containment Strategies For SARS-CoV-2: Isolation, Quarantine

Quarantine is an ancient tool used to prevent the spread of disease. The Bible describes the sequestering of persons with leprosy, and the practice was used widely in 14th-century Europe to control the spread of bubonic and pneumonic plague. To prevent disease transmission, ships were required to stay in harbor for 40 days before disembarkation (thus the term quarantine, which derives from the Latin quadragina or the Italian quaranta, meaning 40).

Quarantine has been used for centuries, but because it was often implemented in a way that equated disease with crime, the practice has negative connotations.

Persons under quarantine were often detained without regard to their essential needs. Those who were exposed but not yet ill were not always separated from the ill, allowing disease to spread within the detained group. Populations targeted for quarantine, such as foreigners, were stigmatized. In some cases, the power of quarantine was abused; for example, at the end of the 19th century, the steerage passengers on arriving ships were frequently quarantined while the first and second-class passengers were allowed to disembark without being examined for illness.

Despite its history, quarantine—when properly applied and practiced according to modern public health principles—can be a highly effective tool in preventing the spread of contagious disease. It may play an especially important role when vaccination or prophylactic treatment is not possible, as was the case with severe acute respiratory syndrome (SARS). Even when direct medical counter-measures are available (e.g., smallpox and pneumonic plague), reducing mobility in the at-risk population may enable the most rapid and efficient delivery of postexposure vaccination and chemoprophylaxis.

Before discussing the role of quarantine as a component of community response and containment for SARS, it is necessary to distinguish, from a public health perspective, between the related practices of isolation and quarantine. Both are usually imposed by health officials on a voluntary basis; however, federal, state, and local officials have the authority to impose mandatory quarantine and isolation when necessary to protect the public's health.

Isolation refers to the separation and restricted movement of ill persons who have a contagious disease in order to prevent its transmission to others. It typically occurs in a hospital setting, but can be done at home or in a special facility. Usually individuals are isolated, but the practice may be applied in larger groups.

Quarantine refers to the restriction of movement or separation of well persons who have been exposed to a contagious disease, before it is known whether they will become ill. Quarantine usually takes place in the home and may be applied at the individual level or to a group or community of exposed persons.

Contact surveillance, in the context of quarantine, is the process of monitoring persons who have been exposed to a contagious disease for signs and symptoms of that disease. Surveillance may be done passively, for example, by informing contacts to seek medical attention if signs or symptoms occur. Contact surveillance can also be performed actively, for example, by having health workers telephone contacts daily to inquire about signs and symptoms or even having health workers directly assess contacts for fever or other symptoms. All quarantined persons should be monitored for development of signs and symptoms of disease to ensure appropriate isolation, management, and/or treatment. For persons without a known contact but believed to be at increased risk for disease or exposure, enhanced surveillance and education can be used for risk assessment monitoring. During the SARS epidemic, this approach was used effectively with airline passengers arriving in the United States from areas of high transmission during the SARS epidemic.

PRINCIPLES OF MODERN QUARANTINE

Quarantine as it is now practiced is a public health tool and a collective action for the common good. Today's quarantines are more likely to involve a few people exposed to contagion

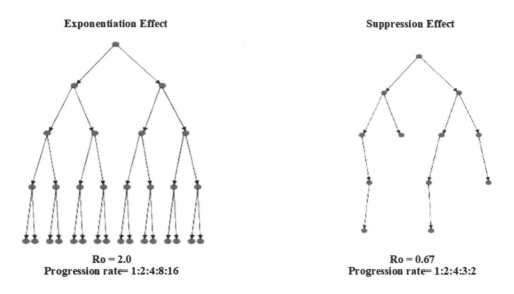

FIGURE 1.7 Effectiveness of vaccination and quarantine to contain a smallpox outbreak after the release of bioengineered, aerosolized smallpox in an airplane carrying 500 people.

in a small area, such as on an airplane or at a public gathering, and only rarely are applied to entire cities or communities. The main goal of modern quarantine is to reduce transmission by increasing the "social distance" between persons; that is, reducing the number of people with whom each person comes into contact (Figure 1.7).

If quarantine is to be used, the basic needs of those infected and exposed must be met. The following key principles of modern quarantine ensure that it strikes the appropriate balance between individual liberties and the public good:

- Quarantine is used when persons are exposed to a disease that is highly dangerous and contagious.
- Exposed well persons are separated from those who are ill.
- Care and essential services are provided to all people under quarantine.
- The "due process" rights of those restricted to quarantine are protected.
- Quarantine lasts no longer than is necessary to ensure that quarantined persons do not become ill. Its maximum duration would be one incubation period from the last known exposure, but it could be shortened if an effective vaccination or prophylactic treatment is available and can be delivered in a timely fashion.
- Quarantine is used in conjunction with other interventions, including—
  - Disease surveillance and monitoring for symptoms in persons quarantined.
  - Rapid diagnosis and timely referral to care for those who become ill.
  - The provision of preventive interventions, including vaccination, or prophylactic antibiotics.

Quarantine encompasses a range of strategies that can be used to detain, isolate, or conditionally release individuals or populations infected or exposed to contagious diseases, and should be tailored to particular circumstances. Quarantine activities can range from only passive or active symptom monitoring or short-term voluntary home curfew, all the way to cancellation of public gatherings, closing public transportation, or, under extreme circumstances, to a cordon sanitaire: a barrier erected around a geographic area, with strict enforcement prohibiting movement in or out. In a "snow day" or "sheltering in place" scenario, schools may be closed, work sites may be closed or access to them restricted, large public gatherings may be cancelled, and public transportation may be halted or restricted. People who become ill under these conditions would need specific instructions for seeking evaluation and care; they would only expose others in their households—or perhaps no one at all, if precautions are taken as soon as symptoms develop. The fact that most people understand the concept of sheltering at home during inclement weather, regarding home in these circumstances as the safest and most sensible place to be, increases the likelihood that similar conditions of quarantine will be accepted. "Snow day" measures can be implemented instantaneously, and most essential services can be met without inordinate additional resources, especially if the quarantine lasts only a few days.

Another important feature of quarantine is that it need not be absolute to be effective. Even a partial or "leaky" quarantine, such as occurs with voluntary compliance, can reduce the transmission of disease. Voluntary measures, which rely on the public's cooperation, reduce or remove the need for legal enforcement and leverage the public's instinct to remain safely sheltered. In contrast, compulsory confinement may precipitate the instinct to "escape." If an effective vaccine is available, partial quarantine can be an effective supplement to vaccination, further reducing transmission of disease. For example, Figure 1.7 shows a model illustrating various outcomes of a hypothetical scenario of 500 people, all of whom are vaccinated against smallpox, exposed to an intentional aerosol release of that contagion on an airplane. In the model, all 500 people are offered postexposure smallpox vaccine; the model assumes that the vaccine is 95% effective. Even under these unlikely and theoretical circumstances, the addition of even partial (50–90%) quarantine to vaccination can have a profound effect on reducing the number of eventual cases in the community. This trend remains significant even at low rates of transmission ("reproductive rates").

COMPUTATIONAL TECHNIQUE OF ANALYSIS EFFECT OF CONTAINMENT STRATEGIES

COVID-19 has an incubation period and exposed people with no symptoms can carry SARS-CoV-2, unlike SARS-CoV. COVID-19 is contagious during the incubation period; therefore, mathematical models can be incorporated to evaluate the nature and impact of global pandemics in the society. There is a long history of mathematical models in epidemiology, going back to the eighteenth century. Bernoulli (1760) used a mathematical method to evaluate the effectiveness of the techniques of variation against smallpox, with the aim of influencing public health policy. Most of the models are compartmental models, with the population divided into classes and with assumptions being made about the rate of transfer from one class to another (Hethcote, 2000).

SIR Model for Pandemics

The SIR (Susceptible, Infected, and Recovered individuals) model is the classically adopted mathematical model to analyse and predict evolution of a spread of a disease in a population.

SIR model divides the (fixed) population of N individuals into the "compartments" which may vary as a function of time t.

Steps of Modeling SIR Model of Spread of Disease

1. Identify the independent and dependent variables. The independent variable is time t (measured in days). Consider two related sets of dependent variables.
    a. First set of dependent variables counts people in each of the groups, each as a function of time:
    S = S(t) is the number of susceptible individuals,
    I = I(t) is the number of infected individuals, and
    R = R(t) is the number of recovered individuals.
    b. Second set of dependent variables represents the fraction of the total population in each of the three categories. So, if N is the total population (7,900,000 in our example), we have
    s(t) = S(t)/N, the susceptible fraction of the population,
    i(t) = I(t)/N, the infected fraction of the population, and
    r(t) = R(t)/N, the recovered fraction of the population.
    It may seem more natural to work with population counts, but some of this calculation will be simpler if it uses the fractions instead. The two sets of dependent variables are proportional to each other, so either set will give us the same information about the progress of the epidemic.

2. Assumptions about the rates of change of our dependent variables:
    a. No one is added to the susceptible group, since we are ignoring births and immigration. The only way an individual leaves the susceptible group is by becoming infected. Assuming that the time-rate of change of $S(t)$, the number of susceptible, depends on the number already susceptible, the number of individuals already infected, and the amount of contact between susceptible and infected. In particular, suppose that each infected individual has a fixed number β of contacts per day that are sufficient to spread the disease. Not all these contacts are with susceptible individuals. If we assume a homogeneous mixing of the population, the fraction of these contacts that are with susceptible is $s(t)$. Thus, on average, each infected individual generates $\beta s(t)$ new infected individuals per day. (With a large susceptible population and a relatively small-infected population, model can ignore tricky counting situations such as a single susceptible encountering more than one infected in a given day.)
    b. Assuming that a fixed fraction γ of the infected group will recover during any given day. For example, if the average duration of infection is three days, then, on average, one-third of the currently infected population recovers each day. (Strictly speaking, what we mean by "infected" is really "infectious," that is, capable of spreading the disease to a susceptible person. A "recovered" person can still feel miserable, and might even die later from pneumonia.)

3. Derivatives of the dependent variables describing this model were first derived by Kermack and McKendrick (Anderson & May, 1992) as follows:
    a. The Susceptible Equation:

$$\frac{dS}{dt} = -\beta s(t) I(t) \tag{1.1}$$

This equation leads to the equation for $s(t)$, i.e.;

$$\frac{ds}{dt} = -\beta s(t) i(t) \tag{1.2}$$

b. The Recovered Equation:

$$\frac{dR}{dt} = \gamma I(t) \tag{1.3}$$

This equation leads to the equation for $r(t)$, i.e.;

$$\frac{dr}{dt} = \gamma i(t) \tag{1.4}$$

c. The Infected Equation:

$$\frac{ds}{dt} + \frac{di}{dt} + \frac{dr}{dt} = 0 \tag{1.5}$$

Therefore,

$$\frac{di}{dt} = -\frac{ds}{dt} - \frac{dr}{dt} = \beta s(t) i(t) - \gamma i(t) \tag{1.6}$$

4. Now, completing the model by giving each differential equation an initial condition. For SARS-CoV-2 particular virus – in US America in 2020 – hardly anyone was immune at the beginning of the epidemic, so almost everyone was susceptible. We will assume that there was a trace level of infection in the population, say, ten people. Thus, our initial values for the population variables are

$$S(0) = 7,900,000; \; I(0) = 10; \; R(0) = 0$$

In terms of the scaled variables, these initial conditions are

$$s(0) = 1; \; i(0) = 1.27 \times 10^{-6}; \; r(0) = 0$$

(Note: The sum of our starting populations is not exactly N, nor is the sum of our fractions exactly one. The trace level of infection is so small that this will not make any difference.) So complete model is

$$\frac{ds}{dt} = -\beta s(t) i(t), \quad s(0) = 1$$

$$\frac{dr}{dt} = \gamma i(t), \quad r(0) = 0$$

$$\frac{di}{dt} = \beta s(t) i(t) - \gamma i(t), \quad i(0) = 1.27 \times 10^{-6}$$

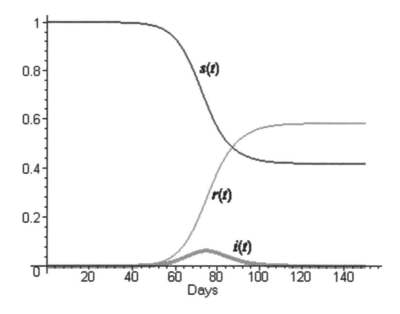

FIGURE 1.8 SIR Model plotting graph.

5. Initially the values for the parameters β and γ not given, but can estimate them, and then adjust them as necessary to fit the excess death data. Model have already estimated the average period of infectiousness at three days, so that would suggest $\gamma = \frac{1}{3}$. Therefore, it can assume that each infected would make a possibly infecting contact every two days, and then β would be $\frac{1}{2}$. Emphasize that this is just a guess. Figure 1.8 shows the solution curves for these choices of b and k.

The experience in China showed that the use of relative extreme isolation measures in conjunction with rapid diagnosis has a strong impact on the dynamics of the epidemic, hence the importance of understanding and quantifying the process to verify the effectiveness of the isolation measures (Chowell et al., 2003).

Different epidemiological models, from the classical SIR model to more sophisticated ones involving population compartments for socially distanced, quarantined, infection aware, asymptomatic infected, and other individuals, share some remarkable dynamic characteristics when contact rates are subject to periodic or one-shot changes. Some advanced variants of SIR mode to evaluate the spread nature of pandemics, some of them are as follows.

SIQR Model

Susceptible Infected Quarantine Recovered (SIQR), a variant of classical SIR model appears to be particularly convenient for the modeling of COVID-19 (Asha & Kumar, 2019) as shown in Figure 1.9. This model considers two categories for infected individuals, one who gets quarantine and others who do not (asymptotic or negligence). Susceptible in the models are the individuals who are at the risk of being infected. Infected are those susceptible whom does the virus affect; they may be asymptotic or have symptoms. Infected individuals who develop signs and gets isolated is considered as quarantine. Recovered are those infectious or quarantine individuals who recovered or died from the disease.

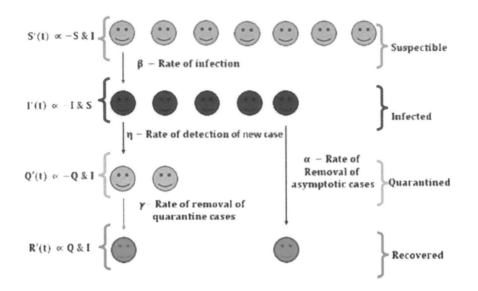

FIGURE 1.9 Pictorial representation of the dependence of each component of the SIQR model, where S stands for Susceptible, I for infected, Q for quarantined, and R for recovered. Left side of the picture represents the dependence of the rate of change on S, I, Q, R. Four proportionality constants relating each parameter of the model is mentioned.

Since the parameters of SIR (and hence SIQR) vary widely depending on the country, anti-epidemic measures, quality of the available data and other factors, if a work do not confine themselves to specific values for the parameters. Instead, SIQR curves for a whole range of the parameters. Derivatives of the dependent variables describing this model as follows:

$$\frac{ds}{dt} = -\frac{\beta SI}{N(1-I)} \tag{1.7}$$

$$\frac{dI}{dt} = \frac{\beta SI}{N(1-I)} - (\alpha + \eta)I \tag{1.8}$$

$$\frac{dQ}{dt} = \eta I - \gamma Q \tag{1.9}$$

$$\frac{dR}{dt} = \gamma Q - \alpha I \tag{1.10}$$

In the previous equations, β denotes the rate of infection; η determines the rate at which new cases are detected from the infected population. γ is the rate at which quarantine are being removed (recovered or died). α is the rate of removal of infectious individuals who are asymptotic (or for any reasons) and didn't get quarantined.

In Figure 1.10, the curve having a black line represents the infected compartment with limited time social distancing, the red line shows the dynamics of the infected compartment with $\beta(t) = \beta_n$ (no social distancing), and the blue line represents the scenario of having the social distancing during an entire epidemic with $\beta(t) = \beta_d$.

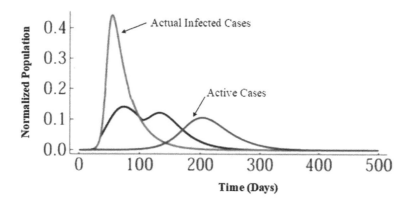

FIGURE 1.10 Temporal evolution of the number of active cases (Q) and actual infected (I) with the day (t) estimate using numerical integration of Equation (1.10) with $\alpha = 0.287$, $\beta = 0.476$, $\gamma = 0.040$, $\eta = 0.020$, $l = 0.99942$, $N = 1.3 \times 10^9$.

SEIR Model

This mathematical model describing the population dynamics of infectious diseases have been playing an important role in a better understanding of epidemiological patterns and disease control for a long time. The differential equations that govern the classic deterministic SEIR (Susceptible – Exposed – Infectious – Recovered) compartmental model have individuals experience a long incubation duration (the "exposed" category), such that the individual is infected but not yet infectious. For example, chicken pox, vector-borne diseases, and even SARS-CoV-2 such as dengue hemorrhagic fever have a long incubation duration where the individual cannot yet transmit the pathogen to others.

The SEIR model diagram shows in Figure 1.11 how individuals move through each compartment in the model.

The infectious rate β, controls the rate of spread which represents the probability of transmitting disease between a susceptible and an infectious individual. The incubation rate, σ, is the rate of latent individuals becoming infectious (average duration of incubation is $\frac{1}{\sigma}$). Recovery rate, $\gamma = \frac{1}{D}$, is determined by the average duration, D, of infection. Λ is the per-capita birth rate, μ is the per-capita natural death rate, α is the virus-induced average fatality rate.

In a closed population with no births or deaths, the SEIR model becomes:

$$\frac{dS}{dt} = \Lambda - \mu S - \frac{\beta SI}{N} \tag{1.11}$$

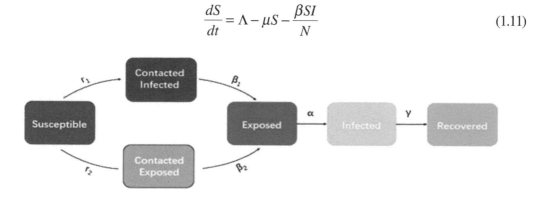

FIGURE 1.11 SEIR Model.

$$\frac{dE}{dt} = \frac{\beta SI}{N} - (\mu + \sigma) E \tag{1.12}$$

$$\frac{dI}{dt} = \sigma E - (\gamma + \mu + \alpha) I \tag{1.13}$$

$$\frac{dR}{dt} = \gamma I - \mu R \tag{1.14}$$

where N = S + E + I + R is the total population.

Let us consider the following base parameters for SEIR model as an example to analyze the results by varying some of them. N_0 = 10 million, α = 0.006/day, β = 0.75/day, γ = (1/8)/day, σ = (1/3)/day, Λ = μN (balance of births and natural deaths), and initial conditions: $S(0) = N_0 - E(0) - I(0)$, $E(0) = 20,000$, $I(0) = 1$ and $R(0) = 0$.

If the isolation precautions have been imposed and that after day 22, R_0 changes from 5.72 to 0.1. Then the changes of the value of the β according;

$$\beta \approx (\gamma + \alpha) R_0$$

The results are shown in Figure 1.12, where the peak has moved from day 30 to day 25, with a significant slowing in the number of new cases.

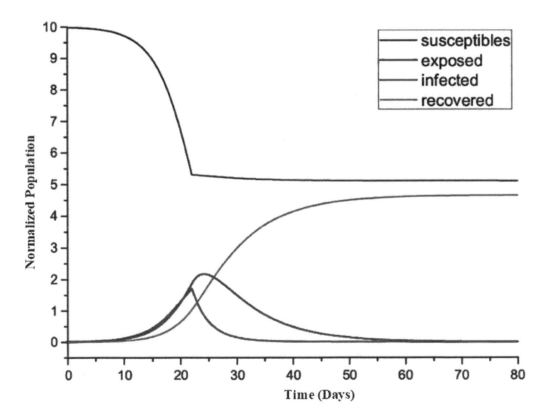

FIGURE 1.12 SEIR Model with 22 days incubation period.

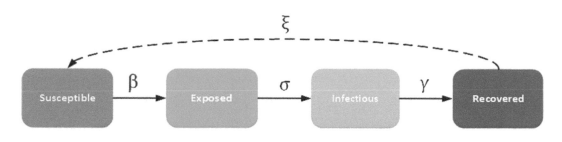

FIGURE 1.13 SEIRS Model.

The total number of dead individuals has decreased, and the number of dead individuals per day at the peak has decreased from 22 to 13 K, approximately. Extreme isolation after imperfect isolation anticipates the process.

SEIRS Model

The SEIRS model is the advanced version of the SEIR model as show in Figure 1.13. The dashed line shows how the SEIR model becomes an SEIRS (Susceptible – Exposed – Infectious – Recovered – Susceptible) model, where recovered people may become susceptible again (recovery does not confer lifelong immunity). For example, rotavirus and malaria are diseases with long incubation durations, and where recovery only confers temporary immunity.

The SEIR model assumes people carry lifelong immunity to a disease upon recovery, but for many diseases the immunity after infection wanes over time. In this case, the SEIRS model is used to allow recovered individuals to return to a susceptible state. Specifically, ξ is the rate which recovered individuals return to the susceptible statue due to loss of immunity. If there is sufficient influx to the susceptible population, at equilibrium the dynamics will be in an endemic state with damped oscillation. The SEIRS ordered differential equations are as follows:

$$\frac{dS}{dt} = -\frac{\beta SI}{N} + \xi R \tag{1.15}$$

$$\frac{dE}{dt} = -\frac{\beta SI}{N} - \sigma E \tag{1.16}$$

$$\frac{dI}{dt} = \sigma E - \gamma I \tag{1.17}$$

$$\frac{dR}{dt} = \gamma I - \xi R$$

where $N = S + E + I + R$ is the total population.

The graph in Figure 1.14 shows the complete trajectory of a fatal SEIRS outbreak: the disease endemicity due to vital process and waning immunity and the effect of vaccination campaigns that eradicate the outbreak after day 500.

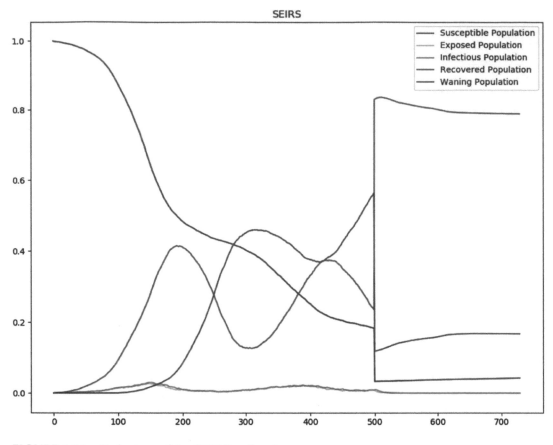

FIGURE 1.14   Trajectory of the SEIRS outbreak.

ADDITIONAL PREVENTIONS TIPS FOR COMMUNITY

The above models will able to estimate the spreading nature of the COVID-19 infection, but in order to prevent from the infection individual community need to follow some preventions. The most important by individual is to avoid sneezing and cough at the public place. The hand cleaning with soap and sanitizer, mouth and nose coverage with mask during sneezing and coughing are essential. Thoroughly washing foodstuff before cocking may help in this regard. The simple housekeeping disinfectants may kill the virus on the surfaces. Regularly cleaning of the surface by the disinfectants may control the virus outbreak. It is always better to avoid the interactions with anyone; suspecting respiratory problems symptoms like sneezing, coughing, breathing problem, etc. It is also advisable to stay at home if anyone has flue and common cold-like symptoms. It is also better not to go to school, work and public places, not use public means of transport (aircraft, train, metro, bus, taxi, etc.). Some important suggestions may include avoiding travel, and collection at a particular place. The drinking of hot water after every hour may be helpful. Plenty of lukewarm water (~5 L per day) may help in this regard. The governments should provide facilities for the decontamination of the hands at the public places. The guidelines are available for healthcare providers, medical staff, researchers and public health individuals (Jin et al., 2020). They can use to control COVID-19 globally. During the entire period of COVID-19, it was realized that this disease is spreading among those who are not taking it seriously and are not following the directions of WHO and the local government. Some people are trying to target one community for the spreading COVID-19 while this virus does not recognize and race, creed, sex, age, and religion. Therefore, it is urgently advised and requested that all the persons should follow the preventive measures, managements and quarantine strictly without any religious discrepancy otherwise the situation may be the worst.

CASE AND CONTACT MANAGEMENT

In the United States, most people with suspected or probable SARS were isolated at home; hospital isolation was reserved for those who required such care or had no suitable home environment. (e.g., homeless, out-of-town visitors). Isolation was continued while symptoms persisted and for ten days thereafter. In some other countries, most persons with suspected or probable SARS were isolated in the hospital. For contact management, the U.S. Centers for Disease Control and Prevention (CDC) recommended quarantine only for health-care workers who had a high-risk exposure to a SARS patient. In several states, however, local health officials "furloughed" health-care workers who were exposed to high-risk probable cases. In general, CDC recommended only passive surveillance. Persons who were exposed to suspected or probable SARS, as well as travelers returning from areas with SARS transmission, were asked to monitor their health for ten days and seek medical attention immediately if fever or respiratory symptoms developed. Active surveillance was reserved for probably and lab-confirmed cases and their high risk close contacts; this was usually conducted by members of the local or state health departments.

In some countries other than the United States (e.g., China, Taiwan [ROC], Singapore, and Canada), home quarantine was used for most close contacts of people with suspected or probable SARS. Designated quarantine facilities were used in some situations for homeless persons, travelers, and people who did not wish to be quarantined at home. In some situations, as a result of staffing shortages and relatively high exposure rates in hospitals, exposed health-care workers and ambulance personnel were placed on "work quarantine," which entailed working during their regular shifts, using comprehensive infection control precautions and personal protective equipment, and staying either at home or in a building near the hospital when off duty. Most persons in home quarantine were asked to monitor their temperature regularly, once or twice a day; health workers called them twice a day to get a report on temperature and symptoms. Other health-care workers had their temperature checked twice a day or more at work. In Singapore, video cameras linked to telephones were occasionally used to monitor patients.

Authorities used a variety of methods to enforce quarantine during the SARS epidemic. In select places, quarantine orders were given to all persons placed in quarantine, while in the majority, only those who demonstrated noncompliance were given orders. Under some orders, noncompliant individuals were isolated in guarded rooms; others were confined at home wearing security ankle bracelets; yet others received fines or even jail sentences. However, these instances of compulsory enforced quarantine orders were clearly the exception rather than the norm during the SARS epidemic.

COMMUNITY CONTAINMENT

In the United States, community containment strategies consisted mainly of coordinating the SARS response activities through emergency operations centers and providing information and education to the public, health workers, and others. This strategy included publishing guidelines and fact sheets on websites, holding press conferences, making presentations to a variety of audiences, and meeting with groups and communities who were experiencing stigmatization.

On some occasions, such as occurred in mainland China, Hong Kong (SAR), Taiwan (ROC), and Singapore, large-scale quarantine was imposed on travelers arriving from other SARS areas, work and school contacts of suspected cases, and, in a few instances, entire apartment complexes where high attack rates of SARS were occurring.

In addition to imposing large-scale quarantine in some cases, many areas with high transmission (e.g., Hong Kong, Singapore, Taiwan, Toronto, and mainland China) used strategies such as mandated fever screening before entry to schools, work, and other public buildings; requiring masks in certain settings; and implementing populationwide temperature monitoring and disinfection campaigns. Community mobilization programs were also developed to educate the public about SARS and what to do to prevent and control it; for example, a populationwide body temperature monitoring campaign and a SARS hotline to promote early detection of fever as a warning sign for SARS. Taiwan and mainland China also undertook a series of community disinfection campaigns in which streets, buildings, and vehicles were sprayed with bleach and bleach was distributed free throughout the community.

Several important lessons can be gained from the experience of countries where large-scale quarantine measures were imposed in response to SARS. First, when the public was given clear messages about the need for quarantine, it was well accepted—far better, in fact, than many public health officials would have anticipated. Indeed, voluntary quarantine was effective in the overwhelming majority of cases. Yet, despite the widespread acceptance of and cooperation with quarantine, it represented a great sacrifice for many people through consequences such as loss of income, concerns for the health of their families, feelings of isolation, and stigma. Finally, large-scale quarantine was found to be complicated and resource intensive to implement, creating enormous logistic, economic, ethical, and psychological challenges for public health authorities. Recent data evaluating the efficacy of quarantine in Taiwan and Beijing, China, during the SARS epidemic suggest that efficiency could be improved by focusing quarantine activities on persons with known or suspected contact with SARS cases. In order to prepare for future epidemics, enhanced systems and personnel will need to be established to deliver essential services to persons in quarantine, to monitor their health and refer them to necessary medical care, and to offer mental health and other support services.

NOTES

1. WHO. Weekly epidemiological record. Available from URL: http://apps.who.int/iris/bitstream/10665/ 252537/1/WER9151_52.pdf?ua=1.
2. A(H3N2)v, A(H3N2) variant; AI, avian influenza; ARDS, acute respiratory distress syndrome; HPAI, highly pathogenic AI; LPAI, low pathogenic AI; MV, mechanical ventilation; N/A, not applicable; URT, upper respiratory tract; WHO, World Health Organization.
3. WHO. 2020. Coronavirus disease 2019 (COVID-19) situation report– 173 (July 11, 2020). https://www.who.int/docs/default-source/coronaviruse/situation-reports/20200711-covid-19-sitrep-173.pdf?sfvrsn=949920b4_2 Accessed on 11 July 2020.
4. CoV, coronavirus; MERS, Middle East respiratory syndrome; SARS, severe acute respiratory syndrome.

REFERENCES

Abdel-Ghafar, A. N., Chotpitayasunondh, T., Gao, Z., Hayden, F. G., Nguyen, D. H., de Jong, M. D., Naghdaliyev, A., Peiris, J. S., Shindo, N., & Soeroso, S. (2008). Writing committee of the second world health organization consultation on clinical aspects of human infection with avian influenza A (H5N1) virus. Update on avian influenza A (H5N1) virus infection in humans. *The New England Journal of Medicine*, *358*(3), 261–273.

Ahmed, W., Angel, N., Edson, J., Bibby, K., Bivins, A., O'Brien, J. W., Choi, P. M., Kitajima, M., Simpson, S. L., & Li, J. (2020). First confirmed detection of SARS-CoV-2 in untreated wastewater in Australia: A proof of concept for the wastewater surveillance of COVID-19 in the community. *Science of The Total Environment*, 138764.

Ali, M., Zaid, M., Saqib, M. A. N., Ahmed, H., & Afzal, M. S. (2020). SARS-CoV-2 and the hidden carriers–sewage, feline, and blood transfusion. *Journal of Medical Virology*, *92*(11), 2291–2292.

Anderson, R. M., & May, R. M. (1992). *Infectious diseases of humans: Dynamics and control.* Oxford University Press.

Asha, K., & Kumar, B. (2019). Emerging influenza D virus threat: What we know so far! *Journal of Clinical Medicine*, *8*(2), 192.

Assiri, A., Al-Tawfiq, J. A., Al-Rabeeah, A. A., Al-Rabiah, F. A., Al-Hajjar, S., Al-Barrak, A., Flemban, H., Al-Nassir, W. N., Balkhy, H. H., & Al-Hakeem, R. F. (2013). Epidemiological, demographic, and clinical characteristics of 47 cases of Middle East respiratory syndrome coronavirus disease from Saudi Arabia: A descriptive study. *The Lancet Infectious Diseases*, *13*(9), 752–761.

Ayittey, F. K., Ayittey, M. K., Chiwero, N. B., Kamasah, J. S., & Dzuvor, C. (2020). Economic impacts of Wuhan 2019-nCoV on China and the world. *Journal of Medical Virology*, *92*(5), 473–475.

Bastola, A., Sah, R., Rodriguez-Morales, A. J., Lal, B. K., Jha, R., Ojha, H. C., Shrestha, B., Chu, D. K. W., Poon, L. L. M., & Costello, A. (2020). The first 2019 novel coronavirus case in Nepal. *The Lancet Infectious Diseases*, *20*(3), 279–280.

Benvenuto, D., Giovanetti, M., Salemi, M., Prosperi, M., De Flora, C., Junior Alcantara, L. C., Angeletti, S., & Ciccozzi, M. (2020). The global spread of 2019-nCoV: A molecular evolutionary analysis. *Pathogens and Global Health*, *114*(2), 64–67.

Bernoulli, D. (1760). Essai d'une nouvelle analyse de la mortalité causée par la petite vérole, et des avantages de l'inoculation pour la prévenir. *Histoire de l'Acad., Roy. Sci.(Paris) Avec Mem*, 1–45.

Biscayart, C., Angeleri, P., Lloveras, S., Chaves, T. do S. S., Schlagenhauf, P., & Rodríguez-Morales, A. J. (2020). The next big threat to global health? 2019 novel coronavirus (2019-nCoV): What advice can we give to travellers?–Interim recommendations January 2020, from the Latin-American society for Travel Medicine (SLAMVI). *Travel Medicine and Infectious Disease*, *33*, 101567.

Blakeman, B. (2020). China must close down "wet markets" now. *The Hill*, 1.

Burrell, C. J., Howard, C. R., & Murphy, F. A. (2016). *Fenner and white's medical virology.* Academic Press.

Chen, J. (2020). Pathogenicity and transmissibility of 2019-nCoV—A quick overview and comparison with other emerging viruses. *Microbes and Infection*, *22*(2), 69–71.

Chen, W.-Q., Ling, W.-H., Lu, C.-Y., Hao, Y.-T., Lin, Z.-N., Ling, L., Huang, J., Li, G., & Yan, G.-M. (2009). Which preventive measures might protect health care workers from SARS? *BMC Public Health*, *9*(1), 81.

Cheng, V. C. C., Wong, S.-C., To, K. K. W., Ho, P. L., & Yuen, K.-Y. (2020). Preparedness and proactive infection control measures against the emerging novel coronavirus in China. *Journal of Hospital Infection*, *104*(3), 254–255.

Choi, W. S., Kang, C.-I., Kim, Y., Choi, J.-P., Joh, J. S., Shin, H.-S., Kim, G., Peck, K. R., Chung, D. R., & Kim, H. O. (2016). Clinical presentation and outcomes of Middle East respiratory syndrome in the Republic of Korea. *Infection & Chemotherapy*, *48*(2), 118–126.

Chowell, G., Fenimore, P. W., Castillo-Garsow, M. A., & Castillo-Chavez, C. (2003). SARS out-breaks in Ontario, Hong Kong and Singapore: The role of diagnosis and isolation as a control mechanism. *Journal of Theoretical Biology*, *224*(1), 1–8.

Christian, M. D., Poutanen, S. M., Loutfy, M. R., Muller, M. P., & Low, D. E. (2004). Severe acute respiratory syndrome. *Clinical Infectious Diseases*, *38*(10), 1420–1427.

Coutard, B., Valle, C., de Lamballerie, X., Canard, B., Seidah, N. G., & Decroly, E. (2020). The spike glycoprotein of the new coronavirus 2019-nCoV contains a furin-like cleavage site absent in CoV of the same clade. *Antiviral Research*, *176*, 104742.

Cowling, B. J., Park, M., Fang, V. J., Wu, P., Leung, G. M., & Wu, J. T. (2015). Preliminary epidemiological assessment of MERS-CoV outbreak in South Korea, May to June 2015. *Eurosurveillance*, *20*(25), 21163.

Cui, J., Li, F., & Shi, Z.-L. (2019). Origin and evolution of pathogenic coronaviruses. *Nature Reviews Microbiology*, *17*(3), 181–192.

Dikid, T., Jain, S. K., Sharma, A., Kumar, A., & Narain, J. P. (2013). Emerging & re-emerging infections in India: an overview. *The Indian Journal of Medical Research*, *138*(1), 19.

Dong, E., Du, H., & Gardner, L. (2020). An interactive web-based dashboard to track COVID-19 in real time. *The Lancet Infectious Diseases*, *20*(5), 533–534.

Donnelly, C. A., Ghani, A. C., Leung, G. M., Hedley, A. J., Fraser, C., Riley, S., Abu-Raddad, L. J., Ho, L.-M., Thach, T.-Q., & Chau, P. (2003). Epidemiological determinants of spread of causal agent of severe acute respiratory syndrome in Hong Kong. *The Lancet*, *361*(9371), 1761–1766.

Elbahesh, H., Saletti, G., Gerlach, T., & Rimmelzwaan, G. F. (2019). Broadly protective influenza vaccines: Design and production platforms. *Current Opinion in Virology*, *34*, 1–9.

Fendrick, A. M., Monto, A. S., Nightengale, B., & Sarnes, M. (2003). The economic burden of non–influenza-related viral respiratory tract infection in the United States. *Archives of Internal Medicine*, *163*(4), 487–494.

Francis, M. E., King, M. L., & Kelvin, A. A. (2019). Back to the future for influenza preimmunity—Looking back at influenza virus history to infer the outcome of future infections. *Viruses*, *11*(2), 122.

Graham, R. L., Donaldson, E. F., & Baric, R. S. (2013). A decade after SARS: Strategies for controlling emerging coronaviruses. *Nature Reviews Microbiology*, *11*(12), 836–848.

Gralinski, L. E., & Menachery, V. D. (2020). Return of the Coronavirus: 2019-nCoV. *Viruses*, *12*(2), 135.

Gu, M., Xu, L., Wang, X., & Liu, X. (2017). Current situation of H9N2 subtype avian influenza in China. *Veterinary Research*, *48*(1), 49.

Guan, W., Ni, Z., Hu, Y., Liang, W., Ou, C., He, J., Liu, L., Shan, H., Lei, C., & Hui, D. S. C. (2020). Clinical characteristics of coronavirus disease 2019 in China. *New England Journal of Medicine*, *382*(18), 1708–1720.

Guan, Y., Zheng, B. J., He, Y. Q., Liu, X. L., Zhuang, Z. X., Cheung, C. L., Luo, S. W., Li, P. H., Zhang, L. J., & Guan, Y. J. (2003). Isolation and characterization of viruses related to the SARS coronavirus from animals in southern China. *Science*, *302*(5643), 276–278.

Hao, W., Li, M., & Huang, X. (2020). First atypical case of 2019 novel coronavirus in Yan'an, China. *Clinical Microbiology and Infection*, *26*(7), 952–953.

Hethcote, H. W. (2000). The mathematics of infectious diseases. *SIAM Review*, *42*(4), 599–653.

Hon, K. L. E., Leung, C. W., Cheng, W. T. F., Chan, P. K. S., Chu, W. C. W., Kwan, Y. W., Li, A. M., Fong, N. C., Ng, P. C., & Chiu, M. C. (2003). Clinical presentations and outcome of severe acute respiratory syndrome in children. *The Lancet*, *361*(9370), 1701–1703.

Honigsbaum, M. (2018). Spanish influenza redux: Revisiting the mother of all pandemics. *The Lancet*, *391*(10139), 2492–2495.

Hui, D. S., Azhar, E. I., Kim, Y.-J., Memish, Z. A., Oh, M., & Zumla, A. (2018). Middle East respiratory syndrome coronavirus: Risk factors and determinants of primary, household, and nosocomial transmission. *The Lancet Infectious Diseases*, *18*(8), e217–e227.

Hui, D. S., Azhar, E. I., Madani, T. A., Ntoumi, F., Kock, R., Dar, O., Ippolito, G., Mchugh, T. D., Memish, Z. A., & Drosten, C. (2020). The continuing 2019-nCoV epidemic threat of novel coronaviruses to global health—The latest 2019 novel coronavirus outbreak in Wuhan, China. *International Journal of Infectious Diseases*, *91*, 264–266.

Hui, D. S. C., Lee, N., & Chan, P. K. S. (2017). A clinical approach to the threat of emerging influenza viruses in the A sia-P acific region. *Respirology*, *22*(7), 1300–1312.

Ison, M. G., & Hirsch, H. H. (2019). Community-acquired respiratory viruses in transplant patients: Diversity, impact, unmet clinical needs. *Clinical Microbiology Reviews*, *32*(4), e00042-19.

Jaijyan, D. K., Liu, J., Hai, R., & Zhu, H. (2018). Emerging and reemerging human viral diseases. *Annals of Microbiology and Research*, *2*(1), 31–44.

Jiang, X., Rayner, S., & Luo, M. (2020). Does SARS-CoV-2 has a longer incubation period than SARS and MERS? *Journal of Medical Virology*, *92*(5), 476–478.

Jones, J. C., Baranovich, T., Marathe, B. M., Danner, A. F., Seiler, J. P., Franks, J., Govorkova, E. A., Krauss, S., & Webster, R. G. (2014). Risk assessment of H2N2 influenza viruses from the avian reservoir. *Journal of Virology*, *88*(2), 1175–1188.

Kang, C. K., Song, K.-H., Choe, P. G., Park, W. B., Bang, J. H., Kim, E. S., Park, S. W., Kim, H. Bin, Kim, N. J., & Cho, S. (2017). Clinical and epidemiologic characteristics of spreaders of Middle East respiratory syndrome coronavirus during the 2015 outbreak in Korea. *Journal of Korean Medical Science*, *32*(5), 744–749.

Karron, R. A., & Black, R. E. (2017). Determining the burden of respiratory syncytial virus disease: The known and the unknown. *The Lancet*, *390*(10098), 917–918.

Khan, S. U., Anderson, B. D., Heil, G. L., Liang, S., & Gray, G. C. (2015). A systematic review and meta-analysis of the seroprevalence of influenza A (H9N2) infection among humans. *The Journal of Infectious Diseases*, *212*(4), 562–569.

Kilbourne, E. D. (2006). Influenza pandemics of the 20th century. *Emerging Infectious Diseases*, *12*(1), 9.

Kjemtrup, A. M., Messenger, S., Meza, A. M., Feiszli, T., Yoshimizu, M. H., Padgett, K., & Singh, S. (2019). New Exposure Location for Hantavirus Pulmonary Syndrome Case, California, USA, 2018. *Emerging Infectious Diseases*, *25*(10), 1962.

Knowles, G. (2020). *Will they ever learn? Chinese markets are still selling bats and slaughtering rabbits on blood-soaked floors as Beijing celebrates' victory'over the coronavirus.*

Körner, R. W., Söderlund-Venermo, M., van Koningsbruggen-Rietschel, S., Kaiser, R., Malecki, M., & Schildgen, O. (2011). Severe human bocavirus infection, Germany. *Emerging Infectious Diseases*, *17*(12), 2303.

Kotsimbos, T., Waterer, G., Jenkins, C., Kelly, P. M., Cheng, A., Hancox, R. J., Holmes, M., Wood-Baker, R., Bowler, S., & Irving, L. (2010). Influenza A/H1N1_09: Australia and New Zealand's winter of discontent. *American Journal of Respiratory and Critical Care Medicine*, *181*(4), 300–306.

Kritas, S. K., Ronconi, G., Caraffa, A., Gallenga, C. E., Ross, R., & Conti, P. (2020). Mast cells contribute to coronavirus-induced inflammation: New anti-inflammatory strategy. *Journal of Biological Regulators and Homeostatic Agents*, *34*(1), 10–23812.

Lai, C.-C., Shih, T.-P., Ko, W.-C., Tang, H.-J., & Hsueh, P.-R. (2020). Severe acute respiratory syndrome coronavirus 2 (SARS-CoV-2) and corona virus disease-2019 (COVID-19): The epidemic and the challenges. *International Journal of Antimicrobial Agents*, 105924.

Lai, S., Qin, Y., Cowling, B. J., Ren, X., Wardrop, N. A., Gilbert, M., Tsang, T. K., Wu, P., Feng, L., & Jiang, H. (2016). Global epidemiology of avian influenza A H5N1 virus infection in humans, 1997–2015: A systematic review of individual case data. *The Lancet Infectious Diseases*, *16*(7), e108–e118.

Li, G., Fan, Y., Lai, Y., Han, T., Li, Z., Zhou, P., Pan, P., Wang, W., Hu, D., & Liu, X. (2020). Coronavirus infections and immune responses. *Journal of Medical Virology*, *92*(4), 424–432.

Li, Q., Zhou, L., Zhou, M., Chen, Z., Li, F., Wu, H., Xiang, N., Chen, E., Tang, F., & Wang, D. (2014). Epidemiology of human infections with avian influenza A (H7N9) virus in China. *New England Journal of Medicine, 370*(6), 520–532.

Li, X., Geng, M., Peng, Y., Meng, L., & Lu, S. (2020). Molecular immune pathogenesis and diagnosis of COVID-19. *Journal of Pharmaceutical Analysis, 10*(2), 102–108.

Lin, L., & Li, T. S. (2020). interpretation of "guidelines for the diagnosis and treatment of novel coronavirus (2019-ncov) infection by the national health commission (trial version 5)." *Zhonghua Yi Xue Za Zhi, 100*, E001–E001.

Liu, D., Shi, W., Shi, Y., Wang, D., Xiao, H., Li, W., Bi, Y., Wu, Y., Li, X., & Yan, J. (2013). Origin and diversity of novel avian influenza A H7N9 viruses causing human infection: Phylogenetic, structural, and coalescent analyses. *The Lancet, 381*(9881), 1926–1932.

Liu, M., Li, X., Yuan, H., Zhou, J., Wu, J., Bo, H., Xia, W., Xiong, Y., Yang, L., & Gao, R. (2015). Genetic diversity of avian influenza A (H10N8) virus in live poultry markets and its association with human infections in China. *Scientific Reports, 5*, 7632.

Liu, S.-L., & Saif, L. (2020). *Emerging viruses without borders: The Wuhan coronavirus.* Multidisciplinary Digital Publishing Institute.

Liu, Y., Gayle, A. A., Wilder-Smith, A., & Rocklöv, J. (2020). The reproductive number of COVID-19 is higher compared to SARS coronavirus. *Journal of Travel Medicine, 27*(2).

Lu, H., Stratton, C. W., & Tang, Y. (2020). Outbreak of pneumonia of unknown etiology in Wuhan, China: The mystery and the miracle. *Journal of Medical Virology, 92*(4), 401–402.

Lu, R., Zhao, X., Li, J., Niu, P., Yang, B., Wu, H., Wang, W., Song, H., Huang, B., & Zhu, N. (2020). Genomic characterisation and epidemiology of 2019 novel coronavirus: Implications for virus origins and receptor binding. *The Lancet, 395*(10224), 565–574.

MacNeil, A., Nichol, S. T., & Spiropoulou, C. F. (2011). Hantavirus pulmonary syndrome. *Virus Research, 162*(1–2), 138–147.

Mahase, E. (2020a). *China coronavirus: What do we know so far?* British Medical Journal Publishing Group.

Mahase, E. (2020b). *Coronavirus: COVID-19 has killed more people than SARS and MERS combined, despite lower case fatality rate.* British Medical Journal Publishing Group.

Menachery, V. D., Yount, B. L., Debbink, K., Agnihothram, S., Gralinski, L. E., Plante, J. A., Graham, R. L., Scobey, T., Ge, X.-Y., & Donaldson, E. F. (2015). A SARS-like cluster of circulating bat coronaviruses shows potential for human emergence. *Nature Medicine, 21*(12), 1508–1513.

Moesker, F. M., Fraaij, P. L. A., & Osterhaus, A. D. M. E. (2013). New, Emerging, and Reemerging Respiratory Viruses. *Viral Infections and Global Change, 355*–375.

Monchatre-Leroy, E., Boué, F., Boucher, J.-M., Renault, C., Moutou, F., Ar Gouilh, M., & Umhang, G. (2017). Identification of alpha and beta coronavirus in wildlife species in France: Bats, rodents, rabbits, and hedgehogs. *Viruses, 9*(12), 364.

Munster, V. J., Koopmans, M., van Doremalen, N., van Riel, D., & de Wit, E. (2020). A novel coronavirus emerging in China—Key questions for impact assessment. *New England Journal of Medicine, 382*(8), 692–694.

Nishiura, H., Kobayashi, T., Yang, Y., Hayashi, K., Miyama, T., Kinoshita, R., Linton, N. M., Jung, S., Yuan, B., & Suzuki, A. (2020). *The rate of underascertainment of novel coronavirus (2019-nCoV) infection: Estimation using Japanese passengers data on evacuation flights.* Multidisciplinary Digital Publishing Institute.

Nishiura, H., Linton, N. M., & Akhmetzhanov, A. R. (2020). *Initial cluster of novel coronavirus (2019-nCoV) infections in Wuhan, China is consistent with substantial human-to-human transmission.* Multidisciplinary Digital Publishing Institute.

Núñez-Delgado, A. (2020). What do we know about the SARS-CoV-2 coronavirus in the environment? *Science of the Total Environment, 138647.*

Park, S., Park, J. Y., Song, Y., How, S. H., Jung, K., & Respiratory Infections Assembly of the APSR. (2019). Emerging respiratory infections threatening public health in the Asia–Pacific region: A position paper of the Asian Pacific Society of Respirology. *Respirology, 24*(6), 590–597.

Parry, J. (2020). *China coronavirus: Cases surge as official admits human to human transmission.* British Medical Journal Publishing Group.

Peeri, N. C., Shrestha, N., Rahman, M. S., Zaki, R., Tan, Z., Bibi, S., Baghbanzadeh, M., Aghamohammadi, N., Zhang, W., & Haque, U. (2020). The SARS, MERS and novel coronavirus (COVID-19) epidemics, the newest and biggest global health threats: What lessons have we learned? *International Journal of Epidemiology, 49*(3), 717–726.

Peiris, M., Guan, Y., & Yuen, K. Y. (2005). *Severe acute respiratory syndrome.* Wiley Online Library.

Philippon, D. A. M., Wu, P., Cowling, B. J., & Lau, E. H. Y. (2020). Avian influenza human infections at the human-animal interface. *The Journal of Infectious Diseases, 222*(4), 528–537.

Qiu, H., Tong, Z., Ma, P., Hu, M., Peng, Z., Wu, W., & Du, B. (2020). *Intensive care during the coronavirus epidemic.* Springer.

Rodriguez-Morales, A. J., Bonilla-Aldana, D. K., Balbin-Ramon, G. J., Rabaan, A. A., Sah, R., Paniz-Mondolfi, A., Pagliano, P., & Esposito, S. (2020). History is repeating itself: Probable zoonotic spillover as the cause of the 2019 novel Coronavirus Epidemic. *Infez Med, 28*(1), 3–5.

Sanchez, J. L., Cooper, M. J., Myers, C. A., Cummings, J. F., Vest, K. G., Russell, K. L., Sanchez, J. L., Hiser, M. J., & Gaydos, C. A. (2015). Respiratory infections in the US military: Recent experience and control. *Clinical Microbiology Reviews, 28*(3), 743–800.

Shen, K., Yang, Y., Wang, T., Zhao, D., Jiang, Y., Jin, R., Zheng, Y., Xu, B., Xie, Z., & Lin, L. (2020). Diagnosis, treatment, and prevention of 2019 novel coronavirus infection in children: Experts' consensus statement. *World Journal of Pediatrics, 16*(3), 1–9.

Song, Z., Xu, Y., Bao, L., Zhang, L., Yu, P., Qu, Y., Zhu, H., Zhao, W., Han, Y., & Qin, C. (2019). From SARS to MERS, thrusting coronaviruses into the spotlight. *Viruses, 11*(1), 59.

Su, Y., Anderson, D., Young, B., Zhu, F., Linster, M., Kalimuddin, S., Low, J., Yan, Z., Jayakumar, J., & Sun, L. (2020). Discovery of a 382-nt deletion during the early evolution of SARS-CoV-2. *BioRxiv.*

Taubenberger, J. K., & Morens, D. M. (2006). 1918 Influenza: The mother of all pandemics. *Emerging Infectious Diseases, 12*(1), 15–22. Available at: https://doi.org/10.3201/eid1201.050979.

Van Doremalen, N., Bushmaker, T., Morris, D. H., Holbrook, M. G., Gamble, A., Williamson, B. N., Tamin, A., Harcourt, J. L., Thornburg, N. J., & Gerber, S. I. (2020). Aerosol and surface stability of SARS-CoV-2 as compared with SARS-CoV-1. *New England Journal of Medicine, 382*(16), 1564–1567.

Velavan, T. P., & Meyer, C. G. (2020). La epidemia de COVID-19. Tropical Medicine & International Health.

Vergara-Alert, J., van den Brand, J. M. A., Widagdo, W., & Muñoz, M. (2017). Livestock susceptibility to infection with Middle East respiratory syndrome coronavirus. *Emerging Infectious Diseases, 23*(2), 232.

Wang, H., Feng, Z., Shu, Y., Yu, H., Zhou, L., Zu, R., Huai, Y., Dong, J., Bao, C., & Wen, L. (2008). Probable limited person-to-person transmission of highly pathogenic avian influenza A (H5N1) virus in China. *The Lancet, 371*(9622), 1427–1434.

Wang, L., Su, S., Bi, Y., Wong, G., & Gao, G. F. (2018). Bat-origin coronaviruses expand their host range to pigs. *Trends in Microbiology, 26*(6), 466–470.

Wang, T. T., Parides, M. K., & Palese, P. (2012). Seroevidence for H5N1 influenza infections in humans: Meta-analysis. *Science, 335*(6075), 1463.

Wei, S.-H., Yang, J.-R., Wu, H.-S., Chang, M.-C., Lin, J.-S., Lin, C.-Y., Liu, Y.-L., Lo, Y.-C., Yang, C.-H., & Chuang, J.-H. (2013). Human infection with avian influenza A H6N1 virus: An epidemiological analysis. *The Lancet Respiratory Medicine, 1*(10), 771–778.

Wichmann, D., Sperhake, J.-P., Lütgehetmann, M., Steurer, S., Edler, C., Heinemann, A., Heinrich, F., Mushumba, H., Kniep, I., & Schröder, A. S. (2020). Autopsy findings and venous thromboembolism in patients with COVID-19: A prospective cohort study. *Annals of Internal Medicine.*

Wilder-Smith, A., & Freedman, D. O. (2020). Isolation, quarantine, social distancing and community containment: Pivotal role for old-style public health measures in the novel coronavirus (2019-nCoV) outbreak. *Journal of Travel Medicine, 27*(2), taaa020.

World Health Organization. (2003a). *Consensus document on the epidemiology of severe acute respiratory syndrome (SARS).* World Health Organization.

World Health Organization. (2003b). Summary of probable SARS cases with onset of illness from 1 November 2002 to 31 July 2003. *Available at:* Http://www. Who. int/csr/sars/country/table2004_04_21/en/index. Html.

World Health Organization. (2004). *WHO guidelines for the global surveillance of severe acute respiratory syndrome (SARS): Updated recommendations, October 2004.* World Health Organization.

World Health Organization. (2017). *WHO MERS-CoV global summary and assessment of risk. Geneva: WHO.*

World Health Organization. (2018). *The top 10 causes of death. Available at:* http://www. who. int/mediacentre/factsheets/fs310/en.

Wu, F., Zhao, S., Yu, B., Chen, Y.-M., Wang, W., Song, Z.-G., Hu, Y., Tao, Z.-W., Tian, J.-H., & Pei, Y.-Y. (2020). A new coronavirus associated with human respiratory disease in China. *Nature, 579*(7798), 265–269.

Wu, Z., & McGoogan, J. M. (2020). Characteristics of and important lessons from the coronavirus disease 2019 (COVID-19) outbreak in China: Summary of a report of 72 314 cases from the Chinese Center for Disease Control and Prevention. *JAMA, 323*(13), 1239–1242.

Xu, Y., Cao, H., Liu, H., Sun, H., Martin, B., Zhao, Y., Wang, Q., Deng, G., Xue, J., & Zong, Y. (2015). Identification of the source of A (H10N8) virus causing human infection. *Infection, Genetics and Evolution, 30*, 159–163.

Yoo, B.-K. (2011). How to improve influenza vaccination rates in the US. *Journal of Preventive Medicine and Public Health, 44*(4), 141.

Yuen, K.-Y., Chan, P. K. S., Peiris, M., Tsang, D. N. C., Que, T. L., Shortridge, K. F., Cheung, P. T., To, W. K., Ho, E. T. F., & Sung, R. (1998). Clinical features and rapid viral diagnosis of human disease associated with avian influenza A H5N1 virus. *The Lancet, 351*(9101), 467–471.

Zaki, A. M., Van Boheemen, S., Bestebroer, T. M., Osterhaus, A. D. M. E., & Fouchier, R. A. M. (2012). Isolation of a novel coronavirus from a man with pneumonia in Saudi Arabia. *New England Journal of Medicine, 367*(19), 1814–1820.

Zhang, R., Chen, T., Ou, X., Liu, R., Yang, Y., Ye, W., Chen, J., Yao, D., Sun, B., & Zhang, X. (2016). Clinical, epidemiological and virological characteristics of the first detected human case of avian influenza A (H5N6) virus. *Infection, Genetics and Evolution, 40*, 236–242.

Zhao, S., Lin, Q., Ran, J., Musa, S. S., Yang, G., Wang, W., Lou, Y., Gao, D., Yang, L., & He, D. (2020). Preliminary estimation of the basic reproduction number of novel coronavirus (2019-nCoV) in China, from 2019 to 2020: A data-driven analysis in the early phase of the outbreak. *International Journal of Infectious Diseases, 92*, 214–217.

Zhou, L., Tan, Y., Kang, M., Liu, F., Ren, R., Wang, Y., Chen, T., Yang, Y., Li, C., & Wu, J. (2017). Preliminary epidemiology of human infections with highly pathogenic avian influenza A (H7N9) virus, China, 2017. *Emerging Infectious Diseases, 23*(8), 1355.

Zhou, P., Yang, X.-L., Wang, X.-G., Hu, B., Zhang, L., Zhang, W., Si, H.-R., Zhu, Y., Li, B., & Huang, C.-L. (2020a). A pneumonia outbreak associated with a new coronavirus of probable bat origin. *Nature, 579*(7798), 270–273.

Zhou, P., Yang, X.-L., Wang, X.-G., Hu, B., Zhang, L., Zhang, W., Si, H.-R., Zhu, Y., Li, B., & Huang, C.-L. (2020b). Discovery of a novel coronavirus associated with the recent pneumonia outbreak in humans and its potential bat origin. *BioRxiv.*

Zhou, T., Liu, Q., Yang, Z., Liao, J., Yang, K., Bai, W., Lu, X., & Zhang, W. (2020c). Preliminary prediction of the basic reproduction number of the Wuhan novel coronavirus 2019-nCoV. *Journal of Evidence-Based Medicine, 13*(1), 3–7.

Zhu, N., Zhang, D., Wang, W., Li, X., Yang, B., Song, J., Zhao, X., Huang, B., Shi, W., & Lu, R. (2020). A novel coronavirus from patients with pneumonia in China, 2019. *New England Journal of Medicine*, *382*(8), 727–733.

Zou, L., Ruan, F., Huang, M., Liang, L., Huang, H., Hong, Z., Yu, J., Kang, M., Song, Y., & Xia, J. (2020). SARS-CoV-2 viral load in upper respiratory specimens of infected patients. *New England Journal of Medicine*, *382*(12), 1177–1179.

Zumla, A., Hui, D. S., Al-Tawfiq, J. A., Gautret, P., McCloskey, B., & Memish, Z. A. (2014). Emerging respiratory tract infections. *The Lancet Infectious Diseases*, *14*(10), 910–911.

Zumla, A., Hui, D. S., & Perlman, S. (2015). Middle East respiratory syndrome. *The Lancet*, *386*(9997), 995–1007.

2 The Origin Molecular Structure, Function, and Evolution Insights of COVID-19

Morphogenesis and Spike Proteins

KEY POINTS

- The recent performance of COVID-19 has affected the whole world, resulting in more than 0.5 million deaths due to the infection.
- A target of potential drug of SARS-CoV-2 is conserved highly, resulting no confirmed drug available for COVID-19.
- A dynamic nature in the structure of the SARS-CoV-2 genomes makes high differences to makes drugs ineffective against SARS-CoV-2.
- The Q-UEL technique is explicitly used for bioinformatics which is strengthening technology to predict the auxiliary structure that is in the form of a coil or cycle.
- Several drugs approved by the FDA are showing positive effects in clinical trials, but further validation is needed in larger subject groups.

INTRODUCTION

Coronaviruses (CoVs) are huge positive-abandoned Ribonucleic Acid (RNA) infections, which are responsible for contaminating a wide variety of mammalian and avian species (Li, 2016). These cloven infections are spherical, oval, or pleomorphic (pleural) in shape and have a measurement between 60 and 140 nm as introduced in Figure 2.1 (Shereen et al., 2020). These infectious viruses have spike-like projections of glycoproteins on their surface, which show up as crowns under the electron magnifying lens; Thus, they are alluded to as coronaviruses (coronum is the Latin expression for the crown). CoVs systematically run under the family Coronaviridae and subfamily Coronavirinae. The subfamily Coronavirina comprises of four genera to specific Alpha-CoVs, Beta-CoVs, Gamma-CoVs, and Delta-CoVs (Cui et al., 2019). COVs are not new to humans and most of them cause mild respiratory diseases in humans and infect pets from decades (Corman et al., 2019).

These cases, since the early days of the 21st century, have been found to pose a major threat to the human population, resulting in excessive increases in demand for immediate and research measures. In view of the phytolanetic evidence, SARS-COV-2 has been considered under the new member of the family Beta coronavirus (Beta-CoVs). This epicardia pathogen infection is the seventh coronavirus that has been identified to infect the humans, and the other six viruses like 229E and NL63 (Alpha-CoVs), OC43, HKU1, SARS-CoV, and MERS-CoV (Beta-CoVs) has been presented in Figure 2.2. In these 229E, NL63, OC43, HKU1 are known as to infect the human population that normally results in mild to one moderate respiratory illness (Corman et al., 2019). However, in some cases, infection of

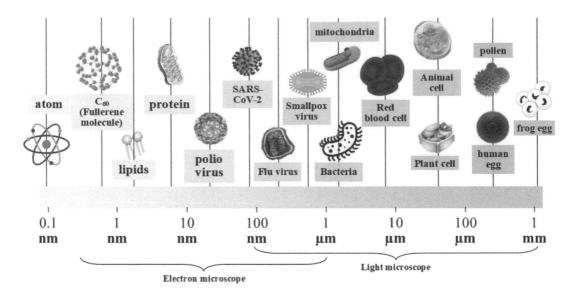

FIGURE 2.1   Virus size compared to different objects under human interaction.

SARS-CoV, MERS-CoV, and SARS-CoV-2 has not only been limited to severe respiratory diseases but also leads to the possibility of damages of human multiple organs, that can cause the loss of human life (Corman et al., 2019).

The genomes of coronavirus are enough capable to encodes several proteins that are structural and non-structural. The auxiliary proteins are liable for have host infections (Lan et al., 2020), membrane fusion (Hofmann & Pöhlmann, 2004), viral gathering (Vennema et al., 1996), morphogenesis, and to release of infection particles (Siu et al., 2008) among different capacities, and the non-structural proteins encourage the viral replication and record (Gao et al., 2020; Snijder et al., 2016). The membrane (M), the envelope (E), and the spike protein (S) are important for basic structure of proteins and are related to the envelope. Among these basic structural proteins, the trimeric spike proteins protrude from the

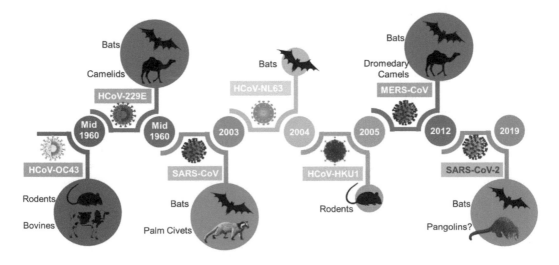

FIGURE 2.2   Human coronaviruses origin and transmission pathogenic.

infection envelope and is a bit of key apparatus that encourages the infection entry section into the host cell (Li, 2016; Wrapp et al., 2020).

The spike proteins are shaped in the form of clover, type-I transmembrane proteins, and have three sections: a huge ectodomain, a solitary pass transmembrane, and an intracellular tail. The ectodomain of spike proteins comprises of a S1 subunit that contains a receptor-binding domain (RBDs) and the membrane combination subunit (S2). The recognition of the host cell held by the RBDs on spike proteins that underlying advance of viral contamination, and restricting communications between spike of coronavirus and its receptor is one of the most basic variables for host range and the transmission of cross-species. The human coronavirus perceive an range of host receptors, in particular HCoV-NL229 perceives aminopeptidase N (APN) (Wentworth & Holmes, 2001) and MERS-CoV bonds dipeptidyl peptidase-4 (DPP4) (Raj et al., 2013), HCoV-OC43 and HCoV-HKU1 bonds specific sorts of O-acetylated sialic acid (Hulswit et al., 2019), and HCoV-NL63 and SARS-CoV perceive angiotensin-converting enzyme 2 (ACE2) (Hofmann et al., 2005; Li et al., 2003). Recent structures alongside utilitarian examinations, have proposed that the SARS-CoV-2 spike proteins use ACE2 and Transmembrane Serine Protease 2 (TMPRSS2) for have cell entry, which is fundamentally the same as the components misused by SARS-CoV (Hoffmann et al., 2020).

Presently, there are more than 100 antibodies that are being created by researchers around the world to give immunity against SARS-CoV-2. The fundamental thought is to uncover the human body to an antigen, which ought not to cause disease however simulation of the immune reaction for creating SARS-CoV-2 explicit immunity (Callaway, 2020). Among all the coronaviruses, spike proteins shows their existence and a significant objective for evoking antibodies; in this way, the details of structure and molecular of spike protein and its connections with related receptors would be fundamental in creating immunizations and antiviral medications against SARS-CoV-2.

In the first section under this chapter discusses the origin, life cycle, and various classification of the coronavirus, then chapter covers the SARS-CoV-2 emergence, morphology and key virulence factors, capacity, and antigenicity of spike glycoproteins and its connections with ACE2 receptor, anti-coronavirus immunization, development of drugs in details, lastly, the chapter covers the computational techniques to understand the structure and emergence of SARS-CoV-2.

EMERGENCE OF SARS-CoV AND SARS-CoV-2

In the month of November 2002, SARS started spreading from the Guangdong region of Southern China, however, its repository was obscure. Before, Nipah and Hendra, both zoonotic infections, begun from bats, and this inspired many researchers to discover if bats are the regular suppliers of SARS-CoV or not (Halpin et al., 2000; Yob et al., 2001). In the year 2005, two groups of researchers autonomously revealed that bats (horseshoe bats specifically) are the regular host of hereditarily differing coronaviruses, and firmly identified with those answerable for the SARS outbreak (Lau et al., 2005; Li et al., 2005). These infections were named SARS-like coronavirus, and they showed impressive hereditary likenesses to one SARS-CoV separated from humans or civets. This recommended the infection answerable for the SARS outbreak that was an individual from the group of SARS-like coronaviruses (Li et al., 2005). One notable point here is that since then SARS has been returned several times (specifically four times): and three times it is reported due to the accidents by research laboratory (Singapore and Taiwan) and once in southern China, where the cause of the disease remains uncertain. In Saudi Arabia, the MERS-CoV peaked in 2012, when people were infected through immediate or trailing contacts with contaminated dromedary camels. In any case, genome examination recommended that MERS-CoV could additionally begin in bats and was sent to camels in the past (Figure 2.2).

In the month of December 2019, serious pneumonia patients of obscure causes were reported in the city Wuhan, China, and a novel strain was identified from the lower respiratory lot tests of four patients (Zhu et al., 2020). From these clinical samples these viruses were disconnected and sequences of their genomes were deep sequencing (Chan et al., 2020; Lu et al., 2020; Zhou et al., 2020). Phylogenetic examination of 2019-nCoVs genomes and different coronaviruses were utilized to build up the developmental history and disease sources. Strikingly, this showed 2019-nCoV (GenBank: MN908947.3) shares about 96% sequence of nucleotide identity to Bat coronavirus RaTG13 (GenBank: MN996532.1), while 79.5% and 55% character identified to SARS-CoV BJ01 (GenBank: AY278488.2) and MERS-CoV HCoV-EMC (GenBank: MH454272.1), respectively and has a place with a similar group of infections that caused SARS and MERS (Figure 2.3).

Despite this that it has high sequence similitudes, barely any generally striking and saved varieties emerged in 2019-nCoVs genomes that were not found previously in beta-coronaviruses. These prominent features, which set up this infection not the same as SARS-CoV and SARS-like coronaviruses are:

1. Numerous transformations in the domains of receptor-bindings of spike protein that may cooperate with ACE2 receptor,
2. Polybasic furin-like protease site (RRAR/S) at the limit of S1/S2 subunits instead of a solitary arginine saw in SARS-CoV, and
3. Expansion of three anticipated O-connected glycans flanking the protease site (Andersen et al., 2020; Coutard et al., 2020).

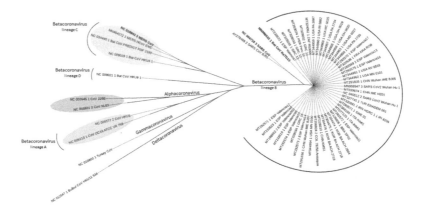

FIGURE 2.3   Phylogenetic connections with the subfamily of coronavirinae: the subfamily is shaped with four genera: Alpha-coronavirus, Beta-coronavirus (lineage A, B, C, and D), Gamma-coronavirus, and Delta-coronavirus. To fulfill the purpose here 43 SARS-CoV-2 genome sequences is selected randomly that covers 15 distinct countries, along with other coronavirinae subfamily individuals. This phylogenetic tree was made utilizing a tool named NgPhylogeny.fr. The investigation demonstrates that SARS-CoV-2 has a cozy relationship with Bat coronavirus RaTG13, and SARS-CoV; consequently named another individual from the heredity B of beta-coronaviruses.

It is worth noting here that the protease 1 site like the furin is a mark of some exceptionally pathogenic avian flu infection and pathogenic Newcastle disease infection (Klenk & Garten, 1994; Steinhauer, 1999). However, sequencing and transformative investigation further recommend that bat is perhaps the host of 2019-nCoV cause, and it may have sent either straightforwardly from the bat or through an obscure intermediate host to contaminate people (Guo et al., 2020; Ou et al., 2020; World Health Organization, 2020; Zhu et al., 2020). Originally this infection was named "2019-novel coronavirus or 2019-nCoV," and afterward the International Committee on Taxonomy of Viruses formally named it "Serious Acute Respiratory Syndrome Coronavirus 2" (SARS-CoV-2) because of its hereditary closeness to SARS-CoV on 11 February, 2020 (World Health Organization, 2020). The point of attention here is that SARS-CoV and SARS-CoV-2 are two distinctive infections. SARS-CoV-2 causes respiratory ailment and WHO named it Corona Virus Disease-2019 (COVID-19). It is an infectious and basically communicated among individuals through respiratory droplets and contact courses (Chan et al., 2020; Liu et al., 2020). SARS-CoV-2 is quickly spreading far and wide and in excess of millions COVID-19 cases are affirmed around the world, and WHO has just declared the COVID-19 outbreak a pandemic.

CLASSIFICATION OF CORONAVIRUSES

International Committee on Taxonomy of Viruses the group of study on coronaviruses has classified coronaviruses under the family Coronaviridae, subfamily Coronavirinae. In light of genotypic and serological portrayal, Coronavirinae is classified into four genera: Alpha-coronavirus, Beta-coronavirus, Gamma-coronavirus, and Delta-coronavirus as presented in Figure 2.4(A) (Coronaviridae Study Group of the International Committee on Taxonomy of Viruses, 2020; Cui et al., 2019; Fung & Liu, 2019; Woo et al., 2012). Till December 2019, six different species of Human Coronavirus (HCoV) has been reported that cause human illness. Four of them cause regular cold manifestations in immunocompromised people, which are HCoV-229E and HCoV-OC43 first distinguished during the 1960s (Hamre & Procknow, 1966; Kahn & McIntosh, 2005; Tyrrell & Bynoe, 1966), HCoV-NL63 in 2004 (Fouchier et al., 2004; Van Der Hoek et al., 2004), and HCoV-HKU1 in 2005 (Lau et al., 2006). The other two strains, which cause deadly disease, are to be specific extreme intense respiratory condition coronavirus (SARS-CoV) first distinguished in 2003 (Holmes, 2003; World Health Organization, 2003; Zaki et al., 2012) and Middle East respiratory syndrome coronavirus (MERS-1 CoV) in 2012 (Zaki et al., 2012). SARS-CoV-2 has 96% nucleotide sequence similarity to Bat coronavirus RaTG13, a SARS-like coronavirus; consequently, has a place with Beta-coronavirus genera (Figure 2.3).

Forster et al. played out a phylogenetic network examination of 160 complete SARS-CoV-2 genomes samples inspected from over the world to comprehend the advancement of this infection in people and disease sources. They named these firmly related genomes in three ancestries, to be specific A, B, and C dependent on amino acid changes. The ancestry A was named for the first bat coronavirus that caused COVID-19, however shockingly it was not the predominant infection type in Wuhan. The A and C types were found prominently in American and Europeans, individually, while the B types were generally predominant in East Asia and required transformations for spreading outside East Asia. The genealogy C contrasts from its parent ancestry B by a change at amino acid position 26,144 and was pervasive in France, Italy, Sweden, England, California, Brazil, Singapore, Hong Kong, Taiwan, and South Korea however, missing from territory Chinese examples.

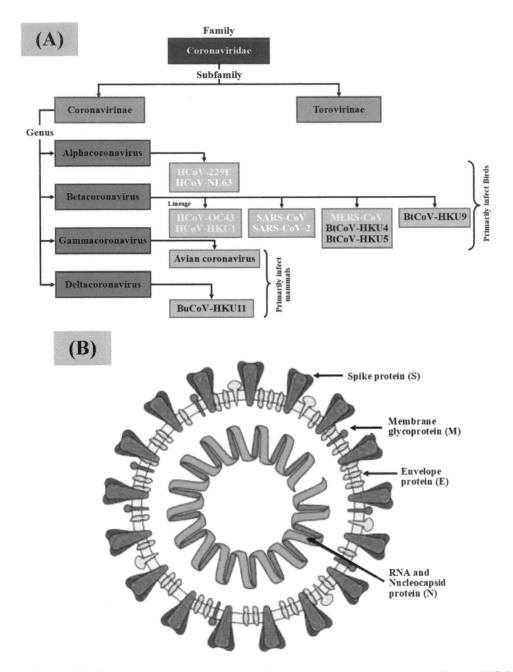

FIGURE 2.4 (A) Classification of coronaviruses: The seven known human coronaviruses (HCoVs) are shown in yellow and white. HCoVs in yellow text the host receptor ACE2. (B) Schematic of the SARS-CoV- 2 structure, the virus illustration is adapted from "Desiree Ho, Innovative Genomics Institute," Accessible at: https://innovativegenomics.org/free-covid-19-illustrations/. (Continued)

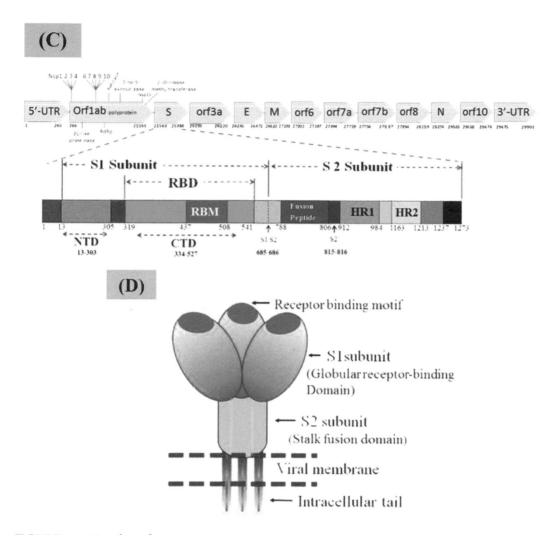

FIGURE 2.4 (Continued) (C) Schematic of SARS-CoV-2 genome (top) and spike protein (base); annotations are adapted from the NCBI (NC_045512.2) and Expasy (https://covid-19.uniprot.org/uniprotkb/P0DTC2), respectively. (D) Cartoon depicts key features and the trimeric structure of the SARS-CoV-2 spike protein.

This sort of phylogenetic characterization can possibly precisely follow the contamination courses and will demonstrate accommodating in planning medicines and immunization advancement (Forster et al., 2020).

KEY FEATURES AND ENTRY MECHANISM OF HUMAN CORONAVIRUSES

Some specific genes in ORF1 downstream regions contains by all the coronaviruses that encode proteins for viral replication, nucleocapsid, and the formation of spikes (van Boheemen et al., 2012). The glycoprotein spikes on the external surface of coronaviruses are liable for the connection and passage of the infection to the host cells (Figure 2.4(B)). The RNA-binding domain (RBD) is inexactly appended among infections, hence, the infection may infect various hosts (Perlman & Netland, 2009; Raj et al., 2013). On the other hands some other coronaviruses generally perceive aminopeptidases or carbohydrates as a main source of receptor as the entrance to the human cells while SARS-CoV and MERS-CoV perceive exopeptidases (Wang et al., 2013). The virus of corona diseases entry mechanism relies on cell proteases that incorporate, human aviation route trypsin (HAT)-like protease, cathepsins, and the transmembrane protease serine 2 (TMPRSS2) that split the spike protein and set up further infiltration changes (Bertram et al., 2011; Glowacka et al., 2011). MERS-CoV utilizes dipeptidyl peptidase 4 (DPP4), while HCoV-NL63 and SARS-CoV require angiotensin-converting enzyme 2 (ACE2) as a main source of receptor (Raj et al., 2013; Wang et al., 2013).

SARS-CoV-2 has the ordinary coronaviruses structure with spike protein and furthermore communicated different polyproteins, nucleoproteins, and membrane proteins, for example, RNA polymerase, 3-chymotrypsin-like protease, papain-like protease, helicase, glycoprotein, and extra proteins (Wu et al., 2020; Zhou et al., 2020). In the region of RDB SARS-CoV-2 virus contains a 3-D structure of spike protein to preserve the van der Waals powers (Xu et al., 2020). The 394 glutamine buildup in the region of RBD for SARS-CoV-2 that perceived by the basic lysine 31 buildup on the human ACE2 receptor (Wan et al., 2020). The existing pattern of pathogenicity of SARS-CoV-2, from connection to replication, is covered with well mentioned form referenced in Figure 2.5.

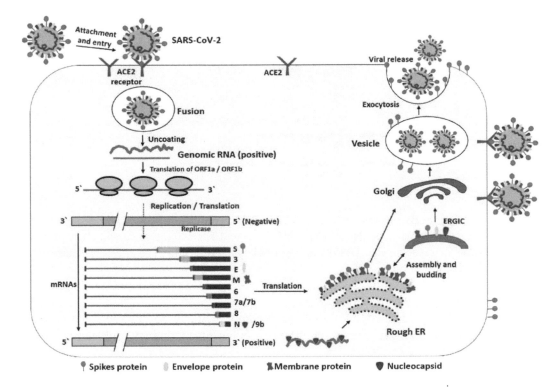

FIGURE 2.5   The patter of SARS-CoV-2 life cycle in host cells; starts its existence pattern when S protein ties to the cell receptor ACE2. After receptor binding, the adaptation change in the S protein encourages viral envelope combination with the cell film through the endosomal pathway. At that point SARS-CoV-2 deliveries RNA into the host cell. Genome RNA is converted into viral replicas polyproteins pp1a and 1ab that are then separated into tiny items by viral proteinases. The polymerase creates a progression of sub genomic mRNAs by irregular record lastly converted into pertinent viral proteins. Viral proteins and genome RNA are accordingly gathered into virions in the ER and Golgi and afterward moved by means of vesicles and delivered out of the cell.[1]

MORPHOLOGY, GENOMIC STRUCTURE, AND ITS VARIATION OF SARS-CoV-2

GENOME SEQUENCING

The SARS-CoV-2 genome sequence began with the early phase of the outbreak at Wuhan, China. The bronchoalveolar lavage liquid examples were gathered from the underlying patients. The quantitative PCR (qPCR) measures with pan CoV primers, including RNA dependent RNA polymerase (RdRp) preliminaries were used as the main stage for affirmation of CoV as a causative microbe or pathogen. Entire genome sequencing completed utilizing cutting edge sequencing stages Illumina sequencer and nanopore sequencing innovation. Zhu and Zhou with their research team announced the early genome sequence of SARS-CoV2 with rough size 29,891 bp. These sequences are submitted to Global Initiative on Sharing All Influenza Data (GISAID) with promotion number: EPI_ISL_402119; EPI_ISL_402120; EPI_ISL_402121; EPI_ISL_402124 and EPI_ISL_402127-402130 (Zhou et al., 2020; Zhu et al., 2020).

After these underlying entries of genome sequences of SARS-CoV2, numerous entries from around the world have shown up in GISAID. The numbers are expanding with the spread of the infection. By the cutoff date of this chapter, in excess of 17,000 genome sequences were submitted to GISAID. With more entries of sequencing information strain 90 varieties, transformations and their effect on pathogenicity can be concentrated for the controlling of this pandemic.

GENOME STRUCTURE

All the coronaviruses including the latest virus SARS-CoV-2 are wrapped infections with a genome size around 30 kb and have jutting spikes for association with the host cells (De Haan et al., 1998). The SARS-CoV-2 contains a positive-sense single-abandoned RNA genome secured by an encompassed structure. As referenced, the state of SARS-CoV-2 is either pleomorphic or circular and is described by club-molded (or crown-like) projections of surface glycoproteins (Wu et al., 2020). The 9860 amino acids have been encoded by genomic RNA. The GC content is exceptionally low for example 38.02%. SARS-CoV-2 genomic RNA comprises of 5′-cap and 3′-poly-A tail structure. This progressive sense RNA is utilized as a format for interpretation in the host. The quantity of open reading frames (ORF) genomic RNA has fluctuated over the CoVs yet at least six ORFs are accounted for this purpose. The first ORF is the longest and possesses right around the two-third segment of the genome encoding polyprotein 1a/b (ppa1a/b). From ppa1a/b polyprotein, 16 nonstructural proteins (NSP) are integrated. The NSP structures a replication-record complex including two proteases papain-like protease (NSP3) and main protease (Mpro) is also called 3CLpro (NSP5) and one RNA dependent RNA polymerase (NSP12). The rest of the part of the genome encodes four crucial structures of the proteins-spike (S), layer (M), envelope (E), and nucleocapsid (N) proteins alongside embellishment proteins (Figure 2.6(A)) (Khailany et al., 2020; Xiao et al., 2020). The examinations between SARS-CoV-2 and the related SARS-CoV uncover around 380 amino acids substitute. These, nsp2 and nsp3 proteins are demonstrated 61 and 102 amino acids substitute individually. Besides, 27 amino acids substitute are likewise situated in spike proteins, while no sub situation happened in nsp7, nsp13, envelope protein, matrix, and accessory proteins p6 and 8b. The assessments of the amino acids substitute in various proteins could illuminate how these distinctions influence the harmfulness and pathogenesis of SARS-CoV 2 (Wu et al., 2020). The different segments of the viral genome are discussed in detail in next section.

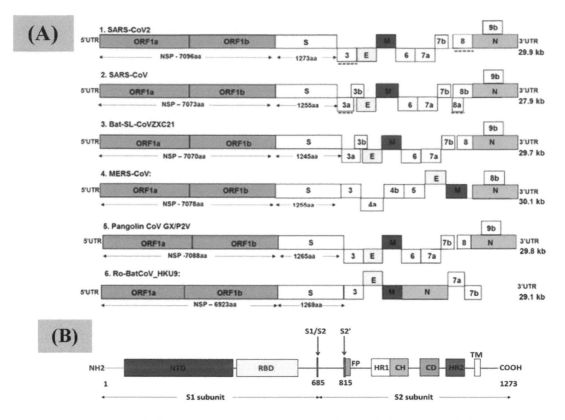

FIGURE 2.6 (A) The viral genome structure and its comparison with different CoVs: Coronaviruses contain a affirmative sense, ssRNA genome fluctuating from 27-32kb in size. The genome includes 5′ and 3′ untranslated regions (UTR), ORF 1a/b (blue boxes) containing two-third of the genome and encodes the polyprotein pp1ab and pp1a which is additionally severed into 16 NSPs engaged with viral RNA replication and record. The auxiliary proteins are encoded by four basic qualities present at 3′ end including Spike (S), Envelope (E), Membrane (M), and Nucleocapsid (N) qualities which are regular highlights to all CoVs. Among these, the S protein assumes a significant part in infection connection and entry; E protein encourages get together and morphogenesis of virions inside the cell; M protein capacities in the recovery of virions in the cell, and N protein assumes a function during virion gathering through its cooperations with viral genome and M protein. Likewise, the adornment qualities interspaced between the basic qualities encode for extra proteins which change in various CoVs regarding the number and are unimportant for infection replication. The examination of coding regions of SARS-CoV-2 with various CoVs demonstrated a comparable genome association to SARS-CoV, Bat SL-CoVZXC21, and Pangolin CoV GX/P2V. There is no amazing contrast in the ORF1 of various CoVs; however, it encodes for NSPs of variable lengths and there is a differentiation in the accessory genes. The red dabbed line shows the remarkable variety between SARS-CoV2 and SARS-CoV; (B) A schematic portrayal of SARS-CoV-2 S protein. The spike protein comprises of S1 and S2 regions. The S1 area contains a N Terminal Domain-NTD (red box) and a C-space or receptor-binding domain (yellow box) answerable for the acknowledgment and authoritative to the host cell receptor (ACE2). The S2 subunit answerable for film combination, contains the combination peptide-FP (dark box), heptad repeat 1 - HR1 (white box), central helix-CH (green), connector domain CD (blue box), heptad repeat 2 - HR2 (earthy colored box), and transmembrane domain TM. Cleavage locales at S1/S2 limit (R685) and S2′ (R815) are demonstrated with dark arrows. (Continued)

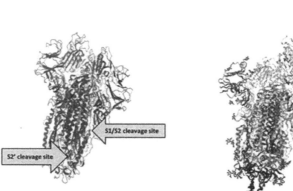

approximate positions of the
cleavage points in the SARS-Cov S1
spike protein superimposed on the
PDB entry 5XLR.

PDB entry 6VYB
SARS-CoV-2 spike ectodomain
structure (open state)

FIGURE 2.6 (Continued)   (C) The Spike Glycoprotein of SARS-CoV (left) and SARS-CoV-2 (right), Showing the two Proteolytic Cleavage Sites settled in SARS-CoV. The Arginine (R) in the monitored theme KRSFIEDLLFNKV is the cleavage point in S2′.

ACCESSORY PROTEINS

Extra genes protein-coding are available in the middle of the structural genes; however, predominantly grouped at 3′ finish of the genome. They are believed to be replaceable however they should have some fundamental part in the life cycle of the virus as they have held their situation in the genome very well over the CoVs. Explicit elements of some extra proteins are tentatively revealed and their conceivable part to counter-attack the immune response of the host. A large portion of the CoVs contains eight extra proteins yet some embellishment proteins are communicated specifically in some coronaviruses only (Lai & Cavanagh, 1997). To encoding the ORFs there have six accessory proteins that are annotated in SARS-CoV-2 including 3, 6, 7a, 7b, 8b, and 9b (Kim et al., 2020). The SARS-CoV and SARS-CoV2 shows variations in accessory proteins (Figure 2.6(A)). For example, 8a protein is absent in SARS-CoV2 and 8b is 37 amino acid longer as compare to SARS-CoV (Shereen et al., 2020; Wu et al., 2020). The impact of these minor variations from the SARS-CoV-2 infectivity and pathogenicity hasn't been built up. In the past investigations there have different CoVs that recognized the functions of extras protein. For instance, 3a and 7a are known to have capacities like particle channel action, up-guideline of host aggravation controllers like NF-$\kappa\beta$, and acceptance of host cell apoptosis (Narayanan et al., 2008). Thus, further investigation may give an association between varieties in embellishment proteins and a serious extent of harmfulness that appeared by SARS-CoV-2. It might likewise feature the capacity of CoV to cross the species hindrances (Song et al., 2005).

   The theory that whether amino acid substitute in spike proteins have the potential for producing SARS-CoV-2 with superinfection capacity is as yet deserving of future examinations.

Structural Proteins Of Viral

S Protein

The spike glycoprotein (or simply called "spike protein") is the natural spike that studs the outside of the coronavirus, its presence provides a crown to electron microscopy, henceforth "corona" (Latin: crown). CoVs makes an entry section in the host cell by emergent in their S protein with the host receptors. The S proteins considered as class 1 transmembrane proteins that distend widely from the infection envelope. These trimeric proteins are made out of three regions named, region of ectodomain, region of transmembrane, and the domain of intracellular. As of late cryo-electron microscopy uncovered the structure of S protein proposing it can make pivot like development bringing about changes among "up" and "down" affirmations (Yuan et al., 2020). The domain of intracellular shows a short intracellular tail. The region of ectodomain has S1 and S2 as subdomains. The subdomain S1 area of spike protein perform like a significant surface antigen. Two subunits contains by this subdomain named, N terminal domain (NTD) and C terminal domain (CTD) (Li, 2016). The subunit of S1-CTD performs like a RBD, and this RBD connects with the 18 deposits of ACE-2 (Lan et al., 2020). Protection of RBDs are done by the glycosylation which is generally seen in viral glycoproteins including S proteins from SARS-CoV and HIV-1. Yet, the glycosylation level of SARS-CoV-2 S protein is low as a contrast with HIV-1 S protein (Watanabe et al., 2020). On the other hand the subdomain S2 having a subunit named membrane fusion. It contains the fusion-peptide-FP, heptad repeat 1-HR1, central helix-CH, connector domain-CD, heptad repeat 2- HR2 and transmembrane domain-TM. There are two sites of cleavage, one site at the boundary of S1/S2 (R685) and second site at S2′ (R815) see Figure 2.6(C) (Coutard et al., 2020; Li, 2016). In addition left side of the Figure 2.6(C) shows the SARS-CoV (past SARS) S1 spike glycoprotein inside the trimer that makes up the spike and right side of the Figure 2.6(C) shows SARS-CoV-2 (present SARS). All the human SARS coronaviruses (and for sure the spike proteins of numerous other related coronaviruses) seem comparable in generally speaking adaptation, and the varieties seen in exploratory structures are most likely more to do with crystallization or other planning strategies, especially in regards to dissolvable subtleties and ligands. SARS-CoV, on the left, has been all around considered and still fills in as the reference model. So as to meld with and infected cells, the spike protein should be in an open state; apparently, the shut state makes it less helpless against antibodies. Likewise on the left Figure 2.6(C) shows the surmised position of the cleavage focuses superimposed on the Protein Data Bank (PDB) entry 5XLR for SARS-CoV. Perusing from the N-terminus of S1, the significant practical components of SARS coronaviruses reasoned from SARS-CoV contemplates and its material is applicable to SARS-CoV-2 that are the S1-NTD, S1-CTD, S1/S2 site as the initial protease sites of cleavage as a cycle between a pleated sheet and a-helix, the fusion peptide (FP) related with an exceptionally cluttered cycle between two a-helices which contains the subsequent site of cleavage S20, and a heptad repeat (HR). The Arginine (R) in the monitored theme KRSFIEDLLFNKV that was of enthusiasm for the past examination that act like a cleavage point in S2′.

The heptad repeat trimerizes to shape a looped coil structure and hauls infection envelope just as the host cell bilayer to closeness, and fusion encouragement (Eckert & Kim, 2001). The boundaries of subunits S1 and S2 presents a furin cleavage site (RRAR). This site recognizes SARS-CoV-2 from SARS-CoV and different coronaviruses. Additional features of SARS-CoV-2 is the expansion of proline buildup toward

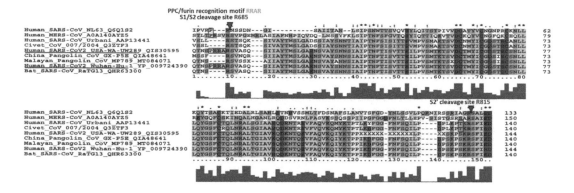

FIGURE 2.7 The numerous sequence arrangements of spike glycoprotein S1/S2 and S2′ sites of cleavage.

the beginning of the furin cleavage site see Figure 2.7 (Bagdonaite & Wandall, 2018; Walls et al., 2020).

The proprotein convertase (PPC) or furin motif RRAR including with the leading proline inclusion is exceptional to SARS-CoV-2 (PRRA inclusion featured in the red box) despite the fact that NL63 and MERS have proline without extra essential buildups. Such a polybasic sites of cleavage is missing in different beta coronaviruses including a bat, Chinese just as Malayan pangolin, and even past human coronaviruses. The cleavage site of S2′, i.e., R815 is moderated over all the arrangements examined, be that as it may, SARS-CoV-2, bat, and pangolin has KPSKR, and civet and hSARS-CoV has KPTKR.

This embedded proline makes a turn that is anticipated to bring about O-linked glycosylation at positions S673, T678, and S686. O-linked glycan may contribute to the solid protection of SARS CoV-2 epitopes (Andersen et al., 2020).

SARS-CoV-2 S protein amino acid sequence is 76% indistinguishable with SARS-CoV while it shows greater character for example 97% with bat coronavirus RaTG13. Curiously, this identity between SARS-CoV and SARS-CoV-2 diminishes in the region of RBD see Figure 2.8. Around 74% of indistinguishable RBD conceivably discloses why they tie to two distinct receptors on the host cells (Ou et al., 2020). For the situation of SARS-CoV,

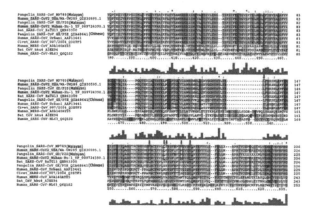

FIGURE 2.8 Multiple sequence arrangements of SARS-CoV-2 receptor binding domain of spike glycoprotein (S) build utilizing Clustal X2.

it has been seen that transformations in RBD can happen to receive with host cells during entry in cell culture (Cui et al., 2019; Sheahan et al., 2008). Thus hypothetically it is conceivable that SARS-CoV-2 picked up the changes in RBD as a transformation during cross-species transmission. Changes in RBD do not just upgrade the auxiliary strength of S protein however it can likewise debilitate the official of the immunizer raised against the strain (Ou et al., 2020). After the underlying collaboration between the domain of S1 space to a 208 and the host receptor Angiotensin-converting enzyme 2 (ACE-2), S2 fragment intercede layer combination of the host, and the viral film that permits the CoV RNA genome to enter inside the host cells (Lan et al., 2020).

Contact amino corrosive residues of RBD, aide of the ACB2 receptor, are separated with red boxes. Each of the six amino acid residues precisely coordinate with Malayan pangolin CoV strains MP789 ((Liu et al., 2020); NCBI acc no: MT084071) and GD/P2S ((Lam, et al., 2020); GISAID acc no: EPI_ISL_410544), both the examples instigated from the Guangdong Wildlife Rescue Center. The protection of these Malayan Pangolins headed by Anti-sneaking Customs Bureau in March 2019. This recommends the hereditary strain of SARS-CoV-2 may have tainted Malayan pangolins.

E Protein

A small form of polypeptide defined the E protein, which comes under the range of 8.4–12 kDa, which comprises under the two specified domains named the hydrophobic transmembrane domain and the charged cytoplasmic tail. The E protein is one of the most preserved proteins over the examined CoVs, henceforth shows normal trademark highlights and capacities among them. For example, SARS-CoV E protein is indistinguishable from SARS CoV-2 aside from four different variations (which are not expected to influence any component or capacity of E protein). Along these features that appeared by SARS-CoV including particle channel movement that are likewise thought to be displayed by SARS-CoV-2 E protein (Alam et al., 2020; Wilson et al., 2004). Coronaviruses E protein has another interesting capacity of "oligomerization" bringing about the development of viroporin (Nieva et al., 2012). The capability of viroporins are to specifically move particles like Ca_2^+ and take an interest in the collecting and arrival of infection particles from host cells (Pham et al., 2017; (Wu et al., 2003; Zhang et al., 2014) The coronavirus E protein is likewise known to add to pathogenesis. It takes an interest in expanding the protein collapsing load on the endoplasmic reticulum (ER). This outcome in mistaken protein collapsing rising into a condition known as unfolded protein reaction (UPR). UPR may at last prompt apoptosis (Fung & Liu, 2014). Such pathogenesis by SARS-CoV E protein is tentatively confirmed in cells contaminated with changed strains rSARS-CoV and rSARS CoV-E and can be investigated for SARS-CoV-2 too (DeDiego et al., 2011). Advance, E protein partakes in the development of specific structure ER–Golgi intermediate compartment (ERGIC) encouraging the arrival of the developed infection (Jiang et al., 2020).

M Protein

The M glycoprotein is one another most important 242 nt constituent of the coronavirus. Being the significant component of the envelope, by connecting with S and E protein the virion envelope accommodates the characteristics shape. The M protein is a multi-spanning membrane protein which is described by three domains of transmembrane having a

C terminal inside and N terminal outside. The third domain of transmembrane contains a region of amphipathic toward the end. This region discovered to be profoundly preserved across coronaviridae individuals. Aside from this region, another region of M protein expressions changeability in protein successions, however strangely these varieties don't affect optional structure of CoV M proteins (Arndt et al., 2010). When the SARS-CoV-2 M protein succession was contrasted and that of bat coronavirus RaTG13 and Malayan pangolin coronavirus MP789, the special inclusion of a Ser residue is seen at N terminal. In addition, arrangement additionally demonstrated replacements at position 70, which is anticipated to be an aspect of the domain of transmembrane. It has been recommended that such transformations in the N-terminal and domain of transmembrane, which are presented to the surface, may have added to the cross-species move of the SARS-CoV-2 (Bianchi et al., 2020). With interactions among various proteins, M protein assumes a significant function in viral gathering and it's inside homeostasis (Lan et al., 2020). Transmembrane is just as endodomain of M protein, partake in protein to protein association (De Haan et al., 2000). It has been likewise realized that coronavirus M proteins can communicate with RNAs, which encodes data about genome pressing signs (Narayanan et al., 2003). These outcomes uphold their focal function in the gathering of the virion particles. As one of the significant proteins of the coronaviruses, it is estimated to be associated with the guideline of replication and pressing of RNA into developed infection particles (Hu et al., 2003). It has been proven that M proteins can embrace two auxiliary affirmations named compact and elongated. Compact M proteins are oftentimes connected with a low thickness of S proteins when contrasted with lengthened ones (Neuman et al., 2011). Such affirmation should be concentrated in SARS-CoV-2. The M protein from SARS-CoV is accounted for to communicate with nuclear factor kappa B (NF-κB) of the host cells, bringing down the quality articulation of cyclooxygenase 2 (Cox 2). Additionally, M protein may add to pathogenesis by commandeering NF-κB and Cox-2 intervened have incendiary reaction (Fang et al., 2007). Being exceptionally like that of SARS-CoV, SARS-CoV-2 M protein may have a comparative part in pathogenesis.

N Protein

The range of N protein considered from 43 to 50 kDa and thought to impasse genomic RNA. On the whole, it is partitioned into three moderated domains named N arm, central linker (CL), and C tail. The N terminal domain (NTD) and C terminal domain (CTD) are the significant structural and utilitarian domain. The functional capacity of the NTD is the binding of RNA and its significant part is involved by decidedly charged amino acids. The CTD intervenes the dimerization of N protein with self-association and contains an atomic limitation signal. The CTD takes a significant part in nucleocapsid protein oligomerization and N-M protein connections. The region of CL is thought to communicate with M protein (Surjit & Lal, 2008). The SARS-CoV-2 N protein sequence of amino acid is roughly 90% indistinguishable with SARS-CoV (Kang et al., 2020). The functional features of N protein incorporate replication and record of viral RNA, arrangement, and support of the ribonucleoprotein (RNP) complex (Lan et al., 2020). Moreover, it is additionally revealed that N proteins are associated with host infection cooperation. They direct host cell cycle including apoptosis to encourage infection augmentation and spread (McBride et al., 2014).

STRUCTURE, FUNCTION, ANTIGENICITY, AND ACE2 RECOGNITION BY THE SARS- CoV-2 SPIKE GLYCOPROTEIN

The spike protein is a multifunctional molecular/sub-atomic machine that assumes key functions in the early strides of viral disease by associating with have vulnerability factors, including receptors and proteases, and in this way tainting human cells containing angiotensin-converting enzyme 2 (hACE2) transmembrane proteins (Lam et al., 2020) The SARS-CoV-2 S protein is a transmembrane glycoprotein composed through the region of S1 that contains the NTD and CTD, S2, a region of transmembrane, and a short cytoplasmic domain see Figure 2.9(c) and (d). Both cryo-EM and crystallographic techniques have been utilized to decide numerous structures of the SARS-CoV-2 spike protein alone, for example, the ectodomain of S protein (SARS-CoV-2 S protein), receptor binding domain of S protein (SARS-CoV-2-S1-CTD), or in complex with full-length ACE2 or dissolvable ACE2/B°AT1, in a brief timeframe. These auxiliary investigations empower to comprehend the fundamentals of molecular of SARS-CoV-2 passage into human cells showing ACE2 receptors (Lan et al., 2020; Wong et al., 2020; Zhang et al., 2020; Zhao et al., 2020). Various structures of SARS-CoV-2-S were seen in numerous states (the pre-fusion, shut, and halfway open compliances and in complex with hACE2 receptor) with the RBDs either in "up" or "down" adaptation see Figure 2.9(a) and (b). The considerable point here is that to draw in the ACE2 receptor,

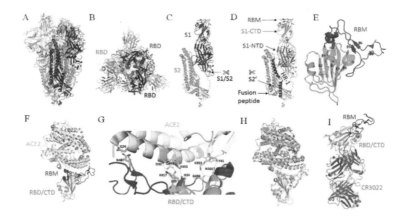

FIGURE 2.9   Spike protein structure of the SARS-CoV-2 individual and with the complex ACE2 receptor. (a) Side perspective on the trimeric SARS-CoV-2 spike ectodomain in the pre-fusion state (PDB ID: 6VSB). The protomer in green is in the "up" compliance and the other two protomers in red and cyan are in "down" adaptation. (b) The top perspective on the trimeric spike protein demonstrating receptor binidn domain (RBDs) in red, blue, and green on each protomer. (c) Structure of a solitary protomer indicating the receptor-restricting subunit S1 in blue and the subunit of membrane fusion is S2 in green. The Furin-like protease site at the limit of S1/S2 subunits is portrayed. (d) The S1 subunit contains the receptor-binding motif (RBM) in the CTD area in blue and the region of NTD is in the sand. The subunit of S2 contains the combination peptide in red, second cleavage site S2′ in dark, and HR1 in pink. (e) RBD structure, center subdomain in green, and RBM in blue (PDB ID: 6LZG). (f) SARS-CoV-2-RBD in complex structure with the ACE2 receptor (PDB ID: 6LZG). (g) SARS-CoV-2-RBD: ACE2 receptor polar interface appeared by explicit deposits. (h) The structural likeness between the SARS-CoV-RBD: hACE2 (green) and SARS-CoV-2-S-CTD: hACE2 (yellow) buildings. (i) Crystal structure of the SARS-CoV-2-RBD (green) in complex with a monoclonal immune response CR3022 (orange). The RBM and CR3022 restricting locales don't cover and are remotely situated on the RBD (PDB ID: 6W41). To prepare these figures utilized Pymol environment.

the RBDs of S1 goes through pivot like developments that either cover up or uncover the regions of receptor bindings, and these adaptations are alluded to as "up" (receptor available) or "down" (receptor unavailable) compliances. SARS-CoV-2 S protein structures show that protein receives a clover molded homotrimeric structure, with three S1 heads that perceive a related cell surface receptor and a membrane tied down trimeric S2 tail, which contains the combination of hardware and is fundamentally α-helical see Figure 2.9(c) and (d) (Lan et al., 2020). During the pre-fusion compliance of SARS-CoV-2 S protein, the RBDs rest over the trimeric S2 tail, showing two protomers in the "down" adaptation and one protomer in the "up" adaptation, which is a state of receptor-accessibility that required for the official to an ACE2 receptor (Lan et al., 2020). In all S ectodomain of the SARS-CoV-2 takes after the firmly related SARS-CoV S protein structure with a root mean square deviation (RMSD) of 3.8 Å more than 959 Cα molecules, with a serious extent of basic homology when singular spaces of SARS-CoV S protein and SARS-CoV-2 S protein were adjusted (Lan et al., 2020).

SARS-CoV-2 S Protein CTD Interactions With Human ACE2 Receptor

Various structures of SARS-CoV-2 S protein CTD in complex with either full-length hACE2 or solvent hACE2 have demonstrated that the extracellular peptidase domain (PD) of ACE2 perceives the RBDs of S protein predominantly through polar communications (Wong et al., 2020; Zhang et al., 2020). Some other beta coronaviruses structure like SARS-CoV-2 S protein CTD recommended that they comprises two subdomains: a center subdomain with twisted five-abandoned antiparallel β sheet (β1, β2, β3, β4, and β7) with a saved disulfide connection between β2-β4, and the other is receptor bending motif (RBM), situated somewhere in the range of β4 and β7 strand as an all-inclusive addition see Figure 2.9(e). The RBM structures a tenderly inward surface that obliges the N-terminal α-helix of the hACE2, and a progression of hydrophilic buildups was seen alongside the interface which shapes a strong organization of H-bond and salt scaffolds connections see Figure 2.9(f). In a nutshell, solid polar contacts incorporate CTD deposits A475, N487, E484, Y453 interfacing with S19, Q24, K31, H34 of α1 helix of hACE2, separately (Lai & Cavanagh, 1997). Residues Q498, T500, N501 on the lump cyclic frames an organization of H-bonds with Y41, Q42, K353, R357 from ACE2 (Wong et al., 2020). Hence, all infection receptor communications are overwhelmed by polar contacts intervened by hydrophilic buildups see Figure 2.9(g) (Lai & Cavanagh, 1997; Wong et al., 2020; Zhang et al., 2020).

Correlation Of The SARS-CoV-2-RBD And SARS-CoV-RBD Interaction With Human ACE2 Receptor

Most of the optional structure components between SARS-CoV-S-RBD (PDB ID: 2AJF) and SARS-CoV-2 S protein CTD (PDB ID: 6LZG, 6M17) are all around superimposed, with a RMSD of 0.475 Å more than 128 Cα molecules, aside from the receptor-binding cycle. Curiously, these structures uncovered that most of the restricting locales of SARS-CoV RBD in hACE2 additionally cover with the SARS-CoV-2 S- protein CTD restricting destinations recommending that the SARS-CoV-2 S protein CTD: hACE2 complex is strikingly like the SARS-CoV-RBD: ACE2 structure with a RMSD of 0.431 Å more than 669 Cα molecules see Figure 2.9(g) and (h). However, in spite of the general similitude, various sequence varieties were seen at the coupling interface that may represent the adjustment in the affinities for hACE2 receptors. The deep examination of the receptor binding interfaces recommended that the SARS CoV-2 S protein CTD: ACE2 complex (PDB ID: 6VW1, 6M17) has bigger covered surface areas (1773 Å2 versus 1686 Å2), has extra contacts (21 versus 17), more Van Der Waals collaborations (288 versus 213) as wells as H-bonds (16 versus 1) than the SARS-CoV-RBD: hACE2 (PDB ID: 2AJF) complex (Zhang et al., 2020). Strikingly, build-ups F486 in SARS-CoV-2 S protein CTD structures more grounded fragrant sweet-smelling associations with Y83 of hACE2 than I472 of SARS-CoV-RBD. Buildup E484 in the SARS-CoV-2 S protein CTD structures more grounded ionic collaborations with K31 contrasted with P470 of SARS-CoV-RBD (Zhang et al., 2020). An example gathered from the province of Kerala, India on January 27, 2020, indicated Arg408→ Ile408 change in the SARS-CoV-2 S protein (GenBank ID: MT012098.1), which in any case is a carefully preserved buildup in SARS-CoV, SARS-CoV-2, and bat SARS-like coronaviruses. The deposits R408 is situated close to the coupling interface of both, the SARS-CoV-2-S-CTD: hACE2 (PDB: 6VW1) and SARS-CoV-RBD: hACE2 (PDB: 2AJF), buildings and shows up not to cooperate legitimately with hACE2 in either case. In any case, R408 structures a H-bond (3.3 Å) with the glycan appended to N90 from hACE2; in this way, adds to higher affinities watched for SARS-CoV-2 S protein CTD: hACE2 complex than the SARS-CoV-RBD: ACE2 complex, where the comparing R395 is found moderately away (6.1 Å) from N90 of hACE2. Arg408→ Ile408 change that rose in the SARS-CoV-2 strain (GenBank ID: MT012098.1) recommended that a higher hydrophobicity with no H-bond framing potential speaks to an example with conceivably decreased ACE2 restricting affinity. Reliable with high auxiliary similitudes, restricting examinations from various labs have announced that balance separation constants (KD) of hACE2 official to SARS-CoV-2-S is 15 nM (Lan et al., 2020) or 94.6 nM (Zhang et al., 2020) or 4.7 nM (Lai & Cavanagh, 1997), which are ~10 or 4 or 6-fold higher affinities, separately than SARS CoV S protein.

By utilizing the cryo-EM strategy for the structure of full-length hACE2 in complex with SARS CoV-2 S protein CTD and B°AT1 (nonpartisan amino acid transporter) was resolved, which uncovered that the ACE2: B°AT1complex is gathered as a dimer of heterodimers, where the collectrin-like area of hACE2 drives homodimerization (PDB ID: 6M17) (Wong et al., 2020). The SARS-CoV-2 S protein CTD is perceived by the extracellular PD of ACE2 as portrayed already. Further, it shows that a homodimeric ACE2 can oblige two S protein trimers, each through a monomer of ACE2 (Wong et al., 2020). Stimulatingly, a superimposition of the ternary complex on RBD in the "down" adaptation has demonstrated that PD conflicts with the S protein, while in the "up" compliance (PDB 6VSB) and no conflicts observed there. So the recommending point is that the "up" affirmation of RBD is a receptor-accessible state and is fundamental for the ACE2-receptor binding. Consider them collectively, then the general interface between SARS-CoV-2 S protein CTD: ACE2 is fundamentally the same as the recently known SARS-CoV-RBD: ACE2 interface, and are overwhelmed by the polar collaborations as announced by various examinations (Lai & Cavanagh, 1997; Wong et al., 2020; Zhang et al., 2020). These bits of proof further recommend that SARS-CoV-2 S protein CTD has expanded nuclear communications with hACE2, which brings about higher affinities contrasted with the SARS-CoV-RBD: hACE2 complex, which may be one of the reasons for improved human-to-human transmission of SARS-CoV-2.

EXHIBITS DISTINCT EPITOPE FEATURES OF SARS-CoV-2 ON THE RBD FROM SARS-CoV

Numerous authoritative and balance epitopes have been recognized in the past time on the spike protein of coronaviruses that makes the S protein a basic objective for antibody plan

(Hussain et al., 2020; Xu et al., 2020; Zou et al., 2020). Shortly after the rise of COVID-19 pandemic, a portion of the underlying endeavors were centered on screening the SARS-CoV S protein explicit antibodies to discover deactivating antibodies for immunization and medication advancement against SARS-CoV-2. The theory behind these examinations depended on the critical arrangement just as structure likenesses and, additionally, both infections tie to similar receptors with covering epitopes. Hence, it was normal that SARS-CoV explicit immune antibodies alone or in the combination can meddle or even hinder SARS-CoV-2 and hACE2 receptor communications.

This has been appeared in vitro also in one animal models that monoclonal antibodies, for example, 80R (Hoffmann et al., 2020), CR3014 (Ziegler et al., 2020), S230.15 and m396 (Lukassen et al., 2020) can impede authoritative of the S1 area and hACE2 receptors by strongly deactivating SARS-CoV. Conversely, CR3022 (Xia et al., 2020) alone didn't show balance yet the blend of CR3022 and CR3014 both demonstrated balance of SARS-CoV in a synergistic manner by perceiving various epitopes on the RBDs (Ziegler et al., 2020). So the considering point here is that, some report proposes that CR3022 can likewise deactivate SARS-CoV alone (Chen & Olsthoorn, 2010). Remarkably, some Chinese researchers tried a few distributed SARS-CoV explicit monoclonal antibodies and found that CR3022 can tie with the RBDs of SARS-CoV-2 with a KD of 6.3 nM, though different antibodies, for example, m396, CR3014, and S230.15 neglected to tie to the SARS-CoV-2 S protein (Lan et al., 2020). However, a low degree of authoritative to SARS-CoV-2-S was seen with a SARS-CoV-S1 explicit polyclonal immune response T62 (#40150-T62, Sino Biological Inc., Beijing, China) and it could ineffectively deactivate SARS-CoV-2 S protein-interceded infection passage. Further examination uncovered that the epitope for T62 likely situated on the RBDs of SARS-CoV-2 S protein, however itemized data is deficient (Krijnse-Locker et al., 1994). In an energizing examination, the Wilson research facility decided the gem structure of CR3022 counter acting agent in complex with SARS-CoV-2-RBD (PDB ID: 6W41) and uncovered that CR3022 ties a profoundly monitored epitope that is indirectly situated from the receptor-restricting site, which empowers cross-responsive authoritative, however, couldn't deactivating SARS-CoV-2 in vitro see Figure 2.9(i) (Chen & Olsthoorn, 2010). However, regardless of whether CR3022 can synergize with different SARS-CoV-2-RBD restricting antibodies for balance requires further assessment and study.

The SARS-CoV (GenBank: AY278488.2) and SARS-CoV-2 (GenBank: MN908947.3) spike proteins both offer about 76% amino acid sequence character proposing that rest 24% amino acids successions, which are non-saved may be answerable for antigenic contrasts between these two proteins. In the journey of discovering novel immunizer restricting epitopes on spike proteins, Zheng et al. performed antibody epitope examination, and surface epitope openness utilizing bioinformatics instruments to distinguish both frail and solid epitopes, which may be generally tentatively disregarded (Fang et al., 2007). Kuo and Masters examine and distinguished five shared epitopes alongside 40 and 29 one of a kind epitopes on the spike proteins of SARS-CoV and SARS-CoV-2, separately. Among these interesting epitopes, 92.7% were begun from non-rationed areas, which may clarify the motivation behind why the vast majority of the SARS-CoV explicit antibodies talked about in this audit didn't predicament to the spike protein of SARS-CoV-2 (Kuo & Masters, 2002). Consider collectively, these outcomes propose the need to create SARS-CoV-2 explicit antibodies and immunization. In next section chapter covers the various computational approaches that can helps to find a better solution to found antibodies and immunization technique through genome structure of SARS-CoV-2.

COMPUTATION APPROACH

Q-UEL METHODS

Theory Behind the General Strategy

Various thoughts and standards, acquired in built-up and plan of synthetic antibodies and petidomimetics, were utilized see Robson (2020a) for detailed description and e.g., Refs. (Westphal, 1986), (Kaliamurthi et al., 2019), (Mehmood et al., 2019), and (Chu et al., 2019), just as a portion of the thoughts that lie behind the mainstream ZINC database.[2] As discussed by researcher Robson in (Robson, 2020a), the current examination began as a utilization case for the Hyperbolic Dirac Net (HDN) and especially the related Q-UEL language for automate implication (Robson et al., 2013, 2016; Robson & Boray, 2015). The hypothesis has been talked about something else, for example, in Robson et al. (2013), Robson and Boray (2015), Robson (2016), and Robson and Boray (2018), which relate more to the useful and general employments of Q-UEL. These contemplations are less significant here in light of the fact that current examinations can be replicated by standard bioinformatics and molecular modeling. In any case, it is farfetched that the examination for Robson (2020a) could have been done and reviewed so quickly without the guide of Q-UEL to interface with sites of the World Wide Web, accumulate information, and encourage the utilization of the publically accessible bioinformatics instruments (Robson, 2020a).

Fundamental Principles of Epitope Prediction for Design of Synthetic Immunizations

The test is eventually one of molecular acknowledgment but in practice, several key standards for hapten configuration identify with recognizing kinds of the normally happening epitope. By the expression, "epitope" in this section is signified "continuous epitope," however, a few littler epitopes might be joined to speak to a broken epitope in which compliance and the relative situation in range can now and then be significant. While a synthetic build suggests the utilization of synthetic science normally joined with a sensible transporter protein to which the peptide is connected artificially, develops can likewise be acquired by cloning, utilizing the principle of protein engineering (Robson & Garnier, 1986). The B-epitope and T-epitope identify with the conventional image of a bone marrow B or thymus T reaction. B-cell epitopes happen at the outside of the protein against which a resistant framework reaction is required. They are perceived by B-cell receptors or antibodies in their local structure and are worried about the bone marrow reaction and antibodies creation. T epitopes might be covered inside protein structures and delivered by proteolysis, and are customarily considered as worried about a cell reaction and immune system memory, for example, dynamic invulnerability. Persistent B cell epitope forecast is fundamentally the same as T-cell epitope expectation. The attention is on B-epitopes here, however, a B-epitope can likewise be (or cover with) a T-epitope particularly in the event that it has a significant substance of hydrophobic deposits. The expectation of these has customarily been based and has principally been founded on the amino acids properties, for example, hydrophilicity, charge, uncovered surface zone, an auxiliary structure. There are numerous prescient algorithms accessible, yet the current creator favors a more "expert system" sort of approach that incorporates test information, however, the above biophysical contemplations surely still assume a solid job.

Q-UEL: A KNOWLEDGE REPRESENTATION TOOLKIT

The primary techniques are basically standard bioinformatics approaches as utilized by Robson (2020a,b). A few strategies, for example, rules for predicting epitope, are best talked about in setting in Results section. The Q-UEL techniques explicitly for bioinformatics are examined by Robson (2020b), and those for computational science and docking of mixes are those utilizing KRUNCH as depicted in Robson (2020a) and the informative supplement in Robson et al. (2011). They are to some degree unconventional by focusing on heuristics to deal with the numerous energy minimization issue, however, the end impact is most likely that of long runs utilizing high-grade of algorithms to calculate the molecular dynamics, given an opportunity for alignment Robson et al. (2011). Prediction of epitope lie in more conventional "one-dimensional" bioinformatics, and in this section and the past researches relied upon expectations utilizing a GOR4 auxiliary structure for prediction of α-helix (h), expanded chain, or β-sheet (e), and coil or circle (c). The explanation behind this and the specific utilization of GOR4 is examined by Robson (2020a), but in short, it is to a limited extent since area predicted by runs of c will in general be immunogenic regardless of whether they are wrong as structure prediction (Robson, 2020a). Conversely, the residues changes in α-helices and β-sheets are accepted to be incidentally B-epitopes, and short area broadened chain can successfully suggest cycles. The center and introductory standards for B-epitope forecast utilized in the current examination consider these

a. surface presentation when a three-dimensional structure is known, however taking into account conformational change in accordance with uncovering buildup when in a probably confused or adaptable cycle, scores ±2,
b. realized introduction dependent on different sorts of investigation, which likewise perceives the likelihood that an incompletely covered site by the above standards can be brought to the surface on authoritative, remarkably for proteolytic cleavage (Robson, 2020a), scores ±2,
c. runs of amino acid from the set [STNQY] score +1, from the set [DEKHR] they score ±2, and from the set [LIVFCM] they score −1,
d. runs of prediction auxiliary structure as coil or cycle c, however, runs of three or less e and the first and last three of helix h can be considered as c for this reason, score ±1, and
e. the motif NX(S/T)X of asparagine (N) serine (S) or threonine (T), where X signifies "not a proline" (P) scores ±2. However, this won't license a comparing peptidomimetic or immunization without considering glycopeptide synthesis innovation. See the conversation underneath, which would legitimize a negative score, contingent upon the innovation accessible.

Likewise, these might be joined with the predication based on critical homology with demonstrated epitopes in databases, which has just been finished by several groups for SARS-CoV-19 (Grifoni et al., 2020).

Sources Data and Material

For wellsprings of required data concerning about COVID-19 infection spike proteins, GenBank and the Protein Data Bank were the principle sources. There was some utilization of in-house pool of data, for example of ordinary B-epitopes and T-epitopes, albeit publically accessible database would presumably serve a similar capacity. There was likewise use additionally of a database of non-peptide ligand molecules of potential intrigue previously created during and since the work depicted by Robson et al. (2011), that was utilized this in proper manner. A considerable set of molecules (counting emodin) are likewise found on the public ZINC database[3] as demonstrated in results section, but few subordinates includes of carbenoxelone, are not, and these subordinates are of enthusiasm as potential coronaviruses antagonists. By considering an entry section of the ZINC database by the codes utilized during this section can go to http://zinc15.docking.org/substances/ and for example, that supported by Q-UEL, a variable, (for example, a Perl variable $mol) to ZINC00011032 and is set at the Q-UEL application goes to http://zinc15.docking.org/substances/search/?q=$mol. Any references to exploratory restricting outcomes concern data from Khan and Kumar (2019) for normal techniques utilized for common natural herbal compounds. As examined by Robson (2020a), Q-UEL helped assemble these as the knowledge representation tags of Q-UEL, so they become part of the developing information representation store.

Important Notation

Concerning peptides and proteins, Table 2.1 utilized by Robson (2020a) that shows the standard IUPAC one-letter codes utilized for sequences of amino acid residues in throughout the computation process under this section.

Traditionalist substitutions are those normal replacements from a peptide plan viewpoint, however, for instance, phenylalanine (F), isoleucine (I), and alanine (An) are viewed as common replacements that show up in the conversation through the sequence of spike

---

TABLE 2.1

One Letter Amino Acid Codes Used in the Text

One Letter Code	Amino Acid	Conservative Replacements
A	alanine	A, E, S, T
C	cysteine/cysteine	S, T, V
D	aspartic acid	E
E	glutamic acid	A, D
F	phenylalanine	M, W, Y
G	glycine	N, P
H	histidine	K, R
I	isoleucine	L, V
K	Lysine	H, R
L	leucine	I, V
M	methionine	F, W, Y
N	asparagine	G, D, Q
P	proline	G
Q	glutamine	N, E
R	arginine	H, K
S	serine	A, T
T	threonine	A, I, S
V	valine	A, I, L
W	tryptophan	F, M, Y
Y	tyrosine	F. M,

protein motifs. These amino acid buildups have hydrophobic sidechains yet they are not traditionalist substitutions but instead significantly various sizes. A sensible clarification is concern that sidechain size preservation matters less when the sidechains are uncovered at the outside of the protein. Comparable ideas underlie the possibility that what can promptly supplant what isn't generally an equivalent likelihood toward every path. In that regard, Table 2.1 will reflect the general progressions that are utilized in the current undertaking for the plan, when beginning from epitopes.

Results

Epitope Prediction

Researcher Robson (2020a) not considered the particular motifs (especially KRSFIEDLLFNKV), they discussed only section like the SARS-CoV-2 spike protein to be of enthusiasm for the above regard. The inclination for one decision depended on

a. protection across numerous strains, proposing that the site has significant capacity and is likely at the spike surface, and
b. maintaining a strategic distance from the protection of the spike protein by broad glycosylation.

The impact of loosening up these limitations is a significant purpose of this section, where countless candidates are found. Over-prediction isn't really a terrible thing, in light of the fact that once a research facility has a peptide synthesizer and different apparatuses for developing and testing plans, it is generally simple and modest to test and reject thoughts, and riskier to botch chances. The goal here is likewise to cover most prospects, to empower index numbers to be relegated to them as per their request in the sequence (putative epitope 1, and so forth). Subsequently, later on, one may then promptly allude to the index number, or talk about another proposition or exploratory epitope broadening, covering, or in any event, lying between two of these epitopes. They are principal to be viewed as B-epitope predictions, however, they are supported if some T-epitopic character is likewise anticipated.

As the practical approach, there was likewise some sensible utilization of ability and an epitope information base trying to refine tasks. Review that the trimeric SARS-CoV spike glycoprotein comprises of three S1–S2 heterodimers. A portion of these will be protected by that arrangement during the vast majority of the life cycle of the infection, however not really in each S protein monomer, and furthermore protected by glycosylation. The prediction of higher scoring epitopes in the sequence underneath are underlined and in bold font and are essentially to be considered as B-epitopes however with some expansion to incorporate T-epitope character where conceivable. Likewise remembered for these forecasts are those utilizing the Immune Epitope Database and Analysis Resource (IEDB) and the Virus Pathogen Resource (ViPR) which have been discussed in next sections. In Figure 2.10 these are appeared in underlined, bold, and in italics in the accompanying, and since some are contiguous sections that resemble a solitary long portrayal in the accompanying, they are likewise expressed independently below. It is evident that while the emphasis was on just KRSFIEDLLFNKV on the off chance that strain variety and glycosylation are overlooked, at that point a great part of the spike protein arrangement contains epitope candidates.

```
        10        20        30        40        50        60        70
         |         |         |         |         |         |         |
MFVFLVLLPLVSSQCVNLTTRTQLPPAYTNSFTRGVYYPDKVFRSSVLHSTQDLFLPFFSNVTWFHAIHV
cceeeeeecccccccccccccccccccccccccccccccceeecccccccccccccccccccceeeee
SGTNGTKRFDNPVLPFNDGVYFASTEKSNIIRGWIFGTTLDSKTQSLLIVNNATNVVIKVCEFQFCNDPF
ccccccccccccccccccccceeeccccccceeeeeeeecccccccceeeeecccceeeeeeecccccccce
LGVYYHKNNKSWMESEFRVYSSANNCTFEYVSQPFLMDLEGKQGNFKNLREFVFKNIDGYFKIYSKHTPI
eeeeeeecccceeeeeeeeeccccccceeeeccchhhhhhcccchhhhhheeecccccceeeccccccc
NLVRDLPQGFSALEPLVDLPIGINITRFQTLLALHRSYLTPGDSSSGWTAGAAAYYVGYLQPRTFLLKYN
ceeeccccccccccccccchhhhhhhhhhhhccccccccccchhhhhhhhhcccccchhhhhcc
ENGTITDAVDCALDPLSETKCTLKSFTVEKGIYQTSNFRVQPTESIVRFPNITNLCPFGEVFNATRFASV
cccceeeeeeccccccccccccccccccceecccccccccccccccccceecccccccccccceechh
YAWNRKRISNCVADYSVLYNSASFSTFKCYGVSPTKLNDLCFTNVYADSFVIRGDEVRQIAPGQTGKIAD
hhhhhhceeccccccccceeecccccccceeeecccccccccccccccccceeeccccceeeccccccceec
YNYKLPDDFTGCVIAWNSNNLDSKVGGNYNYLYRLFRKSNLKPFERDISTEIYQAGSTPCNGVEGFNCYF
cccccccceeeeeeecccccccccccchhhhhhhcccccccccceeeeeeecccccccccccccccee
PLQSYGFQPTNGVGYQPYRVVVLSFELLHAPATVCGPKKSTNLVKNKCVNFNFNGLTGTGVLTESNKKFL
cccccccccccccccceeeeecccccccccccceecccceeeecccccccceeeeeecccccc
PFQQFGRDIADTTDAVRDPQTLEILDITPCSFGGVSVITPGTNTSNQVAVLYQDVNCTEVPVAIHADQLT
cccccccccccccccccccccccccccccceeeecccccccccccceeecccccccceeccccc
PTWRVYSTGSNVFQTRAGCLIGAEHVNNSYECDIPIGAGICASYQTQTNSPRRARSVASQSIIAYTMSLG
S1/S2 SARS spike cleavage        PIGAGICASYHTVSLL----RSTSQKSIVAYTMSLG
                                                   ^
ceeeeeeccccceeeeecccceeccccccccccceecccccccccccccccccccccchhhhhhhccc
AENSVAYSNNSIAIPTNFTISVTTEILPVSMTKTSVDCTMYICGDSTECSNLLLQYGSFCTQLNRALTGI
cccceecccccccccccccccceeeeeeeeeccccccceeeeeecccccceeecccccceeecccchh
AVEQDKNTQEVFAQVKQIYKTPPIKDFGGFNFSQILPDPSKPSKRSFIEDLLFNKVTLADAGFIKQYGDC
S2' SARS spike cleavage          SGFNFSQILPDPLKPTKRSFIEDLLFNKVTLADAGFMKQYGEC
                                               ^
hhhhcchhhhhhhhhhhccccccccccccceeecccccccccchhhhhhhhhhhhhhhcchhhhcccc
LGDIAARDLICAQKFNGLTVLPPLLTDEMIAQYTSALLAGTITSGWTFGAGAALQIPFAMQMAYRFNGIG
cchhhhhhhhhhhhcccceecccccchhhhhhhhhhhhhcceeecccccccchhhhhhhhhhhhhhhcccc
VTQNVLYENQKLIANQFNSAIGKIQDSLSSTASALGKLQDVVNQNAQALNTLVKQLSSNFGAISSVLNDI
eeehhhhhhhhhhhhhcccccceeecchhhhhhhhhhhhhhhhhhhhhhhhhhhhhhcccccchhhhhhh
LSRLDKVEAEVQIDRLITGRLQSLQTYVTQQLIRAAEIRASANLAATKMSECVLGQSKRVDFCGKGYHLM
hhhhhhhhhhhhhhhhhhccccchhhhhhhhhhhhhhhhhhhhhhhhhhhhhhhhhccccceecccccccceee
SFPQSAPHGVVFLHVTYVPAQEKNFTTAPAICHDGKAHFPREGVFVSNGTHWFVTQRNFYEPQIITTDNT
ccccccccccceeeeeecccccccccccccccccccccccceeeeccccceeecccccceeecccce
FVSGNCDVVIGIVNNTVYDPLQPELDSFKEELDKYFKNHTSPDVDLGDISGINASVVNIQKEIDRLNEVA
eecccccceeeeeecccccccccchhhhhhhhhhhcccccccccccccccchhhhhhhhhhhhhh
KNLNESLIDLQELGKYEQYIKWPWYIWLGFIAGLIAIVMVTIMLCCMTSCCSCLKGCCSCGSCCKFDEDD
hhhhhhhhhhhhhhheeeeeecceeeeeeecceeeeeeeeeeeeeeeeecccccccccccccccccc
SEPVLKGVKLHYT
cceeeeeeeccee
```

FIGURE 2.10 Underline, bold, and italic results presents the Virus Pathogen Resource (ViPR). (Continued)

```
NP_073551.1    MFVLLVAYALL-------HIAGCQTTNGLNTSYSVCN-GCVGYSE---------NVFAVE      43
MN908947.3     MFVFL-VLLPLVSSQCVNLTTRTQLPPAYTNSFTR-------------------GVYY-P      39
AIV41987.1     MFLILLISLPTAF--AVIGDLNCPLDPRLKGSFNNRDTGPPSISTDTVDVTNGLGTYYVL      58
               **::*        .  *:.               .               ..:

NP_073551.1    SGGYIPSDFAFNNWFLL---TNTSSVVDGVVRSFQPLLLNCLWSVSGL-----------      88
MN908947.3     DKV---------------FRSSVLHSTQDLFLPFFSNVTWFHAIHVSGT-NGTKRFD      80
AIV41987.1     DRVYLNTTLFLNGYYPTSGSTYRNMALKGTDKL------STLWFKPPFLSDFINGIFAKV     112
               .                      . .:...      .    *

NP_073551.1    ----RFTTGFVYFNGTGRGDCKGFSSDVLSDVIRYNLNFEENLRRGTILFKTSYGVVVFY     144
MN908947.3     NPVLPFNDGVYFASTEKSNIIRGWI---FG-----T--TLDSKTQSLLIVNNATNVVIKV     130
AIV41987.1     KNTKVFKDGVMYSEFPAITIGSTFVNTSYSVVVQPR--TINSTQDGV--NKLQGLLEVSV     168
               *. *. :.         :        :         :.      . :  .

NP_073551.1    CTNNT----------------------LVSGDAHIPFGTVLGNFYCFVNTTIGNETTSA     181
MN908947.3     CEFQFCNDPFLGVYYHKNNKSWMESEFRVYSSANNCTFEYVSQPFLMDLEGKQGN-----     185
AIV41987.1     CQYNMCEYPHTICHP--KLGNHFKELWHLDTGVVSCLYK---RNFTYDVNATY-------     216
               *  :                     :  :.       :    *    :: .

NP_073551.1    FVGALPKTVREFVISRTGHFYINGYRYFTLGNVEAV-----NF------------NVT-     222
MN908947.3     -----FKNLREFVFKNIDGYFK---IYSKHTPINLVRDLPQGFSALEPLVDLPIGINITR     237
AIV41987.1     ---------LYFHFYQEGGTFY---AYFTDT----------GFV-TKFLFNVYLGMALS-     252
               *  :  .:.    *.          .*              ::

NP_073551.1    ----------------------TAETTDFCTVALASYADVLVNVSQTSIANIIYC-NSVI     259
MN908947.3     FQTLLALHRSYLTPGDSSSGWTA-GAAAYYVGYLQPRTFLLKYNENGTITDAVDCALDPL     296
AIV41987.1     --------HYYVMPLTCISRLDIGFTLEYWVTPLTPRQYLLAFNQDGIIFNAVDCMSDFM     304
                             :  :*  .: * :: .   *: :

NP_073551.1    NRLRCDQLSFDVPDGFYSTSPIQSVELPVS--------------------IVSLPVYHKH     299
MN908947.3     SETKCTLKSFTVEKGIYQTSNFRVQPTESIVRFPNITNLCPFGEVFNATRFASVYAWNRK     356
AIV41987.1     SEIKCKTQSIAPPTGVYELNGYTVQPIADVYRRKPDLPNCNIEAWLNDKSVPSPLNWERK     364
               ..:*   *:    *.*.  .                      .  *   :.::

NP_073551.1    TFIVLYVDFKP--QSGGGKCFNCYP---AGVN------ITLANFN---ETKGPLCVDT--     343
MN908947.3     RISNCVADYSVLYNSASFSTFKCYGVSPTKLNDLCFTNVYADSFVIRGDEVRQIAPGQTG     416
AIV41987.1     TFSNCNFNMSSLMSFIQADSFTCNNIDAAKIYGMCFSSITIDKFAIPNRRKVDLQLGNLG     424
               :      :.    . *.*    ::       :     .*        :   :.

NP_073551.1    ----SH------FTT-----KYVAVYANVGRWSAS-------------------------     363
MN908947.3     KIADYNYKLPDDFTGCVIAWNSNNLDSKVGG----NYNYLYRLFRKSNLKPFERDIST--     470
AIV41987.1     YLQSSNYRIDTTATSCQLYYNLPAANVSVSRFNPSTWNKRFGFIEDSVFVPQPTGVFTNH     484
               :          *   .     .*.

NP_073551.1    ----------INTGNCPFS--FGK------------------------------------     375
MN908947.3     ------EIYQA--GSTPCNGVEGFN-----------------------------------     487
AIV41987.1     SVVYAQHCFKAPKNFCPCSSCPGKNNGIGTCPAGTNYLTCDNLCTLDPITFKAPDTYKCP     544
               .  *.   *

NP_073551.1    -VNNFVKFGSVCFSLKDIPGGCAMPIVANWAYSKYYTIGSLYVSWSDGDGITGV------     428
MN908947.3     --------------------CYF--------PLQSYGFQPTNGVGYQPYRV------VVLS     514
AIV41987.1     QTKSLVGIGEHCSGLAVKSDYC--------GNNSCTCQPQAFLGWSADSCLQGDKCNIFA     596
                                             ..        :.:.

NP_073551.1    -----------PQPVEGVSSFMNVTLDKCTKYNIYDVSGVGVIRVSNDTFLNGITY--TS     475
MN908947.3     FELLHA--PATVCG---PKKSTNLVKNKCVNFNFNGLTGTGVLTESNKKFLP-FQQFGRD     568
AIV41987.1     NFILHDVNNGLTCSTDLQKANTEIELGVCVNYDLYGISGQGIFVEVNATYYNSWQNLLYD     656
               .       *.:::: .::* *::   * .:

NP_073551.1    TSGNLLGFKDVTKGTIYSITPCNPPDQLVVYQQAVVGAM---LSENF-TSYGFSNVV---     528
MN908947.3     IADTTDAVRDPQTLEILDITPCSFGGVSVITPGTNTSNQVAVLYQDVNCTEVPVAIHADQ     628
AIV41987.1     SNGNLYGFRDYITNRTFMIHSCYSGRVSAAYH--ANSSEPALLFRNIKCNYVFNNSLTRQ     714
               ..  ..:*  .   *  *  .          .       *  .:.

NP_073551.1    ELPKFFY--------------------ASNGTYNCTDAVLTYSSFGVCADGSIIAVQPR     567
```

FIGURE 2.10 (Continued) Underline, bold, and italic results presents the Virus Pathogen Resource (ViPR). (Continued)

```
MN908947.3     LTPTWRVYSTGSNVFQTRAGCLIGAEH--VNNSYECDIP----IGAGICASYQTQTNSPR    682
AIV41987.1     LQPI-------NYSFDSYLGCVVNAYNSTAISVQTCDLT----VGSGYCVDYSKNRRSRR    763
               *                .  *         . * *...  .     *


NP_073551.1    NVS----------------YDSVSAIVTANLSIPSNWTTSVQVEYLQITSTPIVVDCST    610
MN908947.3     RARSVAS-QSIIAYTMS-LGAENSVAYSNNSIAIPTNFTISVTTEILPVSMTKTSVDCTM    740
AIV41987.1     AITTGYRFTNFEPFTVNSVNDSLEPVGGLYEIQIPSEFTIGNMEEFIQTSSPKVTIDCAA    823
                         .:  **:::* .  * :    .   *:**:


NP_073551.1    YVCNGNVRCVELLKQYTSACKTIEDALRNSARLESADVSEMLTFD-KKAFTLANV-----    664
MN908947.3     YICGDSTECSNLLLQYGSFCTQLNRALTGIAVEQDKNTQEVFAQV-KQIYKTPPIKDF--    797
AIV41987.1     FVCGDYAACKLQLVEYGSFCDNINAILTEVNELLDTTQLQVANSLMNGVTLSTKLKDGVN    883
                ::*... *   * :* * *   ::  *        ::      :


NP_073551.1    SSFGDYNLSSVIPSLPTSGSRVAGRSAIEDILFSKLVTSGLGTVDADYKKCTKGLSIADL    724
MN908947.3     ---GGFNFSQI----LPDPSKPSKRSFIEDLLFNKVTLADAGFIK-QYGDCLGDIAARDL    849
AIV41987.1     FNVDDINFSPVLGCLGSECSKASSRSAIEDLLFDKVKLSDVGFVE-AYNNCTGGAEIRDL    942
                .. *:* :     .  *: : ** ***:**.*:  :. * :.  * .*      **


NP_073551.1    ACAQYYNGIMVLPGVADAERMAMYTGSLIGGIALGGLTSA----VSIPFSLAIQARLNYV    780
MN908947.3     ICAQKFNGLTVLPPLLTDEMIAQYTSALLAGTITSGWTFGAGAALQIPFAMQMAYRFNGI    909
AIV41987.1     ICVQSYKGIKVLPPLLSENQISGYTLAATSASLFPPWTAAAG----VPFYLNVQYRINGL    998
                *.* ::*: ***  :  :: ** :.     *.      :**  :: *  *:*  :


NP_073551.1    ALQTDVLQENQKILAASFNKAMTNIVDAFTGVNDAITQTSQALQTVATALNKIQDVVNQQ    840
MN908947.3     GVTQNVLYENQKLIANQFNSAIGKIQDSLS--------------STASALGKLQDVVNQN    955
AIV41987.1     GVTMDVLSQNQKLIASAFNNALHAIQQGFD--------------ATNSALVKIQAVVNAN    1044
                .:  :** :***::* **.*:  * :.:            :.  :** *:* *** :


NP_073551.1    GNSLNHLTSQLRQNFQAISSSIQAIYDRLDTIQADQQVDRLITGRLAALNVFVSHTLTKY    900
MN908947.3     AQALNTLVKQLSSNFGAISSVLNDILSRLDKVEAEVQIDRLITGRLQSLQTYVTQQLIRA    1015
AIV41987.1     AEALNNLLQQLSNRFGAISASLQEILSRLDALEAEAQIDRLINGRLTALNAYVSQQLSDS    1104
                .::** * .** ..* ***: ::  * .*** ::*: *;****.*** :*:..:*:: *


NP_073551.1    TEVRASRQLAQQKVNECVKSQSKRYGFCGNGTHIFSIVNAAPEGLVFLHTVLLPTQYKDV    960
MN908947.3     AEIRASANLAATKMSECVLGQSKRVDFCGKGYHLMSFPQSAPHGVVFLHVTYVPAQEKNF    1075
AIV41987.1     TLVKFSAAQAMEKVNECVKSQSSRINFCGNGNHIISLVQNAPYGLYFIHFNYVPTKYVTA    1164
                : ::  *   *   *:.*** .**.*.:***:*  *::*: : ** *: :*   :*:


NP_073551.1    EAWSGLCVDGTNGYVLRQPNLALYKEGNYYRITSRIMFEPRIPTMADFVQIENCNVTFVN    1020
MN908947.3     TTAPAICHDGKA-HFPREGV--FVSNGTHWFVTQRNFYEPQIITTDNTFVSGNCDVVIGI    1132
AIV41987.1     KVSPGLCIAGNRGIAPKSGY--FVNVNNTWMYTGSGYYYPEPITENNVVVMSTCAVNYTK    1222
                .  .:*  *.   :.    :  : ...:  *    :  *. * : ..   .* *


NP_073551.1    ISRSELQTIVPEYIDVNKTLQELSYKLPNYTVPDLVVEQYNQTILNLTSEISTLENKSAE    1080
MN908947.3     VNNTVYDPLQPELDSFKEELDKY---FKNHTSPDVDL-----------GDISGINASVVN    1178
AIV41987.1     APYVMLNTSIPNLPDFKEELDQW---FKNQTSVAPDL-----------S-LDYINVTFLD    1267
                 :   *:  ..:: *::     : * *          :        . :. :: .  :


NP_073551.1    LNYTVQKLQTLIDNINSTLVDLKWLNRVETYIKWPWWVWLCISVVLIFVVSMLLLCCCST    1140
MN908947.3     IQKEIDRLNEVAKNLNESLIDLQELGKYEQYIKWPWYIWLGFIAGLIAIVMVTIMLCCMT    1238
AIV41987.1     LQVEMNRLQEAIKVLNHSYINLKDIGTYEYYVKWPWYVWLLICLAGVAMLVLLFFICCCT    1327
                ::  :::*:   .:* :::*: :.  * *:****::** :   : :: : :: ** *


NP_073551.1    GCCGFFSCFASSIRGCCESTKLPYYD-VEKIHIQ--    1173
MN908947.3     SCC-SCLKGCCSCGSCCKFDEDDSEPVLKGVKLHYT    1273
AIV41987.1     GCGTSCFKK---CGGCCDDYTGYQELVIKTSHDD--    1358
                .*            .**.      ::  : .
```

Trypsin: S1/S2 HTVSLLRSTSQKSIVAYTMSL, S2' LPDPLKPTKRSFIEDLLFNKV; cathepsin: S1/S2 HTVSLLRSTSQKSIVAYTMSL;
Elastase: S2' LPDPLKPTKRSFIEDLLFNKV,
Plasmin: S1/S2 HTVSLLRSTSQKSIVAYTMSL, S2' LPDPLKPTKRSFIEDLLFNKV,
TMPRSS1: S1/S2 HTVSLLRSTSQKSIVAYTMSL;
TMPRSS2: Multiple sites;
TMPRSS11a: S1/S2 HTVSLLRSTSQKSIVAYTMSL, S2' LPDPLKPTKRSFIEDLLFNKV.

FIGURE 2.10 (Continued) Underline, bold, and italic results presents the Virus Pathogen Resource (ViPR). (Continued)

```
CLUSTAL O(1.2.4) multiple sequence alignment


MN908947.3     -----MFVFLVLLPLVSSQ----------------------------------------- 14
KX266757       MLVKSLFLVTLLFALSSASLYD--------------------------------------- 22
KC119407.1     MLGKSLLIVTVLFALCSATLYT--------------------------------------- 22
KM454473       MLGKSLLIVTVLFALCSATLYT--------------------------------------- 22
NC016991       -MQRIILISTILYCARALTLADKMLDLLTFPGAHHYFR---GDLQTLHSRISAESYSVN-- 55
NC016993       -MRGAILTLILVTSVKASPLADSVLDFLTFPGAHSYLHPRRGDLGALGNRMRANIRNSQT 59
                   ::     ::       :


MN908947.3     --CVN------------------------------------------------------- 17
KX266757       ------------------------------------------------------------ 22
KC119407.1     ------------------------------------------------------------ 22
KM454473       ------------------------------------------------------------ 22
NC016991       ----------------PYDQYNYQTDSDYYINKSVHLIAPLTNLTLPISGLHRSMQPLRV 99
NC016993       DVCTTIQQGGFIPSTFTFPQWYVLTNGSTFLQGE----------------YTLSQPLLA 102


MN908947.3     ---LTTRTQLPPAYTNSFTRGVYYPDKVFRSSVLHSTQDLFLPFFSNVTWFHAIHVSGTN 74
KX266757       --------------------------NDTY---------------VYYYQ-------- 31
KC119407.1     --------------------------H-DY---------------VYYYQ-------- 30
KM454473       --------------------------H-DY---------------VYYYQ-------- 30
NC016991       GCIFGASNKIDQGFT---ISGMTYPLAYCV---------------PPFYQ-------- 131
NC016993       NAHFCPRKNSDGYWRYSFNNSCLFPDHRCQ---------------DHWYD-------- 137
                                                            ::.


MN908947.3     GTKRFDNPVLPFNDGVYFASTEKSNIIRGWIFGTTLDSKTQSLLIVNNA-------TNVV 127
KX266757       --------------------SAFRPPNGWHLNGGAYAVVNVSSQTNNAGIAPECTVGII 70
KC119407.1     --------------------SAYRPPNGWHLQGGAYAVVNSTNKFNNAGAASECSVGVL 69
KM454473       --------------------SAYRPPNGWHLQGGAYAVVNSTNKFNNAGAASECSVGVL 69
NC016991       --------------------VTNVTYDA-----------------------MRLL 143
NC016993       --------------------SQNPICLGWNNTFGLSDN--------------IRININ 161
                                     .                              :


MN908947.3     IKVCEFQF--------------------CNDPFLGVYYHKNNKSWMESEFRVYSSANNCT 167
KX266757       SGDTV----------------FNASSIAMTAPVGQG-----MQW--------SKSQFCT 100
KC119407.1     FNYTN----GNDVGYN------NSASSVAMTAPL-PG-----MSW--------SKTQFCT 105
KM454473       FNYTN----GNDVGYN------NSASSVAMTAPL-PG-----MSW--------SKTQFCT 105
NC016991       FAFADLNSTGDFLRINTKTMGMLNVSCSASPTPLGHQDADR---TF----YGYNKQLYCY 196
NC016993       ISHDEYQSHGGYVSLTLESGSVVNITCTNNSDPSTVTLATSLLPWA----RAIDQPMYCF 217
                                                                .. *


MN908947.3     FEYVSQPFLMDLEGKQGNFKNLREFVFKNIDGYFKIYSKHTPINLVRDLPQGFSALEPLV 227
KX266757       AHC--------------NFSDITVFVTHCYA------SGAGKCPLTGLIPKGHIRISAMR 140
KC119407.1     AHC--------------NFSDFTVFVTHCFA--------NSCPLTGRIEENHIRVSAMR 142
KM454473       AHC--------------NFSDFTVFVTHCFA--------NSCPLTGRIEENHIRVSAMR 142
NC016991       LDT-------------P--------------------AGMQYMGPLPANLTEITLFR 220
NC016993       ANL-------------T------------T------GTASQLDFMGMLPPLVSELAFDR 245
                .                                      :    :     :


MN908947.3     DL----PIGINITRFQTL-------------LALHRSYLTPGDSSS-----GW-TAGAAA 264
KX266757       NHTLFYNLTVSVSKYPTFKSLQCVDNFTAVYLNGDLVFTSNQTTDVISAGVYFKSGGPIT 200
KC119407.1     NGSLFYNLTVSVSKYPKFKSLQCVNNFTSVYLNGDLVFTSNKTTDVIGAGVYFKAGGPIT 202
KM454473       NGSLFYNLTVSVSKYPKFKSLQCVNNFTSVYLNGDLVFTSNKTTDVIGAGVYFKAGGPIT 202
NC016991       TG------------------------QIYTNGFHLGTIPSELTYVY----LDKLAFQN 250
NC016993       TG------------------------GIYINGYRYYLTSALRDVDF---KLKRNDTAE 276


MN908947.3     YYVGYLQPRTFLLKYNENGTITDAVDCALDPLSETKCTLKSFTVEKGIYQTSNFRVQP-T 323
```

FIGURE 2.10 (Continued)   Underline, bold, and italic results presents the Virus Pathogen Resource (ViPR). (Continued)

```
KX266757     Y--KVMK-EFKVLAYFVNGTAQDVILCDDTPRGLLACQYNTGNFSDGFYPFTNSSLV--K    255
KC119407.1   Y--KIMK-EFKVLAYFVNGTVQDVILCDNSPRGLLACQYNTGNFSDGFYPFTNFSLV--K    257
KM454473     Y--KIMK-EFKVLAYFVNGTVQDVILCDNSPRGLLACQYNTGNFSDGFYPFTNFSLV--K    257
NC016991     KTVCMMANLTDTLITLNHTVIQQVTYCEKDAVQALACQQSTHQLQDGFYSDPAPAVNNLP    310
NC016993     YFAVTWANYTDVHLSVDAGAIEKIKYCNT-PLDRLACDMNVFNLSDGVYSYTSLEKASVP    335
                                    .  .    *      *    . ...*.*

MN908947.3   ESIVRFPNITNLC----------PFGEVFNATRFAS-VYAWNRKRISNCVADYSV-----    367
KX266757     QRFVVY---RENSVNTTLTLTNYTFHNETNAQPNSGGVYTI-STYQTKTAQSGYYNFNLS    311
KC119407.1   DRFIVY---RESSTNTTLELTNFTFTNVSNASPNSGGVDTF-QLYQTHTAQDGYYNFNLS    313
KM454473     DRFIVY---RESSTNTTLELTNFTFTNVSNASPNSGGVDTF-QLYQTHTAQDGYYNFNLS    313
NC016991     KTLVTLPKIAESSTLQINVSATYSYGSASGSI----KLSYNGSSNNSHCVQTPYFKLEQN    366
NC016993     ETFVTLPVYSNHTYVTINTS--YTVGSCVNCPPISSTIDIMHARNDTLCVNSRQFTVRLN    393
             . ::          :           . ..        :           :  .

MN908947.3   -----LYNSASF----STFKCYGVSPTKL-----NDLCFTNVYADSFVIRGDEVRQIAPG    413
KX266757     FLSSFVYKESNYMYGSYHPRCSFRPETINNGLWFNSLAVSLAYGP--------------    356
KC119407.1   FLSSFVYKPSDFMYGSYHPNCNFRPENINNGLWFNSLSVSLTYGP--------------    358
KM454473     FLSSFVYKPSDFMYGSYHPNCNFRPENINNGLWFNSLSVSLTYGP--------------    358
NC016991     LVC-----SGGCSVRIETLTCPFDLNAVSNGMSFQQFCVSTVSG--------------    405
NC016993     THHHAQY-PQYFSTAFVAGTCPFTLPNINNYLTFGSVCFSTVNN--------------    436
                  *                          ....:. .

MN908947.3   QTGKIADYNYKLPDDFTGCVIAWNSNNLDSKVGGNYNYLYRLFRKSNLKPFERDISTEIY    473
KX266757     --------------LQGGCKQSVFQG----RATCCYAYSYN----------------    379
KC119407.1   --------------IQGGCKQSVFSN----KATCCYAYSYR----------------    381
KM454473     --------------IQGGCKQSVFSN----KATCCYAYSYR----------------    381
NC016991     ----------------QCSMQAIVN----TGQ-PWGYV----------------    422
NC016993     ----------------GGCTIHV-------QK-VWNHQY----------------    451
                           *              : :

MN908947.3   QAGSTPCNGVEG------FNCYFPLQSYGFQPTNGVGYQPYRVVVLSFELLHAP-ATVCG    526
KX266757     --GPRMCKGVYSGQLLQDFECGLL-----------VYVTKS---DGSRIQTATKPPVIT    422
KC119407.1   --GPTRCRGVYRGELMQYFECGLL-----------VYVTKS---DGSRIQTRSEPLVLT    424
KM454473     --GPTRCRGVYRGELMQYFECGLL-----------VYVTKS---DGSRIQTRSEPLVLT    424
NC016991     ---------------TST-----------LYVTYV---EGQSFTGT--S-SDQ    443
NC016993     -----------------HTFGT-----------IYVAYQ---DGNYITALPQP-STG    476
                                              *         .

MN908947.3   PKKSTNLVKNKCVNFNFNGLTGTGVLTESNKKFLPFQQFG---RDIADTTD-----AVRD    578
KX266757     QHNYNNITLNTCVDYNIYGRVGQGFITNVTDSAASYNYLADAGLAILDTSGAIDIFVVQG    482
KC119407.1   QYNYNNITLNKCVEYNIYGRVGQGFITNVTEATANYSYLADGGLAILDTSGAIDIFVVRG    484
KM454473     QYNYNNITLNKCVEYNIYGRVGQGFITNVTEATANYSYLADGGLAILDTSGAIDIFVVRG    484
NC016991     IEDLTVLHLDQCTSYTIYGVSGTGVITLSDLQLP-------HGITFRAANGELS--AFKN    494
NC016993     VADISTVHLDVCTKYSIYGKTGTGVIRETNQSYT-------AGLYYTSSSGDLL--AFKN    527
             . . .   :   *..:.:  *   * *.:              :..      ..:.

MN908947.3   PQTLEILDITPCSFGGVSVITPGTNTSNQVAVLYQDVNCTEVPVAIHADQLTPTWRVYS-    637
KX266757     EYGLNYYKVNPCEDVNQQFVVSGGKL---VGILTSRNETGSQ--PLE-----NQFYIKLT    532
KC119407.1   AYGPNYYKVNPCEDVNQQFVVSGGNL---VGILTSHNETDSE--FIE-----NQFYIKLT    534
KM454473     AYGPNYYKVNPCEDVNQQFVVSGGNL---VGILTSHNETDSE--FIE-----NQFYIKLT    534
NC016991     TTTGDVYTIQPCSLPAQLA-IIDSTI---VGAITSTNE--SY--GFSNTIVTPTFYY---    543
NC016993     VTTQKVYSVTPCTLASQVA-VYNNSI---LAAFTSTANLTAI--DFNYTIATPTFYY---    578
             . : ** 	     ..      :.:. :       :         :

MN908947.3   TGSNVFQTRAGCLIGAEHVNNSYECDIPI----GAGICASYQTQTNSPRRARSVASQSII    693
KX266757     NGSRR---------LRRSISSNVTICPYVSYGRYCIEPDGSLKQIVPQELQH------    575
KC119407.1   NGTRR---------SRRSVTENVTNCPYVSYGKFCIKPDGSLSIIVPQELKQ------    577
KM454473     NGTRR---------SRRSVTENVTNCPYVSYGKFCIKPDGSLSIIVPQELKQ------    577
NC016991     ------------------STNATSNCTAPKISYGELGVCADGSIGAVSQLQDSK------    579
NC016993     ------------------HSIGNETCEQPVITYGSIGLCPGGGLRLAHPTEDAA------    614
                              *              .
```

FIGURE 2.10 (**Continued**)   Underline, bold, and italic results presents the Virus Pathogen Resource (ViPR). (Continued)

```
MN908947.3   AYTMSLGAENSVAYSNNSIAIPTNFTISVTTEILPVSMTKTSVDCTMYICGDSTECSNLL   753
KX266757     -------FVAPLLNVTEHVLIPNSFNLTVTDEYIQTRMDKVQINCLQYVCGNSIECRKLF   628
KC119407.1   -------FVSPLLNVTEHVLIPNSFNLTVTDEYIQTRMDKVQINCLQYVCGNSLNCRKLF   630
KM454473     -------FVSPLLNVTEHVLIPNSFNLTVTDEYIQTRMDKVQINCLQYVCGNSLNCRKLF   630
NC016991     ------PSIVP--LYTGEIEIPASFKLSVQTEYLQVQTEQVVIDCPKYVCNGNPRCLQLL   631
NC016993     ------PILVP--ISTSNISIPKNFTVSIQTEYIQIEQQPVVVDCRQYVCNGNPRCLQLL   666
                  : **  .*.::: *  .  .::* :*.... * :*:

MN908947.3   LQYGSFCTQLNRALTGIAVEQDKNTQEVFA-QVKQIYKTPPIKDFG--GFNFSQILP-DP   809
KX266757     RQYGPVCDNILSVVNSVGQKEDMELLNFYSSTKPKGFDTPVLSNVSTGAFNISLLLT-PP   687
KC119407.1   QQYGPVCENILSIVNSVGQKEDMELLSFYSSTKPAGYNAPVFSNISTGDFNISLLLT-PP   689
KM454473     QQYGPVCENILSIVNSVGQKEDMELLSFYSSTKPAGYNAPVFSNISTGDFNISLLLT-PP   689
NC016991     AQYTSACSNIESALHSSAQLDSREITMMFQ-TSSQSVELANITNFQG---DYNFSMILPT   687
NC016993     QQYTSACSTIEQALSLNARLEASSIQDLLT-YSPETLVLANISNFDSGDLNYNLSSLLPK   725
                 :.  :.: .: :            :.:   :. :.

MN908947.3   SKPSKRSFIEDLLFNKVTLADAGF-IKQYGDCLGDI--AARDLICAQKFNGLTVLPPLLT   866
KX266757     SSPSGRSFIEDLLFTSVETVGLPT-DAEYKKCTAGPLGTLKDLICAREYNGLLVLPPIIT   746
KC119407.1   SSPRGRSFIEDLLFTSVETVGLPT-DAEYKKCTAGPLGTLKDLICAREYNGLLVLPPIIT   748
KM454473     SSPRGRSFIEDLLFTSVETVGLPT-DAEYKKCTAGPLGTLKDLICAREYNGLLVLPPIIT   748
NC016991     LPGKDRSAIEDLLFDKVVTNGLGTVDQDYKSCSCKGI--AVADLVCAQYYNGIMVLPGVVD   745
NC016993     E-LYGKSAIEDLLFNKVTNGLGTVDQDYKACTNGM--SIADLVCAQYYNGIMVLPGVAG   782
               :*.****** .*    .    ::*   .:. :**.:  ***  .

MN908947.3   DEMIAQYTSALLAGTITSGWTFGAGAALQIPFAMQMAYRFNGIGVTQNVLYENQKLIANQ   926
KX266757     ADMQTMYTASLVGAMAFGG----ITSAAAIPFATQIQARINHLGITQSLLMKNQEKIAAS   802
KC119407.1   ADMQTMYTASLVGSMAFGG----ITAAGAIPFATQIQARINHLGITQSLLLKNQEKIAAS   804
KM454473     ADMQTMYTASLVGSMAFGG----ITAAGAIPFATQIQARINHLGITQSLLLKNQEKIAAS   804
NC016991     AEKMAMYTGSLTGAMVFGG----LTAAAAIPFSTAVQARLNYVALQTNVLQENQKILAES   801
NC016993     PEKMAQYTASLTGAMVFGG----ITAASAIPFSLAVQSRLNYVALQTDVLQQNQQLLADS   838
                :  :**.:* ..  .*       *** :: *.:  ..:  .:* :**:.*.

MN908947.3   FNSAIGKIQDSLSSTASA--------------LGKLQDVVNQNAQALNTLVKQLSSNFGA   972
KX266757     FNKAIGHMQEGFRSTSLA--------------LQQVQDVVNKQSAILMETMNSLNKNFGA   848
KC119407.1   FNKAIGHMQEGFRSTSLA--------------LQQVQDVVNKQSAILTETMNSLNKNFGA   850
KM454473     FNKAIGHMQEGFRSTSLA--------------LQQVQDVVNKQSAILTETMNSLNKNFGA   850
NC016991     FNQAVGNISLALSNVNTAIQQTSEALLTVSNAINKIQTVVNQQGEALAHLTAQLSQNFGA   861
NC016993     FNNAIGNITLAFKEVSEGLSQVSGAVATVANALTKVQTVVNEQGHALATLTQQLANNFQA   898
               **.*:*::  .:  ..    :      ::* ***::.  *    .** *:.**

MN908947.3   ISSVLNDILSRLDKVEAEVQIDRLITGRLQSLQTYVTQQLIRAAEIRASANLAATKMSEC   1032
KX266757     ISSVIQDIYAQLDAIQADAQVDRLITGRLSSLSVLASAKQSEYIRVSQQRELATQKINEC   908
KC119407.1   ISSVIQDIYAQLDVIQADAQVDRLITGRLSSLSVLASAKQSEYIRVSQQRELATQKINEC   910
KM454473     ISSVIQDIYAQLDVIQADAQVDRLITGRLSSLSVLASAKQSEYIRVSQQRELATQKINEC   910
NC016991     ISTSIQDIYNRLDQIQADQQVDRLITGRLAALNAYVTQLLNKLSQVRSQRILAEQKINEC   921
NC016993     ISASISDIYNRLNQLEADAQVDRLITGRLASLNAFVTQTLSKLAEVRQQRQLATDKVNEC   958
               **:  :.** .:*: :*: *:********* :*. ..:  .    .   ** *:.**

MN908947.3   VLGQSKRVDFCGKGYHLMSFPQSAPHGVVFLHVTYVPAQEKNFTTAPAICHDGKAHF---   1089
KX266757     VKSQSTRYGFCGSGRHVLSIPQNAPNGIVFIHFTYTPESFVNVTAIVGFCVNPPNASQYA   968
KC119407.1   VKSQSNRYGPCGSGRHVLSIPQNAPNGIVFIHFSYTPESFVNVTAIVGFCVQPANASQYA   970
KM454473     VKSQSNRYGFCGSGRHVLSIPQNAPNGIVFIHFSYTPESFVNVTAIVGFCVQPANASQYA   970
NC016991     VKSQSSRYGFCGNGTHLFSLTQAAPNGIFFMHAVLVPQTFQPVVAYAGICVDGYGYS---   978
NC016993     VKSQSPRYGFCGNGTHLFSIVNAAPQGLLFFHTVLLPTQYAYVQAFSGICYNGIALA---   1015
               * .** *  .***.*  *:::*: : **:*:.*:*    .     .:  .:* :

MN908947.3   ----PREGVFVSNGTHWFVTQRNFYEPQIITTDNTFVSGNCDVVIGIVNNTVYDPLQPE-   1144
KX266757     IVPVNDRGVFIQVNGTYYITSRDMYMPRDITAGDIVTLTSCQANYVSVNKTVITTFVDND   1028
KC119407.1   IVPVNSRGIFIQVNGSYYITARDMYMPRDITAGDIVTLTSCQANYVNVNKTYITTFVEDD   1030
KM454473     IVPVNSRGIFIQVNGSYYITARDMYMPRDITAGDIVTLTSCQANYVNVNKTVITTFVEDD   1030
NC016991     --L-QPQLVLYNLNDSYRITPRNMFEPRTPTQSVFIPLTTCSVDFVNVTANNVSIIIPD-   1034
NC016993     --LNDPTLALFKNGDKYLVSPRNMYQPRVPAQADFVYIETCTITYLNLTDLTIDVVIPD-   1072
               :. .  : :: *::: *:  .    .*   .  .
```

```
MN908947.3   LDSFKEELDKYFKN-------HTSPDVDL-----------GDISGINASVVNIQKEIDRL   1186
KX266757     DFDFYDELSKWWNDTKHELPDF-----DEFNYTIPVLNISN-------------EIDRI   1069
KC119407.1   DFDFDDELSKWWNDTKHELPDF-----DDFNYTVPILNISG-------------EIDRI   1071
KM454473     DFDFDDELSKWWNDTKHELPDF-----DDFNYTVPILNISG-------------EIDRI   1071
NC016991     YVD----VNKTVSDIINGLPNYSYPELSLDRFNHTILNLSQEIEDLQIRSQNLSATAELL   1090
NC016993     YVD----VNQTVNDILSKLPNSTGPSLTIDQYNNTILNLTTEIADLNNRTQNLSDVVQNL   1128
                .    ::.:  .:                                        : :
```

```
MN908947.3   NEVAKNLNESLIDLQELGKYEQYIKWPWYIWLGFIAGLIAIVMVTIMLCCMTSCCSCLKG   1246
KX266757     QEVIQGLNDSLIDLETLSILKTYIKWPWYVWLAIAFAVIIFILILGWVFFMTGCCG----   1125
KC119407.1   QGVIQGLNDSIINLEELSIIKTYIKWPWYVWLAIGFAIIIFILILGWVFFMTGCCG----   1127
KM454473     QGVIQGLNDSIINLEELSIIKTYIKWPWYVWLAIGFAIIIFILILGWVFFMTGCCG----   1127
NC016991     QQYIDNLNNTLVDLEWLNRVETYLKWPWYIWLLIFLAIAAFATILVTIFLCTGCCGGCFG   1150
NC016993     EEYIHKLNATLVDLDWLNRVETYIKWPWWVWLLITLAIVAFVILVTIFLCTGCCGGCFG   1188
               :   . ** ::::*:*: *.  :  *:****::** .  .:  .   :       *.**.
```

```
MN908947.3   CC-SCGSCCKFDEDDSE-PV-LKGVK-----LHYT-----   1273
KX266757     CCCGCFGIIPLMSKCGKKSSYYTTFDNDVVTEQYRPKKSV   1165
KC119407.1   CCCGCFGIIPLMSKCGKKSSYYTTFDNDVVTEQYRPKKSV   1167
KM454473     CCCGCFGIIPLMSKCGKKSSYYTTFDNDVVTEQYRPKKSV   1167
NC016991     CCGGCFGLFSKKRRLSSEPT-PVSFK---------LKEW-   1179
NC016993     CCGGCFGLFSHNKRNTESIP-ITSFK---------LKEW-   1217
               **  .*  .                   ..
```

FIGURE 2.10 (Continued) Underline, bold, and italic results presents the Virus Pathogen Resource (ViPR). (Continued)

```
MN908947.3     NRALTGIAVEQDKNTQEVFAQVKQIYKTPPIKDFGGFNFSQILPDPSKPSKRSFIEDL--    821
YP_009666261.1 VQS-----------------IAQILETEPLPST-KLDFRTEENNVT-KITLSFTQEVAS    560
                 ::                  :  ** :* *: .    ::*     : :    . ** :::

QEG08239.1     VLPQTYATAMLTRFIPPPVSISGTLYWLDYPDVFV--YSGNVAFDQPT------------    817
MN908947.3     ILPD------------PSKPSKRSFIEDL-------LFNKVTLAD--AGFIKQYGDCLG    842
YP_009666261.1 EENN------------VT-KITLSFTQEVASTLTQRTINSKQLATPKLNQLKAWYQMTK    588
                   : :                : :           .. :

QEG08239.1     VLPQTYATAMLTRFIPPPVSISGTLYWLDYPDVFV--YSGNVAFDQPT------------    817
MN908947.3     ILPD------------PSKPSKRSFIEDL-------LFNKVTLAD--AGFIKQYGDCLG    842
YP_009666261.1 EENN------------VT-KITLSFTQEVASTLTQRTINSKQLATPKLNQLKAWYQMTK    588
                   :                : :           .. :
```

FIGURE 2.10 (Continued) Underline, bold, and italic results presents the Virus Pathogen Resource (ViPR).

A significant number of the epitopes predicted in the current investigation cover with the expectation made utilizing the Immune Epitope Database and Analysis Resource (IEDB) and the Virus Pathogen Resource (ViPR) (Grifoni et al., 2020), and these included as follows;

1. DAVDCALDPLSETKCTLKS FTVEKGIYQTSN
2. VCGPKKSTNLVKNKCVNFNFNGLTGTGVLTESNKKFLPFQQFGRDIADT TDAVRDP
3. QTLEILDITPCSFGGVSVIGTNTSNQVAVLYQDVNCTEVPVAIHADQLT PTWRVYSTGS
4. FSQILPDPSKPSKRSFIE
5. FGAGAALQIPFAMQMAYRFNGI

Review that one reason for the first single favored candidate KRSFIEDLLFNKV was that a significant number of the predicted epitopes contain a proof of glycosylation, reflecting the standard number (e) in the methods section discussed above. That standard has a special status as considered in this section as manufactured immunization or symptomatic development. It demonstrates likely glycosylation of the protein. The cumbersome oligosaccharides so appended that can be immunogenic, but they are fairly hard to work with synthetically, generally expected to make mass production costly, and might be variable in a structure which can't regularly be found in detail in exploratory three-dimensional protein structures (normally as obtained by X-ray crystallography or high-grade electron microscopy). Antibodies that are raised against the glycosylated surface fix to the protein or relating manufactured glycopeptides that might be explicit for their carbohydrate units. These can be perceived independently of the peptides or with regards to the nearby amino acid deposits. Affirmation and introduction of B-peptide epitopes of glycoproteins might be regulated by glycosylation due to intramolecular starch protein interactions. The helpful versus unwanted impacts of glycosylation in synthetic antibodies is likewise a complex matter. Glycosylation might be basic for reactivity with the immune response, however alternately, it might be in actuality inactivate the abilities of a part of amino acid sequence to work as a B-epitope, which is by all accounts an excellent explanation behind giving the glycosylation motif as a solid negative that opposed to positive score. Sadly, this will rely upon the structure of the antigenic site and immunizer fine specificity, and the included recognition mechanism are not completely clear. There is a (normally) positive perspective in the momentum to see that the comparative impacts of glycosylation that apply to the T-cell-subordinate cell immune and IgG antibody reactions, and that glycosylated peptides can evoke glycopeptide-explicit T-cell clones in the wake of being bound and introduced by MHC class I or II molecules. It is obviously just a positive viewpoint if the expected impact is acquired by the synthetic development.

The Constancy of the KRSFIEDLLFNKV Motif With Minor Varieties in Usual Cold Coronaviruses

The general spike glycoprotein protein sequence appeared above changes over the coronaviruses, but the KRSFIEDLLFNKV subsequence is generally outstanding among the special cases. It reaches out to the regular cold coronaviruses with minor variations and may imply a better focused way to deal with stimulate immunity. For basic colds caused by the rhinovirus, ongoing examination recommends confusion of counteracting antibody responses against a non-defensive epitope as an instrument of how the infection gets away from invulnerability thus allows intermittent infections (Niespodziana et al., 2012). A more clear comprehension of preserved subsequences in coronaviruses may help in tune the activity of Toll-like receptors to start the proper response. These are a class of proteins that assume a key function in the inborn insusceptible system. They are single-pass layer traversing receptors generally communicated on sentinel cells (for example macrophages and dendritic cells) that perceive fundamentally rationed molecular features of pathogens (Morris et al., 2006).

Without concerning the two or more strains of COVID-19 infection showing up that there is no large changes for current purposes. It is adequate to consider the succession of the origin Wuhan isolate as a kind of perspective in examinations for current purposes, for example comparing the sequence of spike protein with the different coronaviruses. Review that at the time of the examination in late February and early March 2020, the sequences of the spike proteins of COVID-19 separates from various states and countries, for example, Brazil, Taiwan, California and India stay indistinguishable or so. For instance, regarding the original Wuhan isolate (Lu et al., 2020), phenylalanine (F) is supplanted by cysteine (C) as buildup 797 out of a Swedish isolate, and alanine (A) is supplanted by valine (V) as buildup 990 out of an Indian isolate. Neither of these identifies with the sequence motif KRSFIEDLLFNKV exceptionally compelling here.

In the underlying investigations by Robson (2020a,b), the genome of the normal cold coronavirus, and especially the succession of the spike protein, was considered adequately a long way from that of the COVID-19 infection in order to be less applicable to that issue. While considering a gander at varying sequences is fundamental for the direction of monitored motifs, altogether different and less relevant pathogens are probably not going to preserve them, except perhaps as example matches including very unpredictable replacement rules. Be that as it may in the presence of the COVID-19 KRSFIEDLLFNKV motif shows up in like manner cold coronavirus and with commonly at most two moderately traditionalist replacements. The traditionalist aspartate (D) and asparagine (N) substitution are likewise genuinely regular in the motif in the sequence analyzed. A model appeared below is a Clustal Omega arrangement of the COVID-19 infection spike protein original Wuhan Seafood Market isolate (GenBank passage MN908947.3) with spike protein agents individuals from the two significant normal cold coronavirus strains 229E and OC43 (GenBank Entries NP_073551.1 and AIV41987.1). In spite of extremist sequence differences for the spike protein sequences generally (just

12.8% identity, well inside the range for an irregular match), the underlined sequence motif KRSFIEDLLFNKV of COVID-19 infection is basically held as that sequence, except actually alanine (A) replaces phenylalanine (F) in the normal cold coronavirus (which is decently moderate at the outside of a protein) and a traditionalist leucine for valine substation in one case. In the sequence (not appeared) of HCoV-HKU1 which is regularly connected with more genuine instances of cold-like diseases, the above motif is as yet observable as RSFFEDLLFDKV in which the isoleucine (I) is supplanted by phenylalanine (F). The "A for F" adjusted motif RSAIEDLLFDKV is likewise found in the coronaviruses of canines, felines, rodents, pigs, rabbits, camels, ferret badgers, raccoon canines, among others. These may be eaten by people in specific countries and remarkably, they are, generally, species that live in nearness to people.

The "PIGAG" motif doesn't appear in the above arrangement, as it is additionally the situation in numerous other indirectly related coronaviruses (Robson, 2020a,b). However a subsequence PIGTNYRSCESTT is exists in the HCoV-HKU1 spike protein that seems to identify with PIGAGICASYQTQ in the COVID-19 infection (a review that HCoV-HKU1 is a typical cold infection, though as a rule related with more extreme, lower respiratory parcel cases). Conversely, not exclusively does the KRSFIEDLLFNKV motif stand apart as conceivably imperative to the COVID-19 infection by virtue of such correlations, but it is also a match with motif that nearly to the main continuous stretch of amino acid deposits in many arrangements like cases discussed above. The subsequence KWPWYIWL is a special case that is of intrigue and a trademark highlight of numerous SARS-CoVs. It isn't, considered as further in this chapter, but to take note of that it doesn't seem to be related with a COVID-19 infection spike protein proteolytic cleavage site.

Variations in the KRSFIEDLLFNKV Motif over More Extensive Range of Coronaviruses

Once looks out to the inaccessible members, there are various variations in the KRSFIEDLLFNKV motif in which enormous varieties occurred in overall spike protein sequence, that are still conspicuous in the spike proteins of coronaviruses of differing different host species, some examples have listed in Table 2.2. The most recognizable variety is a periodic substitution of the cleavage point arginine (R) by a G. As opposed to interrupt the chance of cleavage, it is apparently dislodging that part to an arginine (R) or lysine (K) that deceives to the N-terminal (left half) of the motif. It is intriguing this ordinarily holds immovably the IEDLLF center of the motif.

With these overall discussions a notation comes that the KRSFIEDLLFNKV motif plays a significant role, and apparently a typical or comparable capacity across in any large amount of known coronaviruses that still appears to be a sensible one. Generally a significant role is that it considers any case for the SARS-CoV-2 infection and it's close to the coronavirus family members. As of now, no match with a coronavirus in GeneBank has been recognized in this section by BLAST-p utilizing queries with no phenylalanine (F), for example, RSAIEDLLLDKV, RSAIEDLLIDKV, RSAIEDLLADKV, RSAIEDLLMDKV, RSAIEDLLWDKV, and RSAIEDLLYDKV as queries, But the pursuit has not been thorough on the grounds that it would not be excessively conflicting to any of the current hypothesis if some were found. In the grouping with the inserted glycine (G) substitution of initial arginine (R) by the comparative decidedly charged lysine (K) is normal. In any case, as long as the motif is fundamentally conspicuous, no histidine (H) instead of initial arginine (R) has been found.

TABLE 2.2

Some Modifications of the RSFIEDLLFNKV Motif in Coronaviruses of Mammalian Hosts

Motif	Example	Description
RSFIEDLLFNKV	MN908947.3	SARS-CoV-2 and related coronaviruses, especially bat, civet, pig
RSIIEDLLFNKV	AJD09591.1	Porcine epidemic diarrhea virus
RSFFEDLLFDKL	ADX59495.1	Chaerephon bat coronavirus/Kenya/KY22/2006
RSFVEDLLFDKV	APD51483.1	NL63-related bat coronavirus
RSFIEDLLFDKI	YP_009336484.1	Lucheng Rn rat coronavirus
RSVLEDLLFDKI	ASF90465.1	Wencheng Sm shrew coronavirus
RSAIEDLLFNKV	AAP72150.1	Canine Coronavirus
RSAVEDLLFNKV	ADC35472.1	Feline coronavirus
RSAVEDLLFDKV	ABI14448.1	Feline coronavirus
RSAIEDLLFDKV	AIV41987.1	Common cold, also found in the coronaviruses of dogs, cats, rodents, pigs, rabbits, camels, ferret badgers, raccoon dogs, etc.
RSAIEDILFSKL	NP_073551.1	Common cold
RSAIEDLLFSKV	ASV64340.1	Porcine coronavirus (transmissible gastroenteritis of pigs, TGEV).
RSAIEDLLFAKV	ABG89301.1	Porcine TGEV Miller M6
RSAIEDILFSKV	ALK28767.1	229E-related bat coronavirus
RSFFEDLLFDKV	NC_006577.2	Human HCoV-HKU1 "Flu-ish" cold
RKYRSAIEDLLFDKV	ADU17734.1	Canine coronavirus
RKYRSAIEDLLFDKV	BAN67909.1	Feline coronavirus
RKYRSTIEDLLFDKV	BAP19067.1	Feline coronavirus
RKYGSAIEDLLFDKV	AAY32596.1	Feline coronavirus
ENKGSFIEDLLFDKV	AZF86124.1	Bat-CoV/P.kuhlii/Italy/3398-19/2015
EGKGSFIEDLLFDKV	YP_009201730.1	Bat - [BtNv-AlphaCoV/SC2013]
DNRGSFIEDLLFDKV	QGX41957.1	Western Australian microbat
VQKGSFIEDLLFNKV	AHA61268.1	Porcine epidemic diarrhea virus
VQKRSFIEDLLFNKV	QGA88709.1	Porcine epidemic diarrhea virus

Avian Coronaviruses KRSFIEDLLFNKV Motif Variations

The motif can't stretch out to the different strains uncertainly as recognizable fact that eventually point to the hierarchy that will raise infections and hosts subject to very unique particular weights, and the motif isn't the meaning of coronaviruses. In many cases it is actually perseveres as conspicuous in flying creatures, for example, duck (e.g., GenBank KX266757, KC119407 white-eye fowl CoV HKU (NC016991), magpie-robin (shama) CoV HKU18 (NC016993)) strains, a choice which traverses an enormous scope of coronavirus genome sizes. For detail description can see the arrangements below contrasted and the Wuhan fish market isolate Genbank MN908947.3 that indicating the theme underlined and in bold font.

Traces of the KRSFIEDLLFNKV Motif in Nidoviruses of Reptiles and Fish

Some sign of the constraint of endurance about the RSFIEDLLFNKV motif as the analyst leaves from SARS-CoV-19 may be given by the nidoviruses other than coronaviruses. Fairly coronavirus like nidoviruses is normal as for example reptile infections. The order Nidovirales contains wrapping, positive-strand RNA viruses with the biggest known RNA genomes. Nidoviruses have been recognized in snakes. They have all the earmarks of being most firmly identified with coronaviruses subfamily Torovirinae, and maybe best spoken to as a genus in this subfamily. Sequences suggestive of RSFIEDLLFNKV, for example KNFIDLLLAGF do happen in genomes, for example, the ball python genome, however, these truly lie beyond the restriction of genuine recognition. For instance, Clustal Omega gives 18% of definite match between the Wuhan isolate and spike protein nidovirus one of the reptile shingleback (GenBank ID YP_009666261.1), but the motif is scarcely unmistakable.

Counting fish nidovirus of the Pacific salmon (GenBank QEG08239.1) is striking here on the grounds that it underpins to the above arrangement since it is protected, but GTLYWLDY of the salmon nidovirus is a long way from KRSFIEDL and the closest going before conceivable cleavage point is arginine (R) 10 residues in the N-terminal (to the left side) direction. However, a comparative change happens in some mammalian coronaviruses thus that residue may even now assume as a comparative part of an actuation cleavage.

Theoretical Matches of the KRSFIEDLLFNKV Motif With Human Proteins

Looking for tantamount motif in human proteins that has a genuinely exceptional method of motive. It provide good results, if there is an important match with subsequences outcomes, they may address features of proteins to which both the spike protein and other human proteins may tie, autonomous of some other diversion for shared commonality. Whether or not extrinsic, as epitopes like those in a proposed synthetic vaccine they are steady of possible interest for assessing the peril of cross-reaction and impelling autoimmunity inbuilt inoculation plans, and on a specific occasion with peptidomimetics that brief a sheltered response, perhaps by a coupling vehemently to a human protein that the designer didn't anticipate. As discussed by Robson (2020a), there is a motif organize at 56% identity with 77% consideration is with tumor protein D55 isoform 2 [Homo sapiens], ID: NP_001001874.2, and correspondingly with Tumor protein D52-like 3 [Homo sapiens] ID: AAH33792.1. The accompanying match is concerning neprilsyn entries at simply 56% match and 55% consideration. None of these are satisfactorily close to worry concerning the acknowledgment of a resistant autoimmune response. Some really close matches of KRSFIEDLLFNKV and of the "A for F" modified motif RSAIEDLLFDKV have become noticeable that may possibly have a natural biological significance if point maintained by biological relevance, but they will be unpredictable matches. Concern about the human proteins only that hits a move from 100% spread with half identity to 62% spread with 92% identity. These hits can't be seen as basic for peptides of this length in isolation from other verification. In any case, some evidences seem to be justifying recording for future reference as for a probable regular biological function with respect to the disease. As viably noted by Robson (2020a) that RRSFIDELAFGRG is a portion of a human semaphorin (GenBank NP_001243276.1) that conveyed to consider the lung issues. Running RSAIEDLLFDKV itself in BLAST-p produces 100 coronaviruses hits. RNAREELLFD is found in human MHC class II antigen, GenBank AXN55588.1. RNAREELLFD is found in human immunoglobulin generous chain convergence region GenBank MCG49633.1. DLLFEKV is found in human tubulin, gamma complex related protein 6, isoform CRA_d GenBank EAW73510.1. E3 is excited with 75% identity and 87% matches for SFLEELLF in KHKSFLEELLF in ubiquitin. The cellular E3 ubiquitin ligase ring-finger and CHY zinc-finger domain containing 1 (RCHY1) have been perceived as associating accessories of the viral SARS-unique domain (SUD) and papain-like protease (PLpro), with the consideration of cell p53 as an antagonist of coronaviral replication. The Down-rule of p53 is a huge piece of antiviral innate immunity (Ma-Lauer et al., 2016). Again, these matches remain questionable. GenBank has of the solicitation for 0.2 billion nucleic acid sequences but a 13 residue peptide can have sequences up to 81,920,000 billion.

Fundamental Consideration of Spike Glycoprotein ACE2 Binding Region Features

As KRSFIEDLLFNKV motif stays supported and considered in this section now the focus is to recognizing the amino acid residues in ACE2 and the significance of spike protein. It might for instance include rationed residues that are not together in a constant sequence. While a preserved run of amino acid residue is adequate to be on the list of candidates for a significant site, significant destinations are not really saved runs of amino acid residues. This section is demonstrated that there is some protection, but a huge variety of compositions and RSFIEDLLFNKV. Subsequence RSFIEDLLFNKV and PIGAGICASY ... R examined by Robson (2020a) as the motifs that are related to initiation cleavage sites that don't lie in the receptor (ACE2) binding domain of the SARS-CoV-2 Spike glycoprotein. The connections between the entire spike protein and the receptor-binding domain in PDB entries 6M17 and PDB 6VW1 that appear in the arrangement below. Here a notable point is that the above receptor binding domain goes before the above motif in the sequence. A three-dimensional viewpoint is required for a valuation for the significant sequence features. See Figure 2.11, that have the PDB 6VW1 binding domain is on the right while the bound to ACE2 on the left.

Obviously, not all the receptor-binding domains are cooperating personally with ACE2. The segments of the receptor-binding domain that do associate with ACE2 likewise appear (underlined). To encourage further examination, the cyclic procedure on the spike protein receptor-binding domain were at first delegated cycle a, b, c, d, e, and f arranged by visual viewpoint, at that point joined into three subsequences 1, 2, and 3 that contain these cycles. The aspect of the spike glycoprotein sequences that expresses to the receptor

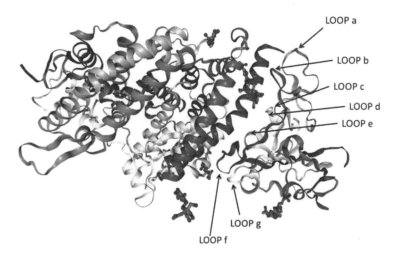

FIGURE 2.11 ACE2 structure connecting with spike glycoprotein receptor domain (protein databank entry 6VW1). (Continued)

```
CLUSTAL O(1.2.4) multiple sequence alignment
WuhanSeafood       MFVFLVLLPLVSSQCVNLTTRTQLPPAYTNSFTRGVYYPDKVFRSSVLHSTQDLFLPFFS   60
PDB6M17            ------------------------------------------------------------    0
PDB6VW1            ------------------------------------------------------------    0


WuhanSeafood       NVTWFHAIHVSGTNGTKRFDNPVLPFNDGVYFASTEKSNIIRGWIFGTTLDSKTQSLLIV  120
PDB6M17            ------------------------------------------------------------    0
PDB6VW1            ------------------------------------------------------------    0


WuhanSeafood       NNATNVVIKVCEFQFCNDPFLGVYYHKNNKSWMESEFRVYSSANNCTFEYVSQPFLMDLE  180
PDB6M17            ------------------------------------------------------------    0
PDB6VW1            ------------------------------------------------------------    0


WuhanSeafood       GKQGNFKNLREFVFKNIDGYFKIYSKHTPINLVRDLPQGFSALEPLVDLPIGINITRFQT  240
PDB6M17            ------------------------------------------------------------    0
PDB6VW1            ------------------------------------------------------------    0


WuhanSeafood       LLALHRSYLTPGDSSSGWTAGAAAYYVGYLQPRTFLLKYNENGTITDAVDCALDPLSETK  300
PDB6M17            ------------------------------------------------------------    0
PDB6VW1            ------------------------------------------------------------    0


WuhanSeafood       CTLKSFTVEKGIYQTSNFRVQPTESIVRFPNITNLCPFGEVFNATRFASVYAWNRKRISN  360
PDB6M17            ------------------RVVPSGDVVRFPNITNLCPFGEVFNATKFPSVYAWERKKISN   42
PDB6VW1            ------------------RVVPSGDVVRFPNITNLCPFGEVFNATKFPSVYAWERKKISN   42
                                     ** *: .:********************:* *****:**:***
                                                   LOOP 1e        LOOP 1d
WuhanSeafood   361 CVADYSVLYNSASFSTFKCYGVSPTKLNDLCFTNVYADSFVIRGDEVRQIAPGQTGKIAD  420
PDB6M17            CVADYSVLYNSTFFSTFKCYGVSATKLNDLCFSNVYADSFVVKGDDVRQIAPGQTGVIAD  102
PDB6VW1            CVADYSVLYNSTFFSTFKCYGVSATKLNDLCFSNVYADSFVVKGDDVRQIAPGQTGVIAD  102
                   **********: ********** *********:*********::**:********** ***
                   LOOP 1c           LOOP 2g                          LOOP 3a
WuhanSeafood   421 YNYKLPDDFTGCVIAWNSNNLDSKVGGNYNYLYRLFRKSNLKPFERDISTEIYQAGSTPC  480
PDB6M17            YNYKLPDDFMGCVLAWNTRNIDATSTGN-------------KPFERDISTEIYQAGSTPC  149
PDB6VW1            YNYKLPDDFMGCVLAWNTRNIDATSTGNYNYKYRLFRKSNLKPFERDISTEIYQAGSTPC  162
                   ********* ***:***:.*:*:.  **              *****************
                   LOOP 3b    LOOP 3f
WuhanSeafood   481 NGVEGFNCYFPLQSYGFQPTKGVGYQPYRVVVLSFELLHAPATVCGPKKSTNLVKNKCVN  540
PDB6M17            NGVEGFNCYFPLQSYGFQPTNGVGYQPYRVVVLP-------------KLSTDLIK-----  191
PDB6VW1            NGVEGFNCYFPLQSYGFQPTNGVGYQPYRVVVLSFELLNAPATVCGPKLSTDLIK-----  217
                   ********************:***********      * **:*:.*


WuhanSeafood       FNFNGLTGTGVLTESNKKFLPFQQFGRDIADTTDAVRDPQTLEILDITPCSFGGVSVITP  600
PDB6M17            ------------------------------------------------------------  191
PDB6VW1            ------------------------------------------------------------  217


WuhanSeafood       GTNTSNQVAVLYQDVNCTEVPVAIHADQLTPTWRVYSTGSNVFQTRAGCLIGAEHVNNSY  660
PDB6M17            ------------------------------------------------------------  191
PDB6VW1            ------------------------------------------------------------  217


WuhanSeafood       ECDIPIGAGICASYQTQTNSPRRARSVASQSIIAYTMSLGAENSVAYSNNSIAIPTNFTI  720
PDB6M17            ------------------------------------------------------------  191
PDB6VW1            ------------------------------------------------------------  217


WuhanSeafood       SVTTEILPVSMTKTSVDCTMYICGDSTECSNLLLQYGSFCTQLNRALTGIAVEQDKNTQE  780
PDB6M17            ------------------------------------------------------------  191
PDB6VW1            ------------------------------------------------------------  217


WuhanSeafood       VFAQVKQIYKTPPIKDFGGFNFSQILPDPSKPSKRSFIEDLLFNKVTLADAGFIKQYGDC  840
PDB6M17            ------------------------------------------------------------  191
PDB6VW1            ------------------------------------------------------------  217


WuhanSeafood       LGDIAARDLICAQKFNGLTVLPPLLTDEMIAQYTSALLAGTITSGWTFGAGAALQIPFAM  900
PDB6M17            ------------------------------------------------------------  191
```

FIGURE 2.11 (Continued) ACE2 structure connecting with spike glycoprotein receptor domain (protein databank entry 6VW1). (Continued)

```
PDB6VW1             ---------------------------------------------------------  217

WuhanSeafood        QMAYRFNGIGVTQNVLYENQKLIANQFNSAIGKIQDSLSSTASALGKLQDVVNQNAQALN  960
PDB6M17             ---------------------------------------------------------  191
PDB6VW1             ---------------------------------------------------------  217

WuhanSeafood        TLVKQLSSNFGAISSVLNDILSRLDKVEAEVQIDRLITGRLQSLQTYVTQQLIRAAEIRA  1020
PDB6M17             ---------------------------------------------------------  191
PDB6VW1             ---------------------------------------------------------  217

WuhanSeafood        SANLAATKMSECVLGQSKRVDFCGKGYHLMSFPQSAPHGVVFLHVTYVPAQEKNFTTAPA  1080
PDB6M17             ---------------------------------------------------------  191
PDB6VW1             ---------------------------------------------------------  217
```

```
LOOP 3a 3b 1c 1d 1e 3f                                    LOOP 3f 2g LOOP 1d
STIEEQAKTFLDKFNHEAEDLFYQSSLASWNYNTNITEENVQNMNNAGDKWSAFLKEQSTLAQMYPLQEIQNLTVKLQLQ
ALQQNGSSVLSEDKSKRLNTILNTMSTIYSTGKVCNPDNPQECLLLEPGLNEIMANSLDYNERLWAWESWRSEVGKQLRP
LYEEYVVLKNEMARANHYEDYGDYWRGDYEVNGVDGYDYSRGQLIEDVEHTFEEIKPLYEHLHAYVRAKLMNAYPSYISP
                                                              LOOP 2f 3G
IGCLPAHLLGDMWGRFWTNLYSLTVPFGQKPNIDVTDAMVDQAWDAQRIFKEAEKFFVSVGLPNMTQGFWENSMLTDPGN
        LOOP 3f
VQKAVCHPTAWDLGKGDFRILMCTKVTMDDFLTAHHEMGHIQYDMAYAAQPFLLRNGANEGFHEAVGEIMSLSAATPKHL
KSIGLLSPDFQEDNETEINFLLKQALTIVGTLPFTYMLEKWRWMVFKGEIPKDQWMKKWWEMKREIVGVVEPVPHDETYC
DPASLFHVSNDYSFIRYYTRTLYQFQFQEALCQAAKHEGPLHKCDISNSTEAGQKLFNMLRLGKSEPWTLALENVVGAKN
MNVRPLLNYFEPLFTWLKDQNKNSFVGWSTDWSPYAD
```

```
MSSSSWLLLSLVAVTAAQSTIEEQAKTFLDKFNHEAEDLFYQSSLASWNYNTNITEENVQNMNNAGDKWSAFLKEQSTLAQMYPLQEIQNLTV
KLQLQALQQNGSSVLSEDKSKRLNTILNTMSTIYSTGKVCNPDNPQECLLLEPGLNEIMANSLDYNERLWAWESWRSEVGKQLRPLYEEYVVLK
NEMARANHYEDYGDYWRGDYEVNGVDGYDYSRGQLIEDVEHTFEEIKPLYEHLHAYVRAKLMNAYPSYISPIGCLPAHLLGDMWGRFWTNLY
SLTVPFGQKPNIDVTDAMVDQAWDAQRIFKEAEKFFVSVGLPNMTQGFWENSMLTDPGNVQKAVCHPTAWDLGKGDFRILMCTKVTMDD
FLTAHHEMGHIQYDMAYAAQPFLLRNGANEGFHEAVGEIMSLSAATPKHLKSIGLLSPDFQEDNETEINFLLKQALTIVGTLPFTYMLEKWRWM
VFKGEIPKDQWMKKWWEMKREIVGVVEPVPHDETYCDPASLFHVSNDYSFIRYYTRTLYQFQFQEALCQAAKHEGPLHKCDISNSTEAGQKLF
NMLRLGKSEPWTLALENVVGAKNMNVRPLLNYFEPLFTWLKDQNKNSFVGWSTDWSPYADQSIKVRISLKSALGDKAYEWNDNEMYLFRSSV
AYAMRQYFLKVKNQMILFGEEDVRVANLKPRISFNFFVTAPKNVSDIIPRTEVEKAIRMSRSRINDAFRLNDNSLEFLGIQPTLGPPNQPPVSIWLIVF
GVVMGVIVVGIVILIFTGIRDRKKPTPLLGKSWLTAILKD
```

S̲T̲IE**EQ**AKTF*L**DKF**N*HE*A̲E̲D̲L̲F*Y̲Q̲S̲SLAS**WN**
GFNCYFPLQSYGFQPT

```
NCYFPLRGYGF - Wuhan seafood market isolate Genbank ID: MN908947.3
NCYWPLRGYGF - [SARS coronavirus C028] Civet GenBank ID: AAV98001.1
NCYWPLKGYGF - [SARS coronavirus PC4-137] palm civet GenBank ID:AAV49720.1
NCYWPLNGYGF - [SARS coronavirus CS21] Civet GenBank ID: ABF68958.1
NCYWPLNDYGF - [Bat SARS-like coronavirus] Bat GenBank ID: ATO98218.1
NCTWP----GF - [Feline coronavirus] Feline GenBank ID: AMD11161.1
NCYP---AGVN - [Human common cold coronavirus 229E] GenBank ID: NP_073551.1
TCNNIDAAKIY - [Human common cold coronavirus OC43] GenBank ID: AIV41987.1
```

```
MN908947.3    RDISTEIYQAGSTPCNGVEGFNCYFPLQSYGFQPTNGVGYQPYRVVVLSFELLHAPATVC  525
NP_073551.1   -------------PIVANWAYSKYYTIGSLYVSWSDGD------------GITGVPQVPE   433
              *     . .:.  *: : *   .. ::*          :  .* *

MN908947.3    YNSASFSTFKCYGVSP------------TKLNDLCFTNVYADSFVIRGDEVRQIAPG--  413
NP_073551.1   PQSGGGKCFNCYPAGVNITLANFNETKGPLCVDTSHFTTKYVAVYANVGRWSASINTGNC  369
              :*.. .. *:** ..           ::  **. *. :.  *    .* *
```

FIGURE 2.11 (**Continued**) ACE2 structure connecting with spike glycoprotein receptor domain (protein databank entry 6VW1).

(ACE2) binding domain that can be appeared by considering the proteins utilized in the two auxiliary determinations 6M17 and 6VW1 in the Protein Data Bank, appeared below in an arrangement made utilizing Clustal Omega arrangement.

The amino acids residues in the underline and bold text are the subsequences of ACE2 that cooperate with the above spike protein ACE2 binding domain cycles, which are demonstrated over every subsequence. These incorporate some longer range electrostatic connections and expected dissolvable impacts. Those additionally in italics *DKFNHEAEDLFY, DKFNHEAEDLFY and KGDFR* have especially solid connections.

The perspective point of view is that the full sequence for ACE2 as angiotensin-converting enzyme 2 isoform X1 [Homo sapiens] GenBank passage XP_011543851.1, is as per the following. The chunk in the three-dimensional structure above is in the striking underlined text.

A notable point here is that in all tests structures there is an association of "glycosylation-like" molecules. For instance, in 6VW1 there are very much confined N-acetyl-D-glucosamine, β-D-mannose, and 1,2-ethanediol molecules that make critical collaborations in a glue-like way, and basically "glue around the edges." Anyway, there is no undeniable sign of association of glycosylation in the principle inside the cooperation face of the complex. For example in between amino acid residues there are cozy connections among protein-protein.

Association of ACE2 and spike glycoprotein includes cooperation between the twisted α-helix residues 19–54 (STIEE ... NYNTN) of ACE2 and an all-encompassing chain configuration, viably an extended cycle that runs from residue 485–500 (GFNCY ... YGQPT) of the spike glycoprotein and includes or finishes in cycle 3a, 3b, and 3f. On accounting the communication of ACE2 with the ACE2 binding domain of the spike glycoprotein, one could on a fundamental imagine blocking the ACE2 as a receptor with a copy of the spike protein surface or blocking the receptor-binding site of the spike glycoprotein protein with a copy of the ACE2 receptor surface. In different types of infections, the previous is generally viewed as more conceivable, but the last would not meddle with the typical capacity of ACE2 and it is obviously essential for the manners by which the immune system, and quite antibodies, work. Potentially the fundamental contention against this subsequent option is that it is essentially identical to utilizing antibodies raised against the spike protein, for example in actuality, uninvolved vaccination.

During the phase of final writing, different news stories are causing to notice the possible utilization of the upper sequence or parts of it, which is that of the α-helix of ACE2.[4] In the above "arrangement," 35 residues contains by the helix and the all-inclusive chain contains 16. They have a comparable length as will be true to form for such structures. A α-helix has an ascent of 1.5 Å per residue along with its axis and there are in common protein helices with turn varieties that suggest up to 2.0 Å. The β-strand or a comparable expanded chain in the spike glycoprotein that cooperates with it has an ascent of around 3.5 Å per residue. A notable point is here that this is not expected to be a representation of sequence match; these chains need to cooperate. In that case, there is an absence of charged residues (acidic and essential side chains) in the extended chain of the spike glycoprotein in structure 6VW1, although an aspartic acid (D) replaces the serine (S) in certain strains, arginine (R) replaces asparagine (N) in others, and so on. A backbone view in detail is confusingly cluttered, but one may identify residue that connect to the boundary region of the ACE2 and spike protein. All sidechains in the above spike protein subsequence GFNCYFPLQSYGFQPT either connect or are probably going to have some impact at the interface. It is maybe helpful to have the underlying mental picture that, generally, the planes of the peptide groups are tangential to the abovementioned α-helix surface, instead of establishing an extended chain that makes an edge-on approach. As even Figure 2.11 does the trick to clarify, the extended chain, similar to any alleged broadened chain in proteins, is basically an obvious helix of the bigger pitch, resembling a very loosened up α-helix, and is itself somewhat supercoiled to fold over the ACE2 α-helix. For this situation, this will in general follow the elbow or twist in the α-helix, remaining generally corresponding to the neighborhood hub of the α-helix, in order to make intimate contact overall.

ACE2 Binding Region for Synthetic Vaccine and Antagonist Design

On the off chance that GFNCYFPLQSYGFQPT is to be utilized as an epitope simple, the cysteine (C) might be tried as an advantageous linker to a carrier protein, otherwise it will be supplanted by serine (S) as a close analogue. By concerning the peptide antagonist, the trouble with utilizing the above sequences STIEE … And, GFNCY … is that they are promptly degraded by having proteases. This would not happen if the peptide is made completely of Domino-acid restudies. A retro-Inverso peptide (Rai, 2019; Robson, 2020a) is comprised of D-amino acids in a switched sequence to the subsequence which tries to copy, and in the extended adaptation accept a side chain geography like to the original native peptide, however with backbone $N-H$ and carbonyl $C=O$ groups interchanged.

$$\left(NH_3^+\right) - dextro - \left[NWSALSSQYFLDEAEHNFKDLFTKAQEEITS\right] - \left(COO^-\right)\left(NH_3^+\right)$$

$$- dextro - \left[TPQFGYSQLPFYSNFG\right] - \left(COO^-\right)$$

These are peptidomimetics of the subsequences sequences STIEE … in ACE2 and GFNCY … in the spike glycoprotein respectively. The cysteine (C) in … CNFG in the subsequent molecule might be a helpful linker for an epitope for an antibody but it should be supplanted by serine (S) in an antagonist. Review that the issue of having the backbone amide $N-H$ and carbonyl $C=O$ groups interchanged is that if the original segment of the backbone being copied, any $N-H$ and $C=O$ groups structure a hydrogen bond with recipient and donor groups in the protein, those hydrogen bonds are now disrupted in the proposed competitive antagonist, e.g., they would be unstable $N-H\cdots H-N$ or $C=O\cdots O=C$ connections. It would be in this manner appear to be significant advantage in utilizing the ACE2 copy, because that is basically an α-helix that utilization up its backbone amide and carbonyl groups. However, retro-inverso α-helices are not normally found in the region that have given some level of accomplishment (Rai, 2019), for example antigenic mimicry. It would be in any case appear to be a value to test both of the retro-inverse peptides in laboratory studies.

As per the above development further both are comes as the basic of a synthetic antibody, or as a peptidomimetic, and concerning the value of extending out the examinations to little natural drug molecules, everything in the above relies upon the degree to which GFNCYFPLQSYGFQPT can deliver escape transformations which may useless before long rend. As in the previous studies, this can relate to the varieties of the above sequence that bother in nearer and considerably more distant relatives. As the accompanying shows, utilizing BLAST-p that don't allow to go extremely far from SARS-CoV-2 to discover matches with just aspect of this sequence (coverage) and the differences inside that region of a partial match.

From the Wuhan seafood market the original pneumonia infection isolated named Wuhan-Hu-1, GenBank ID MN908947.3, FNCYFPLQSYGF is the subsequence in these regions, and the subsequence coverage as example presented in the blow figure that found by BLAST-p.

The remainder of the above subsequence founded by BLAST-p at https://blast.ncbi.nlm. nih.gov/Blast.cgi that matched outcomes differ in an absolute arrangement by Clustal Omega at https://www.ebi.ac.uk/Tools/msa/clustalo/, as follows, obviously, this shows the high degree of variety that happens as one continues on to coronaviruses less identified with the Wuhan seafood market isolation that is accepted to be related with the initial point of COVID-19.

For process culmination, it should note that the arrangement acquired in the region that BLAST-p showed is as per the following.

Phenylalanine (F) normally promptly precedes before a large number of these coordinating subsequences NCYFP... NCYWP... and so on., and the moderate substitution tryptophan (W) substitution for the subsequent phenylalanine (F) is additionally normal, so it might be important that FNCTWP is an subsequence in the mammalian vomeronasal type-2 receptor 1 on sensory cells inside the primary nasal chamber that identifies hefty moisture borne scent particles, and FNCTWP is also found in dynein. Numerous infections require the short end–direction dynein motor complex transport on microtubules from the cell surface toward the core, and dynein notwithstanding kinesins for the transport toward the plasma membrane. However, an immediate association with viral disease, while tempting, is a long way from clear concerning any mechanistic or transformative clarification. Likewise, dynein atomic transport might be less pertinent to the coronavirus (a RNA infection), but certain RNA infections can depend on the dynein system (for example Hantavirus utilizes it for endoplasmic reticulum-Golgi middle compartment). At any rate, the above shows the sorts of further, maybe promptly more subtle, capacities that the above ACE2 binding domain of the spike glycoprotein, and the above motif, may have.

Inside the coronaviruses, there is some level of preservation that recommends that NCYWPLNDYGF is a portion for the infection to save and an insight that FNCTWPGF is the key measure, but there are soon obviously critical varieties across coronaviruses of various hosts as withdraw from the Wuhan seafood market disengage contrasted and the RSFIEDLLFNKV motif in the region of S2′ cleavage (Robson, 2020a). Small natural medications configuration to emulate this segment, or essentially intended to antagonize ACE2 binding, are hence conceivably powerless to get away from changes, for example, quick appearance of medication resistance.

Binding Studies With 11β-Hydroxysteroid Dehydrogenase Type 1 as Model Pharmacaphore

An internal model of pharmacophore decision hindered by emodin is the 11β-hydroxysteroid dehydrogenase type 1 (Robson, 2020a). Here the advancement of the contention for ideal focuses for immunizations and therapeutic antagonists, the above objective fits in as follows. While the above with respect to ACE2 binding must be remembered for antagonists, as noted over the motif isn't well monitored, thus could be inclined to the improvement of escape mutations, for example, obtained protection from immunizations and therapeutic antagonists. Due to the predominant topic of an ACE2 α-helix communicating with an extended chain cycle of the spike glycoprotein, the structure of the cooperation region is genuinely simple to the reason for different SARS strains, and there was so far no undeniable firmly repetitive topic of huge saved residues that are irregular (for example not together in a similar subsequence) that could be interfacing intimately with ACE2. Simultaneously, while emodin seems to act at the ACE2 binding site (Ho et al., 2007).

Prominently, the ACE2 binding region of the spike protein and the binding sequence describe about human proteins and might have different capacities that emodin and related compounds, related in the sense that they are in any event reliable with features of pharmacophore, may restrain. From the earlier, the binding properties of emodin, and the decision of 11β-hydroxysteroid dehydrogenase type 1 as model pharmacophore could similarly identify with the RSFIEDLLFNKV site, or some other site, or a blend of a few. The case for collaboration vomeronasal type-2 receptor 1 and dynein is a best case for marginal, however, these models represented the decent variety of different sorts of capacities, critical to the infection, that may apply. Regardless, any relations among emodin and comparable and possibly related atoms survive from enthusiasm to obstructing the SARS-CoV-2 section and the worse casualty would be the progression of the story created above, which is expected to represent a progression of reasoning in utilizing the standard tools of bioinformatics.

11β-hydroxysteroid dehydrogenase type 1 is intriguing as obliging an extraordinary variation of ligands at the steroid-binding site, however not without a level of particularity as to general features of the ligands, thus these have a potential of SARS-CoV-2 therapeutics. Remembering the refutation standard (Robson, 2020a) that a pharmacophore (or contribution to an ensemble of pharmacophore) the dehydrogenase is deserve to utilizing until another ligand or other data demonstrates something else. So far pharmacophore validation here, for example, a show that it is an appropriate pharmacophore model until demonstrated something else, has been founded fortuitously on emodin and compounds looking synthetically, that is known as practically speaking or contended hypothetically to cooperate with SARS infection entry in some way and bind at least weakly, tentatively or computationally, to 11β-hydroxysteroid dehydrogenase type 1 (Robson, 2020a). A review of compounds that are known tentatively to restrain the dehydrogenase and known tentatively inhibit coronavirus entry, replication and development are being prepared. In any case, validation is broadly dependent on a more vulnerable however bigger assemblage of fundamental binding examinations including an variation of antagonist of coronavirus disease and regularly different sorts of infection contamination, that likewise bind at any rate weakly to the dehydrogenase. The greater part of these, emodin-like and something else, was first found by Q-UEL information gathering instruments as utilized in the underlying coronavirus study (Robson, 2020a) combined with "very early candidate selection principles" in light of evaluations of the mean restricting the quality of grouping when restricting admirably. Note that a hydrogen bond worth around 4 kcal/mol is regardless viably zero when restricting great since it is comparative with binding to water.

Interestingly, aromatic and huge aliphatic and are worth circa 3 kcal/mol because of hydrophobic associations that rcly upon being viewed as comparative with water. There are more perplexing electrostatic and intramolecular entropic contemplations past the current extension. Weak and powerless candidates are additionally considered on the grounds that there might be multiple binding modes that will take a lot of computation time to investigate but which could yield lower restricting binding free energies.

This creates a genuinely "mixed bag" of compounds, in light of the contention that infections and coronavirus specifically may utilize every one of its predetermined number of uncovered or exposable locales for a few purposes, and the coronavirus seems to promptly acclimate to new mechanisms under the particular pressure of medications and antibodies. The subtleties of these particles and studies are the subject of a further studies that will likewise discussed more about some interesting binding together topics. In short, they incorporate numerous names as hoped-for medications fight against the coronavirus that show up in the news and social media conversation. It is helpful to consider them to be separating into three classes.

Quinone-Like

A "quinone" is a class of aromatic compounds that have two carbonyls or ketone C=O utilitarian groups in a similar six-membered ring, however, in "quinone-like" the section incorporates numerous compounds looking like steroid pieces that may have numerous or only one carbonyl grouping and a few rings. This gruping incorporates 9,10-anthraquinone and subsidiaries that identify with numerous significant medications some with laxative and anti-inflammatory capacities, collectively it named anthracenediones. They incorporate ubiquinone as coenzyme Q, and different shorter aliphatic chain structures hydroxyl-decyl-ubiquinone and shorter aliphatic chain structures, laxatives (for example, dantron, emodin, and aloe-emodin, and a portion of the senna glycosides), antimalarials (for example, rufigallol, antineoplastics) utilized in the therapy of disease, for example, mitoxantrone, pixantrone, and the anthracyclines. Alert is required in perusing this list as an expected therapeutics, on the grounds that anthraquinone subordinates rhein, aloe-emodin or anthrone that does not have the methyl gathering, parietin (physcion), somewhat emodin itself, and chrysophanol extricated from Cassia occidentalis are poisonous and known to cause hepatomyoencephalopathy in kids. It is a clinical term viably characterized to cover laziness, jaundice, and adjusted senses of kids in India after utilization of Cassia.

Steroid-Like

This group incorporates some plant steroid-like compounds, for example, carbenoxolone itself from liquorish (licorice) and others found in soy and sprouts.17β-estradiol (the endogenous ligand liable for the development and improvement of numerous tissues) diethylstilbestrol (a manufactured estrogen); 7-methyl-benz[a] anthracene-3,9-diol (a potential characteristic item from a typical polyaromatic hydrocarbon) is likewise of intrigue. This group resembles as follows (1), however the concern for this group (2) is that molecules like emodin that are known to antagonize viral or different diseases are commonly smaller, so it conceivable that a more pertinent pharmacophore would sterically bar a huge steroid-like ring.

Quinine-Like

Should not get confuse between "quinone-like" and "quinine-like." Quinine is an alkaloid derived from cinchona bark, used to treat intestinal sickness like malaria and as an element of carbonated water. A typical element is, regardless of the plenitude of fragrant and different rings that in the quinine-like case incorporate nitrogen, so differently taking after pyrimidines, purines, histidine, and tryptophan. This group is of current impressive enthusiasm as possible therapeutics for COVID-19. Specifically interests are Chloroquine, Theophylline, Tavipiravir, Baloxavir marboxil. Some ACE and ACE2 inhibitors can be ordered in this group. Camostat, a serine protease inhibitor that has been considered as an expected restorative for COVID-19 is advantageous to put in this class on account of its analogs but it doesn't itself incorporate a nitrogen iota inside a ring.

There are a few potential biological associations that will be examined somewhere else. One may be quickly referenced while thinking about the consolidated restorative utilization of an individual from each set. Ubiquinone-like compound can restrain ubiquinone locales that work together with NADH and NADPH cofactor destinations. The last thusly are regularly hindered by the quinine-like individuals.

Numerous other compounds commonly bind "feebly," however, steroid-like compounds are solid fasteners and numerous quinine-like mixes are medium covers: these are examined beneath. Binding quality is obviously a matter of degree. RT (where R is the gas constant and T the total temperature) is 0.593 at 298 K, for example circa 0.6 at biological temperatures, so 1 kcal/mol isn't critical to the thermal noise. Free energies of 2, 3, 4, and 5 compare to restricting affiliation constants of 5, 148, 786, and 4160. The free energies are normally communicated as negative, for the viewpoint from the related system. Taking into account that supreme qualities are substantially less reliable than relative qualities in this field, one may moderately consider restricting energy of 3.5 kcal/mol as a commendable defense for keeping a compound on a list, if one doesn't wish to dismiss rashly, and this appears to be sensible on the off chance that one actually has as a primary concern the invalidation rule. This incorporates the psychological picture that a model pharmacophore, for example, 11β-hydroxysteroid dehydrogenase type 1 has a genuinely enormous pit which doesn't give solid steric inhibition to the candidate ligands, but new proofs may show that a huge ligand, for example, a steroid may be too large to fit the genuine objective which the exploratory data is describing. As such, inadequacies in the pharmacophore model will begin to show up while thinking about bigger potential medications.

The additional advantage of utilizing 11β-hydroxysteroid dehydrogenase type 1 as a model pharmacophore that the data base of experimental and computational investigations on compounds that bind to it. It should be stated that in any case for any basic transformative connection between this dehydrogenase and the spike protein binding receptor ACE2 would be at their best marginal. 11β-hydroxysteroid dehydrogenase type 1 has 292 residues and ACE2 has 613. There is a 24% identity match of amino acid residues in the region of the most ideal match of the dehydrogenase. Additionally there is a 19% conservative substitution (CLUSTAL ":", for example, protection between groups of firmly comparative properties with a score more than 0.5 on the PAM 250 matrix). Whenever it consider individually, this would give some premise to additionally investigating a relationship. Certainly, the regular general guideline is that any two successions are viewed as homologous if they are over 30% accurate amino acid residue matches, and carefully this ought to apply over their whole lengths. In any case, an attention is required on the grounds that the 30% definite match basis is notable to miss numerous easily distinguished homologs and 15–20% is in some cases founds supported by proof of the evolutionary and practical relationship. For instance, arrangements between the basic cold and SARS-CoV-2 spike proteins discussed in previously section are in this range, however, there are lots of valid justification to accept a typical ancestry, there is general conformational similarity, and fundamental features of some sequence motifs are conserved. There are some logics of practically fold motifs with ACE2 that containing two 11β-hydroxysteroid dehydrogenase type 1 folds. The dehydrogenase is a heap of exactly 12 well defined, parallel and antiparallel α-helices of up to around 30 residues, mixed by seven short β-pleated sheet strands. ACE2 has approximately 20 well defined, predominantly, and generally equal and antiparallel α-helices of up to around 30 residues, scattered by six short β-pleated sheet strands. If there is typical developmental origin of 11β-hydroxysteroid dehydrogenase type 1 and ACE2 domains, it is inaccessible, however, it remains barely conceivable, and the more broad conformational investigation is in progress.

Few proofs are available to support the similarity between 11β-hydroxysteroid dehydrogenase type 1 and TMPRSS2, although a serine residue is exceptionally saved in the catalytic site in both cases, which seemingly makes it deserving of some underlying investigation. TMPRSS2 contains a particular cysteine-rich scavenger domain (residues 150–242) and a serine protease domain (residues 255–484). CLUSTAL O(1.2.4) multiple sequence arrangement gives an accurate match of amino acid of just 17.5%. Further they have 17.5% traditionalist sub substitution (CLUSTAL ":", see above). For TMPRSS2 there are some intriguing short-area that are matches with a similar order of appearance, for example, AQYYYS with AYYYYS, VVSHC with VVSHC, LYHSD with LFHDD, and GILRQS with GALRQE, by which certain arguments increased statistical worth slightly. No significant conformational homology is apparent, so it is considered bound to be an opportunity match, and any argument for the similarity between the proteins would be based on some sort of convergent development depends on the certain regular ligands, reviewing again that the coronavirus may profit by repressing the inflammatory reaction.

Fundamental examinations based on the ligands discussed below recommend some level of the binding (4.5 kcal/mol and better, for example, more negative) to both the abovementioned and 11β-hydroxysteroid dehydrogenase type 1, however, these examinations are as yet not fully complete, and low energies may yet be obtained. The most generous database of results that can sensibly be viewed as last is in huge part from the first examinations (Robson et al., 2011). Their carbenoxolone was naturally advanced (via programmed altering of its synthetic structure) under the joined particular pressure of improving binding to 11β-hydroxysteroid dehydrogenase type 1 while avoiding a significant match with compounds secured by all US patents (Robson et al., 2011), and subsequent docking and high evaluation molecular dynamic simulations were done on IBM's Blue Gene (Robson et al., 2011). Many subsequent examinations have been completed on utilizing KRUNCH on a computing system, on the grounds that in the underlying investigation it predicted well that the Blue Gene results giving the KRUNCH binding energies obtained were corrected to fit the Blue Gene outcomes by a linear regression formula (Robson et al., 2011).

Review again that it is based on similarities between certain aggravates that antagonize SARS infection entry and bind the steroid dehydrogenase, in addition to a notable shared trait on account of emodin (for example it binds both), that this model pharmacophore was picked. Since emodin and numerous different compounds of interest that contain two or more aromatic rings, it is sensible, at any rate as an underlying strategy, that one may view them as bits of the steroid ring system and start them in the equivalent steroid-binding cavity on same "plane" as the steroid ring. Such cases that includes minor varieties as sidechains on the first steroid center, the best approach to make initial fit to utilizing carbenoxolone as a guide is self-evident. However, the level perspective on the steroid is misdirecting. The steroid ring system can "buckle" in different cis-trans arrangements of bonds in the rings, and the larger sidechain adaptations favored based on intramolecular energy are maybe not self-evident. In spite of the fact that the revolution boundaries for the vast majority of the advances are obviously over the thermal energy (kT) conformations (0.6 kcal/mol), the related energy demands for clasping of parts of the steroid ring system of differently and generally 2.5–5.0 kcal/mol is not exactly the ligand-receptor binding the related energy demands are underneath the gain in energy from ligand-receptor official to the protein target. This has appeared in the high-grade quantum mechanical Hartree–Fock GAMESS estimations on Blue Gene in the first investigation however which have not been depicted in the literature. Limited energy conformers of steroid-like compounds considered appear in Figure 2.12.

Such counts in vacuo are less dependable for the charged species, but one may get a quantitative evaluation from relative qualities and comparative uncharged species. These compounds are likewise indicated all more obvious chemist's viewpoint in the format of two-dimensional formula. Figure 2.13 shows one of the early analogs of carbenoxolone

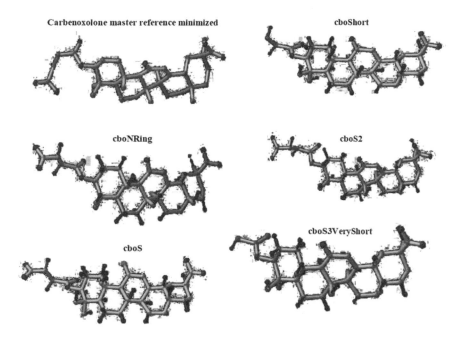

FIGURE 2.12 Preferred conformers of model steroid-like analogs by Hartree–Fock calculations.

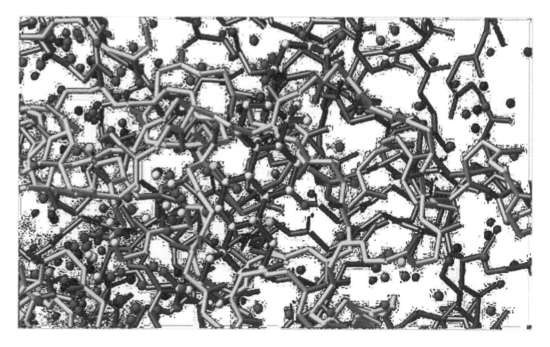

FIGURE 2.13 A Carbenoxolone Analog in site the 11β-hydroxysteroid dehydrogenase type 1 Steroid Binding Cavity. It is the stronger binder in the KRUNCH Modeling System.

in the 11βhydroxysteroid dehydrogenase type 1 steroid-binding site. The specific enthusiasm for this compound is as per the following. Since the first investigation (Robson et al., 2011) KRUNCH made a decision about this as the most grounded cover at 16.8 kcal/mol, this compound was regularly utilized as a beginning template for initial docking arrangements when utilizing KRUNCH. This is despite the fact that (1) it is presumably an impossible decision for a physicist to use in practice because likely oligomerization of the thioketone groups, (2) Corphos (also called Cortisol 21-phosphate, Cortisol, phosphate, Hydrocortisone-21-phosphate or 21-Hydrocortisonephosphoric acid) was the most strongest molecule at 16.8 kcal when utilizing the AMBER power field for molecular dynamics on IBM's Blue Gene (Robson et al., 2011). The thioketone still held sensible binding energy of 16.3 kcal/mol in the last examination, for example effectively a similar restricting quality inside the state of art. Figure 2.13 doesn't gives itself subtleties of any ligand-protein associations, although it does delineates the most secure of fit. That means, except to the lower right of the thioketone ring of the ligand, which seems to identify with genuine opportunities for extra groups to be added to carbenoxolone at that position.

Carbenoxolone and introductory closely related subordinates determined in that review (Robson et al., 2011) are appeared in Figure 2.13, authoritative in the range, 17 to 14 kcal/mol. Exactness and restricted authenticity of such strategies don't generally legitimize more exact explanations on binding energy, and the classification of binding below is an as solid medium, and powerless that observed by Robson et al. (2011). Authors differently consider binding energies from five to nine as a safe prerequisite for significant binding, ng, but again this is dependent upon the contemplations of precision, and practically all concur that it is just the relative qualities that are significant. The notable point is that while they are regularly deciphered as assessments of binding free energy, the entropy segment, especially of the watery dissolvable and solute-dissolvable interactions, is hard to estimate. Test restricting estimations of ligands as a rule in biological system normally range from 4 to 16 kcal/mol, however over 95% lie in the range from 7 to 13 kcal/mol. These ketone subsidiaries are all the more of hypothetical enthusiasm for restricting examinations in light of the fact that practically speaking they may cause oligomerization.

Recall that the two peptide analogs of features of the spike protein of interest are as follows;

$$Original \; L-Mimetic. \left(NH_3^+\right)-GPSKRSFIEDLLFNKVTL$$

$$-\left(COO^-\right) retroinverso \; mimetic \left(NH_3^+\right)$$

$$-dextro-[GNFLLDEIFSRKSRKS]-\left(COO^-\right)$$

Simulations is the only presentational way to be bind relatively weak molecules of range 10 and 8 kcal/mol, respectively, but these compounds are exceptionally flexible with a hypothetical internal in vacuo conformational entropy comparing to about 19.5 kcal/mol that show different binding modes and conformers on binding, and may not be finished yet. A high performance computer system like IBM's Blue Gene utilized in the prior medication configuration study (Robson et al., 2011) that would be surely help.

Figures 2.14 and 2.15 indicate lots of compounds from the ZINC database (Khan & Kumar, 2019), and most were distinguished from the first 11β-hydroxysteroid

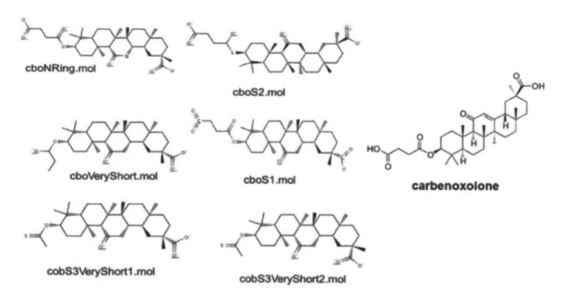

FIGURE 2.14 Pharmacophore Organic Compounds Binding as the solid binders. The assessed restricting energy is in the range of –17 to –14 kcal/mol. These were deigned from carbenoxolone with the goal to have a more strong or equivalent solid binding (–16 kcal/mol), Corphos, cboNRing, and cboS2 bind at –17 kcal/mol.

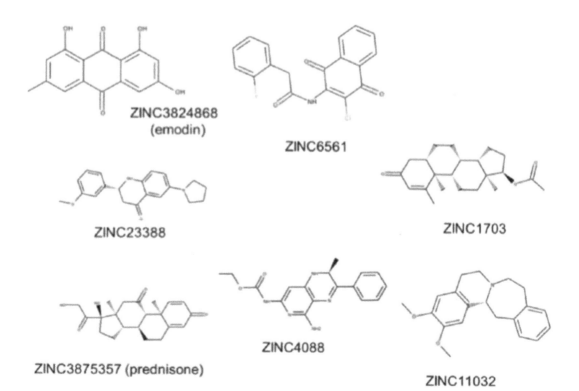

FIGURE 2.15 Pharmacophore Organic Compounds Binding as the Medium Binders. From the ZINC database. The assessed binding energy is in the range of –9 to –11 Kcal/mole.

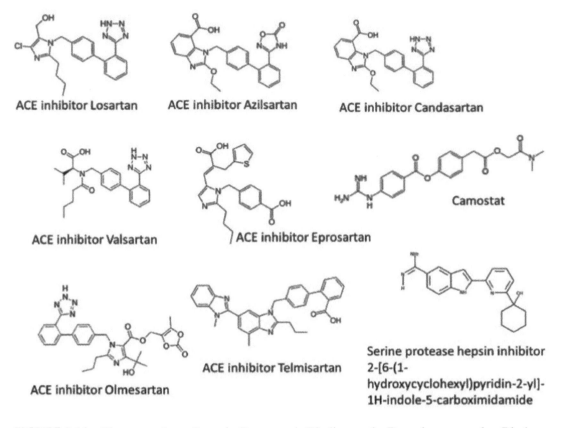

FIGURE 2.16 Pharmacophore Organic Compounds Binding as the Powerless or weaker Binders. Selection known medications or recommendations (alert: utilization of ACE inhibitors may be counterproductive). The assessed binding energy is in the range of –5 to –7 kcal/mol.

dehydrogenase type 1 examination (Robson et al., 2011) and resulting studies. These significant binds are found form normal rules, but they are weaker. They are in the range found for the synthetic peptides of intrigue however they have significant less conformational opportunity.

Figure 2.16 indicates some more weaker binding outcomes by utilizing KRUNCH (Robson et al., 2011). A quick alert is required in reaching conclusions from the compounds as in Figure 2.16. Camostat is certainly of interest as an inhibitor of the ACE2 protein to which the spike protein at first bind for cell entry and appears to be a powerful binding entry (Hoffmann et al., 2020), and likewise, hepsin results are interesting relatively, for example, as it is a potential elective entry point. The ACE inhibitors likewise looked at first fascinating by ideals of specific similitudes to the next possible ligands, and obviously due to their binding in this hypothetical investigation section, the majority of the traditional ACE inhibitors are normally seen as not inhibiting ACE2. Considering about a medication, for example, Valsartan that follows up on ACE may up-regulate ACE2, so encouraging infection entry (Di Guardo, 2020), however emerging information is uncovering a complex picture. There are potential clarifications that would even now consider rivaling spike protein binding; however, these appear to be fairly improbable. Most probably, the binding is adequately powerless that the typical substrate, and furthermore the spike protein, displace it. Communications with aromatic group might be significant here (Loeffler et al., 2020).

Some thought has been given to the forecast of ligand binding site motifs, but so far these have demonstrated basically negative as respects to the interesting outcomes that may reveal any further insight into the abovementioned, although few signs may well have been missed. Binding sites are frequently contained preserved residues that are not contiguous (constant in a sequence), which will require further and more definite investigation, despite the fact that subsequences of two to six amino acid residues length are deserving of a quick primer examination since they are normally engaged with ligand communications. The matches required here as decided by BLAST-p and Clustal Omega are not statistically significant, however, one may consider powerless matches as ligand binding site forecasts similarly that one considers epitope predictions. In a significant part of the this approach considered in this section, the structure of emodin, carbenoxolone, and related compounds that have included conversation of aromatic rings and consequently phenylananine (F), tyrosine (Y), and tryptophan (W) and more broad amino acid residues with hydrophobic character. Polar subsequences are likewise solid binders of charged ligands or have a function for charged atoms or inorganic particles in some ways. To the extent such subsequences in the coronaviruses spike protein are concerned, polar charge-pattern motifs such DRETS and DREDS are regular in ligand binding a portion of the atoms that might be of enthusiasm as antagonizing SARS entry, activation, or replication in some ways. In particular, motifs like SARS-CoV NSPs have zinc finger motifs, while RET and particularly RED are normal in PROSITE motifs[5] including zinc-finger motifs.

This isn't considered straightforwardly applicable to the spike protein in any case, for instance separately in GenBank entry, AIA62240.1 and DREDS and DRETS line up with SRLDKV in three-manner Clustal Omega arrangement with SRLDK of the first Wuhan spike protein sequence MN908947.3 and DRLDT of NP_073551.1 spike protein. These and numerous comparative arrangements additionally represent the significant sequence varieties, and the weak matches are not close in the sequence to the subsequence of interest neither for coronavirus spike protein nor human proteins of potential discussed already. As per the ACE2 concern, the closes coordinate with DRETS, and DREGS is DRKKPS, but this weak match again lays well away from regions of current interest, for example in the arrangement from the region that connects with the spike glycoprotein. DTETA and DRFIN do occur in the C-terminal portion of human 11β-hydroxysteroid dehydrogenase type 1, but again these are required to be unplanned matches.

MACHINE LEARNING CLUSTERING TECHNIQUE

Genome Sequence Analysis

Genome sequencing makes sense for requests to DNA nucleotides or targets in a genome: thus, requests for As, Cs, Gs, and Ts that make up the DNA of a living creature. The genome of human is prepared of over 3 billion of hereditary, i.e., genetic letters. This current

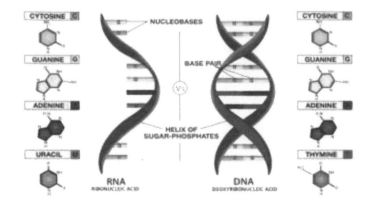

FIGURE 2.17   Polymer structure of RNA (ribonucleic acid) and DNA (deoxyribonucleic acid).

research input sequence consists of Fast Adaptive Shrinkage Threshold Algorithm (FASTA) data format. FASTA is essentially a coded text language of nucleotide and amino acid arrays useful in bioinformatics. Since the spread of input information is FASTA (DNA) and coronavirus is an RNA type of infection, we need to convert DNA into RNA.

DNA 's twisted double helix structure (as seen in Figures 2.17 and 2.18) helps it to loosen as a form of a ladder. This ladder structure consists of synthetic composite lines, called bases. DNA contains only four of these: adenine, thymine, guanine, and cytosine. Adenine binds to cytosine through thymine and guanine. Those bases are addressed with As, Ts, Gs, and Cs separately.

Following steps are used to convert DNA to CAN as follows;

1. Transcribe DNA into mRNA (ATTAAAGGTT… => AUUAAAGGUU…), where T (thymine) is replaced by U (uracil), so we start with AUUAGGGUU using translation function, i.e., transcribe () from the biopython library.

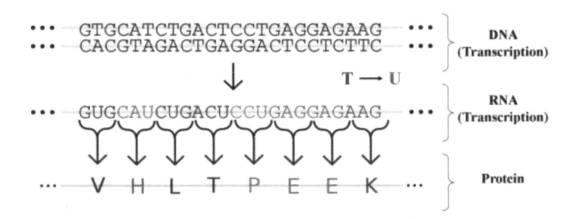

FIGURE 2.18   Transmission of information from FASTA (DNA) to coronavirus RNA and subsequent proteins.

2. Translate the mRNA sequence into amino-acid sequence using a biopython library function translate()-called the STOP codon, a successful protein separator.

DNA basically controls how the infection unfolds.

K-Means Cluster Algorithm

Machine Learning *K*-means cluster algorithm is a non-hierarchical method of clustering which searches for object partition in some clusters. The basic idea of a clustering calculation with *k*-means is to decide the number of clusters that will form the most over time.

The clustering process starts with specific information $X_{ij} \| (i = 1...n; j = 1...m)$, where n is the amount of clustering information to be done and m is the number of attributes/variables (Han et al., 2011). *K*-mean clustering technique is a three step process. In the first step, the center of each cluster $C_{kj} \| (k = 1...n; j = 1...m)$ is determined discretionary. At that point, we compute the distance between each group for each data known as the centroid. To calculate the distance of *data* − *i* to centroid k, called d_{ik} we use Euclidean distance as formulated in Equation (2.1).

$$d_{ik} = \sqrt{\sum_{j=1}^{m} \left(x_{ij} - C_{kj} \right)^2} \tag{2.1}$$

where, d_{ik} defines the distance of object i and centroid k, m represents the data dimensions, x_{ij} defines the coordinates of object i in dimension j, and C_{kj} represents the coordinates of object k in dimension j.

In the second step, the data will be a member of the cluster k if, when compared to the distance to another centroid, the distance of that data to centroid k has the least value. It is set as formulated in Equation (2.2).

$$min \sum_{k=1}^{n} d_{ik} = \sqrt{\sum_{j=1}^{m} \left(x_{ij} - C_{kj} \right)^2} \tag{2.2}$$

In the third stage, the data belonging to each cluster is categorized. The average value of the data which are members of the cluster can be calculated by using the formula in Equation (2.3).

$$C_{kj} = \frac{\Sigma_i^p x_{ij}}{p} \tag{2.3}$$

where, $x_{ij} \in cluster\ k$, p represents the number of cluster k member.

TABLE 2.3

Sample of SARS CoV-2 Isolates 2019-nCoV/USA-AZ1/2020 Complete Genome 12 Variables

Query Acc.ver	Subject Acc.Ver	Identity (%)	Alignment Length	Mismatch	Gap Opens	Q.start	Q.end	S.start	29882	evalue	Bit Score
MN997409.1	MN997409.1	100	29,882	0	0	1	29,882	1	29,882	0	55,182
MN997409.1	MT020881.1	99.99	29,882	3	0	1	29,882	1	29,882	0	55,166
MN997409.1	MT020880.1	99.99	29,882	3	0	1	29,882	1	29,882	0	55,166
MN997409.1	MN985325.1	99.99	29,882	3	0	1	29,882	1	29,882	0	55,166

TABLE 2.4

SARS CoV-2 Isolates 2019-nCoV/USA-AZ1/2020 Data Variable Description

Variable Name	Description
Query Acc.ver	Signifies the code for the original virus.
Subject Aacc.ver	Signifies the Virus mutation identifier.
Identity (%)	Signifies which percentage of the sequence is similar to the original virus.
Alignment Length	Represents how many objects are the same, or similar, in the series
Mismatches	Specify the number of items on which the mutation and the original differ.
Bit score	A metric reflecting how good alignment is; the higher the score, the better the alignment is.

Dataset

Sequences of all available severe acute respiratory syndrome coronavirus 2 isolate 2019-nCoV/USA-AZ1/2020 complete genome available till February 11, 2020 were downloaded from GISAID database (genome data head sample with variable details are presented in Table 2.3 and Table 2.4) on March 31, 2020. The 3CLpro gene sequences were separated from the complete genome sequence and converted into protein arrays using the ExPASy Server decryption device. The adjusted genes are localized by the SARS-CoV-2 reference genome (USA-AZ1; NCBI Reference Sequence/GSAID: MN997409). Total 29,903 bp complete genomic sequences of SARS-CoV-2 strains are available in referenced dataset. Only the complete genomes of high-coverage are included in the dataset.

Results

The reference coronavirus genome sequence represents 263 mutations of itself to increase survival rates within few weeks. Data consist of 263×12 size rows and columns respectively, head data is describe as follows;

Descriptions of some important columns of data are as follows;

Heat map of correlation matrix among the variables of the data is as follows:

Heat map of the data in Figure 2.19 represents that the data is highly correlated with one to another. The alignment length of the array is high correlated with bit score. Now preprocess the data and applying the k-mean clustering with total number of five clusters that are bet fit on the data. These clusters represent a numerical evaluation of the five main types of mutations.

Heatmap in Figure 2.20 represents each cluster's attributes, by column. Because the points were scaled, the actual annotated values do not quantitatively mean anything. The scaled properties can be considered in each section. If scientists somehow managed to develop a vaccine, it should address these major clusters of virus.

Figure 2.21 represents the five clusters of virus mutations those are represents with numeric number. The cluster's higher value means a higher alignment length, which represents a cluster similar to the original virus while lower cluster values reflect the cluster allele further from the original virus genetically. The vast majority of the clusters of viruses differ considerably from the original virus. Therefore, scientists seeking to develop a vaccine should be mindful that the virus is quite mutating.

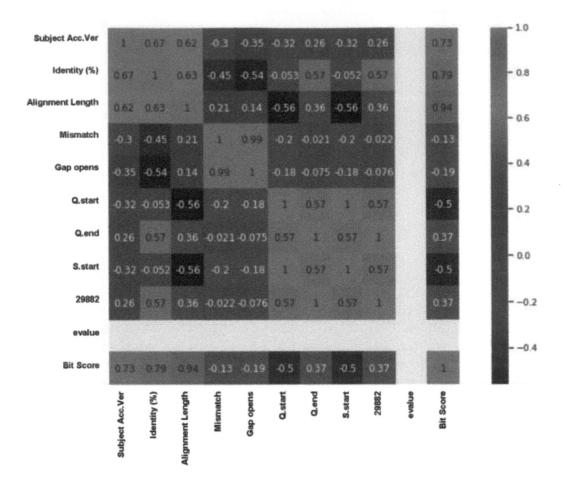

FIGURE 2.19   Heat map of complex matrix of 11 variables of the COVID genomes mutations data.

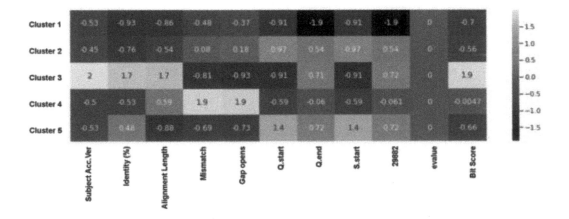

FIGURE 2.20   Heat map of complex matrix of 11 variables of the COVID genomes mutations data and k-means computed clusters.

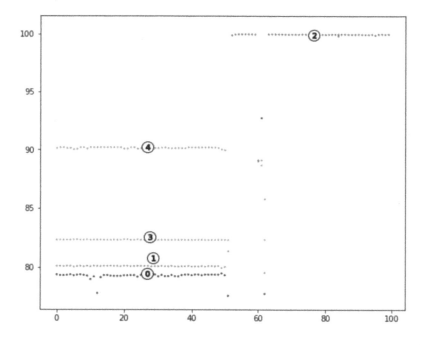

FIGURE 2.21 Clustered data visualization.

NOTES

1. ACE2: angiotensin-converting enzyme 2; ER: endoplasmic reticulum; ERGIC: ER–Golgi intermediate compartment.
2. ZINC15 database (last acessed March 9, 2020), https://zinc.docking.org/.
3. ZINC15 database (last acessed March 9, 2020), https://zinc.docking.org/.
4. https://scitechdaily.com/mit-chemists-have-developed-a-peptide-that-could-block-covid-19/
5. https://prosite.expasy.org/cgi-bin/prosite/prosite_search_full.pl

REFERENCES

Adedeji, A. O., Severson, W., Jonsson, C., Singh, K., Weiss, S. R., & Sarafianos, S. G. (2013). Novel inhibitors of severe acute respiratory syndrome coronavirus entry that act by three distinct mechanisms. *Journal of Virology*, *87*(14), 8017–8028.

Alam, I., Kamau, A. K., Kulmanov, M., Arold, S. T., Pain, A. T., Gojobori, T., & Duarte, C. M. (2020). Functional pangenome analysis suggests inhibition of the protein E as a readily available therapy for COVID-2019. *BioRxiv*.

Andersen, K. G., Rambaut, A., Lipkin, W. I., Holmes, E. C., & Garry, R. F. (2020). The proximal origin of SARS-CoV-2. *Nature Medicine*, *26*(4), 450–452.

Arndt, A. L., Larson, B. J., & Hogue, B. G. (2010). A conserved domain in the coronavirus membrane protein tail is important for virus assembly. *Journal of Virology*, *84*(21), 11418–11428.

Bagdonaite, I., & Wandall, H. H. (2018). Global aspects of viral glycosylation. *Glycobiology*, *28*(7), 443–467.

Bertram, S., Glowacka, I., Müller, M. A., Lavender, H., Gnirss, K., Nehlmeier, I., Niemeyer, D., He, Y., Simmons, G., & Drosten, C. (2011). Cleavage and activation of the severe acute respiratory syndrome coronavirus spike protein by human airway trypsin-like protease. *Journal of Virology*, *85*(24), 13363–13372.

Bianchi, M., Benvenuto, D., Giovanetti, M., Angeletti, S., Ciccozzi, M., & Pascarella, S. (2020). Sars-CoV-2 envelope and membrane proteins: Structural differences linked to virus characteristics? *BioMed Research International, 2020.*

Callaway, E. (2020). The race for coronavirus vaccines: A graphical guide. *Nature, 580*(7805), 576.

Chan, J. F.-W., Kok, K.-H., Zhu, Z., Chu, H., To, K. K.-W., Yuan, S., & Yuen, K.-Y. (2020). Genomic characterization of the 2019 novel human-pathogenic coronavirus isolated from a patient with atypical pneumonia after visiting Wuhan. *Emerging Microbes & Infections, 9*(1), 221–236.

Chan, J. F.-W., Yuan, S., Kok, K.-H., To, K. K.-W., Chu, H., Yang, J., Xing, F., Liu, J., Yip, C. C.-Y., & Poon, R. W.-S. (2020). A familial cluster of pneumonia associated with the 2019 novel coronavirus indicating person-to-person transmission: A study of a family cluster. *The Lancet, 395*(10223), 514–523.

Chen, S.-C., & Olsthoorn, R. C. L. (2010). Group-specific structural features of the 5′-proximal sequences of coronavirus genomic RNAs. *Virology, 401*(1), 29–41.

Chu, Y., Kaushik, A. C., Wang, X., Wang, W., Zhang, Y., Shan, X., Salahub, D. R., Xiong, Y., & Wei, D.-Q. (2019). DTI-CDF: A cascade deep forest model towards the prediction of drug-target interactions based on hybrid features. *Briefings in Bioinformatics.*

Corman, V. M., Lienau, J., & Witzenrath, M. (2019). Coronaviruses as the cause of respiratory infections. *Der Internist, 60*(11), 1136–1145.

Coronaviridae Study Group of the International Committee on Taxonomy of Viruses. (2020). The species Severe acute respiratory syndrome-related coronavirus: Classifying 2019-nCoV and naming it SARS-CoV-2. *Nature Microbiology, 5*(4), 536.

Coutard, B., Valle, C., de Lamballerie, X., Canard, B., Seidah, N. G., & Decroly, E. (2020). The spike glycoprotein of the new coronavirus 2019-nCoV contains a furin-like cleavage site absent in CoV of the same clade. *Antiviral Research, 176,* 104742.

Cui, J., Li, F., & Shi, Z.-L. (2019). Origin and evolution of pathogenic coronaviruses. *Nature Reviews Microbiology, 17*(3), 181–192.

De Haan, C. A. M., Kuo, L., Masters, P. S., Vennema, H., & Rottier, P. J. M. (1998). Coronavirus particle assembly: Primary structure requirements of the membrane protein. *Journal of Virology, 72*(8), 6838–6850.

De Haan, C. A. M., Vennema, H., & Rottier, P. J. M. (2000). Assembly of the coronavirus envelope: Homotypic interactions between the M proteins. *Journal of Virology, 74*(11), 4967–4978.

DeDiego, M. L., Nieto-Torres, J. L., Jiménez-Guardeño, J. M., Regla-Nava, J. A., Alvarez, E., Oliveros, J. C., Zhao, J., Fett, C., Perlman, S., & Enjuanes, L. (2011). Severe acute respiratory syndrome coronavirus envelope protein regulates cell stress response and apoptosis. *PLoS Pathog, 7*(10), e1002315.

Di Guardo, G. (2020). *SARS-CoV-2, hypertension and ACE-inhibitors.*

Eckert, D. M., & Kim, P. S. (2001). Mechanisms of viral membrane fusion and its inhibition. *Annual Review of Biochemistry, 70*(1), 777–810.

Fang, X., Gao, J., Zheng, H., Li, B., Kong, L., Zhang, Y., Wang, W., Zeng, Y., & Ye, L. (2007). The membrane protein of SARS-CoV suppresses NF-κB activation. *Journal of Medical Virology, 79*(10), 1431–1439.

Forster, P., Forster, L., Renfrew, C., & Forster, M. (2020). Phylogenetic network analysis of SARS-CoV-2 genomes. *Proceedings of the National Academy of Sciences, 117*(17), 9241–9243.

Fouchier, R. A. M., Hartwig, N. G., Bestebroer, T. M., Niemeyer, B., De Jong, J. C., Simon, J. H., & Osterhaus, A. D. M. E. (2004). A previously undescribed coronavirus associated with respiratory disease in humans. *Proceedings of the National Academy of Sciences, 101*(16), 6212–6216.

Fung, T. S., & Liu, D. X. (2014). Coronavirus infection, ER stress, apoptosis and innate immunity. *Frontiers in Microbiology, 5,* 296.

Fung, T. S., & Liu, D. X. (2019). Human coronavirus: Host-pathogen interaction. *Annual Review of Microbiology*, *73*, 529–557.

Gao, Y., Yan, L., Huang, Y., Liu, F., Zhao, Y., Cao, L., Wang, T., Sun, Q., Ming, Z., & Zhang, L. (2020). Structure of the RNA-dependent RNA polymerase from COVID-19 virus. *Science*, *368*(6492), 779–782.

Glowacka, I., Bertram, S., Müller, M. A., Allen, P., Soilleux, E., Pfefferle, S., Steffen, I., Tsegaye, T. S., He, Y., & Gnirss, K. (2011). Evidence that TMPRSS2 activates the severe acute respiratory syndrome coronavirus spike protein for membrane fusion and reduces viral control by the humoral immune response. *Journal of Virology*, *85*(9), 4122–4134.

Grifoni, A., Sidney, J., Zhang, Y., Scheuermann, R. H., Peters, B., & Sette, A. (2020). Candidate targets for immune responses to 2019-Novel Coronavirus (nCoV): Sequence homology-and bioinformatic-based predictions. *CELL-HOST-MICROBE-D-20-00119.*

Guo, Y.-R., Cao, Q.-D., Hong, Z.-S., Tan, Y.-Y., Chen, S.-D., Jin, H.-J., Tan, K.-S., Wang, D.-Y., & Yan, Y. (2020). The origin, transmission and clinical therapies on coronavirus disease 2019 (COVID-19) outbreak–an update on the status. *Military Medical Research*, *7*(1), 1–10.

Halpin, K., Young, P. L., Field, H. E., & Mackenzie, J. S. (2000). Isolation of Hendra virus from pteropid bats: A natural reservoir of Hendra virus. *Journal of General Virology*, *81*(8), 1927–1932.

Hamre, D., & Procknow, J. J. (1966). A new virus isolated from the human respiratory tract. *Proceedings of the Society for Experimental Biology and Medicine*, *121*(1), 190–193.

Han, J., Pei, J., & Kamber, M. (2011). *Data mining: concepts and techniques*. Elsevier.

Ho, T.-Y., Wu, S.-L., Chen, J.-C., Li, C.-C., & Hsiang, C.-Y. (2007). Emodin blocks the SARS coronavirus spike protein and angiotensin-converting enzyme 2 interaction. *Antiviral Research*, *74*(2), 92–101.

Hoffmann, M., Kleine-Weber, H., Schroeder, S., Krüger, N., Herrler, T., Erichsen, S., Schiergens, T. S., Herrler, G., Wu, N.-H., & Nitsche, A. (2020). SARS-CoV-2 cell entry depends on ACE2 and TMPRSS2 and is blocked by a clinically proven protease inhibitor. *Cell.*

Hofmann, H., & Pöhlmann, S. (2004). Cellular entry of the SARS coronavirus. *Trends in Microbiology*, *12*(10), 466–472.

Hofmann, H., Pyrc, K., Van Der Hoek, L., Geier, M., Berkhout, B., & Pöhlmann, S. (2005). Human coronavirus NL63 employs the severe acute respiratory syndrome coronavirus receptor for cellular entry. *Proceedings of the National Academy of Sciences*, *102*(22), 7988–7993.

Holmes, K. V. (2003). SARS-associated coronavirus. *New England Journal of Medicine*, *348*(20), 1948–1951.

Hu, Y., Wen, J., Tang, L., Zhang, H., Zhang, X., Li, Y., Wang, J., Han, Y., Li, G., & Shi, J. (2003). The M protein of SARS-CoV: Basic structural and immunological properties. *Genomics, Proteomics & Bioinformatics*, *1*(2), 118–130.

Hulswit, R. J. G., Lang, Y., Bakkers, M. J. G., Li, W., Li, Z., Schouten, A., Ophorst, B., Van Kuppeveld, F. J. M., Boons, G.-J., & Bosch, B.-J. (2019). Human coronaviruses OC43 and HKU1 bind to 9-O-acetylated sialic acids via a conserved receptor-binding site in spike protein domain A. *Proceedings of the National Academy of Sciences*, *116*(7), 2681–2690.

Hussain, M., Jabeen, N., Amanullah, A., Baig, A. A., Aziz, B., Shabbir, S., & Raza, F. (2020). Structural basis of SARS-CoV-2 spike protein priming by TMPRSS2. *BioRxiv.*

Jiang, S., Hillyer, C., & Du, L. (2020). Neutralizing antibodies against SARS-CoV-2 and other human coronaviruses. *Trends in Immunology.*

Kahn, J. S., & McIntosh, K. (2005). History and recent advances in coronavirus discovery. *The Pediatric Infectious Disease Journal*, *24*(11), S223–S227.

Kaliamurthi, S., Selvaraj, G., Chinnasamy, S., Wang, Q., Nangraj, A. S., Cho, W., Gu, K., & Wei, D.-Q. (2019). Exploring the papillomaviral proteome to identify potential candidates for a chimeric vaccine against cervix papilloma using immunomics and computational structural vaccinology. *Viruses*, *11*(1), 63.

Kang, S., Yang, M., Hong, Z., Zhang, L., Huang, Z., Chen, X., He, S., Zhou, Z., Zhou, Z., & Chen, Q. (2020). Crystal structure of SARS-CoV-2 nucleocapsid protein RNA binding domain reveals potential unique drug targeting sites. *Acta Pharmaceutica Sinica B*.

Khailany, R. A., Safdar, M., & Ozaslan, M. (2020). Genomic characterization of a novel SARS-CoV-2. *Gene Reports*, 100682.

Khan, M. Y., & Kumar, V. (2019). Mechanism & inhibition kinetics of bioassay-guided fractions of Indian medicinal plants and foods as ACE inhibitors. *Journal of Traditional and Complementary Medicine*, 9(1), 73–84.

Kim, D., Lee, J.-Y., Yang, J.-S., Kim, J. W., Kim, V. N., & Chang, H. (2020). The architecture of SARS-CoV-2 transcriptome. *Cell*.

Klenk, H.-D., & Garten, W. (1994). Host cell proteases controlling virus pathogenicity. *Trends in Microbiology*, 2(2), 39–43.

Krijnse-Locker, J., Ericsson, M., Rottier, P. J., & Griffiths, G. (1994). Characterization of the budding compartment of mouse hepatitis virus: Evidence that transport from the RER to the Golgi complex requires only one vesicular transport step. *The Journal of Cell Biology*, 124(1), 55–70.

Kuo, L., & Masters, P. S. (2002). Genetic evidence for a structural interaction between the carboxy termini of the membrane and nucleocapsid proteins of mouse hepatitis virus. *Journal of Virology*, 76(10), 4987–4999.

Lai, M. M. C., & Cavanagh, D. (1997). The molecular biology of coronaviruses. In *Advances in virus research* (Vol. 48, pp. 1–100). Elsevier.

Lam, T. T.-Y., Jia, N., Zhang, Y.-W., Shum, M. H.-H., Jiang, J.-F., Zhu, H.-C., Tong, Y.-G., Shi, Y.-X., Ni, X.-B., & Liao, Y.-S. (2020). Identifying SARS-CoV-2-related coronaviruses in Malayan pangolins. *Nature*, 1–4.

Lam, T. T.-Y., Shum, M. H.-H., Zhu, H.-C., Tong, Y.-G., Ni, X.-B., Liao, Y.-S., Wei, W., Cheung, W. Y.-M., Li, W.-J., & Li, L.-F. (2020). Identification of 2019-nCoV related coronaviruses in Malayan pangolins in southern China. *BioRxiv*.

Lan, J., Ge, J., Yu, J., Shan, S., Zhou, H., Fan, S., Zhang, Q., Shi, X., Wang, Q., & Zhang, L. (2020). Structure of the SARS-CoV-2 spike receptor-binding domain bound to the ACE2 receptor. *Nature*, 581(7807), 215–220.

Lau, S. K. P., Woo, P. C. Y., Li, K. S. M., Huang, Y., Tsoi, H.-W., Wong, B. H. L., Wong, S. S. Y., Leung, S.-Y., Chan, K.-H., & Yuen, K.-Y. (2005). Severe acute respiratory syndrome coronavirus-like virus in Chinese horseshoe bats. *Proceedings of the National Academy of Sciences*, 102(39), 14040–14045.

Lau, S. K. P., Woo, P. C. Y., Yip, C. C. Y., Tse, H., Tsoi, H., Cheng, V. C. C., Lee, P., Tang, B. S. F., Cheung, C. H. Y., & Lee, R. A. (2006). Coronavirus HKU1 and other coronavirus infections in Hong Kong. *Journal of Clinical Microbiology*, 44(6), 2063–2071.

Li, F. (2016). Structure, function, and evolution of coronavirus spike proteins. *Annual Review of Virology*, 3, 237–261.

Li, W., Moore, M. J., Vasilieva, N., Sui, J., Wong, S. K., Berne, M. A., Somasundaran, M., Sullivan, J. L., Luzuriaga, K., & Greenough, T. C. (2003). Angiotensin-converting enzyme 2 is a functional receptor for the SARS coronavirus. *Nature*, 426(6965), 450–454.

Li, W., Shi, Z., Yu, M., Ren, W., Smith, C., Epstein, J. H., Wang, H., Crameri, G., Hu, Z., & Zhang, H. (2005). Bats are natural reservoirs of SARS-like coronaviruses. *Science*, 310(5748), 676–679.

Liu, J., Liao, X., Qian, S., Yuan, J., Wang, F., Liu, Y., Wang, Z., Wang, F.-S., Liu, L., & Zhang, Z. (2020). *Community transmission of severe acute respiratory syndrome coronavirus 2, Shenzhen, China, 2020*.

Liu, Z., Xiao, X., Wei, X., Li, J., Yang, J., Tan, H., Zhu, J., Zhang, Q., Wu, J., & Liu, L. (2020). Composition and divergence of coronavirus spike proteins and host ACE2 receptors predict potential intermediate hosts of SARS-CoV-2. *Journal of Medical Virology*, 92(6), 595–601.

Loeffler, J. R., Fernández-Quintero, M. L., Schauperl, M., & Liedl, K. R. (2020). STACKED–S olvation T heory of A romatic C omplexes as K ey for E stimating D rug Binding. *Journal of Chemical Information and Modeling*, 60(4), 2304–2313.

Lu, R., Zhao, X., Li, J., Niu, P., Yang, B., Wu, H., Wang, W., Song, H., Huang, B., & Zhu, N. (2020). Genomic characterisation and epidemiology of 2019 novel coronavirus: Implications for virus origins and receptor binding. *The Lancet, 395*(10224), 565–574.

Lukassen, S., Chua, R. L., Trefzer, T., Kahn, N. C., Schneider, M. A., Muley, T., Winter, H., Meister, M., Veith, C., & Boots, A. W. (2020). SARS-CoV-2 receptor ACE 2 and TMPRSS 2 are primarily expressed in bronchial transient secretory cells. *The EMBO Journal, 39*(10), e105114.

Ma-Lauer, Y., Carbajo-Lozoya, J., Hein, M. Y., Müller, M. A., Deng, W., Lei, J., Meyer, B., Kusov, Y., Von Brunn, B., & Bairad, D. R. (2016). p53 down-regulates SARS coronavirus replication and is targeted by the SARS-unique domain and PLpro via E3 ubiquitin ligase RCHY1. *Proceedings of the National Academy of Sciences, 113*(35), E5192–E5201.

McBride, R., Van Zyl, M., & Fielding, B. C. (2014). The coronavirus nucleocapsid is a multifunctional protein. *Viruses, 6*(8), 2991–3018.

Mehmood, A., Kaushik, A. C., & Wei, D. (2019). Prediction and validation of potent peptides against herpes simplex virus type 1 via immunoinformatic and systems biology approach. *Chemical Biology & Drug Design, 94*(5), 1868–1883.

Morris, G. E., Parker, L. C., Ward, J. R., Jones, E. C., Whyte, M. K. B., Brightling, C. E., Bradding, P., Dower, S. K., Sabroe, I., & Morris, G. E. (2006). Cooperative molecular and cellular networks regulate Toll-like receptor-dependent inflammatory responses. *The FASEB Journal, 20*(12), 2153–2155.

Narayanan, K., Chen, C.-J., Maeda, J., & Makino, S. (2003). Nucleocapsid-independent specific viral RNA packaging via viral envelope protein and viral RNA signal. *Journal of Virology, 77*(5), 2922–2927.

Narayanan, K., Huang, C., & Makino, S. (2008). SARS coronavirus accessory proteins. *Virus Research, 133*(1), 113–121.

Neuman, B. W., Kiss, G., Kunding, A. H., Bhella, D., Baksh, M. F., Connelly, S., Droese, B., Klaus, J. P., Makino, S., & Sawicki, S. G. (2011). A structural analysis of M protein in coronavirus assembly and morphology. *Journal of Structural Biology, 174*(1), 11–22.

Niespodziana, K., Napora, K., Cabauatan, C., Focke-Tejkl, M., Keller, W., Niederberger, V., Tsolia, M., Christodoulou, I., Papadopoulos, N. G., & Valenta, R. (2012). Misdirected antibody responses against an N-terminal epitope on human rhinovirus VP1 as explanation for recurrent RV infections. *The FASEB Journal, 26*(3), 1001–1008.

Nieva, J. L., Madan, V., & Carrasco, L. (2012). Viroporins: Structure and biological functions. *Nature Reviews Microbiology, 10*(8), 563–574.

Ou, J., Zhou, Z., Zhang, J., Lan, W., Zhao, S., Wu, J., Seto, D., Zhang, G., & Zhang, Q. (2020). RBD mutations from circulating SARS-CoV-2 strains enhance the structural stability and human ACE2 affinity of the spike protein. *BioRxiv*.

Ou, X., Liu, Y., Lei, X., Li, P., Mi, D., Ren, L., Guo, L., Guo, R., Chen, T., & Hu, J. (2020). Characterization of spike glycoprotein of SARS-CoV-2 on virus entry and its immune cross-reactivity with SARS-CoV. *Nature Communications, 11*(1), 1–12.

Perlman, S., & Netland, J. (2009). Coronaviruses post-SARS: Update on replication and pathogenesis. *Nature Reviews Microbiology, 7*(6), 439–450.

Pham, T., Perry, J. L., Dosey, T. L., Delcour, A. H., & Hyser, J. M. (2017). The rotavirus NSP4 viroporin domain is a calcium-conducting ion channel. *Scientific Reports, 7*, 43487.

Rai, J. (2019). Peptide and protein mimetics by retro and retroinverso analogs. *Chemical Biology & Drug Design, 93*(5), 724–736.

Raj, V. S., Mou, H., Smits, S. L., Dekkers, D. H. W., Müller, M. A., Dijkman, R., Muth, D., Demmers, J. A. A., Zaki, A., & Fouchier, R. A. M. (2013). Dipeptidyl peptidase 4 is a functional receptor for the emerging human coronavirus-EMC. *Nature, 495*(7440), 251–254.

Robson, B. (2016). Studies in using a universal exchange and inference language for evidence based medicine. Semi-automated learning and reasoning for PICO methodology, systematic review, and environmental epidemiology. *Computers in Biology and Medicine, 79*, 299–323.

Robson, B. (2020a). Computers and viral diseases. Preliminary bioinformatics studies on the design of a synthetic vaccine and a preventative peptidomimetic antagonist against the SARS-CoV-2 (2019-nCoV, COVID-19) coronavirus. *Computers in Biology and Medicine*, 103670.

Robson, B. (2020b). Extension of the Quantum Universal Exchange Language to precision medicine and drug lead discovery. Preliminary example studies using the mitochondrial genome. *Computers in Biology and Medicine*, *117*, 103621.

Robson, B., & Boray, S. (2015). Implementation of a web based universal exchange and inference language for medicine: Sparse data, probabilities and inference in data mining of clinical data repositories. *Computers in Biology and Medicine*, *66*, 82–102.

Robson, B., & Boray, S. (2018). Studies in the extensively automatic construction of large odds-based inference networks from structured data. Examples from medical, bioinformatics, and health insurance claims data. *Computers in Biology and Medicine*, *95*, 147–166.

Robson, B., Caruso, T. P., & Balis, U. G. J. (2013). Suggestions for a web based universal exchange and inference language for medicine. *Computers in Biology and Medicine*, *43*(12), 2297–2310.

Robson, B., & Garnier, J. (1986). *Introduction to proteins and protein engineering*. Elsevier Publishing Company.

Robson, B., Li, J., Dettinger, R., Peters, A., & Boyer, S. K. (2011). Drug discovery using very large numbers of patents. General strategy with extensive use of match and edit operations. *Journal of Computer-Aided Molecular Design*, *25*(5), 427–441.

Schwarz, S., Wang, K., Yu, W., Sun, B., & Schwarz, W. (2011). Emodin inhibits current through SARS-associated coronavirus 3a protein. *Antiviral Research*, *90*(1), 64–69.

Sheahan, T., Rockx, B., Donaldson, E., Sims, A., Pickles, R., Corti, D., & Baric, R. (2008). Mechanisms of zoonotic severe acute respiratory syndrome coronavirus host range expansion in human airway epithelium. *Journal of Virology*, *82*(5), 2274–2285.

Shereen, M. A., Khan, S., Kazmi, A., Bashir, N., & Siddique, R. (2020). COVID-19 infection: Origin, transmission, and characteristics of human coronaviruses. *Journal of Advanced Research*.

Siu, Y. L., Teoh, K. T., Lo, J., Chan, C. M., Kien, F., Escriou, N., Tsao, S. W., Nicholls, J. M., Altmeyer, R., & Peiris, J. S. M. (2008). The M, E, and N structural proteins of the severe acute respiratory syndrome coronavirus are required for efficient assembly, trafficking, and release of virus-like particles. *Journal of Virology*, *82*(22), 11318–11330.

Snijder, E. J., Decroly, E., & Ziebuhr, J. (2016). The nonstructural proteins directing coronavirus RNA synthesis and processing. In *Advances in virus research* (Vol. 96, pp. 59–126). Elsevier.

Song, H.-D., Tu, C.-C., Zhang, G.-W., Wang, S.-Y., Zheng, K., Lei, L.-C., Chen, Q.-X., Gao, Y.-W., Zhou, H.-Q., & Xiang, H. (2005). Cross-host evolution of severe acute respiratory syndrome coronavirus in palm civet and human. *Proceedings of the National Academy of Sciences*, *102*(7), 2430–2435.

Steinhauer, D. A. (1999). Role of hemagglutinin cleavage for the pathogenicity of influenza virus. *Virology*, *258*(1), 1–20.

Surjit, M., & Lal, S. K. (2008). The SARS-CoV nucleocapsid protein: A protein with multifarious activities. *Infection, Genetics and Evolution*, *8*(4), 397–405.

Tyrrell, D. A. J., & Bynoe, M. L. (1966). Cultivation of viruses from a high proportion of patients with colds. *Lancet*, 76–77.

van Boheemen, S., de Graaf, M., Lauber, C., Bestebroer, T. M., Raj, V. S., Zaki, A. M., Osterhaus, A. D. M. E., Haagmans, B. L., Gorbalenya, A. E., & Snijder, E. J. (2012). Genomic characterization of a newly discovered coronavirus associated with acute respiratory distress syndrome in humans. *MBio*, *3*(6).

Van Der Hoek, L., Pyrc, K., Jebbink, M. F., Vermeulen-Oost, W., Berkhout, R. J. M., Wolthers, K. C., Wertheim-van Dillen, P. M. E., Kaandorp, J., Spaargaren, J., & Berkhout, B. (2004). Identification of a new human coronavirus. *Nature Medicine*, *10*(4), 368–373.

Vennema, H., Godeke, G. J., Rossen, J. W., Voorhout, W. F., Horzinek, M. C., Opstelten, D. J., & Rottier, P. J. (1996). Nucleocapsid-independent assembly of coronavirus-like particles by co-expression of viral envelope protein genes. *The EMBO Journal*, *15*(8), 2020–2028.

Walls, A. C., Park, Y.-J., Tortorici, M. A., Wall, A., McGuire, A. T., & Veesler, D. (2020). Structure, function, and antigenicity of the SARS-CoV-2 spike glycoprotein. *Cell.*

Wan, Y., Shang, J., Graham, R., Baric, R. S., & Li, F. (2020). Receptor recognition by the novel coronavirus from Wuhan: An analysis based on decade-long structural studies of SARS coronavirus. *Journal of Virology, 94*(7).

Wang, N., Shi, X., Jiang, L., Zhang, S., Wang, D., Tong, P., Guo, D., Fu, L., Cui, Y., & Liu, X. (2013). Structure of MERS-CoV spike receptor-binding domain complexed with human receptor DPP4. *Cell Research, 23*(8), 986–993.

Watanabe, Y., Allen, J. D., Wrapp, D., McLellan, J. S., & Crispin, M. (2020). Site-specific analysis of the SARS-CoV-2 glycan shield. *BioRxiv.*

Wentworth, D. E., & Holmes, K. V. (2001). Molecular determinants of species specificity in the coronavirus receptor aminopeptidase N (CD13): Influence of N-linked glycosylation. *Journal of Virology, 75*(20), 9741–9752.

Westphal, U. (1986). Hydrophobicity and hydrophilicity of steroid binding sites. In *Steroid-Protein Interactions II* (pp. 265–275). Springer.

Wilson, L., Mckinlay, C., Gage, P., & Ewart, G. (2004). SARS coronavirus E protein forms cation-selective ion channels. *Virology, 330*(1), 322–331.

Wong, M. C., Cregeen, S. J. J., Ajami, N. J., & Petrosino, J. F. (2020). Evidence of recombination in coronaviruses implicating pangolin origins of nCoV-2019. *BioRxiv.*

Woo, P. C. Y., Lau, S. K. P., Lam, C. S. F., Lau, C. C. Y., Tsang, A. K. L., Lau, J. H. N., Bai, R., Teng, J. L. L., Tsang, C. C. C., & Wang, M. (2012). Discovery of seven novel Mammalian and avian coronaviruses in the genus deltacoronavirus supports bat coronaviruses as the gene source of alphacoronavirus and betacoronavirus and avian coronaviruses as the gene source of gammacoronavirus and deltacoronavi. *Journal of Virology, 86*(7), 3995–4008.

World Health Organization. (2003). Coronavirus never before seen in humans is the cause of SARS. In *Coronavirus never before seen in humans is the cause of SARS* (p. 2), WHO.

World Health Organization. (2020). *Naming the coronavirus disease (COVID-19) and the virus that causes it*, WHO.

Wrapp, D., Wang, N., Corbett, K. S., Goldsmith, J. A., Hsieh, C.-L., Abiona, O., Graham, B. S., & McLellan, J. S. (2020). Cryo-EM structure of the 2019-nCoV spike in the prefusion conformation. *Science, 367*(6483), 1260–1263.

Wu, A., Peng, Y., Huang, B., Ding, X., Wang, X., Niu, P., Meng, J., Zhu, Z., Zhang, Z., & Wang, J. (2020). Genome composition and divergence of the novel coronavirus (2019-nCoV) originating in China. *Cell Host & Microbe.*

Wu, F., Zhao, S., Yu, B., Chen, Y.-M., Wang, W., Song, Z.-G., Hu, Y., Tao, Z.-W., Tian, J.-H., & Pei, Y.-Y. (2020). A new coronavirus associated with human respiratory disease in China. *Nature, 579*(7798), 265–269.

Wu, Q., Zhang, Y., Lü, H., Wang, J., He, X., Liu, Y., Ye, C., Lin, W., Hu, J., & Ji, J. (2003). The E protein is a multifunctional membrane protein of SARS-CoV. *Genomics, Proteomics & Bioinformatics, 1*(2), 131–144.

Xia, S., Liu, M., Wang, C., Xu, W., Lan, Q., Feng, S., Qi, F., Bao, L., Du, L., & Liu, S. (2020). Inhibition of SARS-CoV-2 (previously 2019-nCoV) infection by a highly potent pan-coronavirus fusion inhibitor targeting its spike protein that harbors a high capacity to mediate membrane fusion. *Cell Research, 30*(4), 343–355.

Xiao, K., Zhai, J., Feng, Y., Zhou, N., Zhang, X., Zou, J.-J., Li, N., Guo, Y., Li, X., & Shen, X. (2020). Isolation and characterization of 2019-nCoV-like coronavirus from Malayan pangolins. *BioRxiv.*

Xu, H., Zhong, L., Deng, J., Peng, J., Dan, H., Zeng, X., Li, T., & Chen, Q. (2020). High expression of ACE2 receptor of 2019-nCoV on the epithelial cells of oral mucosa. *International Journal of Oral Science, 12*(1), 1–5.

Xu, X., Chen, P., Wang, J., Feng, J., Zhou, H., Li, X., Zhong, W., & Hao, P. (2020). Evolution of the novel coronavirus from the ongoing Wuhan outbreak and modeling of its spike protein for risk of human transmission. *Science China Life Sciences, 63*(3), 457–460.

Yob, J. M., Field, H., Rashdi, A. M., Morrissy, C., van der Heide, B., Rota, P., bin Adzhar, A., White, J., Daniels, P., & Jamaluddin, A. (2001). Nipah virus infection in bats (order Chiroptera) in peninsular Malaysia. *Emerging Infectious Diseases*, *7*(3), 439.

Yuan, M., Wu, N. C., Zhu, X., Lee, C.-C. D., So, R. T. Y., Lv, H., Mok, C. K. P., & Wilson, I. A. (2020). A highly conserved cryptic epitope in the receptor binding domains of SARS-CoV-2 and SARS-CoV. *Science*, *368*(6491), 630–633.

Zaki, A. M., Van Boheemen, S., Bestebroer, T. M., Osterhaus, A. D. M. E., & Fouchier, R. A. M. (2012). Isolation of a novel coronavirus from a man with pneumonia in Saudi Arabia. *New England Journal of Medicine*, *367*(19), 1814–1820.

Zhang, H., Kang, Z., & Gong, H. (2020). The digestive system is a potential route of 2019-nCov infection: A bioinformatics analysis based on single-cell transcriptomes [published online ahead of print January 31, 2020]. *BioRxiv*.

Zhang, R., Wang, K., Lv, W., Yu, W., Xie, S., Xu, K., Schwarz, W., Xiong, S., & Sun, B. (2014). The ORF4a protein of human coronavirus 229E functions as a viroporin that regulates viral production. *Biochimica et Biophysica Acta (BBA)-Biomembranes*, *1838*(4), 1088–1095.

Zhao, Y., Zhao, Z., Wang, Y., Zhou, Y., Ma, Y., & Zuo, W. (2020). Single-cell RNA expression profiling of ACE2, the putative receptor of Wuhan 2019-nCov. *BioRxiv*.

Zhou, P., Yang, X.-L., Wang, X.-G., Hu, B., Zhang, L., Zhang, W., Si, H.-R., Zhu, Y., Li, B., & Huang, C.-L. (2020). A pneumonia outbreak associated with a new coronavirus of probable bat origin. *Nature*, *579*(7798), 270–273.

Zhu, N., Zhang, D., Wang, W., Li, X., Yang, B., Song, J., Zhao, X., Huang, B., Shi, W., & Lu, R. (2020). A novel coronavirus from patients with pneumonia in China, 2019. *New England Journal of Medicine*.

Ziegler, C. G. K., Allon, S. J., Nyquist, S. K., Mbano, I. M., Miao, V. N., Tzouanas, C. N., Cao, Y., Yousif, A. S., Bals, J., & Hauser, B. M. (2020). SARS-CoV-2 receptor ACE2 is an interferon-stimulated gene in human airway epithelial cells and is detected in specific cell subsets across tissues. *Cell*.

Zou, X., Chen, K., Zou, J., Han, P., Hao, J., & Han, Z. (2020). Single-cell RNA-seq data analysis on the receptor ACE2 expression reveals the potential risk of different human organs vulnerable to 2019-nCoV infection. *Frontiers of Medicine*, 1–8.

Part II

COVID-19 Screening, Testing and Detection Systems: Different Paths to the Same Destination

3 Real Time-Polymerase Chain Reaction (RT-PCR) and Antibody Tests

KEY POINTS

- A polymeric molecule essential in various biological roles in coding, decoding, regulation, and expression of genes.
- The bulk of knowledge about the sensitivity and specificity of RT-PCR is based on laboratory measurements.
- The reconstruction of the sensitivity and specificity of RT-PCR in the context of clinical decision-making.
- Nucleic acid detection is one of the essential indicators of COVID-19.
- Digital polymerase chain reaction (dPCR) enables the absolute quantification of target nucleic acids present in a sample.

INTRODUCTION

Polymerase chain reaction (PCR) tests are used to directly detect the presence of an antigen, rather than the presence of the body's immune response, or antibodies. By detecting viral Ribonucleic Acid (RNA), which will be present in the body before antibodies form or symptoms of the disease are present, the tests can tell whether or not someone has the virus very early on.

Rapid detection coupled with high sensitivity and specificity, RT-PCR and digital PCR (dPCR) is well placed in the disease detection and control efforts during this pandemic – which has claimed almost a quarter-million lives as of May 3, 2020, and vaccines and specific treatments are experimental at best.

Early detection is critical in breaking the viral transmission chain. Speedy identification of an infected person, subsequent tracing, and no recent close contact with the infected person have proven to be the key in epidemic control and sealing off the cluster from the populace. High throughput testing meaning the capability of performing a high number of samples within a short time frame—and reliable test results are of paramount importance to the testing capabilities of COVID-19; a role in which RT-PCR and dPCR fulfills.

The RT-PCR is performed by obtaining a sample from the throat or nasopharynx of a patient using a swab designated to maximize the collection of viral particles to enable meaningful extraction of its genetic material. What is meant by virus genetic material? A virus can loosely be described as a protein container for nucleic acids such as Deoxyribonucleic Acid (DNA) or RNA that are specific to it. This material is unique to the virus and helps researchers to identify the virus. One would be able to identify the pathogen by looking into the DNA or RNA that is obtained from a patient sample. So, when we say genetic material, we are talking about the DNA or RNA fragments, which are also referred to as genes that are unique to the virus such as x-, y-, or z gene. RT-PCR is designed to specifically and sensitively detect the presence of these genes.

Whilst there is no perfect test, instead, a diagnostic result is used by the clinician to corroborate findings from other evaluations that result in a full, if not perfect, clinical picture. The same can be said for RT-PCR in COVID-19 diagnosis which has been shown to have varied detection accuracy ranging from 50 to 90%. The false results—positives and negatives—may be due to various factors. A false positive is the erroneous detection of disease in a healthy person whilst a false negative is a failure of identifying a person having the disease. Like all test kits, the ability to detect the SARS-CoV-2 varies according to the gene targets selected by manufacturers. Generally, the gene targets for the detection of COVID-19 are the S, E, N, RdRP, Orf1ab, or Nsp genes. The different gene selection may affect the sensitivity and specificity of an RT-PCR test. In addition to that, other factors such as the design of the test, the quality of the test, and the sample, the operator performing the testing, are among the contributing factors to inaccurate results by RT-PCR.

Immunoassays that are antigen- or antibody-based testing is another alternative for COVID-19 screening. The fast detection rate of immunoassays which is often packaged as rapid test kits enables results to be obtained within 30 min and consequently makes this method attractive for use in the point of care diagnostic setting. Instead of detecting the presence of viral genetic material, antigen-based immunoassays detect the presence of virus-specific antigens, usually proteins, from a patient's sample. The antibody-based test kits, on the other hand, detect the presence of specific antibodies produced by the immune system during an infection. The antibody tests are designed to detect one of two types of molecules—Immunoglobulin M and G (IgM and IgG)—from a blood sample.

The antigen-based rapid test is similar to RT-PCR wherein it facilitates detection in the early phases of an infection, usually a few days after the onset of symptoms before the production of antibodies but with a relatively lower accuracy as it is limited by the amount of viral antigen. Antibody-based rapid test, on the other hand, detects the presence of the specific antibodies—an individualized defense agent against an invading pathogen—produced by the immune system during an infection. It is usually detectable beginning at day seven after the onset of symptoms. However, it is subject to two important factors: individual ability to mount an immune response against the infection and clinical performance of the test kit. Antibody immunoassay can only determine if a person has at some point, been infected with COVID-19, further testing would be needed to check if a person is currently infected. Detail about the antigen based detection and its computational techniques will cover in Chapter 5.

RT-PCR testing is recommended by World Health Organization (WHO) for the screening of COVID-19 as it can be used to detect the presence of the SARS-CoV-2 as long as the body has not completely shed the virus. In other words, it is the tool of choice in the early phases of the disease; a critical juncture to guide efforts in disease controls. Next section will cover the RTPCR and dPCR in detail.

REAL TIME RT-PCR

The COVID-19 RT-PCR test is a real-time reverse transcription polymerase chain reaction (rRT-PCR) test for the qualitative detection of nucleic acid from SARS-CoV-2 in upper and lower respiratory specimens (such as nasopharyngeal or oropharyngeal swabs, sputum, lower respiratory tract aspirates, bronchoalveolar lavage, and nasopharyngeal wash/aspirate) collected from individuals suspected of COVID-19 by their healthcare provider (HCP), as well as upper respiratory specimens (such as nasopharyngeal or oropharyngeal swabs, nasal swabs, or mid-turbinate swabs) collected from any individual, including from individuals without symptoms or other reasons to suspect COVID-19 infection. It is a nuclear-derived method for detecting the presence of specific genetic material in any pathogen, including a virus. Originally, the method used radioactive isotope markers to detect targeted genetic materials, but subsequent refining has led to the replacement of isotopic labeling with special markers, most frequently fluorescent dyes. This technique allows scientists to see the results almost immediately while the process is still ongoing, whereas conventional RT-PCR only provides results at the end of the process.

This test is also for use with individual nasal swab specimens that are self-collected using the Pixel by LabCorp COVID-19 test home collection kit by individuals when determined by a HCP to be appropriate based on results of a COVID-19 questionnaire and the LabCorp At Home COVID-19 test home collection kit when directly ordered by a HCP. This is one of the most widely used laboratory methods for detecting the COVID-19 virus. While many countries have used real time RT-PCR for diagnosing other diseases, such as Ebola virus and Zika virus, many need support in adapting this method for the COVID-19 virus, as well as in increasing their national testing capacities.

The COVID-19 RT-PCR test is also for the qualitative detection of nucleic acid from the SARS-CoV-2 in pooled samples, using a matrix pooling strategy (i.e., group pooling strategy), containing up to five individual upper respiratory swab specimens (nasopharyngeal, mid-turbinate, anterior nares or oropharyngeal swabs) per pool and 25 specimens per matrix, where each specimen is collected under observation or by a HCP using individual vials containing transport media. Negative results from pooled testing should not be treated as definitive. If a patient's clinical signs and symptoms are inconsistent with a negative result or results are necessary for patient management, then the patient should be considered for individual testing. Specimens included in pools where the positive sample cannot be identified using the matrix must be tested individually prior to reporting a result. Specimens with low viral loads may not be detected in sample pools due to the decreased sensitivity of pooled testing.

RT-PCR METHOD IN TESTING

- Real time RT-PCR (reverse transcription-polymerase chain reaction) is now one of the most accurate laboratory methods for detecting, tracking, and studying the coronavirus.
- RT-PCR is a nuclear-derived method for detecting the presence of specific genetic material from any pathogen, including a virus.
- It uses markers to detect the presence targeted genetic materials.
- Originally, radioactive isotope markers were used.
- Subsequent refining has led to the replacement of the isotopic labeling with special markers, most frequently fluorescent dyes.
- With real time RT-PCR, scientists can see the results almost immediately while the process is still ongoing. [Conventional RT-PCR only provides results at the end.]

Testing is limited to laboratories designated by LabCorp that are also certified under CLIA and meet the requirements to perform high complexity tests.

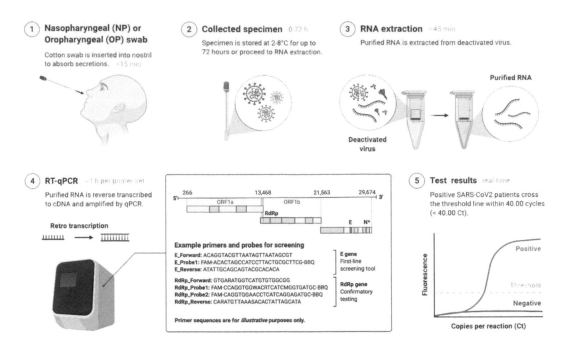

FIGURE 3.1   The general workflow of COVID-19 diagnostic RT-PCR swab tests.

Results are for the identification of SARS-CoV-2 RNA. The SARS-CoV-2 RNA is generally detectable in respiratory specimens during the acute phase of infection. Positive results are indicative of the presence of SARS-CoV-2 RNA; clinical correlation with patient history and other diagnostic information is necessary to determine patient infection status. Positive results do not rule out bacterial infection or co-infection with other viruses. The agent detected may not be the definite cause of disease. Laboratories within the United States and its territories are required to report all positive results to the appropriate public health authorities.

Negative results do not preclude SARS-CoV-2 infection and should not be used as the sole basis for patient management decisions. Negative results must be combined with clinical observations, patient history, and epidemiological information.

Testing with the COVID-19 RT-PCR test is intended for use by trained clinical laboratory personnel specifically instructed and trained in the techniques of real-time PCR and in vitro diagnostic procedures as shown in Figure 3.1. The COVID-19 RT-PCR is only for use under the Food and Drug Administration's Emergency Use Authorization.

PRINCIPLE BEHIND RT-PCR TESTING

- In order for a virus like the coronavirus to be detected early in the body, using real time RT-PCR, scientists need to convert the RNA to DNA.
- This is a process called "reverse transcription."
- They do this because only DNA can be copied—or amplified—which is a key part of the real time RT-PCR process for detecting viruses.
- Scientists amplify a specific part of the transcribed viral DNA hundreds of thousands of times.

- By this amplification, instead of trying to spot a minuscule amount of the virus among millions of strands of genetic information, scientists have a large enough quantity of the target sections of viral DNA.
- This facilitates in the accurate confirmation that the virus is present.

How Does RT-PCR Work In Coronavirus Case?

- A sample is collected from parts of the body where the coronavirus gathers, such as a person's nose or throat.
- The sample is treated with several chemical solutions.
- This remove the substances, such as proteins and fats, and extracts only the RNA present in the sample.
- This extracted RNA is a mix of a person's own genetic material and, if present, the coronavirus' RNA.
- The RNA is reverse transcribed to DNA using a specific enzyme.
- Then, additional short fragments of DNA are added that are complementary to specific parts of the transcribed viral DNA.
    - Some of the added genetic fragments are for building DNA strands during amplification.
    - The others are for building the DNA and adding marker labels to the strands, which are then used to detect the virus.
- These fragments attach themselves to target sections of the viral DNA if the virus is present in a sample.
- The mixture is then placed in a RT-PCR machine.
- The machine cycles through temperatures that heat and cool the mixture to trigger specific chemical reactions.
- These reactions then create new, identical copies of the target sections of viral DNA, and the cycle repeats over and over to continue copying.
- [Each cycle doubles the previous amount: two copies become four, four copies become eight, and so on.
- A standard real time RT-PCR setup usually goes through 35 cycles.
- So, by the end of the process, around 35 billion new copies of the sections of viral DNA are created from each strand of the virus present in the sample.]
- As new copies of the viral DNA sections are built, the marker labels attach to the DNA strands and then release a fluorescent dye.
- This is measured by the machine's computer and presented in real time on the screen.
- The computer tracks the amount of fluorescence in the sample after each cycle.
- When the amount goes over a certain level of fluorescence, this confirms that the virus is present.
- Scientists also monitor how many cycles it takes to reach this level in order to estimate the severity of the infection.

Nucleic Acid Testing

Nucleic acid testing is the primary method of diagnosing COVID-19. A number of reverse transcription polymerase chain reaction (RT-PCR) kits have been designed to detect SARS-CoV-2 genetically (Figure 3.2). RT-PCR involves the reverse transcription of SARS-CoV-2

Institution	Gene target	Forward Primer (5'-3')	Reverse Primer (5'-3')	Probe (5'-3')
U.S. CDC [=]	N gene	N1: GACCCCAAAATCAGCGAAAT	N1: TCTGGTTACTGCCAGTTGAATCTG	N1: FAM-ACCCCGCATTACGTTTG GTGGACC-BHQ1
		N2: TTACAAACATTGGCCGCAAA	N2: GCGCGACATTCCGAAGAA	N2 FAM-ACAATTTGCCCCCAGC GCTTCAG-BHQ1
		N3: GGGAGCCTTGAATACACCAAAA	N3: TGTAGCACGATTGCAGCATTG	N3: FAM-AYCACATTGGCACCCGC AATCCTG-BHQ1
		RP-F RNAse: AGATTTGGACCTGCGAGCG	RP-RRNAse: GAGCGGCTGTCTCCACAAGT	RP-P RNAse: FAM-TTCTGACCTGAAGGCTC TGCGCG– BHQ-1
China CDC [=]	ORF1ab and N gene	ORF1ab: CCCTGTGGGTTTTACACTTAA	ORF1ab: ACGATTGTGCATCAGCTGA	ORF1ab: FAM- CCGTCTGCGGTATGTGGAAAG GTTATGG-BHQ1
		N: GGGGAACTTCTCCTGCTAGAAT	N: CAGACATTTTGCTCTCAAGCTG	N: FAM-TTGCTGCTGCTTGA CAGATT-TAMRA
Charité, Germany [=]	RdRp, E, N gene	RdRp: GTGARATGGTCATGTGTGGCGG	RdRp: CARATGTTAAASACACTATTAGCATA	RdRp 1: FAM-CAGGTGGAACCTCATC AGGAGATGC-BBQ RdRp 2: FAM-CCAGGTGGWACRTCATC MGGTGATGC-BBQ
		E: ACAGGTACGTTAATAGTTAATAGCGT	E: ATATTGCAGCAGTACGCACACA	E: FAM-ACACTAGCCATCCTTA CTGCGCTTCG-BBQ
Hong Kong University [=]	ORF1b- nsp14, N gene	ORF1b-nsp14: TGGGGYTTTACRGGTAACCT	ORF1b-nsp14: AACRCGCTTAACAAAGCACTC	ORF1b-nsp14: FAM-TAGTTGTGATGCWATC ATGACTAG-TAMRA
		N: TAATCAGACAAGGAACTGATTA	N: CGAAGGTGTGACTTCCATG	N: FAM-GCAAATTGTGCA ATTTGCGG-TAMRA
National Institute of Infectious Diseases, Japan [=]	N gene	N: AAATTTTGGGGACCAGGAAC	N: TGGCAGCTGTGTAGGTCAAC	N: FAM-ATGTCGCGCAT TGGCATGGA-BHQ
National Institute of Health, Thailand [=]	N gene	N: CGTTTGGTGGACCCTCAGAT	N: CCCCACTGCGTTCTCCATT	N: FAM- CAACTGGCAGTAACCABQH1

FIGURE 3.2 Polymerase Chain Reaction (PCR) Tests/Primers for SARS-CoV-2

RNA into complementary DNA (cDNA) strands, followed by amplification of specific regions of the cDNA (Freeman et al., 1999; Kageyama et al., 2003). The design process generally involves two main steps: (1) sequence alignment and primer design, and (2) assay optimization and testing. Corman et al. aligned and analyzed a number of SARS-related viral genome sequences to design a set of primers and probes (Corman et al., 2020). Among the SARS-related viral genomes, they discovered three regions that had conserved sequences: (1) the RdRP gene (RNA-dependent RNA polymerase gene) in the open reading frame ORF1ab region, (2) the E gene (envelope protein gene), and (3) the N gene (nucleocapsid protein gene). Both the RdRP and E genes had high analytical sensitivity for detection (technical limit of detection of 3.6 and 3.9 copies per reaction), whereas the N gene provided poorer analytical sensitivity (8.3 copies per reaction). The assay can be designed as a two-target system, where one primer universally detects numerous coronaviruses including SARS-CoV-2 and a second primer set only detects SARS-CoV-2.

After designing the primers and probes, the next step involves optimizing assay conditions (e.g., reagent conditions, incubation times, and temperatures), followed by PCR testing. RT-PCR can be performed in either a one-step or a two-step assay. In a one-step assay, reverse transcription and PCR amplification are consolidated into one reaction. This assay format can provide rapid and reproducible results for high-throughput analysis. The challenge is the difficulty in optimizing the reverse transcription and amplification steps as they occur simultaneously, which leads to lower target amplicon generation. In the two-step assay, the reaction is done sequentially in separate tubes (Wong & Medrano, 2005). This assay format is more sensitive than the one-step assay, but it is more time-consuming and requires optimizing additional parameters (Bustin, 2004; Wong & Medrano, 2005). Lastly, controls need to be carefully selected to ensure the reliability of the assay and to identify experimental errors.

Nucleic Acid Testing for SARS-CoV-2

At least 11 nucleic-acid-based methods and eight antibody detection kits have been approved in China by the National Medical Products Administration (NMPA) for detecting SARS-CoV-2. However, RT-PCR is the most predominantly used method for diagnosing COVID-19 using respiratory samples (World Health Organization, 2020). Upper respiratory samples are broadly recommended, although lower respiratory samples are recommended for patients exhibiting productive cough (Centers for *Disease* Control and Prevention, 2020a). Upper respiratory tract samples include nasopharyngeal swabs, oropharyngeal swabs, nasopharyngeal washes, and nasal aspirates. Lower respiratory tract samples include sputum, BAL fluid, and tracheal aspirates. Both BAL and tracheal aspirates can be high risk for aerosol generation. The detectable viral load depends on the days after illness onset. In the first 14 days after onset, SARS-CoV-2 could most reliably be detected in sputum followed by nasal swabs, whereas throat swabs were unreliable eight days after symptom onset (Pan et al., 2020; Yang et al., 2020). Given the variability in the viral loads, a negative test result from respiratory samples does not rule out the disease. These negatives could result from improper sampling techniques, low viral load in the area sampled, or mutations in the viral genome (Winichakoon et al., 2020). Winichakoon et al. recommended multiple lines of evidence for patients linked epidemiologically even if the results are negative from nasopharyngeal and/or oropharyngeal swab (Winichakoon et al., 2020).

The United States Centers for Disease Control and Prevention (CDC) uses a one-step real time RT-PCR (rRT-PCR) assay, which provides quantitative information on viral loads, to detect the presence of SARS-CoV-2 (Centers for *Disease* Control and Prevention, 2020b). To perform the assay, the viral RNA is extracted and added to a master mix. The master mix contains nuclease-free water, forward and reverse primers, a fluorophore-quencher probe, and a reaction mix (consisting of reverse transcriptase, polymerase, magnesium, nucleotides, and additives). The master mix and extracted RNA are loaded into a PCR thermocycler, and the incubation temperatures are set to run the assay. The CDC has recommended cycling conditions for rRT-PCR (Centers for Disease Control and Prevention, 2020b). During rRT-PCR, the fluorophore-quencher probe is cleaved, generating a fluorescent signal. The fluorescent signal is detected by the thermocycler, and the amplification progress is recorded in real time. The probe sequence used by Guan et al. was Black Hole Quencher-1 (BHQ1, quencher) and fluorescein amidite (FAM, fluorophore). This reaction takes ~45 min and can occur in a 96-well plate, where each well contains a different sample or control. There must be both a positive and a negative control to interpret the final results properly when running rRT-PCR. For SARS-CoV-2, the CDC provides a positive control sequence called nCoVPC (Centers for Disease Control and Prevention, 2020b). A number of SARS-CoV-2 RT-PCR primers and probes from different research groups and agencies are listed in Figure 3.2.

Integrating Nucleic Acid Detection With Clinical Management

There are different implementation workflows for RT-PCR tests in clinical settings. Corman et al. proposed a three-step workflow for the diagnosis of SARS-CoV-2 (Corman et al., 2020). They define the three steps as first line screening, confirmation, and discriminatory assays. To maximize the number of infected patients identified, the first step detects all SARS-related viruses by targeting different regions of the E gene. If this test is positive, then they propose the detection of the RdRP gene using two different primers and two different probes. If these results are also positive, then they conduct the discriminatory test with one of the two probe sequences (Corman et al., 2020). See Figure 3.2 (Charité, Germany). Chu et al. proposed a slightly different assay workflow (Chu et al., 2020). They screened samples using primers for the N gene and used those from the ORFlb gene for confirmation. A diagnosis where the patient sample is positive with N gene primer and negative with the ORFlb gene would be inconclusive. In such situations, protein tests (i.e., antibody tests) or sequencing would be required to confirm the diagnosis (Chu et al., 2020).

DEVICE DESCRIPTION AND TEST PRINCIPLE

The COVID-19 RT-PCR Test is an rRT-PCR test. The test can be run in a singleplex format (three individual assays) or multiplexed into a single reaction and amplification set up. In a singleplex format, the test uses three primer and probe sets to detect three regions in the SARSCoV-2 nucleocapsid (N) gene and one primer and probe set to detect human RNase P (RP) in a clinical sample. When multiplexed into a single reaction, the test uses two primer and probe sets to detect two regions in the SARS-CoV-2 N gene and one primer and probe set to detect RP. RNA isolated from upper and lower respiratory specimens (such as nasal, nasopharyngeal or oropharyngeal swabs, sputum, lower respiratory tract aspirates, bronchoalveolar lavage, and nasopharyngeal wash/aspirate or nasal aspirate) is reverse transcribed to cDNA and subsequently amplified using Applied Biosystems QuantStudio7 Flex (QS7) instrument with software version 1.3. During the amplification process, the probe anneals to a specific target sequence located between the forward and reverse primers. During the extension phase of the PCR cycle, the 5′ nuclease activity of Taq polymerase degrades the bound probe, causing the reporter dye to separate from the quencher dye, generating a fluorescent signal. Fluorescence intensity is monitored at each PCR cycle by QS7.

The Pixel by LabCorp COVID-19 Test Home Collection Kit will only be dispensed to patients meeting the inclusion criteria based on the information provided through the Pixel website COVID-19 questionnaire and reviewed by the Physician Wellness Network (PWN). The PWN will determine test eligibility and write prescriptions for testing. PWN will also follow up all positive and inconclusive test results by contacting the patients. Negative patients will be notified by email, phone message and through the website portal.

The LabCorp At Home COVID-19 Test Home Collection Kit will be dispensed to patients when prescribed by their physician using the LabCorp provider interface to order diagnostic tests. Once the physician order is placed, LabCorp will mail the home collection kit to the patient, who will perform the sample collection and mail it back to LabCorp. LabCorp will then report test results back to the ordering physician and to the patient via the LabCorp patient portal.

The Pixel by LabCorp COVID-19 Test Home Collection Kit and the LabCorp At Home COVID-19 Test Home Collection Kit is composed of a shipping box, pre-labeled return envelope, directions, specimen collection materials (nasal swab and saline tube), and specimen biohazard bag. Instructions are included in the kit to direct the home users on how to appropriately collect the nasal swab specimen and place it in the saline transport tube, how to properly package the specimen and how to mail the specimen back to the laboratory using the pre-labeled FedEx return envelope.

DESCRIPTION OF POOLING

Traditionally, pooling employs a two-stage approach where samples are tested as pools and then any positive pools are retested at a later time to determine which individual was positive. While this approach saves reagents, it is not practical to implement in a high throughput testing environment where many thousands of samples would need to be pulled and retested every day. Matrix based pooling strategies allow the lab to test samples as pools while preventing the need to retest individual samples as long as the expected (and observed) number of positive samples per matrix is less than or equal to one (Table 3.1). To combat the retest problem, LabCorp will employ a matrix pooling strategy where samples will be tested twice in pools of four samples which increases lab efficiency by a factor of two if the tested population prevalence remains < 6% (Table 3.1).

Matrix based pooling as described below will be performed in the laboratory using liquid handling robots and will not be performed or analyzed by hand. Using a 4×4 matrix as an example (Figure 3.3), 16 samples are arranged in a 4×4 grid. Each sample is then combined into horizontal (rows) and vertical (columns) pools to create X and Y positional information for each sample. As long as no more than one sample per matrix is positive, an individual positive can be ascertained without retesting any of the pools (Figure 3.4). If there are two positives in a matrix, 12.5% of the time (1/8), both positives can be ascertained if they fall in either the same row or the same column (Figure 3.5) while 87.5% of the time they will result in an equivocal result (Figure 3.6). If four or more pools (two per row or column set) return positive, all samples in each equivocal pool must be retested to determine which are positive (Figure 3.6). If one or more row or column pools returns positive without a corresponding row or column pool returning positive (No X/Y intersection), then all samples within the positive pools must be retested as individuals (Figure 3.7 and Figure 3.8).

TABLE 3.1

Matrix-Based Pooling Strategies Increase Throughput Without Requiring Retesting. Green—One Positive Per Matrix at Indicated Prevalence

	Expected Positives			
Prevalence (%)	3×3	4×4	5×5	10×10
0.1	0.009	0.016	0.025	0.1
0.5	0.045	0.08	0.125	0.5
1.0	9	0.16	0.25	1
3.0	27	0.48	0.75	3
5.0	45	0.8	1.25	5
10	0.9	1.6	2.5	10
15	1.35	2.4	3.75	15
Throughput	1.5	2	2.5	5

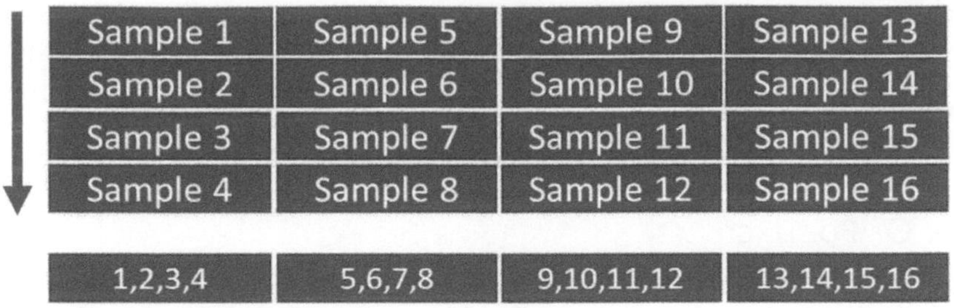

Sample 1	Sample 5	Sample 9	Sample 13
Sample 2	Sample 6	Sample 10	Sample 14
Sample 3	Sample 7	Sample 11	Sample 15
Sample 4	Sample 8	Sample 12	Sample 16

1,2,3,4	5,6,7,8	9,10,11,12	13,14,15,16

FIGURE 3.3 4×4 Matrix Example. Arrows—Indicate pooling direction. Boxes outside matrix grid represent the final pools.

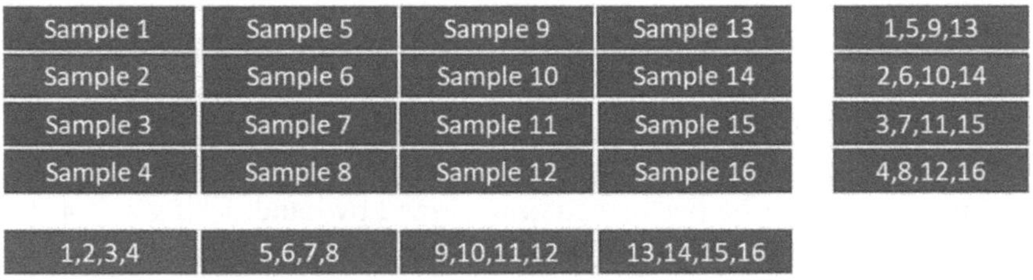

Sample 1	Sample 5	Sample 9	Sample 13	1,5,9,13
Sample 2	Sample 6	Sample 10	Sample 14	2,6,10,14
Sample 3	Sample 7	Sample 11	Sample 15	3,7,11,15
Sample 4	Sample 8	Sample 12	Sample 16	4,8,12,16

1,2,3,4	5,6,7,8	9,10,11,12	13,14,15,16

FIGURE 3.4 Unequivocal Identification in a 4×4 matrix. Red—positive sample or pool.

Sample 1	Sample 5	Sample 9	Sample 13	1,5,9,13
Sample 2	Sample 6	Sample 10	Sample 14	2,6,10,14
Sample 3	Sample 7	Sample 11	Sample 15	3,7,11,15
Sample 4	Sample 8	Sample 12	Sample 16	4,8,12,16

1,2,3,4	5,6,7,8	9,10,11,12	13,14,15,16

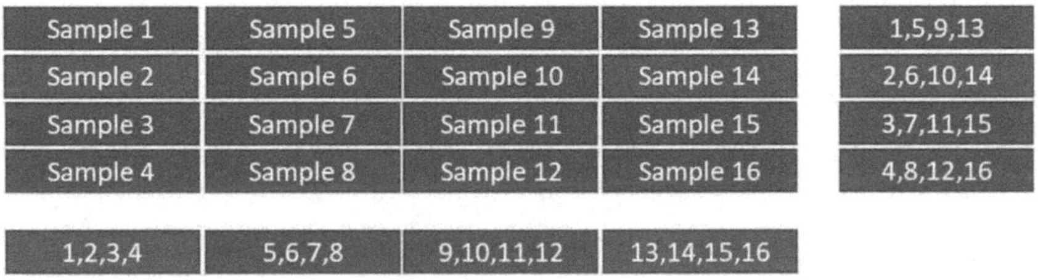

FIGURE 3.5 Unequivocal identification in a 4×4 matrix when two samples are positive. Red—positive sample or pool.

Sample 1	Sample 5	Sample 9	Sample 13	1,5,9,13
Sample 2	Sample 6	Sample 10	Sample 14	2,6,10,14
Sample 3	Sample 7	Sample 11	Sample 15	3,7,11,15
Sample 4	Sample 8	Sample 12	Sample 16	4,8,12,16

1,2,3,4	5,6,7,8	9,10,11,12	13,14,15,16

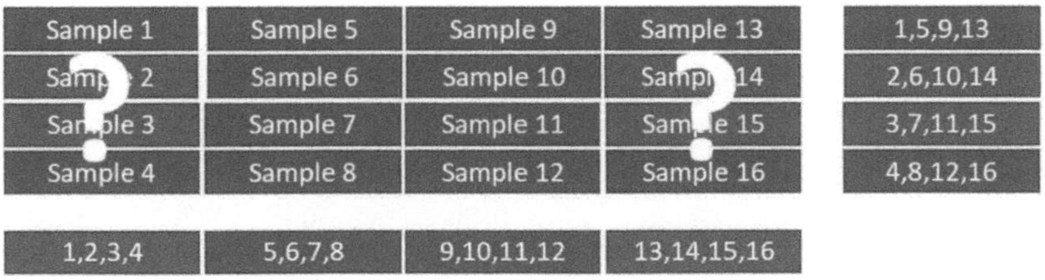

FIGURE 3.6 Equivocal identification in a 4×4 matrix when two samples are positive. Red—positive sample or pool. Question Marks—Row and column pools are equivocal, and must be repeated as individuals.

Sample 1	Sample 5	Sample 9	Sample 13	1,5,9,13
Sample 2	Sample 6	Sample 10	Sample 14	2,6,10,14
Sample 3	Sample 7	Sample 11	Sample 15	3,7,11,15
Sample 4	Sample 8	Sample 12	Sample 16	4,8,12,16

1,2,3,4	5,6,7,8	9,10,11,12	13,14,15,16

FIGURE 3.7 Equivocal identification in a 4×4 matrix when no samples are positive. Occurs when one or two pools are positive without a corresponding row or column resulting positive. Red—positive sample or pool, Question Marks—Column pools are equivocal, and must be repeated as individuals.

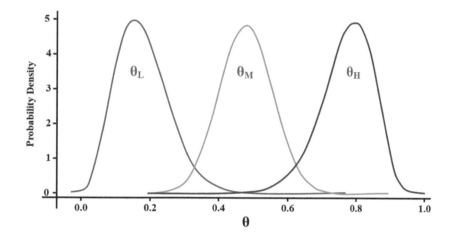

FIGURE 3.8 Distributions corresponding to low, medium, and high confidence of identification of diagnostic errors. The beta distribution for θ_L has parameters a = 5, b = 20. The beta distribution for θ_M has parameters a = 20, b = 20. The beta distribution for θ_H has parameters a = 20, b = 5.

COMPUTATIONAL TECHNIQUE OF RT-PCR TEST DIAGNOSTIC SENSITIVITY AND SPECIFICITY RECONSTRUCTION FOR COVID-19

The rapid development and deployment of RT-PCR tests has been essential for the ability to measure and control the spread of SARS-CoV-2. However, the urgency of the pandemic has not allowed time for reliable and adequately powered clinical studies to be conducted to measure the diagnostic limitations of the RT-PCR test. At present, the bulk of knowledge about the sensitivity and specificity of RT-PCR is based on laboratory measurements that have goals related to the minimum threshold of detection of viral loads and the required number of thermal cycles of the chain reaction (Pfefferle et al., 2020). Some attention has been given to the viral distribution by physical location, such as the differences in positive rates of RT-PCR in nasopharyngeal versus oropharyngeal swabs, or in the sputum and bronchoalveolar lavage fluid (Wang et al., 2020; Yang et al., 2020). Other factors that can impact the diagnostic success of RT-PCR include the timing of the test relative to disease onset, adequacy of the volume of fluids collected in the swab, and deviations from the laboratory recommended protocol under real-world conditions.

In terms of clinical decision-making, any of the causes of failure of the test can lead to incorrect diagnoses due to false positives and false negatives. This issue has received media attention and a recent editorial written by a professor of medicine in an influential US newspaper (Krumholz, 2020) urged physicians to beware of false negatives of diagnostic testing for COVID-19 while acknowledging that reliable data on rates of false negatives were not yet available.

This section provides a timely assessment of the diagnostic sensitivity and specificity of RT-PCR that is based on a sample of 1014 patients in Wuhan, China (Ai et al., 2020). The original study had the aim of measuring the accuracy of chest CT imaging for diagnosis of COVID-19 and they assumed that RT-PCR was the gold standard. However, the authors provided additional information about the status of patients that allows for the reconstruction of the sensitivity and specificity of RTPCR in the context of clinical decision-making. The knowledge of the efficacy and limitations of RT-PCR, even if known for only the Chinese version of the test at this time, can be expected to provide a valuable reference for medical practitioners and researchers at the frontlines of the fight against the pandemic. The findings have implications for policy makers as well, because policies for pandemic control in conditions of limited availability of tests that have a high rate of false negatives can be starkly different from policies in the presence of an abundant supply of a diagnostic test with excellent predictive values.

DATA AND METHODS

Data

Data from published findings (Ai et al., 2020) have been used in this study. The study included 1014 patients suspected of having COVID-19 in Wuhan, China, who underwent RT-PCR and chest CT imaging diagnostic tests during a 30-day period in the months of January and February, 2020. The mean age was reported to be 51 ± 15 years, and 46% were male. Throat swab samples were collected and the RT-PCR assays were reported to have used TaqMan One-Step RT-PCR kits from Shanghai Huirui Biotechnology Co., Ltd., or Shanghai BioGerm Medical Biotechnology Co., Ltd., both of which were reported to have been approved for use by China Food and Drug Administration. RT-PCR tests were positive for 601 patients (59.3%) and negative for the other 413 patients (40.7%). Although these tests were treated as the gold standard for comparison with chest CT imaging, the study authors provided valuable additional information. Patients who had negative RT-PCR tests but positive tests from chest CT were reassessed on the basis of clinical symptoms, CT features, and serial CT scans. The study staff concluded that among patients with negative RT-PCR tests, 147 could be classified as highly likely cases of COVID-19 and another 103 could be classified as probable cases of COVID-19. Moreover, among the 601 patients with positive RT-PCR tests, 21 patients were classified negative for COVID-19 from chest CT imaging. In this study, these 21 cases are assumed to have a low chance of being false positives, which is in alignment with the implicit assumption of the original study, indicated by their choice of RT-PCR as the reference for comparison with chest CT imaging. Apart from its role in the identification of probable false positives and negatives of RT-PCR, the chest CT imaging data is ignored in this study. In summary, the data are composed of firm knowledge of RT-PCR test results and probabilistic knowledge of the numbers of false positives and false negatives. The ranges and notations used for the true and false positives and negatives are presented in Table 3.2.

TABLE 3.2

Counts and Notation for the Joint Distribution of RT-PCR Test Result and Presence or Absence of COVID-19

	COVID-19 Present	COVID-19 absent	Row Sums
Positive RT-PCR	N1 − n1	n1	N1 = 601
Negative RT-PCR	n2	N2 − n2	N2 = 413
Column Sums	N1 − n1 + n2	N2 − n2 + n1	N1 + N2 = 1014

Note: Maximum range of variation for n1 is [0, 21] and the maximum range for n2 is [0, 250], but probable ranges are much narrower. The 95% ci for n1 was found to be [0, 9] and for n2 it was [136, 197]

Statistical Analysis

A modified Bayesian approach was adopted to estimate the uncertainty that arose from imprecise knowledge of the data. The data, denoted X, consisted of the 2×2 contingency table that represented the observed joint distribution of the RT-PCR decision (positive or negative) and the binary disease status (COVID-19 present or absent). Since the number of positive and negative tests were known, the data were uniquely defined from the number of false positives, n1, and number of false negatives, n2, i.e., X = X(n1, n2). The uncertainty in the data stemmed from the uncertainty in values of the random variables, n1 and n2. The distributions of n1 and n2 were estimated from the level of confidence expressed about false identifications. This procedure has similarities to fuzzy logic in which linguistic uncertainties about terms such as highly likely and probable are represented by membership functions (Zadeh, 1975). Although it is motivated by fuzzy logic, the treatment used here is strictly based in probability theory. The starting point was an informative distribution defined on the probability space of a diagnostic error. Upon calculating the resulting distributions of n1 and n2, the estimated values and distributions of sensitivity and specificity were derived from the joint distribution of n1 and n2. More details are given below.

The approach is thus Bayesian in the computational sense; it starts with an informative distribution, akin to an informative prior distribution, and ends with a distribution of the desired parameters (Gelman et al., 2013). However, the terminal points of the analysis do not describe the distribution of the same parameters, so use of the terms prior and posterior distributions has been avoided. Moreover, the likelihood function of the data that is calculated here has a different interpretation than the one obtained in normal conditions when the data are firmly known. For any given probability of false identification, the likelihood of the number of false positives or negatives is obtained from the binomial distribution. The number of trials for the binomial distribution are known from the data, while the binomial probability parameter, denoted here by θ, arises from a distribution that represents the degree of confidence expressed about the false identifications. Thus, the distribution of n1 is expressed by:

$$\Pr(n_1) = \sum_{\theta_L} \Pr(n_1|\theta_L)\Pr(\theta_L)$$

where θ_L is the chance of a case being false positive, the subscript L refers to a low chance, $Pr(\theta_L)$ is the distribution of that chance over the probability space [0, 1], and $\mathrm{Pr}(n_1|\theta_L)$ is the binomial distribution with probability θ_L and number of trials given by the maximum range for n_1, which is known to be 21. Similarly, the distribution of n_2 is expressed by:

$$\mathrm{Pr}(n_2) = \sum_{\theta_H \theta_M} \mathrm{Pr}(n_H|\theta_H)\mathrm{Pr}(\theta_H)\mathrm{Pr}(n_M|\theta_H)\mathrm{Pr}(\theta_M)$$

where θ_H and θ_M are the high and medium chances of a case being highly likely to be a false negative and probable false negative, respectively. The sum of n_H and n_M equals n_2 and the distributions of n_H and n_M are binomial, given values of θ_H and θ_M along with the number of binomial trials, which are known to be 147 and 103, respectively. Beta distributions, which often serve as conjugate distributions for the binomial distribution, were used for θ_L, θ_M, and θ_H to describe low, medium, and high levels of confidence in the diagnostic errors that were identified.

The data $X(n_1, n_2)$ were uniquely specified by n_1 and n_2, as were the sensitivity, S_1, and specificity, S_2. In particular,

$$S_1(n_1, n_2) = \frac{(N_1 - n_1)}{(N_1 - n_1 + n_2)} \text{ and } S_2(n_1, n_2) = \frac{(N_2 - n_2)}{(N_2 - n_2 + n_1)}$$

where the values of N_1 and N_1 are known. Therefore, the joint distribution $Pr(n_1, n_2)$ provided a mapping to the distributions of the sensitivity and specificity. The careful considerations described up to this point resulted in estimates of the expected values of sensitivity, specificity and a measure of the uncertainty in their values that arose from imperfect knowledge of the data. Another source of uncertainty is due to sampling error, which was estimated using established methods for the standard error for proportions.

Lastly, this study evaluated the predictive values of the test that provide the chance of disease in a patient conditional upon results of the diagnostic test. Sensitivity is a conditional probability that can be reversed using the Bayes formula to provide the positive predictive value of the test:

$$\mathrm{Pr}(COVID-19|Positive\ RT-PCR) = \frac{S_1 Pr(COVID-19)}{S_1 Pr(COVID-19) + (1 - S_2)(1 - \mathrm{Pr}(COVID-19))}$$

A similar formula can be expressed for the probability of COVID-19 in a patient even if the test is negative, i.e., $\mathrm{Pr}(COVID-19|Negative\ RT-PCR)$. In the above equation, Pr(COVID-19) on the right hand side can be interpreted as the prevalence of the disease when the testing is being done in the general population. More generally, $Pr(COVID-19)$ is the prior probability of presence of the disease. This is also the more appropriate interpretation in the present circumstances in which the testing is reserved largely for symptomatic patients. The medical professional may suspect that a patient has COVID-19, which could be quantified into the prior probability. The RT-PCR test is then carried out and the test result decides the posterior probability. Statistical analysis was done using the R programming language in the RStudio software environment (R Core Team, 2013; RStudio Team, 2019).

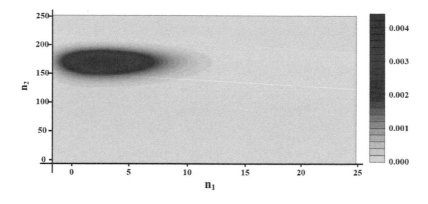

FIGURE 3.9 Joint distribution of false positives, n_1, and false negatives, n_2. The color scale refers to the probability of observing any pair of values of n_1 and n_2.

RESULTS

Shape parameters of the beta distributions for low, medium, and high confidence levels for being a false test result were a=5, b=20 for $Pr(\theta_L)$, a=20, b=20 for $Pr(\theta_M)$, and a=20, b=5 for $Pr(\theta_H)$. The median value of θ_L was 0.192, with 10th and 90th percentiles given by 0.105 and 0.306, respectively. The median value of θ_M was 0.500, with 10th and 90th percentiles equal to 0.399 and 0.601, respectively. For θ_H, the median value was 0.808, with 10th and 90th percentiles given by 0.694 and 0.895, respectively. The distributions for θ_L, θ_M, and θ_H are shown in Figure 3.9.

The maximum likelihood of the joint distribution of n_1 and n_2 (Figure 3.9) was located at $n_1 = 3$ and $n_2 = 172$. This solution corresponds to an estimate of 770 patients with COVID-19 and 244 without the disease. Due to the low number of false positives, the expectation value of specificity was high: $\hat{S}_2 = 0.988$. In contrast, the high false negative count was reflected in the lower expectation value of sensitivity: $\hat{S}_1 = 0.777$. The 95% confidence intervals for $Pr(n_1,n_2)$ led to the corresponding limits for $Pr(S_1 \mid n_1,n_2)$ and $Pr(S_2 \mid n_1,n_2)$. Sensitivity had a 95% confidence interval from 0.746 to 0.821, while the 95% confidence interval for specificity ranged between 0.958 and 1.000. Figure 3.10 depicts the distributions of sensitivity and specificity.

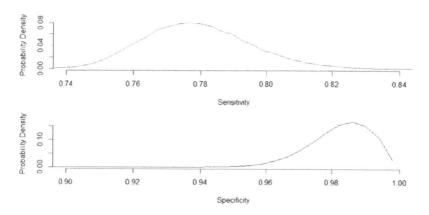

FIGURE 3.10 Distributions of sensitivity, $Pr(S_1 \mid n_1,n_2)$, and specificity $Pr(S_2 \mid n_1,n_2)$ estimated by the modified Bayesian method described in the study.

TABLE 3.3

Estimated Values of Sensitivity and Specificity of RT-PCR for Diagnosis of COVID-19

		Value (est.)	95% CI (Data Uncertainty)		95% CI (incl. sampling error)	
			Lower	Upper	Lower	Upper
Set 1	Sensitivity	0.777	0.746	0.821	0.715	0.849
	Specificity	0.988	0.958	1	0.933	1
Set 2	Sensitivity	0.778	0.757	0.805	0.727	0.833
	Specificity	0.984	0.963	1	0.94	1
Set 3	Sensitivity	0.779	0.74	0.842	0.709	0.869
	Specificity	0.983	0.95	1	0.923	1

Note: Set 1 refers to the primary choice of beta distributions for low, medium, and high confidence levels of the identified diagnostic errors, while set 2 and set 3 are explorations resulting from the assumption of narrower and wider beta distributions. Among columns, the first 95% ci represents the uncertainty arising from imperfect data. The second 95% ci includes sampling error in addition to the data uncertainty

The 95% confidence intervals mentioned above provided a measure of the uncertainty that arose from imperfect knowledge of the data. Additionally, the sampling error was estimated from the standard error for proportions evaluated at each of the endpoints of the 95% confidence interval for the data-related uncertainty. The overall 95% confidence intervals that incorporate the two sources of error are shown in Table 3.3.

The impact was explored of selecting different shape parameters for the beta distributions that describe low, medium, and high confidences. First, narrower beta distributions were defined by using shape parameters a=20, b=80 for $Pr(\theta_L)$, a=80, b=80 for $Pr(\theta_M)$, and a=80, b=20 for $Pr(\theta_H)$. The median values of θ_L, θ_M, and θ_H were 0.198, 0.500, and 0.802, respectively. The span between the 10th and 90th percentiles was approximately 0.1, which may be compared to 0.2 for the distributions described previously. Second, wider beta distributions were defined by using shape parameters a=3, b=10 for $Pr(\theta_L)$, a=10, b=10 for $Pr(\theta_M)$, and a=10, b=3 for $Pr(\theta_H)$. The median values of θ_L, θ_M, and θ_H were 0.217, 0.500, and 0.783, respectively. The span between the 10th and 90th percentiles was approximately 0.29. The estimated values of sensitivity, specificity, and their 95% confidence intervals are shown in Table 3.3. Point estimates of the parameters showed very little variation, but the choice of narrower/wider beta distributions resulted in somewhat narrower/wider confidence intervals.

The predictive values of the RT-PCR diagnostic test are shown in Figure 3.11 for prior probabilities ranging from zero to one. The two curves in the figure show the posterior probabilities of the presence of COVID-19 when test results are positive or negative. Additionally, Table 3.4 displays the number of confirmatory tests that are needed to establish presence or absence of COVID-19 at confidence levels of 90 and 95%. For example, if the prior probability of presence of COVID-19 in a patient is judged to be 0.6, a single negative RT-PCR test would reduce that probability to 0.253. A second negative test would reduce it further to 0.070, which would be sufficient if at least 90% confidence is required to establish absence of the disease. However, for the confidence level of 95%, a third negative test would be needed to lower the probability of COVID-19 below 0.05.

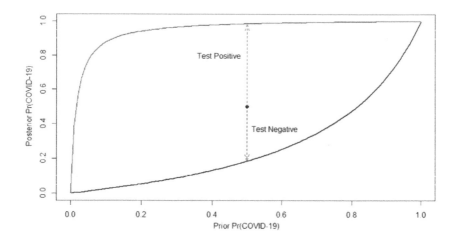

FIGURE 3.11 Probability of having COVID-19 after RT-PCR test as a function of the prior probability, or suspected chance that a patient may have the disease. The upper (light yellow) curve applies for a person who tests positive, while the lower (purple) curve applies when the test is negative. The diagonal is the line of equality of prior and posterior probabilities; any point on it may be considered the predicted probability before the diagnostic test is done. The arrows show an example of the changes induced by test results: the prior value of 0.50 jumps to the posterior value of 0.98 after a positive test and drops to 0.18 after a negative test result. The horizontal dashed lines mark 90% and 95% confidences at the top and bottom.

TABLE 3.4

Predictive Values of the RT-PCR Diagnostic Test for COVID-19

Prior Probability of COVID-19	Posterior Probability of COVID-19		Num. Tests to Establish Presence of COVID-19		Num. Tests to Establish Absence of COVID-19	
	Positive Test	Negative Test	P > 0.90	P > 0.95	P < 0.10	P < 0.05
0.1	0.875	0.025	2	2	1	1
0.2	0.94	0.054	1	2	1	2
0.3	0.964	0.088	1	1	1	2
0.4	0.977	0.131	1	1	2	2
0.5	0.984	0.184	1	1	2	2
0.6	0.99	0.253	1	1	2	3
0.7	0.993	0.345	1	1	3	3
0.8	0.996	0.475	1	1	3	3
0.9	0.998	0.671	1	1	3	4

Note: Posterior probabilities are shown for prior probabilities ranging from 0.1 To 0.9, Along with the number of confirmatory tests needed to establish presence or absence of covid-19 with confidence levels of 90 and 95%

RT-PCR tests are commonly used for the diagnosis of many influenza viruses and coronaviruses, including the viruses responsible for the 2002-04 SARS coronavirus outbreak, the 2009 H1N1 influenza pandemic, and the 2012 MERS coronavirus outbreak. RT-PCR tests are often treated as the gold standard in comparisons of diagnostic methods, which has led to few sources of reliable data about their diagnostic accuracy in clinical practice. The virus culture process is considered a better standard, but it takes several days in comparison to the few hours needed for RT-PCR tests. In one such comparison (Roa et al., 2011), RT-PCR was found to have sensitivity greater than 96% relative to virus culture for the diagnosis of H1N1 influenza. High accuracy of RT-PCR has also been reported for MERS (Huh et al., 2017). On the other hand, low accuracy has been reported for detection of SARS with real-time RT-PCR (Lau et al., 2003; Peiris et al., 2003) although rates of detection were improved with the refinement of laboratory methods (Poon et al., 2003).

In the current COVID-19 pandemic, it has been a great boon to have had the rapid development of several versions of RT-PCR diagnostic tests that target the detection of different genes from the viral RNA. Laboratory testing has shown that at least one version of the RT-PCR assay can detect viral loads as small as 3.2 RNA copies per reaction (Corman et al., 2020) and that it does not cross-react to other known coronaviruses, particularly when the primer for the assay is well-chosen (Chan, et al., 2020) However, there is widespread doubt about how well the tests work in practice (Krumholz, 2020). One source of error arises from the uncertain distribution of the virus in the body at various times during the COVID-19 disease trajectory (Ai et al., 2020). Comparisons of specimens from nasal and throat swabs indicate better sensitivity in nasal swabs and diminished sensitivity in throat swabs, particularly after the first few days of disease onset (Yang et al., 2020). The variation in the severity of the viral infection between subjects is another source of error; milder infections are more likely to escape detection. Other sources of error include sample collection, storage and transportation errors, such as collecting a low volume of fluid in swabs and depletion of the sample. Laboratory errors during assay processing are possible too.

The sensitivity and specificity of diagnostic testing using RT-PCR for COVID-19 that were estimated in this study may be considered to provide the cumulative impact of the various possible sources of error. It is clear that the sensitivity of the test is its weakest aspect while the specificity appears to be very good. Between 15 and 29% of COVID-19 cases may have gone undetected by the RT-PCR diagnostic test designed by China CDC that was implemented with TaqMan One-Step RT-PCR kits. As far as the medical practitioner is concerned, the predictive values of the diagnostic test are of utmost importance. For COVID-19, if a medical practitioner suspected that there was a 50% chance that a patient had the disease, a subsequent positive RTPCR test would increase that chance to 98.4%. On the other hand, after a negative RT-PCR test the patient still has 18.4% chance of the disease. A second confirmatory negative test would be needed to bring the chance of disease below 5%.

It is possible that some of the diagnostic errors were mitigated by the actions of medical professionals who might have taken a critical view of negative test results for symptomatic patients. Nevertheless, the false negative rate is still likely to be among the main reasons for the difficulty in controlling the breakout in its early stages. The problem of false negatives implies that public health measures that rely on singling out and isolating the cases of COVID-19 are unlikely to be successful on large scales. For instance, if the true prevalence is 1% in a population, testing would miss approximately 22 cases of COVID-19 for every 10,000 people tested. A highly transmissible virus can continue to propagate through the misdiagnosed cases.

The proportion of throat swab specimens that were positive for SARS-CoV-2 in RT-PCR tests conducted on patients with confirmed COVID-19 have been reported as being a mere 32% (Wang et al., 2020) and almost twice as much—60% in severe cases and 61% in mild cases—in another study (Yang et al., 2020). Neither of those values is equivalent to sensitivity as defined in this study because multiple specimens were drawn from a smaller set of participants in the mentioned studies. Nonetheless, it seems reasonable to conclude that the sensitivity estimated in this study is higher than what was suggested by the mentioned studies. A possible reason might be that viral loads may have been higher for data collected in the epicenter of the pandemic. On the other hand, it is worth noting that the sensitivity of RT-PCR for SARS-CoV-2 that was estimated in this study is in close alignment with the value of 0.80 reported for the sensitivity of detection of SARS with RT-PCR (Poon et al., 2003). Perhaps the similarity is not too surprising since the genomes of the two viruses have been reported to be 82% similar (Chan, et al., 2020)

The primary limitation of this study is that the estimated sensitivity and specificity apply to the particular version of the RT-PCR test that was urgently created and that was being used in Wuhan, China, during January and February, 2020. Laboratories around the world reacted rapidly to the pandemic and created their own versions of the RT-PCR test, as well as tests of other types. It may be expected that experimentation was done with protocols and procedures that resulted in changes in the performance of RT-PCR tests that were developed later. Another limitation of the study is that it is a retrospective study based on probabilistic knowledge of diagnostic errors. A study that is designed to compare the diagnostic accuracy of RT-PCR with a better gold standard method would be able to provide more definitive estimates and narrower confidence intervals. Data about the severity of infections of sampled patients and measures of viral load that were found in the RT-PCR tests, such as cycle threshold, were not available, which is another limiting factor of study covered in this section.

The diagnostic sensitivity and specificity of the RT-PCR test for COVID-19 were reconstructed from data on 1014 patients in Wuhan, China. Uncertainty that arose from incomplete knowledge of the joint distributions of test results and disease status was quantified with a modified Bayesian analysis, along with the quantification of uncertainty due to sampling error. The results indicated that the RT-PCR test administered via throat swabs had a conspicuous rate of false negative results, likely missing between 15 and 29% of patients with COVID-19. For any patient who is suspected to have COVID-19 with higher than a roughly one-in-five chance, at least two confirmatory negative RT-PCR tests would be necessary to reduce the likelihood of disease below 5%. The limitation of the study findings is that they apply to one version of the RT-PCR diagnostic test for COVID-19 that was developed and distributed urgently by China CDC. Study findings may not generalize to other versions of the RT-PCR test that are being used in diverse geographic regions.

DIGITAL POLYMERASE CHAIN REACTION

Digital polymerase chain reaction (dPCR) enables the absolute quantification of target nucleic acids present in a sample (Kalinina et al., 1997; Sykes et al., 1992). In dPCR, the sample is first partitioned into many independent PCR sub-reactions such that each

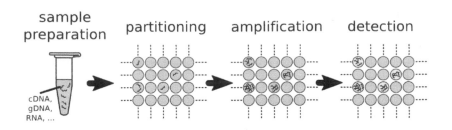

FIGURE 3.12 Principles of digital PCR. The sample is divided into many independent partitions such that each contains either a few or no target sequences. The distribution of target sequences in the partitions can be approximated with a Poisson's distribution. Each partition acts as an individual PCR micro reactor and partitions containing amplified target sequences are detected by fluorescence. The ratio of positive partitions (presence of fluorescence) over the total number allows to determine the concentration of the target in the sample.

partition contains either a few or no target sequences (Figure 3.12). After PCR, the fraction of amplification-positive partitions is used to quantify the concentration of the target sequence with a statistically defined accuracy using Poisson's statistics (Dube et al., 2008; Whale et al., 2013). Interestingly, sample partitioning efficiently concentrates the target sequences within the isolated microreactors. This concentration effect reduces template competition and thus enables the detection of rare mutations in a background of wild-type sequences. Furthermore, it may also allow for a higher tolerance to inhibitors present in a sample.

Statistical Foundations Of dPCR

dPCR benefits from statistical foundations that permit to infer both the target concentration and the accuracy of the quantification. This section reviews the statistical approaches underlying quantification by dPCR. Those approaches depend directly on the specific applications of the dPCR assay, e.g., absolute quantification or copy number variant analysis.

Binomial Probability and Poisson Approximation

To estimate the probability p of a partition to contain at least one target sequence, we should consider the case of the random distribution of m molecules into n partitions. This situation corresponds to a binomial process where the outcome of each drawing is either present or absent and the drawing is repeated m times. The chance of a target sequence to be present in a partition is $\frac{1}{n}$ because it results from random or independent events. The probability p is the complementary chance of the partition to be empty after the m target sequences are distributed. A partition has m chances, or attempts, to receive one target sequence. The chance for a partition to be empty is then $\left(1-\frac{1}{n}\right)$ after one drawing, and $\left(1-\frac{1}{n}\right)^m$ after m attempts, finally $p = 1-\left(1-\frac{1}{n}\right)^m$. In the situations where n is large ($\frac{1}{n}$ *very small*), one can consider the term $\left(1-\frac{1}{n}\right)$ as the first order approximation of $e^{-\frac{1}{n}}$, hence the probability p can be approximated to $p = 1 - e^-$ where $\lambda = \frac{m}{n}$. This formulation defines the probability function of a Poisson distribution of parameter lambda. Poisson distribution describes the probability distribution of independent events where the average number of events (λ) is known. The Poisson distribution predicts the proportion of partitions containing a given number of target sequences. Conversely, knowing the distribution permits to calculate the average number of a target sequence in the sample. Even though target partitioning follows a Poisson distribution, dPCR does not provide a detailed distribution and only indicates whether target sequences are present or not in a partition. Nonetheless, the ratio of positive partitions k (containing some target sequences) over the total number of partitions n is sufficient to predict the initial concentration of the target sequence in the sample with $\lambda = -ln\left(1 - \frac{k}{n}\right)$.

Quantification Accuracy

Intuitively, the confidence in the estimation of the target concentration depends on the number of empty partitions. In extreme cases, i.e., when most of the partitions are either empty or full, the confidence in the estimated concentration is very low because the pattern empty/full is not very informative.

The confidence interval is typically estimated using functions that can be directly calculated. Those estimations rely on assumptions that have direct consequences on the estimation. For instance, the Wald method approximates the binomial distribution (a discrete function with finite support) with a normal distribution (a continuous function with infinite support) (Brown et al., 2001; Wallis, 2013). As already noted (Shen et al., 2010), this approximation provides inaccurate results if most of the partitions are empty or if more than half of the partitions are filled. The Wilson method or interval (Wilson, 1927) is thus preferred for direct calculation. In this case, the confidence interval is given by:

$$p + \frac{\alpha^2}{2n} \pm \sqrt[\alpha]{\left(\frac{p(1-p)}{n} + \frac{\alpha^2}{4n^2}\right)} \Big/ \left(1 + \frac{\alpha^2}{4n^2}\right)$$

where p is the probability that a partition is empty, n the total number of partitions and α is equal to 1.96 for a 95% confidence interval. Other methods, including the direct or Clopper-Pearson method, demonstrate better approximation but the equations must be numerically solved (Wallis, 2013). Furthermore, these numerical-based methods are rarely used for dPCR (Shen et al., 2010).

The previous considerations suggest that there exists a value of lambda for which the initial template concentration can be estimated with the highest confidence. In cases of 10,000 or more partitions, the maximal confidence is obtained for a λ value of about 1.6, which corresponds to a proportion of 20% of empty partitions (Figure 3.13). As noted previously, the precision is poor for low values of λ, reaches an optimal for a λ of 1.6 before slowly declining with increasing values of λ, which corresponds to a saturation of the partitions. The accuracy of the estimation of λ increases with the number of partitions and the optimal precision $\left(at \ \lambda = 1.6\right)$ scales as the inverse square root of the number of partitions.

Most Probable Number (MPN)

For over a century, digital assays were conducted to estimate the concentration of microorganisms of public health concern (Halvorson & Ziegler, 1933; Ziegler & Halvorson, 1935). These estimations were based on repeatedly sampling a specimen at different dilutions to optimize the chances of estimating the concentration of microorganisms with the greatest

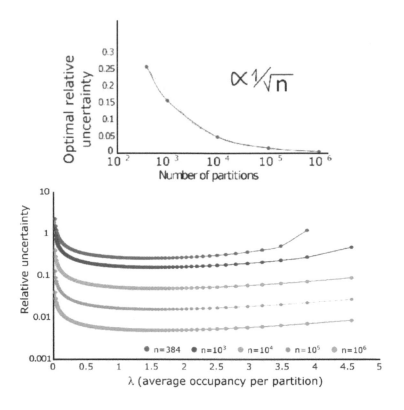

FIGURE 3.13 Quantification accuracy of dPCR. The precision of dPCR is non-uniform and depends on the average occupancy of target sequence per partition. The precision of dPCR also increases with an increasing number of partitions (distinct colors). The inset shows that the evolution of the relative uncertainty $\left(taken\ at\ \lambda \approx 1.6\right)$ decays as an invert square root of the number of partitions.

confidence. However, such methods take into account the values from the entire dilution series and treat the concentration of the target as a parameter to optimize the probability of observing those experimental values (method of maximum likelihood) (Cochran, 1950). The probability function can be numerically optimized with various approaches, which gives rise to different MPN methods. The values are usually tabulated according to the dilution ratios, number of samples and estimation strategies (Taubenberger & Morens, 2006). Those MPN methods provide comparable results to the Poisson approximation while being more cumbersome to implement in digital PCR applications (Kiss et al., 2008; Shen et al., 2010. However, the MPN method is the appropriate approach when analyzing multi-volume dPCR (Kreutz et al., 2011; Shen, et al., 2011).

Copy Number Variant (CNV) Applications

dPCR has been extensively used to measure genetic imbalances, or Copy Number Variant (CNV), that result from the deletion or amplification of genomic regions or locus. In CNV analysis, the copy number of a locus relative to another is the relevant information. The statistics to estimate the presence of a genetic imbalance using dPCR employs various methods. One such method relies on the Sequential Probability Ratio Test (SPRT), initially developed for quality control. It continuously tests two concurrent hypothesis while accumulating data until a hypothesis is considerably more probable than the other (Wald, 2004). In dPCR, SPRT was used to distinguish between homozygosity and heterozygosity in specific cell types in the presence of a homozygous background (Shih et al., 2001; Singer et al., 2002; Zhou et al., 2001). Other studies directly considered the statistical analysis of the ratio of two λ estimated for two loci (Whale et al., 2012). The ratio of λ was log transformed to normalize its distribution and to enable the derivation of its confidence. Alternatively, the confidence interval of the ratio was derived with an algorithm based on Fieller's theorem (Dube et al., 2008).

Absolute Limit of Quantification Due to Specimen Sampling

The analysis is only performed on a sample, which is a small portion of a specimen. This imposes a fundamental limit on the quantification accuracy. The concentration of an analyte in the tested sub-volume may differ greatly from the concentration of the analyte in the entire specimen due to statistical sampling (Debski & Garstecki, 2016). In other words, even a perfect quantification cannot properly determine the true concentration of the analyte in the specimen. The variability between samples can also be estimated using a Poisson distribution. For instance, if the average number of the target sequence in a sample is one, the chance of quantifying the true concentration in any sample is only a third. This highlights two critical aspects: (1) low values of λ are not correctly quantified, which is a fundamental inaccuracy that exists for all sampling techniques; and (2) this sampling error or noise is not systematic but random and can be only reduced by analyzing multiple samples of a same specimen.

Hypothesis and Technological Implications

Poisson statistics relies on two assumptions: (1) target sequences are randomly distributed across partitions and (2) all partitions have the same volume. The random distribution of target sequences has been validated experimentally by deriving the Ripley's K function that measures the randomness of the spatial distribution of partition occupancy (Bhat et al., 2009; Heyries et al., 2011) or by confirming that the estimated concentrations using sub-arrays are consistent (Shen et al., 2010). However, precautions are necessary when quantifying target sequences localized in same genomic regions. For instance, this is the case when estimating the copy number of the HER-2 oncogene that amplifies within a short region of chromosome 17 (Kallioniemi et al., 1992). If the target sequences are not physically separated, they end up in the same partition and lead to an underestimation of the gene copy number in the sample (Whale et al., 2012). Conversely, the assumption of random distribution has also been used to measure the linkage of different genes by dPCR (Roberts et al., 2014). This approach relies on the multiplexed detection of different targets that produce specific fluorescent signals. The co-amplification of two target sequences in the same partition produces a dual-colored signal that indicates their presence on the same DNA template. Interestingly, linked targets (i.e., a single molecule with two different target sequences) have been used to assess the prevalence of molecular dropout, i.e., the absence of amplification despite the presence of a target sequence in a partition (Whale et al., 2013). The rate of molecular dropout was estimated from the number of single color partitions compared to the number of two-color partitions.

Quantification by dPCR assumes that partitions possess identical volumes; however, a large degree of variability in volume may be observed. The latter directly depends on the methods used to create the partitions. The effect of this variation in partition volume has been experimentally assessed and considered a potential source of dPCR imprecision (Bhat et al., 2009). For λ higher than one, an increased variance in partition volume results in the over-estimation of empty partitions. In this situation, the proportion of empty partitions is lower than the proportion of partitions that contain a single molecule. As a result, the number of partitions that should be empty but capture a molecule due to a volume increase is lower than the number of partitions that should contain one molecule but end up empty due to a decrease in partition volume. In contrast to statistical uncertainty, the effect of partition volume variability on quantification accuracy does not decrease with the number of partitions. This inaccuracy will thus dominate the dPCR imprecision at high number of partitions (Pinheiro et al., 2012). A theoretical analysis concluded that the variability of the partition volume has a minimal impact when it is below 10% or when λ is lower than one, but its effect should be considered otherwise (Huggett et al., 2015). Volume variation of commercial systems have been reported to be lower than 3% (Dong et al., 2015), but research prototypes can suffer from high volume variation depending on the type of fabrication used and on the physical principles underlying the partitioning step.

Conclusion of the Statistical Foundations of dPCR

dPCR is a statistical method that divides a sample into numerous partitions and enables the enumeration of empty and occupied partitions to determine the concentration of a target sequence present in a sample. dPCR is an absolute quantification method that does not rely on calibration curves and whose accuracy is more easily predictable (Huggett et al., 2015). The theoretical foundations of dPCR are well established but it is critical to appreciate the inherent statistical limitations of this method. The precision of dPCR is limited by the uncertainty of the measurement due to: (1) specimen sampling, whose effect is prevalent for low target concentrations and can only be minimized by using technical replicates; (2) its statistical nature whose effect on precision can be reduced by increasing the number of partitions (Pinheiro et al., 2012). dPCR's intrinsic precision is not constant across its dynamic range and can be quite poor at the extremes. This is the case when most of the partitions are either positive or negative. Another technical limitation of dPCR stems from the variation in partition volume, which can have a detrimental effect at high average occupancy λ and can dominate quantification uncertainty at very high number of partitions. Those statistical considerations highlight the importance of the number of partitions, their volume and the standard deviation of their volume (Huggett et al., 2015).

PERFORMANCE METRICS

Sensitivity of Detection

The sensitivity or lower limit of detection corresponds to the detection of a single molecule in a single partition. Hence, the minimal concentration that can be detected depends on the total volume of the reaction or on the number of partitions and their volume. This simple reasoning underlines the limits of sensitivity of dPCR because dPCR techniques rely on partitions with volumes in the pL-nL range and their number is limited in practice. By contrast, the reaction volume of RT-PCR is typically much larger and can also be easily adjusted to reach higher sensitivity.

TABLE 3.5

Design Parameters and Performance Metrics of dPCR

Metrics	Accuracy	Sensitivity	Upper Limit
Design parameter	Number of partitions Variation in partition volume	Total assay volume or -Number of partitions $\times$ volume of partition	Volume of partition
Comments	Relative accuracy scales like $1/\sqrt{number\ of\ partitions}$ Variation in partition volume dominates inaccuracy at very high number of partitions	$1/(Total\ assay\ volume)$	Benefits from small partition volume

Dynamic Range of Detection

The dynamic range of detection is defined by the difference between the highest and the lowest detectable concentration of a molecule. The highest molecule concentration directly depends on the partition volume, i.e., partitions with smaller volumes correspond to higher molecule concentrations for a given λ. Interestingly, the highest number of target sequences detected can be far greater than the number of partitions. This value is estimated by solving λ for a given precision and number of partitions in the situation of high partition occupancy. For instance, given a precision of 12.6%, the highest number of target sequences detected can be 5-fold greater than 20,000 droplets generated (Pinheiro et al., 2012), or 11-fold greater than 106 partitions created (Heyries et al., 2011).

From those considerations, a large dynamic range of detection creates opposing constraints on the volume of partitions; with larger partition volumes improving the lower detection limit and smaller partition volumes improving the higher detection limit (Table 3.5). This conundrum can be addressed by using dPCR designs with multi-volume partitions, where a series of large volume partitions assure high sensitivity while a series of small volume partitions allows high detection limit, and a few series of partitions with intermediate volume provide high precision (Shen, et al., 2011; Wald, 2004). Interestingly, this approach is equivalent to performing a series of different dilutions followed by a quantification using the MPN method. Furthermore, multi-volume dPCR allows to uncouple dynamic range and measurement precision (Kreutz et al., 2011). On a practical aspect, this approach reduces the overall number of partitions required to reach a given dynamic range and hence the overall footprint of devices.

Practical Considerations in the Reliability of dPCR
Measurements-False-Negative/Positive Signals

Sensitivity is highly dependent on the rates of false positive and false negative events. Although dPCR is a digital assay, the signal detected is initially analog and a threshold needs to be applied to separate true signal from background signal (see Hatch et al., 2011 for a statistical thresholding method). False positives can arise from poor assay design or from the detection of spurious amplification at high number of PCR cycles. Additionally, they may also stem from cross-contamination during experimental set-up (Pinheiro et al., 2012).

While false positives can be minimized by proper assay design and optimization (Taylor et al., 2017), false negative or molecular dropout are less tractable. The intrinsic design of dPCR assays makes it prone to molecular dropout for various reasons: (1) the increased surface to volume ratio due to the small volume (pL-nL range) partitions increases the chance of PCR inhibition due to interactions of the reagents with surfaces or interfaces (Zhu et al., 2012); (2) it has been observed that single molecule amplification is often less efficient than amplification with higher number of molecules (Bhat et al., 2009); (3) the amplification efficiency is highly dependent on the source of DNA (i.e., genomic vs. plasmid, fragmented vs. long DNA molecules) (Bhat et al., 2009; Dong et al., 2015), and can be impaired by exposure of DNA molecules to heating (Bhat et al., 2011).

The mathematical framework introduced previously covers the statistical nature or intrinsic uncertainty of dPCR; however, the exact variance of dPCR assays should include the effect of upstream processes such as DNA extraction and pre-amplification (Kiss et al., 2008). For instance, it could be tempting to pre-amplify a sample with low target concentration to reach the optimal λ value of 1.6. However, the variance associated with the pre-amplification reaction is not systematic and cannot be corrected. As a result, direct quantification of low target concentration is still preferable (Kiss et al., 2008; Whale et al., 2013). The sensitivity of dPCR to molecular dropout or the variability of the sample preparation (extraction and/or pre-amplification) needs to be considered when assessing assay accuracy. Proper assay design and validation are critical to minimize typical issues arising from molecular dropout, false positives, or poor signal thresholding (Dong et al., 2015; Huggett et al., 2013).

MINIATURIZATION AND HYPER-COMPARTMENTALIZATION

Although the recent development of dPCR has been supported by advances in device miniaturization, the concept of dPCR has been developed (Huang et al., 2015; Sykes et al., 1992) using microtubes (Sykes et al., 1992) or 384-well microplates (Huang et al., 2015; Shih et al., 2001; Zhou et al., 2001). These formats suffer from limited number of partitions, limited automation and from the cost associated with the large amount of reagent needed. Microfluidics, i.e., miniaturization of fluid-handling (Hong & Quake, 2003), has enabled the massively-parallel sample partitioning and the advent of dPCR platforms. Microfluidics relies on microfabrication techniques adapted from microelectronics and its implementation relies either on fast prototyping by soft lithography in Polydimethylsiloxane (PDMS) (Duffy et al., 1998), glass etching (Du et al., 2009), or injection molding (Hindson et al., 2011). Numerous active and passive microfluidic methods have been used to compartmentalize samples, from physical partitions to liquid droplets. Most of those methods allow for simple automation and limited reagent use.

Before reviewing the different principles and methods employed to create partitions, it is worth mentioning some partition-free approaches. For instance, an early approach utilized a fused-silica capillary, typically used for capillary electrophoresis, as a reaction vessel to perform PCR on diluted DNA molecules. The number of amplified molecules was counted after electro-migration using an inline fluorescence detector (Li et al., 2001). This strategy relies on the limited diffusion of the amplicons generated, which migrate altogether as a plug during electrophoresis. The signal is a succession of peaks that corresponds to the number of target sequences in the sample. A more recent approach is based on the transformation of target sequences into 1 μm DNA nanoballs by Rolling Circle Amplification

(RCA) (Jarvius et al., 2006). The DNA nanoballs can then be enumerated under a microscope or a microfluidic cytometer.

In the following section, we distinguish physical partitions where the reaction is partitioned into isolated chambers or microwells from droplet emulsions that can be collected outside the microfluidic devices.

Chamber Formats

Performing dPCR with physical partitions or chambers involves device filling, sample partitioning, thermocycling and assay readout. We differentiate active partitioning methods that involve either device reconfiguration or mechanical actuation from passive partitioning methods that are driven by fluidic effects or properties. We further distinguish self-partitioning methods that include both passive filling and partitioning.

Active Partitioning Platforms

One of the first microfluidic dPCR device relied on microfluidic valves that were created by superimposing a fluidic and a control networks of microfluidic channels made of the elastomeric material PDMS (Unger et al., 2000). Those networks are separated by a thin membrane that can be deformed into a microfluidic channel by applying pressure into the opposing control channel to create an "on-off" valve (Figure 3.14a). The workflow includes: (1) filling all the chambers with the reaction; (2) pressuring the control layer, which closes the connection between the chambers, thus isolating the chambers from one another. Such a device enabled the creation of $14,112 \times 6.25 \ nL$ partitions. The volume variation of the partitions depends on the precision of the soft-lithography process (Duffy et al., 1998) used for the microfabrication.

The SlipChip platform (Du et al., 2009) also uses an active partitioning approach (Figure 3.14(b)). The device is composed of two chip halves, each etched with two independent arrays of microwells (Shen et al., 2010). The chip is assembled by putting into contact and aligning the two open-faced halves such that the chambers from the opposite halves form temporary continuous serpentine microfluidic channels. The sample and reaction mix are then flowed through independent microfluidic networks and are subsequently compartmentalized into arrays of independent chambers by slipping the chip halves. Further slipping assures superimposition of the sample and the PCR arrays creating a single array of independent microreactors. The chip is assembled in mineral oil, which lubricates the system during slipping and ensures the isolation of partitions. Partitioning is effectively achieved by mechanical shearing applied during the slipping motion. This strategy enabled the creation of 1280 partitions of 2.6 nL without the need for pumps and valves. Additionally, the authors mention that they could create up to 16,384 microwells of picoliter volume using the same footprint (Shen et al., 2010).

Passive Partitioning Platforms

Passive partitioning uses fluidic effects to create sub-volumes and does not rely on mechanical methods. Arrays of microwells have been used to create partitions with either active or passive methods. This format can be considered as a direct miniaturization of a 384-well microplate, where the volume of individual microwells ranges from pL to nL (Jackman et al., 1998; Morrison et al., 2006). The key difference from its macroscale counterpart is that microwells are usually loaded all at once to fully exploit the parallelization offered by the format. This in turn necessitates a method that isolates microwells from one another and

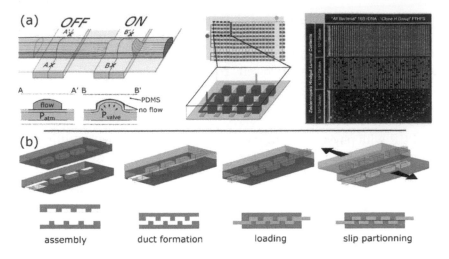

FIGURE 3.14 Active partitioning platforms. (a) Schematic of a push-up valve in a microfluidic chip made of PDMS. Left panel: The control channels (red) are separated from the fluidic channels (blue) by a thin flexible membrane (yellow). The flow through the fluidic channel is unobstructed if the control channel is not pressurized (OFF valve). When the control channel is pressurized, the thin PDMS membrane deforms and bulges into the fluidic channel, obstructing the flow (ON valve). As depicted in the bottom panel, a tight seal is obtained if the top of the fluidic channel is rounded. Central panel: Schematic diagram showing many parallel chambers (blue) connected through channels to a single input. The network of control channels (red) creates valves between each chamber allowing the partitioning of their content into independent PCR microreactors. Right panel: Three panels of 1176 chambers each, show the results of dPCR on samples harvested from a single termite (Z. nevadensis). (Figure adapted from Ottesen et al., 2006 with permission.); (b) SlipChip device relies on two chip halves that contain arrays of open chambers. Temporary ducts or channels are formed when the two parts are aligned and put in contact while submerged in mineral oil. Sample and reagents are injected before the device is reconfigured by slipping. The slipping motion creates arrays of independent microreactors. The device can be further slipped to bring the two independent arrays (containing reagent and sample) in contact to trigger mixing (not shown). (Figure adapted from Shen et al., 2011 with permission.)

avoids rapid evaporation of minuscule volumes. To support efficient microwell filling and partitioning, it is necessary to have differential surface properties between the interior of the microwell that needs to be hydrophilic and the top face of the array (in between the microwells) that needs to be hydrophobic (Akagi et al., 2004; Cohen et al., 2010).

The open version of the array of microwells has been the foundation of both active and passive partitioning platforms. Partitions were actively created by injecting the aqueous phase in the microwells, which were pre-layered with an immiscible oil, using a micro-dispenser (Matsubara et al., 2004). Alternatively, the partitioning can be performed by the apposition of a glass slide (Kinpara et al., 2004), a deformable membrane (Wiktor et al., 2015), or pressure-sensitive tape (Dimov et al., 2014) after assay loading.

In contrast to these active strategies, partitioning with this format can be performed passively by using an overlay of immiscible oil after loading of the aqueous phase into the microwells. The oil phase preferentially wets the top of the array and creates a meniscus that displaces the aqueous phase; however, the oil/aqueous phase/solid triple line gets pinned at transitions between hydrophobic and hydrophilic areas (Jackman et al., 1998;

Ostuni et al., 2001). The liquid-liquid interface then extends from the pinned triple line until it reaches another hydrophobic patch where another propagating triple line will be created (Reddy et al., 2005). The oil progresses on the hydrophobic surface of the array and around the well orifices to generate a sweeping motion that displaces the excess of aqueous phase.

Pinning also exists when a triple line encounters an abrupt change of topology or channel direction (Sposito & DeVoe, 2017; Vulto et al., 2011). Pinning can thus be used to isolate dead-end chambers within a microfluidic network thanks to the topology of the main channel and the chambers (Figure 3.15(a)) (Heyries et al., 2011). In this configuration, the oil film gets pinned at the chamber orifices. This strategy greatly increases the chamber density by reducing the size of the main channel compared to microfluidic valves that require a minimum span or width to be efficiently deformed. This method resulted in the generation of up to 1 million partitions in the pL range with a standard deviation of the volume equal to a few percent (Heyries et al., 2011). The very high number of partitions allows unparalleled precision and a theoretical dynamic range of up to seven logs. In addition to a much higher density of chambers, the strategy requires a simpler fabrication process than pneumatic valves.

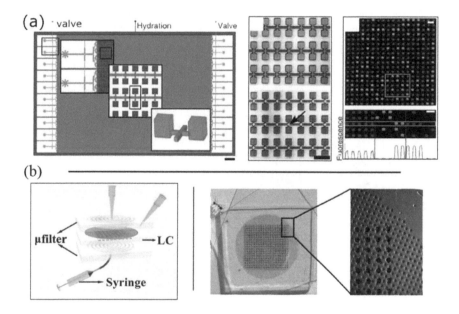

FIGURE 3.15 Passive partitioning platforms. (a) Megapixel digital PCR using planar emulsion arrays. Left panel: Schematic of the megapixel digital PCR device, with insets showing the array and chambers at increasing magnification. Scale bar: 3 mm. Central panel: The chambers are loaded with a blue dye. The arrow indicates chambers isolated by immiscible oil. Scale bar: 50 μm. Right panel: Multiplexed detection of HLCS (green) and RPPH1 (blue) over 342 chambers. (top). A close-up view shows the signals of the boxed chambers in the different fluorescence channels (middle), with the corresponding intensity profile of the middle row (bottom). Scale bars: 50 μm. (Figure adapted from (Heyries et al., 2011) with permission.); (b) Vacuum-assisted reagent loading in a PDMS-based array of microwells. Left panel: The schematic of the microfluidic chip depicts the process of reagent loading into the lamina chip layer via a μ filter layer. The syringe is used to create a temporary vacuum through the PDMS layer and drive liquid into the microwells. Right panel: Device loaded with the reagent (red) and water (blue). (Figure adapted from Tian et al., 2015 with permission.)

Critically, the filling of chambers at small scale is not trivial and is constrained by capillary effects (Reddy et al., 2005). In practical terms, the injected liquid needs to let the air exit the volume in a coordinated fashion. This requirement is alleviated using PDMS, an elastomer permeable to gases. Chambers are filled by pushing the air out through the material, by pressuring the incoming liquid. Alternatively, the device can be packaged under vacuum (Zhu et al., 2012) or vacuum can be applied to a chamber located underneath an array of microwells to drive filling (Figure 3.15(b)) (Tian et al., 2015). This approach avoids the risk of losing the sample through a small leak. PDMS presents however several drawbacks: (1) DNA and protein tends to absorb onto its hydrophobic surface if not properly pre-incubated with a solution of BSA (Ma et al., 2018), which in turn may affect its surface properties; (2) it is permeable to water and evaporation must be mitigated by incorporating water reservoirs (Gansen et al., 2012) and vapor barriers made of parylene C (Heyries et al., 2011) or glass (Hatch et al., 2011), which complicates device fabrication; (3) it suffers from a high cost of production, which impedes its use in large-scale manufacturing.

Self-Digitization Platforms

Self-digitization platforms combine both passive filling and partitioning. Passive filling can be enabled by harnessing the pinning effect to efficiently displace the air with a liquid during filling. This has been achieved by staggering two series of chambers across a main channel (Figure 3.16(a)) (Sposito & DeVoe, 2017). In this contraption, the liquid alternately

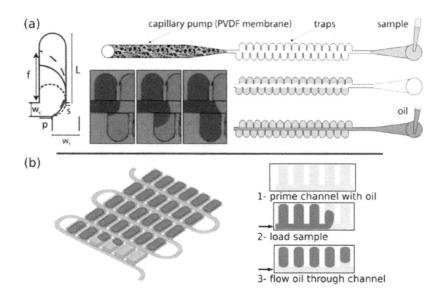

FIGURE 3.16 Self-filling and partitioning platforms. (a) Geometry for a staggered trap configuration where filling is controlled by pinning. The design enables an efficient filling by the sweeping motion of the solution through the traps and thus avoids trapping air within the chambers. The pinning offset is different on each side of the main channel thanks to a barrier wall. The loading process of the staggered device is shown in the pictures. The device incorporates a capillary pump that passively aspirates the excess of liquid. (Figure adapted from Sposito & DeVoe, 2017 with permission); (b) Schematic of the self-digitization device that contains 1020 wells. The device is first primed with oil, then filled with the reaction mix and injected with another stream of oil to create an array of droplets trapped in the structures. (Figure adapted from Thompson et al., 2014 with permission.)

sweeps through the chambers without trapping air because one extremity of the interface is pinned thanks to a barrier wall. The staggered configuration is critical to allow alternate pinning between the two sides of the main channel. The wetting of the aqueous phase on the plastic surface is increased by the addition of a surfactant and glycerol, which facilitates the filling phase. This platform also includes a capillary pump that pulls the excess of liquid from the device and simplifies the actuation of the system. The partitioning is completed by injection of an immiscible oil phase. This proof of principle generated an array of 768×11 nL partitions with a volume variation of 12%.

The actuation can also play a key role in simplifying an experimental set-up. For instance, spinning can distribute fluid into chambers located along a spiraling channel (Sundberg et al., 2010). Unfortunately, this format does not permit a direct observation of the filling and partitioning steps, which would be useful to improve the channel design. Overall, this platform generated a series of 1000×33 nL partitions but with a volume variation of up to 16%.

In the self-digitization approach (Cohen et al., 2010; Gansen et al., 2012), the device consists of a main channel with side chambers (Figure 3.16(b)) (Thompson et al., 2014). The device is first primed with immiscible oil that wets the channel and chamber walls. The aqueous sample is then injected followed by another plug of oil to create partitions. The filling involves the displacement of the immiscible oil by the aqueous solution and requires the walls to be hydrophobic, which may appear counterintuitive (Cohen et al., 2010). The hydrophobicity of the wall assures the presence of a thin film of oil at its surface (Tice et al., 2003), which acts as the draining conduit during the phase displacement. In the case of hydrophilic walls, the aqueous phase interacts strongly with the walls and creates a plug that prevents the oil from leaking out of the chambers.

The process contrasts with passive partitioning because it involves the formation of droplets that are generated through the splitting of a plug through a network of chambers (Boukellal et al., 2009), and it does not rely on pinning and differential surface properties between the main channel and the chambers. Droplet splitting is indeed governed by the capillary number that characterizes the relative effect of viscous and capillary forces (Link et al., 2004; Tan et al., 2004). The partition volume is mostly set by the chamber volume, but it also depends on the geometry of the chamber, flow rate, capillary number, contact angle, and oil viscosity. A refined version of the self-digitization platform yielded arrays of 535×6 nL partitions with a partition volume variation of 10–15% (Gansen et al., 2012). The same group further applied the same principles to a network of microwells located at the bottom of a main channel (Schneider et al., 2013). This strategy yielded a higher density of partitions (38,400 partitions of 2 nL). It also enabled optimization of the droplet formation by adjusting the design of the main channel.

Droplet-Based Platforms

The first goal of emulsification is to create isolated microreactors of aqueous droplets within immiscible oil. A critical component of this technology is the surfactant and oil formulation that assures both the stability of those microreactors and their compatibility with molecular reactions such as PCR or isothermal amplification (Holtze et al., 2008).

Encapsulation does not always perform sample partitioning and it can be used just to create independent microreactors such as in BEAMing (Beads, Emulsion, Amplification, Magnetics) (Diehl et al., 2006; Li et al., 2006). In this method, partitioning is achieved with magnetic beads that capture the target sequences by limiting dilution such that a single molecule is captured per bead. Encapsulation is performed to generate single-bead droplets used as independent microreactors to amplify the target sequence and saturate the bead surface. Emulsions can be easily and quickly obtained by mechanical shearing, which generates polydisperse droplets. After bead recovery, bead-bound sequences tagged with a fluorescent label are identified by flow cytometry at very high throughput. The magnetic beads allow for a simple and efficient sample purification and manipulation. This approach is applied to quantify genetic imbalance of specific genetic loci (Dressman et al., 2003; Li et al., 2006). The strength of this method resides in the transformation of a molecular signal into a cytometric readout with minimal constraints on the emulsification process.

Microfluidic droplet methods differ from BEAMing by using droplets as true partitions. They are enabled by microfluidic emulsification techniques that generate monodisperse droplets with very limited volume variation. Microfluidic droplets can be created with different techniques such as T-junction (Thorsen et al., 2001), nozzle (Figure 3.17(a)) (Anna et al., 2003), or step emulsification (Sugiura et al., 2001). Droplet formation with T-junctions and microfluidic nozzles relies on the viscous shearing that overcomes capillary effects at

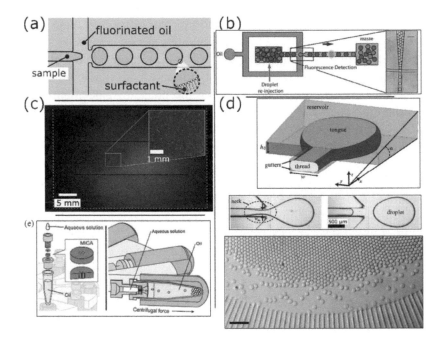

FIGURE 3.17 Microfluidic droplet-based platforms. (a) Schematic illustrating the generation of droplets with a nozzle or droplet generator. The aqueous phase is pinched by two streams of immiscible oil that stretch the interface via viscous forces until a capillary instability develops and the droplet detaches. Droplets are very stable thanks to surfactants that stabilize their interface; (b) The fluorescence signal from droplets can be sequentially detected in a single-file configuration. This arrangement is reminiscent of the optical and fluidic configurations used in flow cytometry. (Figure adapted from Dangla et al., 2013 with permission.); (c) Droplet signal can also be interrogated using a wide field detection that allows up to 1 million droplets to be analyzed simultaneously. (Figure adapted from Hatch et al., 2011 with permission.); (d) Microfluidic droplets can be generated with a simplified experimental setup that relies on a gradient of confinement (a type of step emulsification). (Figure adapted from Dangla et al., 2013 with permission.); (e) Alternatively, highly parallel droplet generators have been adapted to actuation by centrifuge, which allows concurrent encapsulation of several samples. Scale bar: 500 μm. (Figure adapted from Chen et al., 2017 with permission.)

the interface. Droplet generation via flow-focusing thus depends on the capillary number of the system. On the contrary, step emulsification is driven by an imbalance of Laplace pressure controlled by the geometry of the channel. Those droplet generation techniques result in the generation of streams of droplets with volumes ranging from pL to nL and a throughput of up to tens of thousands of droplets per second. In contrast to droplets generated in solid chambers, microfluidic droplets are not static but manipulated within networks of channels. Droplets can be collected off-chip for thermocycling and re-injected into a microfluidic device for readout. In droplet microfluidics, the sample does not interact with the channel walls once encapsulated, even though this may not preclude cross-contamination (Pinheiro et al., 2012) or interfacial inhibition (Beverung et al., 1999; Courtois et al., 2009).

dPCR applications based on microfluidic droplets have been enabled by single molecule amplification (Beer et al., 2008; Kumaresan et al., 2008). Using droplet-based microfluidics, the number of partitions can be adjusted to meet the requirement of an application, with for example devices capable of generating over 1 million droplets (Hatch et al., 2011). Furthermore, the volume variation of microfluidic droplets resides within a few percent (Dong et al., 2015). It also does not depend on the homogeneity of the microfabrication over a large array of features because all the droplets are usually generated using a single generator. This tight volume distribution remained lower than 3% when measured from droplets generated with 16 independent generators from five different eight-channel commercial cartridges (Huggett et al., 2015). The throughput of droplet generation can be increased with multi-nozzle systems (Schaerli et al., 2009) or through droplet splitting (Hatch et al., 2011); however, the effects of those techniques on the variation of droplet volume are unknown. Finally, multi-volume assays cannot be easily implemented in a single run using droplet microfluidics because the droplet size depends mostly on the nozzle dimensions, and manipulation of droplets in channels is complicated if droplets are polydisperse.

The throughput of droplet digital PCR (ddPCR) is often limited by the readout that is typically performed by interrogating droplets sequentially in a configuration inherited from flow cytometry (Figure 3.17(b)). The readout throughput is lower than in cytometry because droplets cannot withstand high shear rates. This limitation can be overcome by converting droplets into cytometry-compatible particles such as magnetic (Diehl et al., 2006; Li et al., 2006) or agarose beads (Zhang et al., 2012), or by using a double emulsion format (Zinchenko et al., 2014). Alternatively, a 3D particle counter (IC 3D) has been developed for rapid enumeration of positive droplets directly in the collection vial, which alleviates the need for further manipulation of the emulsion (Kang et al., 2014). IC 3D is based on a horizontal microscope whose confocal volume scans the whole emulsion by rotating and moving the collection vial. More classic approaches include wide field detection strategies that have been implemented to image droplets arranged in 2D arrays or crystals (Figure 3.17(c)) (Dangla et al., 2013; Kiss et al., 2008). This approach is cheaper and easier to implement, as it does not require any optical alignment. This format also permits real-time detection and melting-curve analysis, which provide efficient strategies to reject any spurious amplification that may be present at high number of thermal cycles.

Minimizing the need for specialized equipment to perform partitioning represents an important technological trend. Microfluidic droplets have been generated using gradient of confinement, a method similar to step emulsification that permits to simplify actuation of the oil phase (Figure 3.17(d)) (Dangla et al., 2013). Interestingly, both step emulsificators (Schuler et al., 2015) and droplet generators (Chen et al., 2017) have been adapted to actuation by centrifuges typically found in laboratories (Figure 3.17(e)). In addition to simplifying

TABLE 3.6

Summary of Partitioning Platforms for dPCR

Partitioning Method	Number of Partitions	Volume of Partitions	Principles
Microfluidic valving	10^4	10 nL	Relies on the elasticity of the material
SlipChip	10^4	10 nL	Slipping for partitioning
Open arrays of microwells	10^5	10 pL	Both active and passive strategies demonstrated
Microfluidic chambers	10^6	10 pL	Pinning of the oil interface to isolate chambers
Self-digitization	10^4	10 nL	Plug splitting within a network of chambers pre-wet with immiscible oil
Self-filling	10^3	10 nL	Control of the pinned interfaces for controlled filling
Spinning disk	10^3	10 nL	
Droplet generator	10^4–10^6	10^1–10^2 pL	Droplets used as partitions

the set-up and streamlining the workflow, those approaches can increase sample throughput by enabling simultaneous encapsulation of multiple samples.

A wide range of microfluidic approaches has been used to implement dPCR (Table 3.6). dPCR platforms aim at providing the optimal performance for dPCR by delivering a high number of partitions with limited volume variations and a large total reaction volume. dPCR technologies can be classified according to the format of the partitions and the methods used to create them. The partition formats include physical partitions and droplets. The principles underlying partitioning inform on the source of volume variation, the density of partitions that can be achieved and the simplicity of the set-up to perform partitioning. The basic principles involved in partitioning include: (1) direct mechanical shearing in micro-valve-based arrays or in some cases of open arrays of microwells; (2) viscous shearing in the case of the SlipChip format and droplet generators; (3) pinning to control partitioning by immiscible oil in arrayed chambers or arrays of microwells, as well as to control passive filling of arrays of staggered traps; and (4) gradient of Laplace pressure to generate droplets.

Cost-effective manufacturing is also a critical factor for high volume or commercial applications, and plastic injection molding is preferred over PDMS. There is a trend towards simplifying the actuation, which will lower the cost of those platforms, reduce the hands-on time and support the widespread adoption of dPCR. dPCR platforms currently lack the sample multiplexing capability of RT-PCR.

COMPUTATIONAL TECHNIQUE OF ddPCR TEST FOR SENSITIVITY ASSESSMENT OF COVID-19

The ddPCR technology is based on the absolute quantification of targets using the principles of dilution and partition of the reaction mix in 20,000 nanodroplets obtained by using oil-water emulsion. This methodology improves the accuracy and detection of targets in a low-cost and high-sensitive PCR approach (Dong et al., 2020). Currently, ddPCR is

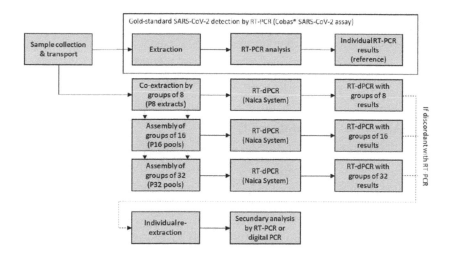

FIGURE 3.18 Schematic of the structure of the comparative study.

effectively used for the absolute quantification of viral load, for the analysis of circulating DNA, gene and microRNA expression and analysis of gene copy number variation (Suo et al., 2020; Visseaux et al., 2020; Vogels et al., 2020).

MATERIALS AND METHODS

Summary of the method of the comparative study Overall, 448 patient samples are tested for SARS-CoV-2 by (1) individual RT-PCR (local gold standard method), (2) DPCR in 56 groups of eight samples, (3) DPCR in 28 groups of 16 samples, and (4) DPCR in 14 groups of 32 samples and results are compared between all four test protocols. In case of discordance between the results of individual RT-PCR testing and group testing in DPCR, samples were re-analyzed individually by DPCR, by the gold-standard RT-PCR and a confirmatory RT-PCR assay. The whole protocol is illustrated in Figure 3.18.

SPECIMENS COLLECTION, STORAGE, AND POOLING

Nasopharyngeal swabs of 448 patients screened for Covid-19 at the Bichat university hospital (Paris, France), one of the two Paris reference centers for emerging diseases, between May 6 and May 26, 2020 were included. All samples were collected in universal transport medium (UTM) (Virocult® or eSwabTM) and tested, within 15 Hrs maximum upon collection, for SARS-CoV-2 detection according to the local standards. Briefly, 400 μL of transport medium were tested by RT-PCR (Cobas SARS-CoV-2 test, Roche). All the remaining volume of transport medium of all specimens was kept at +5°C.

No later than 24 Hrs after routine screening, all samples with a leftover UTM volume above 600 μL were systematically included in the group testing analysis. Thus, 125 μL of each included specimen were sampled and randomly mixed with seven others to generate a total of 56 groups of eight specimens with a final volume of 1 mL per group. Nucleic acids were extracted from each group prior to viral titration by DPCR. The remaining volume of transport medium was stored at +5°C for further investigations if required.

According to the current French ethical laws, samples used in the current study were only included after the completion of all analysis required for the patient's care.

PREPARATION OF GROUPS OF 16 AND 32 INDIVIDUALS

After extraction of the 56 groups of eight specimen (P8 extracts) and prior to viral titration by DPCR, 28 groups of 16 individual samples (P16 groups) were obtained by mixing 15 μL of two P8 extracts and 14 groups of 32 (P32 groups) were obtained by mixing 10 μL of two P16 groups.

Detection of SARS-CoV-2 by Grouped DPCR Testing

SARS-CoV-2 titration of the grouped samples by DPCR was performed on the Naica system (Stilla Technologies, France) (as shown in Figure 3.19) within the next three hours after extraction, using the COVID-19 Multiplex Digital PCR Detection Kit (Stilla Technologies, France/Apexbio, China). This one-step reverse transcription PCR kit is a triplex PCR allowing amplification, detection and quantification of one sequence in the N gene, one sequence in the ORF1ab region of SARS-CoV2 and an endogenous internal control (IC) to assess the quality of the sample and extraction. These sequences are targeted by three TaqMan probes respectively labeled with a FAM, HEX and Cy®5 fluorophore.

As recommended by the kit manufacturer, the PCR mix for a single reaction contained 12.5 μL of dPCR MasterMix 1, 1 μL of dPCR Mix 2, 1 μL of COVID-19 Assay and 10.5 μL of either, P8, P16, P32, positive control, negative control or individual extract. The 25 μL of this PCR mix were loaded in the inlet ports of the Sapphire chips (Stilla Technologies, France). The chips were placed in the Naica Geode (Stilla Technologies, France) for droplets generation, reverse transcription and PCR amplification following the kit manufacturer's instructions.

After amplification, the chips were transferred to the Naica Prism3 (Stilla technologies, France) for fluorescence reading in the three detection channels (Figure 3.18) and data were analyzed with Crystal Miner Software (Stilla Technologies, France) following the kit manufacturer's instructions.

Detection of SARS-CoV-2 by Routine Individual RT-PCR Testing

All 448 specimens were analyzed individually on a Cobas® 6800 system (Roche, Switzerland) for COVID-19 screening using the Cobas® SARS-CoV-2 Test kit targeting conserved regions for ORF-1a/b and Egene (Figure 3.20). For each specimen, 400 μL of transport medium were mixed with 400 μL of Cobas® lysis buffer and loaded on the robot. During the run, extracts were eluted in 50 μL of which 27 μL were used in the RT-PCR amplification of E and ORF-1a/b. A sample was considered positive for routine screening of COVID-19 ("RT-PCR+") if either target had a Ct value below 40 PCR cycles.

Within 11 days maximum (and 20 days for "Sample_25659") upon storage at +5°C, some samples which had different results for RT-PCR and DPCR were reassessed on the Cobas® 6800 system. To compensate for the low remaining amounts of transport medium, the nasal swabs were vortexed once more into the remaining transport medium diluted one to ten with new transport medium.

Extraction of Total NAs on Grouped Samples

All nucleic acids extractions for DPCR assays were performed on a MagNA Pure LC 2.0 (Roche, Switzerland) using the MagNA Pure LC Total Nucleic Acid Isolation Kit (Roche, Switzerland) following manufacturer's instructions. For all sample groups, the

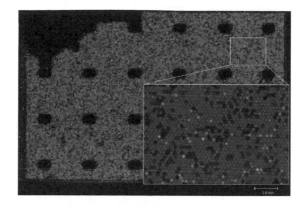

FIGURE 3.19 Image of the droplet crystal obtained using the Naica System on grouped extracts P8_22, including a zoom on a sub-region of the crystal. Droplet color code: dark grey = negative for all targets; blue: positive for N gene only; green: positive for ORF1ab only; red: positive for IC only; cyan: positive for N and ORF1ab genes; magenta: positive for N gene and IC; yellow: positive for ORF1ab gene and IC; white/mixed: positive for all. The droplet crystal contains 25,820 analyzable droplets, out of which 1,057, 883 and 21,121 were positive for the N, ORF1ab and IC, respectively.

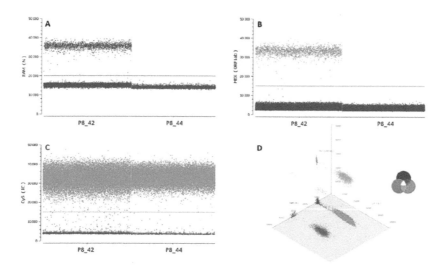

FIGURE 3.20 Fluorescence results as displayed in the Crystal Miner software showing 1D dot-plots of a positive (P8_42) and a negative (P8_44) pool of eight samples in the FAM (a), HEX (b) and Cy5 (c) channels. The horizontal line marks the threshold above which droplets (represented as dots) are considered positive for the amplification of N, ORF1ab and for the endogenous internal control respectively. The thresholds are set by manufacturer at 20 000 RFUs, 15 000 RFUs and 15 000 RFUs for the FAM, HEX and Cy5 channels. (d) 3D dot-plots of P8_42: if the concentration of either target is high enough, co-encapsulation of several targets can occur in a droplet leading to the apparition of clusters for double positive droplets (cyan, yellow and purple) and triple positive droplets (light grey). Triple negative droplets, containing no target, are shown in the dark grey cluster.

total volume of 1 mL was used for the extraction. For individual samples, 200 μL was diluted with 800 μL of buffer before extraction. Nucleic acids were eluted from 1 mL to 50 μL of the elution buffer provided with the kit and stored at +5°C for a maximum of 12 Hrs before analysis.

INDIVIDUAL CONFIRMATORY TESTING FOR SARS-CoV-2 BY RT-PCR AND DPCR

In case of discrepancies between individual RT-qPCR and grouped DPCR, DPCR results were confirmed by extracting individually each sample of the group and retesting them individually according to the previously described DPCR protocol. Confirmatory RT-qPCR test were also performed on individual samples as previously described with the Cobas SARS-CoV-2 assay and a third method, RealStar® SARS CoV-2 RT-PCR Kit (Altona Diagnostics, Germany), was also performed on an ABI 7500 thermocycler (ThermoFisher Scientific, United-States) from the same individual extraction as for the confirmatory DPCR assay. Briefly, this latter assay targets all lineage B-betacoronaviruses by amplifying a sequence of the E gene and a sequence of the S gene specific to SARS-CoV-2 as well as a heterologous internal control. A sample was considered positive to SARS-CoV-2 if the Ct value of either target is below 40 PCR cycles.

LoB/LoD EVALUATION FOR SARS-CoV-2 DETECTION USING DPCR

The Limit of Blank (LoB) and Limit of Detection (LoD) were evaluated for SARS-CoV-2 detection using the group testing approach used in the study on a cohort of 256 pre-epidemic nasal swab samples (negative control samples) that were collected between December 1, 2019 and January 31, 2020 and for which transport medium was stored at –20 °C within 48 Hrs after sampling.

Specimens were randomly grouped into 32 groups of eight negative controls which were co-extracted and analyzed by DPCR using the same protocol described above. The results for all 32 groups are given in Table 3.7. The LoB at 95% confidence level for the N target and the ORF1ab target is determined to be of two and zero positive droplets, respectively. The LoD at 95% confidence level for each target is of 0.49 copies/μL (7 copies/PCR) and 0.24 copies/μL (three copies/PCR), respectively.

Consequently, a threshold of a least three positive droplets in aggregate between both the N target and ORF1ab target is used to classify a sample as positive to SARS-CoV-2 by DPCR in this study.

RESULTS

Cohort Description From Routine RT-PCR Testing

Using routine RT-PCR testing, 25 samples were identified as positive out of the 448 samples tested, corresponding to an average test positivity rate of 5.5%. The positivity rate decreased during the study period from 8.5% for the first 224 samples to 2.5% for the last 224 samples, in correlation with the decreasing disease prevalence observed during the month of May in France.

The average Ct value was of 30.0 and 27.3 for the E gene and ORF gene, respectively, with minimum values of 16.5 and 16.3 and maximum values of 38.7 and >40 (not detected) (Figure 3.21).

TABLE 3.7

Detection Results in Number of Positive Droplets for N, ORF1ab, N+ORF1ab and IC by DPCR in 32 Groups of Eignt Pre-Epidemic Samples

Sample ID	Number of Droplets	Pos. Droplets (N + ORF1ab)	Pos. Droplets (N)	Pos. Droplets (ORF1ab)	IC (cp/μL)
Group 1	19,460	0	0	0	31,430
Group 2	20,641	0	0	0	10,985
Group 3	21,449	0	0	0	4054
Group 4	20,983	0	0	0	15,143
Group 5	19,881	1	1	0	7401
Group 6	20,609	0	0	0	8783
Group 7	19,044	0	0	0	6249
Group 8	20,787	0	0	0	8759
Group 9	21,470	0	0	0	10,271
Group 10	18,952	0	0	0	17,578
Group 11	23,424	0	0	0	8222
Group 12	22,748	0	0	0	9875
Group 13	23,747	0	0	0	10,275
Group 14	24,886	0	0	0	4266
Group 15	24,079	0	0	0	10,264
Group 16	24,718	0	0	0	13,219
Group 17	24,228	0	0	0	10,186
Group 18	23,742	0	0	0	8431
Group 19	23,880	0	0	0	7628
Group 20	23,613	0	0	0	3111
Group 21	25,723	0	0	0	8987
Group 22	25,522	0	0	0	7411
Group 23	24,781	0	0	0	6894
Group 24	7074	0	0	0	5884
Group 25	27,003	0	0	0	8911
Group 26	27,138	0	0	0	5552
Group 27	24,425	0	0	0	7886
Group 28	27,017	0	0	0	7484
Group 29	26,722	0	0	0	9963
Group 30	26,088	0	0	0	2492
Group 31	26,747	0	0	0	5703
Group 32	26,728	0	0	0	5825

Results From Grouped DPCR Testing

All results for the detection of SARS-CoV-2 by DPCR for the grouped extracts (P8) and the subsequent groups of 16 (P16) and 32 (P32) are presented in Table 3.8.

Because sample pooling was performed systematically as samples came in the laboratory for routing RT-PCR testing, the groups contain variable numbers of RT-PCR positive samples (as shown in table 3.10) ("RT-PCR+" samples).

Given the positivity rate of RT-PCR at the time of the study, the majority of P8 extracts had no RT-PCR+ samples (35 out of 56) and 21 groups contained at least one RT-PCR+ sample, including 18 that had one single RT-PCR+ sample.

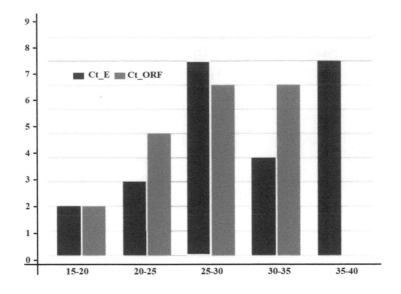

FIGURE 3.21 Distribution of Ct values for the E gene and ORF gene, as measured using individual reference RT-PCR with Cobas® 6800 SARS-CoV-2 assay, for the 25 positive samples.

For the largest group size of 32 samples, only 2 P32 groups had no RT-PCR+ samples. 12 P32 groups had at least one RT-PCR+ sample, including 6 with only one single RT-PCR+ sample.

Detailed Results for DPCR in Groups of 8

The results for SARS-CoV-2 detection by DPCR in groups of eight samples, detailed in Table 3.8 and Figure 3.22, are in concordance with the reference individual RT-PCR

TABLE 3.8

Distribution of the Samples Identified as Positive by the Routine RT-PCR Method (Cobas® SARS-CoV-2 assay) in the Groups of 8, 16, and 32 and Corresponding DPCR Detection of SARS-CoV-2 in the Groups

Number of RT-PCR Positive Sample(s) in the Group	Results for P8 Extracts			Results for P16 Groups			Results for P32 Groups		
	Total	dPCR–	dPCR+	Total	dPCR–	dPCR+	Total	dPCR–	dPCR+
0	35	32	3	12	11	1	2	2	0
1	18	1	17	10	2	8	6	0	6
2	2	0	2	4	0	4	3	0	3
3	1	0	1	1	0	1	1	0	1
4	0	0	0	1	0	1	1	0	1
5	0	0	0	0	0	0	0	0	0
6	0	0	0	0	0	0	1	0	1
Total	56	33	23	28	12	16	14	2	12

Top table — P8 extracts (reference RT-PCR + grouped DPCR)

Sample_ID	Ct_E	Ct_ORF	P8_##	# of droplets	Pos droplets N	Pos droplets ORF	IC [C] (cp/µL)	COBAS/dPCR status
8 COBAS negative samples			P8_25	25585	1	0	13405	-/-
27309	36.65	ND	P8_26	25498	5	1	18210	+/+
+ 7 COBAS negative samples								
8 COBAS negative samples			P8_27	25770	0	0	14721	-/-
56075	ND	ND	P8_28	25667	32	19	16170	-/+
+ 7 COBAS negative samples								
8 COBAS negative samples			P8_29	25568	0	0	11813	-/-
8 COBAS negative samples			P8_30	25757	0	0	12565	-/-
8 COBAS negative samples			P8_31	25476	0	0	8230	-/-
8 COBAS negative samples			P8_32	25324	0	0	17214	-/-
8 COBAS negative samples			P8_33	25765	1	0	17060	-/-
8 COBAS negative samples			P8_34	25803	0	0	17915	-/-
59120	24.1	23.28	P8_35	26095	14584	11406	9821	+/+
+ 7 COBAS negative samples								
8 COBAS negative samples			P8_36	25774	0	0	13463	-/-
8 COBAS negative samples			P8_37	24635	1	0	10338	-/-
8 COBAS negative samples			P8_38	24082	1	0	17996	-/-
60401	ND	ND	P8_39	26374	1	3	15263	-/+
+ 7 COBAS negative samples								
60611	28.14	27.86	P8_40	26259	979	757	7136	+/+
+ 7 COBAS negative samples								
74465	16.5	16.3	P8_41	26883	26883	26883	8581	+/+
+ 7 COBAS negative samples								
75547	31.3	29.4	P8_42	27389	2045	1905	11346	+/+
+ 7 COBAS negative samples								
8 COBAS negative samples			P8_43	26105	0	0	5791	-/-
8 COBAS negative samples			P8_44	25839	0	0	14504	-/-
8 COBAS negative samples			P8_45	27194	0	1	12374	-/-
8 COBAS negative samples			P8_46	26285	0	0	22379	-/-
8 COBAS negative samples			P8_47	25420	0	0	24184	-/-
8 COBAS negative samples			P8_48	26010	0	0	14457	-/-
8 COBAS negative samples			P8_49	24858	0	0	12808	-/-
79484	35.73	34.45	P8_50	25900	7	7	13425	+/+
8 COBAS negative samples			P8_51	24696	0	0	16954	-/-
8 COBAS negative samples			P8_52	25416	0	0	4837	-/-
8 COBAS negative samples			P8_53	25625	0	0	12554	-/-
8 COBAS negative samples			P8_54	23544	0	0	6078	-/-

Top table — P16 groups

P16_##	# of droplets	Pos droplets N	Pos droplets ORF	IC [C] (cp/µL)	COBAS/dPCR status
P16_13	25257	0	0	15031	-/+
P16_14	25364	13	5	13146	-/+
P16_15	27217	0	0	12192	-/-
P16_16	27198	0	0	12741	-/-
P16_17	26670	0	0	17539	-/-
P16_18	25884	8381	6405	11333	+/+
P16_19	28555	0	0	14937	-/-
P16_20	27345	506	415	11245	+/+
P16_21	24825	24825	24825	9690	+/+
P16_22	26078	0	0	9354	-/-
P16_23	25239	0	0	17469	-/-
P16_24	26470	0	0	19399	-/-
P16_25	25065	4	3	13301	+/+
P16_26	25356	0	0	11840	-/-
P16_27	22665	0	0	9484	-/-

Top table — P32 groups

P16_##	# of droplets	Pos droplets N	Pos droplets ORF	IC [C] (cp/µL)	COBAS/dPCR status
P32_07	25105	7	2	13330	+/+
P32_08	26284	0	0	11980	-/-
P32_09	26986	4628	3336	13335	+/+
P32_10	25842	230	184	12290	+/+
P32_11	26391	26391	26391	9388	+/+
P32_12	26536	0	0	18153	-/-
P32_13	26706	2	6	12266	+/+
P32_14	26044	2	1	6664	+/+

Bottom table — P8 extracts (reference RT-PCR + grouped DPCR)

Sample_ID	Ct_E	Ct_ORF	P8_##	# of droplets	Pos droplets N	Pos droplets ORF	IC [C] (cp/µL)	COBAS/dPCR status
25652	21.2	20.9	P8_01	25340	25340	25128	15556	+/+
25653	38.01	0						
+ 6 COBAS negative samples								
25659	34.02	32.26	P8_02	25685	0	0	3642	+/-
+ 7 COBAS negative samples								
8 COBAS negative samples			P8_03	22995	1	0	5530	-/-
8 COBAS negative samples			P8_04	26245	0	0	14896	-/-
27241	34	32.1	P8_05	26634	63	42	24859	+/+
+ 7 COBAS negative samples								
27304	28.8	28.12	P8_06	27184	1767	650	8160	+/+
+ 7 COBAS negative samples								
27316	27.71	27	P8_07	25752	3597	2667	13527	+/+
+ 7 COBAS negative samples								
27342	26.27	25.24	P8_08	26060	26059	26056	28478	+/+
+ 7 COBAS negative samples								
30923	38.27	ND	P8_09	25655	4	1	16784	+/+
+ 7 COBAS negative samples								
8 COBAS negative samples			P8_10	25511	0	0	19934	-/-
8 COBAS negative samples			P8_11	22083	0	0	17689	-/-
25736	34.5	32	P8_12	22503	418	256	29721	+/+
+ 7 COBAS negative samples								
31173	38.73	ND	P8_13	22408	3	2	13871	+/+
+ 7 COBAS negative samples								
31271	18.71	17.81	P8_14	22982	22982	22974	14204	+/+
31278	36.52	34.83						
31417	25.04	24.61						
+ 5 COBAS negative samples								
8 COBAS negative samples			P8_15	22883	0	0	17210	-/-
31397	21.6	21.16	P8_16	24406	23431	21878	12568	+/+
31415	25.04	24.61						
+ 6 COBAS negative samples								
8 COBAS negative samples			P8_17	25825	0	0	13476	-/-
51318	28.35	27.89	P8_18	25304	1543	1189	15304	+/+
+ 7 COBAS negative samples								
51958	35.15	32.25	P8_19	25088	40	39	16078	+/+
+ 7 COBAS negative samples								
52042	ND	ND	P8_20	25083	5	2	14024	-/+
+ 7 COBAS negative samples								
8 COBAS negative samples			P8_21	24808	0	2	18935	-/-
52408	28.81	28.22	P8_22	25820	1057	883	7399	+/+
+ 7 COBAS negative samples								
8 COBAS negative samples			P8_23	23991	0	0	12420	-/-
8 COBAS negative samples			P8_24	25510	0	0	16601	-/-

Bottom table — P16 groups

P16_##	# of droplets	Pos droplets N	Pos droplets ORF	IC [C] (cp/µL)	COBAS/dPCR status
P16_01	25262	25196	22657	9080	+/+
P16_02	24508	0	0	10026	-/-
P16_03	26718	980	350	15988	+/+
P16_04	26735	26497	26315	19941	+/+
P16_05	26446	4	1	18236	+/+
P16_06	27274	224	125	21805	+/+
P16_07	23420	23420	23418	13459	+/+
P16_08	21923	17166	14218	14676	+/+
P16_09	24573	739	554	13055	+/+
P16_10	26314	32	25	16918	+/+
P16_11	24624	468	360	12282	+/+
P16_12	25837	0	0	14885	-/-

Bottom table — P32 groups

P16_##	# of droplets	Pos droplets N	Pos droplets ORF	IC [C] (cp/µL)	COBAS/dPCR status
P32_01	17348	16047	11332	9237	+/+
P32_02	4298	3890	3693	17412	+/+
P32_03	21285	83	54	19589	+/+
P32_04	24222	24222	24221	14252	+/+
P32_05	23569	319	202	12648	+/+
P32_06	26550	305	212	13244	+/+

FIGURE 3.22 Results for (A) Individual Reference RT-PCR Testing; (B) Grouped Testing by DPCR for P8 Extracts; (C) Grouped Testing by DPCR for P16 Groups; and (D) Grouped Testing by DPCR for P32 Groups. Highlighted in Light Green: Results are in Concordance (–/– or +/+). Highlighted in Light Orange: COBAS+/dPCR– Discordance. Highlighted in Light Red: COBAS–/dPCR+ Discordance. ND= "Not Detected"

TABLE 3.9

Confusion Matrix for P8 Extracts

Confusion Matrix for P8 Extracts	Expected Negatives (RT-PCR)	Expected Positives (RT-PCR)	Total
Negatives in DPCR	32	1	33
Positives in DPCR	3	20	23
Total	35	21	56

testing for 52 groups (corresponding for 416 samples), out of which 32 were RT-PCR negative groups and 20 groups contained at least one RT-PCR+ sample.

For the remaining four groups with discording results, three RT-PCR negative groups tested positive by DPCR ("RT-PCR-/dPCR+" discordances – group IDs: P8_20, P8_28 and P8_39) and one RT-PCR+ group was found negative by DPCR (RT-PCR+/dPCR- discordance – group ID: P8_02). The Ct values for the sample associated with the RT-PCR+/dPCR- discordance was of 34 and 32.3 for the E gene and ORF1ab with the Cobas® SARS-CoV-2 assay, respectively. This sample is referred to as Sample 25659 for later discussion.

Complementary analysis of the discordances are depicted below.

Of note, out of the eight individual samples with Ct > 35 for the E gene, six ended up to be the only positive sample in a P8 extract and all the corresponding groups were detected positive by DPCR. The highest detected Ct values for the E gene and ORF1ab were 38.7 and >40 (not detected), respectively.

Detailed Results for DPCR in Groups of 16

The results for SARS-CoV-2 detection by DPCR in groups of 16 samples, detailed in Tables 3.8, 3.9, and 3.10, are in concordance with individual RT-PCR testing for 25 groups (corresponding for 400 samples), out of which eleven are RT-PCR- groups and 14 are RT-PCR+ groups. Among the three groups with discording results, one presented a RT-PCR-/dPCR+ discordance (Group ID: P16_14) and two RT-PCR+/dPCRdiscordances (Group IDs: P16_13 and P16_28).

Of note, out of the eight individual samples with Ct > 35 for the E gene, five ended up to be the only positive sample in a P16 group. Two of these groups are responsible for the 2 RT-PCR+/dPCR– discordances. The E gene and OFR1ab Ct values for these two samples were of [36.7; >40 (not detected)] and [36.3; 34.2], while the highest Ct values for a detected single positive sample were [38.3; >40 (not detected)].

TABLE 3.10

Confusion Matrix for P16 Groups

Confusion Matrix for P16 Groups	Expected Negatives (RT-PCR)	Expected Positives (RT-PCR)	Total
Negatives in DPCR	11	2	13
Positives in DPCR	1	14	15
Total	12	16	28

TABLE 3.11
Confusion Matrix for P32 Groups

Confusion Matrix for P32 Groups	Expected Negatives (RT-PCR)	Expected Positives (RT-PCR)	Total
Negatives in DPCR	2	0	2
Positives in DPCR	0	12	12
Total	2	12	14

Detailed Results for DPCR in Groups of 32

The results for SARS-CoV-2 detection by DPCR in groups of 32 are in concordance with individual RT-PCR testing for all 14 groups (corresponding for 448 samples) and are depicted in Tables 3.8 and 3.11.

Out of the eight individual samples with Ct >35 for the E gene, three ended up to be the only positive sample in a P32 group. All such three P32 groups tested positive by DPCR. The highest detected Ct values for the E gene and ORF1ab is of [36.7; >40 (not detected)].

Investigation of RT-PCR–/dPCR+ Discordances

As detailed above, three P8 extracts (P8_20, P8_28, & P8_39) and one P16 group (P16_14) tested positive by DPCR while containing only RT-PCR negative samples. P16_14 originates from a combination of groups with opposite discordances: P8_27 (RT-PCR+/dPCR–) and P8_28 (RT-PCR–/dPCR+) groups.

To further investigate these RT-PCR–/dPCR+ discordances, confirmatory testing DPCR was performed on all individual samples from corresponding groups. For each group, one sample tested positive by individual DPCR, with measured concentrations of viral RNA ranging from 128 copies per reaction to two copies per reaction for the N gene, and from 106 to 1 copies for the ORF1ab gene. The three corresponding dPCR+ samples (sample IDs: 52,042, 56,075, and 60,401) were retested on the Cobas® 6800 system and by confirmatory individual RT-qPCR using the Altona assay. All results are presented in the Table 3.12.

Two samples were found positive using the Altona assay with Ct values ranging between 28.4 and 33 for the E and S genes. Among them, the sample presenting the highest viral load by DPCR (Sample 56,075) was also found positive by the Cobas® confirmatory assay with a high Ct value of 36.7 for the E gene while the ORF gene was not detected. The remaining sample tested negative with both the confirmatory Cobas assay and the Altona assay. It had borderline levels of positive droplets in DPCR (N=2; ORF1ab=1).

Based on these results and for further sensitivity discussions, samples 52,042 and 56,075 that tested positive by both DPCR and Altona RT-PCR are considered as true positive samples. Sample 60,401 is considered a DPCR false positive pending further analysis.

Investigation of the Sample RT-PCR+/dPCR

One group of 8 (P8_02) was tested negative by DPCR and contained one RT-PCR+ sample (Sample 25659) with Ct values of 34 and 32.3 for the E gene and ORF1ab, respectively. Sample 25,659 was subsequently retested by RT-PCR on the Cobas protocol and was also re-extracted individually and retested by individual DPCR.

TABLE 3.12

Results of the Individual Reassessment by Both DPCR and RT-PCR (Altona and Cobas®) for the Samples From the Three "COBAS-/dPCR+" Discordant Groups. NT = "Not tested." ND= "Not detected"

Sample ID	COBAS reference	P8 extract number	dPCR+/ dPCR-	N cp / rnx	ORF1ab cp / rnx	IC cp / rnx	Altona E gene	Altona S gene	COBAS N	COBAS OFR
51996	COBAS-	20	dPCR-	1	0	7502	NT	NT	NT	NT
52019	COBAS-	20	dPCR-	0	0	25944	NT	NT	NT	NT
52031	COBAS-	20	dPCR-	0	0	68983	NT	NT	NT	NT
52035	COBAS-	20	dPCR-	0	0	28215	NT	NT	NT	NT
52042	COBAS-	20	dPCR+	16	19	a89747	33	31.9	ND	ND
52047	COBAS-	20	dPCR-	0	0	122825	NT	NT	NT	NT
52060	COBAS-	20	dPCR-	0	0	17237	NT	NT	NT	NT
52062	COBAS-	20	dPCR-	0	0	105711	NT	NT	NT	NT
56075	COBAS-	28	dPCR+	128	106	69268	29	28.4	36.7	ND
56077	COBAS-	28	dPCR-	0	0	34656	NT	NT	NT	NT
56083	COBAS-	28	dPCR-	0	0	71410	NT	NT	NT	NT
56191	COBAS-	28	dPCR-	0	0	22471	NT	NT	NT	NT
56211	COBAS-	28	dPCR-	0	0	21185	NT	NT	NT	NT
56275	COBAS-	28	dPCR-	0	0	22771	NT	NT	NT	NT
56303	COBAS-	28	dPCR-	0	0	56797	NT	NT	NT	NT
56307	COBAS-	28	dPCR-	0	0	59159	NT	NT	NT	NT
60241	COBAS-	39	dPCR-	0	0	46988	NT	NT	NT	NT
60281	COBAS-	39	dPCR-	1	0	73581	NT	NT	NT	NT
60310	COBAS-	39	dPCR-	0	0	11420	NT	NT	NT	NT
60334	COBAS-	39	dPCR-	0	0	32663	NT	NT	NT	NT
60345	COBAS-	39	dPCR-	0	0	814	NT	NT	NT	NT
60362	COBAS-	39	dPCR-	0	0	36943	NT	NT	NT	NT
60389	COBAS-	39	dPCR-	0	0	825	NT	NT	NT	NT
60401	COBAS-	39	dPCR+	2	1	43651	ND	ND	ND	ND

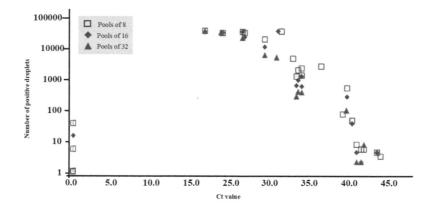

FIGURE 3.23 Plot of the number of positive droplets measured by DPCR for the N gene target in the groups of 8, 16, and 32 versus the predicted equivalent Ct value of the E gene of an RT-PCR measurement of the group using the Cobas® SARS-CoV-2 assay. The predicted equivalent Ct value of a group is defined as an average of the Ct values of the positive samples included in the group, taking into account the logarithmic scale of the Ct value.

Sample_25659 was found to be borderline negative by DPCR (N=2; ORF1ab=0) but Ct values of 37.3 and 34.9 were found for E and ORF, respectively, in the second Cobas® assessment.

Based on these results and for further sensitivity discussions, sample 25,659 is considered as a true positive sample.

Correlation between DPCR Measurements and Ct Values

A good correlation was observed between the number of positive droplets observed in DPCR and the Ct values of the positive samples contained in the groups. See Figures 3.23 and 3.24.

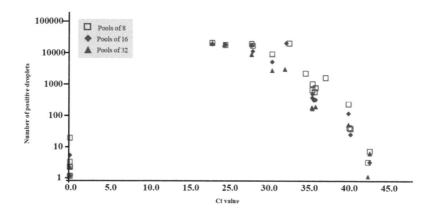

FIGURE 3.24 Plot of the number of positive droplets measured by DPCR for the ORF1ab gene target in the groups of 8, 16, and 32 versus the predicted equivalent Ct value of the ORF gene of an RT-PCR measurement of the group using the Cobas® SARS-CoV-2 assay. The predicted equivalent Ct value of a group is defined as an average of the Ct values of the positive samples included in the group, taking into account the logarithmic scale of the Ct value.

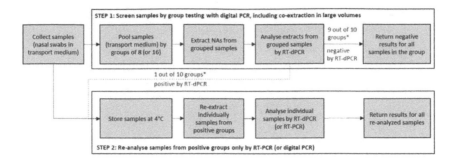

FIGURE 3.25 Graph of the suggested practical protocol for implementation of group testing by DPCR.

In this work, we assessed the sensitivity and specificity of group testing combined with digital PCR for SARS-CoV-2 detection. Three different group sizes were investigated using a commercially available digital PCR assay, the COVID-19 Multiplex Digital PCR Detection Kit (Stilla Technologies, France/Apexbio, China). This assay demonstrated a low LoB (at two and zero positive droplets per PCR for N and ORF1ab genes, respectively) and low LoD (at five and three copies/PCR for N and ORF1ab genes, respectively). This LoD is lower than most estimation for WHO and other reference RT-PCR assays typically ranging between 5 and 500 copies/PCR (Visseaux et al., 2020; Vogels et al., 2020).

For our analysis, we proposed a protocol of group screening performed by DPCR with secondary individual re-testing of positive groups as illustrated in Figure 3.25.

We assessed this protocol by assessing in real-life condition 448 consecutive samples grouped by 8, 16, and 32 samples.

We observed a better sensitivity than individual RT-PCR testing for groups of eight samples. Indeed, a total of 23 groups of eight samples tested positive and included 26 true positive samples. Only 25 samples were identified as positive using reference individual RT-PCR testing, corresponding to a +4% improvement in sensitivity. Two among the three samples associated with RT-PCR-/dPCR+ discordances were confirmed as true positive by RT-PCR using a SARS-CoV-2 specific assay from Altona. The last one was not confirmed as positive by RT-PCR and is undergoing further investigations. One sample was associated to a RT-PCR+/dPCR- discrepant results and is also considered a true positive sample as confirmed by RT-PCR retesting. Further investigation by sequencing is underway on these four samples in an effort to rigorously assess the existence and nature of nucleic acids variations responsible for the discording results.

Grouped testing by DPCR has similar sensitivity to individual RT-PCR testing for a group size of 16 samples. 15 groups of 16 samples tested by DPCR positive and included a total of 25 true positive samples, of which 23 are RT-PCR positive samples and two are RT-PCR-/dPCR+ samples. However, two RTPCR+ groups tested negative with grouped DPCR. This is likely explained by high Ct values of the single positive sample included in each of these two groups.

Testing in the 14 groups of 32 samples by DPCR has 100% concordance with the reference RT-PCR testing. Re-testing positive groups by DPCR would have likely led to better sensitivity than RT-PCR. However, we are careful in drawing conclusions for groups of 32 given the limited data points in this case as only 14 groups, including only two RT-PCR negative groups.

An alternative and even more cost-effective group testing protocol could be to perform the re-testing steps using RT-PCR with Cobas or Altona assays. In these protocols, the sensitivity becomes dependent on the RT-PCR kit used, leading to potential discrepancies with DPCR as observed in our results for groups of eight samples. However, our data suggest that performing the individual tests for groups of 8 and 16 with a RT-PCR assay would still have a similar sensitivity.

Overall, our data indicates that COVID-19 group testing combined with digital PCR for large group sizes of 8 and 16 samples, followed by individual re-testing of positive groups, has better or similar sensitivity than individual RT-PCR testing. Groups of 32 samples could also be considered, but our analysis needs to be confirmed in the future as, due to the epidemiological situation at the time, a low number of negative groups and groups containing a single positive sample were assessed.

The gain in sensitivity of the proposed method is likely due to a combination of (1) a concentration effect due to performing the pooling prior extraction and performing the extraction step from a large volume of 1 mL of pooled transport medium, and (2) the intrinsic superior sensitivity of digital PCR compared to RT-PCR, as demonstrated previously for SARS-CoV-2 (Dong et al., 2020; Yu et al., 2020) and other viruses (Gupta et al., 2019; Huang et al., 2015) detection.

Below standard sensitivity is one of the main reasons why group testing has not been widely adopted for COVID-19 testing, whilst research groups have advocated for its implementation as a solution to the world-wide un-met demand for tests and reagent shortage (Anderson et al., 2020; Gollier & Gossner, 2020; Hogan et al., 2020; Yelin et al., 2020).

The current study suggests that the high sensitivity of group testing could be achieved using by digital PCR instead of RT-PCR in the first group screening step. It makes the approach viable for large-scale, low cost patient screening with minimum reagent consumption. For a test positivity rate of 1%, our group testing protocol would save 79%, 80%, and 69% of reagents compared to individual testing, for group sizes of 8, 16, and 32 samples. Group size does not significantly impact cost or reagent consumption for group sizes above eight samples and test positivity rates below 1%. Consequently, the choice of group size (8, 16, or 32) is mostly a balance of sensitivity and test capacity. Our results indicate that group testing by digital PCR and a group size of 16 would increase testing capabilities by more than 10-fold while having a sensitivity comparable to the current standard of individual testing by RTPCR.

Group testing can be used in various context where testing is not currently put in place due to testing capacity or with strong economic constraints and where SARS-CoV-2 prevalence is low. In countries where the pandemic is not yet under control or could re-emerge, enhancing testing capacity is essential to winning the battle against COVID-19. In countries where the first wave is fading, the fight against COVID-19 goes through a combination between a test/trace/isolate strategy and social distancing. Increasing the range of people tested amongst contacts with positive cases, but also periodic testing of population in frequent contact with others (e.g., nurses, transportation workers, clerks, etc...) as well as in fragile populations such as nursing homes can be part of a strategy against COVID-19 while allowing a relaxation of social distancing measures at the same time. Group testing can help in all of these situations.

REFERENCES

Ai, T., Yang, Z., & Hou, H. (2020). Correlation of chest CT and RT-PCR testing in coronavirus Disease 2019 (COVID-19) in China: A report of 1014 cases [e-pub ahead of print]. *Radiology, 296*(2).

Akagi, Y., Rao, S. R., Morita, Y., & Tamiya, E. (2004). Optimization of fluorescent cell-based assays for high-throughput analysis using microchamber array chip formats. *Science and Technology of Advanced Materials, 5*(3), 343.

Anderson, C., Castillo, F., Koenig, M., & Managbanag, J. (2020). Pooling nasopharyngeal swab specimens to increase testing capacity for SARS-CoV-2. *BioRxiv.*

Anna, S. L., Bontoux, N., & Stone, H. A. (2003). Formation of dispersions using "flow focusing" in microchannels. *Applied Physics Letters, 82*(3), 364–366.

Beer, N. R., Wheeler, E. K., Lee-Houghton, L., Watkins, N., Nasarabadi, S., Hebert, N., Leung, P., Arnold, D. W., Bailey, C. G., & Colston, B. W. (2008). On-chip single-copy real-time reverse-transcription PCR in isolated picoliter droplets. *Analytical Chemistry, 80*(6), 1854–1858.

Beverung, C. J., Radke, C. J., & Blanch, H. W. (1999). Protein adsorption at the oil/water interface: Characterization of adsorption kinetics by dynamic interfacial tension measurements. *Biophysical Chemistry, 81*(1), 59–80.

Bhat, S., Herrmann, J., Armishaw, P., Corbisier, P., & Emslie, K. R. (2009). Single molecule detection in nanofluidic digital array enables accurate measurement of DNA copy number. *Analytical and Bioanalytical Chemistry, 394*(2), 457–467.

Bhat, S., McLaughlin, J. L. H., & Emslie, K. R. (2011). Effect of sustained elevated temperature prior to amplification on template copy number estimation using digital polymerase chain reaction. *Analyst, 136*(4), 724–732.

Boukellal, H., Selimović, Š., Jia, Y., Cristobal, G., & Fraden, S. (2009). Simple, robust storage of drops and fluids in a microfluidic device. *Lab on a Chip, 9*(2), 331–338.

Brown, L. D., Cai, T. T., & DasGupta, A. (2001). Interval estimation for a binomial proportion. *Statistical Science*, 101–117.

Bustin, S. A. (2004). *AZ of quantitative PCR*. International University Line La Jolla, CA.

Centers for Disease Control and Prevention. (2020a). Interim guidelines for collecting, handling, and testing clinical specimens from persons under investigation (PUIs) for coronavirus disease 2019 (COVID-19). *COVID-19.*

Centers for Disease Control and Prevention. (2020b). *Research Use Only Real-Time RT-PCR Protocol for Identification of 2019-nVoV*. CDCP.

Chan, J. F.-W., Kok, K.-H., Zhu, Z., Chu, H., To, K. K.-W., Yuan, S., & Yuen, K.-Y. (2020). Genomic characterization of the 2019 novel human-pathogenic coronavirus isolated from a patient with atypical pneumonia after visiting Wuhan. *Emerging Microbes & Infections, 9*(1), 221–236.

Chan, J. F.-W., Yip, C. C.-Y., To, K. K.-W., Tang, T. H.-C., Wong, S. C.-Y., Leung, K.-H., Fung, A. Y.-F., Ng, A. C.-K., Zou, Z., & Tsoi, H.-W. (2020). Improved molecular diagnosis of COVID-19 by the novel, highly sensitive and specific COVID-19-RdRp/Hel real-time reverse transcription-PCR assay validated in vitro and with clinical specimens. *Journal of Clinical Microbiology, 58*(5).

Chen, Z., Liao, P., Zhang, F., Jiang, M., Zhu, Y., & Huang, Y. (2017). Centrifugal micro-channel array droplet generation for highly parallel digital PCR. *Lab on a Chip, 17*(2), 235–240.

Chu, D. K. W., Pan, Y., Cheng, S. M. S., Hui, K. P. Y., Krishnan, P., Liu, Y., Ng, D. Y. M., Wan, C. K. C., Yang, P., & Wang, Q. (2020). Molecular diagnosis of a novel coronavirus (2019-nCoV) causing an outbreak of pneumonia. *Clinical Chemistry, 66*(4), 549–555.

Cochran, W. G. (1950). Estimation of bacterial densities by means of the" most probable number". *Biometrics, 6*(2), 105–116.

Cohen, D. E., Schneider, T., Wang, M., & Chiu, D. T. (2010). Self-digitization of sample volumes. *Analytical Chemistry, 82*(13), 5707–5717.

Corman, V., Bleicker, T., Brünink, S., Drosten, C., Zambon, M., & World Health Organization. (2020). Diagnostic detection of Wuhan coronavirus 2019 by real-time RT-PCR. *Geneva: World Health Organization, January, 13.*

Corman, V. M., Landt, O., Kaiser, M., Molenkamp, R., Meijer, A., Chu, D. K. W., Bleicker, T., Brünink, S., Schneider, J., & Schmidt, M. L. (2020). Detection of 2019 novel coronavirus (2019-nCoV) by real-time RT-PCR. *Eurosurveillance*, *25*(3), 2000045.

Courtois, F., Olguin, L. F., Whyte, G., Theberge, A. B., Huck, W. T. S., Hollfelder, F., & Abell, C. (2009). Controlling the retention of small molecules in emulsion microdroplets for use in cell-based assays. *Analytical Chemistry*, *81*(8), 3008–3016.

Dangla, R., Kayi, S. C., & Baroud, C. N. (2013). Droplet microfluidics driven by gradients of confinement. *Proceedings of the National Academy of Sciences*, *110*(3), 853–858.

Debski, P. R., & Garstecki, P. (2016). Designing and interpretation of digital assays: Concentration of target in the sample and in the source of sample. *Biomolecular Detection and Quantification*, *10*, 24–30.

Diehl, F., Li, M., He, Y., Kinzler, K. W., Vogelstein, B., & Dressman, D. (2006). BEAMing: Single-molecule PCR on microparticles in water-in-oil emulsions. *Nature Methods*, *3*(7), 551–559.

Dimov, I. K., Lu, R., Lee, E. P., Seita, J., Sahoo, D., Park, S., Weissman, I. L., & Lee, L. P. (2014). Discriminating cellular heterogeneity using microwell-based RNA cytometry. *Nature Communications*, *5*(1), 1–12.

Dong, L., Meng, Y., Sui, Z., Wang, J., Wu, L., & Fu, B. (2015). Comparison of four digital PCR platforms for accurate quantification of DNA copy number of a certified plasmid DNA reference material. *Scientific Reports*, *5*(1), 1–11.

Dong, L., Zhou, J., Niu, C., Wang, Q., Pan, Y., Sheng, S., Wang, X., Zhang, Y., Yang, J., & Liu, M. (2020). Highly accurate and sensitive diagnostic detection of SARS-CoV-2 by digital PCR. *MedRxiv*.

Dressman, D., Yan, H., Traverso, G., Kinzler, K. W., & Vogelstein, B. (2003). Transforming single DNA molecules into fluorescent magnetic particles for detection and enumeration of genetic variations. *Proceedings of the National Academy of Sciences*, *100*(15), 8817–8822.

Du, W., Li, L., Nichols, K. P., & Ismagilov, R. F. (2009). SlipChip. *Lab on a Chip*, *9*(16), 2286–2292.

Dube, S., Qin, J., & Ramakrishnan, R. (2008). Mathematical analysis of copy number variation in a DNA sample using digital PCR on a nanofluidic device. *PloS One*, *3*(8), e2876.

Duffy, D. C., McDonald, J. C., Schueller, O. J. A., & Whitesides, G. M. (1998). Rapid prototyping of microfluidic systems in poly (dimethylsiloxane). *Analytical Chemistry*, *70*(23), 4974–4984.

Freeman, W. M., Walker, S. J., & Vrana, K. E. (1999). Quantitative RT-PCR: Pitfalls and potential. *Biotechniques*, *26*(1), 112–125.

Gansen, A., Herrick, A. M., Dimov, I. K., Lee, L. P., & Chiu, D. T. (2012). Digital LAMP in a sample self-digitization (SD) chip. *Lab on a Chip*, *12*(12), 2247–2254.

Gelman, A., Carlin, J. B., Stern, H. S., Dunson, D. B., Vehtari, A., & Rubin, D. B. (2013). *Bayesian data analysis*. CRC press.

Gollier, C., & Gossner, O. (2020). Group testing against Covid-19. *Covid Economics*, *2*.

Gupta, R. K., Abdul-Jawad, S., McCoy, L. E., Mok, H. P., Peppa, D., Salgado, M., Martinez-Picado, J., Nijhuis, M., Wensing, A. M. J., & Lee, H. (2019). HIV-1 remission following CCR5Δ32/Δ32 haematopoietic stem-cell transplantation. *Nature*, *568*(7751), 244–248.

Halvorson, H. O., & Ziegler, N. R. (1933). Application of statistics to problems in bacteriology: III. A Consideration of the accuracy of dilution data obtained by using several dilutions. *Journal of Bacteriology*, *26*(6), 559.

Hatch, A. C., Fisher, J. S., Tovar, A. R., Hsieh, A. T., Lin, R., Pentoney, S. L., Yang, D. L., & Lee, A. P. (2011). 1-Million droplet array with wide-field fluorescence imaging for digital PCR. *Lab on a Chip*, *11*(22), 3838–3845.

Heyries, K. A., Tropini, C., VanInsberghe, M., Doolin, C., Petriv, I., Singhal, A., Leung, K., Hughesman, C. B., & Hansen, C. L. (2011). Megapixel digital PCR. *Nature Methods*, *8*(8), 649–651.

Hindson, B. J., Ness, K. D., Masquelier, D. A., Belgrader, P., Heredia, N. J., Makarewicz, A. J., Bright, I. J., Lucero, M. Y., Hiddessen, A. L., & Legler, T. C. (2011). High-throughput droplet digital PCR system for absolute quantitation of DNA copy number. *Analytical Chemistry*, *83*(22), 8604–8610.

Hogan, C. A., Sahoo, M. K., & Pinsky, B. A. (2020). Sample pooling as a strategy to detect community transmission of SARS-CoV-2. *JAMA*, *323*(19), 1967–1969.

Holtze, C., Rowat, A. C., Agresti, J. J., Hutchison, J. B., Angile, F. E., Schmitz, C. H. J., Köster, S., Duan, H., Humphry, K. J., & Scanga, R. A. (2008). Biocompatible surfactants for water-in-fluorocarbon emulsions. *Lab on a Chip*, *8*(10), 1632–1639.

Hong, J. W., & Quake, S. R. (2003). Integrated nanoliter systems. *Nature Biotechnology*, *21*(10), 1179–1183.

Huang, J.-T., Liu, Y.-J., Wang, J., Xu, Z.-G., Yang, Y., Shen, F., Liu, X., Zhou, X., & Liu, S.-M. (2015). Next generation digital PCR measurement of hepatitis B virus copy number in formalin-fixed paraffin-embedded hepatocellular carcinoma tissue. *Clinical Chemistry*, *61*(1), 290–296.

Huggett, J. F., Cowen, S., & Foy, C. A. (2015). Considerations for digital PCR as an accurate molecular diagnostic tool. *Clinical Chemistry*, *61*(1), 79–88.

Huggett, J. F., Foy, C. A., Benes, V., Emslie, K., Garson, J. A., Haynes, R., Hellemans, J., Kubista, M., Mueller, R. D., & Nolan, T. (2013). The Digital MIQE Guidelines: M inimum I nformation for Publication of Q uantitative Digital PCR E xperiments. *Clinical Chemistry*, *59*(6), 892–902.

Huh, H. J., Kim, J.-Y., Kwon, H. J., Yun, S., Lee, M.-K., Ki, C.-S., Lee, N. Y., & Kim, J.-W. (2017). Performance evaluation of the PowerChek MERS (upE & ORF1a) real-time PCR kit for the detection of Middle East respiratory syndrome coronavirus RNA. *Annals of Laboratory Medicine*, *37*(6), 494–498.

Jackman, R. J., Duffy, D. C., Ostuni, E., Willmore, N. D., & Whitesides, G. M. (1998). Fabricating large arrays of microwells with arbitrary dimensions and filling them using discontinuous dewetting. *Analytical Chemistry*, *70*(11), 2280–2287.

Jarvius, J., Melin, J., Göransson, J., Stenberg, J., Fredriksson, S., Gonzalez-Rey, C., Bertilsson, S., & Nilsson, M. (2006). Digital quantification using amplified single-molecule detection. *Nature Methods*, *3*(9), 725–727.

Kageyama, T., Kojima, S., Shinohara, M., Uchida, K., Fukushi, S., Hoshino, F. B., Takeda, N., & Katayama, K. (2003). Broadly reactive and highly sensitive assay for Norwalk-like viruses based on real-time quantitative reverse transcription-PCR. *Journal of Clinical Microbiology*, *41*(4), 1548–1557.

Kalinina, O., Lebedeva, I., Brown, J., & Silver, J. (1997). Nanoliter scale PCR with TaqMan detection. *Nucleic Acids Research*, *25*(10), 1999–2004.

Kallioniemi, O.-P., Kallioniemi, A., Kurisu, W., Thor, A., Chen, L.-C., Smith, H. S., Waldman, F. M., Pinkel, D., & Gray, J. W. (1992). ERBB2 amplification in breast cancer analyzed by fluorescence in situ hybridization. *Proceedings of the National Academy of Sciences*, *89*(12), 5321–5325.

Kang, D.-K., Ali, M. M., Zhang, K., Huang, S. S., Peterson, E., Digman, M. A., Gratton, E., & Zhao, W. (2014). Rapid detection of single bacteria in unprocessed blood using Integrated Comprehensive Droplet Digital Detection. *Nature Communications*, *5*(1), 1–10.

Kinpara, T., Mizuno, R., Murakami, Y., Kobayashi, M., Yamaura, S., Hasan, Q., Morita, Y., Nakano, H., Yamane, T., & Tamiya, E. (2004). A picoliter chamber array for cell-free protein synthesis. *Journal of Biochemistry*, *136*(2), 149–154.

Kiss, M. M., Ortoleva-Donnelly, L., Beer, N. R., Warner, J., Bailey, C. G., Colston, B. W., Rothberg, J. M., Link, D. R., & Leamon, J. H. (2008). High-throughput quantitative polymerase chain reaction in picoliter droplets. *Analytical Chemistry*, *80*(23), 8975–8981.

Kreutz, J. E., Munson, T., Huynh, T., Shen, F., Du, W., & Ismagilov, R. F. (2011). Theoretical design and analysis of multivolume digital assays with wide dynamic range validated experimentally with microfluidic digital PCR. *Analytical Chemistry*, *83*(21), 8158–8168.

Krumholz, H. M. (2020). If you have coronavirus symptoms, assume you have the illness, even if you test negative. *The New York Times*, 1.

Kumaresan, P., Yang, C. J., Cronier, S. A., Blazej, R. G., & Mathies, R. A. (2008). High-throughput single copy DNA amplification and cell analysis in engineered nanoliter droplets. *Analytical Chemistry*, *80*(10), 3522–3529.

Lau, L. T., Fung, Y.-W. W., Wong, F. P.-F., Lin, S. S.-W., Wang, C. R., Li, H. L., Dillon, N., Collins, R. A., Tam, J. S.-L., & Chan, P. K. S. (2003). A real-time PCR for SARS-coronavirus incorporating target gene pre-amplification. *Biochemical and Biophysical Research Communications*, *312*(4), 1290–1296.

Li, H., Xue, G., & Yeung, E. S. (2001). Selective detection of individual DNA molecules by capillary polymerase chain reaction. *Analytical Chemistry*, *73*(7), 1537–1543.

Li, M., Diehl, F., Dressman, D., Vogelstein, B., & Kinzler, K. W. (2006). BEAMing up for detection and quantification of rare sequence variants. *Nature Methods*, *3*(2), 95–97.

Link, D. R., Anna, S. L., Weitz, D. A., & Stone, H. A. (2004). Geometrically mediated breakup of drops in microfluidic devices. *Physical Review Letters*, *92*(5), 54503.

Ma, Y.-D., Chang, W.-H., Luo, K., Wang, C.-H., Liu, S.-Y., Yen, W.-H., & Lee, G.-B. (2018). Digital quantification of DNA via isothermal amplification on a self-driven microfluidic chip featuring hydrophilic film-coated polydimethylsiloxane. *Biosensors and Bioelectronics*, *99*, 547–554.

Matsubara, Y., Kerman, K., Kobayashi, M., Yamamura, S., Morita, Y., Takamura, Y., & Tamiya, E. (2004). On-chip nanoliter-volume multiplex TaqMan polymerase chain reaction from a single copy based on counting fluorescence released microchambers. *Analytical Chemistry*, *76*(21), 6434–6439.

Morrison, T., Hurley, J., Garcia, J., Yoder, K., Katz, A., Roberts, D., Cho, J., Kanigan, T., Ilyin, S. E., & Horowitz, D. (2006). Nanoliter high throughput quantitative PCR. *Nucleic Acids Research*, *34*(18), e123–e123.

Ostuni, E., Chen, C. S., Ingber, D. E., & Whitesides, G. M. (2001). Selective deposition of proteins and cells in arrays of microwells. *Langmuir*, *17*(9), 2828–2834.

Ottesen, E. A., Hong, J. W., Quake, S. R., & Leadbetter, J. R. (2006). Microfluidic digital PCR enables multigene analysis of individual environmental bacteria. *Science*, *314*(5804), 1464–1467.

Pan, Y., Zhang, D., Yang, P., Poon, L. L. M., & Wang, Q. (2020). Viral load of SARS-CoV-2 in clinical samples. *The Lancet Infectious Diseases*, *20*(4), 411–412.

Peiris, J. S. M., Chu, C.-M., Cheng, V. C.-C., Chan, K. S., Hung, I. F. N., Poon, L. L. M., Law, K.-I., Tang, B. S. F., Hon, T. Y. W., & Chan, C. S. (2003). Clinical progression and viral load in a community outbreak of coronavirus-associated SARS pneumonia: A prospective study. *The Lancet*, *361*(9371), 1767–1772.

Pfefferle, S., Reucher, S., Nörz, D., & Lütgehetmann, M. (2020). Evaluation of a quantitative RT-PCR assay for the detection of the emerging coronavirus SARS-CoV-2 using a high throughput system. *Eurosurveillance*, *25*(9), 2000152.

Pinheiro, L. B., Coleman, V. A., Hindson, C. M., Herrmann, J., Hindson, B. J., Bhat, S., & Emslie, K. R. (2012). Evaluation of a droplet digital polymerase chain reaction format for DNA copy number quantification. *Analytical Chemistry*, *84*(2), 1003–1011.

Poon, L. L. M., Chan, K. H., Wong, O. K., Yam, W. C., Yuen, K. Y., Guan, Y., Lo, Y. M. D., & Peiris, J. S. M. (2003). Early diagnosis of SARS coronavirus infection by real time RT-PCR. *Journal of Clinical Virology*, *28*(3), 233–238.

R Core Team. (2013). *R: A language and environment for statistical computing*. Vienna, Austria.

Reddy, S., Schunk, P. R., & Bonnecaze, R. T. (2005). Dynamics of low capillary number interfaces moving through sharp features. *Physics of Fluids*, *17*(12), 122104.

Roa, P. L., Catalán, P., Giannella, M., de Viedma, D. G., Sandonis, V., & Bouza, E. (2011). Comparison of real-time RT-PCR, shell vial culture, and conventional cell culture for the detection of the pandemic influenza A (H1N1) in hospitalized patients. *Diagnostic Microbiology and Infectious Disease*, *69*(4), 428–431.

Roberts, C. H., Jiang, W., Jayaraman, J., Trowsdale, J., Holland, M. J., & Traherne, J. A. (2014). Killer-cell Immunoglobulin-like Receptor gene linkage and copy number variation analysis by droplet digital PCR. *Genome Medicine*, *6*(3), 1–9.

RStudio Team. (2019). *RStudio: Integrated Development for R [Internet]*. Boston, MA: RStudio, Inc.

Schaerli, Y., Wootton, R. C., Robinson, T., Stein, V., Dunsby, C., Neil, M. A. A., French, P. M. W., DeMello, A. J., Abell, C., & Hollfelder, F. (2009). Continuous-flow polymerase chain reaction of single-copy DNA in microfluidic microdroplets. *Analytical Chemistry*, *81*(1), 302–306.

Schneider, T., Yen, G. S., Thompson, A. M., Burnham, D. R., & Chiu, D. T. (2013). Self-digitization of samples into a high-density microfluidic bottom-well array. *Analytical Chemistry*, *85*(21), 10417–10423.

Schuler, F., Schwemmer, F., Trotter, M., Wadle, S., Zengerle, R., von Stetten, F., & Paust, N. (2015). Centrifugal step emulsification applied for absolute quantification of nucleic acids by digital droplet RPA. *Lab on a Chip*, *15*(13), 2759–2766.

Shen, F., Davydova, E. K., Du, W., Kreutz, J. E., Piepenburg, O., & Ismagilov, R. F. (2011). Digital isothermal quantification of nucleic acids via simultaneous chemical initiation of recombinase polymerase amplification reactions on SlipChip. *Analytical Chemistry*, *83*(9), 3533–3540.

Shen, F., Du, W., Kreutz, J. E., Fok, A., & Ismagilov, R. F. (2010). Digital PCR on a SlipChip. *Lab on a Chip*, *10*(20), 2666–2672.

Shen, F., Sun, B., Kreutz, J. E., Davydova, E. K., Du, W., Reddy, P. L., Joseph, L. J., & Ismagilov, R. F. (2011). Multiplexed quantification of nucleic acids with large dynamic range using multivolume digital RT-PCR on a rotational SlipChip tested with HIV and hepatitis C viral load. *Journal of the American Chemical Society*, *133*(44), 17705–17712.

Shih, I.-M., Zhou, W., Goodman, S. N., Lengauer, C., Kinzler, K. W., & Vogelstein, B. (2001). Evidence that genetic instability occurs at an early stage of colorectal tumorigenesis. *Cancer Research*, *61*(3), 818–822.

Singer, G., Kurman, R. J., Chang, H.-W., Cho, S. K. R., & Shih, I.-M. (2002). Diverse tumorigenic pathways in ovarian serous carcinoma. *The American Journal of Pathology*, *160*(4), 1223–1228.

Sposito, A. J., & DeVoe, D. L. (2017). Staggered trap arrays for robust microfluidic sample digitization. *Lab on a Chip*, *17*(23), 4105–4112.

Sugiura, S., Nakajima, M., Iwamoto, S., & Seki, M. (2001). Interfacial tension driven monodispersed droplet formation from microfabricated channel array. *Langmuir*, *17*(18), 5562–5566.

Sundberg, S. O., Wittwer, C. T., Gao, C., & Gale, B. K. (2010). Spinning disk platform for microfluidic digital polymerase chain reaction. *Analytical Chemistry*, *82*(4), 1546–1550.

Suo, T., Liu, X., Feng, J., Guo, M., Hu, W., Guo, D., Ullah, H., Yang, Y., Zhang, Q., & Wang, X. (2020). ddPCR: A more accurate tool for SARS-CoV-2 detection in low viral load specimens. *Emerging Microbes & Infections, just-accepted*, 1–30.

Sykes, P. J., Neoh, S. H., Brisco, M. J., Hughes, E., Condon, J., & Morley, A. A. (1992). Quantitation of targets for PCR by use of limiting dilution. *Biotechniques*, *13*(3), 444–449.

Tan, Y.-C., Fisher, J. S., Lee, A. I., Cristini, V., & Lee, A. P. (2004). Design of microfluidic channel geometries for the control of droplet volume, chemical concentration, and sorting. *Lab on a Chip*, *4*(4), 292–298.

Taubenberger, J. K., & Morens, D. M. (2006). 1918 Influenza: The mother of all pandemics. *Emerging Infectious Diseases*, *12*(1), 15–22. https://doi.org/10.3201/eid1201.050979

Taylor, S. C., Laperriere, G., & Germain, H. (2017). Droplet Digital PCR versus qPCR for gene expression analysis with low abundant targets: From variable nonsense to publication quality data. *Scientific Reports*, *7*(1), 1–8.

Thompson, A. M., Gansen, A., Paguirigan, A. L., Kreutz, J. E., Radich, J. P., & Chiu, D. T. (2014). Self-digitization microfluidic chip for absolute quantification of mRNA in single cells. *Analytical Chemistry*, *86*(24), 12308–12314.

Thorsen, T., Roberts, R. W., Arnold, F. H., & Quake, S. R. (2001). Dynamic pattern formation in a vesicle-generating microfluidic device. *Physical Review Letters*, *86*(18), 4163.

Tian, Q., Song, Q., Xu, Y., Zhu, Q., Yu, B., Jin, W., Jin, Q., & Mu, Y. (2015). A localized temporary negative pressure assisted microfluidic device for detecting keratin 19 in A549 lung carcinoma cells with digital PCR. *Analytical Methods*, *7*(5), 2006–2011.

Tice, J. D., Song, H., Lyon, A. D., & Ismagilov, R. F. (2003). Formation of droplets and mixing in multiphase microfluidics at low values of the Reynolds and the capillary numbers. *Langmuir*, *19*(22), 9127–9133.

Unger, M. A., Chou, H.-P., Thorsen, T., Scherer, A., & Quake, S. R. (2000). Monolithic microfabricated valves and pumps by multilayer soft lithography. *Science*, *288*(5463), 113–116.

Visseaux, B., Le Hingrat, Q., Collin, G., Bouzid, D., Lebourgeois, S., Le Pluart, D., Deconinck, L., Lescure, F.-X., Lucet, J.-C., & Bouadma, L. (2020). Evaluation of the QIAstat-Dx Respiratory SARS-CoV-2 Panel, the first rapid multiplex PCR commercial assay for SARS-CoV-2 detection. *Journal of Clinical Microbiology*.

Vogels, C. B. F., Brito, A. F., Wyllie, A. L., Fauver, J. R., Ott, I. M., Kalinich, C. C., Petrone, M. E., Landry, M.-L., Foxman, E. F., & Grubaugh, N. D. (2020). Analytical sensitivity and efficiency comparisons of SARS-COV-2 qRT-PCR assays. *MedRxiv*.

Vulto, P., Podszun, S., Meyer, P., Hermann, C., Manz, A., & Urban, G. A. (2011). Phaseguides: A paradigm shift in microfluidic priming and emptying. *Lab on a Chip*, *11*(9), 1596–1602.

Wald, A. (2004). *Sequential analysis*. Courier Corporation.

Wallis, S. (2013). Binomial confidence intervals and contingency tests: Mathematical fundamentals and the evaluation of alternative methods. *Journal of Quantitative Linguistics*, *20*(3), 178–208.

Wang, W., Xu, Y., Gao, R., Lu, R., Han, K., Wu, G., & Tan, W. (2020). Detection of SARS-CoV-2 in different types of clinical specimens. *JAMA*, *323*(18), 1843–1844.

Whale, A. S., Cowen, S., Foy, C. A., & Huggett, J. F. (2013). Methods for applying accurate digital PCR analysis on low copy DNA samples. *PloS One*, *8*(3), e58177.

Whale, A. S., Huggett, J. F., Cowen, S., Speirs, V., Shaw, J., Ellison, S., Foy, C. A., & Scott, D. J. (2012). Comparison of microfluidic digital PCR and conventional quantitative PCR for measuring copy number variation. *Nucleic Acids Research*, *40*(11), e82–e82.

Wiktor, P., Brunner, A., Kahn, P., Qiu, J., Magee, M., Bian, X., Karthikeyan, K., & LaBaer, J. (2015). Microreactor array device. *Scientific Reports*, *5*, 8736.

Wilson, E. B. (1927). Probable inference, the law of succession, and statistical inference. *Journal of the American Statistical Association*, *22*(158), 209–212.

Winichakoon, P., Chaiwarith, R., Liwsrisakun, C., Salee, P., Goonna, A., Limsukon, A., & Kaewpoowat, Q. (2020). Negative nasopharyngeal and oropharyngeal swabs do not rule out COVID-19. *Journal of Clinical Microbiology*, *58*(5).

Wong, M. L., & Medrano, J. F. (2005). Real-time PCR for mRNA quantitation. *Biotechniques*, *39*(1), 75–85.

World Health Organization. (2020). *Laboratory testing for coronavirus disease 2019 (COVID-19) in suspected human cases: interim guidance, 2 March 2020*. World Health Organization.

Yang, Y., Yang, M., & Shen, C. (2020). Evaluating the accuracy of different respiratory specimens in the laboratory diagnosis and monitoring the viral shedding of 2019-nCoV infections. Posted February 17, 2020. *Available at: Doi: Https://Doi. Org/10.1101/2020.02, 11*.

Yelin, I., Aharony, N., Shaer-Tamar, E., Argoetti, A., Messer, E., Berenbaum, D., Shafran, E., Kuzli, A., Gandali, N., & Hashimshony, T. (2020). Evaluation of COVID-19 RT-qPCR test in multi-sample pools. *MedRxiv*.

Yu, F., Yan, L., Wang, N., Yang, S., Wang, L., Tang, Y., Gao, G., Wang, S., Ma, C., & Xie, R. (2020). Quantitative detection and viral load analysis of SARS-CoV-2 in infected patients. *Clinical Infectious Diseases*.

Zadeh, L. A. (1975). The concept of a linguistic variable and its application to approximate reasoning—I. *Information Sciences*, *8*(3), 199–249.

Zhang, H., Jenkins, G., Zou, Y., Zhu, Z., & Yang, C. J. (2012). Massively parallel single-molecule and single-cell emulsion reverse transcription polymerase chain reaction using agarose droplet microfluidics. *Analytical Chemistry*, *84*(8), 3599–3606.

Zhou, W., Galizia, G., Goodman, S. N., Romans, K. E., Kinzler, K. W., Vogelstein, B., Choti, M. A., & Montgomery, E. A. (2001). Counting alleles reveals a connection between chromosome 18q loss and vascular invasion. *Nature Biotechnology*, *19*(1), 78–81.

Zhu, Q., Gao, Y., Yu, B., Ren, H., Qiu, L., Han, S., Jin, W., Jin, Q., & Mu, Y. (2012). Self-priming compartmentalization digital LAMP for point-of-care. *Lab on a Chip*, *12*(22), 4755–4763.

Zhu, Z., Jenkins, G., Zhang, W., Zhang, M., Guan, Z., & Yang, C. J. (2012). Single-molecule emulsion PCR in microfluidic droplets. *Analytical and Bioanalytical Chemistry*, *403*(8), 2127–2143.

Ziegler, N. R., & Halvorson, H. O. (1935). Application of Statistics to Problems in Bacteriology: IV. Experimental Comparison of the Dilution Method, the Plate Count, and the Direct Count for the Determination of Bacterial Populations. *Journal of Bacteriology*, *29*(6), 609.

Zinchenko, A., Devenish, S. R. A., Kintses, B., Colin, P.-Y., Fischlechner, M., & Hollfelder, F. (2014). One in a million: Flow cytometric sorting of single cell-lysate assays in monodisperse picolitre double emulsion droplets for directed evolution. *Analytical Chemistry*, *86*(5), 2526–2533.

4 Antigen–Antibody Reaction-Based Immunodiagnostics Method

KEY POINTS

- Laboratories need to acquire multiple assays to meet SARS-CoV-2 testing demand.
- Four polypeptide chains-two light chains and two longer heavy chains compose the immunoglobulin molecule.
- Immunology is the study of molecules, cells, and organs that make up the immune system.
- The use of specific antibodies enable the detection of pathogen-specific antigens and, consequently, the direct detection of pathogens.
- ABCpred and LBtope methods are based on artificial neural networks trained on similar B-cell epitope positive data.

INTRODUCTION

As the rapidly progressing COVID-19 pandemic and the limited laboratory-based molecular testing capacities, new point-of-care (POC), scalable rapid diagnostic tests have been invented recently as easy-to-use tools to allow COVID-19 diagnostics outside of laboratory settings. What is more, the urgent need to multiply testing for COVID-19 has been clearly identified as an essential element of the anti-coronavirus strategy all over the world.

The diagnostic sensitivity, specificity and accuracy concerning suspected COVID-19 infection, based on controlled testing and performance data from clinical settings, is of substantial importance in the context of limiting the scope of coronavirus epidemics. Unreliable and unproved tests may not detect patients with active infection or may incorrectly indicate COVID-19-negative patients as positive, hampering healthcare efforts. The diagnostic laboratory and point-of-care tests (POCTs) used in order to detect SARS-CoV-2 are, first of all, reference tests based on molecular technique real-time quantitative reverse transcriptase polymerase chain reaction assay (RT-qPCR) as well as serological antibody-detecting and antigen-detecting tests, for auxiliary purposes. At present, only molecular quantitative reverse transcription PCR (RT-qPCR) testing of respiratory tract samples is the recommended method for the identification and laboratory confirmation of COVID-19 cases, as these methods were evaluated for their quality and safety through the World Health Organization (WHO) protocols. On the other hand, based on current scientific evidence, WHO recommends the use of POC immunodiagnostic tests for research purposes and, at present, they should not be utilized in a clinical decision-making setting and in patient care until fully validated, with supporting data available. However, they can be useful in epidemiologic research or disease surveillance and further evolve as a critical step to develop COVID-19 vaccine in future. At the time of increased demand for hospital services, clinicians, governments and health services urgently need a fast, sensitive, but at the same time inexpensive diagnostic test, in order to rapidly manage patients, regarding admissions to hospitals meant for COVID-19 treatment. Therefore, the role of an approved and reliable diagnostic test in the COVID-19 care pathway is of the utmost importance.

Immunodiagnostic assays are procedures that utilize products of the immune response as integral parts of the test. Basically, immunodiagnostic assays use antibodies generated either against a single antigen or antigens associated with a specific analyte, pathogen, or disease condition. Historically, polyclonal antibodies generated against antigens of interest were produced in small living being, by injecting the antigen preparation with an adjuvant (such as Freund's complete or incomplete adjuvant), according to a schedule previously determined to give a maximum immune response. The direct detection of analyte, pathogens or disease conditions has been the gold standard for diagnosing infectious diseases ever since the establishment of the Henle Koch Postulates in 1882. However, in practical laboratory diagnostic testing, using indirect serological methods to test for infectious diseases is still important for detecting specific antibodies and to immunologically detect pathogen antigens in blood and liquor, despite advances in the direct detection of pathogens in culture and the use of molecular biological techniques. The test typically responds to the antigen preparation by producing antibodies to every recognizable antigenic epitope, thus inducing a polyclonal immunoglobulin response. Immunoglobulins are composed of two sets of identical amino acid chains; two heavy chains and two shorter light chains. Heavy chains are connected to each other by two or more disulfide bonds, whereas each light chain is connected to a heavy chain by one disulfide bond. The amino (N) terminus of a light and heavy chain compose the hypervariable amino acid region, or the "Fab" portion of the antibody molecule, whereas the carboxylic acid (COOH) terminus of both heavy chains compose the crystallizable, or Fc portion of the antibody see Figure 4.1.

The first immunoglobulin class to be generated by antibody-producing B cells is IgM, a pentavalent antibody molecule with high affinity for antigen epitopes. The IgM response decreases with time and is replaced by a second, high avidity immunoglobulin class termed IgG antibodies. After serial bleedings to determine that a strong immune response has occurred, blood is collected and the antibody fraction isolated using any of a variety of methods. Although such polyclonal antibody preparations can be highly sensitive in detecting the presence of pathogens, they tend to bind to other related microorganisms (cross-react), confusing test results.

DEFINITION OF BASIC TERMS OF IMMUNOASSAYS FOR DISEASE

THE IMMUNE SYSTEM

Immunology is the study of molecules, cells, and organs that make up the immune system. The function of the immune system is to recognize self-antigens from non-self-antigens and defend the body against non-self (foreign) agents. Through specific and non-specific defense mechanisms, the body's immune system is able to react to microbial pathogens and protect against disease. The first line of defense against infection is intact skin, mucosal membrane surfaces, and secretions that prevent pathogens from penetrating into the body.

When a foreign agent penetrates the first line of resistance, an immune reaction is elicited and immune cells are recruited into the site of infection to clear microorganisms and damaged cells by phagocytosis. If the inflammation remains aggravated, antibody-mediated

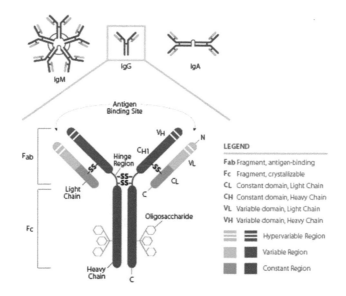

FIGURE 4.1 The structure of an immunoglobulin molecule. Four polypeptide chains-two light chains and two longer heavy chains compose the immunoglobulin molecule. Though each light chain is attached to a heavy chain by a single disulfide linkage, the two heavy chains are connected to each other through two or more disulfide linkages. Intrachain disulfide linkages within the heavy and light chains also determine the conformation of the molecule. Pepsin digestion was shown to cleave the molecule into two distinct fragments, the Fab (antigen binding fragment), and the Fc (crystallizable fragment) whereas papain digestion cleaved the molecule into three fragments. Both heavy and light chains are composed of a constant amino acid region and a variable amino acid region. The Fab fragment contains the hypervariable portions of the variable amino acid regions, which identifies and binds the antigen to which it is elicited. The Fc fragment consists of amino acid sequences important in a number of immunologically important events, such as complement fixation, macrophage fixation, membrane transmission, and antibody catabolism. Carbohydrate moieties are attached to the Fc portion of the antibody molecule.

immune reaction is activated and different types of immune cells are engaged to resolve the disease. The immune system is composed of cellular and humoral elements. The cellular component includes mast cells, neutrophils, macrophages, T and B lymphocytes, and plasma cells. The humoral component includes complement, lyzozyme, interferon, antibodies, and cytokines. All work cooperatively to eliminate immunogenic foreign substances from the body.

IMMUNOASSAYS

To aid in the diagnosis of disease caused by infectious microorganisms, immunoassays have been developed. These biochemical and serological techniques are based on the detection and quantitation of antibodies generated against an infectious agent, a microbe, or non-microbial antigen.

Because antibodies can be produced against any type of macromolecule, antibody-based techniques are useful in identifying molecules in solution or in cells. A blood sample is collected from the patient during the acute phase of the disease when antibody levels are high. Serum is then isolated and the concentration of antibodies is measured through various methods. Most assays rely on the formation of large immune complexes when an antibody binds to a specific antigen which can be detected in solution or in gels. Recent methods employ pure antibodies or antigens that have been immobilized on a platform and that can be measured using an indicator molecule. These methods provide high sensitivity and specificity and have become standard techniques in diagnostic immunology.

SEROLOGY TESTING

Serology testing allows the determination of immunity against different infecting organisms via the dosage of IgG. In the context of science and laboratory medicine, it is concerned with antigen–antibody reactions as the major carrier of humoral immunity. Antigen–antibody binding reactions occur in a highly specific way using the lock-and-key principle. Therefore, the use of specific antibodies enable the detection of pathogen-specific antigens and, consequently, the direct detection of pathogens. In the same respect, when pathogen-specific antigens are used, the pathogen can be detected based on the immune response specifically directed at it.

Individuals are deemed reactive or seropositive when their testing material (e.g., blood or urine) is found to contain pathogen-specific antigens or antigen-specific antibodies that are an expression of an acute or, under certain circumstances, past confrontation between the immune system and the pathogen in question. On the other hand, individuals are considered non-reactive or seronegative when neither pathogen-specific antigens, nor a pathogen-specific immune response can be detected. The immune system of immunologically health individuals stores every significant incident of contact with immunologically relevant pathogen antigens in the organism's immunological memory. This is done in the form of a specific immune response. Thus, contact with most pathogens can be detected months or even years later as evidenced by a specific immune response. Thus, contact with other, non-detectable pathogens and pathogens that are difficult to cultivate or cannot be cultivated can be detected. An organism's antibody response functions as an amplifier after it has come into contact with even a tiny amount of pathogenic and non-pathogenic microorganism.

At the same time, it becomes evident that serological testing for infectious diseases requires an immune system response in order to achieve diagnostic detection, at least when detecting pathogenspecific antibodies. The specific immune response frequently correlates to the incubation period of the infection and the type of pathogen, however it also depends on the individual's own immunology. Depending on the length of incubation time, diagnostic antibody reactions can also be negative in the early phase of an infection due to a delayed immune response. At the same time, a persisting immunological antibody response in the low reactive range, which can be diagnostically detected for months or even years after an acute infection, is not evidence per se of a current infection. Both constellations constitute a limitation of serological antibody detection. On the one hand, it is not possible to make a diagnosis during the acute stage of an infection because there is a delayed immune response. On the other hand, no clear statement can be made as to whether the detected antibodies are a result of an acute infection or an infection that happened a while back since, in the case of many diseases, antibodies persist long after an infection occurs.

The same holds true for pathogen-specific antigen detection in different bodily fluids. In this case the kinetics of the diagnostically useable antigens also crucially depends on the pathogen, the length of the infection and the type of testing material. As with pathogen-specific antibody detection, antigen detection in the early stage of an infection can be negative or can remain positive for days or weeks (in certain circumstances for months) following a healed or adequately treated infection.

For a clinically sound and diagnostically accurate interpretation of pathogen-specific antigen or antibody detection there needs to be a fundamental understanding in everyday clinical practice of serological and immunological correlations and the varying pathogen-specific kinetics of humoral immunity. This will briefly be touched on below.

Antigens

In serological testing for infectious diseases, antigens are molecules that react with the effector cells of the immune response (T and B cells, or antibodies). They trigger a specific immune response. These usually include proteins, lipoproteins and polysaccharides, less commonly lipids or nucleic acids. In the case of whole-cell antigens, a distinction should be made with regard to so-called haptens. Haptens are unable to trigger a targeted immune response due to their low molecular size. Instead, they become immunologically effective after binding to the carrier substances, preferably proteins. The parts of the antigen that determine the specific immune response are called epitopes. They are responsible for binding to the specific antibodies directed against them in line with the lock and key principle. Epitopes are usually made up of segments of around six to eight amino acids or polysaccharides.

Antibodies

The specifically acquired humoral immunity is essentially borne by immunoglobulins or antibodies. Synthesis occurs in plasma cells that are produced from clonally expanding B lymphocytes after antigen contact. Plasma cells are responsible for the monoclonal, class-specific and antigen-specific production of antibodies. Even when there is no longer any antigen stimulus, the production of specific antibodies can continue for months or even years thanks to memory cells which can be stimulated into producing an intensified immune response (secondary response) based on a renewed rapid clonal expansion after repeated contact with the antigen.

The structure of the immunoglobulins as shown in Figure 4.1 follows constant principles. All classes of antibodies (IgG, IgA, IgM, IgD, and IgE) are made up of two identically heavy chains and two identically light chains. These chains are connected by disulfide bonds. Light and heavy chains are individually present in two and five varieties respectively. These determine the class of antibody. They consist of a constant region and a variable region. At the molecular level, the variable region of the light and heavy chains is equipped with specific bonding sites for the immunologically recognized epitopes of the respective antigens. The molecular weights of the antibody classes fluctuate between 150 kD for IgG and 970 kD for the pentamer-shaped IgM (10% of the entire serum immunoglobulin). IgM is typically the carrier of the early immune response, while IgG is the carrier of the late immune response or the secondary response. The immunoglobulin classes IgD and IgE act as membrane receptors on B cells or mast cells, eosinophils and basophils. IgA is a secretory antibody that is found in both monomeric and dimeric forms. It is the main carrier of humoral immunity in mucosal secretions and bodily fluids. In the serum of healthy individuals, IgG constitutes 70–75% of the total amount of immunoglobulin. Though rarely relevant from a diagnostic perspective, IgG can be divided into various subclasses (IgG 1 – 4) that perform different tasks. In terms of the serological diagnosis of infectious diseases, these subclasses play a particular role with regard to complement activation and in terms of their proportional distribution pattern in serum. Accordingly, antibody deficiency syndrome or even IgG subclass defects can lead to a reduction in the informative value of diagnostic detection reactions. The same applies to potentially acquired, genetically determined defects at the B cell level.

Usually the antibodies that have formed as part of a specific immune reaction to an antigen are polyclonal, i.e., they are formed by various B cell clones, since most antigens carry very different epitopes and can, thus stimulate various B cell clones. Monoclonal antibodies, on the other hand, are antibodies that are produced from a clonally generated B cell line and are completely identical. These types of antibodies are mostly produced for industrial or research purposes and play a crucial role in serologically diagnosing infectious diseases and in treatment.

Antibody Functions

Differentiated plasma cells are crucial players in the humoral immunity response. The antibodies they secrete are particularly significant against extracellular pathogens and toxins. Once secreted, antibodies circulate freely and act independently of plasma cells. Sometimes, antibodies can be transferred from one individual to another. For instance, a person who has recently produced a successful immune response against a particular disease agent can donate blood to a non-immune recipient, confering temporary immunity through antibodies in the donor's blood serum. This phenomenon, called passive immunity, also occurs naturally during breastfeeding, which makes breastfed infants highly resistant to infections during the first few months of life.

Antibodies coat extracellular pathogens and neutralize them by blocking key sites on the pathogen that enhance their infectivity, such as receptors that "dock" pathogens on host cells. Antibody neutralization can prevent pathogens from entering and infecting host cells, as opposed to the cytotoxic T-cell-mediated approach of killing cells that are already infected to prevent progression of an established infection. The neutralized antibody-coated pathogens can then be filtered by the spleen and eliminated in urine or feces.

Antibodies also mark pathogens for destruction by phagocytic cells, such as macrophages or neutrophils, because they are highly attracted to macromolecules complexed with antibodies. Phagocytic enhancement by antibodies is called opsonization. In another process, complement fixation, IgM and IgG in serum bind to antigens, providing docking sites onto which sequential complement proteins can bind. The combination of antibodies and complement enhances opsonization even further, promoting rapid clearing of pathogens.

Affinity, Avidity, and Cross Reactivity

Not all antibodies bind with the same strength, specificity, and stability. In fact, antibodies exhibit different affinities (attraction) depending on the molecular complementarity between antigen and antibody molecules. An antibody with a higher affinity for a particular antigen would bind more strongly and stably. It would be expected to present a more challenging defense against the pathogen corresponding to the specific antigen.

The term avidity describes binding by antibody classes that are secreted as joined, multivalent structures (such as IgM and IgA). Although avidity measures the strength of binding, just as affinity does, the avidity is not simply the sum of the affinities of the antibodies in a multimeric structure. The avidity depends on the number of identical binding sites on the antigen being detected, as well as other physical and chemical factors. Typically, multimeric antibodies, such as pentameric IgM, are classified as having lower affinity than monomeric antibodies, but high avidity. Essentially, the fact that multimeric antibodies can bind many antigens simultaneously balances their slightly-lower-binding strength for each antibody/antigen interaction.

Antibodies secreted after binding to one epitope on an antigen may exhibit cross reactivity for the same or similar epitopes on different antigens. Cross reactivity occurs when an antibody binds not to the antigen that elicited its synthesis and secretion, but to a different antigen. Because an epitope corresponds to such a small region (the surface area of about four to six amino acids), it is possible for different macromolecules to exhibit the same molecular identities and orientations over short regions.

Cross reactivity can be beneficial if an individual develops immunity to several related pathogens despite having been exposed to or vaccinated against only one of them. For instance, antibody cross reactivity may occur against the similar surface structures of various Gram-negative bacteria. Conversely, antibodies raised against pathogenic molecular components that resemble self-molecules may incorrectly mark host cells for destruction, causing autoimmune damage. Patients who develop systemic lupus erythematosus (SLE) commonly exhibit antibodies that react with their own DNA. These antibodies may have been initially raised against the nucleic acid of microorganisms, but later cross-reacted with self-antigens. This phenomenon is also called molecular mimicry.

EMERGED RAPID IMMUNODIAGNOSTIC (SEROLOGY IMMUNOASSAYS) TESTS

Immunological methods are, most often, the chemiluminescent assaying of immunoglobulin IgG and IgM for SARS-CoV-2 from blood on an analyzer, or immunochromatographic assessment in the form of rapid POCTs, not requiring additional equipment. The methods of detecting anti-SARS-CoV-2 antibodies, despite the ongoing research to develop them further, may or even should be applied during the coronavirus epidemics (Hsueh et al., 2004; Lippi et al., 2020). After about a week from the first clinical manifestations, the sensitivity of molecular diagnostics (PCR) diminishes gradually for SARS-CoV-2 infections, due to the decreasing amount of virus particles in the respiratory tract epithelium. In such cases, patients may have false negative results, despite the ongoing infection.

LATERAL FLOW IMMUNOASSAY

Among the many contemporary technologies available, special attention should be paid to rapid lateral flow immunoassay (LFIA), also referred to as immunochromatographic tests. Perhaps they are not so much appreciated in the scientific community as PCR methods or Enzyme-Linked Immunosorbent Assay (ELISA tests), despite the fact that they do find application in diagnostics more and more often. They differ, depending on the type of test, but the basic principle of their action is invariably the same—they make use of the unique property that antibodies possess, that of selective binding to a specific particle or group of similar particles (antigen). LFIAs provide an uncomplicated and relatively inexpensive tool meant for detecting the presence (or absence) of a given component in the examined specimen, such as the presence of a virus in an analyzed blood sample. Examination with the use of those tests is possible for various types of test material—whole human blood, blood plasma, serum, stool, urine, sweat, cerebrospinal fluid, or even tears (Vashist, 2020). The test principle is based on an immunological method, using specific antibodies, most often in

TABLE 4.1

The Brief Comparison of Advantages and Disadvantages of Immunochromatographic Tests (Guan et al., 2004; Koczula & Gallotta, 2016; Kogaki et al., 2005)

Advantages	Disadvantages
Short reaction time for most tests, amounting to 5–20 min	Suboptimal sensitivity, results often false negative, particularly during enhanced activity of the virus
Simple and comfortable to use and perform. Some tests may be performed in outpatient clinics or at patient's bed.	Despite substantial specificity sometimes the results are false negative, particularly when the virus is not much active.
Reading most often possible with "naked eye."	It is necessary to verify positive or doubtful results.
Small amount of material to be collected, variety of material.	Increased risk of operator becoming infected
"best before" date distant (usually 18 months from manufacturing date)	

complex with colloidal gold, where a drop of the examined substance first moves along the nitrocellulose membrane using capillary phenomena. After the sample is absorbed by the membrane, the antigen (should the test prove to be positive) binds to the colloidal gold complex and respective antibodies. Consequently, the effect of that reaction is the formation of a complex, which will be detected by the test. The interpretation of results consists of confirmation or ruling out of the presence of antigens in the examined sample, based on color test strips that appear in the test (Lippi et al., 2020; West et al., 2020). The brief comparison of advantages and disadvantages of immunochromatographic tests is presented in Table 4.1.

At present, most immunoenzymatic tests available are based on the immunochromatic technique. The difference between those tests depends upon the molecule assayed (p/c or antigens), structure, performance time, and diagnostic material. It may be supposed that, in future, rapid tests will enable easier and quicker diagnostics of many diseases, without the necessity of performing tedious and complicated procedures. This would reduce the waiting time for obtaining results, and accelerate decision making regarding suitable treatment. (Oh et al., 2006; Posthuma-Trumpie et al., 2009)

IMMUNOENZYMATIC AND IMMUNOFLUORIMETRIC ASSAYS

The detection of specific SARS-CoV-2 serum antibodies allows for a rapid, cost-effective, and reasonably sensitive clinical diagnosis of COVID-19, as immunoglobulins such as IgM provide the initial humoral response during the first stage of viral infection, prior to the onset of the adaptive, high-affinity IgG response essential for long-term immunological memory. Research indicates that after SARS infection, antibodies of the IgM class may be detected in patient's blood about six days after the infection, while IgG may be already detected after eight days. As SARS-CoV-2 belongs to the same large family of viruses, which includes those causing Middle East Respiratory Syndrome (MERS) and Severe Acute Respiratory Syndrome (SARS), it should be assumed that the process of producing antibodies will be similar to that in case of other viruses belonging to that family, while the detection of IgG antibodies and IgM antibodies acting against SARS-CoV-2 may be an

TABLE 4.2

Clinical Significance of an IgM/IgG Serological Test Result

Phase of Infection	Type of Test		
	PCR	IgM	IgG
The window period for a test designed to detect a specific disease	P(+)	N(−)	N(−)
Early stage of infection	P(+)	P(+)	N(−)
Active phase of infection	P(+)	P(+)	P(+)
Late or recurrent stage of infection	P(+)	N(−)	P(+)
Early stage of infection. PCR result may be false negative[a]	N(−)	P(+)	N(−)
Past infection (recover)[a]	N(−)	N(−)	P(+)
The recovery stage of infection, or PCR result may be false negative[a]	N(−)	P(+)	P(+)
No infection and no special symptoms	N(−)	N(−)	N(−)

Note: P(+)—positive; N(−)—negative.

[a] Human coronaviruses (HCoV) OC43, 229E, NL63, and HKU1 may cause false positive ELISA results.

indication of infection. Moreover, the detection of IgM antibodies usually indicates a recent exposure to SARS-CoV-2, whereas the detection of IgG antibodies in case of COVID-19 indicates exposure to the virus some time ago (Li et al., 2020).

Serological tests, detecting solely the IgM class of antibodies, should find applications for diagnostic purposes. When using tests which detect both IgM and IgG antibodies, one should remember that a positive result may be the evidence of past infection, not active infection (Table 4.2). Negative results from serological tests do not exclude SARS-CoV-2 infection, as the "window period" (delay in the production of antibodies) may exceed seven days. Serological tests may also give false positive results. This may be the case of past or ongoing infection with virus strains other than SARS-CoV-2, such as coronavirus HKU1, NL63, OC43, or 229E. Moreover, the first tests assessing the titer of IgA class antibodies have been launched, which, from the perspective of immunology, is of extreme importance, as it provides the possibility of testing for antibodies in a material other than blood samples collected from patients, e.g., respiratory tract secretions.

Serological tests are thus applied as an adjunctive method, for monitoring the epidemiological situation, yet they may be performed faster and are less costly than genetic tests. This diagnostic method has a limited sensitivity, yet efforts to improve it are ongoing, as it is useful for monitoring the infection. Due to insufficient data concerning, among others, the dynamics of immunological response to infection and the diagnostic value of available tests for detecting IgM and IgG class antibodies (comprising sensitivity, specificity, positive, and negative predictive value), in many countries, it is currently not recommended to use serological tests for diagnostic purposes. Table 4.3 displays the evaluation of serological tests validated by the FDA.

SARS-CoV-2 INFECTIVITY AND IMMUNE RESPONSE

The detection of SARS-CoV-2 infection and immune response has been described in relation to different diagnostic tests. In this section, we summaries the evidence from studies to date.

TABLE 4.3

Evaluations of Coronavirus Disease 2019 (COVID-19) Serological Tests, Including Sensitivity, Specificity, and Predictive Value

Test Name	Euroimmun SARS-COV-2 ELISA (IgG)	Healgen COVID-19 IgG/IgM Rapid Test Cassette	Biomedomics COVID-19 IgM-IgG Rapid Test kit	Phamatech COVID-19 RAPID TEST	Tianjin Beroni Biotechnology SARS-COV-2 IgG/ IgM Antibody Detection Kit
Clinical Sensitivity IgM		100%	86.70%	26.70%	83.30%
Clinical Specificity IgM		100%	97.10%	97.50%	100%
Clinical Sensitivity IgG	90%	96.70%	73.30%	86.70%	30%
Clinical Specificity IgG	100%	97.50%	100%	96.20%	100%
Clinical Sensitivity IgM+IgG		100%	96.70%	86.70%	90%
Clinical Specificity IgM+IgG		97.50%	97.10%	93.80%	100%
Positive Predictive Value at prevalence = 5% (IgM+IgG or IgG)	100%	67.80%	63.70%	42.40%	100%
Negative Predictive Value at prevalence = 5% (IgM+IgG or IgG)	99.50%	100%	99.80%	99.30%	99.50%

VIRAL INFECTIVITY

Studies have shown that SARS-CoV-2 RNA can be detected two to three days before onset of symptoms and can remain detectable up to 25–50 days after the onset of symptoms, particularly in patients who remain symptomatic for an extended period. SARS-CoV-2 RNA can be detected for longer in respiratory samples from patients with severe disease than in samples from patients with mild illness. Viral RNA concentrations peak within the first five days after onset of symptoms and decrease slowly with rising antibody concentrations. However, RNA clearance is not always associated with rising antibody concentrations, particularly in patients who were critically ill. An important question for the potential for spread of COVID-19 is whether individuals who are RNA-positive are shedding infectious virus. A small study in nine patients found that viral replication stopped five to seven days after onset of symptoms but patients remained RNA-positive for one to two weeks after this point. Hence, there remains some uncertainty as to whether a patient who is RNA-positive is shedding live virus or not.

IMMUNE RESPONSE TO COVID-19 DISEASE

Maturation of the immune response typically takes 40 days with variations in the dynamics of the antibody response depending on disease severity and other factors still to be discovered. In most studies of laboratory confirmed COVID-19 cases, IgM antibodies start to be detectable around five to ten days after onset of symptoms and rise rapidly. IgG antibody concentrations follow the IgM response closely. Seroconversion is typically within the first three weeks with the mean time for seroconversion being 9–11 days after onset of symptoms for total antibody, 10–12 days for IgM, and 12–14 days for IgG.

COVID-19 ANTIBODY RESPONSE: PATHOGENIC OR PROTECTIVE?

Antibodies against the receptor-binding domain of the spike protein and the nucleocapsid protein have been associated with neutralising activity. Neutralising antibodies to these domains can be detected approximately seven days after onset of symptoms and rise steeply over the next two weeks. Several studies showed that patients can remain RNA-positive despite high concentrations of IgM and IgG antibodies against the nucleocapsid protein and the receptor-binding domain of the spike protein. Whether the presence of neutralising antibodies translates into protective immunity in patients with COVID-19 is unclear. Some researchers speculate that antibodies can enhance infectivity as higher antibody concentrations have been observed in patients with severe disease than in those with mild disease. In one study (n = 222), a greater proportion of patients with high IgG concentrations had severe disease than did those with low IgG concentrations (52% vs 32%, $p = 0.008$). The role of antibody response in the pathogenesis of COVID-19 remains unclear pending further studies.

COMPUTATIONAL METHOD

IMMUNOINFORMATICS-BASED ANALYSIS

An immunoinformatics-based computational approach to mine the proteome of SARS-CoV-2 and subsequently identify immunodominant epitopes of SARS-CoV-2. Detecting immune responses that are based on specific immunodominant epitopes enables generating both antibody- and cell-mediated immunity against a specific pathogen. This can facilitate the fast and effective elimination of the pathogen. Using a variety of computational tools, we predicted all possible B- and T-cell epitope regions in SARS-CoV-2 protein sequences, and selected those regions where both B- and T-cell epitopes mapped. Notably, despite evidence that SARS-CoV-2 originated from bats, it phylogenetically diverged from SARS-CoV (Cui et al., 2020; Moran et al., 2020). Therefore, we selected and mapped regions that positively predicted protective antigens to the experimentally validated epitopes of SARS-CoV. We then only selected epitopes that were 100% identical between SARS-CoV and SARS-CoV-2. We thus identified 15 potential immunogenic regions and 25 immunodominant epitopes from SARS-CoV-2 proteins. The global distribution of these epitopes was analyzed to estimate the percentage of infected individuals that express an MHC molecule that is capable of binding a particular epitope. Interestingly, seven epitopes were found to cover more than 87% of the worldwide virus-affected population. Further structural molecular docking analyses were carried out to estimate the binding interactions of these potential epitopes with human major histocompatibility complexes (MHC) proteins. Thus, our study has identified a set of potential immunodominant epitopes from the SARS-CoV-2 proteome that are capable of generating both antibody- and cell-mediated immune responses. To conclude, our findings may be useful in developing effective peptide vaccines against COVID-19 infections.

Data and Material

The whole genome and proteome data of SARS-CoV-2 isolates from different geographic locations is retrieved from Genbank (NCBI). Protein sequences of SARS-CoV and MERS-CoV were also collected from Genbank. The experimentally determined B- and T-cell epitopes of SARS-CoV were retrieved from the publicly available Immune Epitope Database (IEDB) (Vita et al., 2019) with the filtering criteria of at least one positive assay: (1) positive B-cell assays, (2) positive T-cell assays, and (3) positive MHC binding assays.

Predicting Potential Linear B-Cell Epitopes in SARS-CoV-2

Linear B-cell epitopes are peptides with antigenic abilities that are bound by receptors on the surface of B lymphocytes and, thus, generate immune responses (Van Regenmortel, 2009). We used multiple approaches to predict the linear B-cell epitopes from the protein sequences of SARS-CoV-2. These included three machine learning-based methods, namely, BepiPred (Jespersen et al., 2017), ABCpred (Saha & Raghava, 2006b), and LBtope (Singh et al., 2013). BepiPred utilizes data that are obtained from three-dimensional (3D)-structures of the antigen–antibody complex, based on random forests that were trained on the B-cell epitope. We set a cutoff of 0.5 for detecting B-cell epitopes using BepiPred. The ABCpred and LBtope methods are based on artificial neural networks trained on similar B-cell epitope positive data. ABCpred relies on random peptides for the training of negative data, in contrast to LBtope, which uses negative data that are based on experimentally validated non-B-cell epitopes from IEDB (Vita et al., 2019). We used a cutoff of 0.51 and chose all window lengths of 10–20 for predicting B-cell epitopes using the ABCpred search tool.

Prediction of Potential T-Cell Epitopes in SARS-CoV-2

Predicting T-cell epitopes is important for identifying the smallest peptide in an antigen that is able to stimulate CD4 or CD8 T-cells to generate immunogenicity. Thus, the aim here is to identify peptides within antigens that are potentially immunogenic. MHC-peptide binding is considered to be the most important determinant of T-cell epitopes (Davis & Bjorkman, 1988). MHC binds to the antigenic region and becomes more available on the cell surface, where T-cells can recognize them. The accurate prediction of these binders is crucial for efficient vaccine design due to the importance of MHC binders for the activation of T-cells of the immune system (Patronov & Doytchinova, 2013). MHC class I and II epitopes were predicted using Tepitool (Paul et al., 2016), available at IEDB (Fleri et al., 2017). For predicting MHC class-I epitopes, the parameter for selecting predicted peptides was set as equal or less than 500 median inhibitory concentrations (IC50), while for MHC class-II epitope prediction, the same parameter was set to equal or less than 1000 nM IC50 (Paul et al., 2013; Wang et al., 2008). NetMHCpan-4.0 (Jurtz et al., 2017) and nHLAPred (Lata et al., 2007) were also used to predict the MHC class-I binding epitope, and potential T-cell epitopes were predicted using CTLPred (Bhasin & Raghava, 2004). CTLPred predicts T-cell epitopes (CTL) from antigen sequences instead of using the intermediate step in which MHC Class I binders are predicted.

Prediction of Protective Antigens

It is important to identify epitopes that are crucial for inducing protection and eliminate others in order to develop peptide-based vaccines. Protective antigens are able to induce an immune response. Thus, Vaxijen V2.0 (Doytchinova & Flower, 2007) was used to predict the ability of the predicted SARS-CoV-2 epitopes to protect antigens. The default threshold of Vaxijen V2.0 (0.4) was used to predict the protection potential of antigens.

Analysis of Epitope Conservation and Population Coverage of T-Cell Epitopes

An IEDB conservancy analysis tool was utilized in order to analyze the degree of conservation of SARS-CoV-2 B- and T-cell epitopes. The population coverage of T-cell epitopes was analyzed using tools available at the IEDB (Dimitrov et al., 2014). The predicted population coverage represents the percentage of individuals within a defined population which are likely to elicit an immune response to a T-cell epitope.

Prediction of Allergenicity, Toxicity, and Possibilities of Autoimmune Reactions

The allergenicity of immunodominant epitopes were predicted using AllerTOP v. 2.0 (Dimitrov et al., 2014) and AlgPred (Saha & Raghava, 2006a). AllerTOP v. 2.0 classified allergens and non-allergens based on the vk-nearest neighbours (kNN) method within an accuracy of 88.7%. AlgPred classified allergens and non-allergens using a hybrid approach (SVMc, IgE epitope, ARPs BLAST, and MAST) within an accuracy of 85%. The toxicity of the epitopes was predicted by means of the ToxinPred (Gupta et al., 2013) web-server, which applies machine learning approaches using different properties of the peptides. Further, we performed a BLAST search (with a criteria of >90% identity) of all of the potential epitopes vs. all the available human antigens from positive B-cell/T-cell/MHC ligand assays for autoimmune diseases in IEDB to determine the risks of potential predicted epitopes triggering a cascade of autoimmune reactions.

Result

Identification of Immunodominant Epitopes from the Proteins of SARS-CoV-2 Immunodominant epitopes, which can generate both antibody- and cell-mediated immunity, were identified to generate memory cells against SARS-CoV-2. We first predicted B- and T-cell epitopes and their possible MHC alleles from the SARS-CoV-2 protein using a variety of tools described in the Methods in order determine immunodominant epitopes. All of the B- and T-cell epitopes that were predicted from the different SARS-CoV-2 protein sequences were selected for further analysis. Subsequently, using a combinatorial screening approach, we analyzed all of the predicted B-cell and T-cell epitope (MHC-I and MHC-II) libraries of different lengths, from all protein sequences. The aim was to identify the immunogenic regions that could potentially act as both B-cell and T-cell epitopes. We compared the libraries of predicted B-cell epitopes vs. T-cell epitopes and selected those epitopes with 100% sequence coverage. The lengths of the immunogenic regions were selected based on the maximum coverage of B-cell or T-cell epitopes in the mapped regions. Figure 4.2 depicts the pipeline used in the study for detecting immunodominant epitopes.

We predicted the abilities of the epitopes to serve as protective antigens using Vaxijen and to understand the immunomodulatory effect of epitopes identified from immunogenic regions (Doytchinova & Flower, 2007). Unique epitopes were selected accordingly for further analysis. We identified a total of 17 immunogenic regions from the viral membrane glycoprotein, spike glycoprotein, and nucleocapsid phosphoprotein, onto which both B-cell and T-cell epitopes were mapped. Although immunoinformatics approaches were established to identify potential epitopes from pathogens, some computationally predicted epitopes may not be optimally immunogenic in vivo. Therefore, it is necessary to test the predicted epitopes in vivo to ensure that they can generate B-cell and/or T-cell responses. Detailed understanding of protective immune responses against SARS-CoV might be

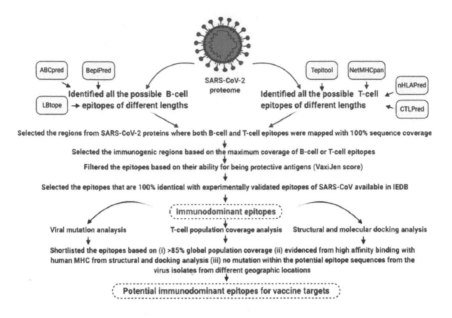

FIGURE 4.2 Computational approaches used to identify potential immunodominant epitopes from the proteome of severe acute respiratory syndrome coronavirus 2 (SARS-CoV-2).

presumably important for developing a vaccine against SARS-CoV-2 (Grifoni et al., 2020). For this reason, the 100% identical and experimentally confirmed epitopes between SARS-CoV and SARS-CoV-2 were chosen in this study. Accordingly, we mapped all of the epitopes that were predicted from the 17 regions of three proteins of SARS-CoV-2 with the experimentally validated epitopes of SARS-CoV, and only selected the 100% identical epitopes. The lengths of the epitopes were adjusted based on the mapped experimentally-determined epitopes of SARS-CoV. To define the immunodominant epitopes, the core parts of both B-cell and T-cell epitopes were verified within those mapped epitope sequences. Finally, we found 15 potential immunogenic regions of SARS-CoV-2 that explicitly include 25 mapped immunodominant epitopes, which can generate immune responses by both B-cells and T-cells (Table 4.4, Figure 4.3).

Interestingly, the mapping of immunogenic regions onto the structure of SARS-CoV-2 spike glycoprotein (Figure 4.3(c)) revealed a number of potential epitopes that were not exposed to solvent. For example, the beta-strand spanning Val1060–Val1068, composed of hydrophobic residues (VVFLHVTYV), is not a solvent-accessible region in the multi-sub-unit spike glycoprotein (Figure 4.3(d)). Indeed, the solvent-accessible surface area (SASA) was estimated to be ~0 for all residues of this epitope, with the only exception of the-Val1068 (SASA ~24 A2). This region contrasts with the nearby region of another epitope, Asp663–Leu680 (DIPIGAGICASYHTVSLL, Table 4.4), which was mostly exposed to solvent (Figure 4.3(e)). This implies the "recognition-after-proteolysis" pathway of protein interactions with the immune system.

We predicted the abilities of the epitopes to serve as protective antigens using Vaxijen and to understand the immunomodulatory effect of epitopes identified from immunogenic regions (Doytchinova & Flower, 2007). Unique epitopes were selected accordingly for further analysis. We identified a total of 17 immunogenic regions from the viral membrane glycoprotein, spike glycoprotein, and nucleocapsid phosphoprotein, onto which both

TABLE 4.4

Potential Immunodominant Regions of SARS-CoV-2 and the Mapped Epitopes in Those Regions

Potential Immunogenic Regions from Proteins of SARS-CoV-2, Isolated in Wuhan-Hu-1 (NC_045512.2)	The Number of Epitopes Mapped	Potential Immunodominant Epitopes
Membrane glycoprotein (61–70)	1	TLACFVLAAV
Membrane glycoprotein (157–187)	3	GRCDIKDLPKEITVATSR
		PKEITVATSRTLSYYKL
		TSRTLSYYKLGASQRV
Nucleocapsid phosphoprotein (176–191)	1	SRGGSQASSRSSSRSR
Nucleocapsid phosphoprotein (240–264)	2	QQQGQTVTKKSAAEASKK
		KKSAAEASKKPRQKRTA
Nucleocapsid phosphoprotein (268–286)	1	YNVTQAFGRRGPEQTQGNF
Nucleocapsid phosphoprotein (292–330)	3	IRQGTDYKHWPQIAQFA
		QFAPSASAFFGMSRIGM
		FFGMSRIGMEVTPSGTW
Nucleocapsid phosphoprotein (360–375)	1	YKTFPPTEPKKDKKKK
Spike glycoprotein (327–343)	1	VRFPNITNLCPFGEVFN
Spike glycoprotein (663–680)	1	DIPIGAGICASYHTVSLL
Spike glycoprotein (817–833)	1	FIEDLLFNKVTLADAGF
Spike glycoprotein (891–918)	3	GAALQIPFAMQMAYRFN
		PFAMQMAYRFNGIGVTQ
		MAYRFNGIGVTQNVLYE
Spike glycoprotein (1019–1041)	2	RASANLAATKMSECVLG
		AATKMSECVLGQSKRVD
Spike glycoprotein (1060–1068)	1	VVFLHVTYV
Spike glycoprotein (1157–1209)	3	KNHTSPDVDLGDISGIN
		DLGDISGINASVVNIQK
		EIDRLNEVAKNLNESLIDLQELGKYEQY
Spike glycoprotein (1254–1273)	1	CKFDEDDSEPVLKGVKLHYT

B-cell and T-cell epitopes were mapped. Although immunoinformatics approaches were established to identify potential epitopes from pathogens, some computationally predicted epitopes may not be optimally immunogenic in vivo. Therefore, it is necessary to test the predicted epitopes in vivo to ensure that they can generate B-cell and/or T-cell responses. Detailed understanding of protective immune responses against SARS-CoV might be presumably important for developing a vaccine against SARS-CoV-2 (Grifoni et al., 2020). For this reason, the 100% identical and experimentally confirmed epitopes between SARS-CoV and SARS-CoV-2 were chosen in this study. Accordingly, we mapped all of the epitopes that were predicted from the 17 regions of three proteins of SARS-CoV-2 with the experimentally validated epitopes of SARS-CoV, and only selected the 100% identical epitopes. The lengths of the epitopes were adjusted based on the mapped experimentally-determined epitopes of SARS-CoV. To define the immunodominant epitopes, the core parts of both B-cell and T-cell epitopes were verified within those mapped epitope sequences. Finally, we found 15 potential immunogenic regions of SARS-CoV-2 that explicitly include

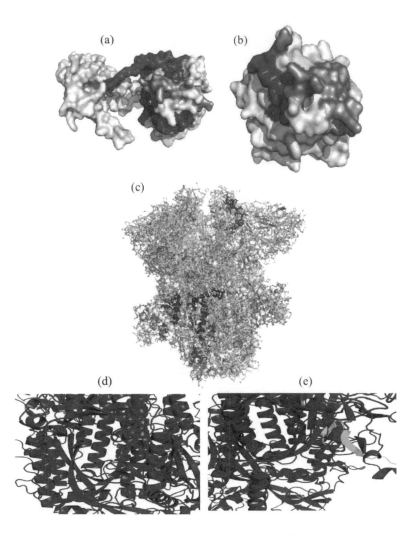

FIGURE 4.3 Potential immunogenic regions mapped onto SARS CoV-2 proteins. (a) Nucleocapsid phosphoprotein: residues 176–191 (orange), 240–264 (salmon), 268–286 (lime), 292–330 (sand), 360–375 (sky-blue). (b) Membrane glycoprotein: residues 61–70 (orange), 157–187 (salmon). (c) Spike glycoprotein: residues 327–343 (orange), 663–680 (yellow), 817–833 (wheat), 891–918 (green), 1019–1041 (lime), 1060–1068 (red), 1157–1209 (cyan), and 1254–1273 (sky-blue). In all of these regions, both B-cell and T-cell epitopes are mapped. (d) The region Val1060–Val1068 (orange beta-strand) of the spike glycoprotein (green cartoon) is mostly composed of hydrophobic residues (VVFLHVTYV) which are not exposed to solvent. (e) Residues Asp663–Leu680 (DIPIGAGICASYHTVSLL, blue) of the spike glycoprotein (green cartoon) are mostly solvent-exposed, with the exception of Cys671 and Ala672.

25 mapped immunodominant epitopes, which can generate immune responses by both B-cells and T-cells (Table 4.4, Figure 4.3(a)–(c)).

Interestingly, the mapping of immunogenic regions onto the structure of SARS-CoV-2 spike glycoprotein (Figure 4.3(c)) revealed a number of potential epitopes that were not exposed to solvent. For example, the beta-strand spanning Val1060–Val1068, composed of hydrophobic residues (VVFLHVTYV), is not a solvent-accessible region in the multi-subunit spike glycoprotein (Figure 4.3(d)). Indeed, the solvent-accessible surface area (SASA) was estimated to be ~0 for all residues of this epitope, with the only exception of the-Val1068 (SASA ~24 A2). This region contrasts with the nearby region of another epitope, Asp663–Leu680 (DIPIGAGICASYHTVSLL, Table 4.4), which was mostly exposed to solvent (Figure 4.3(e)). This implies the "recognition-after-proteolysis" pathway of protein interactions with the immune system.

Analysis of Viral Mutations Within the Potential Epitope Regions

Selection pressure of the human immune system has been shown to drive viral point mutations that evade immune surveillance (Lucas et al., 2001). Therefore, patterns of mutational events need to be examined in order to understand the epitope escape that is important for the transmission of viruses between different sub-populations. Potential immunogenic epitopes with a low chance of mutation are thus optimal candidates for generating effective vaccines. We analyzed mutations within the immunodominant epitopes identified in SARV-CoV-2 isolates from different geographic locations. We found a few single point mutations within the immunodominant regions of a few SARS-CoV-2 sequences isolates from the United States of America (Figure 4.4). Despite the low number of point mutations in the immunodominant epitopes, they reflect the severity of mutated viral genomes within the American population. Our observations highlight that immune pressure-induced genetic drifts play an important role in the evolution of SARS-CoV-2. This might be essential for evading immune surveillance by the host. The correlation of patterns of mutations and human immune pressure-induced genetic evolution of SARS-CoV-2 will be understood in detail with the availability of more sequenced viruses from different countries.

Population Coverage of Immunodominant Epitopes

Human leukocyte antigens (HLAs) are the most polymorphic genes in humans, and their allele distributio and expression vary by ethnic group and geographical location. The classical HLA loci are class I (HLA-A, B, C, E, F, and G) and class II (HLA-DR, DQ, DM, and DP) molecules, which provide antigen presentation to CD8 and CD4 T-cells (Blackwell et al., 2009). Therefore, the identification of epitopes that can be recognized by multiple HLA alleles and cover most of the world's population is important for the development of successful vaccines. Thus, we analyzed population coverage by HLAs of all of the epitopes

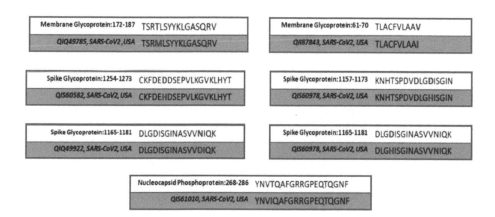

FIGURE 4.4 The point mutations found within the potential epitopes of American SARS-CoV-2 isolates. The mutated regions are highlighted in red.

from the immunogenic regions of SARS-CoV-2 using the IEDB population coverage analysis tool (Vita et al., 2019). We identified seven epitopes from five immunogenic regions, which cover more than 87% of the world's population (Table 4.5). Among these seven potential immunodominant epitopes, six are 17 amino acids in length. We found that the residue 891–918 region of the spike glycoprotein contains three potential immunodominant epitopes. Of these, two have world population coverages of 97.46% and 92.52%, respectively. Similarly, the residue 292–330 region of the nucleocapsid phosphoprotein contains three potential immunodominant epitopes. Of these, two have 87.42 and 92.81% world population coverages, respectively. These results indicate that the seven immunodominant epitopes could be potential candidates for designing vaccines against SARS-CoV-2 that can cover almost the entire world population.

Analysis of Allergenicity, Toxicity, and Autoimmune Reactivity

Epitope allergenicity is a prominent obstacle for vaccine development. We thus verified that the identified epitopes are not allergens. The allergenicity analysis results of the seven immunodominant epitopes (Table 4.5) highlighted that six of these epitopes were not predicted as allergens using both AllerTOP (Dimitrov et al., 2014) and AlgPred (Saha & Raghava, 2006a). Only one epitope ("FIEDLLFNKVTLADAGF") was predicted as an allergen by AllerTOP, whereas the AlgPred method predicted it as a non-allergen. Therefore, the proper classification of allergens was not possible for this epitope due to the limitation of computational prediction methods. Toxicity profiling of these predicted epitopes revealed that all were safe and possibly non-toxic. Epitope spreading is a process where diversification of the immune response is induced by an antigen to meet both B-cell and T-cell specificities during a chronic autoimmune or infectious response (Powell & Black, 2001; Vanderlugt & Miller, 1996). Thus, we analyzed the possibility that the seven predicted immunodominant epitopes (Table 4.5) would generate autoimmune reactions. For this purpose, we performed a BLAST search of our epitopes against the database of epitope sequences of human antigens for autoimmune diseases, which were validated by positive B-cell/T-cell/MHC ligand assays. Consequently, we found that none of the human epitopes for autoimmune disease share significant sequence identity with our predicted SARS-CoV-2 immunodominant epitopes (Table 4.5). This result indicates that the seven epitopes have a very low risk for generating autoimmune reactions in humans.

Structural Analysis and Modeling of Epitope Presentation by MHC Class I and II Systems

Epitopes are faced with extremely complex and competitive environments that include the multitude of HLA proteins that bind immunogenic peptides with different affinities, and present selected epitopes to surface receptors on immune cells. Therefore, we performed molecular docking analysis to understand the binding interactions of the identified immunodominant epitopes with human MHC complexes

Structures of different HLA-peptide complexes from MHC class I and II were collected and aligned, as described in Methods. Structures of HLAs are fairly similar within each group (I and II) and share the same canonical fold. The epitopes were clustered in similar conformations in the HLA antigen binding grooves created by two helices in parallel orientation (Figure 4.5 (a) and (b)). For the most part, backbone "traces" of peptides were similar (Figure 4.5 (a)). The N- and C-termini occupied essentially the same positions inpockets A and F of HLA binding sites (Figure 4.5 (c) and (d)). This suggests that conformational

TABLE 4.5

Epitopes With More Than 85% World Population Coverage

Epitopes	Epitope Location	World Population Coverage (%)	Predicted HLA Locus
PKEITVATSRTLSYYKL	Membrane glycoprotein:165–181	95.82%	HLA-A, HLA-B, HLA-DRB1, HLA-DRB3, HLA-DRB4, HLA-DRB5, HLA-DQA1, HLA-DQB1
QFAPSASAFFGMSRIGM	Nucleocapsid phosphoprotein:306–322	92.81%	HLA-A, HLA-B, HLADRB1, HLA-DRB3, HLADRB4, HLA-DRB5, HLA-DQB1
FFGMSRIGMEVTPSGTW	Nucleocapsid phosphoprotein:314–330	87.42%	HLA-A, HLA-B, HLA-DRB1, HLA-DRB4, HLA-DRB5, HLA-DQA1, HLA-DQB1
FIEDLLFNKVTLADAGF	Spike glycoprotein:817–833	94.26%	HLA-A, HLA-B, HLA-DRB1, HLA-DRB3, HLA-DRB4, HLA-DRB5, HLA-DQA1, HLA-DQB1, HLA-DPA1, HLA-DPB1
GAALQIPFAMQMAYRFN	Spike glycoprotein:891–907	97.46%	HLA-A, HLA-B, HLA-DRB1, HLA-DRB4, HLA-DRB5, HLA-DQA1, HLA-DQB1, HLA-DPA1,HLA-DPB1
PFAMQMAYRFNGIGVTQ	Spike glycoprotein:897–913	92.52%	HLA-A, HLA-B, HLA-DRB1, HLA-DRB3, HLA-DRB4, HLA-DRB5, HLA-DQA1, HLA-DQB1, HLA-DPA1
EIDRLNEVAKNLNESLIDLQELGKYEQY	Spike glycoprotein:1182–1209	88.57%	HLA-A, HLA-B, HLA-DRB1, HLA-DRB3, HLA-DQA1, HLA-DQB1

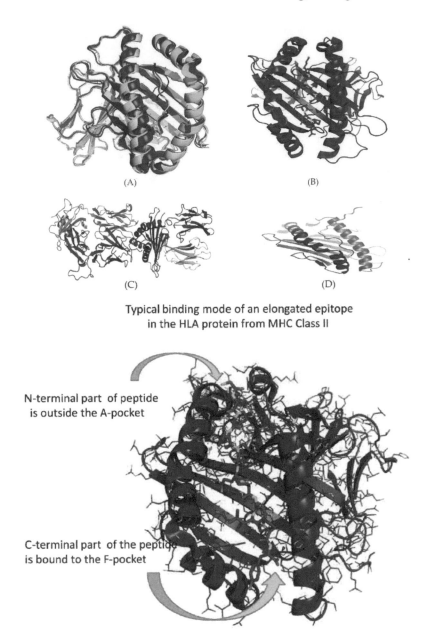

FIGURE 4.5 (A) Structures of aligned major histocompatibility complexes (MHC) (Class I) HLA-peptide complexes are fairly similar, sharing the same canonical fold and peptide binding mode. (B) A typical 9-mer peptide molecule (orange sticks) arranged in the binding site of a HLA protein (green cartoon) from MHC Class I. The N- (upper side) and C- (down side) termini occupy essentially the same positions in the A- and F-pockets, respectively (C) A typical 13-mer peptide in "bulged" conformation (orange chain) confined to the interface area between its cognate HLA-B*35:08 protein (alpha chain, green; beta-micro-globulin, blue) and the T-cell receptor (alpha chain, wheat; beta-chain, lemon). PDB ID: 2ak4 (D) The elongated 17-residue epitope (blue chain, LNKHIDAYKTFPPTEPK) bound to HLA from MHC Class I (green ribbon), with the N-terminal part arranged outside the A-pocket. The C-terminal part is bound in the F-pocket of the binding groove. The binding mode of the core epitope KTFPPTEPK (orange chain) is also shown. (Bottom) Typical binding mode of an elongated epitope in the HLA protein from MHC class II.

flexibility was mostly concentrated in the middle part of the epitope sequences, whereas the motion of terminal residues was restricted, in agreement with the possibility of "bulged" conformations. Based on these similarities and common canonical structural properties in HLA-peptide binary complexes, we generated 3D structures of the epitopes that are listed in Table 4.4 in their bound conformations. These epitope molecules were built using ~150 residue backbone templates taken from epitope structures that were collected in SCEptRe and AutoPeptiDB, and available in the PDB.

Theoretically, six types of peptide-MHC structures were possible: (1) peptide-HLA (MHC I), (2) peptide-HLA (MHC II), (3) peptide-HLA-TCR (MHC I), (4) peptide-HLA-TCR (MHC II), (5) peptide-HLA-BCR (MHC I), and (6) peptide-HLA-BCR (MHC II). In this study, types 1, 2, and 3 were considered. We modeled the binding of the epitopes to different HLA proteins from MHC class I and II, and to HLA-TCR (MHC I). In the peptide-HLA-TCR type of binding, the docking scores were mostly higher (as compared to the binary peptide-HLA complexes). This was because epitope molecules were confined to the interface area between their cognate HLA/TCR proteins (Figure 4.5(c)). This mode of binding implies that that N- and C-termini are bound to the HLA surface, whereas middle residues interact with TCR. Using the crystal structure of the nonapeptide KTFPPTEPK bound to HLA-A*1101 (PDB ID 1×7q) as the reference state, we performed an extensive conformational sampling and docking study of this complex. We demonstrated that the top-score docking peptide conformations were clustered around the native conformation, with an estimated energy −9.97 kcal/mol (corresponding to the nanomolar affinity range). Moreover, we found similar binding energies (~−9.5 kcal/mol) in docking simulations of KTFPPTEPK binding with HLA-A*02:01 (epitopes from Table 4.4). Therefore, the computational protocol we used (see Methods) enabled: (1) the generation of a library of immunogenic sequences, and (2) structure-based selection of appropriate candidates using docking to multiple HLA structural templates. This approach was applied to all of the epitopes listed in Table 4.4. Some of these immunogenic sequences constitute overlapping sites. For example, the sequence of the reference nonapeptide (KTFPPTEPK) was identical to region Lys362–Lys370 in the SARS-CoV nucleocapsid protein. In the SARS-CoV-2 variant, this motif was predicted in the epitope sequences LNKHIDAYKTFPPTEPK, KHIDAYKTFPPTEPKKDKKK, and YKTFPPTEPKKDKKKK, corresponding to positions Lys361 to Lys369 (Figure 4.5(a), sky-blue area on the nucleocapsid protein surface). The nonapeptide KTFPPTEPK has demonstrated high-affinity binding to the protein from MHC Class I, whereas its interaction with the HLA-DRB1 (from MHC Class II) is less pronounced (estimated binding energy is ~−6–7 kcal/mol). Vice versa, extended peptides LNKHIDAYKTFPPTEPK (length 17), KHIDAYKTFPPTEPKKDKKK (length 20), and YKTFPPTEPKKDKKKK (length 16) do not fit HLA binding sites in HLAs from MHC Class I. Interestingly, we found that the core part (KTFPPTEPK) of the LNKHIDAYKTFPPTEPK peptide can bind to the recognition site of HLA proteins from MHC Class I (~−7 to 8 kcal/mol), whereas the N-terminal part of this 17-residue peptide is arranged outside the A-pocket. The C-terminal part was found to occupy the F-pocket of the binding site (Figure 4.5(d)). In agreement with the well-known binding mode in the peptide-MHC class II system, the 17-residue peptide LNKHIDAYKTFPPTEPK demonstrated high-affinity docking scores, ~−9 to 10 kcal/mol, in interaction with DRB1 proteins. Accordingly, our molecular docking studies imply that peptides consisting of 9–11 amino acids were mostly recognized by MHC Class I molecules, whereas longer sequences tend to target the MHC Class II system (Figure 4.5(e)). We predicted the MHC-I processing of identified immunodominant epitopes (Table 4.4) for all of the available MHC alleles of HLA-A, HLA-B, and HLA-Cusing the IEDB tool (http://tools.iedb.org/processing/) (Vita et al., 2019), and found that all of the immunodominant epitopes can undergo further proteolysis and recognition by MHC class I molecules (considering a processing score >1). Therefore, the core part of immunodominant epitopes with longer sequence lengths can be presented by MHC class I molecules after proteasomal processing.

SUPPORT VECTOR MACHINE TO PREDICT B-CELL

A method for predicting linear B-cell epitopes using a support vector machine (SVM) a machine learning method used in this section. Although the performance of SVM-based classifiers largely depends on the selection of the kernel function, there are no theoretical foundations for choosing good kernel functions in a data-dependent way. Therefore, one objective of this study was to explore a class of kernel methods, namely string kernels, in addition to the widely used radial bias function (RBF) kernel. Our choice of string kernels was motivated by their successful application in a number of bioinformatics classification tasks, including protein remote homology detection (Leslie et al., 2004) protein structure prediction (Rangwala et al., 2007), protein binding site prediction (Wu et al., 2006), and major histocompatibility complex (MHC) binding peptide prediction (Salomon & Flower, 2006). In addition, we introduce the subsequence kernel (SSK), which has been successfully used in text classification (Lodhi et al., 2002), but has been under-explored in macromolecular sequence classification applications. Our empirical results demonstrate superior performance of SSK over other string kernels and the RBF kernel. Hence, we employed the SSK in building SVM classifiers for our proposed linear B-cell epitope prediction method, BCPred.

Data and Material

We obtained 2019-nCoV (SARS-CoV-2019) and SARS-CoV reference sequence data from NCBI GeneBank (NC_045512 and NC_004718) (Fan Wu et al., 2020; Lu et al., 2020). We then extracted the 2019-nCoV protein sequences of ORF1AB, S, ORF3A, E, M, ORF6, ORF7A, ORF7B, ORF8, N, and ORF10 based on the reference genome. Genomes with single protein are not included in the analysis.

Methodology

Support vector machines (SVMs) (Vapnik, 1995) are a class of supervised machine learning methods used for classification and regression. Given a set of labeled training data (x_i, y_i), where $x_i \in R^d$ and $y_i \in \{+1, -1\}$, training an SVM classifier involves finding a hyperplane that maximizes the geometric margin between positive and negative training data samples. The hyperplane is described as $f(x) = \langle w, x \rangle + b$, where w is a normal vector and b is a bias term. A test instance, x, is assigned a positive label if $f(x) > 0$, and a negative label otherwise. When the training data are not linearly separable, a kernel function is used to map nonlinearly separable data from the input space into a feature space. Given any two data samples x_i and x_j in an input space $\in R^d$, the kernel function K returns $K(x_i, x_j) = \langle \phi(x_i), \phi(x_j) \rangle$ where Φ is a nonlinear map from the input space X to the corresponding feature space. The kernel function K has the property that $K(x_i, x_j)$ can be computed without explicitly mapping x_i and x_j into the feature space, but instead, using their dot product $\langle x_i, x_j \rangle$ in the input space. Therefore, the kernel trick allows us to train a linear classifier, e.g., SVM, in a high-dimensional feature space where the data are assumed to be linearly separable without explicitly mapping each training example from the input space into the feature space. This approach relies implicitly on the selection of a feature space in which the training data are likely to be linearly separable (or nearly so) and explicitly on the selection of the kernel function to achieve such separability. Unfortunately, there is no single kernel that is guaranteed to perform well on every data set. Consequently, the SVM approach requires some care in selecting a suitable kernel and tuning the kernel parameters (if any).

String Kernels

String kernels (Haussler, 1999; Lodhi et al., 2002) are a class of kernel methods that have been successfully used in many sequence classification tasks (Leslie et al., 2004; Saigo et al., 2004). In these applications, a protein sequence is viewed as a string defined on a finite alphabet of 20 amino acids. In this work, we explore four string kernels: spectrum (Leslie et al., 2001), mismatch (Leslie et al., 2004), local alignment (Saigo et al., 2004), and subsequence (Leslie et al., 2001), in predicting linear B-cell epitopes. The subsequence kernel has proven useful in text classification and natural language processing (Clark et al., 2006). However, to the best of our knowledge, this kernel has not been previously explored in the context of macromolecular sequence classification problems. A brief description of the four kernels follows.

Spectrum Kernel

Let A denote a finite alphabet, e.g., 20 amino acids. x *and* y denote two strings defined on the alphabet A. For $k \geq 1$, the k−spectrum is defined as (Leslie et al., 2001):

$$\phi_k = \left(\varphi_\alpha (x) \right)_{\alpha \in A^k} \tag{4.1}$$

where φ_α is the number of occurrences of the k-length substring α in the sequence x. The k-spectrum kernel of the two sequences x and y is obtained by taking the dot product of the corresponding k spectra:

$$K_k^{spct} (x, y) = \langle \phi_k (x), \phi_k (y) \rangle \tag{4.2}$$

Intuitively, this kernel captures a simple notion of string similarity: two strings are deemed similar (i.e., have a high k-spectrum kernel value) if they share many of the same k-length substrings.

Mismatch Kernel

The mismatch kernel (Leslie et al., 2004) is a variant of the spectrum kernel in which inexact matching is allowed. Specifically, the (k, m)-mismatch kernel allows up to $m \leq k$ mismatches to occur when comparing two k-length substrings. Let α be a k-length substring, the (k, m)-mismatch feature map is defined on α as:

$$\phi_{(k,m)} (\alpha) = (\varphi_\beta (\alpha))_{\beta \in A^k} \tag{4.3}$$

where $\varphi_\beta(\alpha) = 1$ if $\beta \in N_{(k,m)(\alpha)}$, where β is the set of k-mer substrings that differs from α by at most m mismatches. Then, the feature map of an input sequence x is the sum of the feature vectors for k-mer substrings in x:

$$\phi_{(k,m)}(x) = \sum_{k-\text{mean } \alpha \text{ in } x} \phi_{(k,m)}(\alpha) \tag{4.4}$$

The (k, m)-mismatch kernel is defined as the dot product of the corresponding feature maps in the feature space:

$$K_k^{msmtch}(x,y) = \left\langle \phi_{(k,m)}(x), \phi_{(k,m)}(y) \right\rangle \tag{4.5}$$

It should be noted that the $(k, 0)$-mismatch kernel results in a feature space that is identical to that of the k-spectrum kernel. An efficient data structure for computing the spectrum and mismatch kernels in $O(|x|+|y|)$ and $O(k^{m+1}|A|^m(|x|+|y|))$, respectively, has been provided by Leslie et al. (2004).

Local Alignment Kernel

Local alignment (LA) kernel (Saigo et al., 2004) is a string kernel adapted for biological sequences. The LA kernel measures the similarity between two sequences by summing up scores obtained from gapped local alignments of the sequences. This kernel has several parameters: the gap opening and extension penalty parameters, d and e, the amino acid mutation matrix s, and the factor β, which controls the influence of suboptimal alignments on the kernel value. Detailed formulation of the LA kernel and a dynamic programming implementation of the kernel with running time complexity in $O(|x||y|)$ have been provided by Saigo et al. (2004).

Subsequence Kernel

The subsequence kernel (Leslie et al., 2004) generalizes the k-spectrum kernel by considering a feature space generated by the set of all (contiguous and non-contiguous) k-mer subsequences. For example, if we consider the two strings "act" and "acctct," the value returned by the spectrum kernel with k = 3 is 0. On the other hand, the (3, 1)-mismatch kernel will return 3 because the 3-mer substrings "acc," "cct," and "tct" have at most one mismatch when compared with "act." The subsequence kernel considers the set ("ac-t," "a-ct," "ac—t" "a-c– t," "a—ct") of non-contiguous substrings and returns a similarity score that is weighted by the length of each non-contiguous substring. Specifically, it uses a decay factor, $\lambda \leq 1$, to penalize non-contiguous substring matches. Therefore, the subsequence kernel with k = 3 will return $2\lambda^4 + 3\lambda^6$ when applied to "act" and "acctct" strings. More precisely, the feature map ϕ_k of a string x is given by

$$\phi_{(k,\lambda)}(x) = \left(\sum_{i:u=x[i]} \lambda^{l(i)} \right)_{u \in A^k} \tag{4.6}$$

where $u = x(i)$ denotes a substring in x where $1 \leq i_1 < \cdots < i_{|u|} \leq |x|$ such that $u_j = s_{ij}$, for $j = 1,\ldots, |u|$ and $l(i) = i_{|u|} - i_1 + l$ is the length of the subsequence in x. The subsequence kernel for two strings x and y is determined as the dot product of the corresponding feature maps:

$$K(x,y)^{sub}_{(k,\lambda)} = \langle \phi_{(k,\lambda)}(x), \phi_{(k,\lambda)}(y) \rangle$$

$$= \sum_{u \in A^k} \sum_{i:u=x[i]} \lambda^{l(i)} \sum_{j:u=y[j]} \lambda^{l(j)}$$

$$= \sum_{u \in A^k} \sum_{i:u=x[i]} \sum_{j:u=y[j]} \lambda^{l(i)+l(j)} \qquad (4.7)$$

This kernel can be computed using a recursive algorithm based on dynamic programming in $O(k|x||y|)$ time and space. The running time and memory requirements can be further reduced using techniques described by Seewald & Kleedorfer (2005).

Amino Acid Pairs Propensity Scale

Amino acid pairs (AAPs) are obtained by decomposing a protein/peptide sequence into its 2-mer subsequences (Chen et al., 2007) observed that some particular AAPs tend to occur more frequently in B-cell epitopes than in non-epitope peptides. Based on this observation, they developed an AAP propensity scale defined by:

$$\theta(\alpha) = log\left(\frac{f^+_\alpha}{f^-_\alpha}\right) \qquad (4.8)$$

where f^+_α and f^-_α are the occurrence frequencies of AAP α in the epitope and non-epitope peptide sequences, respectively. These frequencies have been derived from Bcipep (Saha et al., 2005) and Swissprot (Bairoch & Apweiler, 2000) databases, respectively. To avoid the dominance of an individual AAP propensity value, the scale in Equation (4.8) has been normalized to a $(-1, +1)$ interval through the following conversion:

$$\theta(\alpha) = 2\left(\frac{\theta(\alpha)-min}{max-min}\right) - 1 \qquad (4.9)$$

where max and min are the maximum and minimum values of the propensity scale before the normalization.

Chen et al. (2007) explored SVMs using two kernels: a dot product kernel applied to the average of the AAP scale values for all the AAPs in a peptide and an RBF kernel defined in a 400-dimensional feature space as follows:

$$\phi_{AAP}(x) = \left(\varphi_\alpha(x).\theta(\alpha)\right)_{\alpha \in A^2} \qquad (4.10)$$

where $\varphi_\alpha(x)$ is the number of occurrences of the 2-mer α in the peptide x. The optimal performance was obtained using the RBF kernel and a window of 20 amino acids (Chen et al., 2007).

Performance Evaluation

The prediction accuracy (ACC), sensitivity (Sn), specificity (Sp), and correlation coefficient (CC) are often used to evaluate prediction algorithms (Baldi et al., 2000). The CC measure has a value in the range from -1 to $+1$, and the closer the value to $+1$, the better the predictor. ACC, S_n, S_p, and CC are defined as follows:

$$ACC = \frac{TP + TN}{TP + FP + TN + FN} \tag{4.11}$$

$$S_n = \frac{TP}{TP + FN} \text{ and } S_p = \frac{TN}{TN + FP} \tag{4.12}$$

$$CC = \frac{TP \times TN - FP \times FN}{\sqrt{(TN + FN)(TN + FP)(TP + FN)(TP + FP)}} \tag{4.13}$$

where TP, FP, TN, and FN are the numbers of true positives, false positives, true negatives, and false negatives, respectively.

Although these metrics are widely used to assess the performance of machine learning methods, they all suffer from the important limitation of being threshold-dependent. Threshold-dependent metrics describe the classifier performance at a specific threshold value. It is often possible to increase the number of true positives (equivalently, sensitivity) of the classifier at the expense of an increase in false positives (equivalently, false alarm rate). The receiver operating characteristic (ROC) curve describes the performance of the classifier over all possible thresholds. The ROC curve is obtained by plotting the true positive rate as a function of the false positive rate or, equivalently, sensitivity versus (1-specificity) as the discrimination threshold of the binary classifier is varied. Each point on the ROC curve describes the classifier at a certain threshold value, i.e., at a particular choice of tradeoff between true positive rate and false positive rate. The area under ROC curve (AUC) is a useful summary statistic for comparing two ROC curves. AUC is defined as the probability that a randomly chosen positive example will be ranked higher than a randomly chosen negative example. An ideal classifier will have an AUC = 1, while a classifier assigning labels at random will have an AUC = 0.5, any classifier performing better than random will have an AUC value that lies between these two extremes.

Result

Potential B-Cell Epitopes of 2019-nCoV

We predicted likely human antibody binding sites (B-cell epitopes) on SARS and 2019-nCoV S protein with Disctope2. Our analysis focused on neutralizing binding sites by only examining residues 1–600. We scanned both spike protein structures with Discotope2 to identify potential antibody binding sites on the protein surface (Figure 4.6). For the SARS-CoV S protein, we identified a strong cluster of antibody sites (>30 residues, pink or red) on the receptor binding domain (RBD, the ACE2 interacting surface). Three independent studies (Guo et al., 2004; Hua et al., 2004; Yu et al., 2007) discovered B-cell epitopes in this region (blue) with a combination of in vitro and ex vivo approaches. Additionally, Discotope2 identifies residue 541–555 as another binding site, which was supported by two independent studies (Figure 4.6a, blue) (Guo et al., 2004; Yu et al., 2007. This gives us

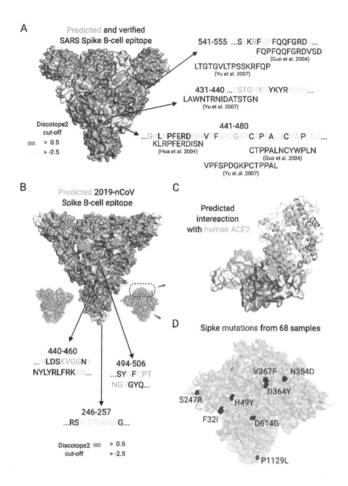

FIGURE 4.6 Predicted B-cell epitopes on SARS-CoV and 2019-nCoV spike (S) protein. 3D structures of both spike protein were scanned with Discotope2 to assess potential antibody binding sites (B-cell epitopes). Red indicates residues with score > 0.5 (cut-off for specificity of 90%), and pink indicates residues with score > –2.5 (cut-off for specificity of 80%). (A) The receptor binding domain (RBD) of SARS spike protein has concentrated high score residues and is comprised of two linear epitopes. One additional binding site is predicted to be around residue 541–555. Three independent experimental studies (Guo et al., 2004;Hua et al., 2004; Yu et al., 2007) identify patient antibodies recognize these three linear epitopes (blue). (B) 2019-nCoV spike protein is predicted to have a similar strong antibody binding site near RBD and an additional site around residue 246–257. (C) The predicted antibody binding site on 2019-nCov RBD potentially overlaps with the interacting surface for the known human entry receptor ACE2 (yellow). (D) Eight 2019-nCoV spike protein point mutations are present in a cohort of 68 viral samples. No mutations are near the ACE2 interacting surface. One mutation (S247R) occurs near one of the predicted antibody binding sites (residue 246–257).

some confidence in the ability of Discotope2 to predict B-cell epitopes if given an unknown protein structure.

For the 2019-nCoV S protein, Discotope2 identified a similar antibody binding site on S protein potential RBD, but with fewer residues (17 residues, Figure 4.6(b)). With computational protein-protein docking, we predicted one potential interacting conformation between the 2019-nCoV S protein and the human ACE2 entry receptor (Figure 4.6(c)). The

TABLE 4.6

Top Potential Epitopes for Key 2019-nCoV Proteins

Gene	Sequence	Position	MHC-I Cov.		MHC-II Cov.		Antibody
S	SYGFQPTNGVGYQPY	494	Yes	52%	Yes	100%	Yes
	SQSIIAYTMSLGAEN	689	Yes	74%	Yes	100%	No
	IPTNFTISVTTEILP	714	Yes	70%	Yes	100%	No
	AAAYYVGYLQPRTFL	262	Yes	65%	Yes	100%	No
	APHGVVFLHVTYVPA	1056	Yes	65%	Yes	100%	?
ORF1ab	DGEVITFDNLKTLLS	1547	Yes	83%	Yes	100%	No
	EVRTIKVFTTVDNIN	1564	Yes	78%	Yes	100%	No
	IINLVQMAPISAMVR	2368	Yes	78%	Yes	100%	No
	NPTTFHLDGEVITFD	1540	Yes	74%	Yes	100%	No
	VAAIFYLITPVHVMS	2783	Yes	74%	Yes	100%	No
M	IASFRLFARTRSMWS	97	Yes	65%	Yes	100%	?
N	ATKAYNVTQAFGRRG	264	Yes	74%	Yes	100%	?
E	VKPSFYVYSRVKNLN	52	Yes	74%	Yes	100%	?

Note: We ranked epitopes based on their likely coverage of presentation by MHC-I and MHC-II alleles. S protein 494–508 is highly ranked based on MHC presentation and is also one of the predicted top B-cell epitopes, localized near the S protein receptor binding domain (**Figure 4.6**). MHC-I coverage is calculated by the 9mer with the highest MHC-I coverage for each epitope (highlighted in orange). All candidates are likely to be presented by both MHC-I and MHC-II. A question mark (?) under the antibody column indicates that one or more SARS homolog of this peptide is a known B-cell epitope

main antibody binding site substantially overlaps with the interacting surface where ACE2 binds to S protein, and an antibody binding to this surface is likely to block viral entry into cells. Discotope2 identified anther antibody binding site (residue 246–257) different from SARS-CoV but with lower scores (>–2.5 raw scores).

We identified eight point mutation sites on S protein from a cohort of 68 2019-nCoV samples (Figure 4.6d). All mutations are apart from the protein S RBD, and one mutation (S247R) occurs near one of the predicted minor antibody binding site (residue 246-257) as shown in Table 4.6. In summary, we observed major structural and B-cell epitope similarity between SARS-CoV and 2019-nCoV spike proteins. A recent Cryo-EM study of 2019-nCoV S protein supports such structural similarity, and it would be informative to rerun our analysis once the Cryo-EM crystal structure becomes publicly available. RBDs in both proteins seem to be important B-cell epitopes for neutralizing antibodies, however, SARS-CoV appears to have larger attack surface than 2019-nCoV (Figure 4.6(a) and (b)). Fortunately, we have not observed any mutations altering binding sites for this major B-cell epitope in 2019-nCoV.

SVM Using the Subsequence Kernel Outperforms Other Kernel Methods and the AAP Method

In the first set of experiments, we used our homology-reduced data sets to evaluate SVMs trained using the spectrum kernel *at* $k = 1, 2,$ *and* 3, the (k, m)–mismatch kernel at (k, m) = (3, 1), (4, 1), (5, 1), and (5, 2), the LA kernel, and the subsequence kernel at $k = 2, 3,$ *and* 4. We compared

TABLE 4.7

Performance of Different Methods on Our BCP20 Homology-Reduced Data Set Using Fivefold Cross-Validation. BCPred Method Denotes

Method	ACC(%)	Sn(%)	Sp(%)	CC	AUC
K_1^{spct}	62.62	60.63	64.62	0.253	0.681
K_2^{spct}	58.56	59.49	57.63	0.171	0.614
K_3^{spct}	64.12	63.2	65.05	0.283	0.66
$K_{(3,1)}^{\text{msmtch}}$	48.86	50.5	47.22	−0.023	0.468
$K_{(4,1)}^{\text{msmtch}}$	55.35	54.64	56.06	0.107	0.593
$K_{(5,1)}^{\text{msmtch}}$	64.91	62.05	67.76	0.299	0.683
$K_{(5,2)}^{\text{msmtch}}$	55.85	55.35	56.35	0.117	0.584
LA	64.76	61.63	67.9	0.296	0.696
$K_{(2,0.5)}^{\text{sub}}$	62.62	62.34	62.91	0.253	0.664
$K_{(3,0.5)}^{\text{sub}}$	65.83	67.48	64.19	0.317	0.722
BCPred	67.9	72.61	63.2	0.36	0.758
RBF	57.28	57.49	57.06	0.146	0.617
AAP	64.05	52.92	75.18	0.288	0.7

the performance of the four string kernels to that of the RBF kernel trained using a binary representation of the data in which each amino acid is represented by a 20-bit binary string. In addition, we evaluated our implementation of the AAP method (Chen et al., 2007) on our data sets. For all methods, the performance was evaluated using fivefold cross validation. Because it is not feasible to include the complete set of results in this paper, we report only the results on the 20-mer peptides data set, BCP20, and provide the results on data sets BCP18, BCP16, BCP14, and BCP12 in the Supplementary Materials.

Table 4.7 compares the performance of different kernel-based SVM classifiers on BCP20 data set. The subsequence kernel has the best overall performance, in terms of AUC. The $(5, 1)-$ mismatch kernel performs slightly better than the k-spectrum kernel, and the performance of k-spectrum kernel with $k = 1$ and $k = 3$ is much better than its performance with $k = 2$. The performance of both the k-spectrum and (k, m)-mismatch kernels appears to be very sensitive to the choice of k and m parameters, because for some choices of k and m, the classifier performance deteriorates to that expected for random assignment of labels to test instances. In contrast, the performance of the subsequence kernel appears to be much less sensitive to the choice of parameter k.

Our implementation of the AAP method (Chen et al., 2007) has the second best overall performance and demonstrates the highest specificity. The LA kernel is very competitive in performance with AAP. Interestingly, the AAP significantly outperforms the RBF kernel trained using data in its binary representation. The AAP method is essentially an RBF kernel trained on the same data but using a different representation in which each peptide is represented by a vector of 400 numeric values computed based on the AAP propensity scale. The significant difference observed in performance of these two RBF-based methods highlights the importance of the data representation in kernel methods. All of these observations hold not only for the BCP20 data set but also for the homology-reduced data sets of peptides with different lengths (see Supplementary Materials). Most of the methods

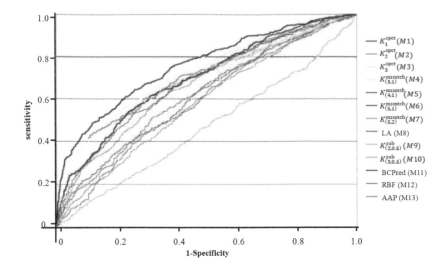

FIGURE 4.7 ROC curves for different prediction methods on BCP20 homology-reduced data set. BCPred method denotes $K_{(4,0.5)}^{sub}$. The BCPred ROC curve dominates all other ROC curves for any user selected threshold corresponding to specificity in the range of 100 to 20%.

have their best performance on BCP20 data set and show slight decreases in performance on data sets with decreasing peptide length.

Figure 4.7 shows the ROC curves for all methods evaluated in this experiment. The ROC curve for the subsequence kernel, $K_{(4,0.5)}^{sub}$, dominates the other ROC curves over a broad range of choices for the tradeoff between true positive and false positive rates. For any user-selected threshold corresponding to specificity in the range 100 to 20%, $K_{(4,0.5)}^{sub}$, has the best corresponding sensitivity. We conclude that BCPred, SVM-based classifier trained using the subsequence kernel $K_{(4,0.5)}^{sub}$, outperforms all other methods tested in predicting linear B-cell epitopes.

Statistical Analysis

We summarize statistical analysis of the results and conclusions presented in the preceding subsection. Specifically, we attempt to answer, from a statistical prospective, the following questions: is the performance of BCPred significantly different from those of other methods? Or more generally, how do the different B-cell epitope prediction methods compare with each other?

To answer these questions, we utilized multiple hypothesis comparisons (Fisher, 1956; Friedman, 1940) for comparing a set of classifiers on multiple data sets. We chose to use the AUC as the performance metric in these tests. Table 4.8 shows the AUC values of 13 classifiers on the five homology-reduced data sets.

One approach for performing multiple hypothesis comparisons over the results in Table 4.8, is to perform paired t-tests between each pair of classifiers at *p*-value equal to 0.05. However, when the number of classifiers being compared is large compared to the number of datasets, paired *t*-tests are susceptible to type I error, i.e., falsely concluding that the two methods significantly differ from each other in terms of performance when in fact they do not. To reduce the chance of type I errors, we used Bonferroni adjustments (Neter et al., 1996) in performing multiple comparisons. Specifically, two classifiers are considered different at 0.05 significance level, if the null hypothesis (that they are not different)

TABLE 4.8
AUC Values for Different Methods Evaluated on Homology-Reduced Data Sets

Method	BCP20	BCP18	BCP16	BCP14	BCP12	Avg
K_1^{spct}	0.681(6)	0.588(11)	0.652(7)	0.582(11)	0.591(10)	0.619(9)
K_2^{spct}	0.614(10)	0.636(8)	0.612(9)	0.597(9)	0.606(8)	0.613(8.8)
K_3^{spct}	0.660(8)	0.675(6)	0.645(8)	0.675(3)	0.636(6)	0.658(6.2)
$K_{(3,1)}^{msmtch}$	0.468(13)	0.465(13)	0.460(13)	0.506(13)	0.450(13)	0.470(13)
$K_{(4,1)}^{msmtch}$	0.593(11)	0.599(10)	0.569(11)	0.596(10)	0.548(11)	0.581(10.6)
$K_{(5,1)}^{msmtch}$	0.683(5)	0.691(4.5)	0.667(6)	0.649(6)	0.594(9)	0.657(6.1)
$K_{(5,2)}^{msmtch}$	0.584(12)	0.568(12)	0.563(12)	0.574(12)	0.535(12)	0.565(12)
LA	0.696(4)	0.691(4.5)	0.686(4)	0.671(4)	0.662(4)	0.681(4.1)
$K_{(2,0.5)}^{sub}$	0.664(7)	0.668(7)	0.681(5)	0.647(7)	0.643(5)	0.661(6.2)
$K_{(3,0.5)}^{sub}$	0.722(2)	0.726(2)	0.718(2)	0.697(2)	0.687(2)	0.710(2)
BCPred	0.758(1)	0.751(1)	0.730(1)	0.733(1)	0.709(1)	0.736(1)
RBF	0.617(9)	0.601(9)	0.594(10)	0.603(8)	0.620(7)	0.607(8.6)
AAP	0.700(3)	0.699(3)	0.689(3)	0.665(5)	0.663(3)	0.683(3.4)

Note: For each data set, the rank of each classifier is shown in parentheses

is rejected by a paired t-test at $0.05/12 = 0.0042$ confidence level (12 denotes the number of comparisons). Table 4.9 summarizes the results of Bonferroni-corrected tests comparing the performance of the classifiers. Significantly different pairs of classifiers are indicated with $a^{\times}$. The results in Table 4.9 show that the reported performance of BCPred is significantly different from the performance of other classifiers. On the other hand, the

TABLE 4.9
Results of Bonferroni Adjustments Using p-value = 0.0042

	M1	M2	M3	M4	M5	M6	M7	M8	M9	M10	M11	M12
K_1^{spct} (M1)												
K_2^{spct} (M2)	0											
K_3^{spct} (M3)	0	0										
$K_{(3,1)}^{msmtch}$ (M4)	0	×	×									
$K_{(4,1)}^{msmtch}$ (M5)	0	×	×	×								
$K_{(5,1)}^{msmtch}$ (M6)	0	0	0	×	×							
$K_{(5,2)}^{msmtch}$ (M7)	0	×	×	×	×	×						
LA (M8)	×	×	0	×	×	0	×					
$K_{(2,0.5)}^{sub}$ (M9)	0	×	0	×	×	0	×	×				
$K_{(3,0.5)}^{sub}$ (M10)	×	×	×	×	×	×	×	×	×			
BCPred (M11)	×	×	×	×	×	×	×	×	×	×		
RBF (M12)	0	0	0	×	0	0	×	×	0	×	×	
AAP (M13)	×	×	0	×	×	0	×	0	×	0	×	×

Note: "×" Indicates that the corresponding pair of methods is significantly different differences between the performance of K_3^{spct}, $K_{(5,1)}^{msmtch}$, LA, and $K_{(3,0.5)}^{sub}$ classifiers and the performance of AAP are not statistically significant.

A second approach for performing multiple hypothesis comparisons over the results in Table 4.8 is to use non-parametric tests. Demšar (2006) has suggested that non-parametric tests should be preferred over parametric tests for comparing machine learning algorithms because the non-parametric tests, unlike parametric tests, do not assume normal distribution of the samples (e.g., the data sets). Demšar suggested a three-step procedure for performing multiple hypothesis comparisons using non-parametric tests. First, the classifiers being compared are ranked on the basis of their observed performance on each data set (see Table 4.8). Second, Friedman test is applied to determine whether the measured average ranks are significantly different from the mean rank under the null hypothesis. Third, if the null hypothesis can be rejected at 0.05 significance level, the Nemenyi test is used to determine whether significant differences exist between any given pair of classifiers. Unfortunately, this procedure requires the number of data sets to be greater than ten and the number of methods to be greater than five (Demšar, 2006). Because we have 13 classifiers to compare and only five data sets, we cannot use this procedure. However, as noted by Demšar (2006), the average ranks by themselves provide a reasonably fair comparison of classifiers. Hence, we use average ranks to compare BCPred with the other methods. As shown in Table 4.8, BCPred and $K_{(3,0.5)}^{sub}$ have average ranks 1 and 2, respectively, followed by AAP and LA kernel with average ranks 3.4 and 4.1.

In summary, the results reported in Table 4.8 along with the statistical analysis of the results lend support to the conclusion summarized in the preceding subsection that the performance of BCPred is superior to that of the other 12 methods.

Identifying B-cell Epitopes in the Receptor-Binding Domain of SARS-CoV Spike Protein

Since its outbreak in 2002, the development of an effective and safe vaccine against Severe Acute Respiratory Syndrome Coronavirus (SARS-CoV) has become an urgent need for preventing future worldwide outbreak of SARS, a life threatening disease (Drosten et al., 2003; Fouchier et al., 2003; Ksiazek et al., 2003). Infection by SARS-CoV is initiated by the binding of its spike (S) protein to its functional receptor, angiotensin-converting enzyme 2 (ACE2), which is expressed on the surface of host cells (Dimitrov, 2003). The S protein comprises 1255 amino acids and consists of two functional domains: S1 (residues 1–667) and S2 (residues 668–1255) (Feihong Wu et al., 2006). The S1 domain is responsible for binding to receptors on target cells (Li et al., 2003) and the S2 domain contributes to the subsequence fusion between viral envelope and cellular membrane (Beniac et al., 2006). In addition, the S2 domain contains two highly conserved heptad repeat (HR) regions, HR1 and HR2 correspond to amino acid residues 915–949 and 1150–1184, respectively (Sainz et al., 2005). Several studies reported that the receptor-binding domain (RBD), residues 318–510, is an attractive target for developing SARS-CoV vaccine because blocking the binding of S1 domain to cellular receptors can prevent envelope fusion and virus entry mediated by the S2 domain (Prabakaran et al., 2006; Sui et al., 2004). Based on these findings, we surveyed the literature to collect previously identified epitopes within the RBD fragment of the SARS-CoV S protein. The collected epitopes are summarized in Table 4.8. None of these epitopes appears in our training data sets. Because epitope SP3 is included within the epitope (434–467) (GNYNYKYRYLKHGKLRPFERDISNVPFSPDGKPC) reported by Lien et al. (2007), we omitted the longer epitope.

```
  1        11        21        31        41        51        60
  |         |         |         |         |         |         |
NITNLCPFGEVFNATKFPSVYAWERKKISNCVADYSVLYNSTFFSTFKCYGVSATKLNDL 60
...............EEEEEEEEEEEEEEEEEE........................
CFSNVYADSFVVKGDDVRQIAPGQTGVIADYNYKLPDDFMGCVLAWNTRNIDATSTGNYN 120
..........................................EEEEEEEEEEEEEEEEEE
YKYRYLKHGKLRPFERDISNVPFSPDGKPCTPPALNCYWPLNDYGFYTTTGIGYQPYRVV 180
..................EEEEEEEEEEEEEEEE.EEEEEEEEEEEEEEEEEE......
VLSFELLNAPATV 193
.............


  1        11        21        31        41        51        60
  |         |         |         |         |         |         |
NITNLCPFGEVFNATKFPSVYAWERKKISNCVADYSVLYNSTFFSTFKCYGVSATKLNDL 60
...............EEEEEEEEEEEEEEEEEE........................
CFSNVYADSFVVKGDDVRQIAPGQTGVIADYNYKLPDDFMGCVLAWNTRNIDATSTGNYN 120
..EEEEEEEEEEEEEEEE....................................EEEEEEE
YKYRYLKHGKLRPFERDISNVPFSPDGKPCTPPALNCYWPLNDYGFYTTTGIGYQPYRVV 180
EEEEEEEE........EEEEEEEEEEEEEEEE...........EEEEEEEEEEEEEEEE
VLSFELLNAPATV 193
E............
```

FIGURE 4.8 BCPREDS server predictions of epitopes within the RBD of SARS-CoV S protein, made using BCPred (top) and AAP (bottom). Experimentally identified epitopes are underlined. "E" indicates that the corresponding amino acid residue lies in a predicted linear B-cell epitope.

We submitted 193 residues comprising the RBD region of SARS-CoV S protein (residues 318–510 according to accession AAT74874) to the BCPREDS, ABCPred, and Bepipred servers. For BCPREDS, we used the default specificity threshold (75%) and set the epitope length to 16 residues. For the other two servers, we used the default settings. Figure 4.8 shows the BCPred (top) and AAP (bottom) predictions returned by BCPREDS. Four of the B-cell epitopes predicted by BCPred overlap with epitopes that have been identified in the antigenic regions of RBD of SARS-CoV S protein through experiments. Three of the five epitopes predicted by AAP have substantial overlap with the SP1, SP2, and SP5 epitopes, and the fourth partially overlaps epitopes SP2 and SP3; the fifth does not overlap with any experimentally reported epitopes. In contrast, the ABCPred server, using default parameters, returned 22 predictions covering almost the entire query sequence. BepiPred returned nine predicted variable-length epitopes, but only three of them are longer than four residues in length. Two out of these four epitopes overlap with experimentally reported epitopes. The complete ABCPred and BepiPred predictions are provided in the Supplementary Materials. In evaluating these results, it is worth noting that a high false positive rate is more problematic than an occasional false negative prediction in the B-cell epitope prediction task (Söllner & Mayer, 2006), because a major goal of B-cell epitope prediction tools is to reduce the time and expense of wet lab experiments.

REFERENCES

Bairoch, A., & Apweiler, R. (2000). The SWISS-PROT protein sequence database and its supplement TrEMBL in 2000. *Nucleic Acids Research, 28*(1), 45–48.

Beniac, D. R., Andonov, A., Grudeski, E., & Booth, T. F. (2006). Architecture of the SARS coronavirus prefusion spike. *Nature Structural & Molecular Biology, 13*(8), 751–752.

Bhasin, M., & Raghava, G. P. S. (2004). Prediction of CTL epitopes using QM, SVM and ANN techniques. *Vaccine, 22*(23–24), 3195–3204.

Blackwell, J. M., Jamieson, S. E., & Burgner, D. (2009). HLA and infectious diseases. *Clinical Microbiology Reviews, 22*(2), 370–385.

Chen, J., Liu, H., Yang, J., & Chou, K.-C. (2007). Prediction of linear B-cell epitopes using amino acid pair antigenicity scale. *Amino Acids*, *33*(3), 423–428.

Clark, A., Florêncio, C. C., Watkins, C., & Serayet, M. (2006). Planar languages and learnability. *International Colloquium on Grammatical Inference*, 148–160.

Cui, Z., Chang, H., Wang, H., Lim, B., Hsu, C.-C., Yu, Y., Jia, H., Wang, Y., Zeng, Y., & Ji, M. (2020). Development of a rapid test kit for SARS-CoV-2: An example of product design. *Bio-Design and Manufacturing*, 1.

Davis, M. M., & Bjorkman, P. J. (1988). T-cell antigen receptor genes and T-cell recognition. *Nature*, *334*(6181), 395–402.

Demšar, J. (2006). Statistical comparisons of classifiers over multiple data sets. *Journal of Machine Learning Research*, *7*(Jan), 1–30.

Dimitrov, D. S. (2003). The secret life of ACE2 as a receptor for the SARS virus. *Cell*, *115*(6), 652–653.

Dimitrov, I., Bangov, I., Flower, D. R., & Doytchinova, I. (2014). AllerTOP v. 2—A server for in silico prediction of allergens. *Journal of Molecular Modeling*, *20*(6), 2278.

Doytchinova, I. A., & Flower, D. R. (2007). VaxiJen: a server for prediction of protective antigens, tumour antigens and subunit vaccines. *BMC Bioinformatics*, *8*(1), 4.

Drosten, C., Günther, S., Preiser, W., Van Der Werf, S., Brodt, H.-R., Becker, S., Rabenau, H., Panning, M., Kolesnikova, L., & Fouchier, R. A. M. (2003). Identification of a novel coronavirus in patients with severe acute respiratory syndrome. *New England Journal of Medicine*, *348*(20), 1967–1976.

Fisher, R. A. (1956). *Statistical methods and scientific inference.*

Fleri, W., Paul, S., Dhanda, S. K., Mahajan, S., Xu, X., Peters, B., & Sette, A. (2017). The immune epitope database and analysis resource in epitope discovery and synthetic vaccine design. *Frontiers in Immunology*, *8*, 278.

Fouchier, R. A. M., Kuiken, T., Schutten, M., Van Amerongen, G., Van Doornum, G. J. J., Van Den Hoogen, B. G., Peiris, M., Lim, W., Stöhr, K., & Osterhaus, A. D. M. E. (2003). Koch's postulates fulfilled for SARS virus. *Nature*, *423*(6937), 240.

Friedman, M. (1940). A comparison of alternative tests of significance for the problem of m rankings. *The Annals of Mathematical Statistics*, *11*(1), 86–92.

Grifoni, A., Sidney, J., Zhang, Y., Scheuermann, R. H., Peters, B., & Sette, A. (2020). A sequence homology and bioinformatic approach can predict candidate targets for immune responses to SARS-CoV-2. *Cell Host & Microbe.*

Guan, M., Chen, H. Y., Foo, S. Y., Tan, Y.-J., Goh, P.-Y., & Wee, S. H. (2004). Recombinant protein-based enzyme-linked immunosorbent assay and immunochromatographic tests for detection of immunoglobulin G antibodies to severe acute respiratory syndrome (SARS) coronavirus in SARS patients. *Clinical and Diagnostic Laboratory Immunology*, *11*(2), 287–291.

Guo, J.-P., Petric, M., Campbell, W., & McGeer, P. L. (2004). SARS corona virus peptides recognized by antibodies in the sera of convalescent cases. *Virology*, *324*(2), 251–256.

Gupta, S., Kapoor, P., Chaudhary, K., Gautam, A., Kumar, R., Raghava, G. P. S., & Consortium, O. S. D. D. (2013). In silico approach for predicting toxicity of peptides and proteins. *PloS One*, *8*(9), e73957.

Haussler, D. (1999). *Convolution kernels on discrete structures.* Technical report, Department of Computer Science, University of California.

Hsueh, P.-R., Huang, L.-M., Chen, P.-J., Kao, C.-L., & Yang, P.-C. (2004). Chronological evolution of IgM, IgA, IgG, and neutralisation antibodies after infection with SARS-associated coronavirus. *Clinical Microbiology and Infection*, *10*(12), 1062–1066.

Hua, R., Zhou, Y., Wang, Y., Hua, Y., & Tong, G. (2004). Identification of two antigenic epitopes on SARS-CoV spike protein. *Biochemical and Biophysical Research Communications*, *319*(3), 929–935.

Jespersen, M. C., Peters, B., Nielsen, M., & Marcatili, P. (2017). BepiPred-2.0: Improving sequence-based B-cell epitope prediction using conformational epitopes. *Nucleic Acids Research*, *45*(W1), W24–W29.

Jurtz, V., Paul, S., Andreatta, M., Marcatili, P., Peters, B., & Nielsen, M. (2017). NetMHCpan-4.0: Improved peptide–MHC class I interaction predictions integrating eluted ligand and peptide binding affinity data. *The Journal of Immunology*, *199*(9), 3360–3368.

Koczula, K. M., & Gallotta, A. (2016). Lateral flow assays. *Essays in Biochemistry*, *60*(1), 111–120.

Kogaki, H., Uchida, Y., Fujii, N., Kurano, Y., Miyake, K., Kido, Y., Kariwa, H., Takashima, I., Tamashiro, H., & Ling, A. (2005). Novel rapid immunochromatographic test based on an enzyme immunoassay for detecting nucleocapsid antigen in SARS-associated coronavirus. *Journal of Clinical Laboratory Analysis*, *19*(4), 150–159.

Ksiazek, T. G., Erdman, D., Goldsmith, C. S., Zaki, S. R., Peret, T., Emery, S., Tong, S., Urbani, C., Comer, J. A., & Lim, W. (2003). A novel coronavirus associated with severe acute respiratory syndrome. *New England Journal of Medicine*, *348*(20), 1953–1966.

Lata, S., Bhasin, M., & Raghava, G. P. S. (2007). Application of machine learning techniques in predicting MHC binders. In *Immunoinformatics* (pp. 201–215). Springer.

Leslie, C., Eskin, E., & Noble, W. S. (2001). The spectrum kernel: A string kernel for SVM protein classification. In *Biocomputing 2002* (pp. 564–575). World Scientific.

Leslie, C. S., Eskin, E., Cohen, A., Weston, J., & Noble, W. S. (2004). Mismatch string kernels for discriminative protein classification. *Bioinformatics*, *20*(4), 467–476.

Li, W., Moore, M. J., Vasilieva, N., Sui, J., Wong, S. K., Berne, M. A., Somasundaran, M., Sullivan, J. L., Luzuriaga, K., & Greenough, T. C. (2003). Angiotensin-converting enzyme 2 is a functional receptor for the SARS coronavirus. *Nature*, *426*(6965), 450–454.

Li, Z., Yi, Y., Luo, X., Xiong, N., Liu, Y., Li, S., Sun, R., Wang, Y., Hu, B., & Chen, W. (2020). Development and clinical application of a rapid IgM-IgG combined antibody test for SARS-CoV-2 infection diagnosis. *Journal of Medical Virology*.

Lien, S.-P., Shih, Y.-P., Chen, H.-W., Tsai, J.-P., Leng, C.-H., Lin, M.-H., Lin, L.-H., Liu, H.-Y., Chou, A.-H., & Chang, Y.-W. (2007). Identification of synthetic vaccine candidates against SARS CoV infection. *Biochemical and Biophysical Research Communications*, *358*(3), 716–721.

Lippi, G., Salvagno, G. L., Pegoraro, M., Militello, V., Caloi, C., Peretti, A., Gaino, S., Bassi, A., Bovo, C., & Cascio, G. Lo. (2020). Assessment of immune response to SARS-CoV-2 with fully automated MAGLUMI 2019-nCoV IgG and IgM chemiluminescence immunoassays. *Clinical Chemistry and Laboratory Medicine (CCLM)*, *1*(ahead-of-print).

Lodhi, H., Saunders, C., Shawe-Taylor, J., Cristianini, N., & Watkins, C. (2002). Text classification using string kernels. *Journal of Machine Learning Research*, *2*(Feb), 419–444.

Lu, R., Zhao, X., Li, J., Niu, P., Yang, B., Wu, H., Wang, W., Song, H., Huang, B., & Zhu, N. (2020). Genomic characterisation and epidemiology of 2019 novel coronavirus: implications for virus origins and receptor binding. *The Lancet*, *395*(10224), 565–574.

Lucas, M., Karrer, U. R. S., Lucas, A., & Klenerman, P. (2001). Viral escape mechanisms–escapology taught by viruses. *International Journal of Experimental Pathology*, *82*(5), 269–286.

Moran, A., Beavis, K. G., Matushek, S. M., Ciaglia, C., Francois, N., Tesic, V., & Love, N. (2020). The detection of SARS-CoV-2 using the cepheid xpert xpress SARS-CoV-2 and Roche cobas SARS-CoV-2 assays. *Journal of Clinical Microbiology*.

Neter, J., Kutner, M. H., Nachtsheim, C. J., & Wasserman, W. (1996). *Applied linear statistical models*.

Oh, J.-S., Ha, G.-W., Cho, Y.-S., Kim, M.-J., An, D.-J., Hwang, K.-K., Lim, Y.-K., Park, B.-K., Kang, B., & Song, D.-S. (2006). One-step immunochromatography assay kit for detecting antibodies to canine parvovirus. *Clinical and Vaccine Immunology*, *13*(4), 520–524.

Patronov, A., & Doytchinova, I. (2013). T-cell epitope vaccine design by immunoinformatics. *Open Biology*, *3*(1), 120139.

Paul, S., Sidney, J., Sette, A., & Peters, B. (2016). TepiTool: A pipeline for computational prediction of T cell epitope candidates. *Current Protocols in Immunology*, *114*(1), 18–19.

Paul, S., Weiskopf, D., Angelo, M. A., Sidney, J., Peters, B., & Sette, A. (2013). HLA class I alleles are associated with peptide-binding repertoires of different size, affinity, and immunogenicity. *The Journal of Immunology*, *191*(12), 5831–5839.

Posthuma-Trumpie, G. A., Korf, J., & van Amerongen, A. (2009). Lateral flow (immuno) assay: its strengths, weaknesses, opportunities and threats. A literature survey. *Analytical and Bioanalytical Chemistry*, *393*(2), 569–582.

Powell, A. M., & Black, M. M. (2001). Epitope spreading: Protection from pathogens, but propagation of autoimmunity? *Clinical and Experimental Dermatology*, *26*(5), 427–433.

Prabakaran, P., Gan, J., Feng, Y., Zhu, Z., Choudhry, V., Xiao, X., Ji, X., & Dimitrov, D. S. (2006). Structure of severe acute respiratory syndrome coronavirus receptor-binding domain complexed with neutralizing antibody. *Journal of Biological Chemistry, 281*(23), 15829–15836.

Rangwala, H., DeRonne, K., & Karypis, G. (2007). Protein structure prediction using string kernels. *Knowledge Discovery in Bioinformatics: Techniques, Methods, and Applications* (pp. 145–168). *Hoboken, NJ: John Wiley & Sons, Inc.*

Saha, S., Bhasin, M., & Raghava, G. P. S. (2005). Bcipep: A database of B-cell epitopes. *BMC Genomics, 6*(1), 1–7.

Saha, S., & Raghava, G. P. S. (2006a). AlgPred: Prediction of allergenic proteins and mapping of IgE epitopes. *Nucleic Acids Research, 34*(suppl_2), W202–W209.

Saha, S., & Raghava, G. P. S. (2006b). Prediction of continuous B-cell epitopes in an antigen using recurrent neural network. *Proteins: Structure, Function, and Bioinformatics, 65*(1), 40–48.

Saigo, H., Vert, J.-P., Ueda, N., & Akutsu, T. (2004). Protein homology detection using string alignment kernels. *Bioinformatics, 20*(11), 1682–1689.

Sainz, B., Rausch, J. M., Gallaher, W. R., Garry, R. F., & Wimley, W. C. (2005). Identification and characterization of the putative fusion peptide of the severe acute respiratory syndrome-associated coronavirus spike protein. *Journal of Virology, 79*(11), 7195–7206.

Salomon, J., & Flower, D. R. (2006). Predicting Class II MHC-Peptide binding: a kernel based approach using similarity scores. *BMC Bioinformatics, 7*(1), 501.

Seewald, A. K., & Kleedorfer, F. (2005). *Lambda pruning: an approximation of the string subsequence kernel*. Technical report, Technical Report, Osterreichisches Forschungsinstitut fur.

Singh, H., Ansari, H. R., & Raghava, G. P. S. (2013). Improved method for linear B-cell epitope prediction using antigen's primary sequence. *PLoS One, 8*(5), e62216.

Söllner, J., & Mayer, B. (2006). Machine learning approaches for prediction of linear B-cell epitopes on proteins. *Journal of Molecular Recognition: An Interdisciplinary Journal, 19*(3), 200–208.

Sui, J., Li, W., Murakami, A., Tamin, A., Matthews, L. J., Wong, S. K., Moore, M. J., Tallarico, A. S. C., Olurinde, M., & Choe, H. (2004). Potent neutralization of severe acute respiratory syndrome (SARS) coronavirus by a human mAb to S1 protein that blocks receptor association. *Proceedings of the National Academy of Sciences, 101*(8), 2536–2541.

Van Regenmortel, M. H. V. (2009). What is a B-cell epitope? In *Epitope Mapping Protocols* (pp. 3–20). Springer.

Vanderlugt, C. J., & Miller, S. D. (1996). Epitope spreading. *Current Opinion in Immunology, 8*(6), 831.

Vapnik, V. N. (1995). The nature of statistical learning. *Theory.*

Vashist, S. K. (2020). *In vitro diagnostic assays for COVID-19: Recent advances and emerging trends.* Multidisciplinary Digital Publishing Institute.

Vita, R., Mahajan, S., Overton, J. A., Dhanda, S. K., Martini, S., Cantrell, J. R., Wheeler, D. K., Sette, A., & Peters, B. (2019). The immune epitope database (IEDB): 2018 update. *Nucleic Acids Research, 47*(D1), D339–D343.

Wang, P., Sidney, J., Dow, C., Mothé, B., Sette, A., & Peters, B. (2008). A systematic assessment of MHC class II peptide binding predictions and evaluation of a consensus approach. *PLoS Computational Biology, 4*(4), e1000048.

West, C. P., Montori, V. M., & Sampathkumar, P. (2020). COVID-19 testing: The threat of false-negative results. *Mayo Clinic Proceedings, 95*(6), 1127–1129.

Wu, F., Olson, B., Dobbs, D., & Honavar, V. (2006). Comparing kernels for predicting protein binding sites from amino acid sequence. *The 2006 IEEE International Joint Conference on Neural Network Proceedings*, 1612–1616.

Wu, F., Zhao, S., Yu, B., Chen, Y.-M., Wang, W., Song, Z.-G., Hu, Y., Tao, Z.-W., Tian, J.-H., & Pei, Y.-Y. (2020). A new coronavirus associated with human respiratory disease in China. *Nature, 579*(7798), 265–269.

Yu, H., Jiang, L.-F., Fang, D.-Y., Yan, H.-J., Zhou, J.-J., Zhou, J.-M., Liang, Y., Gao, Y., Zhao, W., & Long, B.-G. (2007). Selection of SARS-coronavirus-specific B cell epitopes by phage peptide library screening and evaluation of the immunological effect of epitope-based peptides on mice. *Virology, 359*(2), 264–274.

Part III

COVID-19 Detection: Advanced Image Processing with Artificial Intelligence Techniques

5 Lung Function Testing (LFT) With Normal CT Scans and AI Algorithm

KEY POINTS

- A COVID-19 holistic, highly compact signature integrating imaging and clinical/biological attributes is presented.
- An automatic Short and Long-term prognosis is presented, offering complementary means to facilitate triage for COVID-19.
- Validation of model over multiple sites is important to establish its generalizablity.
- Both volume and radiomic features of pulmonary opacities are key to quantifying the extent of lung involvement.
- Autoencoders, unsupervised learning generative models, are used to reconstruct the input image.

INTRODUCTION

Coronavirus Disease 2019 (COVID-19) has become a global pandemic with an exponential growth rate and an incompletely understood transmission process. The virus is harbored most commonly with little or no symptoms, but can also lead to a rapidly progressive and often fatal pneumonia in 2–8% of those infected (Hoehl et al., 2020; Lai et al., 2020; Sohrabi et al., 2020). The exact mortality, prevalence, and transmission dynamics remain somewhat ill-defined in part due to the unique challenges presented by SARS-CoV-2 infection, such as peak infectiousness at or just preceding symptom onset and a poorly understood multi-organ pathophysiology with dominant features and lethality in the lungs (He et al., 2020). The rapid rate of spread has strained healthcare systems worldwide due to shortages in key protective equipment and qualified providers (Ranney et al., 2020), partially driven by variable access to point-of-care testing methodologies, including reverse transcription polymerase chain reaction (RT-PCR). As rapid RT-PCR testing becomes more available, challenges remain, including high false negative rates, delays in processing, variabilities in test techniques, and sensitivity sometimes reported as low as 60–70% (Fang et al., 2020; Yang et al., 2020).

Computed tomography (CT) is a test that provides a window into pathophysiology that could shed light on several stages of disease detection and evolution (Fang et al., 2020; Xie et al., 2020; Yu et al., 2020). While challenges continue with rapid diagnosis of COVID-19, frontline radiologists report a pattern of infection that is somewhat characteristic with typical features including ground glass opacities in the lung periphery, rounded opacities, enlarged intra-infiltrate vessels, and later more consolidations that are a sign of progressing critical illness. While CT and RT-PCR are most often concordant (Xie et al., 2020), CT can also detect early COVID-19 in patients with a negative RT-PCR test (Xie et al., 2020), in patients without symptoms, or before symptoms develop or after symptoms resolve (Ai et al., 2020; Jin et al., 2020). CT evaluation has been an integral part of the initial evaluation of patients with suspected or confirmed COVID-19 in multiple centers in Wuhan China and northern Italy (Sverzellati et al., 2020; Li & Xia, 2020; Zhao et al., 2020). A recent international expert consensus report supports the use of chest CT for COVID-19 patients with worsening respiratory status or in resource constrained environments for medical triage of patients who present with moderate–severe clinical features and a high pretest probability of COVID-19 (Rubin et al., 2020). However, these guidelines also recommend against using chest CT in screening or diagnostic settings in part due to similar radiographic presentation with other influenza-associated pneumonias. Techniques for distinguishing between these entities may strengthen support toward use of CT in diagnostic settings.

Due to the rapid increase in number of new and suspected COVID-19 cases, there may be a role for artificial intelligence (AI) approaches for the detection or characterization of COVID-19 on imaging. CT provides a clear and expeditious window into this process, and deep learning of large multinational CT data could provide automated and reproducible biomarkers for classification and quantification of COVID-19 disease. Artificial Intelligence using Deep Learning has been advocate for automated reading of COVID-19 CT scans, including diagnosing COVID-19 (Butt et al., 2020; Bai, et al., 2020b; Jin et al., 2020; Li et al., 2020; Ouyang et al., 2020; Song et al., 2020; Wang et al., 2020; Wang et al., 2020) and quantifying parenchymal involvement (Gozes et al., 2020; Mei et al., 2020; Shan et al., 2020; Zhang et al., 2020). Prior single center studies have demonstrated the feasibility of AI for the detection of COVID-19 infection, or even differentiation from community acquired pneumonia (Li et al., 2020; Wang et al., 2020). AI models are often severely limited in utility due to homogeneity of data sources, which in turn limits applicability to other populations, demographics, or geographies. While these studies illustrate the potential of AI algorithms, their practical value is debatable (Kundu et al., 2020). Without adhering to radiological reporting standards, it is doubtful whether these algorithms provide any real benefit in addition to or instead of manual reading, limiting their adoption in daily practice. Also, algorithms that follow a standardized scoring system need validation to confirm that they assign scores in a similar way to radiologists and can identify COVID-19 positive patients with similar or even better performance. The purpose of this study is to develop, evaluate and validate various deep learning techniques that automatically scores chest CT scans of patients using data from a globally diverse, multi-institution dataset with suspected COVID-19 according to the CT severity score systems.

GENERAL CONSIDERATION OF PFT FOR COVID-19

Pulmonary function tests (PFTs) are noninvasive tests that show how well the lungs are working. It is an important tool in the investigation and monitoring of patients with respiratory pathology. They provide important information relating to the large and small airways, the pulmonary parenchyma and the size and integrity of the pulmonary capillary bed. Although they do not provide a diagnosis per se, different patterns of abnormalities are seen in various respiratory diseases which helps to establish a diagnosis. Table 5.1 describe the indications for performing PFTs, describe abnormal results and correlate these with underlying pathology.

TABLE 5.1

Indications for Pulmonary Function Tests

S. No.	Indications	Examples
1	Investigation of patients with symptoms/ signs/ investigations that suggest pulmonary disease	Cough Wheeze Breathlessness Crackles Abnormal chest x-ray
2	Monitoring patients with known pulmonary disease for progression and response to treatment	Interstitial fibrosis COPD Asthma Pulmonary vascular disease
3	Investigation of patients with disease that may have a respiratory complications	Connective tissue disorders Neuromuscular diseases
4	Preoperative evaluation prior	Lung resection Abdominal surgery Cardiothoracic surgery
5	Evaluation patients a risk of lung diseases	Exposure to pulmonary toxins such a radiation, medication, or environmental or occupational exposure
6	Surveillance following lung transplantation to assess for	Acute rejection Infection Obliterate bronchiolitis

LUNG STRUCTURE

Lung structure was evaluated using CT scans. In children, a single detector CT scanner (Philips LX, Philips Medical Systems, Best, The Netherlands) was used from 1997 to 1999, and a multidetector row (four or eight rows of detectors) CT scanner after 1999 (General Electric Light Speed Ultra, GE Medical Systems, Milwaukee, WI, USA). Scans were obtained using a beam current of 120 mA, an exposure time of 0.5 s, and a beam potential of 120 kV from lung apex to base at 15 mm intervals using 1.25 mm thick slices. In adults, a PQ 6000 scanner (Picker International Inc, Highland Heights, OH, USA) was used throughout the study period. Scans were obtained using a beam current of 160 mA, a 1 s exposure time, and a beam potential of 120 kV from lung apex to lung base at 10 mm intervals using 1.5 mm thick slices.

All scans were reconstructed with a high spatial frequency algorithm (bone), printed (window width 1400 Hounsfield units (HU), window level 2400 HU), blinded to date and patient identification, and scored in random order by two independent experienced observers using an adapted scoring system recently developed by Brody et al. (2004). This scoring system evaluates the five lung lobes and the lingula as a sixth lobe for severity and extent of central and peripheral bronchiectasis, extent of central and peripheral mucous plugging, severity and extent of central and peripheral airway wall thickening, extent of opacities (atelectasis or consolidations), and extent of cysts and bullae. Hyperinflation (gas trapping) was excluded from scoring since not all scans had expiratory images and mosaic perfusion was scored instead. Ground glass pattern was not scored in this study. The maximum composite CT score without air trapping and ground glass pattern and with mosaic perfusion was 180 (Brody et al., 2004). In addition, component CT scores were calculated by adding the component scores from the six lobes. Maximal component scores for central bronchiectasis, peripheral bronchiectasis, central mucus, peripheral mucus, central airway wall thickening, peripheral airway wall thickening, opacities, mosaic perfusion, and cysts or bullae were 18. For statistical analysis the mean composite and component CT scores of both observers were expressed on a scale of 0–100 (percentage of maximum possible score).

LUNG FUNCTION

Conventional PFTs were done using a dry rolling seal spirometer (MasterLab, Jaeger, Wurzburg, and Germany). Forced vital capacity (FVC), forced expiratory volume in 1 second (FEV1), mid expiratory flow at 25% and 50% of VC (MEF25 and MEF50), residual volume (RV), and total lung capacity (TLC) were expressed as percentage of predicted values and as Z scores. The ratio between FEV1 and FVC and between RV and TLC was calculated and expressed as a percentage, as percentage predicted, and as a Z score. For children, prediction equations developed by Quanjer et al. (1995) were used for FEV1 and FVC and prediction equations developed by Zapletal et al. (1987) were used for MEF25, MEF50, RV, and TLC. For adults, prediction equations from the European Respiratory Society (Tammeling et al., 1993) were used for all parameters. Spirometric tests (FEV1, FVC, MEF25, and MEF50) were performed in all patients at each annual checkup. Plethysmography (RV and TLC) was performed in 106 of 119 patients (89%), 81 of 92 (88%), and 21 of 24 patients (88%) at the first, second, and third checkup, respectively.

REVIEW OF CHEST CT FINDINGS IN EARLY COVID-19 STUDIES

Numerous studies of COVID-19 cases have reported the appearance of typical imaging features on chest CT of confirmed cases that may be helpful in future screening. In addition, these features can be monitored through subsequent scans for determination of the effectiveness of the treatment. An initial study of 41 patients in Wuhan indicated that all patients demonstrated abnormalities in chest CT images, with 98% of the patients having bilateral involvement. Patients that had been admitted to the ICU exhibited bilateral multiple lobular and subsegmental areas of consolidation, while non-ICU patients showed bilateral ground-glass opacities (GGOs) and subsegmental areas of consolidation. Subsequent CT images showed bilateral GGOs but resolved consolidation (Huang et al., 2020). Another initial study of 81 patients admitted to one of two hospitals in Wuhan reported abnormal chest CT findings even in asymptomatic cases, with rapid evolution from focal unilateral to diffuse bilateral GGOs that progressed or coexisted with consolidations within one to three weeks (Shi et al., 2020). A study of 101 cases of COVID-19 from four institutions in Hunan, China also determined that most patients had GGOs or mixed GGOs and consolidation, vascular enlargement in the lesion(s), and traction bronchiectasis. In addition, lesions present were more likely to have a peripheral distribution and bilateral involvement, as well as exhibit lower lung predominance and a multifocal tendency (Zhao et al., 2020b). A study of an early casualty of a staff member of the Wuhan seafood market suspected of being the origin of the disease indicated patchy bilateral GGOs with peribronchial and peripheral/subpleural distribution (Qian et al., 2020). Another early study indicated multifocal nodular opacities in multiple lobes, and confirmed decreased density of the opacities and development of GGOs and reversed halo signs following six days of treatment. This study also reported that the initial laboratory testing was negative but a subsequent test was positive, which suggests that the CT may be more indicative in the early stages of the infection (Wu et al., 2020). A study of the passengers onboard the Diamond Princess cruise ship, on which the disease spread rapidly in early February of 2020, even found GGOs with partial consolidation on numerous asymptomatic patients that tested positive for COVID-19 (Inui et al., 2020).

Of 21 patients in another study, 71% had involvement of more than two lobes in the chest CT, 57% had GGOs, 33% had opacities with a rounded morphology, 33% had a peripheral distribution of disease, 29% had consolidation with GGOs, and 19% had crazy-paving patterns. A total of 14% of patients had normal CT scans, which likely supports the WHO statement that many cases are mild and asymptomatic. Another important note to make is the complete absence of lung cavitation, discrete pulmonary nodules, pleural effusions, and lymphadenopathy on all of the CT scans (Chung et al., 2020). Building upon that study, 121 patients were evaluated in a subsequent study and the results indicated that 56% of patients had a normal CT scan within the first two days of symptom onset. However, after a longer time, the CT findings were more frequent and consistent, including consolidation, bilateral and peripheral disease, greater total lung involvement, linear opacities, crazy-paving pattern, and the reverse halo sign. Bilateral lung involvement was observed in 28% of early patients (zero to two days after symptom onset), 76% of intermediate patients (3–5 days), and 88% of late patients (6–12 days) (Bernheim et al., 2020). One study found that chest CT demonstrated a low rate of 3.9% of missed diagnosis of COVID-19. The results also confirmed the above findings in reporting that 90% of scans in positive COVID-19 cases showed GGOs, with or without consolidation, as well as vascular enlargement in 82% of cases, interlobular septal thickening in a crazy-paving pattern in 70.6% of cases, and air bronchogram signs in 69% of cases (Li & Xia, 2020). A summary study of 919 patients with COVID-19 indicated GGOs in 88% of the cases, bilateral involvement in 87.5%, posterior involvement in 80.4%, multilobar involvement in 78.8%, peripheral distribution in 76%, and consolidation in 31.8% (Salehi et al., 2020). A study of 108 patients indicated GGOs in 60%, GGOs with consolidation in 41%, vascular thickening in 80%, crazy-paving pattern in 40%, air bronchogram in 48%, and halo sign in 64%. The distribution of the lung legions in 90% of cases was peripheral and the shape was patchy in 86% of the cases (Han et al., 2020). One study evaluated the difference in CT scans based on patient age groups. The stud confirmed that the most common features were patchy lesions and GGOs with or without consolidation in the 98 patients in their study. Patients older than 45 years of age had more bilateral lung, lung lobe, and lung field involvement as well as greater lesion numbers than patients less than 18. In addition, GGOs accompanied by interlobular septa thickening or a crazy-paving pattern, consolidation, and air bronchogram were more common in patients above 45 years than those less than 45 (Chen et al., 2020). These results may explain some of the small inconsistencies in the above studies, as the results are not differentiated by patient age. A recent study that compiled 147 publications from the China outbreak reported that of 8711 patients with COVID-19, over 95% of the patients had abnormal presentations on chest CT, with approximately 74% having bilateral infiltration, 73% peripheral distribution, 70% GGOs, and 30% consolidation. In addition, the reported mortality rate among all the patients in the studies was only 3% (Tang et al., 2020).

MONITORING THE SEVERITY AND PROGRESSION OF COVID-19 WITH CHEST CT

Studies investigating the CT imaging features based on the severity of the disease found that the severity is evident on the CT images based on the proliferation of the features. For example, bilateral involvement was seen in 50% of mild cases, 65% of common cases, and 100% of severe and critical cases. Also, GGOs, consolidation, and other typical COVID-19 markers ranged from not being seen in the mild cases to appearing in 100% of the critical cases (Liu et al., 2020). Studies specifically evaluating the use of CT in monitoring the progression of the disease over time emphasized the importance of follow-up CT scans, by demonstrating that the CT scans could be used to predict the prognosis of patients, as well as evaluate the treatment response of patients over the course of the disease. CT images from the studies indicated the typical features of COVID-19 in early scans and the alleviation of those features confirming the recovery of the patients. For example, in one study (Shi et al., 2020) evaluating the CT findings for 81 early patients in Wuhan details the progression of the disease for a 42-year-old woman from presentation at day three through the last image before discharge on day 18. The first image demonstrates multifocal consolidations affecting the bilateral, sub pleural lung parenchyma. By day seven, the extent of the lesions had increased, and they had become heterogeneous, with internal bronchovascular bundle thickening. Day 11 demonstrates previous opacifications dissipating into GGOs and irregular linear opacities. Finally, day 18 indicates further resolution of the lesions, and the patient was discharged two days later (Shi et al., 2020). Another study monitoring the progression of the disease in 21 rRT-PCR confirmed COVID-19 cases reported GGOs, crazy-paving patterns, and consolidation in the majority of patients, with a peak of disease around 10 days from the onset of initial symptoms. After the peak, they reported gradual resolution of consolidation and crazy-paving patterns (Pan et al., 2020). Another disease progression study also agreed with the studies above in finding GGOs in 85.6% of cases, mixed GGOs with consolidation in 62.7%, vascular enlargement in 78%, and bilateral lung involvement in 79.7% of the cases (Zhao et al., 2020a). One study presented a 36-week pregnant woman in Wuhan, China, in which comparison of the CT scan acquired two days after admission with the initial CT scan showed the progression of the disease. The decision was made from the scans to perform a Caesarean section, a decision which would have been much more difficult to make in the absence of CT (Chen et al., 2020).

CORRELATION OF TESTING WITH rRT-PCR AND CHEST CT

Specifically evaluating the effectiveness of rRT-PCR and chest CT, one study reported positive rates of 59 and 88%, respectively. Positive chest CT was identified through the existence of the typical features detailed in the previous sections. Using rRT-PCR as a reference, the sensitivity of chest CT was 97%. Analyzing both tests, 60–93% of patients had initial positive chest CT consistent with COVID-19 before the initial positive rRT-PCR test results. A total of 42% of patients showed improvement on follow-up chest CT scans before the rRT-PCR results turned negative. Another study presented findings of five patients who initially tested negative by rRT-PCR but eventually tested positive through repeated tests. All patients exhibited chest CTs with GGOs and/or mixed GGOs and consolidation (Ai et al., 2020). A third study reported similar findings, with 97% sensitivity by the initial CT scan, as compared to the initial rRT-PCR sensitivity of 83.3%. Among the patients for which the rRT-PCR test was initially negative, half tested positive in the second round of testing after a few days, while the other half finally tested positive in the third round of testing after several days (Long et al., 2020). A recent study compiled results from over 4000 patients and reported that the sensitivity of CT was 86%, while rRT-PCR needed to be repeated up to three times before giving an accuracy of 99%. These studies indicate the potential of chest CT to provide more accurate results than rRT-PCR in the early stages of the COVID-19 disease, which is critical in terms of ensuring treatment and isolation begin immediately. Therefore, the use of both chest CT and rRT-PCR has proven important in ensuring that cases are not missed and are identified as early as possible. Patients with CT findings typical of COVID-19 but negative rRT-PCR results should be isolated, and rRT-PCR testing should be repeated to avoid misdiagnosis.

THE ABILITY TO DIFFERENTIATE BETWEEN COVID-19 PNEUMONIA AND OTHER PNEUMONIAS

One study compared the chest CT scans of 11 patients with COVID-19 pneumonia with scans of 22 patients having non-COVID-19 pneumonia. The study found no statistical difference in imaging features between the two sets of scans. The typical COVID-19 imaging features were found in both groups in similar percentages: GGOs in 100% of COVID-19 and 90% of non-COVID-19, mixed GGOs in 63.6% versus 72.7%, and consolidation in 54.5% versus 77.3%. However, the chest CT scans for patients testing positive for COVID-19 demonstrated GGOs predominantly located in the peripheral zone in 100% of patients, as compared to 31.8% of the negative patients. Therefore, the study concluded that findings highly suspicious of COVID- 19 were imaging patterns of multifocal, peripheral, pure GGOs, mixed GGOs, or consolidation with slight predominance in the lower lung and findings of more extensive GGOs than consolidation during the first week of illness (Cheng et al., 2020). In a recent study investigating the ability of both Chinese and American radiologists to differentiate between more than 200 COVID-19 cases and 200 non-COVID-19 pneumonia cases, six of the seven radiologists demonstrated a specificity greater than 93%. In addition, a peripheral distribution was found to distinguish COVID-19 from other viral pneumonia in 63–80% of the cases (Bai, et al., 2020a).

DEEP LEARNING ARCHITECTURES FOR CT SCAN

Computed Tomography Scans produces tomographic images allowing users to see the object of interest from inside without cutting. This technique is broadly used for medical diagnostics in many different situations. Tomographic images from human body displays internal organs and requires a specialist for identifying and segmenting the area of interest. For the current COVID-19 pandemic, chest CT images captured from COVID-19 patients frequently show bilateral patchy shadows or ground glass opacity in the lung, CT has become a vital complementary tool for detecting the lung associated with COVID-19. Chest CT is relatively easy to operate and has a high sensitivity for screening COVID-19 infection. Therefore, CT could serve as a practical approach for early screening and diagnosis of COVID-19 in China. However, as the increment of confirmed and suspected cases of COVID-19, manually contouring of lung lesions is a tedious and labor-intensive task.

To speed up diagnosis and improve access to treatment, developing a fast automatically segmentation for COVID-19 infection is critical for the disease assessment.

Recently, with the rapid development of artificial intelligence, deep learning technology has been widely used in medical image processing due to its powerful feature representation. Several techniques based on deep learning have published to detect COVID-19 pneumonia from CT images. In this section we are exploring various deep learning models effectively contribute in the detection of COVID-19 infection using CT scan images.

DETECTION OF COVID-19 USING UNET ConvNet

UNET ConvNet

The UNet architecture is built upon the Fully Convolutional Network and modified in a way as show in Figure 5.1 that it yields better segmentation in medical imaging. Compared to FCN-8, the two main differences are (1) UNet is symmetric and (2) the skip connections between the downsampling path and the upsampling path apply a concatenation operator instead of a sum. These skip connections intend to provide local information to the global information while upsampling. Because of its symmetry, the network has a large number of feature maps in the upsampling path, which allows to transfer information. By comparison, the basic FCN architecture only had number of classes feature maps in its upsampling path.

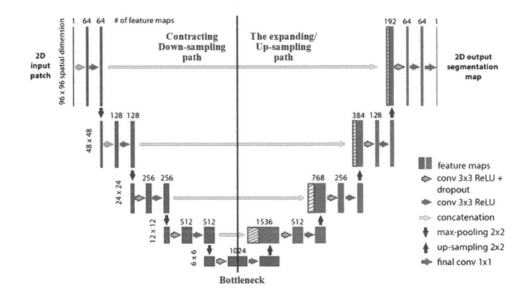

FIGURE 5.1 The figure illustrates the U-net architecture with the largest patch-size of 96 × 96 voxels. The displayed U-net is an encoder-decoder network with a contracting path (encoding part, left side) that reduces the height and width of the input images and an expansive path (decoding part, right side) that recovers the original dimensions of the input images. Each box corresponds to a multi-channel feature map. The dashed boxes stand for the concatenated copied feature maps from the contractive path. The arrows stand for the different operations as listed in the right legend. The number of channels is denoted on top of the box and the image dimensionality (x-y-size) is denoted on the left edge. The half U-net is constructed likewise, with the only difference given by the halved number of channels throughout the network.

The UNet owes its name to its symmetric shape, which is different from other FCN variants. UNet architecture is separated in three parts:

1. The contracting/downsampling path
2. Bottleneck
3. The expanding/upsampling path

(1) Contracting/downsampling path

- The contracting path is composed of four blocks. Each block is composed of
- 3 × 3 Convolution Layer + activation function (with batch normalization)
- 3 × 3 Convolution Layer + activation function (with batch normalization)
- 2 × 2 Max Pooling

The number of feature maps doubles at each pooling, starting with 64 feature maps for the first block, 128 for the second, and so on. The purpose of this contracting path is to capture the context of the input image in order to be able to do segmentation. This coarse contextual information will then be transfered to the upsampling path by means of skip connections.

(2) Bottleneck

This part of the network is between the contracting and expanding paths. The bottleneck is built from simply two convolutional layers (with batch normalization), with dropout.

(3) Expanding/upsampling path

The expanding path is also composed of four blocks. Each of these blocks is composed of

- Deconvolution layer with stride two
- Concatenation with the corresponding cropped feature map from the contracting path
- 3 × 3 Convolution layer + activation function (with batch normalization)
- 3 × 3 Convolution layer + activation function (with batch normalization)

The purpose of this expanding path is to enable precise localization combined with contextual information from the contracting path.

Data and Material

We used COVID-19-positive and non-COVID data from GitHub (Zhao et al., 2020) and consolidation and healthy CT scans from a private Indian hospital. The data obtained contained 275 CT scans labeled as COVID-19-positive. The ground truth in these images was decided on the basis of their RT-PCR test results. These CT images had different sizes from 143 patient cases (Zhao et al., 2020). In total, the data contained 5212 slices and was split into training, validation, and test sets. The prevalence of positive cases in each of the sets was kept at 20%. As the available open-source data had varied resolutions, we decided to fix our input size to 512×512 pixels. The original images were in the unsigned int8 format, in the range of [0, 255]. We converted these images to floating-point 16, in the range of [0, 1]. The output masks were in the binary form [0, 1] at pixel-level, where 1s indicated the region of interest. Table 5.2 shows the detailed distribution of data.

The CT slices were annotated, classified, and marked positive by a group of trained expert radiologists. The positive CT slices had typical findings including bilateral pulmonary

TABLE 5.2
Slice-Level Dataset Splits

Dataset	COVID-19	Non-COVID	Total Slices
Training	657	2628	3285
Validation	120	477	597
Test	266	1064	1330

parenchymal ground-glass and consolidative pulmonary opacities, sometimes with a rounded morphology and a peripheral lung distribution (Chung et al., 2020). Ground-glass opacification was defined as hazy increased lung attenuation with preservation of bronchial and vascular margins, and consolidation was defined as opacification with obscuration of margins of vessels and airway walls (Hansell et al., 2008). Notably, lung cavitation, discrete pulmonary nodules, pleural effusions, and lymphadenopathy were marked as negative. Our radiologists used an open source tool called VIA (Dutta & Zisserman, 2019) for annotating the images, as it supports various shapes, including ellipses, circles, and polygons, for marking the ROI. Figure 5.2 shows an example of the annotation.

Methodology

In this section, we give a brief overview of our training and the inference algorithms.

We used UNet for medical image segmentation, which uses the concept of deconvolution (Ronneberger et al., 2015; Zeiler & Fergus, 2014). UNets are built on the architecture of fully convolutional networks as discussed above. The most important property of UNet is the short-cut connections between the layers of equal resolution in the encoder path and the decoder path. These connections provide essential high resolution features to the deconvolution layers (Hesamian et al., 2019). Here, we used Xception (Chollet, 2017) as the encoder for UNet.

We used transfer learning by fine-tuning a network pretrained on CXRs for the same problem but a different task (Shin et al., 2016). Transfer learning is proven to give better performance when the tasks of source and target network are more similar, and yet even transferring the weights of far and distant tasks has been proved to be better than random initialization (Yosinski et al., 2014).

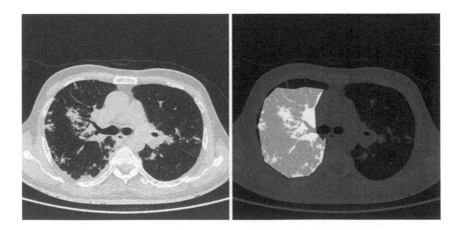

FIGURE 5.2 (left) original image and (right) annotated ROI.

Here, we have tried to solve the problem of distinguishing COVID-19 cases from non-COVID-19 by using weights from our COVID-19 vs Healthy model, as pre-trained weights for this model already gave a sensitivity of 0.9 with a specificity of 0.8. Initially, we built a CT model for consolidation vs healthy and later fine-tuned our model for COVID-19 vs nonCOVID-19.

In the training stage, we use binary cross entropy as the loss function and the standard Adaptive Adam Optimizer with a batch size of four. We set the max epochs to 50 and set the learning rate to 10−4, which is decayed on the plateau after patience of four epochs. We resize each training image to a fixed size of 512 × 512 pixels. To alleviate the over fitting of our model on the training data from a particular source, we try to include data from varied sources. One of the drawbacks of having a 2D CT model is that the inference tends to be slow. Our model has a sensitivity of 0.964, hence we plan to use specific slices for inference.

Results

We tested our model using varied sets of data from different sources. We initially evaluated the model on our test set, consisting of 1330 images, in which COVID-19-positive samples had a prevalence of 20%. Our model gave a sensitivity of 0.963 (95% CI: 0.94-0.98) and a specificity of 0.936 (95% CI: 0.92-0.95). The dice coefficient on positive samples was 0.561. Figures 5.3 and 5.4 show the superimposed masks on one of the slices.

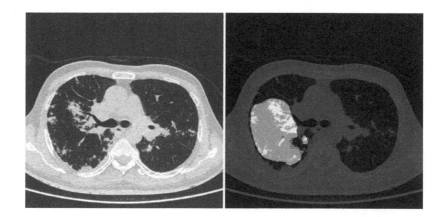

FIGURE 5.3   (left) original image and (right) corresponding predicted mask.

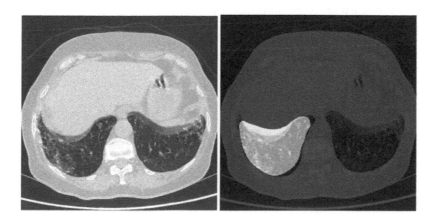

FIGURE 5.4   (left) original image and (right) corresponding predicted mask.

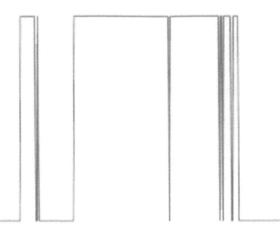

FIGURE 5.5   Trend of predictions of Slice No. 0 to 300 from CT no. 16.

Apart from this, we evaluated the model on a total of 140 scans with a prevalence of 20% for positive cases. These scans were tested on data from three sources. One source contained Italian and Chinese scans, while the remaining came from two separate private Indian hospitals. After passing these images through our model, we sorted the slices as per the position of the slice in the CT scan. We observed a pattern wherein the consecutive slices had the same predictions which is expected from a radiology perspective. Figure 5.5 provides an example of the predictions for a positive CT scan. Here we see the expected pattern of consecutive slices, predicted as positive by the model.

Hence, we convert the slice-level prediction to scan-level prediction using the logic that if 15 consecutive slices in a scan are marked as positive, then we mark the scan as positive. Table 5.3 shows the results obtained at scan-level.

Advantages of UNet

- The UNet combines the location information from the downsampling path with the contextual information in the upsampling path to finally obtain a general information combining localisation and context, which is necessary to predict a good segmentation map.
- No dense layer, so images of different sizes can be used as input (since the only parameters to learn on convolution layers are the kernel, and the size of the kernel is independent from input image' size).
- The use of massive data augmentation is important in domains like biomedical segmentation, since the number of annotated samples is usually limited.

TABLE 5.3

Scan-Level Performance of the Model on the Test Set

Performance Metric	Value	95% C.I.
Sensitivity	0.964	(0.88,1)
Specificity	0.884	(0.82,0.94)
F1-score	0.794	(0.68,0.89)

ENSEMBLE OF CONVOLUTIONAL AUTOENCODER AND RANDOM FOREST

Advancement in the deep learning feature extraction methodologies makes it a potential tool especially in the field of medical imaging. An autoencoder is a neural network model, trained to reconstruct its input in an unsupervised way. Usually hidden network layers reduce the input size, and learn relevant features that allow better reconstruction. However, deep auto-encoders use several nonlinear layers to learn complex hierarchical functions from highly insightful results. To generate meaningful features particularly for image processing and natural language processing applications, approaches such as Sparse auto-encoders (Deng et al., 2013), Denoising autoencoders (Vincent et al., 2008), Contractive autoencoders (Rifai et al., 2011) and Variational autoencoders (Goodfellow et al., 2014). Nevertheless, these approaches only amount for data reconstruction.

This framework employs the extraction of two feature sets, the first feature set being extracted using an unsupervised learning approach, the convolutional autoencoders as generic feature extractor while the second set of features has been extracted, keeping in mind the importance of textural features for images, using Gray Level Co-occurrence matrix as hand-crafted feature to build a better performing classifier. Analysis have been performed on both sets of features to find out that the ensemble of both these feature sets can be useful for the classification of the SARS-CoV-2 when employed via a random forest classifier. Results showed that the proposed approach could be used to diagnose COVID-19 as an assistant framework. The details are discussed in the subsequent sections.

Data and Material

The dataset consists of 2482 CT scans, out of which 1252 images belong to patients tested positive with SARS-CoV-2 infection, and 1230 images for patients not infected with coronavirus (but infected with other pulmonary diseases). The dataset selected for the verification of proposed concept is already openly available.[1]

Methodology

Deep learning generally refers to application of CNN for feature extraction and object classification. The layers of CNN process information in a nonlinear fashion which transforms the data into a more abstract level. The neurons in a particular layer are selectively attached to some of the neurons in the next layer. Higher layers essentially enhance parts of the given data that are significant for segregation from unimportant attributes. Finally, the output is diminished to a single vector of probability scores. For COVID-19 infection detection, features of chest CT images are used for classification whether they belong to infected class or not.

Convolutional Autoencoder

Autoencoders, unsupervised learning generative models, are used to reconstruct the input image. They employ a symmetric model consisting of two blocks, viz. encoder and decoder. The encoder compresses input image into a lower dimension output that contains only the informative features of input, then the decoder reconstructs the image from the features extracted by the encoder. So once the training is completed the encoder becomes a powerful tool for the extraction of features from the input. These autoencoders can be created using different type of neural networks.

In this study, we employed a convolutional autoencoder architecture which is shown in Figure 5.6. In Table 5.4, the layers one to nine constitute the encoder which operates on

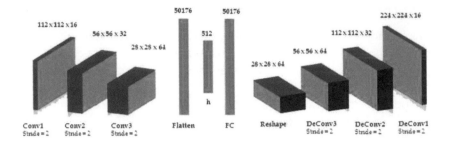

FIGURE 5.6   Flowchart of the ensemble framework.

224 × 224 × 3 pixels to convert it to a 512 feature vector, and the layers 10 to 18 constitute the decoder part which is useful for training but is not required for deployment.

The objective here was to keep minimum possible features so the encoder can be tested with greater depth and multiple convolutional layers at each step. It was found that architecture of layers one to nine gave the best results. Experimentation was conducted to compare 512 and 256 features, in which we found that one with 512 features performed better.

The network was trained using a batch size of 32 for a maximum of 200 epochs with Adam optimizer and mean squared error (MSE) as loss function. The model was trained using early stopping which ensured that if the validation loss remained non-decreasing consistently for 30 epochs then the training stopped. The objective remains to avoid overfitting of the model and storing the best model at model checkpoint by minimizing the validation loss.

TABLE 5.4

Description of Autoencoder Architecture Layers

Layer	Kernel Size	Width	Activation	Output Size
Input	–	3	–	224 × 224 × 3
Conv2D	3 × 3	16	ReLu	224 × 224 × 16
max-pool	2 × 2			112 × 112 × 16
Conv2D	3 × 3	32	ReLu	112 × 112 × 32
max-pool	2 × 2			56 × 56 × 32
Conv2D	3 × 3	64	ReLu	56 × 56 × 64
max-pool	2 × 2			28 × 28 × 64
Flatten				50176
Dense				512
Dense				50176
Reshape				28 × 28 × 64
Conv2D	3 × 3	64	ReLu	28 × 28 × 64
up-sample	2 × 2			56 × 56 × 64
Conv2D	3 × 3	32	ReLu	56 × 56 × 32
up-sample	2 × 2			112 × 112 × 32
Conv2d	3 × 3	16	ReLu	112 × 112 × 16
up-sample	2 × 2			224 × 224 × 16
Conv2D	3 × 3	3	Sigmoid	224 × 224 × 3

Haralick Features

Haralick textural features (Haralick et al., 1973) are a total of 14 features calculated using a Grey Level Co-occurrence Matrix (GLCM). GLCM is used for texture analysis because it can estimate image quality related to second order statistics. The grey level co-occurrence matrix is a two dimensional matrix of joint probabilities between pairs of pixels separated by a distance d in a given direction r.

GLCM texture captures the relationship between two pixels at a time, known as the reference pixel and the neighbor pixel. GLCM shows the distance and angular spatial relationship over a specific size image sub-region. It considers how often the values of a pixel with a grey level (grey scale intensity or grey tone) are levelled horizontally, vertically and diagonally. GLCM is effective for the calculation of haralick features if the images are of same resolution and are grey-scaled (Brynolfsson et al., 2017).

In our study, we have used only the first 13 of haralick features because of the instability of 'maximum instability coefficient' (14th feature). The distance d is fixed at one and the direction r is varied as 0°, 45°, 90°, 135°. Mahotas (Coelho, 2012), a computer vision python library, has been used to calculate the Haralick features in all the above mentioned directions. From the given dataset, each image is resized to 224 × 224 pixels and converted to a grey scaled image, to get the images into same resolution and use grey levels, which is then passed through mahotas and a feature vector of 13 × 4 is extracted for each image.

Classification Using Random Forest

Random forest (RF) is an ensemble (i.e., a collection) of tens or hundreds of decision trees (Liaw & Wiener, 2002). Ensemble models are often robust to variance and bias. The algorithm is efficient with respect to a large number of variables since it repeatedly subsets the variables available. Consequently, the deep spatial features generated by the auto-encoder and the spatial-temporal features produced by GLCM are concatenated and fed into the RF for classification.

Result Analysis

Applying the proposed procedure on the input, two new datasets are generated, that is, one with features retrieved using autoencoders and other from Haralick features. From these datasets, a composite dataset is formed that contains the combination of these features as shown in Figure 5.7. A total of 564 relevant features are obtained which are used to train a random forest model with ntree = 100.

Parameters of Results Assessment

For the assessment of the results obtained from the above process, certain quantities need to be evaluated, which are widely used for comparison of the performance of binary classification models. In the given equations, follow the notation: TP be true positive, FP be false positive, FN be false negative, and TN be true negative.

Accuracy

It is used to convey the percentage of images correctly identified. It is defined as the ratio of correct predictions to the total number of predictions and is given as

$$Accuracy = \frac{TP + TN}{TP + TN + FP + FN}$$

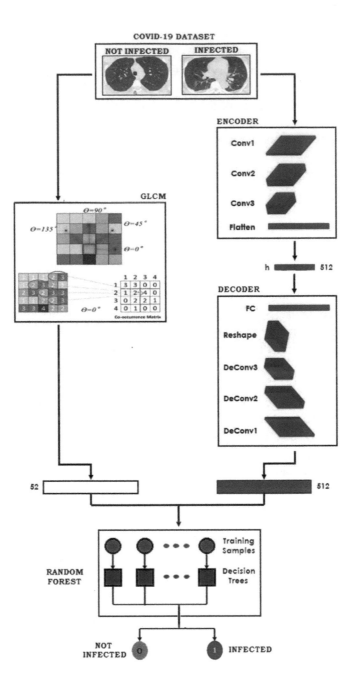

FIGURE 5.7   Diagrammatic Representation of Entire Process.

Precision

It is used to convey how many predicted as positive by the model were actually supposed to be predicted as positive. It is defined as the ratio of predicted true positives to the total number of predicted positives, and is given as

$$Precision = \frac{TP}{TP + FP}$$

Recall

It is used to convey how well the model has classified the positive examples. It is defined as the ratio of predicted true positives to the actual positives, and is given as

$$Recall = \frac{TP}{TP + FN}$$

F1-Score

It is the harmonic mean of precision and recall whose value is high if precision and recall are close and vice versa. It conveys how well the model is fitted, and is given as

$$F1 - score = \frac{TP}{TP + 0.5(TP + FN)}$$

Specificity

It is used to convey how many predicted negative by the model were actually supposed to be predicted as negative. It is defined as the ratio of predicted true negatives to the total negatives predicted by the model, and is given as

$$Specificity = \frac{TP}{TN + FP}$$

Area under Curve

AUC conveys how well the model can distinguish between the positive and the negative class of the data.

The input dataset was split into 80% training and 20% testing, that is, 1984 training and 497 testing images. Consequently, confusion matrices were generated for the classification models given in Table 5.5. This helps us to realize whether the model is confusing between two classes or not. Each row of the matrix represents the instances in a predicted class, while each column represents the instances in an actual class.

Using the values obtained from the confusion matrices, the assessment of the model is done by calculating the performance metrics, summarized in Table 5.6.

The column marked in bold is the proposed model which performed relatively better. Furthermore, the superior classification ability is also well demonstrated by Figures 5.8 and 5.9 which are illustrations of prediction variability.

TABLE 5.5

Confusion Matrices of Dataset Formed at Each Stage for 497 Number of Testing Data Points

	GLCM		Autoencoder		Composite	
	AP	AN	AP	AN	AP	AN
PP	236	12	234	14	245	3
PN	11	238	26	223	8	241

Note: AP Refers to Actual Positive, AN is Actual Negative, PP is Predicted Positive, and PN is Predicted Negative

TABLE 5.6

Performance Metrics for Each Method

	GLCM	Convolutional Encoder	Composite
Accuracy	95.37%	91.95%	97.78%
Precision	95.20%	94.09%	98.77%
Recall	95.58%	89.55%	96.78%
F1-score	95.39%	91.76%	97.77%
Specificity	95.20%	94.09%	98.77%
AUC	95.37%	91.95%	97.78%

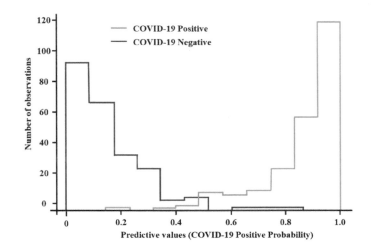

FIGURE 5.8   Plot of number of observations vs. prediction probability.

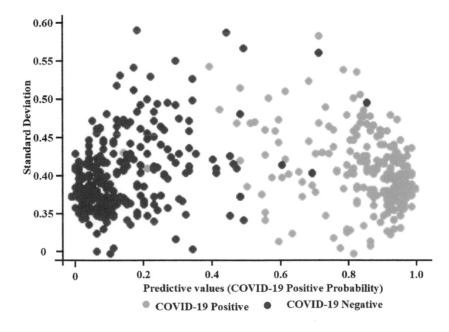

FIGURE 5.9   Scatter plot of standard deviation vs. prediction probability.

These figures show the degree of influence the training set has for producing the observed random forest predictions and provides additional information about prediction accuracy. Forest-confidence-interval is a Python module for calculating variance and adding confidence intervals to scikit-learn random forest classification objects The package's random forest error function uses the random forest object (including training and test data) to create variance estimates that can be plotted (such as confidence intervals or standard deviations).

The classification accuracy, F1-score, precision, recall, specificity and AUC for the developed framework is 97.78%, 97.77%, 98.77%, 96.78%, 98.77% and 97.78%, respectively. The time taken by the model to predict 50 training examples is 13.4 s, that is, 0.268 seconds per testing image. Thus, the results demonstrate that the fusion of texture features with deep feature can provide a representative description for COVID-19 detection in a fast and efficient manner. We also performed the whole analysis with support vector machine as a classifier but its performance was poor as compared to random forest based model. We can therefore conclude that the proposed model is indeed a better model with discriminatory features for the classification of COVID-19 from CT images.

FULLY CONNECTED SEGMENTATION NEURAL NETWORK (FCSegNet)

The FCSegNet is a new tailored deep convolutional neural network (CNN) for segmenting the chest CT images with COVID-19 infections. Figure 5.10 shows the chest CT images with COVID-19 infection, which contain ground glass opacities (GGOs), areas of consolidation,

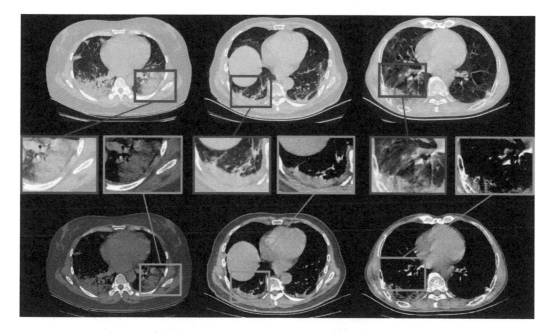

FIGURE 5.10 Chest CT images of three patients with laboratory proven COVID-19 pneumonia. As shown in the top row, patchy ground-glass opacities (GGOs) and areas of consolidation bilaterally exist in all lung lobes (highlighted with red bounding box). It is hard to distinguish COVID-19 infection regions from the chest wall. The boundaries of COVID-19 infection regions are highlighted (as indicated by green bounding box), after carefully adjusting the window breadth and window locations for each CT image

and a mix of both in all lung lobes. Most lesions were located peripherally, with a slight preponderance of dorsal lung areas. Due to the special structure and visual characteristics, the boundaries of COVID-19 infection regions are difficult to distinguish from the chest wall, making accurate segmentation for COVID-19 infection regions difficult. We observe that the boundaries of COVID-19 infection regions will be revealed by adjusting different parameters of window breadth and window locations in annotation processing, as shown in Figure 5.10, which can be beneficial for the COVID-19 infection image segmentation.

So FCSegNet consist three-dimensional (3D) convolution based deep learning method for automatic segmentation of COVID-19 infection regions as well as the entire lung from chest CT images. This method can be hugely beneficial for the early screening of patients with COVID-19. Inspired by the observation in annotation processing, the boundaries of COVID-19 infection regions are highlighted by adjusting the window breadth and window locations, a Feature Variation (FV) block to handle the confusing boundaries. The central idea of the FV block is to implicitly enhance the contrast and adjust the intensity in the feature level automatically and adaptively for different images. Based on the captured features of previous layers, the FV block employs channel attention to obtain the global parameter to generate new features. In addition to the channel attention, the FV block uses spatial attention to guide the feature extraction from inputs in the encoder. Aggregating these features can effectively enhance the capability of feature representation for the segmentation of COVID-19. Furthermore, we propose a Progressive Atrous Spatial Pyramid Pooling (PASPP) to handle the challenging shape variations of COVID-19 infection areas. PASPP consists of a base convolution module followed by a cascade of atrous convolutional layers, which uses multistage parallel fusion branches to obtain the final features. Each atrous convolutional layer in PASPP only uses atrous filters with a reasonable dilation rate to cover different receptive fields. And by the progressively aggregated information from atrous convolutional layers, the information from multiple scales is effectively fused, which further promotes the performance of COVID-19 pneumonia segmentation.

Data and Material

We used a publicly available CT image dataset about COVID-19, to foster the development of AI methods for using CT to screen and test COVID-19 patients. To assemble the COVID-CT dataset (Zhao et al., 2020). CT images of patients infected with COVID-19 were collected from scientic articles (pre-prints) deposited in the medRxiv and biRxiv repositories, from January 19 to March 25 and also some images were donated by hospitals (http://medicalsegmentation. com/covid-19/). The PyMuPDF software was used to extract images from the manuscripts, in order to maintain high quality. Meta data were manually ex- tracted and associated with each image: patient age, gender, location, medical history, scan time, severity of COVID-19, and medical report. The dataset contains 349 COVID-19 CT images from 216 patients and 463 non-COVID-19 CT images (used as negative training examples). Regarding healthy and non-covid patients, the authors collected images from two other datasets (MedPix dataset, LUNA dataset), from the Radiopaedia website and from other articles and texts available at PubMed Central (PMC). A total of 463 images were collected from 55 patients.

Analogous to the previous dataset, the COVID-CT dataset has denied standard for image size and contrast. Figure 5.11 shows some examples. It is also important to highlight that some images contain textual information which may interfere with model prediction. See Figure 5.12.

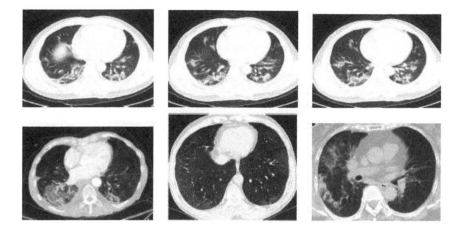

FIGURE 5.11 Examples of CT images that are: positive for COVID-19 (top) and non-COVID-19 (bottom) from COVID-CT dataset.

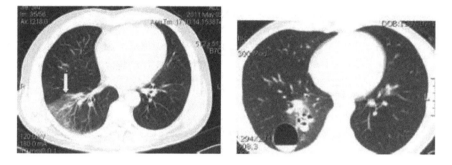

FIGURE 5.12 Example of images with textual information.

A protocol is proposed for the creation of training, validation, and test sets. The COVID-19 images that were donated by hospitals and extracted directly from medical equipment (LUNA and Radiopaedia) were selected to compose the validation and test sets. The remaining—extracted from scientic articles and manuscripts—were reserved to compose the training set. The dataset is available at https://github.com/UCSD-AI4H/COVID-CT.

In the Table 5.7 is possible to observe the issues indented in the datasets, and the relation between the number of patients and the amount of images of each class (COVID and Non-COVID).

All imaging data were reconstructed by using a medium sharp reconstruction algorithm with a thickness of 0.625–10 mm (81% under 2 mm). To protect privacy, we deleted the personally identifiable information (PII) from all CT scans. A total of 189 patient's CT images were randomly extracted for training. The remaining CT images of 82 patients were used as the testing set.

Dataset Annotation

Although we captured enough data of the COVID-19 chest CT images, accurate annotated labels are also indispensable. To enable the model to learn on accurate annotations, we build a team of six annotators with deep radiology background and proficient annotating skills to annotate the areas and boundaries of the lung and COVID-19 infection regions.

TABLE 5.7

Summarizes the Datasets Presented in This Section

Dataset	COVID-19		Non-COVID-19		Issues
	# Patients	# Images	# Patients	# Images	
COVID-CT	216	349	55	463	non-standard size of images non-standard contrast of images textual information on images

Also, the quality of the final annotations is assessed by a senior radiologist with frontline clinical experience of COVID-19

Methodology

FCSegNet

This is a unified high-accuracy network for the segmentation of COVID-19 infection from chest CT images. This network consists of two parts: Encoder and Decoder. As shown in Figure 5.13, the encoder with four layers (i.e., E1, E2, E3, E4) obtains robust information via feature extractor and PASPP. Each layer employs residual and FV blocks as the basic operations for feature extractors, except the E4 layer. The residual block adds up the input features and the results after two convolutional layers, which effectively alleviates the vanishing gradient. To preserve multiple contextual information and enlarge the receptive field, we use PASPP with different dilate rates on the final E4 layer. After obtaining the encoded features, the decoder tries to restore the features to its original input size, which can remove the information loss induced by down-sampling from Encoder. The decoder has three layers (D3, D2, D1). Each decoder layer allows the networks to gradually propagate the global

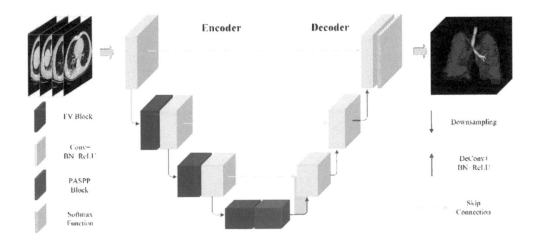

FIGURE 5.13 The architecture of the proposed FCSegNet. The network includes encoder part for feature extraction and decoder part for estimating the segmentation results. The FV block is adopted to highlight contrast and position of COVID-19, the PASSP block is built based on progressively fusing the output of different arous convolutional layers. The visualized final result is a presentation of the 3D segmentation of lung and the regions associated with COVID-19 infection.

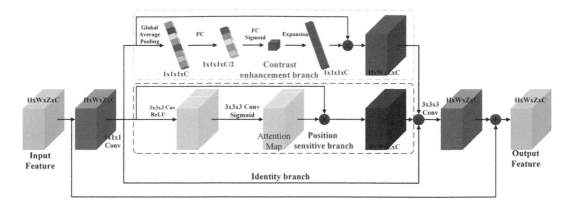

FIGURE 5.14 FV block consists of contrast enhancement branch, position sensitive branch, and identity branch. The features of these branches are concatenated to decrease the number of the channel via a $3 \times 3 \times 3$ convolutional layer. The output features are obtained after residual learning with input.

contextual information to a higher resolution layer. After a sigmoid activation function, we obtain the final segmentation of COVID-19 infection regions.

In addition, the skip connection is adopted to concatenate the output features of the encoder and input features of the decoder. In this paper, the main contribution is we improve the encoder by adding FV block and PASPP block to better capture effective features. The overview of these two blocks is as follows.

1. The architectures of FV block by considering a material fact, the boundaries of COVID-19 infection regions are highlighted by adjusting the window breadth and window locations. As shown in Figure 5.14, the proposed FV block includes three branches, e.g., contrast enhancement branch, position sensitive branch, identity branch, which can automatically change the parameter to display the boundaries and position of COVID-19. Specifically, the contrast enhancement branch learns a global parameter via a channel attention unit to highlight useful boundary information. The position sensitive branch obtains a weight map by spatial attention unit to focus on the COVID-19 regions. Finally, the FV block preserves more useful information by fusing these refined features.
2. The PASPP block takes the featured extracted with FV block as input and acquires semantic information with different receptive fields showing in Figure 5.15.

Although ASPP has been proposed to capture global information for semantic segmentation, we claim that aggregating information progressively is a more reasonable approach to get effective features. The PASPP block adopts atrous convolutions with different dilation rates to obtain features with various scales. The final output is generated straightforwardly to assemble residual branches in parallel.

Feature Variation

As mentioned before, the boundaries of COVID-19 infection regions are highlighted by adjusting the window breadth and window locations. In Figure 5.14, the designed FV block, which includes contrast enhancement branch, position sensitive branch and

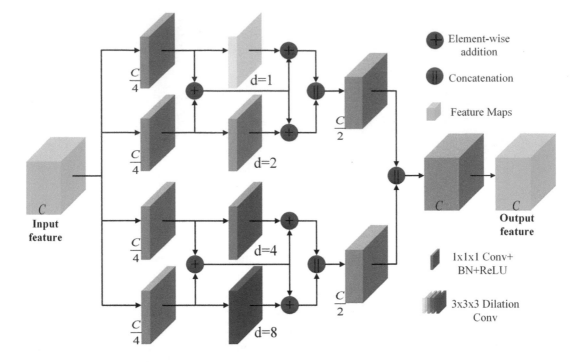

FIGURE 5.15　The structure of PASPP block. We assemble two residual branches in parallel and sum up the outputs from two $1\times1\times1$ convolutional layers, then the outputs of two branches are progressively blended. Note that, compared to input features, the number of the channel decreases to quarter after each $1\times1\times1$ convolutional layer.

identity branch, tries to enhance the contrast of features and highlight the useful regions. Let Fv denotes the input feature, the features after $1\times1\times1$ represent Fv_1. The output feature Fv_{out} is given as,

$$Fv_{out} = Fv + Cov_3\big(Conca\big(C(Fv_1), P(Fv_1), Fv_1\big)\big) \tag{5.1}$$

where $Cov_3(\cdot)$ denotes the $3\times3\times3$ convolutional layer, $Conca(\cdot)$ is the concatenation operation, $C(\cdot)$ represents the contrast enhancement branch, $P(\cdot)$ is the position sensitive branch. The form of residual learning in Equation (5.1) implies that the information from the early blocks can quickly flow to the later blocks, and the gradient can be quickly back-propagated to the early blocks from the later blocks (Zhao et al., 2016). The details of each sub-module are as follows

1. Contrast Enhancement Branch: To enhance the contrast of features, the contrast enhancement branch $Con(\cdot)$ in Equation (5.1) attempts to learn a global parameter F_g for input feature Fv (See Figure 5.14). The corresponding function is given as,

$$F_g = Cov_1\big(Cov_3\big(GAP(Fv_1)\big)\big) \tag{5.2}$$

where $Cov1(\cdot)$ denotes the $1\times1\times1$ convolutional layer, $GAP(\cdot)$ represents global average pooling. The values of F_g is in the range [0, 1]. We obtain a channel weight map F_g' via expansion, thus the number of F_g' is consistent with Fv. Finally, the output of contrast enhancement branch F_c can be formulated as below

$$F_c = F_g' \otimes Fv_1 \tag{5.3}$$

where $\otimes$ denotes the element-wise multiplication. Note that, instead of calculating a sequence of weight for feature Fv_1, we generate one weight for all the features of Fv_1. This process is exactly corresponding to adjust the window breadth and window locations. Thus we deem it has the ability to generate enhanced features.

2. Position Sensitive Branch: The goal of position sensitive branch is to discard harmful information and highlight the helpful features, which are used to segmentation of COVID-19 infection. This branch $P(\cdot)$ in Equation (5.1) is a small network. The architecture of position sensitive branch is displayed in Figure 5.14. The attention map A is calculated using input feature Fv_1 after two convolutional layers. Each layer adopts $3 \times 3 \times 3$ convolution. The two convolutional layers are followed by a ReLU function and a sigmoid function, respectively. In the end, the output of this branch F_P is obtained by element-wise multiplication between Fv_1 and the attention map

$$F_P = A \otimes Fv_1 \tag{5.4}$$

The values in A are still in the range [0, 1]. The attention map has same size as input feature.

Progressive Atrous Spatial Pyramid Pooling

In this subsection, we start with preliminary knowledge of atrous spatial pyramid pooling, then introduce the proposed PASPP block

1. Atrous Spatial Pyramid Pooling: Global information captured by a large receptive field is essential for medical semantic segmentation. To increase the receptive field size and decrease the number of convolutional layers, arous convolution is first proposed in (Chen et al., 2017) to obtain enough global information while keeping the size of the feature map unchanged. In one dimensional case, let $y[i]$ represents output and $x[i]$ denotes input, atrous convolution can be formulated as follows:

$$y[i] = \sum_{k=1}^{K} x[i + d.k].w[k] \tag{5.5}$$

where K denotes the filter size, d represents the dilation rate, and $w[k]$ is the $k-th$ parameter of filter. A larger dilation rate will capture a larger receptive field. To produce different receptive fields, atrous spatial pyramid pooling taking atrous convolutions with different dilation rates to generate features with various scales. These features are concatenated together. Thus the outputs are indeed a sampling of the input with different scales information.

2. The PASPP Block: In COVID-19 segmentation task, the infection regions often has different sizes (See Figure 5.12). To alleviate this dilemma, the features must be

able to include different receptive fields. For this goal, we employ ASPP in our network and progressively fuse the features with different receptive fields. The structure of PASPP is illustrated in Figure 5.15. Given the input feature of PASPP F_p, we obtain four features $F_{p_1}, F_{p_2}, F_{p_3}, F_{p_4}$ by four $1\times1\times1$ convolutional layers in parallel. Note that, compared to input features, the number of the channel decreases to quarter after each $1\times1\times1$ convolutional layer (See the second column in Figure 5.15). Then each branch feeds the feature into different atrous convolutional layer, respectively. The corresponding function is given as,

$$Fd_t = Cov_3^d \left(F_p \right), t = 1,2,3,4; d = 2^{t-1} \tag{5.6}$$

where Cov_3^d denotes the $3\times3\times3$ atrous convolutional layer with dilation rate d, Fd_t represents the output feature of the $i-th$ branch after Cov_3^d. Sum the inputs of two adjacent atrous convolution branches, and add the sum to the output of each residual branch as the input of the subsequent layer. It is formulated as below,

$$\begin{cases} Fd_t' = Fd_t + Fd_1 + Fd_2 & t = 1,2 \\ Fd_t' = Fd_t + Fd_3 + Fd_4 & t = 3,4 \end{cases} \tag{5.7}$$

where Fd_t' denotes the output features of $t-th$ branch. To get effective features, $Fd_t', t = 1,2,3,4$ will be progressively aggregated based on adjacent features in parallel.

$$\begin{cases} Fd_1'' = Cov_1 \left(Conca \left(Fd_1', Fd_2' \right) \right) \\ Fd_2'' = Cov_1 \left(Conca \left(Fd_3', Fd_4' \right) \right) \end{cases} \tag{5.8}$$

The Fd_1'' tends to fuse the information with small receptive field, Fd_2'' prones to capture features with larger receptive field. The channel's number of Fd_1'' and Fd_2'' is half of the input feature. All the information is assembled by:

$$F_{Pout} = Cov_1 \left(Conca \left(Fd_1'', Fd_1'' \right) \right) \tag{5.9}$$

where F_{Pout} denotes the output features of PASPP block.

Evaluation Metrics

The screening performance of the proposed method is conducted by the Dice similarity coefficient, sensitivity, and precision. The Dice similarity coefficient (Dice) represents a similarity metric between the ground truth, and the prediction score maps (Milletari et al., 2016). It is calculated as follows:

$$Dic(A, B) = \frac{2|A \cap B|}{|A| + |B|} \tag{5.10}$$

where A is the segmented infection region, B denotes the corresponding reference region, $A \cap B \vee$ represents the number of pixels common to both images. Sensitivity denotes the number of correctly identified positives with respect to the number of positives. Precision is the fraction of positive instances among the retrieved instances.

Implementation Details

The Parameters of the Network

For the proposed framework, the encoding layers are residual blocks, FV blocks, PASSP blocks, and down sampling, while the decoding layers are residual blocks and deconvolution layers kernels with a stride of 1/2. The last layer is a softmax activation function to produce the segmentation results. All layers use $3 \times 3 \times 3$ kernels, if not specified otherwise. Each convolutional layer is followed by batch normalization and ReLU. The channel numbers are doubled each layer from 64 to 512 during encoding and halved from 512 to 64 during decoding. We set the combination of dice loss L_d and cross-entropy loss L_c as the loss function using the ground-truth label map. The final loss function is

$$Lossfunction = 0.5 \times L_d + 0.5 \times L_c$$

Training Details

Working framework of FCSegNet using Pytorch. For network training, we train all models from scratch with random initial parameters. The entire models are conducted on intel-i7 processor with Nvidia 16 GB memory. We randomly crop the $128 \times 128 \times 64$ patches as the training samples. For optimization, we use Adam optimizer by setting $\beta_1 = 0.9, \beta_2 = 0.999, \epsilon = 10^{-8}$ and batch size is two. In experiments, the initial learning rate is $1 \times e^{-4}$, and the learning rate decay of $1 \times e^{-6}$. The proposed network will preform both lung and COVID-19 segmentation tasks.

Result

Comparison With the State-of-the-art Methods

We compare our FCSegNet against the previous state-of-the-art methods on two datasets (the collected domestic test set and Germany data). Specifically, we evaluate the proposed method with FCN (Yang & Zhang, 2019), UNet (Çiçek et al., 2016), and UNet++ (Zhao et al., 2016). Note that all methods employ 3D convolution in the framework. The same training dataset and setting are used for all methods.

1. Qualitative Results on the Domestic Datasets: We compare our method with several state-of-the-art methods on the test set (Figures 5.16, 5.17, and 5.18), which contains some challenging samples with different contrast and pathogenic conditions.
   - COVID-19 segmentation task: Figure 5.16(a)–(d) illustrate the results of different methods, red line denotes the COVID-19 segmentation result of ground truth. Since the contrast (COVID-19 and lung) of this case is not enough, these methods cannot obtain approving results. The FCN method cannot obtain the whole edge of COVID-19. The results of UNet++ are often scattered and overlook the overall structures of COVID-19. The proposed method and UNet achieve better results; however, UNet result products flaw in the center of the lung (white points in (b)). Since the proposed method employs FV blocks which adaptively enhance the global contrast of features, the proposed method can avoid the scattered artifacts. In addition, the PASPP blocks further improve the performance of our method.

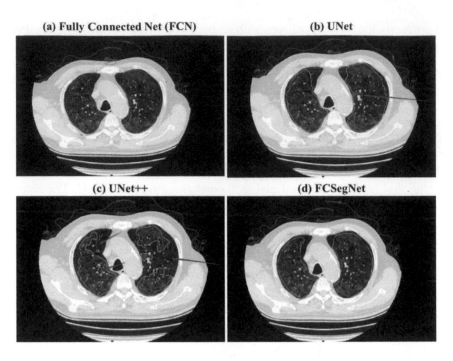

FIGURE 5.16 Visual comparisons on the testing data for COVID-19 segmentation. (a)–(d) show the results of the state-of-the-art methods and the proposed method, respectively. The red arrows indicate the flows of different methods. Ground truth is shown with the red line, other methods are displayed with different colors.

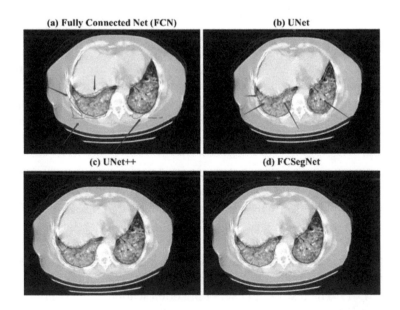

FIGURE 5.17 Figure (a)–(d) shows the results of the state-of-the-art methods and the proposed method, respectively when typical infection segmentation results of CT scans of COVID-19 patient (severe). The contrast of this case is too low to segment COVID-19 infection. The proposed method still can handle this difficulty sample. The red arrows indicate the flows of different methods. Ground truth is shown with the red line, other methods are displayed with different colors.

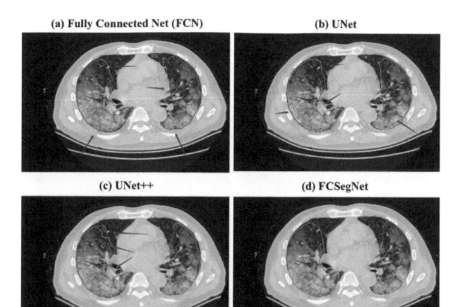

FIGURE 5.18   Figure (a)–(d) shows the results of the state-of-the-art methods and the proposed method, respectively with comparisons on the chest CT example of non-severe infection COVID-19 on the test set. The infection regions are not easily to peeling from the chest wall. The red arrows indicate the flows of different methods. Ground truth is shown with the red line, other methods are displayed with different colors.

Figure 5.17(a)–(d) display the example of low contrast CT images, COVID-19 infection regions are similar with chest wall. Most of the methods can obtain massive structures of COVID-19. However, the proposed method generates a more reasonable edge for infection regions due to the contributions of FV blocks.

Figure 5.18 shows a different case captured from a non-severe patient, but the COVID-19 infection regions still hard to distinguish from the chest wall. Thus, the methods of FCN and UNet++, generate dissatisfying results. The proposed method combined global and local information effectively obtains well-pleasing segmentation results for COVID-19 infection.

- Lung segmentation task: For the lung segmentation task, we test the performance of the proposed network on the test set. Figure 5.19(a) and (b) display the results of different methods. From Figure 5.19, we can easily observe that all results can close to the precision like manually annotated. UNet++ method often miss the boundary of the lung.

2. Qualitative Results on the Germany Data: To verify the generalization ability of all methods, we use ten cases of data captured from Brainlab Co. Ltd. in Germany to test the segmentation of COVID-19 infection and the lung.

- COVID-19 segmentation task: Figure 5.20 shows the comparisons on the chest CT images on the Germany data. The intensity of COVID-19 infection regions is very similar to that of the lung, which is a very challenging example. As displayed in Figure 5.20, all state-of-the-art methods (i.e., FCN, UNet, UNet++)

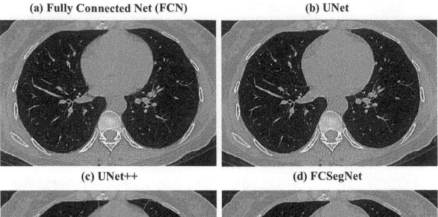

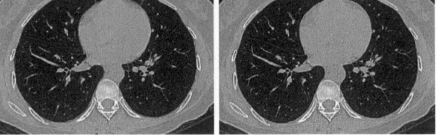

FIGURE 5.19 Visual comparisons on the testing data for lung segmentation. (a)–(d) show the results of the state-of-the-art methods and the proposed method, respectively.

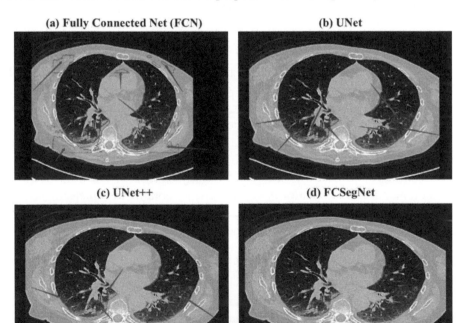

FIGURE 5.20 Figure (a)–(d) shows the results of the state-of-the-art methods and the proposed method, respectively with comparisons on the chest CT example of non-severe infection COVID-19 on the Germany data. The red arrows indicate the flows of different methods. Ground truth is shown with the red line, other methods are displayed with different colors.

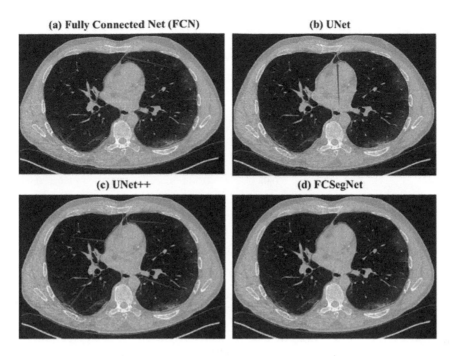

FIGURE 5.21 Figure (a)–(d) shows the results of the state-of-the-art methods and the proposed method, respectively with the lung segmentation results on the Germany data. The red arrows indicate the flows of different methods. Ground truth is shown with the red line, other methods are displayed with different colors.

generate perishing and over-segmentation. Different from others, the proposed methods can obtain perfect results, which like a manual annotation (See Figure 5.20(d)).

- Lung segmentation task: The segmentation results of all methods on the Germany data are shown in Figure 5.21. Most of all methods can generate a distinct outline of the lung. However, from the regions marked with the red arrow, our method has a stronger segmentation ability than other state-of-the-art methods. These perfect results demonstrate the effectiveness of the FV and PASPP blocks.

Quantitative Results

Based on the ground truths manually contoured by the radiology experts, we conduct the evaluations and comparisons to evaluate the accuracy of segmentation quantitatively. The results are reported in Table 5.8, which includes lung segmentation and COVID-19 infection segmentation.

For the segmentation of COVID-19, as shown in Table 5.8, the results of the proposed method achieves best in all the metrics. Thanks to the FV and PASPP block, the COVID-SegNet can effectively segment COVID-19 infection regions and significantly improve the segmentation performance over the UNet by 3.8% in term of Dice. All these metrics demonstrate the effectiveness of our model.

For the lung segmentation task, the average Dice similarity coefficient is 0.987. The average sensitivity and precision are 0.986 and 0.990, respectively. Although the existing methods have achieved enough promotion and the performance is hard to improve, the proposed

TABLE 5.8

Quantitative Comparison between Methods on the Test Dataset

Tasks	Metrics	FCN	UNet	UNet++	FCSegNet
COVID-19	Dice	0.659	0.688	0.681	0.726
	Sensitive	0.719	0.736	0.735	0.751
	Precision	0.597	0.662	0.719	0.726
Lung	Dice	0.865	0.987	0.986	0.987
	Sensitive	0.986	0.987	0.988	0.986
	Precision	0.983	0.984	0.985	0.99

FCSegNet still surpasses state of-the-art methods on the term of precision. We consider these results are attributed to the contributions of the proposed FV and PASPP blocks.

Ablation Studies

As shown in Table 5.9, the baseline model is a UNet structure with four layers in the encoder. We conduct the contrast enhancement branch (CEB), position-sensitive branch (PSB), and FV block, respectively. In addition, we also replace CEB with the original channel attention block (CAB, removed the global parameter in CEB) to verify the function of global contrast enhancement. For verifying the PASPP block, we use ASPP and ResASPP, which removes the concatenation in PASPP to prove the advantage of possessively fusing features.

1. Study on the FV block: The quality of the FV block, which is the combination of the contrast, global and position information, is critical for enhancing the ability of accurate COVID-19 segmentation. In this section, we first evaluate the performance of the contrast enhancement branch (CEB) from both lung and COVID-19 segmentation. Then, we study the function of the position sensitive branch (PSB). All the comparisons are both preformed on two tasks (lung and COVID-19 segmentation). All the results in Table 5.9 demonstrate the effectiveness of the FV blocks.

   Context information is of great significance for segmenting the confusing boundary and position of COVID-19 infection regions. To verify the performance of CEB, we employ the original channel attention block (CAB) to replace the CEB and PSB in the FV block. From Table 5.9, we can see that the ASPP improves the segmentation performance over the UNet4. The reason is that the features have redundant information. However, the performance is further improved when we replace the CAB with CEB. Since the CAB merely learns the weights for each channel, the CEB uses global information to guide feature enhancement, which proves the ability of the CEB.

   For PSB, it is actually a spatial attention module which has proved the effectiveness in many tasks. This branch focuses on the positions of features which are helpful to detect and segment COVID-19 infection regions. As we expected, the network with PSB generates satisfying numerical results. Combining these two branches in parallel, we obtain the FV block which consists of global (ECB) and local (PSB) information to improve the segmentation task.

2. Study on the PASPP block: PASPP consists of multiple atrous convolutional layers with different dilation rates and progressive concatenations. In this part, we

TABLE 5.9

Performance of Network With Different Blocks

	Blocks							COVID-19 Lesion			Lung Segmentation		
UNet4	CAB	CEB	PSB	FV	ASPP	ResASPP	PASPP	Dice	Sensitive	Precision	Dice	Sensitive	Precision
X								0.658	0.67	0.651	0.959	0.956	0.951
X	X							0.675	0.683	0.665	0.96	0.954	0.956
X		X						0.682	0.692	0.674	0.966	0.961	0.97
X			X					0.684	0.695	0.677	0.962	0.963	0.969
X				X				0.708	0.729	0.704	0.975	0.97	0.981
X					X			0.663	0.684	0.672	0.968	0.965	0.971
X						X		0.679	0.701	0.681	0.977	0.973	0.975
X							X	0.711	0.732	0.707	0.98	0.982	0.983
X				X			X	0.726	0.751	0.726	0.987	0.986	0.99

conduct experiments to study how different settings of PASPP influence the performance quantitatively. We compare the PASPP block with original ASPP and modified ResASPP (removed progressive concatenations). The results are reported in Table 5.9, from which we obtain several conclusions. First, progressively fusing strategy is very effective for COVID-19 segmentation. We deem the reason is different scale features should not be fused at once for the sophisticated COVID-19 segmentation. With the progressively fusing, the adjacent information can better supplement the missing details. Second, compared with ASPP and ResASPP, sine the ResASPP includes residual learning, it obtains reasonably high performances. This implies that the information from the early blocks can quickly flow to the output of atrous convolutional layers, and the gradient can be quickly back-propagated to the early blocks from the atrous convolutional layers. Third, the ASPP significantly improves the segmentation performance over the UNet.

In general, to extract compacted features and obtain semantic information from COVID-19 CT images, we insert FV blocks into the encoder and employ PASPP for enlarging the receptive fields. As reported in Table 5.9, the proposed network not only achieves the best performance on lung segmentation but also on COVID-19 segmentation.

NOTE

1. www.kaggle.com/plameneduardo/sarscov2-ctscan-dataset.

REFERENCES

Ai, T., Yang, Z., & Hou, H. (2020). Correlation of chest CT and RT-PCR testing in coronavirus Disease 2019 (COVID-19) in China: A report of 1014 cases [e-pub ahead of print]. *Radiology*.

Bai, H. X., Hsieh, B., Xiong, Z., Halsey, K., Choi, J. W., Tran, T. M. L., Pan, I., Shi, L.-B., Wang, D.-C., & Mei, J. (2020a). Performance of radiologists in differentiating COVID-19 from viral pneumonia on chest CT. *Radiology*.

Bai, H. X., Wang, R., Xiong, Z., Hsieh, B., Chang, K., Halsey, K., Tran, T. M. L., Choi, J. W., Wang, D.-C., & Shi, L.-B. (2020b). AI augmentation of radiologist performance in distinguishing COVID-19 from pneumonia of other etiology on chest CT. *Radiology*.

Bernheim, A., Mei, X., Huang, M., Yang, Y., Fayad, Z. A., Zhang, N., Diao, K., Lin, B., Zhu, X., & Li, K. (2020). Chest CT findings in coronavirus disease-19 (COVID-19): relationship to duration of infection. *Radiology*, 200463.

Brody, A. S., Klein, J. S., Molina, P. L., Quan, J., Bean, J. A., & Wilmott, R. W. (2004). High-resolution computed tomography in young patients with cystic fibrosis: distribution of abnormalities and correlation with pulmonary function tests. *The Journal of Pediatrics*, *145*(1), 32–38.

Brynolfsson, P., Nilsson, D., Torheim, T., Asklund, T., Karlsson, C. T., Trygg, J., Nyholm, T., & Garpebring, A. (2017). Haralick texture features from apparent diffusion coefficient (ADC) MRI images depend on imaging and pre-processing parameters. *Scientific Reports*, *7*(1), 1–11.

Butt, C., Gill, J., Chun, D., & Babu, B. A. (2020). Deep learning system to screen coronavirus disease 2019 pneumonia. *Applied Intelligence*, 1.

Chen, L.-C., Papandreou, G., Kokkinos, I., Murphy, K., & Yuille, A. L. (2017). Deeplab: Semantic image segmentation with deep convolutional nets, atrous convolution, and fully connected crfs. *IEEE Transactions on Pattern Analysis and Machine Intelligence*, *40*(4), 834–848.

Chen, R., Chen, J., & Meng, Q. (2020). Chest computed tomography images of early coronavirus disease (COVID-19). *Canadian Journal of Anesthesia/Journal Canadien d'anesthésie*, *67*(6), 754–755.

Chen, Z., Fan, H., Cai, J., Li, Y., Wu, B., Hou, Y., Xu, S., Zhou, F., Liu, Y., & Xuan, W. (2020). High-resolution computed tomography manifestations of COVID-19 infections in patients of different ages. *European Journal of Radiology*, 108972.

Cheng, Z., Lu, Y., Cao, Q., Qin, L., Pan, Z., Yan, F., & Yang, W. (2020). Clinical features and chest CT manifestations of coronavirus disease 2019 (COVID-19) in a single-center study in Shanghai, China. *American Journal of Roentgenology*, 1–6.

Chollet, F. (2017). Xception: Deep learning with depthwise separable convolutions. *Proceedings of the IEEE Conference on Computer Vision and Pattern Recognition*, 1251–1258.

Chung, M., Bernheim, A., Mei, X., Zhang, N., Huang, M., Zeng, X., Cui, J., Xu, W., Yang, Y., & Fayad, Z. A. (2020). CT imaging features of 2019 novel coronavirus (2019-nCoV). *Radiology*, 295(1), 202–207.

Çiçek, Ö., Abdulkadir, A., Lienkamp, S. S., Brox, T., & Ronneberger, O. (2016). 3D U-Net: learning dense volumetric segmentation from sparse annotation. *International Conference on Medical Image Computing and Computer-Assisted Intervention*, 424–432.

Coelho, L. P. (2012). Mahotas: Open source software for scriptable computer vision. *ArXiv Preprint ArXiv:1211.4907*.

Deng, J., Zhang, Z., Marchi, E., & Schuller, B. (2013). Sparse autoencoder-based feature transfer learning for speech emotion recognition. *2013 Humaine Association Conference on Affective Computing and Intelligent Interaction*, 511–516.

Dutta, A., & Zisserman, A. (2019). The VIA annotation software for images, audio and video. *Proceedings of the 27th ACM International Conference on Multimedia*, 2276–2279.

Fang, Y., Zhang, H., Xie, J., Lin, M., Ying, L., Pang, P., & Ji, W. (2020). Sensitivity of chest CT for COVID-19: Comparison to RT-PCR. *Radiology*, 200432.

Goodfellow, I., Pouget-Abadie, J., Mirza, M., Xu, B., Warde-Farley, D., Ozair, S., Courville, A., & Bengio, Y. (2014). Generative adversarial nets. *Advances in Neural Information Processing Systems*, 2672–2680.

Gozes, O., Frid-Adar, M., Greenspan, H., Browning, P. D., Zhang, H., Ji, W., Bernheim, A., & Siegel, E. (2020). Rapid ai development cycle for the coronavirus (covid-19) pandemic: Initial results for automated detection & patient monitoring using deep learning ct image analysis. *ArXiv Preprint ArXiv:2003.05037*.

Han, R., Huang, L., Jiang, H., Dong, J., Peng, H., & Zhang, D. (2020). Early clinical and CT manifestations of coronavirus disease 2019 (COVID-19) pneumonia. *American Journal of Roentgenology*, 1–6.

Hansell, D. M., Bankier, A. A., MacMahon, H., McLoud, T. C., Muller, N. L., & Remy, J. (2008). Fleischner Society: Glossary of terms for thoracic imaging. *Radiology*, 246(3), 697–722.

Haralick, R. M., Shanmugam, K., & Dinstein, I. H. (1973). Textural features for image classification. *IEEE Transactions on Systems, Man, and Cybernetics*, 6, 610–621.

He, X., Lau, E. H. Y., Wu, P., Deng, X., Wang, J., Hao, X., Lau, Y. C., Wong, J. Y., Guan, Y., & Tan, X. (2020). Temporal dynamics in viral shedding and transmissibility of COVID-19. *Nature Medicine*, 26(5), 672–675.

Hesamian, M. H., Jia, W., He, X., & Kennedy, P. (2019). Deep learning techniques for medical image segmentation: Achievements and challenges. *Journal of Digital Imaging*, 32(4), 582–596.

Hoehl, S., Rabenau, H., Berger, A., Kortenbusch, M., Cinatl, J., Bojkova, D., Behrens, P., Böddinghaus, B., Götsch, U., & Naujoks, F. (2020). Evidence of SARS-CoV-2 infection in returning travelers from Wuhan, China. *New England Journal of Medicine*, 382(13), 1278–1280.

Huang, C., Wang, Y., Li, X., Ren, L., Zhao, J., Hu, Y., Zhang, L., Fan, G., Xu, J., & Gu, X. (2020). Clinical features of patients infected with 2019 novel coronavirus in Wuhan, China. *The Lancet*, 395(10223), 497–506.

Inui, S., Fujikawa, A., Jitsu, M., Kunishima, N., Watanabe, S., Suzuki, Y., Umeda, S., & Uwabe, Y. (2020). Chest CT findings in cases from the cruise ship "Diamond Princess" with coronavirus disease 2019 (COVID-19). *Radiology: Cardiothoracic Imaging*, 2(2), e200110.

Jin, S., Wang, B., Xu, H., Luo, C., Wei, L., Zhao, W., Hou, X., Ma, W., Xu, Z., & Zheng, Z. (2020). AI-assisted CT imaging analysis for COVID-19 screening: Building and deploying a medical AI system in four weeks. *MedRxiv.*

Kundu, S., Elhalawani, H., Gichoya, J. W., & Kahn Jr, C. E. (2020). *How Might AI and Chest Imaging Help Unravel COVID-19's Mysteries?* Radiological Society of North America.

Lai, C. C., Liu, Y. H., Wang, C. Y., Wang, Y. H. & Hsueh, P. R. (2020). Asymptomatic carrier state, acute respiratory disease, and pneumonia due to severe acute respiratory syndrome coronavirus 2 (SARSCoV-2): Facts and myths. *Journal of Microbiology, Immunology and Infection.*

Li, L., Qin, L., Xu, Z., Yin, Y., Wang, X., Kong, B., Bai, J., Lu, Y., Fang, Z., & Song, Q. (2020). Artificial intelligence distinguishes COVID-19 from community acquired pneumonia on chest CT. *Radiology.*

Li, Y., & Xia, L. (2020). Coronavirus disease 2019 (COVID-19): Role of chest CT in diagnosis and management. *American Journal of Roentgenology, 214*(6), 1280–1286.

Liaw, A., & Wiener, M. (2002). Classification and regression by randomForest. *R News, 2*(3), 18–22.

Liu, K.-C., Xu, P., Lv, W.-F., Qiu, X.-H., Yao, J.-L., & Jin-Feng, G. (2020). CT manifestations of coronavirus disease-2019: A retrospective analysis of 73 cases by disease severity. *European Journal of Radiology,* 108941.

Long, C., Xu, H., Shen, Q., Zhang, X., Fan, B., Wang, C., Zeng, B., Li, Z., Li, X., & Li, H. (2020). Diagnosis of the Coronavirus disease (COVID-19): rRT-PCR or CT? *European Journal of Radiology,* 108961.

Mei, X., Lee, H.-C., Diao, K., Huang, M., Lin, B., Liu, C., Xie, Z., Ma, Y., Robson, P. M., & Chung, M. (2020). Artificial intelligence–enabled rapid diagnosis of patients with COVID-19. *Nature Medicine,* 1–5.

Milletari, F., Navab, N., & Ahmadi, S.-A. (2016). V-net: Fully convolutional neural networks for volumetric medical image segmentation. *2016 Fourth International Conference on 3D Vision (3DV),* 565–571.

Ouyang, X., Huo, J., Xia, L., Shan, F., Liu, J., Mo, Z., Yan, F., Ding, Z., Yang, Q., & Song, B. (2020). Dual-Sampling Attention Network for Diagnosis of COVID-19 from Community Acquired Pneumonia. *IEEE Transactions on Medical Imaging.*

Pan, F., Ye, T., Sun, P., Gui, S., Liang, B., Li, L., Zheng, D., Wang, J., Hesketh, R. L., & Yang, L. (2020). Time course of lung changes on chest CT during recovery from 2019 novel coronavirus (COVID-19) pneumonia. *Radiology,* 200370.

Qian, L., Yu, J., & Shi, H. (2020). Severe acute respiratory disease in a Huanan seafood market worker: Images of an early casualty. *Radiology: Cardiothoracic Imaging, 2*(1), e200033.

Quanjer, P. H., Borsboom, G., Brunekreef, B., Zach, M., Forche, G., Cotes, J. E., Sanchis, J., & Paoletti, P. (1995). Spirometric reference values for white European children and adolescents: Polgar revisited. *Pediatric Pulmonology, 19*(2), 135–142.

Ranney, M. L., Griffeth, V., & Jha, A. K. (2020). Critical supply shortages—the need for ventilators and personal protective equipment during the Covid-19 pandemic. *New England Journal of Medicine, 382*(18), e41.

Rifai, S., Vincent, P., Muller, X., Glorot, X., & Bengio, Y. (2011). Contractive auto-encoders: Explicit invariance during feature extraction. *Icml.*

Ronneberger, O., Fischer, P., & Brox, T. (2015). U-net: Convolutional networks for biomedical image segmentation. *International Conference on Medical Image Computing and Computer-Assisted Intervention,* 234–241.

Rubin, G. D., Ryerson, C. J., Haramati, L. B., Sverzellati, N., Kanne, J. P., Raoof, S., Schluger, N. W., Volpi, A., Yim, J.-J., & Martin, I. B. K. (2020). The role of chest imaging in patient management during the COVID-19 pandemic: A multinational consensus statement from the Fleischner Society. *Chest.*

Salehi, S., Abedi, A., Balakrishnan, S., & Gholamrezanezhad, A. (2020). Coronavirus disease 2019 (COVID-19): a systematic review of imaging findings in 919 patients. *American Journal of Roentgenology,* 1–7.

Shan, F., Gao, Y., Wang, J., Shi, W., Shi, N., Han, M., Xue, Z., & Shi, Y. (2020). Lung infection quantification of covid-19 in ct images with deep learning. *ArXiv Preprint ArXiv:2003.04655*.

Shi, H., Han, X., Jiang, N., Cao, Y., Alwalid, O., Gu, J., Fan, Y., & Zheng, C. (2020). Radiological findings from 81 patients with COVID-19 pneumonia in Wuhan, China: A descriptive study. *The Lancet Infectious Diseases*.

Shin, H.-C., Roth, H. R., Gao, M., Lu, L., Xu, Z., Nogues, I., Yao, J., Mollura, D., & Summers, R. M. (2016). Deep convolutional neural networks for computer-aided detection: CNN architectures, dataset characteristics and transfer learning. *IEEE Transactions on Medical Imaging*, *35*(5), 1285–1298.

Sohrabi, C., Alsafi, Z., O'Neill, N., Khan, M., Kerwan, A., Al-Jabir, A., Iosifidis, C., & Agha, R. (2020). World Health Organization declares global emergency: A review of the 2019 novel coronavirus (COVID-19). *International Journal of Surgery*.

Song, Y., Zheng, S., Li, L., Zhang, X., Zhang, X., Huang, Z., Chen, J., Zhao, H., Jie, Y., & Wang, R. (2020). Deep learning enables accurate diagnosis of novel coronavirus (COVID-19) with CT images. *MedRxiv*.

Sverzellati, N., Milanese, G., Milone, F., Balbi, M., Ledda, R. E., & Silva, M. (2020). Integrated radiologic algorithm for COVID-19 pandemic. *Journal of Thoracic Imaging*.

Tammeling, G. J., Cotes, J. E., Pedersen, O. F., Peslin, R., & Yernault, J. C. (1993). Standardized lung function testing. *Eur Respir J*, *6*(Suppl 16), 5–40.

Tang, C., Zhang, K., Wang, W., Pei, Z., Liu, Z., Yuan, P., Guan, Z., & Gu, J. (2020). Clinical Characteristics of 20,662 Patients with COVID-19 Described in 147 Articles: A Systemic Review and Meta-Analysis. *Available at SSRN 3571542*.

Vincent, P., Larochelle, H., Bengio, Y., & Manzagol, P.-A. (2008). Extracting and composing robust features with denoising autoencoders. *Proceedings of the 25th International Conference on Machine Learning*, 1096–1103.

Wang, J., Bao, Y., Wen, Y., Lu, H., Luo, H., Xiang, Y., Li, X., Liu, C., & Qian, D. (2020). Prior-Attention Residual Learning for More Discriminative COVID-19 Screening in CT Images. *IEEE Transactions on Medical Imaging*.

Wang, S., Kang, B., Ma, J., Zeng, X., Xiao, M., Guo, J., Cai, M., Yang, J., Li, Y., & Meng, X. (2020). A deep learning algorithm using CT images to screen for Corona Virus Disease (COVID-19). medRxiv. *Published Online April*, *24*, 2002–2020.

Wu, Y., Xie, Y., & Wang, X. (2020). Longitudinal CT findings in COVID-19 pneumonia: case presenting organizing pneumonia pattern. *Radiology: Cardiothoracic Imaging*, *2*(1), e200031.

Xie, X., Zhong, Z., Zhao, W., Zheng, C., Wang, F., & Liu, J. (2020). Chest CT for typical 2019-nCoV pneumonia: Relationship to negative RT-PCR testing. *Radiology*, 200343.

Yang, B., & Zhang, W. (2019). FD-FCN: 3D Fully Dense and Fully Convolutional Network for Semantic Segmentation of Brain Anatomy. *ArXiv Preprint ArXiv:1907.09194*.

Yang, Y., Yang, M., & Shen, C. (2020). Evaluating the accuracy of different respiratory specimens in the laboratory diagnosis and monitoring the viral shedding of 2019-nCoV infections. Posted February 17, 2020. *Available at: Doi: Https://Doi. Org/10.1101/2020.02*, *11*.

Yosinski, J., Clune, J., Bengio, Y., & Lipson, H. (2014). How transferable are features in deep neural networks? *Advances in Neural Information Processing Systems*, 3320–3328.

Yu, M., Xu, D., Lan, L., Tu, M., Liao, R., Cai, S., Cao, Y., Xu, L., Liao, M., & Zhang, X. (2020). Thin-section Chest CT Imaging of Coronavirus Disease 2019 Pneumonia: Comparison Between Patients with Mild and Severe Disease. *Radiology: Cardiothoracic Imaging*, *2*(2), e200126.

Zapletal, A., Samanek, M., & Paul, T. (1987). Lung function in children and adolescents: methods, reference values. *Progress in Respiration Research*, *22*.

Zeiler, M. D., & Fergus, R. (2014). Visualizing and understanding convolutional networks. *European Conference on Computer Vision*, 818–833.

Zhang, K., Liu, X., Shen, J., Li, Z., Sang, Y., Wu, X., Zha, Y., Liang, W., Wang, C., & Wang, K. (2020). Clinically applicable AI system for accurate diagnosis, quantitative measurements, and prognosis of covid-19 pneumonia using computed tomography. *Cell*.

Zhao, J., Zhang, Y., He, X., & Xie, P. (2020). COVID-CT-Dataset: a CT scan dataset about COVID-19. *ArXiv Preprint ArXiv:2003.13865.*

Zhao, L., Wang, J., Li, X., Tu, Z., & Zeng, W. (2016). Deep convolutional neural networks with merge-and-run mappings. *ArXiv Preprint ArXiv:1611.07718.*

Zhao, W., Zhong, Z., Xie, X., Yu, Q., & Liu, J. (2020a). CT scans of patients with 2019 novel coronavirus (COVID-19) pneumonia. *Theranostics, 10*(10), 4606.

Zhao, W., Zhong, Z., Xie, X., Yu, Q., & Liu, J. (2020b). Relation between chest CT findings and clinical conditions of coronavirus disease (COVID-19) pneumonia: a multicenter study. *American Journal of Roentgenology, 214*(5), 1072–1077.

6 Chest X-Ray Image-Based Testing Using Machine Learning Techniques

KEY POINTS

- COVID-19 detection in chest X-ray using multi-graded and hierarchical learners.
- Using a database that represents a real-world scenario with its natural imbalance.
- Textual search from chest X-ray images with pneumonia.
- To evaluate handcrafted and learned features to check their complementarities.
- Ground glass appearance is common in earlier presentations and may precede the appearance of consolidation.

INTRODUCTION

We live in a universe of viruses. It is estimated that there are billions of types of viruses on earth, and ~320,000 types that infect mammals alone. Many viral species exist in our surrounding environment. As we live, breathe, eat, talk, and go about our daily activities, the number of viruses that we come into contact with is virtually infinite. Fortunately, only a relatively small number of viruses are known to infect humans.

COVID-19 is a global challenge that should be addressed by all scientific means. Medical image analysis is a well-known approach that could be beneficial in the diagnosis of COVID-19. Severe Acute Respiratory Syndrome (SARS) and COVID-19 belong to the same family of Coronaviruses, where the detection of SARS cases using chest images proposed by several methods (Hosseini & Zekri, 2012; Quek et al., 2010; Xie et al., 2006) and for pneumonia detection in general (Rajpurkar et al., 2017).

Chest radiography or chest X-ray (CXR) is a fast and relatively inexpensive imaging modality which is available in many resource-constrained healthcare settings. Unfortunately, there is a severe shortage of radiological expertise in these regions to allow for precise interpretation of such images (Mollura & Lungren, 2014). An AI system may be a helpful tool as an adjunct to radiologists or, in the common case that radiological expertise is not available, for the medical team (Annarumma et al., 2019; Hwang, et al., 2019a). Previous work in the related task of tuberculosis (TB) detection on CXR (Hwang, et al., 2019b; Murphy et al., 2020; Qin et al., 2019). has demonstrated that software can perform at the level of an expert radiologist at the task of TB identification.

Machine learning has demonstrated high performance for several image processing applications such as image analysis (Chouhan et al., 2020), image classification (Rawat & Wang, 2017), and image segmentation (Yang et al., 2017). Image classification achieved by extracting the import features from the images by a descriptor (e.g., SIFT (Yang & Newsam, 2008) and image moment (Abd Elaziz et al., 2019), and then these features can be used in the classification task using classifiers such as SVM In contrast to handcrafted features, deep neural network-based methods (Simonyan & Zisserman, 2014) provides high performance in classifying the images according to the extracted features. According to the characteristics of machine learning, several efforts utilized machine learning based methods to classify the chest X-ray images into COVID-19 patient class or normal case class. Imaging procedures are crucial in the COVID-19 pandemic when it comes to assessing suspected cases and the course of the disease. On the basis of the latest scientific evidences we consider the role of X-ray imaging in the current situation. All of these efforts utilized deep learning-based approaches.

CHEST X-RAY IMAGING FOR COVID-19

COVID-19 is likely to remain an important differential diagnosis for the foreseeable future in anyone presenting to hospital with a flu-like illness, lymphopenia on full blood count, and/or a change in normal sense of smell (anosmia) or taste (Zhao et al., 2020). Most people with COVID-19 infection do not develop pneumonia; however, chest radiography of people who are seriously ill with respiratory symptoms (i.e., atypical pneumonia(Kooraki et al., 2020) or organizing pneumonia (Ai et al., 2020; Kanne et al., 2020) when they present to hospital can help to identify those with COVID-19 pneumonia.

This section offer advice to non-radiologists on how to look for changes on chest radiograph that may be suggestive of COVID-19 pneumonia, as prompt review and report from an onsite or remote radiologist is not always available.

GROUND GLASS OPACITY OF COVID-19 PNEUMONIA

No fixed definition of COVID-19 pneumonia exists; in this article the term is used when describing patients with clinical features of COVID-19 infection who have either clinical or radiological evidence of pneumonia, (Ai et al., 2020; Kanne et al., 2020) or acute respiratory distress.

Like other pneumonias, COVID-19 pneumonia causes the density of the lungs to increase. This may be seen as whiteness in the lungs on radiography which, depending on the severity of the pneumonia, obscures the lung markings that are normally seen; however, this may be delayed in appearing or absent.

- When lung markings are partially obscured by the increased whiteness, a ground glass pattern (ground glass opacity, Figure 6.1) occurs. This can be subtle and might need confirmation with a radiologist.
- Peripheral, coarse, horizontal white lines, bands, or reticular changes which can be described, as linear opacities may also be seen in association with ground glass opacity (Figure 6.1).
- When lung markings are completely lost due to the whiteness, it is known as consolidation (this is usually seen in severe disease) (Figures 6.2 and 6.3(c)) (Hansell et al., 2008). A small case series in Korea found that, in polymerase chain reaction (PCR) confirmed COVID-19 infection, in those with radiological abnormalities, 70% of the radiographical opacities (number of lesions, not patients) were consolidation (Yoon et al., 2020).

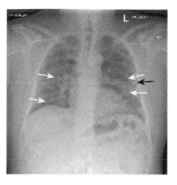

FIGURE 6.1 Ground glass opacity. Posterior-anterior chest radiograph of patient A, a man in his 50s with COVID-19 pneumonia. Features include ground glass opacity in both mid and lower zones of the lungs, which is predominantly peripheral (white arrows) with preservation of lung marking. Linear opacity can be seen in the periphery of the left mid zone (black arrow).

COVID-19 pneumonia can be classed as an atypical pneumonia because of the radiographic appearances of multifocal ground glass opacity, linear opacities, and consolidation. These changes are also seen in other atypical pneumonias, including other coronavirus infections (severe acute respiratory system, SARS, and Middle East respiratory syndrome, MERS) (Hosseiny et al., 2020).

Review the radiograph systematically, looking for abnormalities of the heart, mediastinum, lungs, diaphragm, and ribs (Pezzotti, 2014), and remembering that radiographic changes of COVID-19 pneumonia can be subtle or absent. Compare with previous chest radiographs when available. Look for evidence of ground glass opacity, peripheral linear opacities, or consolidation in the lung.

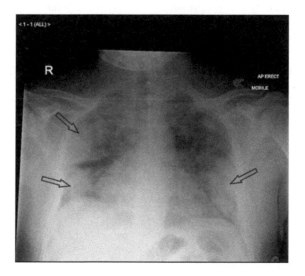

FIGURE 6.2 Consolidation. Anterior-posterior (AP) chest radiograph of patient B, a man in his 50s, with severe COVID-19 pneumonia, showing bilateral dense peripheral consolidation and loss of lung markings in the mid and lower zones (outlined arrows).

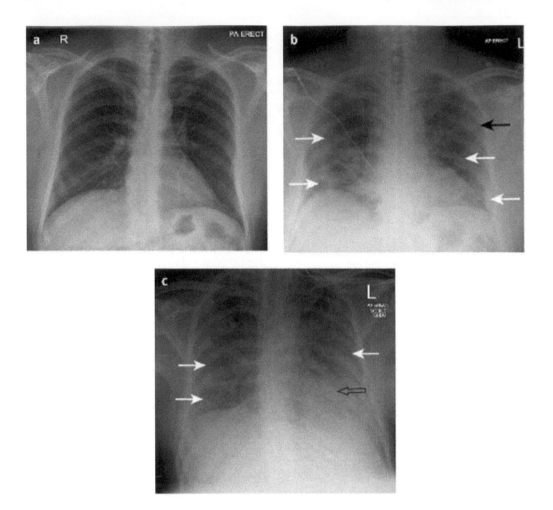

FIGURE 6.3 Serial radiological progression seen with COVID-19 pneumonia. (a) Normal posterior-anterior chest radiograph of patient C, a man in his 50s (taken up to 12 months before admission, included here for comparison). (b) AP chest radiograph of patient C when he developed COVID-19 pneumonia—taken in the emergency department (day zero of admission), showing ground glass opacities in the periphery (outer third of the lung) of both lungs in the mid and lower zones (white arrows), preservation of lung marking, and linear opacity in the periphery of the left mid zone (black arrow). (c) AP chest radiograph of patient C on day ten of admission, showing progression to severe COVID-19 pneumonia: patient intubated with endotracheal tube, central lines, and nasogastric tube in situ. Dense consolidation with loss of lung markings is now seen behind the heart in the left lower zone (outlined arrow). Extension of the peripheral ground glass changes seen in (B) can be seen in the periphery of the right mid and lower zones and the left mid zone (white arrows).

Usually Affected Part Of Lungs With COVID-19

A quantitative meta-analysis covering 2847 patients in China and Australia, and a multinational descriptive analysis of 39 case report articles summarising 127 patients, found that COVID-19 pneumonia changes are mostly bilateral on chest radiographs (72.9%, 95% confidence interval 58.6 to 87.1) and have ground glass opacity in 68.5% of cases (95% CI 51.8 to 85.2) (Figures 6.1 and 6.3(b)); however, these data are pooled so it is not possible to link the radiographic findings to the duration of disease or severity (Rodriguez-Morales et al., 2020).

A retrospective case series of 64 patients hospitalized with COVID-19 infection in Hong Kong found that chest radiograph changes are often peripheral (41%) and lower zone (50%) in distribution (Wong et al., 2020); these findings are supported by a pictorial review from the US describing common manifestations and patterns of lung abnormality seen on portable chest radiography in COVID-19 patients (Jacobi et al., 2020); it does not, however, describe a formal methodology, the geographical location of the patients, or the numbers of patients included.

This pictorial review also suggests that the coarse linear opacities associated with COVID-19 on chest radiography typically appear in the lung peripheries (Figures 6.1 and 6.3(b)) (Jacobi et al., 2020).

A small case series in Korea showed that 80% of radiographical changes (again this relates to the number of radiological lesions seen, not patients) were found peripherally (Yoon et al., 2020).

Potential chest X-ray image findings in COVID-19 pneumonia

- Most patients with COVID-19 infection have a mild illness and do not develop pneumonia (Wu & McGoogan, 2020).
- The chest radiograph may be normal in up to 63% of people with COVID-19 pneumonia, particularly in the early stages (Chen et al., 2020; Ng et al., 2020; Wong et al., 2020; Yoon et al., 2020). (but there is uncertainty around this estimate, ranging from 0 to 63%)
- Changes include ground glass (68.5%) (Rodriguez-Morales et al., 2020), coarse horizontal linear opacities, and consolidation.12 These are more likely to be peripheral and in the lower zones, but the whole lung can be involved (Wong et al., 2020; Yoon et al., 2020).
- Ground glass appearance is common in earlier presentations and may precede the appearance of consolidation (Jacobi et al., 2020; Wong et al., 2020).
- Bilateral lung involvement is most common (72.9%) (but can be unilateral in 25%) (Rodriguez-Morales et al., 2020).
- Signs suggestive of potential comorbidities on chest radiography might be obscured by signs of COVID-19 pneumonia
- The appearance of nodules, pneumothorax, or pleural effusion (1–3%) might be incidental, caused by COVID-19 or by comorbidities

Additionally consider COVID-19 infection in patients with nodular lung lesions, pneumothorax, and pleural effusion as these have been reported in case series of patients with COVID-19 infection in China and Korea (Chen et al., 2020; Wong et al., 2020; Zhao et al., 2020a); however, the evidence within these reports is not strong, making it difficult to be certain when these are incidental findings, a sign of dual pathology, or unusual manifestations of COVID-19. The pictorial review mentioned above also reports this range of radiological abnormalities but cites similar studies (Jacobi et al., 2020).

Look for cardiac outline abnormalities on chest radiography as cardiac complications are reported with COVID-19 (which can be seen on echo (Zeng et al., 2020)); however, no reports of cardiac abnormalities seen on chest radiographs have been published.

It is good practice to look for radiograph features that might indicate comorbidities such as tumors, emphysema, community acquired pneumonia, and bone fracture. Look for misplaced tubes (e.g., endotracheal, nasogastric, pleural drains) and lines (e.g., central venous lines), and evidence of heart disease including sternotomy wires, which could indicate previous cardiac surgery. Not all of these comorbidities have been reported in relation to COVID-19 chest radiographs; (Chen et al., 2020; Chen et al., 2020; Liu et al. 2020). however, in some cases, COVID-19 pneumonia changes might be so widespread that features suggestive of comorbidities are obscured.

RELIABILITY OF DETECTING COVID-19 USING CHEST X-RAY

Avoid relying solely on imaging findings; use them in conjunction with clinical findings to form an overall clinical assessment, because

- No single feature on chest radiography is diagnostic of COVID-19 pneumonia
- Initial chest radiography may be normal but patients may later develop clinical or radiological signs of COVID-19 pneumonia—i.e., early radiographs may be negative (see patient D, Figure 6.4)
- A retrospective case series of 64 patients hospitalized with COVID-19 infection in Hong Kong found that 31% (20 patients) had normal chest radiographs on admission. Of these patients, 35% (n=7) developed radiographical changes on follow-up radiography (Rubin et al., 2020; Wong et al., 2020). This study also suggested that peak radiological severity on chest radiography is seen at days 10–12 of symptom onset (Wong et al., 2020) (see patient c, Figure 6.3).
- On the basis of this study, the multinational consensus statement from the Fleischner Society for thoracic radiology stated that chest radiography can be insensitive in mild or early COVID-19 infection (Guan et al., 2020; Rubin et al., 2020).
- In a series of 1099 hospitalized patients with laboratory confirmed COVID-19 from across China, of the 274 patients who had chest radiography on admission 162 (59.1%) showed abnormalities, most commonly "bilateral patchy

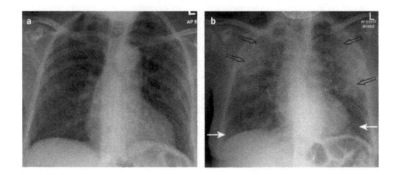

FIGURE 6.4   Serial radiological progression seen with covid 19 pneumonia (a) A normal AP chest radiograph of patient D, a woman in her 70s who is in hospital with COVID-19 infection (day zero of admission). (b) An AP chest radiograph of patient D on day eight, showing ground glass opacification now present at both lung bases (white arrows). Consolidation is also seen in the periphery of the left upper and mid zones (outlined arrows). Increased density (whiteness) is also present in the periphery of the right upper zone; this is not as dense or white as that seen in the left lung, showing progression of lung change of ground-glass opacification to consolidation (outlined arrows).

shadowing" (n=100, 36.5%). Of 1099 patients 975 had computed tomography but it is unclear how many of the chest radiographs were false negatives for covid pneumonia.

- The introduction of a systematic review of case series and case reports covering 919 patients in China and Korea suggests that while chest radiography is of little diagnostic value in the early stages, in intermediate and advanced stages, features suggestive of COVID-19 infection may be seen (Salehi et al., 2020). However, it is unclear in the review how the conclusions regarding chest radiography were reached. A case series of 799 patients from Wuhan China with confirmed COVID-19 looked at a subset of those who died (n=113) or were discharged (n=161) and reported that all patients had abnormalities on chest radiograph on admission (Chen et al., 2020).
- Chest radiographs can be normal in some patients with clinically diagnosed COVID-19 pneumonia, or who have been diagnosed with COVID-19 pneumonia by computed tomography—i.e., there may be false negative radiographs (Ng et al., 2020; Wong et al., 2020; Yoon et al., 2020).
- In the Hong Kong retrospective case series described above, four patients never developed abnormalities on radiography; however one of these patients (25%) had ground glass opacities on chest computed tomography (performed within 48 hours of chest radiography) (Wong et al., 2020).
- A case series of nine patients with PCR confirmed COVID-19 infection in Korea reported that three had abnormal baseline radiographs but eight had changes on baseline computed tomography, suggesting five of eight baseline radiographs (63%) were false negatives (Yoon et al., 2020).
- A case series in China reported that a subset of two of five (40%) patients had normal chest radiographs, but computed tomography done on the same day confirmed COVID-19 pneumonia (Ng et al., 2020).

FEATURES AND LIMITATIONS OF CHEST RADIOGRAPHS IN COVID-19

Features

Normal

- Central mediastinum and heart appear normal.
- Lungs predominantly contain air (appearing black).
- Lung markings are present, representing blood vessels extending from the hilum to the lung periphery (these branch and decrease in calibre, such that few vessels are seen at the lung periphery).
- The diaphragm is curvilinear in outline with sharp costophrenic margins.

Ground Glass Opacity

- The initial abnormalities suggesting COVID-19 pneumonia on a chest radiograph are loss of the normal black appearance in the lung.
- This is seen as increased whiteness, (because of increased density), but not enough to totally obscure lung markings; giving a ground glass appearance.
- Ground glass opacities can be difficult to observe; radiologist confirmation is recommended.

- Horizontal linear opacities may be seen with ground-glass change (Pezzotti, 2014) (Figures 6.1 and 6.3(b)).
- Location: usually bilateral but can be unilateral More often reported in a peripheral lung adjacent to the chest wall and diaphragm and usually with a distribution in the mid and lower zones (Hosseiny et al., 2020; Pezzotti, 2014; Wong et al., 2020). Figure 6.4(b) shows ground glass opacities in the right upper zone, as will be the case in approximately 20% of patients with COVID-19 pneumonia

Consolidation

- Ground-glass opacities become denser (whiter) and progress to consolidation with complete loss of lung markings
- Location: The areas of consolidation are likely to have progressed from sites of ground glass opacities (Figures 6.2 and 6.3(c)).

Limitations

AP images from portable machines produce a poorer quality image when compared with a PA chest radiograph done in a dedicated radiography facility, therefore can be more difficult to interpret. Limitations of AP chest radiograph include reduced inspiratory effort because of the patient's positioning (potentially exacerbated by their illness), resulting in sub-optimal imaging; lung changes may therefore appear more marked or localized infection may be missed; the heart can also appear magnified.

Under-exposure of a chest radiograph can occur with operator factors such inappropriate radiation dose, rotation of the patient, patient factors such high body mass index, chest wall abnormalities (or breast prostheses), and inappropriate processing of the image. In an under-exposed image, the whole radiograph appears whiter. In comparison with a site with pathology or abnormality, the affected site or area will be of increased density (whiter) compared with normal areas (Figure 6.1).

MACHINE LEARNING ARCHITECTURES FOR CHEST X-RAY

ENSEMBLE FEATURE OPTIMIZATION WITH KNN CLASSIFICATION

Orthogonal moments and their variants are providing a powerful tool used in many image processing and pattern recognition applications. Feature extraction using the image moments successfully reported for several applications (Eltoukhy et al., 2018; Hosny et al., 2019). For instance, combining orthogonal quaternion Polar Harmonic Transform moments with optimization algorithms for image representation and feature selection has been successfully reported in color galaxies images classification (Hosny et al., 2020).

The motivation of this ensemble technique is to compute an accurate classification method for COVID-19 chest X-ray image depends on combining the strength of two techniques. First, a new image descriptor, FrMEMs. Second, a modified feature selection technique based on Manta-Ray Foraging Optimization and differential evolution (MRFODE).

This work using a method of COVID-19 chest x-ray image classification. This method extracts the features from chest x-ray images using FrMEMs moment. Then the extracted features are divided into testing and training sets. Followed by using the MRFODE algorithm to reduce these features and remove the redundant and irrelevant features. This process achieved by generating a set of solutions and computing the fitness value for each of them using the KNN classifier based on a training set with determining the best of them. Then applying the operators of MRFO in the exploration phase; however, in the exploitation phase, the probability of each solution is computed using its fitness value. According to specified criteria, the solution updated either using DE or the operators of MRFO. The process of updating solutions stopped when reached to terminal conditions. The best solution used to remove the irrelevant features from the testing set and compute the label of the COVID-19 image dataset.

Image-Based Classification Method

Image moments defined as projections of image functions onto a polynomial basis where the image moments used to extract global and local features from these images (Flusser et al., 2016). Generally, projection of digital images using orthogonal polynomials with fractional orders results in orthogonal moments of fractional orders which able to extract both coarse and fine features from the input digital images. In this paper, new orthogonal Exponent moments of fractional orders derived. Then, these moments utilized to extract high accurate 961 features from each COVID-19 input image. The intrinsic properties of the new image moments are:

1. These orthogonal moments are successfully able to represent digital images for low and high orders.
2. The orthogonal moments are invariants to geometric transformations, which is an essential property for classification and recognition applications.
3. The orthogonal moments are robust to noise.
4. Fast and inexpensive computation requirements make them favorable for real-time applications.

Feature Extraction

A few years ago, Hu et al. (2014) defined the orthogonal exponent moments as:

$$FrM_{pq} = \frac{1}{4\pi} \int_0^{2\pi} \int_0^1 f(r,\theta) \left[E_{pq}(r,\theta) \right] r \, dr \, d\theta \tag{6.1}$$

where the order, p, and the repetition, q, are $0, \pm1, \pm2, \pm3, \ldots; \hat{i} = \sqrt{-1}; (\cdot)$ refers to the complex conjugate process; $E_{pq}(r,\theta)$ refers to the exponent basis functions which defined as:

$$E_{pq}(r,\theta) = T_p(r) e^{-\hat{i}q\theta} \tag{6.2}$$

with

$$T_p(r) = \sqrt{\frac{2}{r}} e^{-\hat{i}2\pi pr} \tag{6.3}$$

We generalized $E_{pq}(r,\theta)$ of integer orders in the domain $[0,1] \times [0,2\pi]$ and converted to the fractional-order form, $W_{pq}^\alpha(r,\theta)$, with a real-values parameter $\alpha \epsilon R^+$ in the same domain as follows:

$$W_{pq}^\alpha(r,\theta) = T_p(r,\alpha) e^{-\hat{i}q\theta} \tag{6.4}$$

$$T_p(r,\alpha) = r^{\alpha-1}\sqrt{\frac{2}{r^\alpha}}e^{-\hat{i}2\pi pr^\alpha} \tag{6.5}$$

The basic functions of fractional-order, $W_{pq}^\alpha(r,\theta)$, are orthogonal

$$\int_0^{2\pi}\int_0^1 W_{pm}^\alpha(r,\theta)\left[W_{qn}^\alpha(r,\theta)\right]\, rdrd\theta = \frac{4\pi}{\alpha}\delta_{pm}\delta_{qn} \tag{6.6}$$

In this section, the authors utilized the multi-channel approach (Hosny & Darwish, 2019; Singh & Singh, 2018) in which the input color images processed using the RGB color model where the $R-, G-B-channels$ are expressed using $f_R(r,\theta), f_G(r,\theta) \wedge f_B(r,\theta)$ respectively. The multi-channel orthogonal fractionalorder exponent moment

$$FrM_{pq} = \frac{\alpha}{4\pi}\int_0^{2\pi}\int_0^1 f_c(r,\theta)r^{\alpha-1}\sqrt{\frac{2}{r^\alpha}}e^{-\hat{i}2\pi pr^\alpha}e^{-\hat{i}q\theta}rdrd\theta \tag{6.7}$$

Assume the rotation of the original image, $f_c(r,\theta)$, with an angle β, then the rotated image, $f_C^\beta(r,\theta)$, is:

$$f_C^\beta(r,\theta) = f_c(r,\theta-\beta) \tag{6.8}$$

Let $\hat{\theta} = \theta - \beta$, then $\theta = \hat{\theta} + \beta$ and $d\theta = d\hat{\theta}$, then using the Equations (6.8) in (6.7) yield

$$FrM_{pq}\left(f_C^\beta(r,\theta)\right) = FrM_{pq}\left(f_c(r,\theta)\right)e^{iq\beta} \tag{6.9}$$

Based on the properties of Euler function, $e^{iq\beta} \vee 1$, So, Equation (6.10) is simplified as

$$\left|FrM_{pq}\left(f_C^\beta(r,\theta)\right)\right| = \left|FrM_{pq}\left(f_c(r,\theta)\right)\right| \tag{6.10}$$

This equation proves that the magnitude values of FrMEMs are unchanged with any rotation in the input image.

Wang et al. (2015) showed that circular orthogonal moments achieved the scaling invariance when the input color images mapped into the unit circle. In this work, the input images interpolated to fit the unit-circle domain. Thus, the computed FrMEMs are scaling invariants. The central FrMEMs, are derived in a similar way to (Suk & Flusser, 2009). The FrMEMs calculated with high accuracy using the kernel-based approach (Hosny & Darwish, 2018; Qin et al., 2012).

Parallel Implementation

The parallel implementation is a recent trend used to accelerate the intensive computing of image moments, especially for large-sized images and high moment orders. The emergence of new parallel architectures enriches the efforts toward this goal. Qin et al. (2012) proposed a parallel recurrence method to accelerate the implementation of the Zernike moment. In this context, Deng et al. (2015) extended the work of Qin and his colleague. They implemented a parallelfriendly method for moment computation and image reconstruction based

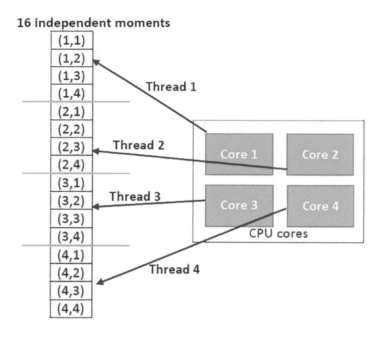

FIGURE 6.5 Parallel implementation of FrMEMs moment on 4-cores CPU.

on Zernike moment. Recently, Salah et al. (2020) proposed a parallel computational method to accelerate the computational process of the polar harmonic transforms of integer-order.

In the same direction, we proposed a parallel implementation of the FrMEMs on multi-core CPU architecture. This parallel implementation provided to cope with the increasing size of the chest x-ray dataset. The FrMEMs consists of $(pmax+1) \times (qmax+1)$ moment component. These moment components computations are independent. Each moment component has a unique combination of p and q values. For instance, for a fractional moment order of 5, there are 36 separate moment component.

In Figure 6.5, the proposed parallel implementation of FrMEMs moment depicted. The multicore CPU has four cores; each core computes a portion of the moment component.

Feature Selection

In this part, we introduced the modified Manta-Ray Foraging Optimization (MRFO) based on Differential Evolution (DE) as a feature selection method. However, the basics of MRFO and DE discussed firstly.

Manta Ray Foraging Optimization (MRFO)

In general, the MRFO simulates the behaviors of three foraging's, including cyclone foraging, Chain foraging, and somersault foraging The details of each foraging given in the following subsections

Chain Foraging

In the MRFO, the foraging chain formed by using the manta rays' line up head-to-tail. Besides, the movement of each agent, except the first one, is in the direction of the food and the agent in front of it which means the current agent $(xi(t), i = 1, 2, ..., N)$ at iteration (t)

is updated depends on the position of best agent and the agent in front of it. This process formulated as in the following equation:

$$x_t^d(t+1) = \begin{cases} x_t^d(t) + r \times \left(x_{best}^d(t) - x_t^d(t)\right) + \alpha \times \left(x_{best}^d(t) - x_t^d(t)\right) & i = 1 \\ x_t^d(t) + r \times \left(x_{t-1}^d(t) - x_t^d(t)\right) + \alpha \times \left(x_{best}^d(t) - x_t^d(t)\right) & otherwise \end{cases} \quad (6.11)$$

where $r \in [0,1]$ refers to random vector and $x_{best}^d(t)$ represents the best agent (in MRFO refers to the plankton with high concentration) at $d - th$ dimension. α is a weight coefficient, and defined as

$$\alpha = 2 \times r \times \sqrt{|log(r)|} \quad (6.12)$$

Cyclone Foraging

In this foraging, the manta rays will construct a long chain foraging, and they are swimming towards the source of the food in a spiral movement. This process means that each agent will follow the front agent, and its movement is in the direction of the solution along the spiral. Therefore, the updating process of the current agent formulated as:

$$x_t^d(t+1) = \begin{cases} x_{best}^d(t) + r \times \left(x_{best}^d(t) - x_i^d(t)\right) + \beta \times \left(x_{best}^d(t) - x_i^d(t)\right) & i = 1 \\ x_{best}^d(t) + r \times \left(x_{i-1}^d(t) - x_i^d(t)\right) + \beta \times \left(x_{best}^d(t) - x_i^d(t)\right) & i = 2,....,N \end{cases} \quad (6.13)$$

$$\beta = 2e^{n\frac{T-t+1}{T}} \times sin(2\pi r_1) \quad (6.14)$$

where $r_1 \in [0,1]$ is a random number, T is the total number of generations.

Followed (Zhao et al., 2020b), the agents forced to find a new position far from $x_{best}^d(t)$ by using a random number as reference to them in the search space instead of the best agent. This can be formulated as:

$$x_t^d(t+1) = \begin{cases} x_{rand}^d(t) + r \times \left(x_{rand}^d(t) - x_i^d(t)\right) + \beta \times \left(x_{rand}^d(t) - x_i^d(t)\right) & i = 1 \\ x_{rand}^d(t) + r \times \left(x_{i-1}^d(t) - x_i^d(t)\right) + \beta \times \left(x_{rand}^d(t) - x_i^d(t)\right) & otherwise \end{cases} \quad (6.15)$$

where $x_{rand}^d(t)$ is a random agent generated in the search space using the following

$$x_{rand}^d(t) = LB^d + rand \times \left(UB^d - LB^d\right) \quad (6.16)$$

Somersault Foraging

In this foraging, each agent swims to and around the position of the food (is called pivot). Thus, the agents update their positions using the following equation

$$x_i^d(t+1) = x_i^d(t) + S \times \left(r_2 \times x_{best}^d(t) - r_3 \times x_i^d(t)\right), i = 1,2,3,...,N \quad (6.17)$$

where r_2 and r_3 are random numbers belong to $[0,1]$.

Differential Evolution

In this section, the mathematical modeling of Differential evolution (DE) introduced one of the most popular The DE, similar to other MHs, begins by setting the initial value for a set of agents X, then calculate the fitness value for each agent. Thereafter, mutation operator is applied to X_i and it is formulated as

$$Z_i = X_{r1} + F \times (X_{r2} - X_{r3}) \qquad (6.18)$$

In Equation (6.18), r_1, r_2 and r_3 refer to random indices, but they are different from i. F represents the mutation scaling factor. The next step is to apply the crossover operator to generate a new agent, and defined as

$$V_i = \begin{cases} Z_i & r < C_r \\ X_i & otherwise \end{cases} \qquad (6.19)$$

In Equation (6.19), C_r is the probability of the crossover, and $r \in [0,1]$ is a random value. The next process is to compute the fitness value of V_i and compared it with $f(X_i)$ to update the value of the current agent X_i as in the following equation:

$$X_i = \begin{cases} V_i & f(V_i) < f(X_i) \\ X_i & otherwise \end{cases} \qquad (6.20)$$

Enhanced MRFO Based on DE as Feature Selection

In this section, the developed COVID-19 x-ray image classification model based on the extracted features using the FrMEMs and implemented an enhanced version from the MRFO based on DE, which called MRFODE presented. The developed method begins by extracting the features from the input images, either COVID-19 or Non-COVID-19, using FrMEMs. Then MRFODE generates a set of N agents; each of them is a solution for the FS problem (i.e., a subset of selected features). After that, the fitness value for each agent is computed, which indicates the quality of the selected features corresponding to the ones in the Boolean version of each agent. The best agent that has the best fitness value is determined and used in updating the position of agents using the operators of the traditional MRFO. Then, the terminal condition (if they reached) checked. Finally, they stop updating or repeat the process. The main steps of the proposed COVID-19 image classification contain three phases where the details of each stage discussed in a separate subsection.

In the first phase, the input x-ray images received then FrMEMs applied to extract a set of features (D_{Feat}) from these images. The extracted features split into two, training and testing sets, which represent 80 and 20%, respectively from the total number of images.

The second phase begins by setting a random value for a set of N agents using Equation (6.21).

$$x_t = LB_t + rand \times (UB_t - LB_t) \qquad (6.21)$$

Each agent is converted to binary using the following equation:

$$x_t = \begin{cases} 1 & if \dfrac{1}{1+e^{-x_t}} > 0.5 \\ 0 & otherwise \end{cases} \qquad (6.22)$$

This sigmoid function is applied since it provides high-quality performance than the traditional Boolean approach. According to the definition modeled in Equation (6.22). The values of ones in binary solution represent the features that should be selected features while removed those that corresponding to zero values.

To illustrate this concept, consider the value of the current agent in binary form is $x_i = [1,0,0,1,1]$, so this indicates that the second and the third features will remove while others selected as relevant features. The process of converting the real solution to Boolean is followed by computing the quality of the selected features using the following equation:

$$f_t = \beta \times \gamma + (1 - \beta) \times \frac{N_{sel}}{D} \tag{6.23}$$

In Equation (6.23), γ refers to the classification error by using the KNN classifier. The N_{sel} represents the number of features selected by the current agent. The $\beta \in [0,1]$ is a random value applied to provides a balance between γ and the selected features. Then the best agent (x_{best}) found in our study, which has the smallest. Then the agents are updated according to the operators of MRFO algorithm or DE, as discussed in Sections C .1 and C. 2, respectively. This process performed by computing the probability (Pr_i) of each agent in Somersault foraging as in Equation (6.24).

$$Pr_i = \frac{f_1}{\sum_{i=1}^{N} f_i} \tag{6.24}$$

In the case of $Pr_i < 0.5$ then the operators of MRFO are used to update x_i; otherwise, the operators of DE used. After reaching the terminal conditions the best agent (x_{best}) is a return from this second phase.

In the third phase, the testing set applied to assess the selected features from the second phase, which performed by removing the irrelevant features—followed by evaluating the performance of classification using a variant set of metrics.

Data and Metrical

The dataset used in this section of work collected by Joseph Paul Cohen and Paul Morrison and Lan Dao in GitHub (Cohen et al., 2020) and images extracted from 43 different publications. References of each image provided in the metadata. Normal and Viral pneumonia images adopted from the chest x-ray Images (pneumonia) database (Mooney, 2020). It contains 216 COVID-19 positive images (some collected from the Twitter account of Italian Cardiothoracic radiologist), 1675 negative COVID-19 images. The data was collected mainly from retrospective cohorts of pediatric patients of one to five years old from Guangzhou Women and Children's medical center. We refer to this dataset as dataset-1.

This dataset shared many characteristics regarding the collecting source. The COVID-19 images collected from a patient with an age range from 40 to 84 from both genders. The data contains 216 COVID-19 positive images and 1,675 COVID-19 negative images. Sample images of both datasets shown in Figure 6.6.

Methodology

Figure 6.7 depicts the flowchart of the proposed classification method of chest x-ray images which summarizes the entire model components. The input to the classifier is a set of images of two classes, COVID-19, and normal cases. The parallel FrMEMs is executed on

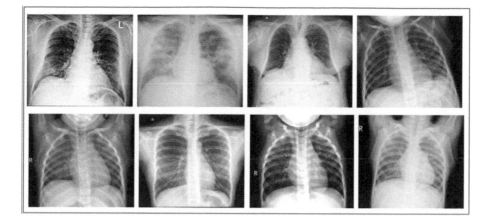

FIGURE 6.6 Sample images of dataset-1.

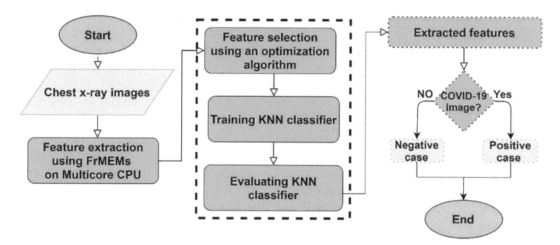

FIGURE 6.7 Flowchart of the proposed method.

multi-core CPUs to extract the image features. Then, an optimization algorithm used for the purposed of feature extraction. Finally, a KNN classifier trained and evaluated.

Model Evaluation

In this study, the results of the proposed COVID-19 x-ray classification image-based method compared with other popular MH techniques that applied as FS. These techniques include sine cosine algorithm (SCA), grey wolf optimization (GWO), Henry Gas Solubility optimization (HGSO), whale optimization algorithm (WOA), and Harris Hawks optimizer (HHO).

These algorithms are used in this comparison since they established their performance in different applications such as global optimization and feature selection methods (Abd El Aziz et al., 2018; Abd Elaziz et al., 2017; Ibrahim et al., 2018). The quality of each FS algorithm assessed by using three measures: Accuracy, the ratio of the selected features, and the fitness value where the accuracy (Acc) defined as:

$$Acc = \frac{T_P + T_N}{T_N + T_P + F_N + F_P} \times 100 \qquad (6.25)$$

TABLE 6.1

The Running Time in Seconds Required to Extract 961 Features From One Image

	1 core (sequential)	2 cores	4 cores	8 cores
Run-time	213	118	55.47	27.1
speedup	–	1.80×	3.83×	7.84×

Results and Discussion

In this subsection, we described the performed experiments and discussed the obtained results. Table 6.1 lists the run-time in seconds and the obtained speedup of the moment computation, i.e., feature extraction phase, at moment order equals and 30 to extract 961 features from each image. The obtained speedup is close to the theoretical limits (2×, 4×, & 8× for 2-, 4-, and 8-multi-core), which prove the efficiency of the utilized parallel approach. The results of Table 6.1 show that the proposed parallel implementation of the moment computation accelerating the feature extraction phase by a factor related to the number of used CPU cores.

The proposed algorithm depends on extracting the features using FrMEMs and using a modified MRFO based on DE as a feature selection method. To find the smallest sub-set of relevant features that leads to increase the classification performance. Besides, the MRFODE compared with other MH methods that used as feature selection models, including such as MRFO, HGSO, HHO, GWO, SCA, and WOA. These FS methods are used the extracted features from FrMEMs as input and aimed to select the most relevant features. The Comparison results according to accuracy, several selected features, and fitness value given in Tables 6.2 and 6.3.

It observed from Table 6.2 that the MRFODE provides better accuracy than other MH methods based on the Best and mean of the accuracy among the two datasets. Since it achieves the first rank in both terms, followed by GWO that has the second rank. Meanwhile, the SCA algorithm is ranked #1 in terms of STD followed by HGSO and GWO at dataset-1 and dataset-2, respectively. As well as, the accuracy of using the extracted features without the feature selection method is the proposed model 0.901 and 0.9309 for Dataset-1 and Dataset-2, respectively. These results indicate the high effect of proposed MRFODE on the quality of classification the COVID-19 x-ray images.

In terms of the fitness value, it is seen from Table 6.3 that the proposed MRFODE has the smallest fitness value overall the mean, STD, Best, and Worst values at Qatar dataset.

TABLE 6.2

Comparison Results of MRFODE and Other MH Methods in Terms of Accuracy

Fn	Measure	MRFO	MRFODE	HHO	HGSO	WOA	SCA	GWO
Dataset-1	Mean	0.9499	0.9609	0.9414	0.9456	0.9541	0.9536	0.9551
	STD	0.0081	0.0106	0.0136	0.0076	0.0048	0.0048	0.0079
	NSel	15.6	16	20	16.8	22	97.2	105.2
	RSF	0.015	0.0166	0.02	0.017	0.022	0.1	0.109

TABLE 6.3

Results of Fitness Value for MRFODE and Other Methods

		MRFO	MRFODE	HHO	HGSO	WOA	SCA	GWO
Dataset-1	Mean	0.0332	0.0278	0.0355	0.0359	0.0344	0.1734	0.1292
	STD	0.003	0.0072	0.0071	0.007	0.0034	0.0648	0.0046
	Best	0.0299	0.0189	0.0284	0.0266	0.0305	0.1291	0.1252
	Worst	0.0365	0.0386	0.0437	0.0426	0.038	0.3516	0.1362

However, at the data1, it provides better results according to the mean and the Best value, which is ranked 1#, while, the traditional MRFO achieves the better at STD, and Worst. These results indicate that the proposed algorithm has a high ability to balance between the error of classification through selected the most relevant features, as well as, and, selecting the smallest number of features.

Moreover, Table 6.2 lists the average of MRFODE and other MH methods in terms of several selected features. It noticed that the proposed MRFODE picks the smallest number of features at the two datasets

Figure 6.8 depicts the average of MRFODE and other MH methods overall the two datasets according to the accuracy, number of selected features, and fitness value. The results shown in Figure 6.8 provide evidence for the superiority of the proposed MRFODE since it has a high value at accuracy. Also, the smallest number of selected features and fitness value. However, the CPU time(s) of it is the third rank, and this the main limitation of it.

Figure 6.9 depicts the confusion matrix for the two datasets using the predicted output from MRFODE. From Figure 6.9, it can notice the high ability of the proposed model to distinguish the COVID-19 from non-COVID X-ray images.

The further analysis presented to evaluate the performance of the proposed model by using a non-parametric test named Friedman test, which ranks the methods. For the accuracy measure, the best algorithm is that it has the highest rank, while for the other measures, the lowest rank preferred.

Table 6.4 lists the mean rank of each algorithm obtained using the Friedman test. From these results, it noticed that the developed MRFODE has the best rank at the accuracy, selected features, and fitness value. Since it has a higher rank at accuracy and the smallest mean rank at the other two measures. This indicates the high ability of MRFODE to select the optimal subset of features that leads to an increase in the classification accuracy for the two tested datasets.

DEEP CONVOLUTIONAL NEURAL NETWORKS

In order to control the spread of COVID-19, a large number of suspected cases need to be screened for proper isolation and treatment. Pathogenic research facility testing is the indicative best quality level however it is tedious with noteworthy bogus negative outcomes. Quick and precise analytic strategies are desperately expected to battle the sickness. In light of COVID-19 radiographically changes in X-ray pictures, we meant to build a deep learning method that could extract COVID-19's graphical features so as to give a clinical

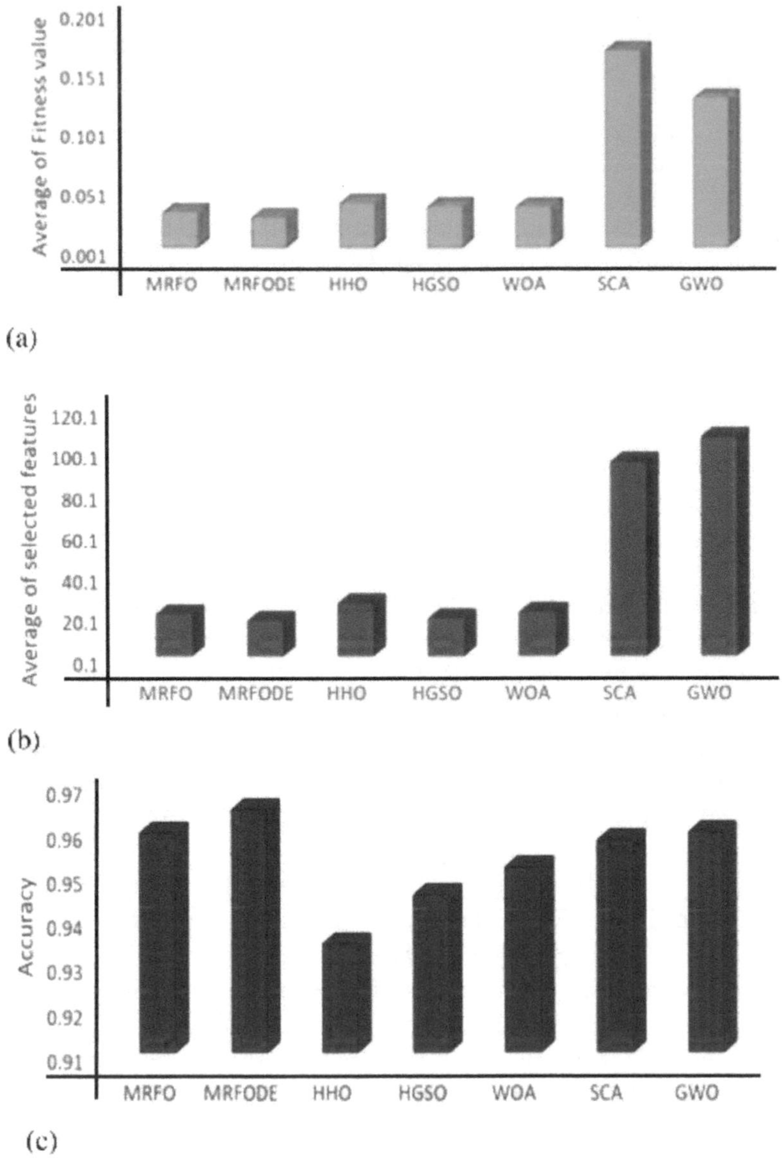

FIGURE 6.8   Average of comparison results between algorithm over (a) accuracy, (b) a number of selected features, and (c) fitness value.

analysis in front of the pathogenic test, thus saving critical time for disease control. In this section, (DCNN) (Peng et al., 2018), a machine learning classification technique is used to classify the Chest X-ray images. As accuracy is the most significant factor in this issue, by taking a more prominent number of pictures for training the network and by increasing the number of iterations, the DCNN accuracy can be improved. Tensor Flow is a large-scale machine learning system developed by Google (Abadi et al., 2016) and Inception V3 is Google's CNN architecture (Szegedy et al., 2016). Here, the DCNN algorithm is executed with Tensor Flow and Inception V3.

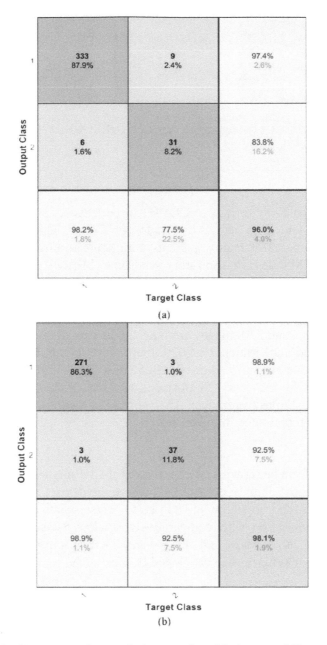

FIGURE 6.9 (a) & (b) presents the confusion matrix with the two different datasets using the predicted output from MRFODE.

TABLE 6.4

Mean Rank Obtained Using Friedman Test for Each Method

	MRFO	MRFODE	HHO	HGSO	WOA	SCA	GWO
Accuracy	5.375	6.625	1.125	1.875	3.625	3.875	5.5
Fitness	2	1.875	4.625	3.875	3.375	6.875	5.375
Attribute	2.5	1.5	4.5	2.5	4	6	7

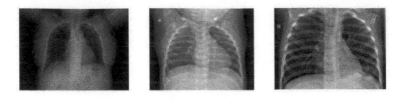

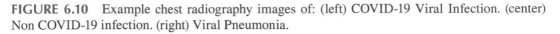

FIGURE 6.10 Example chest radiography images of: (left) COVID-19 Viral Infection. (center) Non COVID-19 infection. (right) Viral Pneumonia.

Data and Material

In this study, 315 chest X-ray images of COVID-19 patients have been obtained from the open source GitHub repository shared by Dr. Joseph Cohen. This repository is containing chest X-ray/CT images of mainly patients with acute respiratory distress syndrome (ARDS), COVID-19, Middle East respiratory syndrome (MERS), pneumonia, severe acute respiratory syndrome (SARS). In addition, 330 COVID-19 positive radiographic images (CXR and CT) were carefully chosen from Italian Society of Medical and Interventional Radiology (SIRM) COVID-19 DATABASE Out of 330 radiographic images, 70 images are chest X-ray images and 250 images are lung CT images. This database is updated in a random manner and until March 29, 2020, there were 63 confirmed COVID-19 cases were reported in this database. In addition, 2905 chest X-ray images were selected from COVID-19 Radiography Database (Platform, 2017). Out of 2905 radiographic images, there are 219 COVID-19 positive images, 1341 normal images and 1345 viral pneumonia images examples are represented in Figure 6.10.

Methodology

DCNN typically perform better with a larger dataset than a smaller one. Transfer learning can be beneficial in those applications of CNN where the dataset is not large. The idea of transfer learning uses the trained model from large datasets such as ImageNet (Platform, 2017) is used for application with comparatively smaller dataset. This eliminates the requirement of having large dataset and also reduces the long training period as is required by the deep learning algorithm when developed from scratch.

Image Pre-Processing

One of the significant phases in the data preprocessing was to resize the X-ray images as the image input for algorithm were different. We implemented some image pre-processing technique to increase the performance to our system by speeding up training time. First, we resized all our images to $299 \times 299 \times 3$ to increase processing time and also to suitable in Inception V3. In the image preprocessing step, we need to label the data since the learning technique of convolution neural network fits into administered learning in machine learning.

Image Augmentation

CNN needs a sufficient amount of data to achieve excellent performance. We apply data augmentation techniques to increase the insufficient data in training, and the techniques used include vertical flip, horizontal flip, noise, translation, blur and rotate the image 60°, 90°, 180°, 270°, showing in Figure 6.11 and Table 6.5. Therefore, the initial dataset consisting

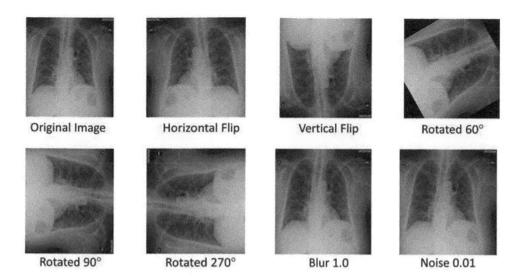

Original Image   Horizontal Flip   Vertical Flip   Rotated 60°

Rotated 90°   Rotated 270°   Blur 1.0   Noise 0.01

FIGURE 6.11 Example of augmented images by rotating, flipping, blur, and noise.

TABLE 6.5

Details of Training, Validation and Test Set

Class	Images	Augmented Total	With Augmentation		
			Training	**Validation**	**Test**
COVID-19	864	8640	7340	500	800
Normal	1341	13410	12000	910	500
Viral Pneumonia	1345	13450	12000	950	500

of 864 COVID-19 images, 1341 normal images, and 1345 viral pneumonia images was expanded to a total of 8640 COVID-19 images, 13,410 normal chest X-ray images, and 13,450 viral pneumonia images.

Transfer Learning

Transfer learning is a machine learning technique (Rachna, 2020) which is based on the concept of reusability Transfer learning is often used with CNN in the way that all layers are kept except the last one, which is trained for the specific problem. This technique can be particularly useful for medical applications since it does not require as much training data, which can be hard to get in medical situations. In the analysis of medical data, one of the biggest difficulties faced by researchers is the limited number of available datasets. Deep learning models often need a lot of data. Labeling this data by experts is both costly and time consuming. The biggest advantage of using transfer learning method is that it allows the training of data with fewer datasets and requires less calculation costs. With the transfer learning method, which is widely used in the field of deep learning, the information gained by the pre-trained model on a large dataset is transferred to the model to be trained.

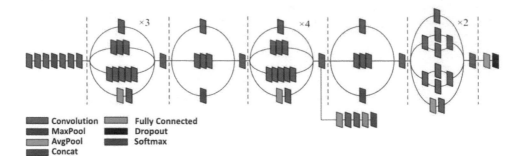

FIGURE 6.12   Inception V3 Architecture.

Figure 6.12 defines the Inception V3 model which performs convolution, pooling, soft-max and fully connected procedures. Here a pre-trained neural network established for one task can be utilized as the initial point of another task. The Inception-v3 architecture comprises two fragments:

 I. Use the feature extraction section of the convolutional neural network.
 II. Classification section utilizing fully-connected and softmax layers.

TensorFlow

It is an artificial neural network there are more than three layers, shown in Figure 6.13. It has single input, single output and many invisible layers. To use transfer learning for clas-sifying chest X-ray images, we used the TensorFlow library to load the Inception V3 model on our local machine, retrain it on the chest X-ray dataset and then classify new images to be one of the three categories normal, viral pneumonia and COVID-19. It is a deep learn-ing framework established by Google that can control all neurons (nodes) in the system and has a library appropriate for image processing. Neural network weights can be changed to improve performance.

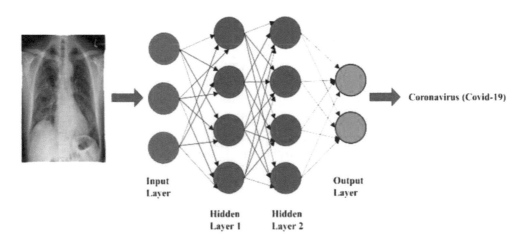

FIGURE 6.13   Neural network classifier.

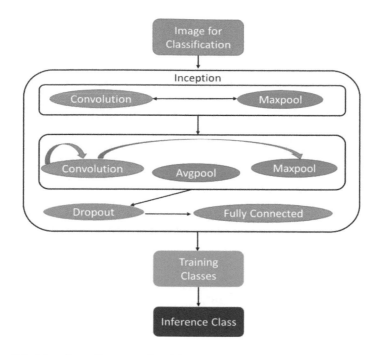

FIGURE 6.14 Working flow diagram of architecture.

Model Evaluation

Figure 6.14 provides a step-by-step procedure for the proposed work model. The steps for the projected classification architecture are as follows:

I. Recursively perform convolution and pooling on images.
II. Apply drop out and fully connected. Now the image must be classified according to the labeled training class.

Convolution is a gradual process. Extracts various features of input. Each kernel is responsible for producing output function. Low-level features of the image, such as edges, lines and corners are determined by the lower layer, and the higher-level features are extracted by the higher layer.

Pooling is applied to make the features obtained from convolution robust against noise. Pooling layers are usually of two types namely, average pooling and max pooling. It is basically a dimensionality reduction or feature extraction step. A simple example of max and average pooling is shown in Figure 6.15.

In this study, we built DCNN based InceptionV3 model for the classification of COVID-19 Chest X-ray images to normal, viral pneumonia and COVID-19 classes. In addition, we applied transfer learning technique that was realized by using ImageNet data to overcome the insufficient data and training time.

The schematic representation of conventional CNN including InceptionV3 model for the prediction of COVID-19 patients, viral pneumonia and normal were depicted in Figure 6.16. Chest X-ray images are taken as input, Inception V3 is applied, convolution, pooling, softmax, and fully connected processes are performed. Upon completing these tasks, they are classified according to different training modules and eventually classified

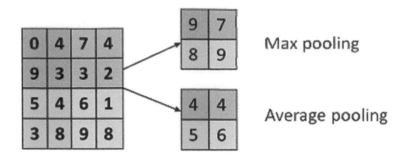

FIGURE 6.15   Example of max and average pooling.

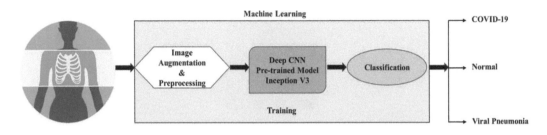

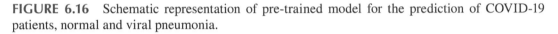

FIGURE 6.16   Schematic representation of pre-trained model for the prediction of COVID-19 patients, normal and viral pneumonia.

as normal, viral pneumonia and COVID-19 classes. Inception V3 is one of the states of art architectures in image classification challenge. The best network for medical image analysis seems to be the Inception V3 architecture and it preforms better than even the more recent architectures. So, we selected Inception V3 model that is implemented using TensorFlow and hence the retraining is done with TensorFlow.

Result

In this study, we had presented a novel method that could screen COVID-19 fully automatically by DCNN. Chest X-ray images have been used for the prediction of COVID-19 infected patients. Popular pre-trained model Inception V3 has been trained and after training, the model was experienced on chest X-ray images of COVID-19, normal and viral pneumonia that are not used in the training phase. We have obtained the best performance as a classification accuracy of more than 98%. The experimental work is done by connecting the docker to the virtual box. The neural network is trained to create bottleneck values. As shown in Figure 6.17(top), create a bottleneck for individual image and save it to a folder. After all the bottlenecks have been created, the last few layers of the model are trained. We have set the training steps to 4000, which is sufficient to generate sufficient outcomes. There are a series of accuracy, cross-entropy, and verification accuracy as shown in Figure 6.17(bottom). Training accuracy indicates a correctly labeled share of the current training image. Cross-entropy indicates how finely the training is performed on the cross-entropy loss function, and validation accuracy is related to training accuracy. Training accuracy increased as training proceeds after 4000 iterations, the final test accuracy was 96%.

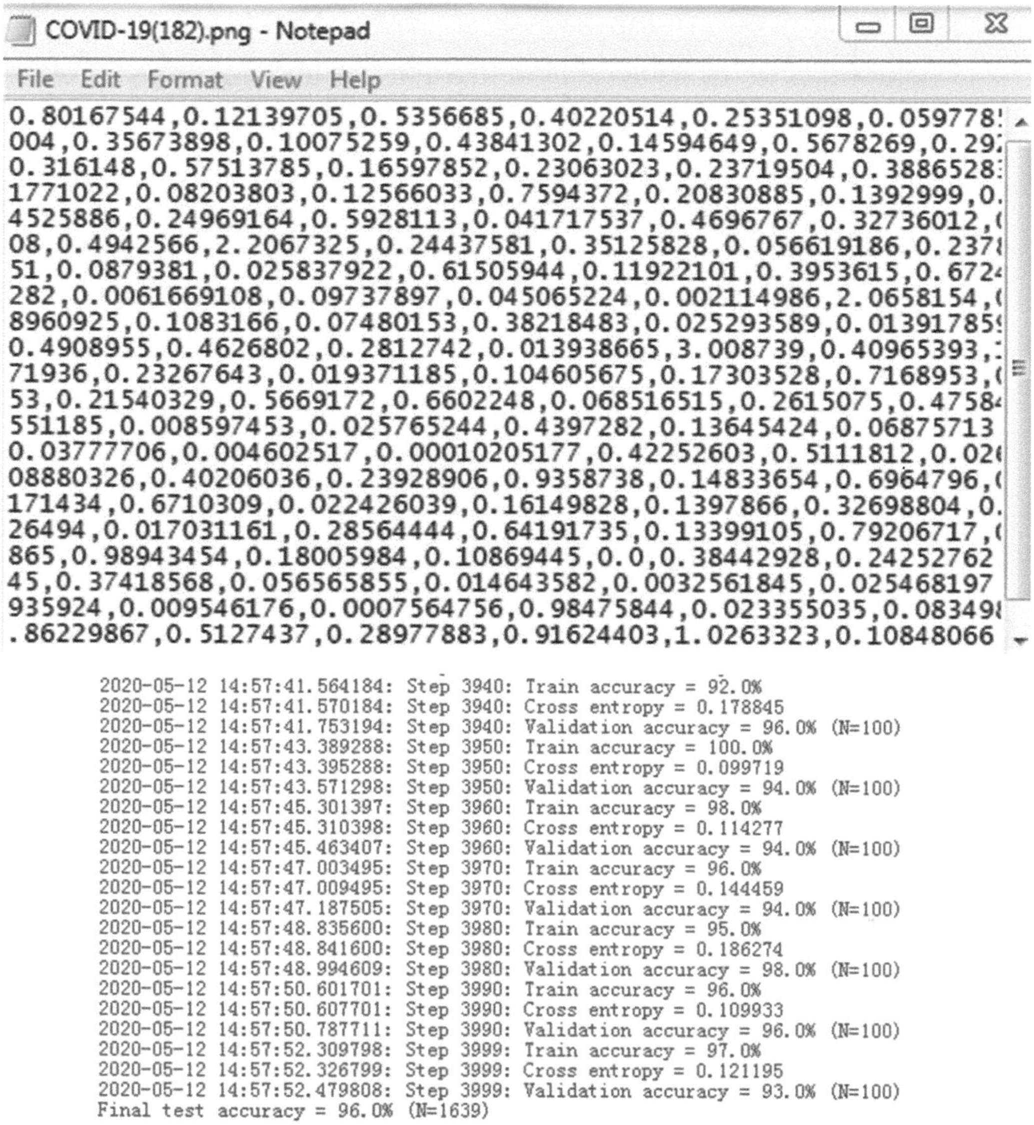

0.80167544,0.12139705,0.5356685,0.40220514,0.25351098,0.059778!
004,0.35673898,0.10075259,0.43841302,0.14594649,0.5678269,0.29;
0.316148,0.57513785,0.16597852,0.23063023,0.23719504,0.3886528:
1771022,0.08203803,0.12566033,0.7594372,0.20830885,0.1392999,0.
4525886,0.24969164,0.5928113,0.041717537,0.4696767,0.32736012,(
08,0.4942566,2.2067325,0.24437581,0.35125828,0.056619186,0.237{
51,0.0879381,0.025837922,0.61505944,0.11922101,0.3953615,0.672<
282,0.0061669108,0.09737897,0.045065224,0.002114986,2.0658154,(
8960925,0.1083166,0.07480153,0.38218483,0.025293589,0.01391785{
0.4908955,0.4626802,0.2812742,0.013938665,3.008739,0.40965393,:
71936,0.23267643,0.019371185,0.104605675,0.17303528,0.7168953,(
53,0.21540329,0.5669172,0.6602248,0.068516515,0.2615075,0.4758<
551185,0.008597453,0.025765244,0.4397282,0.13645424,0.06875713
0.03777706,0.004602517,0.00010205177,0.42252603,0.5111812,0.02(
08880326,0.40206036,0.23928906,0.9358738,0.14833654,0.6964796,(
171434,0.6710309,0.022426039,0.16149828,0.1397866,0.32698804,0.
26494,0.017031161,0.28564444,0.64191735,0.13399105,0.79206717,(
865,0.98943454,0.18005984,0.10869445,0.0,0.38442928,0.24252762
45,0.37418568,0.056565855,0.014643582,0.0032561845,0.025468197
935924,0.009546176,0.0007564756,0.98475844,0.023355035,0.08349{
.86229867,0.5127437,0.28977883,0.91624403,1.0263323,0.10848066

2020-05-12 14:57:41.564184: Step 3940: Train accuracy = 92.0%
2020-05-12 14:57:41.570184: Step 3940: Cross entropy = 0.178845
2020-05-12 14:57:41.753194: Step 3940: Validation accuracy = 96.0% (N=100)
2020-05-12 14:57:43.389288: Step 3950: Train accuracy = 100.0%
2020-05-12 14:57:43.395288: Step 3950: Cross entropy = 0.099719
2020-05-12 14:57:43.571298: Step 3950: Validation accuracy = 94.0% (N=100)
2020-05-12 14:57:45.301397: Step 3960: Train accuracy = 98.0%
2020-05-12 14:57:45.310398: Step 3960: Cross entropy = 0.114277
2020-05-12 14:57:45.463407: Step 3960: Validation accuracy = 94.0% (N=100)
2020-05-12 14:57:47.003495: Step 3970: Train accuracy = 96.0%
2020-05-12 14:57:47.009495: Step 3970: Cross entropy = 0.144459
2020-05-12 14:57:47.187505: Step 3970: Validation accuracy = 94.0% (N=100)
2020-05-12 14:57:48.835600: Step 3980: Train accuracy = 95.0%
2020-05-12 14:57:48.841600: Step 3980: Cross entropy = 0.186274
2020-05-12 14:57:48.994609: Step 3980: Validation accuracy = 98.0% (N=100)
2020-05-12 14:57:50.601701: Step 3990: Train accuracy = 96.0%
2020-05-12 14:57:50.607701: Step 3990: Cross entropy = 0.109933
2020-05-12 14:57:50.787711: Step 3990: Validation accuracy = 96.0% (N=100)
2020-05-12 14:57:52.309798: Step 3999: Train accuracy = 97.0%
2020-05-12 14:57:52.326799: Step 3999: Cross entropy = 0.121195
2020-05-12 14:57:52.479808: Step 3999: Validation accuracy = 93.0% (N=100)
Final test accuracy = 96.0% (N=1639)

FIGURE 6.17   (top) Generation of Bottleneck values. (bottom) Final test accuracy of the retraining.

Training Accuracy & Cross-Entropy

We measured the training accuracy and cross-entropy during the training steps as shown in Figure 6.18.

The training accuracy Figure 6.18(top) illustrates the percentage of the images used in the current dataset that were labeled with the correct class and the validation accuracy Figure 6.18(top) shows the percentage of randomly selected correctly labeled images from a different set. The core difference is that the accuracy of training is based on the images that the network can learn, so the network can over adapt to the noise in the data. Cross entropy Figure 6.18(bottom) is a loss function which gives a sight into how well the process of learning is progressing, lower numbers are better here.

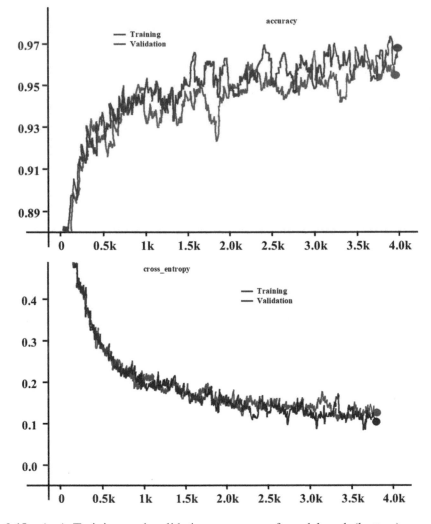

FIGURE 6.18 (top) Training and validation accuracy of model and (bottom) cross entropy. Orange curve indicates the training cross-entropy/accuracy and blue curve indicates the validation cross-entropy/accuracy.

To provide more human-interpretable explanations, we conducted several experiments on the chest X-ray images to evaluate the classification performance of the network investigated, let's consider the following examples.

Example 1: the CXR image is classified to contain a confirmed COVID-19 case with a probability of 99.59%, the true class is COVID-19, as shown in Figure 6.19 (top).
Example 2: the CXR image is classified to contain a confirmed COVID-19 case with a probability of 98.30%, the true class is COVID-19, as shown in Figure 6.19 (bottom).

Figure 6.19 shows the results when the sample test image was taken. Since COVID-19 has a higher score compared to normal and viral pneumonia, the test image is classified as COVID-19. It can be concluded that the proposed technique can classify COVID-19 X-ray images very reliably.

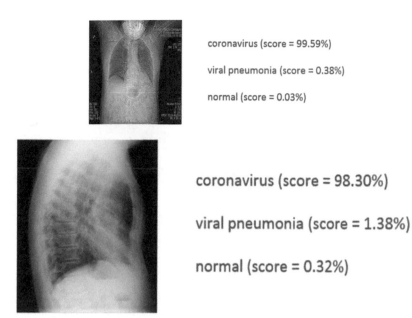

coronavirus (score = 99.59%)

viral pneumonia (score = 0.38%)

normal (score = 0.03%)

coronavirus (score = 98.30%)

viral pneumonia (score = 1.38%)

normal (score = 0.32%)

FIGURE 6.19 Example CXR images of COVID-19 cases from two different patients. (top) Classification performance obtained by testing our trained architecture with first CXR image. (bottom) Classification performance obtained by testing our trained architecture.

ResNet50, InceptionV3, and InceptionResNetV2 Models

X-ray machines are used to scan the affected body such as fractures, bone dislocations, lung infections, pneumonia and tumors. CT scanning is a kind of advanced X-ray machine that examines the very soft structure of the active body part and clearer images of the inner soft tissues and organs (Rachna, 2020). Using X-ray is a faster, easier, cheaper and less harmful method than CT. Failure to promptly recognize and treat COVID-19 pneumonia may lead to increase in mortality.

In this section we used ResNet50, InceptionV3 and Inception-ResNetV2 pre-trained models to obtain a higher prediction accuracy for small X-ray dataset. The summarized follows of work as: (1) The end-to-end structure models without manual feature extraction and selection methods. (2) We show that ResNet50 is an effective pre-trained model among other two pre-trained models. (3) Chest X-ray images are the best tool for the detection of COVID-19. (4) The pre-trained models have been shown to yield very high results in the small dataset (50 COVID-19 vs. 50 Normal).

Data and Material

In this section, chest X-ray images of 50 COVID-19 patients have been obtained from the open source GitHub repository shared by Dr. Joseph Cohen. This repository is consisting chest X-ray/CT images of mainly patients with acute respiratory distress syndrome (ARDS), COVID-19, Middle East respiratory syndrome (MERS), pneumonia, severe acute respiratory syndrome (SARS). In addition, 50 normal chest X-ray images were selected from Kaggle repository called "Chest X-Ray Images (Pneumonia)" (Mooney, 2018).

The experiments based on a created dataset with chest X-ray images of 50 normal (Mooney, 2018) and 50 COVID-19 patients (100 images in total). All images in this dataset

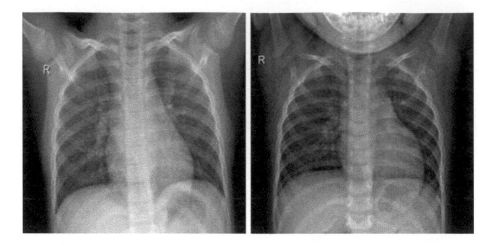

FIGURE 6.20   Representative chest X-ray images of normal.

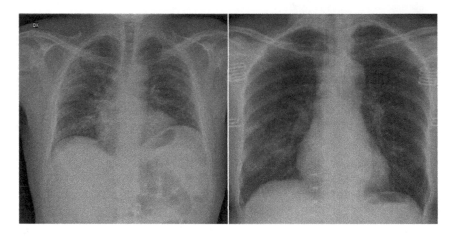

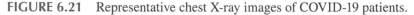

FIGURE 6.21   Representative chest X-ray images of COVID-19 patients.

were resized to 224×224 pixel size. In Figures 6.20 and 6.21, representative chest X-ray images of normal and COVID-19 patients are given, respectively.

Deep Transfer Learning

Deep learning is a sub-branch of the machine learning field, inspired by the structure of the brain. Deep learning techniques used in recent years continue to show an impressive performance in the field of medical image processing, as in many fields. By applying deep learning techniques to medical data, it is tried to draw meaningful results from medical data.

Deep learning models have been used successfully in many areas such as classification, segmentation and lesion detection of medical data. Analysis of image and signal data obtained with medical imaging techniques such as Magnetic Resonance Imaging (MRI), Computed Tomography (CT) and X-ray with the help of deep learning models. As a result of these analyzes, detection and diagnosis of diseases such as diabetes mellitus, brain tumor, skin cancer and breast cancer are provided with convenience (Kassani & Kassani, 2019; Lee et al., 2009; Saba et al., 2020; Yildirim et al., 2019).

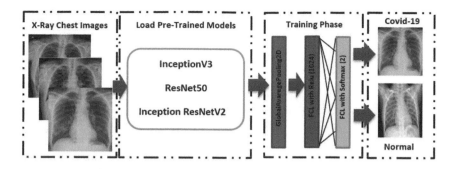

FIGURE 6.22 Schematic representation of pre-trained models for the prediction of COVID-19 patients and normal.

In the analysis of medical data, one of the biggest difficulties faced by researchers is the limited number of available datasets. Deep learning models often need a lot of data. Labeling this data by experts is both costly and time consuming. The biggest advantage of using transfer learning method is that it allows the training of data with fewer datasets and requires less calculation costs. With the transfer learning method, which is widely used in the field of deep learning, the information gained by the pre-trained model on a large dataset is transferred to the model to be trained.

Deep convolutional neural network (CNN) based ResNet50, InceptionV3 and Inception-ResNetV2 models for the classification of COVID-19 Chest X-ray images to normal and COVID-19 classes used in this experiment. In addition, we applied transfer learning technique that was realized by using ImageNet data to overcome the insufficient data and training time. The schematic representation of conventional CNN including pre-trained ResNet50, InceptionV3 and Inception ResNetV2 models for the prediction of COVID-19 patients and normal were depicted in Figure 6.22. It is also available publicly for open access at https://github.com/drcerenkaya/COVID-19-Detection.

Residual neural network (ResNet) model is an improved version of convolutional neural network (CNN). ResNet adds shortcuts between layers to solve a problem. Thanks to this, it prevents the distortion that occurs as the network gets deeper and more complex. In addition, bottleneck blocks are used to make training faster in the ResNet model (Wu et al., 2019). ResNet50 is a 50- layer network trained on the ImageNet dataset. ImageNet is an image database with more than 14 million images belonging to more than 20 thousand categories created for image recognition competitions (Russakovsky et al., 2015). InceptionV3 is a kind of convolutional neural network model. It consists of numerous convolution and maximum pooling steps. In the last stage, it contains a fully connected neural network (Ahn et al., 2018). As with the ResNet50 model, the network is trained with ImageNet dataset. The model consists of a deep convolutional network using the Inception ResNetV2 architecture that was trained on the ImageNet-2012 dataset. The input to the model is a 299×299 image, and the output is a list of estimated class probabilities (Byra et al., 2018).

Experimental Setup

Python programming language was used to train the proposed deep transfer learning models. All experiments were performed on a Google Colaboratory Linux server with Ubuntu 16.04 operating system using Tesla K80 GPU graphics card. CNN models (ResNet50,

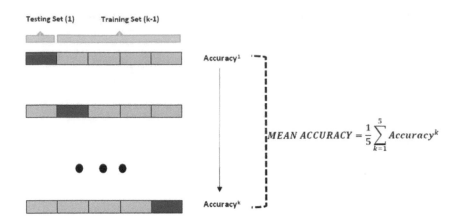

FIGURE 6.23   Visual display of testing and training datasets for 5-fold cross validation.

InceptionV3 and Inception-ResNetV2) were pre-trained with random initialization weights using the Adam optimizer. The batch size, learning rate and number of epochs were experimentally set to 2, 1e-5 and 30, respectively for all experiments. The dataset used was randomly split into two independent datasets with 80% and 20% for training and testing respectively. As cross validation method, k-fold was chosen and results were obtained according to 5 different k values (k=1–5) as shown in Figure 6.23.

Performance Metrics

A total of five criteria were used for the performances of deep transfer learning models. These are:

$$Accuracy = \frac{TN + TP}{TN + TP + FN + FP} \tag{6.26}$$

$$Recall = \frac{TP}{TP + FN} \tag{6.27}$$

$$Specificity = \frac{TN}{TN + FP} \tag{6.28}$$

$$Precision = \frac{TP}{TP + FP} \tag{6.29}$$

$$F1 - Score = 2 \times \frac{Precision \times Recall}{Precision + Recall} \tag{6.30}$$

TP, FP, TN, and FN given in Equations (6.26)–(6.30) represent the number of True Positive, False Positive, True Negative, and False Negative, respectively. Given a test dataset and model, TP is the proportion of positive (COVID-19) that are correctly labeled as COVID-19 by the model; FP is the proportion of negative (normal) that are mislabeled as positive (COVID-19); TN is the proportion of negative (normal) that are correctly labeled as normal and FN is the proportion of positive (COVID-19) that are mislabeled as negative (normal) by the model.

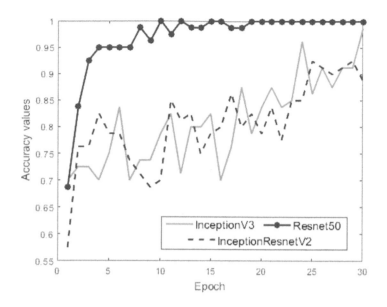

FIGURE 6.24 The performance of three pre-trained models (Training accuracy for fold-3).

Result

In this study, chest X-ray images have been used for the prediction of coronavirus disease patients (COVID-19). Popular pre-trained models such as ResNet50, InceptionV3 and Inception ResNetV2 have been trained and tested on chest X-ray images. Training accuracy and loss values for fold-3 of the pre-trained models are given in Figures 6.5 and 6.6, respectively. The training stage has been carried out up to 30th epoch to avoid overfitting for all pre-trained models. It can be seen from Figure 6.24 that the highest training accuracy is obtained with the ResNet50 model. InceptionV3 and Inception-ResNetV2 models have similar performance.

However, it is seen that ResNet50 shows a fast training process than other models. Although the pre-trained models give very high initial values, the initial values are below 70% due to the low number of data. The training loss values of ResNet50, InceptionV3 and Inception ResNetV2 are shown in Figure 6.25.

When the loss figures are analyzed, it is seen that the loss values decrease in three pre-trained models during the training stage. It can be said that the ResNet 50 model both decreases loss values faster and approaches zero.

In Figure 6.26, confusion matrices of COVID-19 and normal test results of the models are given. First, InceptionV3 pre-trained model classified 10 of the COVID-19 as True Positive for fold-3 and classified 10 of the normal as True Negative. Secondly, ResNet50 model also classified 10 of the COVID-19 as True Positive for fold-3 and classified 10 of the normal as True Negative. Lastly, Inception ResNetV2 classified 10 of the COVID-19 as True Positive for fold-3 and classified 9 of the normal as True Negative. Besides the confusion matrix, receiver operating characteristic curve (ROC) plots and areas for each model are given. InceptionV3 and ResNet50 pre-trained models appear to be very high.

In another detailed performance, comparisons of three models using the test data are shown in Table 6.6. We have obtained the best performance as an accuracy of 98%, recall of 96%, and specificity value of 100% for ResNet50 pre-trained model. The lowest

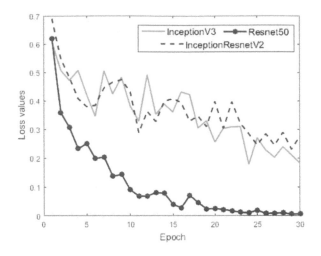

FIGURE 6.25   The performance of three pre-trained models (Training loss values for fold-3).

performance values have been yielded an accuracy of 87%, recall of 84%, and specificity value of 90% for Inception-ResNetV2. As a result, the ResNet50 model provides superiority over the other two models both training and testing stage.

There are very few studies on literature due to the emergence of COVID-19 virus disease. Some of these are as follows: (Sethy & Behera, 2020) proposed a detection of COVID-19 using X-ray images based on deep feature and SVM. They collected X-ray images from GitHub, Kaggle, and Open-I repository. They extracted the deep feature of CNN models and fed to SVM classifier individually. They have obtained 95.38% of accuracy for ResNet50&SVM. Fei et al. (Shan et al., 2020), tried to predict COVID-19 patients using "VB-Net" neural network to segment COVID-19 infection regions in CT scans. They handled the results statistically. They obtained dice similarity coefficients of 91.6%±10.0%. Xiaowei et al. (Butt et al., 2020), proposed an early prediction model to classification COVID-19 pneumonia from Influenza-A viral pneumonia and healthy cases using pulmonary CT images using deep learning techniques. Their CNN model has yielded the highest overall accuracy was 86.7% CT images. Wang et al. (2020), used CT images to predict COVID-19 cases. They also used the Inception transfer-learning model to establish the algorithm. They obtained an accuracy of 89.5% with specificity of 88.0% and sensitivity of 87.0%.

In addition to these studies in the literature, the main advantages of our study can be summarized as follows:

I. Chest X-ray images have been used in the study. X-ray images can be obtained from any hospital very easily, quickly and without difficulty.
II. Our method is a completely end-to-end system. So, it does not have any feature extraction or selection.
III. Three different pre-trained common models are compared such as ResNet50, Inception V3 and Inception-ResNetV2.
IV. Although it is a very new subject and the number of data is limited, the results are quite high.

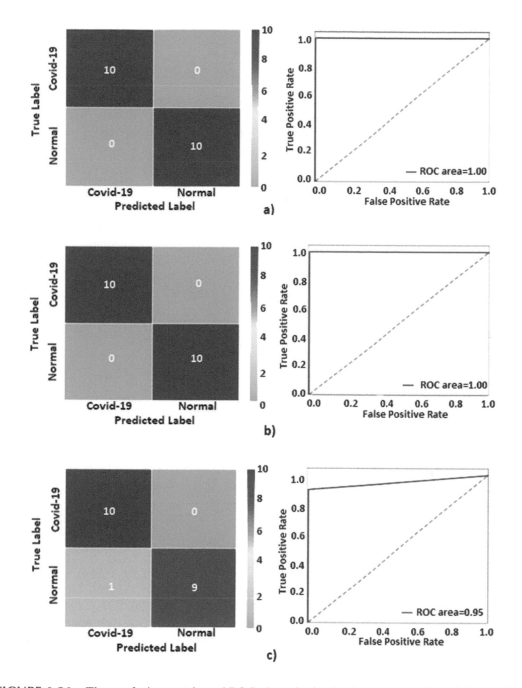

FIGURE 6.26 The confusion matrix and ROC plots obtained using pre-trained models for fold-3 results: (a) InceptionV3, (b) ResNet50, (c) Inception-ResNetV2.

The main problem of our study is the limited number of COVID-19 X-ray images used for the training of deep learning models. In order to overwhelm this problem, we have used deep transfer learning models. If we reach more data in the coming days, we are planning to improve working with different models.

TABLE 6.6

Prediction Performance Results Obtained From Different Pre-Trained CNN Models for 5-Fold Cross Validation Methods

MODELS	FOLD	Confusion Matrix and Performance Results (%)				Confusion Matrix and Performance Results (%)				
		TP	TN	FP	FN	Acc	Rec	Spe	Pre	F1
InceptionV3	Fold-1	7	10	0	3	85	70	100	100	82
	Fold-2	10	10	0	0	100	100	100	100	100
	Fold-3	10	10	0	0	100	100	100	100	100
	Fold-4	10	10	0	0	100	100	100	100	100
	Fold-5	10	10	0	0	100	100	100	100	100
	Mean					97	94	100	100	96
ResNet50	Fold-1	8	10	0	2	90	80	100	100	89
	Fold-2	10	10	0	0	100	100	100	100	100
	Fold-3	10	10	0	0	100	100	100	100	100
	Fold-4	10	10	0	0	100	100	100	100	100
	Fold-5	10	10	0	0	100	100	100	100	100
	Mean					98	96	100	100	98
Inception-ResNetV2	Fold-1	9	7	3	1	80	90	70	75	82
	Fold-2	10	9	1	0	95	100	90	91	95
	Fold-3	10	9	1	0	95	100	90	91	95
	Fold-4	7	10	0	3	85	70	100	100	82
	Fold-5	6	10	0	4	80	60	100	100	75
	Mean					87	84	90	91	86

Note: The Abbreviations in **Table 6.6** are: True Positive (TP), True Negative (TN), False Positive (FP), False Negative (FN), Accuracy (Acc), Recall (Rec), Specificity (Spe), Precision (Pre), F1-Score (F1)

REFERENCES

Abadi, M., Barham, P., Chen, J., Chen, Z., Davis, A., Dean, J., Devin, M., Ghemawat, S., Irving, G., & Isard, M. (2016). Tensorflow: A system for large-scale machine learning. *12th {USENIX} Symposium on Operating Systems Design and Implementation ({OSDI} 16)*, 265–283.

Abd El Aziz, M., Ewees, A. A., & Hassanien, A. E. (2018). Multi-objective whale optimization algorithm for content-based image retrieval. Multimedia Tools and Applications, *77*(19), 26135–26172.

Abd Elaziz, M. E., Ewees, A. A., Oliva, D., Duan, P., & Xiong, S. (2017). A hybrid method of sine cosine algorithm and differential evolution for feature selection. *International Conference on Neural Information Processing*, 145–155.

Abd Elaziz, M., Hosny, K. M., & Selim, I. M. (2019). Galaxies image classification using artificial bee colony based on orthogonal Gegenbauer moments. Soft Computing, *23*(19), 9573–9583.

Ahn, J. M., Kim, S., Ahn, K.-S., Cho, S.-H., Lee, K. B., & Kim, U. S. (2018). A deep learning model for the detection of both advanced and early glaucoma using fundus photography. PloS One, *13*(11), e0207982.

Ai, T., Yang, Z., & Hou, H. (2020). Correlation of chest CT and RT-PCR testing in coronavirus Disease 2019 (COVID-19) in China: A report of 1014 cases [e-pub ahead of print]. *Radiology*.

Annarumma, M., Withey, S. J., Bakewell, R. J., Pesce, E., Goh, V., & Montana, G. (2019). Automated triaging of adult chest radiographs with deep artificial neural networks. Radiology, *291*(1), 196–202.

Butt, C., Gill, J., Chun, D., & Babu, B. A. (2020). Deep learning system to screen coronavirus disease 2019 pneumonia. Applied Intelligence, 1.

Byra, M., Styczynski, G., Szmigielski, C., Kalinowski, P., Michałowski, Ł., Paluszkiewicz, R., Ziarkiewicz-Wróblewska, B., Zieniewicz, K., Sobieraj, P., & Nowicki, A. (2018). Transfer learning with deep convolutional neural network for liver steatosis assessment in ultrasound images. International Journal of Computer Assisted Radiology and Surgery, *13*(12), 1895–1903.

Chen, J., Qi, T., Liu, L., Ling, Y., Qian, Z., Li, T., Li, F., Xu, Q., Zhang, Y., & Xu, S. (2020). Clinical progression of patients with COVID-19 in Shanghai, China. *Journal of Infection.*

Chen, N., Zhou, M., Dong, X., Qu, J., Gong, F., Han, Y., Qiu, Y., Wang, J., Liu, Y., & Wei, Y. (2020). Epidemiological and clinical characteristics of 99 cases of 2019 novel coronavirus pneumonia in Wuhan, China: a descriptive study. The Lancet, *395*(10223), 507–513.

Chen, T., Wu, D., Chen, H., Yan, W., Yang, D., & Chen, G. (2020). Clinical characteristics of 113 deceased patients with coronavirus disease 2019: Retrospective study [published online March 26, 2020]. BMJ.

Chouhan, V., Singh, S. K., Khamparia, A., Gupta, D., Tiwari, P., Moreira, C., Damaševičius, R., & De Albuquerque, V. H. C. (2020). A novel transfer learning based approach for pneumonia detection in chest X-ray images. Applied Sciences, *10*(2), 559.

Cohen, J. P., Morrison, P., & Dao, L. (2020). COVID-19 image data collection. ArXiv Preprint ArXiv:2003.11597.

Deng, A.-W., Wei, C.-H., & Gwo, C.-Y. (2015). Algorithms for computing zernike moments and image reconstruction in parallel process. *2015 2nd International Conference on Information Science and Control Engineering*, 105–109.

Eltoukhy, M. M., Elhoseny, M., Hosny, K. M., & Singh, A. K. (2018). Computer aided detection of mammographic mass using exact Gaussian–Hermite moments. Journal of Ambient Intelligence and Humanized Computing, 1–9.

Flusser, J., Suk, T., & Zitová, B. (2016). 2D and 3D image analysis by moments. John Wiley & Sons.

Guan, W., Ni, Z., Hu, Y., Liang, W., Ou, C., He, J., Liu, L., Shan, H., Lei, C., & Hui, D. S. C. (2020). Clinical characteristics of coronavirus disease 2019 in China. New England Journal of Medicine, *382*(18), 1708–1720.

Hansell, D. M., Bankier, A. A., MacMahon, H., McLoud, T. C., Muller, N. L., & Remy, J. (2008). Fleischner Society: Glossary of terms for thoracic imaging. Radiology, *246*(3), 697–722.

Hosny, K. M., Elaziz, M. A., Selim, I. M., & Darwish, M. M. (2020). Classification of galaxy color images using quaternion polar complex exponential transform and binary Stochastic Fractal Search. Astronomy and Computing, 100383.

Hosny, K. M., & Darwish, M. M. (2018). New set of quaternion moments for color images representation and recognition. Journal of Mathematical Imaging and Vision, *60*(5), 717–736.

Hosny, K. M., & Darwish, M. M. (2019). New set of multi-channel orthogonal moments for color image representation and recognition. Pattern Recognition, *88*, 153–173.

Hosny, K. M., Hamza, H. M., & Lashin, N. A. (2019). Copy-for-duplication forgery detection in colour images using QPCETMs and sub-image approach. IET Image Processing, *13*(9), 1437–1446.

Hosseini, M. S., & Zekri, M. (2012). Review of medical image classification using the adaptive neuro-fuzzy inference system. Journal of Medical Signals and Sensors, *2*(1), 49.

Hosseiny, M., Kooraki, S., Gholamrezanezhad, A., Reddy, S., & Myers, L. (2020). Radiology perspective of coronavirus disease 2019 (COVID-19): lessons from severe acute respiratory syndrome and Middle East respiratory syndrome. American Journal of Roentgenology, *214*(5), 1078–1082.

Hu, H., Zhang, Y., Shao, C., & Ju, Q. (2014). Orthogonal moments based on exponent functions: Exponent-Fourier moments. Pattern Recognition, *47*(8), 2596–2606.

Hwang, E. J., Nam, J. G., Lim, W. H., Park, S. J., Jeong, Y. S., Kang, J. H., Hong, E. K., Kim, T. M., Goo, J. M., & Park, S. (2019a). Deep learning for chest radiograph diagnosis in the emergency department. Radiology, *293*(3), 573–580.

Hwang, E. J., Park, S., Jin, K.-N., Im Kim, J., Choi, S. Y., Lee, J. H., Goo, J. M., Aum, J., Yim, J.-J., & Cohen, J. G. (2019b). Development and validation of a deep learning–based automated detection algorithm for major thoracic diseases on chest radiographs. JAMA Network Open, *2*(3), e191095–e191095.

Ibrahim, R. A., Abd Elaziz, M., & Lu, S. (2018). Chaotic opposition-based grey-wolf optimization algorithm based on differential evolution and disruption operator for global optimization. Expert Systems with Applications, *108*, 1–27.

Jacobi, A., Chung, M., Bernheim, A., & Eber, C. (2020). Portable chest X-ray in coronavirus disease-19 (COVID-19): A pictorial review. *Clinical Imaging.*

Kanne, J. P., Little, B. P., Chung, J. H., Elicker, B. M., & Ketai, L. H. (2020). Essentials for radiologists on COVID-19: An update—radiology scientific expert panel. Radiological Society of North America.

Kassani, S. H., & Kassani, P. H. (2019). A comparative study of deep learning architectures on melanoma detection. Tissue and Cell, *58*, 76–83.

Kooraki, S., Hosseiny, M., Myers, L., & Gholamrezanezhad, A. (2020). Coronavirus (COVID-19) outbreak: What the department of radiology should know. *Journal of the American College of Radiology.*

Lee, H., Pham, P., Largman, Y., & Ng, A. Y. (2009). Unsupervised feature learning for audio classification using convolutional deep belief networks. Advances in Neural Information Processing Systems, 1096–1104.

Liu, Z., Xiang, J., Wang, Y., Song, B., Gu, X., et al. 2020. Clinical course and risk factors for mortality of adult inpatients with COVID-19 in Wuhan, China: A retrospective cohort study. Lancet, *395*, 1054–1062.

Mollura, D., & Lungren, M. P. (2014). Radiology in global health. Springer.

Mooney, P. (2018). Chest x-ray images (pneumonia). *Online],* Https://Www.Kaggle.Com/ Paultimothymooney/Chest-Xray-Pneumonia*, Tanggal Akses.*

Mooney, P. (2020). *"Kaggle Chest x-ray Images (Pneumonia) Dataset.*

Murphy, K., Habib, S. S., Zaidi, S. M. A., Khowaja, S., Khan, A., Melendez, J., Scholten, E. T., Amad, F., Schalekamp, S., & Verhagen, M. (2020). Computer aided detection of tuberculosis on chest radiographs: An evaluation of the CAD4TB v6 system. Scientific Reports, *10*(1), 1–11.

Ng, M.-Y., Lee, E. Y. P., Yang, J., Yang, F., Li, X., Wang, H., Lui, M. M., Lo, C. S.-Y., Leung, B., & Khong, P.-L. (2020). Imaging profile of the COVID-19 infection: radiologic findings and literature review. Radiology: Cardiothoracic Imaging, *2*(1), e200034.

Peng, P., Zhao, X., Pan, X., & Ye, W. (2018). Gas classification using deep convolutional neural networks. Sensors, *18*(1), 157.

Pezzotti, W. (2014). Chest X-ray interpretation: not just black and white. Nursing2019, *44*(1), 40–47.

Platform, G. C. (2017). *Image Classification Transfer Learning with Inception v3.*

Qin, A. K., Huang, V. L., & Suganthan, P. N. (2008). Differential evolution algorithm with strategy adaptation for global numerical optimization. IEEE Transactions on Evolutionary Computation, *13*(2), 398–417.

Qin, H., Qin, L., Xue, L., & Yu, C. (2012). A parallel recurrence method for the fast computation of Zernike moments. Applied Mathematics and Computation, *219*(4), 1549–1561.

Qin, Z. Z., Sander, M. S., Rai, B., Titahong, C. N., Sudrungrot, S., Laah, S. N., Adhikari, L. M., Carter, E. J., Puri, L., & Codlin, A. J. (2019). Using artificial intelligence to read chest radiographs for tuberculosis detection: A multi-site evaluation of the diagnostic accuracy of three deep learning systems. Scientific Reports, *9*(1), 1–10.

Quek, C., Irawan, W., & Ng, E. Y. K. (2010). A novel brain-inspired neural cognitive approach to SARS thermal image analysis. Expert Systems with Applications, *37*(4), 3040–3054.

Rachna, C. (2020). *Difference Between X-ray and CT Scan.*

Rahman, T., Chowdhury, M., & Khandakar, A. (2020). COVID-19 Radiography Database. Kaggle.

Rajpurkar, P., Irvin, J., Zhu, K., Yang, B., Mehta, H., Duan, T., Ding, D., Bagul, A., Langlotz, C., & Shpanskaya, K. (2017). Chexnet: Radiologist-level pneumonia detection on chest x-rays with deep learning. ArXiv Preprint ArXiv:1711.05225.

Rawat, W., & Wang, Z. (2017). Deep convolutional neural networks for image classification: A comprehensive review. Neural Computation, *29*(9), 2352–2449.

Rodriguez-Morales, A. J., Cardona-Ospina, J. A., Gutiérrez-Ocampo, E., Villamizar-Pena, R., Holguin-Rivera, Y., Escalera-Antezana, J. P., Alvarado-Arnez, L. E., Bonilla-Aldana, D. K., Franco-Paredes, C., & Henao-Martinez, A. F. (2020). Latin American Network of Coronavirus Disease 2019-COVID-19 Research (LANCOVID-19). Clinical, Laboratory and Imaging Features of COVID-19: A Systematic Review and Meta-Analysis. Travel Medicine and Infectious Disease, *34*, 101623.

Rubin, G. D., Ryerson, C. J., Haramati, L. B., Sverzellati, N., Kanne, J. P., Raoof, S., Schluger, N. W., Volpi, A., Yim, J.-J., & Martin, I. B. K. (2020). The role of chest imaging in patient management during the COVID-19 pandemic: A multinational consensus statement from the Fleischner Society. Chest.

Russakovsky, O., Deng, J., Su, H., Krause, J., Satheesh, S., Ma, S., Huang, Z., Karpathy, A., Khosla, A., & Bernstein, M. (2015). Imagenet large scale visual recognition challenge. International Journal of Computer Vision, *115*(3), 211–252.

Saba, T., Mohamed, A. S., El-Affendi, M., Amin, J., & Sharif, M. (2020). Brain tumor detection using fusion of hand crafted and deep learning features. Cognitive Systems Research, *59*, 221–230.

Salah, A., Li, K., Hosny, K. M., Darwish, M. M., & Tian, Q. (2020). Accelerated CPU–GPUs implementations for quaternion polar harmonic transform of color images. Future Generation Computer Systems, *107*, 368–382.

Salehi, S., Abedi, A., Balakrishnan, S., & Gholamrezanezhad, A. (2020). Coronavirus disease 2019 (COVID-19): A systematic review of imaging findings in 919 patients. American Journal of Roentgenology, 1–7.

Sethy, P. K., & Behera, S. K. (2020). Detection of coronavirus disease (COVID-19) based on deep features. Preprints, *2020030300*, 2020.

Shan, F., Gao, Y., Wang, J., Shi, W., Shi, N., Han, M., Xue, Z., & Shi, Y. (2020). Lung infection quantification of COVID-19 in ct images with deep learning. ArXiv Preprint ArXiv:2003.04655.

Simonyan, K., & Zisserman, A. (2014). Very deep convolutional networks for large-scale image recognition. ArXiv Preprint ArXiv:1409.1556.

Singh, C., & Singh, J. (2018). Multi-channel versus quaternion orthogonal rotation invariant moments for color image representation. Digital Signal Processing, *78*, 376–392.

Suk, T., & Flusser, J. (2009). Affine moment invariants of color images. *International Conference on Computer Analysis of Images and Patterns*, 334–341.

Suykens, J. A. K., & Vandewalle, J. (1999). Least squares support vector machine classifiers. Neural Processing Letters, *9*(3), 293–300.

Szegedy, C., Ioffe, S., Vanhoucke, V., & Alemi, A. (2016). Inception-v4, inception-resnet and the impact of residual connections on learning. ArXiv Preprint ArXiv:1602.07261.

Wang, S., Kang, B., Ma, J., Zeng, X., Xiao, M., Guo, J., Cai, M., Yang, J., Li, Y., & Meng, X. (2020). A deep learning algorithm using CT images to screen for Corona Virus Disease (COVID-19). medRxiv. *Published Online April, 24*, 2002–2020.

Wang, X., Li, W., Yang, H., Wang, P., & Li, Y. (2015). Quaternion polar complex exponential transform for invariant color image description. Applied Mathematics and Computation, *256*, 951–967.

Wong, H. Y. F., Lam, H. Y. S., Fong, A. H.-T., Leung, S. T., Chin, T. W.-Y., Lo, C. S. Y., Lui, M. M.-S., Lee, J. C. Y., Chiu, K. W.-H., & Chung, T. (2020). Frequency and distribution of chest radiographic findings in COVID-19 positive patients. Radiology, 201160.

Wu, Z., & McGoogan, J. M. (2020). Characteristics of and important lessons from the coronavirus disease 2019 (COVID-19) outbreak in China: Summary of a report of 72 314 cases from the Chinese Center for Disease Control and Prevention. JAMA, *323*(13), 1239–1242.

Wu, Z., Shen, C., & Van Den Hengel, A. (2019). Wider or deeper: Revisiting the resnet model for visual recognition. Pattern Recognition, *90*, 119–133.

Xie, X., Li, X., Wan, S., & Gong, Y. (2006). Mining x-ray images of SARS patients. Data Mining, 282–294.

Yang, L., Zhang, Y., Chen, J., Zhang, S., & Chen, D. Z. (2017). Suggestive annotation: A deep active learning framework for biomedical image segmentation. *International Conference on Medical Image Computing and Computer-Assisted Intervention*, 399–407.

Yang, Y., & Newsam, S. (2008). Comparing SIFT descriptors and Gabor texture features for classification of remote sensed imagery. *2008 15th IEEE International Conference on Image Processing*, 1852–1855.

Yildirim, O., Talo, M., Ay, B., Baloglu, U. B., Aydin, G., & Acharya, U. R. (2019). Automated detection of diabetic subject using pre-trained 2D-CNN models with frequency spectrum images extracted from heart rate signals. Computers in Biology and Medicine, *113*, 103387.

Yoon, S. H., Lee, K. H., Kim, J. Y., Lee, Y. K., Ko, H., Kim, K. H., Park, C. M., & Kim, Y.-H. (2020). Chest radiographic and CT findings of the 2019 novel coronavirus disease (COVID-19): Analysis of nine patients treated in Korea. Korean Journal of Radiology, *21*(4), 494–500.

Zeng, J.-H., Liu, Y., Yuan, J., Wang, F., Wu, W.-B., Li, J.-X., Wang, L.-F., Gao, H., Qu, J.-X., & Wang, Y. (2020). *Clinical characteristics and cardiac injury description of 419 cases of COVID-19 in Shenzhen, China.*

Zhao, Q., Meng, M., Kumar, R., Wu, Y., Huang, J., Deng, Y., Weng, Z., & Yang, L. (2020). Lymphopenia is associated with severe coronavirus disease 2019 (COVID-19) infections: A systemic review and meta-analysis. *International Journal of Infectious Diseases*.

Zhao, W., Zhang, Z., & Wang, L. (2020b). Manta ray foraging optimization: An effective bio-inspired optimizer for engineering applications. Engineering Applications of Artificial Intelligence, *87*, 103300.

Zhao, W., Zhong, Z., Xie, X., Yu, Q., & Liu, J. (2020a). Relation between chest CT findings and clinical conditions of coronavirus disease (COVID-19) pneumonia: A multicenter study. American Journal of Roentgenology, *214*(5), 1072–1077.

7 Blood Cell Microscope Image-Based Testing Using Deep Learning Techniques

KEY POINTS

- Complete blood cell counts (CBCs) is used as a routine indicator to evaluate the bone marrow to produce the necessary cells.
- Blood cell detection methods apply the conventional computer vision techniques such as segmentation algorithms.
- YOLO: "You Only Look Once," in short YOLO, is a state-of-the-art object detection classification algorithm.
- The YOLO method treats object detection as a regression problem.
- A robust algorithm for accurate and efficient segmentation of whole-slide WBC, RBC, and platelet cells based on semantic segmentation.

INTRODUCTION

The microscopic inspection of blood smears provides diagnostic information concerning patients' health status. The inspection results of the differential blood count reveal a wide range of critical hematic pathologies. For example, the presence of infections (like anemia, dengue, COVID-19), and some particular kinds of virus that can be diagnosed based on the results of the classification and the count of white blood cells (WBCs). The expert operatives use the traditional method for the differential blood count. They use a microscope and count the percentage of the occurrence of each type of cell present within an area of interest in smears. This manual counting process is very tedious and slow. Also, cell classification and counting accuracy may depend on the capabilities and experience of the operators. Therefore, the necessity of an automated differential counting system becomes inevitable.

A blood test result more typically seen in the disorders associated with bone marrow diseases was found in a patient with Coronavirus Disease (COVID-19), a viral infection caused by severe acute respiratory syndrome coronavirus 2 (SARS-CoV-2) (Mitra et al., 2020). Leucoerythroblastic reactions in blood usually indicate a significant deviation from the body's normal immune response. They resemble immature red blood cells (RBCs) and bone marrow cells (myeloid cells) circulating in the blood.

COVID-19 AND BLOOD ANALYSIS: A CASE STUDY

A healthy woman in her 40s suddenly developed flu-like symptoms that led to her admission at a local community hospital. Her chest X-ray and Computerized Tomography (CT) scans at the time showed signs of pneumonia. As her respiratory symptoms worsened, the patient needed intubation and ventilation. She was transferred to UC Davis Medical Center for advanced care.

Upon admission, the patient's initial blood tests revealed a normal WBC count, reduced level of lymphocytes (one type of WBCs), insufficient normal-sized RBCs, and a normal platelet count. Three days later, the patient had an increased level of WBCs (leukocytosis) and above normal levels of immature neutrophil cells. Her blood test also showed a mild increase in the number of monocytes (immune cells) and a reduced level of lymphocytes.

The leucoerythroblastic picture reflected normal shape and size of the RBCs but in lower than normal levels (normocytic anemia), occasional immature RBCs (nucleated), a mild presence of RBCs with different sizes (anisocytosis), and rare tear-drop-shaped cells known as dacrocytes. It also showed neutrophilia, highlighting the body's rush to produce WBCs to fight the infection.

As the patient got better, neutrophilia resolved, and the other blood indicators were back to normal ranges. The patient has since been discharged and is recovering at home.

Complete blood cell (CBC) counts are one of the most common diagnostic methods in medical institutions. For example, detection of different WBC counts can help to manage acute radiation syndrome. When a patient undergoes a radiation therapy or chemotherapy, CBCs are used as a routine indicator to evaluate the bone marrow to produce the necessary cells. In addition, inflammation, leukemia, immunodeficiency, etc., can be detected and identified using different WBC counts. Bone marrow fibrosis, lymphoma, aplastic anemia, and lupus erythematosus are closely related to the abnormal platelet counts. Excessive bleeding such as kidney bleeding is related to changes in the number of RBCs.

COMPUTATION TECHNIQUES

YOLO MODEL

Early blood cell detection methods apply the conventional computer vision techniques such as segmentation algorithms and create image descriptors such as SIFT/LBP/HPG (Jiang et al., 2010; Fernyhough, 2016). But a CBC detection needs to overcome challenges such as cell overlap, small sizes, high background noise, and so on. Recently, deep neural networks have attracted vast interest from research community, and from recent studies (Xia et al., 2019; Storey et al., 2017; Storey et al., 2018; Jiang et al., 2019; Jiang & Crookes, 2019) we have found these techniques can be a good answer for data-driven tasks. With benefits from the improvements of computing power and data acquiring technique, deep learning models such as Convolutional Neural Networks (CNNs) show a high performance in computer vision game and real application. Since 2012, several CNN-based object detection algorithms have been proposed such as R-CNN, Fast-RCNN, Faster RCNN, and Mask-RCNN (Girshick et al., 2014; Girshick, 2015; Ren et al., 2015; He et al., 2017). In 2016, Redmon et al. (2016) suggested a new object detection method named YOLO that has a high detection speed but sacrifices some accuracy compared with the CNN region-based approaches.

Data and Material

The dataset contains 364 open-source microscopic blood cell images. These blood smear microscopic pictures illustrate three kinds of species, including RBCs, WBCs, and platelets. Figure 7.1 shows some input samples from the data set.[1]

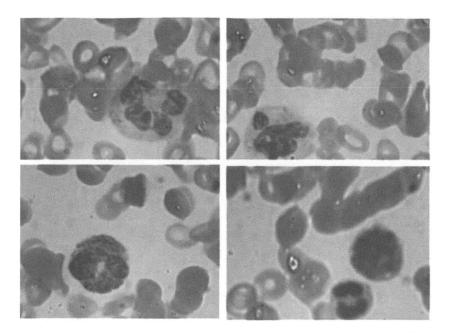

FIGURE 7.1   The sample of blood smear microscopic images.

Methodology

YOLO: "You Only Look Once," in short YOLO, is a state-of-the-art object detection classification algorithm (Redmon et al., 2016). It treats object detection as a regression problem. It requires only one forward propagation pass through the network to make a fast prediction for both image class and location. It resizes the image by 448 × 448 and divides the entire image into a 7 × 7 grid cell, and each grid cell predicts for two bounding boxes and confidence score for the boxes. The grid cell in which the center of the object lies is responsible for detecting that object. The original implementation of the YOLO model as a CNN is evaluated on the Pattern Analysis, Statistical Modeling, and Computational Learning (PASCAL) Visual Object Classes (VOC) dataset. Its network architecture contains 24 convolutional layers and two fully connected layers and is inspired by the GoogLeNet. Among its different versions, we choose to use Tiny YOLO, as it is the fastest of all. Tiny YOLO uses nine instead of 24 convolutional layers; other than that all the parameters are the same (Redmon et al., 2016).

The system pipeline of our model used in this section is presented in Figures 7.2 and 7.3. The obtained microscopic blood smear images are resized using YOLO algorithm into 416 × 416. After that, the localization and classification tasks will be fulfilled by the rest of the deep neural network. The qualified candidate detection network will serve in the last stage of the fast diagnosis process.

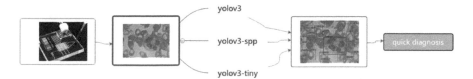

FIGURE 7.2   Scheme diagram of deep learning based diagnosis.

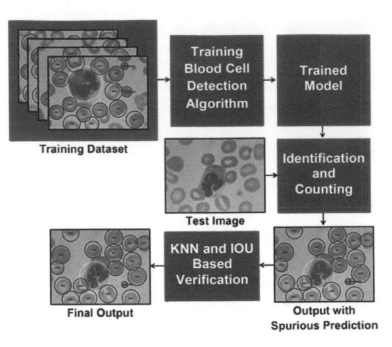

FIGURE 7.3   Block diagram of automatic blood cells identification and counting system.

Considering the privacy of the patients and difficulty of obtaining a large amount of labeled datasets in the medical field, we propose to apply transfer learning into this deep learning diagnosis method. The crucial concept of transfer learning is that the new model can use the previous one's knowledge to quickly master its present learning task. This is because in the processing of deep neural networks, the starting layers always detect lower level features such as curves, angles, and lines no matter what we want to detect. However, for the last several layers we often need to train them separately to achieve a unique classifier in order to meet the required performance. The model uses only seven convolutional and maximum pooling layers as its backbone network to achieve an easier and faster performance. Our framework is shown in Figure 7.2, and the network architecture of the model is shown in Figure 7.4.

Result

Our raw samples are obtained from an open-source dataset on GitHub,[2] which contains 364 blood smear microscopic images. In order to utilize the values of small datasets, we only separate the images into a training set and a test set by a ratio of 8:2. We convert our datasets into the YOLOv3 format datasets and build the network based on the Pytorch framework. Our experiments all run on a remote server with a 4G NVIDIA i7 processor. The training is based on pre-trained weights; thus, the training time is significantly shorter than training from scratch. The analysis using both YOLOv3-SPP and YOLOv3 takes about half an hour to complete 100-epoch training process, whereas YOLOv3-tiny takes only 10 min to finish the training. This is mainly because the size of YOLOv3-tiny is very small to reach a high training and detection speed. Figure 7.5 shows the test results on the Blood Cell Count and Detection (BCCD) dataset, and we can see that the YOLOv3-SPP has achieved the best accuracy when the model becomes converged.

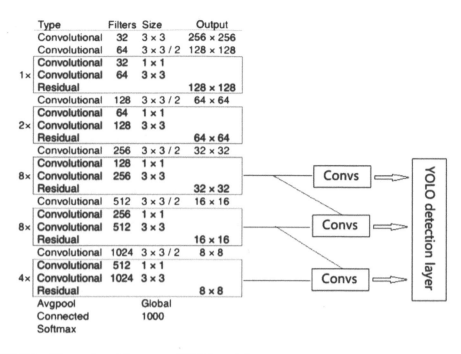

FIGURE 7.4   Network architecture of CNN model.

From the test results, it is obvious that WBCs are easy to detect so that all the three models produce very high mAP and F1 values. However, both the RBCs and platelets represent a low precision with a high recall rate. This result directly indicates that our method generates too many false positives. From the detection of the samples, we can see that there are challenges including the large number and shape overlap of RBCs, the large noises, or low background contrast because of the tiny size of platelets.

The YOLOv3-SPP model shows the best performance among the three methods discussed above. Its mean average precision can reach 0.886, and the precision for three kinds

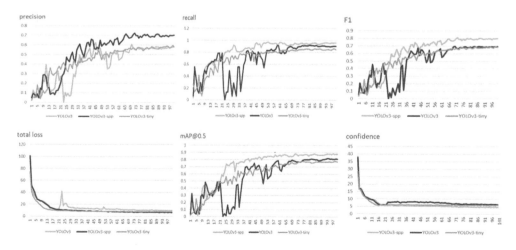

FIGURE 7.5   Test results of three different YOLO networks on the blood cell dataset BCCD.[3] Top row, from left: precision, recall, and F1 measure; Bottom row, from left: total loss, mAP, and confidence.

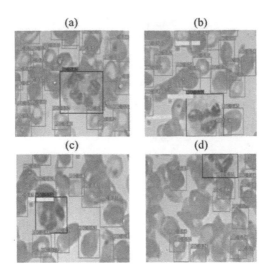

FIGURE 7.6   YOLOv3-SPP detection results on blood smear microscopic images (a), (b), (c), and (d).

of blood cells can exceed 80%, and especially that of the WBCs is about 0.98. The detection time of YOLOv3-SPP can reach 0.132 s for four samples, as shown in Figure 7.6. Although YOLOv3-tiny is much faster with a detection time of about 0.095 s for four samples, its precision and recall become low when applied to a real scenario. The detection examples of the YOLOv3-SPP method are shown in Figure 7.6. Almost all the blood cells can be marked out by different rectangular boxes. The big blue rectangular boxes are WBCs, while the yellow small boxes are platelets, and the targets present in large amount are RBCs.

In Figure 7.7, we further tested our system using the samples from a COVID-19 patient (Mitra et al., 2020), where we can clearly see a blood clot in the first image. The test results show a perfect performance on these COVID-19 samples, implying a potential of this technology for automated hematology for COVID-19 medical analysis.

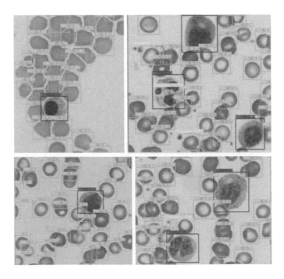

FIGURE 7.7   Further tests on COVID-19 samples from Mitra et al. (2020).

PARASITEMIA EVALUATION METHODS

Machine learning based automated identification of COVID-19 infection cells using microscopic section images can help to reduce the time consumed in traditional ways. Detection of blood cells by a patient's blood mark microscopic examination using different techniques of image processing can support fast and effective detection of infection. White blood cell (WBC) images of suspected and confirmed cases of COVID-19 may be essentially helpful for the three stages of enhancement, segmentation, and classification. These stages of image processing can help to achieve greater quality and accuracy in blood cancer detection. Approaching the conventional segmentation and counting of blood cells is considered an essential step that helps in extracting features to diagnose diseases like leukemia. The image analysis will allow hematology experts to perform faster and more accurately. In this work, the image recognition problem of WBC cancer has been investigated. Different types of WBCs are classified using a Gaussian Feature Convolutional Visual Recognition (GFCVR) method. The most important features or segments of these blood cells are provided as input microscopic images to the neural network. The consequences of this analysis are mainly considering the identification of blood cancer affected region with feature extraction for specific WBC images. In this proposed approach pre-processing the image, classifies multi-level clustering to find the affected area in blood cells. In this proposed simulation, results in time complexity, accuracy, recall, perception, false classification ratio gives better results compared with other existing methods.

Evaluation algorithm for detecting the degree of blood infection, using Python 3.8.0 environment, was designed with respect to plasmodium-infected RBC images. This process enables the algorithm to distinguish between infected and uninfected RBCs images. In order to determine parasitemia values, the proposed algorithm uses a morphological image processing technique to effectively identify the infected and uninfected RBCs. The algorithm also detects the plasmodium penetration into the RBCs, which is a key configuration in the series of processes. The algorithm is made as a standardized test procedure through color image processing based on the hue, saturation, value (HSV) color space technique, providing a quantitative analysis on the blood samples.

Preprocessing

RBC images have some preprocessing steps that involve the conversion of the original image into a grayscale image and the enhancement of its contrast by adaptive histogram equalization (Zuiderveld, 1994; Reza, 2004; Cheng & Shi, 2004). The value of adaptive histogram equalization was determined by Otsu's method. Through these two processes an improved image is obtained for the next stage. Figure 7.8 shows a prior image and subsequent image with respect to the preprocessing. Figure 7.8b shows the grayscale image of the actual microscopic image, which categorically distinguishes the RBCs in the sample (Figure 7.9).

Edge Detection

The Sobel edge detector (SED) uses two 3 9 3 kernels which are convolved with the original image to calculate approximations of the derivatives, one for horizontal changes, and one for vertical. Edge detection is a general term for the mathematical method used to determine the point in the digital image which detects the change in the brightness of the image if it changes rapidly or has a discontinuity. Edge refers to a point which is composed of a set

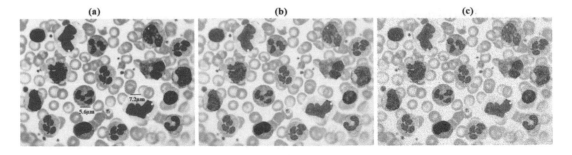

FIGURE 7.8 Adaptive histogram equalization. (a) Original image. (b) Grey scale image. (c) Bitmap image.

of typical curved segment to radically change the brightness of the image. Therefore, applying the image edge detection algorithm can reduce the amount of data to be handled markedly, while maintaining the important structural characteristics of the image and filtering the lower priority information. The SED is a discrete differentiation operator, computing an approximation of the gradient of the image intensity function. At each point in the image, the result of SED is either the corresponding gradient vector or the norm of this vector. SED uses the masks in Figure 7.10 to approximate digitally the first derivatives G_x and G_y. In other words, the gradient at the center point in a neighborhood is computed as followed by SED (Gonzalez et al., 2004) (Vincent & Folorunso, 2009).

$$G = \left[G_x^2 + G_y^2 \right]^{\frac{1}{2}}$$

$$= \left\{ \left[\left(z_7 + 2z_8 + z_9 \right) - \left(z_1 + 2z_2 + z_3 \right) \right]^2 + \left[\left(z_3 + 2z_6 + z_9 \right) - \left(z_1 + 2z_4 + z_7 \right) \right]^2 \right\}^{\frac{1}{2}} \tag{7.1}$$

A pixel at location (x, y) is an edge pixel if $g \geq T$ at that location, where T is a specified threshold.

Edge Link

If the edge detection procedure is successful, the subsequent operations for interpreting the contents of the image information can be substantially simplified. However, it is not possible to obtain an ideal edge, such as the actual image of the appropriate complexity. For

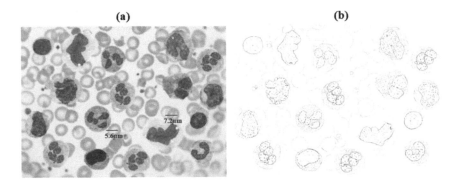

FIGURE 7.9 Edge detection. (a) Grayscale image. (b) Edge image.

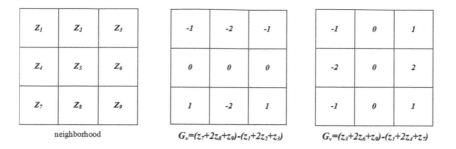

FIGURE 7.10 SED mask.

this reason, it may represent a potential corresponding to the discontinuity of the image brightness. Edges are extracted from the non-trivial image, which do not complicate the subsequent operations to interpret the image data corresponding to the respective conditions of interest in the image. This means it not only the edge segments that are connected by a curved edge as false edges or omissions. Edge detection is a technique of the basic steps in a variety of fields such as image processing, image analysis, image recognition, and computer vision. Therefore, the edge link has been recognized as an essential step in the image processing procedure.

Derived edges are connected to each other at their link points, which forms closed perimeter around the RBCs. Link points close the shape of edge lines using 20 kinds of different 3×3 masks shown in Figure 7.11. Such an edge link mask is connected to each link of all points through the scanning area with respect to the image size of 1300×1030.

Morphological Operation

For RBC images segmentation, the morphological operation included the following three sequential steps: (1) flood-fill operation, (2) removal of invalid RBCs and noise, and (3) detection of overlapping RBCs. As a prerequisite for the processing of the following steps, Figure 7.12 shows the result of each step in the morphological operation.

First, based on the edge image link, a flood-fill operation on background pixels (that is internal pixels of the linked edge contour) of the input binary image was performed.

However, due to the presence of one linked edge contour inside another linked edge contour, the flood-fill operation is not performed accurately. In other words, a black cavity occurs in the image of the white colored RBCs in which the flood-fill operation is

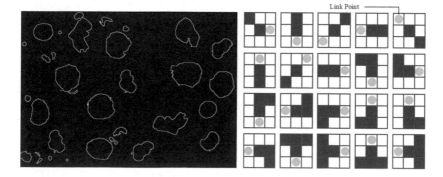

FIGURE 7.11 Edge link image and mask.

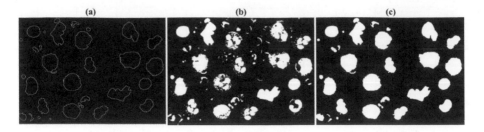

FIGURE 7.12 Morphological operation. (a) Edge linked image. (b) Flood-fill image. (c) Remove invalid RBCs and noise.

performed. The opening and closing operation was carried out to improve this phenomenon. Opening generally smoothens the contour of an object, breaks and narrows isthmuses, and eliminates thin protrusions. Closing also tends to smoothen sections of contours, but, as opposed to opening, it generally fuses narrow breaks and long thin gulfs, eliminates small holes, and fills gaps in the contour (Gonzalez et al., 2004; Goyal, 2011).

The opening of set A by structuring element B, denoted $A \circ B$, is defined as

$$A \circ B = (A \oplus B) \ominus B \qquad (7.2)$$

Thus, the opening A by B is the erosion of A by B, followed by a dilation of the result by B. Similarly, the closing of set A by structuring element B, denoted $A \cdot B$, is defined as

$$A \cdot B = (A \oplus B) \ominus B \qquad (7.3)$$

It means that the closing of A by B is simply the dilation of A by B, followed by the erosion of the result by B.

Second, in order to remove invalid RBCs and the image noise, the following two methods are used. One is the method for removing the edge line contacting the outermost pixel on the image that is to say the removal of invalid RBCs creates the outermost pixel line of the image. It connects the outermost pixel line to the adjacent linked edge line. Then it removes one connected line with the image coordinates of the outermost pixel of the image, the other is the method for removing objects smaller than the size of typical RBCs. In the process of removing noise from the image, the size of the smallest RBC is calculated based on the number of pixels, and the largest noise is calculated. The threshold value is set by the two calculated sizes.

Third, labeling was performed as the first step to detect the overlapping RBCs. As a result of labeling, all RBCs are merged into one object with or without overlapping. The objects that were rolled into one have morphological differences. Identification of distorted values based on the roundness of each object is a criterion of distinguishing the overlapping RBCs. Therefore, the reason for performing the labeling is that it is possible for the roundness to be numerically confirmed. Roundness of overlapping RBCs is close to zero, the roundness of the correct circle is expressed as one, since the roundness means a correct circle. In this research, the RBCs were determined to overlap less than 0.6, because the threshold value of the roundness was set to 0.6 (Figure 7.13).

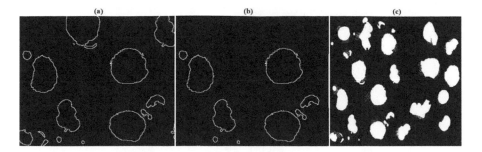

FIGURE 7.13 Remove invalid RBCs and noise. (a) Create the outermost pixel line and connection. (b) Remove one connected line. (c) Images with RBCs and noise coexist.

Clump Split

The purpose to enforce clump split overlap on RBCs is to improve significantly the accuracy in the evaluation process of parasitemia. As shown in Figure 7.14, a problem that arises is that the overlap of two RBCs is recognized as one RBC. In such cases, the clump split method (Kumar et al., 2006; LaTorre et al., 2013; Farhan et al., 2013) is used to split clumps of two or more RBCs into constituent cells. The process is shown in Figure 7.14 and its steps have been explained based on the figure. Results obtained using the clump split method are shown in Figure 7.15.

Concavity depth $\overline{CD}$ is a concaveness measure proposed by Rosenfeld (1985). First, the group K_i of convex hull segment can be obtained from the image boundary. Then, the maximum distance between each segment can be calculated for the four pixels, K_1, K_2, K_3, and K_4. Two tangents $\overline{K_1K_3}$ and $\overline{K_2K_4}$ can be drawn using these four pixels. Each pixel on the boundary between K_1 and K_3 has a concavity depth value, which is the rectilinear distance from the corresponding tangent $\overline{K_1K_3}$. Where the distance from K_1 to C_i is a value that can be seen by the calculation. This calculation process is continued until the maximum value of the concavity depth $\overline{CD_1}$ is achieved. Also, each pixel on the boundary between K_2 and K_4 has a concavity depth value, which is the rectilinear distance from the

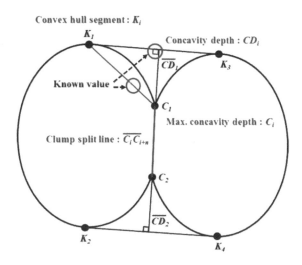

FIGURE 7.14 Clump split method.

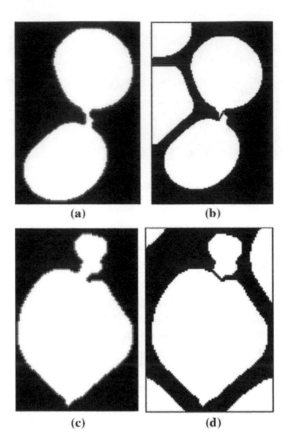

FIGURE 7.15 Clump split image. (a) Before clump spit. (b) After clump split. (c) Before clump split. (d) After clump split.

corresponding tangent $\overline{K_2K_4}$. Where the distance from K_2 to C_i is a value that can be seen by the calculation. This calculation process is continued until the maximum value of the concavity depth $\overline{CD_2}$ is achieved. After performing this iterative process, finally, it turns the value of the closest pixel in clump split line $\overline{C_iC_{i+n}}$.

Parasites Detection

In the Giemsa staining method used for the detection of COVID-19 parasites, Plasmodium is stained with a purple color throughout the process. In order to extract these characteristics through Figures 7.16 and 7.17, compare the Red Green Blue (RGB) image and the HSV image. The results were excellent in the HSV image.

HSV is one of the several color systems used by people to select colors (e.g., of paints or inks) from a color wheel or palette. These color systems are closer to human experience and expression of color sensations than the RGB system (Georgieva et al., 2005; Sural et al., 2002; Deswal & Sharma, 2014).

For parasite detection, it can be divided into the following four sequential steps: (1) HSV conversion, (2) S component analysis, (3) parasites detection, and (4) image registration.

In a color image, the sub-images in red, green, and blue are very analogous to each other. The separation of parasites in gray levels is not proper. The parasites were found to be different in color. Therefore, hue–saturation–value color space is analyzed as shown

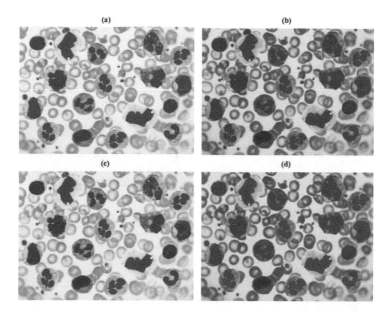

FIGURE 7.16   RGB image and components. (a) RGB image. (b) R component. (c) G component. (d) B component.

in Figure 7.17. A bright object is a viewpoint in hue component, H and saturation, S. This is because Giemsa staining solution colors hexane. That is, RGB colors emphasized in these objects look dark and are colored in purple (Harms et al., 1986; Olivo-Marin, 2002). Therefore, the white cells and parasites that include RGB are much brighter in images than other objects. This is why saturation components are used in color images (Figure 7.18).

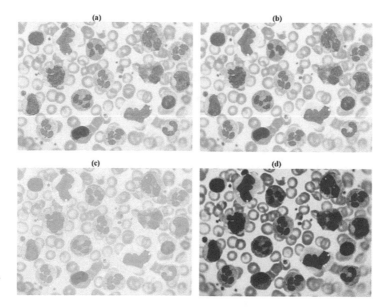

FIGURE 7.17   HSV image and components. (a) HSV image. (b) H component. (c) S component. (d) V component.

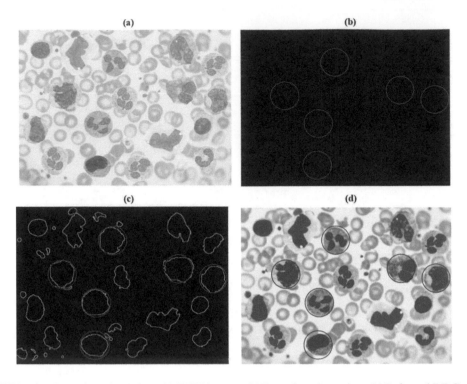

FIGURE 7.18 Parasites detection. (a) HSV image. (b) Parasites detection. (c) Infected RBCs detection. (d) Image registration on RGB image.

Results

Figure 7.18 shows the parasite evaluation results obtained using the Python 3.8.0 environment. The microscopic image of the blood sample is processed through various preprocessing, processing, and post-processing stages. Evaluation algorithm for blood infection degree, using Python software, was designed with respect to the RBCs image infected with parasites of the plasmodium to distinguish it from the uninfected RBCs image. Briefly, this involved the detection of the infected RBCs using preprocessing (which involves the conversion of grayscale and the enhancement of the image contrast by adaptive histogram equalization).

The value of adaptive histogram equalization was determined by Otsu's method; edge detection (which uses two 3×3 kernels that are convolved with the original image to calculate approximations of the derivatives, one for horizontal changes, and one for vertical); edge link (link points close the shape of edge lines using 20 kinds of different 3×3 masks. Such an edge link mask is connected to each link of all points through the scanning area with respect to the image size of 1300×1030); morphological operation (which involves flood-fill operation, removal of invalid RBCs and noise, and detection of overlapping RBCs), the clump split method (which is used to split clumps of two or more RBCs into constituent cells), and parasite evaluation (which can be divided into HSV conversion, S component analysis, parasites detection, and image registration). Subsequently, parasite infection is identified based on the S component analysis of converted the HSV image. These color systems are closer to human experience and expression of color sensations than the RGB method. It was found that all these extensive steps have improved processing of the image and assisted in evaluating the number of cells that are infected with COVID-19. When compared to the existing process to detect COVID-19 infection, this procedure is fast, accurate, economical, and does not require high skills to interpret the results. The interface tool is designed in such a way that the sequencing is given in the order in which the procedure should be executed and therefore reduces the ambiguity in evaluating the results. The result table gives the RBC count, the number of infected RBCs, and the percentage of parasitemia present in the blood sample. The results also indicate that the method is robust and accurate.

NOTES

1. BCCD Dataset, https://github.com/Shenggan/BCCD Dataset.
2. BCCD Dataset, https://github.com/Shenggan/BCCD Dataset.
3. BCCD Dataset, https://github.com/Shenggan/BCCD Dataset.

REFERENCES

Cheng, H. D., & Shi, X. J. (2004). A simple and effective histogram equalization approach to image enhancement. *Digital Signal Processing, 14*(2), 158–170.

Deswal, M., & Sharma, N. (2014). A fast HSV image color and texture detection and image conversion algorithm. *International Journal of Science and Research, 3*(6).

Farhan, M., Yli-Harja, O., & Niemistö, A. (2013). A novel method for splitting clumps of convex objects incorporating image intensity and using rectangular window-based concavity point-pair search. *Pattern Recognition, 46*(3), 741–751.

Fernyhough, E. N. (2016). *Automated segmentation of structures essential to cell movement.* University of Leeds.

Georgieva, L., Dimitrova, T., & Angelov, N. (2005). RGB and HSV colour models in colour identification of digital traumas images. *International Conference on Computer Systems and Technologies, 12*(1).

Girshick, R. (2015). Fast r-cnn. *Proceedings of the IEEE International Conference on Computer Vision,* 1440–1448.

Girshick, R., Donahue, J., Darrell, T., & Malik, J. (2014). Rich feature hierarchies for accurate object detection and semantic segmentation. *Proceedings of the IEEE Conference on Computer Vision and Pattern Recognition,* 580–587.

Gonzalez, R. C., Woods, R. E., & Eddins, S. L. (2004). *Digital image processing using MATLAB.* Pearson Education India.

Goyal, M. (2011). Morphological image processing. *IJCST, 2*(4).

Harms, H., Gunzer, U., & Aus, H. M. (1986). Combined local color and texture analysis of stained cells. *Computer Vision, Graphics, and Image Processing, 33*(3), 364–376.

He, K., Gkioxari, G., Dollár, P., & Girshick, R. (2017). Mask r-cnn. *Proceedings of the IEEE International Conference on Computer Vision,* 2961–2969.

Jiang, R., & Crookes, D. (2019). Shallow unorganized neural networks using smart neuron model for visual perception. *IEEE Access, 7,* 152701–152714.

Jiang, R. M., Crookes, D., Luo, N., & Davidson, M. W. (2010). Live-cell tracking using SIFT features in DIC microscopic videos. *IEEE Transactions on Biomedical Engineering, 57*(9), 2219–2228.

Jiang, Z., Chazot, P. L., Celebi, M. E., Crookes, D., & Jiang, R. (2019). Social behavioral phenotyping of Drosophila with a 2D–3D hybrid CNN framework. *IEEE Access, 7,* 67972–67982.

Kumar, S., Ong, S. H., Ranganath, S., Ong, T. C., & Chew, F. T. (2006). A rule-based approach for robust clump splitting. *Pattern Recognition, 39*(6), 1088–1098.

LaTorre, A., Alonso-Nanclares, L., Muelas, S., Peña, J. M., & DeFelipe, J. (2013). Segmentation of neuronal nuclei based on clump splitting and a two-step binarization of images. *Expert Systems with Applications, 40*(16), 6521–6530.

Mitra, A., Dwyre, D. M., Schivo, M., Thompson III, G. R., Cohen, S. H., Ku, N., Graff, J. P. (2020). Leukoerythroblastic reaction in a patient with COVID-19 infection. *American Journal of Hematology, 95*(8), 999–1000.

Olivo-Marin, J.-C. (2002). Extraction of spots in biological images using multiscale products. *Pattern Recognition, 35*(9), 1989–1996.

Redmon, J., Divvala, S., Girshick, R., & Farhadi, A. (2016). You only look once: Unified, real-time object detection. *Proceedings of the IEEE Conference on Computer Vision and Pattern Recognition*, 779–788.

Ren, S., He, K., Girshick, R., & Sun, J. (2015). Faster r-cnn: Towards real-time object detection with region proposal networks. *Advances in Neural Information Processing Systems*, 91–99.

Reza, A. M. (2004). Realization of the contrast limited adaptive histogram equalization (CLAHE) for real-time image enhancement. *Journal of VLSI Signal Processing Systems for Signal, Image and Video Technology, 38*(1), 35–44.

Rosenfeld, A. (1985). Measuring the sizes of concavities. *Pattern Recognition Letters, 3*(1), 71–75.

Storey, G., Bouridane, A., & Jiang, R. (2018). Integrated deep model for face detection and landmark localization from "In The Wild" images. *IEEE Access, 6*, 74442–74452.

Storey, G., Jiang, R., & Bouridane, A. (2017). Role for 2D image generated 3D face models in the rehabilitation of facial palsy. *Healthcare Technology Letters, 4*(4), 145–148.

Sural, S., Qian, G., & Pramanik, S. (2002). Segmentation and histogram generation using the HSV color space for image retrieval. *Proceedings. International Conference on Image Processing, 2*, II–II.

Vincent, O. R., & Folorunso, O. (2009). A descriptive algorithm for sobel image edge detection. *Proceedings of Informing Science & IT Education Conference, 40*, 97–107.

Xia, T., Jiang, R., Fu, Y. Q., & Jin, N. (2019). Automated blood cell detection and counting via deep learning for microfluidic point-of-care medical devices. *IOP Conference Series: Materials Science and Engineering, 646*(1), 12048.

Zuiderveld, K. (1994). Contrast limited adaptive histogram equalization. *Graphics Gems*, 474–485.

Part IV

Analysis of the Pre- and Post-Impact
of the COVID-19 Pandemic Crisis

8 Direct and Indirect Impacts of Environmental Factors on the COVID-19 Pandemic

KEY POINTS

- The COVID-19 pandemic provides substantial challenges to different socio-ecological systems, with clear impacts on many aspects of the environment.
- Air quality is highly sensitive to anthropogenic emissions.
- NO_2 and coliform reduced due to closure of industrial activities including fisheries.
- Area under industrial use and surface water availability exhibited better imprints.
- Factor analyses illustrated diminishing of water quality contrast following lockdown.

INTRODUCTION

The Earth is a dynamically changing planet, permanently shaped by socio-ecological interactions. Variations and changes are common in a nonlinear and dynamic system such as our planet, but passing certain thresholds may push the stability of the systems into a new regime which can have significant consequences at different spatial and temporal scales. Understanding and early prediction of the impacts of such dramatic changes is a challenge for all sciences (including environmental information science such as zoology, mineralogy, oceanography, limnology, soil science, geology and physical geography, and atmospheric science, etc.) but also for our society as a whole (Cremades et al., 2019; Johnston et al., 2019). Extreme variations in natural processes and phenomena, in many cases, have been enhanced or even caused by human actions, generating hazards that lead to risks for both communities and the environment, and as a result, sometimes disasters occur. The concept of disaster has evolved over time, and here we use an adapted Intergovernmental Panel on Climate Change (IPCC) definition: a disaster is an event, which severely alters the functioning of a community due to hazardous physical, biological, or human-related impacts leading to widespread adverse effects on multiple scales and systems (environment, economic, social). Immediate emergency response, also as external support, is required for recovery (Field et al., 2012). Disasters are often perceived as acute situations, but they can also be chronic (Zibulewsky, 2001). Most researchers currently view social disruption as the key defining feature or essential dimension of a disaster (Perry, 2018). The spatial extent of the immediate impact is usually directly related to the physical characteristics of the hazard, but the longer-term effects can encompass larger regions, depending on the functional relevance of the affected areas. For example, earthquakes may cause instantaneous damage and casualties at the sites where they occur, but their adverse consequences for human health, the environment, cultural heritage, and economic activity may affect regions and last for years (Ripoll Gallardo et al., 2018).

Pandemics are hazards related to large-scale outbreaks of infectious diseases that can greatly increase morbidity and mortality over a wide geographic area and cause significant economic, social, and political disruption (Madhav et al., 2017). The consequences of a pandemic, affecting people on a worldwide scale, with expected long-term impacts and consequences on the coupled socio-ecological systems, can be described as a disaster. On 13 March 2020, the World Health Organization (WHO) declared the novel coronavirus disease (COVID-19) a pandemic (Cucinotta & Vanelli, 2020) pushing humankind into an ongoing global crisis, which is unique in the recent history, at least by its spatial extent, rapid onset and its complexity of consequences.

Governments reacted to the outbreak by restricting people's movements. By 3rd April, with over one million confirmed cases worldwide, many countries implemented lockdown, self-quarantine, and social distancing measures, with close to three billion people asked to stay at home (Insider, 2020), more than one billion people alone in India. These restrictions meant that people were unable to commute to their workplaces, and as a result, offices and factories closed. Internationally, broad entry bans were applied, and flight routes were suspended. It has given the nature a "healing time" with reduced human interference in natural environment.

Given the important role of large coronavirus-a silver lining environment: the grounding of planes and shutdown of factories due to the implementation of travel bans and lockdowns had a beneficial effect on air pollution, water pollution, and noise pollution as well. Major impact of lockdown due to COVID-19 can be observed on air quality, which is being experienced by everyone and recorded in various official reports. By March, the decline in coal use by power plants, oil refining, steel manufacturing, and air travel was estimated to have caused a 250 Mt decrease in $CO2$ emissions (Myllyvirta, 2020a). NASA and the European Space Agency (ESA) reported a dramatic fall in N_2O pollution across North-Eastern China (NASA, 2020) and the lowest average level of N_2O ever recorded in India was a result of the nationwide curfew at the end of March.

The COVID-19 pandemic provides substantial challenges to different socio-ecological systems, with clear impacts on many aspects of the environment. It is caused by the Severe Acute Respiratory Syndrome Coronavirus 2 (SARS-CoV-2), and by 29 April 2020, COVID-19 had affected 213 countries, territories, and areas across five different WHO regions and three international conveyances. SARS-CoV-2 results in apparently high fatality rates and incapacitated health systems and the prevention of further transmission has rapidly become a priority (Ferretti et al., 2020). Considering the obvious impacts on all the components of the Earth system, increasing concerns and assumptions related to the changes and consequences following the COVID-19 pandemic are currently under study.

Significant advances were made in technology (e.g., enhanced monitoring, storage and transmission of information, communication systems, and efficacy of renewables), environment (monitoring and modeling, e.g., enhanced observational systems and advanced weather and climate models), and biodiversity conservation which has improved the quality of life globally. Despite this significant improvement of quality of life, several potentially destructive issues have dominated the global agenda, such as increasing threats derived from terrorist organisations, climate and environmental changes, nuclear proliferation, economic crises, and the democracy backsliding (Cornwall, 2020). In this context, the resilience of cities to pandemic disasters has not been properly prepared.

Six major pandemic and epidemic outbreaks swept the planet between 2000 and 2019, namely Severe Acute Respiratory Syndrome (SARS) (2002–2004), H1N1 influenza (2009),

Middle East respiratory syndrome (MERS) (2012–2020), the West-African Ebola virus epidemic (2013–2016), the Zika fever (2015–2016) and Avian influenza (2008–2014). None of these, however, achieved the spatial extent and the widespread impacts that the novel coronavirus did.

Although the pandemic situation is out of control for human beings, the positive side of it has made us to reconsider our lives and reorganize it in a way that has less impact on our planet. The situation today is a "reset" for nature and mankind, giving us a prospect to observe and analyze in and around. Significant changes in behavior are expected and predicting the impact of the pandemic on different sectors is of highly significant societal interest (Ali & Alharbi, 2020). This chapter aims to present an early overview of the observed and potential consequences of the COVID-19 on the natural and anthropogenic environment with a special focus on rural and urban areas. Since the scientific investigations and pertinent information about the characteristics and impacts of the pandemic exist only in the formative stages, we present the potential impacts of COVID-19 on the environment in the expectation that future research will pursue these avenues of inquiry. The impact on rural and urban areas including the population health has been immediately noticeable, and this chapter includes the most relevant examples available during the development of the events. We argue that the effects of COVID-19 are determined mainly by anthropogenic factors which are becoming obvious as human activity diminishes across the planet (Cramer et al., n.d.).

The impact of air pollution on population and their health was extensively studied in past by several researchers. The Urban air quality management strategies were planned which concentrated on emission inventory, control strategies, monitoring network, and participation of public (Gulia et al., 2015). A general comparison between the major air pollutants was also studied and the impact of industrialization, transportation, and other anthropogenic activities were analyzed (Singh et al., 2007). Several government and non-government agencies have been collected and analyzed to understand the change in quality of various environmental factors such as air and water quality due to lockdown caused by COVID-19. Different tools like satellite images and Air Quality Index (AQI) have been used to study the indirect effect of COVID-19. Outcomes of the study will help the policy-makers to define the Post-COVID strategy for the country, as the pollution level which we were not able to achieve during last decade (even after applying all sort of technological advancement) have become a real thing due to lockdown. This study can also be used as a baseline study to analyse the health impact (specifically on sensitive receptors) due to reduction in air pollution.

COVID-19 AND OTHER LARGE-SCALE EPIDEMIC DISEASES OF THE 21ST CENTURY

The main cause of pandemic events and epidemic diseases is the close interaction between human populations with both domesticated and wildlife pathogens (Woolhouse & Gowtage-Sequeria, 2005). Most pathogens pass from wildlife reservoirs and enter into human populations through hunting and consumption of wild species, wild animal trade, and other contacts with wildlife. Urban areas are especially vulnerable through the high population density and mobility. The COVID-19 dwarfs the six previous large-scale epidemics of the 21st century in terms of spatial extent and societal consequences

(Ali & Alharbi, 2020), and it is the only pandemic with widespread and complex environmental impacts. We briefly present a few characteristics of the other large-scale epidemic events of the 21st century:

a. The SARS occurred in 2003, leading to more than 8000 infections with a mortality rate of approximately 10% and an impact limited only to local and regional economies (LeDuc & Barry, 2004). The epidemic ended abruptly in July 2003 and no human cases of the SARS coronavirus have been detected since.

b. The 2009 H1N1 influenza virus (swine flu) was a pandemic that first appeared in Mexico and the United States in March and April of 2009. It became a global pandemic as a result of global mobility and airline travel and led to an estimated 0.4% case fatality (Al Hajjar & McIntosh, 2010).

c. The MERS was first identified in humans in Saudi Arabia and Jordan in 2012 (Memish et al., 2020). MERS is considered a zoonotic pathogen, with infected dromedary camels being the animal source of infection to humans (El-Kafrawy et al., 2019; Gardner et al., 2019). By contrast to SARS, which was contained within a year of emerging, MERS continues to have a limited circulation and causes human disease with intermittent sporadic cases, community clusters, and nosocomial outbreaks in the Middle East region with a high risk of spreading globally (Zumla et al., 2015).

d. The Ebola virus was first detected in 1976 in Zaire (presently the Democratic Republic of Congo). Since the virus was first detected, over 20 known outbreaks of Ebola have been identified in sub-Saharan Africa, mostly in Sudan, Uganda, Democratic Republic of Congo, and Gabon (Malvy et al., 2019). At present, no vaccine or efficient antiviral management strategy exists for Ebola (Hasan et al., 2019). Although the Ebola virus has substantial epidemic and pandemic potential (due to the ease of international travel), as shown by the 2013–2016 West-African Ebola virus epidemic with approximately 28,000 confirmed cases and 11,000 deaths (Garske et al., 2017; Lo et al., 2017), Ebola outbreaks have been geographically limited (Malvy et al., 2019).

e. The Zika fever (2015–2016) was first isolated in 1947 from a febrile rhesus macaque monkey in the Zika Forest of Uganda. Since 1954, when the first cases in humans were reported, the Zika virus had only limited sporadic infections in Africa and Asia. However, a large outbreak with approximately 440,000–1,300,000 cases spread from Brazil to 29 countries in the Americas in 2015 (Plourde & Bloch, 2016). In November 2016, WHO announced the end of the Zika outbreak.

f. Avian flu (bird flu) was first reported in 1997 in Hong Kong with only 18 infections and six human deaths. More than 700 cases of the avian flu have been reported from over 60 countries (Alexander & Brown, 2009) of the reported outbreaks occurred in 2016 in China (Chatziprodromidou et al., 2018).

A detailed description of the complete timeline of spread of epidemics and infections is covered in Chapter-1 Figure 1.5.

In the absence of any effective treatments, SARS-CoV, MERS-CoV, and SARS coronaviruses are of very high societal concern, since they could unexpectedly become a global pandemic at any time (Memish et al., 2020). As a result, coronaviruses in general have been studied to anticipate their societal and environmental impact. This has immediate

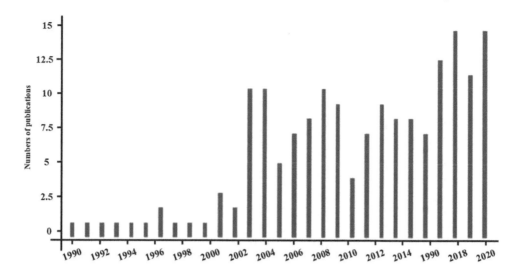

FIGURE 8.1 Number of publications referring to the topic coronaviruses and (Climate or Water or Soil or Ecosystems), retrieved on 30 April 2020. The statistics include studies tackling the bidirectional relation between all types of coronaviruses and the mentioned environmental components. (Data source: Web of Science.)

application to the COVID-19 virus. Furthermore, chapter summarizes the relevant knowledge on the causative agent, pathogenesis and immune responses, epidemiology, diagnosis, treatment and management of the disease, control, and prevention strategies of the COVID-19 (Harapan et al., 2020).

The development and spread of COVID-19 under the control of environmental factors justify the scientific interest for the combined studies of coronaviruses on one side and socio-ecological systems (including the interplay between climate, water, soil) on the other side. The number of scientific publications examining such topics has constantly increased in recent decades, and the COVID-19 pandemic strongly motivates the 2020 record (Figure 8.1).

In general, temperature, humidity, wind, and precipitation may favor either the spread or the inhibition of epidemic episodes. However, while some research found that local weather conditions of lowered temperature, mild diurnal temperature range, and low humidity may favor the transmission (Liu et al., 2020), other studies claim there is no evidence that warmer weather can determine the decline of the case counts of COVID-19 (Zhu & Xie, 2020). Increased ultraviolet light, as occurs particularly during the summer months, leads to inactivation of the coronaviruses and analyses the subject comprehensively and find that warming weather is unlikely to stop the spread of the pandemic (Sagripanti & Lytle, 2007).

To understand the relative importance between physical and social parameters that favor the spread of the virus, an area in which different health and social policies have been equally implemented on a variety of environmental and climatic conditions must be examined. Italy is a viable experimental model to examine the impact of different health policies, as stated by the government authorities themselves (Horowitz et al., 2020). In Italy, the regionalization of public health has addressed the pandemic following completely different schemes from one region to another and represents an important test to verify the scientific hypotheses on the behavior of SARS-CoV-2.

Given that coronaviruses tend to spread in lowered temperatures and drier conditions during the winter months (i.e., during a period of reduced solar radiation), it is surprising that Italy was the first European country severely affected by the pandemic, and its hospitals were suddenly overrun. Northern Italy experienced a very dry and mild winter caused by the presence of a strong polar vortex. The winter of 2019–2020 was one of the driest winters in 60 years (https://www.arpae.it/dettaglio_notizia.asp?idLivello=32 &id=11052). The impact on the social and economic structure of the country immediately gave rise to concerns about the potential transmission pathways of the virus and the spread at European scale.

COVID-19 ENVIRONMENTAL IMPACTS

The impact of the COVID-19 pandemic on the environment raised attention from the very beginning of the crisis, consisting of (a) observations and analysis of the immediate effects, and (b) estimations related to long-term changes. Qualitative assumptions prevail, while consistent quantitative research must wait for relevant data sets and additional knowledge. Most facets of the environmental impact of the COVID-19 pandemic have not directly resulted from the virus itself. The consequence of abruptly limiting or closing economic sectors, such as heavy industry, transport, or hospitality businesses, has affected the environment directly. Moreover, the impact of the COVID-19 pandemic on socio-ecological systems may be highly variable, from radical changes in individual lifestyle, society, and international affairs (Gutérres, 2020) to simply facilitating a faster change than would normally have emerged (Haass, 2020). From an anthropocentric perspective, the pandemic may lead to a more sustainable future, including increased resilience of the socio-ecological systems or shorter supply chains, which is a positive development. However, it is still possible that some nations will opt for less sustainability by pursuing rapid economic growth and focusing less concern on the environment. While negative impacts on the economy and society, in general, are probably huge, it is very likely that the global-scale reduction of economic activities due to the COVID-19 crisis triggers a lot of sensible improvements in environmental quality and climatic systems. However, not all the environmental consequences of the crisis have been or will be positive. This includes an increased volume of non-recyclable waste, the generation of large quantities of organic waste due to diminish ed agricultural and fishery export levels, and difficulties in maintenance and monitoring of natural ecosystems. The temporal resolution of the coronavirus impact ranges from immediate (days to weeks) to short-term (months) and long-term (years), and different examples are provided in a matrix (Figure 8.2). While the first impacts are divided between rapid environmental improvements, such as urban air and water quality, and pollution episodes, such as the ones caused by the sanitary disposals, the estimated short- and long-term impacts are mainly positive.

IMPACTS ON THE PHYSICAL SYSTEMS OF THE ENVIRONMENT

Impacts are rarely limited to a single physical system. However, for the sake of better inventory and understanding, the impact of the COVID-19 on the physical systems focuses on the air, water, and soil individually, with an emphasis on urban areas.

Large cities or megacities are often very centralized structures providing a certain degree of comfort and protection to the citizen, but they increase the exposure to specific

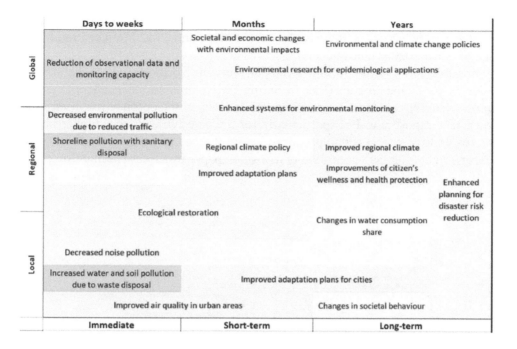

FIGURE 8.2 Matrix of observed and potential impacts of COVID-19 on environment and climate change. Red blocks are negative impacts, green are positive, and grey stands for neutral effects.

threats. For example, the higher population densities favor higher exposure to hazards. In contrast to rural areas, where the population tends to have gardens, the effects of the lockdown conditions in cities showed more severe effects on the mental health of individuals living in close quarters. The COVID-19 crisis is driving toward a new paradigm that brings urban policies closer to present and strengthens the future needs of urban population and public health.

One of the key characteristics of the pandemic event in focus in this study is the spatial extent but also versatility of the scale of the impact. No other disaster has covered the whole planet with comparable intensities over so many urban areas with multifaceted threats that are challenging our cities during the crisis.

Air Quality and Local Climate

Air quality is highly sensitive to anthropogenic emissions. In the European Economic Area countries (EU, Norway, Liechtenstein, and Iceland), the energy used by industrial processes and the road transportation sector is responsible for about 54% of the nonmethane volatile organic compounds (NMVOC), 51% of the NOx, 30% of PM2.5 and 25% of SOx emissions. The COVID-19 crisis has caused severe impacts on the energy and resources, high-tech and communications, retail, manufacturing, and transportation sectors, in terms of personnel, operations, supply chain, and revenue. By mid-April, a 40–50% decline in economic activity was estimated as a result of the draconian disease-suppression policies, and severe multiquarter economic impacts in multiple markets became imminent. Consequently, the impact on air quality was rapidly visible at various spatial scales. Even as early as the end of March 2020, reductions in air pollution were reported in China, Italy, and New York City, and sharp declines in global greenhouse-gas emissions have been predicted for the rest of the year (Tollefson, 2020). Moreover, an overview focused on several European countries reveals that the reduction of the weekly NO_2, PM10, and PM2.5 concentrations during March and April 2020 is quasi-general (Figures 8.3–8.6).

One possible cause of the impact of the pandemic in Northern Italy is that a high concentration of particulate matter (PM, including PM10 and PM2.5) makes the respiratory system more susceptible to infection and complications of the coronavirus disease. Higher and consistent exposure to PM (particularly for the elderly) leads to a higher probability that the respiratory system is compromised before the onset of the virus. This was a serious concern right after the publication of a position paper by SIMA (Italian Environmental

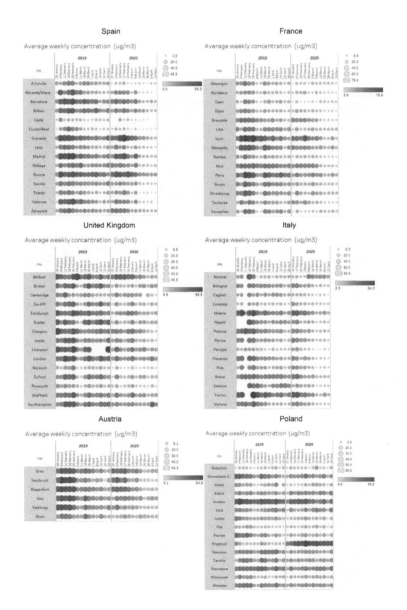

FIGURE 8.3   Average weekly NO_2 concentration between January 2019 and April 2020 in urban areas from Spain, France, United Kingdom, Italy, Austria, and Poland. (Source: https://www.eea. europa.eu/themes/air/air-quality-and-covid19/monitoring-covid-19-impacts-on.)

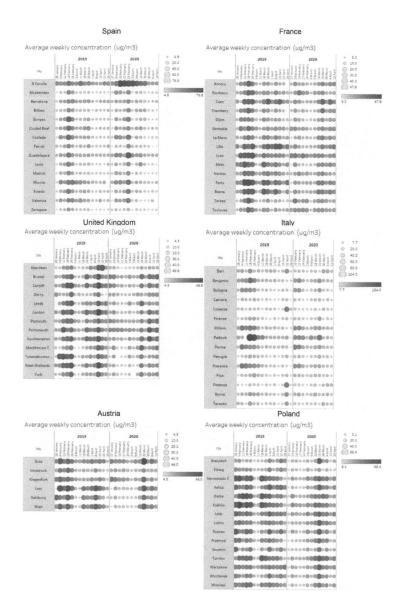

FIGURE 8.4   Average weekly PM10 concentration between January 2019 and April 2020 in urban areas from Spain, France, United Kingdom, Italy, Austria, and Poland. (Source: https://www.eea. europa.eu/themes/air/air-quality-and-covid19/monitoring-covid-19-impacts-on.)

Medical Society), where correlations were found between pollution levels and the spread of the virus (Setti et al., 2020). Strong evidence exists on the greater predisposition of the respiratory system to serious diseases, but the hypothesis that pollutants can be a carrier for the virus in the free atmosphere seems very unlikely. The spread of droplets produced by sneezing or coughing is necessary so that high viral concentration and a lack of air circulation and exchange can be potentially very dangerous (Contini & Costabile, 2020).

The analysis of the demographic and economic characteristics of the two Italian regions most affected by the pandemic help to understand that the spread of the virus is dependent on parameters other than simply air transport. The most affected regions are quite similar

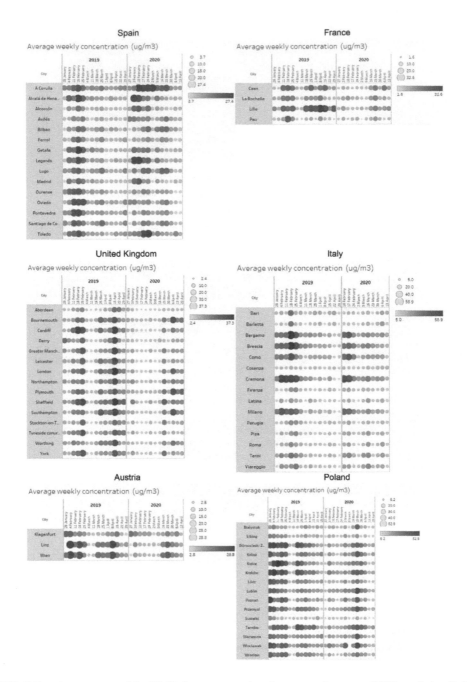

FIGURE 8.5　Average weekly PM2.5 concentration between January 2019 and April 2020 in urban areas from Spain, France, United Kingdom, Italy, Austria, and Poland. (Source: https://www.eea.europa.eu/themes/air/air-quality-and-covid19/monitoring-covid-19-impacts-on.)

demographically; Lombardy has a population density of 420 per km² while Veneto has a density of 270 per km² and the average age of the populations is practically identical. Economic indicators also reveal a gross domestic product of Lombardy of 34,000 €/capita and Veneto of 29,500 €/capita. The number of beds in the healthcare facilities for intensive care are nearly identical in the two regions, while there is a public health laboratory for

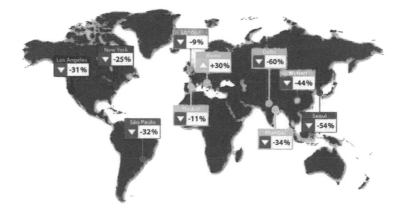

FIGURE 8.6 This map shows the percent reduction in PM2.5 levels when comparing the 2020 shutdown period to the same period in 2019. (Image adapted from: IQ Air 2020.)[1]

every 3,000,000 inhabitants in Lombardy and for every 500,000 people in Veneto. The healthcare structure is a very important aspect that explains the notable difference between the two regions, as the home care service for the elderly and disabled is more than double in Veneto than in Lombardy. For neighboring regions with similar pollution levels, the infection rate is extremely uneven. Thus, it appears unlikely that PM is a viable vector for the virus, but it does illustrate the concern over disparate regional healthcare systems. This also has an important impact on future exit strategies from the pandemic and on the use of personal protective equipment (PPE) as the virus may vector using healthcare workers.

It is very likely that the Italian case provides lessons for other European countries and validates the measures taken to limit the effects of the pandemic. As for the environmental impacts, physical and ecological systems have been affected in many places, as addressed and detailed in the next sections.

The massive lockdowns of entire cities, economies, schools, and social life for weeks led to unknown large-scale and extensive restrictions in mobility as a response to social distancing guidance related to COVID-19 (Figure 8.7). Globally, the largest reductions in mobility are visible for Western and Southern Europe (e.g., Spain—59%, Italy—55%, France—51%) and South America (e.g., Bolivia—60% or Columbia—54%). In South America, mobility in the period 1 April to 17 April showed a mean decrease of 47% compared to the 5-week period 3 January–5 February 2020. Other continents showed a mean decrease of around 30%. South Korea was the only country that showed a slightly positive trend of +1.8% for the analyzed period. The reason here is that the mobility trends for places like national parks, public beaches, marinas, dog parks, plazas, and public gardens increased significantly, although other mobility categories (e.g., workplaces, transit stations) showed a decrease. Even if general mobility characteristics may vary by country and the period of strongest reductions in mobility may not be evident in April, Figure 8.7 shows the global picture of the effects of the COVID-19 pandemic.

In particular, one of the most hit sectors was the aviation that contributes about 1–2% of global greenhouse gas emissions (Harrison et al., 2015) and about 3–5% of global CO_2 emissions (Kivits et al., 2010). Between 23 January 2020 and 21 April 2020, travel restrictions caused air traffic to decline by around 63% in the total number of flights and about 75% in the number of commercial flights (Figure 8.8). The latest scenario of the International

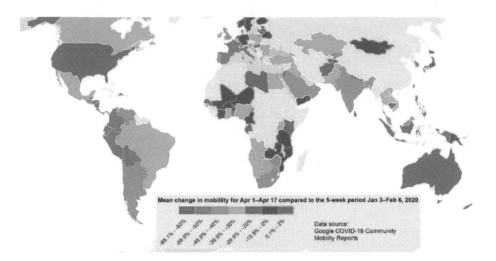

FIGURE 8.7　Mean changes in mobility aggregated to country-level for the period 1 April–17 April 2020 compared to the 5-week period 3 January–6 February 2020. Countries in grey have no data. (Data source: https://www.google.com/covid19/mobility/.)

Air Transport Association (IATA) suggests that air traffic will fall by 48% for 2020. Even if the aviation sector returns to its pre-pandemic levels, 40% of the passengers indicate they will wait at least six months before returning to air travel. Specifically, 70% indicate they will wait for their financial situation to stabilize. The strong decrease in both short-term and mid-term aviation travel will lead to a reduction in greenhouse gas emissions, particularly CO_2. Additionally, the reduction in contrails may increase the daily temperature range (Travis et al., 2002). The reduction of contrails will probably lead to a decrease in air temperature due to the decreasing greenhouse effect (Myllyvirta, 2020b).

The Centre for Research on Energy and Clean Air reported that methods to contain the spread of coronavirus, such as quarantines and travel bans, resulted in a 25% reduction of carbon emission in China (McMahon, 2020; Myllyvirta, 2020a). In the first month of lockdowns, China produced approximately 200 million fewer metric tons of carbon dioxide than the same period in 2019, due to the reduction in air traffic, oil refining, and coal consumption (McMahon, 2020). One Earth systems scientist estimated that this reduction may have saved at least 77,000 lives (McMahon, 2020). However, Sarah Ladislaw from the

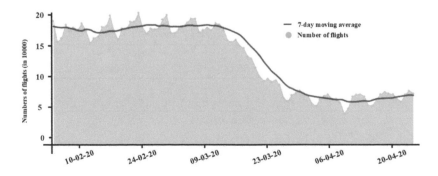

FIGURE 8.8　Commercial flights tracked by Flightradar24 between 31 January and 29 April 2020. (Source: https://www.flightradar24.com/data/statistics.)

Center for Strategic & International Studies argued that reductions in emissions due to economic downturns should not be seen as beneficial, stating that China's attempts to return to previous rates of growth amidst trade wars and supply chain disruptions in the energy market will worsen its environmental impact. Between 1 January and 11 March 2020, the ESA observed a marked decline in nitrous oxide emissions from cars, power plants, and factories in the Po Valley region in Northern Italy, coinciding with lockdowns in the region.

NASA and ESA have been monitoring how the nitrogen dioxide gases dropped significantly during the initial Chinese phase of the COVID-19 pandemic. The economic slowdown from the virus drastically dropped pollution levels, especially in cities like Wuhan, China by 25–40% (Zhang et al., 2020). NASA uses an Ozone Monitoring Instrument (OMI) to analyze and observe the ozone layer and pollutants such as NO_2, aerosols, and others. This instrument helped NASA to process and interpret the data coming in due to the lockdowns worldwide. According to NASA scientists, the drop in NO_2 pollution began in Wuhan, China, and slowly spread to the rest of the world. The drop was also very drastic because the virus coincided with the same time of year as the lunar year celebrations in China (Zhang et al., 2020). During this festival, factories and businesses were closed for the last week of January to celebrate the lunar year festival. The drop in NO_2 in China did not achieve an air quality of the standard considered acceptable by health authorities. Other pollutants in the air such as aerosol emissions remained (Allen et al., 2020).

A joint research led by scientists from China and the United States estimated that nitrogen oxides ($NOx=NO+NO_2$) emissions decreased by 50% in East China from 23 January (Wuhan lockdown) to 9 February 2020 in comparison to the period from 1 to 22 January 2020. Emissions then increased by 26% from 10 February (back-to-work day) to 12 March 2020, indicating possible increasing socioeconomic activities after most provinces allowed businesses to open. It is yet to be investigated what COVID-19 control measures are most efficient in controlling virus spread and least socioeconomic impact (Zhang et al., 2020).

Satellite remote sensing provides real-time evidence for the beneficial effect of the COVID-19 pandemic on air quality over large areas. For example, both NASA and ESA pollution monitoring satellites measured a significant decrease in nitrogen dioxide (NO_2) over North-Eastern China during the economic slowdown of January–February 2020 (Figure 8.9). Moreover, data retrieved by the Moderate Resolution Imaging Spectroradiometer (MODIS) on NASA's Terra satellite show that the February–March 2020 lockdown dramatically reduced the aerosol levels in Northern India (Figure 8.10).

Regarding the transport sector, motor vehicles were responsible for 30% of the 2018 greenhouse gas emissions in Austria, for example. This was the second-largest source of greenhouse gas emissions in Austria, behind the energy and industry sectors, which together contributed 36%. The COVID-19 crisis has led to a substantial reduction in motor vehicle traffic with not only a reduction in greenhouse gas emissions and particulate pollution but also a major reduction in traffic noise and tire wear on road surfaces. In Vienna, with a population of 1.9 million, car and truck traffic were reduced by 52% and 50%, respectively, between 1 March and the first week of April.

These reductions, extrapolated to similar urban areas in Europe, have led to significantly improved air quality. In Milan, average concentrations of NO_2 for the 16–22 March period was 21% lower than for the same week in 2019. In Bergamo, average concentrations of NO_2 in 2020 were 47% lower than in 2019 for the same week, and similar reduction of average NO_2 concentrations have been observed in other major cities (e.g., Barcelona, 55%; Madrid, 41%; Lisbon, 51%) (Contini & Costabile, 2020).

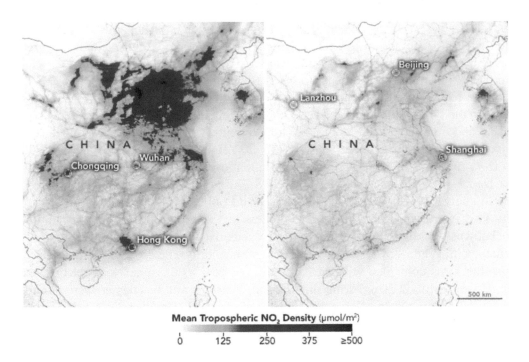

Mean Tropospheric NO$_2$ Density (μmol/m²)

0   125   250   375   ≥500

FIGURE 8.9   Mean tropospheric NO$_2$ values retrieved by NASA Aura and ESA S5TROPOMI pollution monitoring satellites over North-Eastern China in January and February 2020. (Source: https://earthobservatory.nasa.gov/images/146362/airborne-nitrogen-dioxide-plummets.)

Data also show a reduction in the urban PM concentration. Reduced concentrations of PM2.5 in Seoul (South Korea) were 54% lower from 26 February to 18 March 2020 when compared to the same period in 2019. Los Angeles (United States) observed its longest continuous period of clean air on record, lasting over 18 days from March 7 to 28. PM2.5 concentration levels were lower by 31% from the same time last year and down 51% from the average of the previous four years (https://www.iqair.com/blog/air-quality/report-impact-of-covid-19-on-global-air-quality-earth-day). For Barcelona (Tobías et al., 2020), reported approximately 50% reduction of NO$_2$ and black carbon, 30% decrease of PM10, and 33–57% increase of O$_3$ concentrations, very likely due to the lockdown of the city. However, the favorable role of meteorological conditions was also granted.

Well-known for its high level of pollution, Milan is considering a shift from car traffic to pedestrian and bicycle over 35 km of streets, as a result of the coronavirus crisis (https://www.theguardian.com/world/2020/apr/21/milan-seeks-to-prevent-post-crisis-return-of-traffic-pollution). Milan launched on 24 April 2020 a new strategy for adaptation asking for an open contribution from the population where it is clearly stated that the mission is to elaborate a new strategy to exit from pandemic, called Phase 2. The objectives are to remake the city by accounting for problems faced during the pandemic. Public transportation is one of the main foci along with the protection of elderly people.

Impact on Water Resources

It is stated and proved in several studies that anthropogenic activities are considered as one of the key drivers of pollution in all spheres of the environment (Akimoto 2003; Masood et al. 2016; Schlacher et al. 2016; Volkamer et al. 2006). Since all types of industries, vehicle

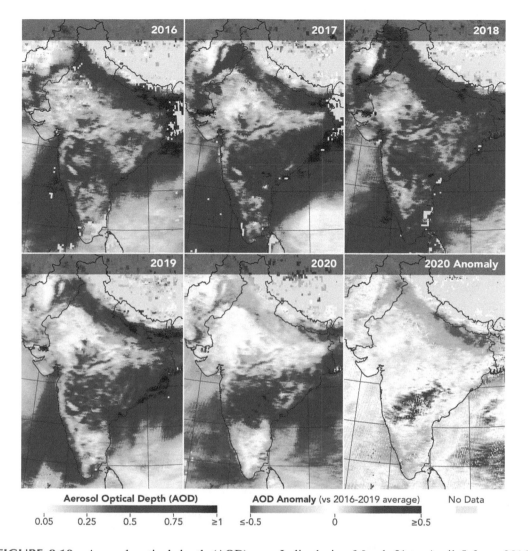

FIGURE 8.10 Aerosol optical depth (AOD) over India during March 31 to April 5 from 2016 through 2020. (Source: https://earthobservatory.nasa.gov/images/146596/airborne-particle-levels-plummet-in-northern-india.)

movement, and people's activity suddenly halted for weeks, perhaps for the first time in modern history, it is expected that pollution loads to the environment may also get decreased. As expected, in a matter of days, the carbon emissions level has dropped significantly (Stone 2020). The immediate impact of the COVID-19 pandemic on aquatic systems and water resources is very limited, but water quality and resources may be affected on monthly and annual perspectives. According to the Ministry of Ecology and Environment, China, the air quality went up 11% in the category "good" in as many as 337 cities (Henriques 2020). Scripps Institute of Oceanography reported that the use of fossil fuel would decline by about 10% around the world owing to the COVID-19 spread (SCRIPPS 2020). While these improvements in environmental pollution are considered to be temporary, the current level of pollution in the atmosphere, biosphere, and hydrosphere could be much lower than the pre-COVID-19 period.

Quantifying the status of pollution during the lockdown period is an important task for researchers to understand the effect of the COVID-19 spread on the environment in the short- and long-term. Satellite-based data from Tropospheric Monitoring Instrument (TROPOMI) on ESA's Sentinel-5 satellite and the OMI on NASA's Aura satellite shows a decreased level of nitrogen dioxide (NO_2) in the atmosphere (ESA 2020). On the other hand, the status of pollution in the hydrosphere that includes lakes, rivers, oceans, and groundwater reservoirs, has not been investigated. For decades, the hydrosphere has been severely polluted because of rapid urbanization, industrialization, and overexploitation. During the lockdown period, the major industrial sources of pollution that affect aquatic ecosystems, such as industrial wastewater disposal, crude oil, heavy metals, and plastics (Häder et al. 2020), have shrunk or completely stopped. Therefore, the level of pollution is expected to be reduced. For example, news media reported that the Grand Canal in Italy, where the COVID-19 crippled the whole nation, turned clear, and reappearances of many aquatic species (Clifford 2020). Similarly, the Ganges, a sacred but severely polluted river in India, turns cleaner at several places during the nationwide lockdown period that started on 25th March 2020 (Mani 2020). The New Indian Express on 24 April 2020 reported that water quality of river Ganga, in India is improved by 40–50% during the time of lockdown. Central Pollution Control Board (CPCB) (2020) reported that Dissolved oxygen (DO) (>6 mg/l), Biochemical oxygen demand (BOD) (<2 mg/l), total coliform (5000 per 100 ml), and pH (range between 6.5 and 8.5) have improved a lot and the identified range of the quality components are within the range of bathing.

Another immediate effect due to less boat traffic and tourist activities has been clearly seen in Venice waters. Waters cleared during the coronavirus lockdown of the city in March and April 2020 (Figure 8.11).

FIGURE 8.11 Comparative view of the Venice area between 13 April 2020 vs. 19 April 2019. Satellite images released by the European Space Agency, Copernicus Sentinel-2 mission. (Available from http://www.esa.int/ESA_Multimedia/Images/2020/04/Deserted_Venetian_lagoon.)

Medema et al. (2020) first detected the presence of the SARS-CoV-2 in sewage and indicated it as a sensitive tool to monitor the circulation of the virus. Although the viral RNA has been detected in wastewater, this does not necessarily imply a risk either to the public or to the environment. Gundy et al. (2009) showed that coronaviruses die off rapidly in wastewater and are inactivated faster in warmer water (i.e., 10 days in water at 23°C and >100 days in water at 4°C).

Disposal of sanitary consumables, such as PPE, is already creating concern about the impact of the pandemic event on water bodies. By May 2020, many reports claimed significant harm on the aquatic environment, especially along the shorelines (e.g., in Hong Kong and Canada) due to sanitary disposal resulting from medical activities or personal protection.

The COVID-19 crisis has and probably will exhibit longer-term impacts on water resources usage and management. The economic effects of the COVID-19 pandemic, changes in national budgets, and changes in funding priorities may lead to lack of funding for water-related infrastructure and water utilities. The impacts of underfunding (e.g., increased forthcoming losses or lack of investments to improve efficiency) may only manifest after a few years.

During lockdown conditions, water utilities from Germany and Austria report that the daily peak in water consumption in the morning is shifted by around 1.5–2 Hrs. Generally, a dampening effect and a more even distribution in water consumption during the day is observed. Regarding the amount of water consumed, increases as well as decreases of around 5% are reported. Increases are explained by higher demands due to watering of gardens—surprisingly, not due to increased handwashing—and decreases by fewer commuters, students, and pupils in supply areas.

By contrast, municipalities with high touristic activity—a leading cause of water demandn (Čenčur Curk et al., 2015)—will exhibit important reduction in water consumption. Reports from the strong tourism heritage of Tirol, Austria, suggest reductions in water consumption of up to 50% in municipalities where tourism plays an important role. Depending on the return of tourism following the end of the pandemic, a noteworthy reduction of water demand and pressures on water resources can be expected.

One another example is Miami Beach that was close its beaches after Florida Gov. Ron DeSantis refused to do so statewide. Its satellite images give a clear picture of the water quality improvement as shown in Figure 8.12.

Industrial water consumption, a generally poorly measured quantity, has certainly decreased. The longer-term impacts on water resources will depend on economic developments following the crisis. In comparison to domestic and industrial water demand, the highest pressures on water resources come from the agricultural sector. Here, long-term forecasts will depend on the return of agriculture following the crisis, although short-term effects are probably visible in reduced irrigation demand.

Impact on Aquatic Systems and Wildlife

This crisis has also had a deep impact on aquatic systems and wildlife. While the world has come to a complete and utter standstill, nature seems to be reclaiming her territory—wild animals near urban cityscapes are taking this opportunity to step beyond the comforts of their forested homes, global wildlife trade has been thrown into the spotlight and wildlife tourism too has felt the impact of this pandemic.

On the other hand demand for seafoods including fish and fish prices have both decreased due to the pandemic (Korten, 2020), and fishing fleets around the world sit mostly idle

FIGURE 8.12   Satellite image of Miami Beach before COVID-19 lockdown and during lockdown on 20th March 2020. (Source: Planet Lab.)

(Reiley, 2020). German scientist Rainer Froese has said the fish biomass will increase due to the sharp decline in fishing, and projected that in European waters, some fish such as herring could double their biomass. As of April 2020, signs of aquatic recovery remain mostly anecdotal.

As people stayed at home due to lockdown and travel restrictions, some animals have been spotted in cities. Sea turtles were spotted laying eggs on beaches they once avoided (such as the coast of the Bay of Bengal), due to the lowered levels of human interference and light pollution. In the United States, fatal vehicle collisions with animals such as deer, elk, moose, bears, mountain lions fell by 58% during March and April (as shown in Figure 8.13).

The pandemic may have created new challenges for various urban-dwelling animals, like rats, gulls, or monkeys, who have become so reliant on food discarded or provided by humans that they may struggle to make ends meet under current conditions. Interestingly, in some countries where lockdowns allow outdoor exercise, humans are flocking to green spaces in or near metropolitan areas, potentially disturbing resident wildlife (Corlett et al., 2020). At the same time, reduced human presence in more remote areas may potentially expose endangered species, such as rhinos or raptors, to increased risk of poaching or persecution (Buckley, 2020). Finally, concerns have been raised that, in low-income countries, economic hardship may force increased exploitation of natural resources (Dong et al., 2020).

"Marine" includes seabirds and other marine species, "avian" refers to all other bird species, and "terrestrial" are non-avian species living mostly on land. Population density

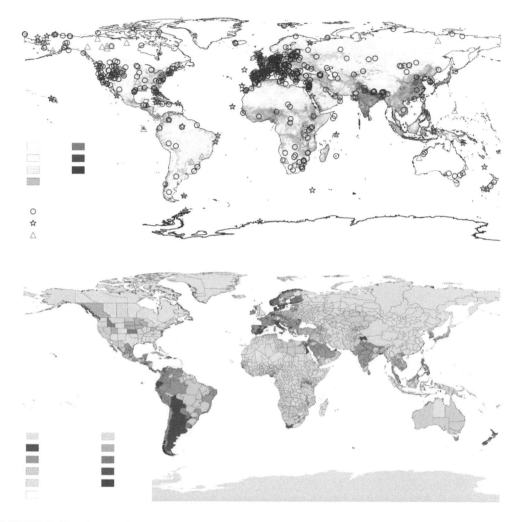

FIGURE 8.13 Illustrating the research potential of the recently launched COVID-19 Bio-Logging Initiative. Top: locations of a subsample of active animal tracking ('bio-logging') studies superimposed on human population density. (Data sources: 801 publicly visible animal tracking studies from the Movebank research platform (www.movebank.org) that are likely to contain data overlapping with the COVID-19 period (data extracted 18 May 2020).)

data sourced from ref. 15 (data accessed 15 May 2020). Bottom: median percentage of change based on daily values (with reference to the data provider's default baseline from the five-week period between 3 January and 6 February 2020) in visits to places like local parks, national parks, public beaches, marinas, dog parks, plazas, and public gardens for the month of April 2020. Data are plotted for 900 subregions within 131 countries (note that for 1.6% of the subregions fewer than five daily values were available for April 2020). This information should be interpreted cautiously, and is shown here merely to provide a preliminary, coarse-scale illustration of some recent changes in human mobility; scientific analyses will require higher-resolution, calibrated data. Data sourced from ref. 16 (data accessed 7 May 2020). Both maps were drawn with the QGIS Geographic Information

System (http://qgis.org), using freely available data (2018) for country borders from GADM (https://gadm.org) (data accessed 6 May 2020).

Conservationists expect that African countries will experience a massive surge in bush-meat poaching. Matt Brown of the Nature Conservancy said that "When people don't have any other alternative for income, our prediction—and we're seeing this in South Africa—is that poaching will go up for high-value products like rhino horn and ivory." (Deliso, 2020). On the other hand, Gabon decided to ban the human consumption of bats and pangolins, to stem the spread of zoonotic diseases, as the novel coronavirus is thought to have trans-mitted itself to humans through these animals. In June 2020, Myanmar allowed breed-ing of endangered animals such as tigers, pangolins, and elephants. Experts fear that the Southeast Asian country's attempts to deregulate wildlife hunting and breeding may create "a New COVID-19."

IMPACTS ON THE ECOLOGICAL SYSTEMS

From an ecological perspective, the COVID-19 crisis is fundamentally related to the relationships between society and ecosphere. While the origin in a Wuhan wet market or industrial livestock or other source is not yet fully clarified (Andersen et al., 2020), it is well known that MERS-CoV, SARS-CoV, and SARS-CoV-2 are all animal coronavi-ruses that infected people and then succeeded to spread in different communities at large scale. Around the globe, more than 2.7 million people are dying from zoonosis in a year (Grace et al., 2012), but the impact is even greater as the zoonosis are also affecting human health, livestock sector, and agriculture and usually the poorer human populations are more affected.

The coronavirus crisis is most probably one of the many challenges our society will have to face in the forthcoming decades as an indirect consequence of the impact of climate change on the ecosphere through many mechanisms, including diminishing species habitats (Corlett et al., 2020), changing species distributions (Zhang et al., 2019) and an increasing influx of alien invasive species (Dukes & Mooney, 1999). Currently, economic development focuses on continuous growth without considering the conservation of natural systems.

In a letter sent to the WHO in April 2020, more than 300 animal welfare and con-servation organizations stressed the need to recognize the link between wildlife markets and pandemics (https://lioncoalition.org/2020/04/04/open-letter-to-world-health-organisa-tion/). However, this is related with the need to act on existing international conventions, such as CITES (the Convention on International Trade in Endangered Species of Wild Fauna and Flora, also known as the Washington Convention) to protect endangered plants and animals from trafficking. As this is not the first time such outbreaks have occurred (see the SARS event between 2002 and 2003), conventions like CITES should be rein-forced. Forest landscape fragmentation also may facilitate more often human contact with wild animals, increasing the likelihood of transmission risk of animal-to-human viruses (Bloomfield et al., 2020).

The pandemic has also had an impact on ecological research, fieldwork, and experi-ments. In many cases, this research activity has been diminished or halted, with important consequences on conservation of species and habitats. There is also a possible economic impact on conservation programs around the globe as a result of pandemic and different programs are assessing their long-term viability (such as the Global Environmental Fund) (Corlett et al., 2020). Even after the pandemic ends, a danger exists that both research

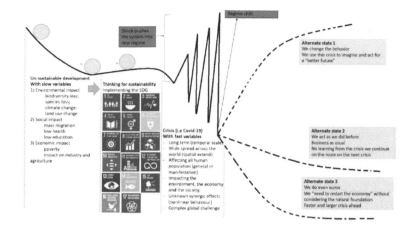

FIGURE 8.14 Possible regime shifts due to the combined impact of slow and fast variables on the system dynamics.

and conservation programs will be diminished mainly due to miscommunication between decision-makers and scientists.

However, perhaps the most important impact of the pandemic on the ecological transition focuses on sustainability and the still possible choices that the society could make to ensure its long-term survivability. As explained in Figure 8.14, the coupled natural-human system is on a path of transitioning from an unsustainable development toward sustainability being under pressure from different drivers. The instability caused by the pandemic is characterized by variables that have sudden and multiple impacts on both the natural environment and on society and could push the system into three different potential states. The fast variables are characterizing the instability phase and the slow variables act as controlling variables (Carpenter & Turner, 2000). Only one of these potential states is the desirable one, moving away from unwanted events and ensuring that the pandemic was a painful but still a "learning event" that drove towards a "better future." The main characteristic of the pandemic is that it is acting like a shock that pushes the system toward a regime shift with difficult to predict consequences.

Nature is part of the solution for recovery and sustainable reconstruction. Nevertheless, the effect of the COVID-19 pandemic on ecological systems has not yet been fully realized, and further monitoring will bring new findings and perspectives.

Impacts On Environmental Dimension Of The Global Affairs

It is very likely that the COVID-19 pandemic will reshape the economic and environmental policies at an international scale.

The strength of some bilateral agreements and international partnerships has been tested by this pandemic. Whereas China persistently invested in Africa's natural resources and infrastructure projects, the treatment of African citizens living in China and the frustration at Beijing's opposition on granting debt relief could deteriorate the Chinese economic and political supremacy in Africa. Ataguba (2020) also discusses the impact of the crisis on African economies with unpredictable environmental consequences. The roles that China and the United States of Americacurrently play for mitigating risk include an ecological emphasis to the pandemic strategy preparedness in order to better protect the global community from zoonotic disease (Evans et al., 2020). The coronavirus epidemic could significantly impact the Italians' relationship with the EU, as indicated by the widely spread perception that the EU was not efficient in supporting the fight against coronavirus, at least in February–March (i.e., 88% of Italians believed so in March 2020). Such changes are expected to generate indirect long-term environmental impacts.

Climate changes are often perceived as a risk driver at the global scale and COVID-19 has offered an excellent example of how a single underestimated threat can challenge the foundations of global security, economic stability, and democratic governance. According to analyses before the COVID-19 pandemic, if countries are unable to implement the nationally determined contributions as ratified through the Paris Agreement, the emissions reduction efforts would cost the whole world about 149.8–792.0 trillion dollars until 2100 (Wei et al., 2020). Plans prepared for reinforcing the emission reduction goals established under the 2015 Paris Agreement are not only postponed until 2021, but they will probably suffer consistent adjustments in the new economic circumstances. In the short term, it is hard to assume that climate change and environmental sustainability will be priorities for the world governments or local authorities, while the long-term cost for emission reduction could be raised. The coronavirus crisis also threatens local commitments to implement climate change adaptation and mitigation measures that have been initiated in the recent period. Both national and international governance will be affected.

The impact of coronavirus on the EU climate plan was already the subject of discussions in several meetings in Brussels and there are concerns that the targets set for 2050 now will be difficult to reach especially due to the necessity for a rapid economic recovery. Poland, in particular, expressed doubts on reaching the targets set for 2050 (http://www.caneurope.org/publications/press-releases/1864-eu-aims-for-net-zero-emissions-by-2050-now-it-needs-to-work-on-raising-the-2030-target). Big industries such as car manufacturers also have expressed concerns about not being able to meet the targets set (https://www.carbonbrief.org/daily-brief/eu-leaders-agree-to-consider-climate-in-coronavirus-recovery-plan).

During the 2010s, environmental efforts have intensively addressed the generous framework of the "Transforming our World: the 2030 Agenda for Sustainable Development." This agenda includes 17 Sustainable Development Goals (SDGs) designed to eradicate poverty and achieve sustainable development by 2030. We argue that most of these goals were immediately impacted by the COVID-19 pandemic, while longer-term effects are also expected (Table 8.1), most of them directly connected to urban areas and population health. It is very likely that the concept and implementation of the agenda must be reconsidered according to the new findings related to our exposure, vulnerabilities, and resilience to global disaster risks.

ENVIRONMENTAL MONITORING AND CLIMATE SERVICES

The COVID-19 crisis has challenged environmental monitoring and climate services, creating both adversities in observations as well as challenges to create better preparedness.

A lack of reliable data on the spread of COVID-19 could lead to not only a once-in-a-century pandemic but also a once-in-a-century decision fiasco. The crisis has revealed the crucial need to access long-term, real-time data for supporting policymakers and reaction at different scales, and it has motivated environmental scientists to reinforce our monitoring capacity to address sustainability issues the pandemic has raised.

TABLE 8.1

Observed and Estimated Impacts of the COVID-19 Pandemic on the Sustainable Development Goals (SDGs)

S.No.	SDGs	COVID-19 Observed and Potential Impacts (Examples)	Time Scales of the Impact	References
1	No Poverty	Deep economic and financial crisis could dramatically increase extreme poverty.	Days to decades	[98]
2	Zero Hunger	The crisis has caused a massive slowdown of the efforts to support investment, including through enhanced international cooperation. Impact on the Water, Energy and Food security nexus.	Days to decades	[2]
3	Good Health and Well-being	Greater attention to the elderly and the fragile population for the growth of dedicated assistance services and access to medical and food resources.	Days to decades	[105]
4	Quality Education	Education systems were forced to abruptly change procedures, shifting from physical to online teaching.	Days to decades	[106]
5	Gender Equality	Pre-existing inequalities in the labor market have been deepened.	Days to years	[107,108]
6	Clean Water and Sanitation	The discovery of the permanence of the virus on surfaces and in aquifers requires a revision of the purification and sanitation systems.	Days to years	[109]
7	Affordable and Clean Energy	Alternative energy sources and backup storage and transport systems should be developed to secure societal needs during crises.	Years to decades	[110]
8	Decent Work and Economic Growth	The pandemic has shown that there are groups of workers most exposed to risk to health and life by requiring a revision of the working methods in industry, commerce and health.	Months to decades	[105,111]
9	Industry, Innovation and Infrastructure	Technological innovation and a close link with the research invention, also to the advantage of a change in production methods, has proved to be an unavoidable condition for the solution of global problems	Months to decades	[112,113]
10	Reduced Inequality	Improvements in access to information technologies to reduce inequalities in poor and large families who have to use remote school systems and access to other resources.	Days to months	[24,114]
11	Sustainable Cities and Communities	Revisions of adaptation plans are foreseen for major cities to increase health resilience in citizens and to better protect elderly population.	Months to decades	[72,115,116]
12	Responsible Consumption and Production	Revision of production systems from the global to the local scale to ensure access and distribution of strategic resources with consequent enhancement of territorial activities.	Months to decades	[117]
13	Climate Action	Transfer of the concepts learned from pandemic evolution to the climate issue.	Months to decades	[118]
14	Life Below Water	No evidence of significant observed or potential impact.	Not the case	[119]
15	Life on Land	Possible financial shortages on protected areas, Increase microplastics in water and soil; Strong support for closing the wildlife trade; Concerns about the influence of habitat loss on epidemic episodes.	Months to decades	[92,93]
16	Peace and Justice Strong Institutions	The importance of strong coordination between institutions has been markedly indicated for national ones but, above all, for international ones where the exchange of exact and punctual information can indicate safe ways for solving problems on a global level.	Months to decades	[99,120]
17	Partnerships to achieve the Goal	The efficiency of international agreements have been dramatically challenged, and the need for rethinking regional and global partnerships emerged.	Days to decades	[103]

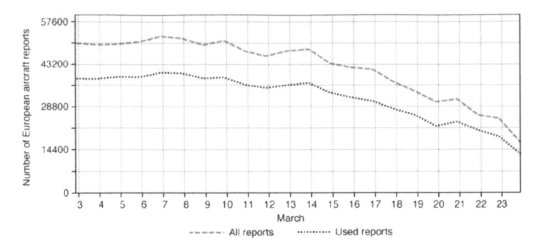

FIGURE 8.15   Number of daily aircraft reports over Europe received and used at ECMWF. (Source: https://www.ecmwf.int/en/about/media-centre/news/2020/drop-aircraft-observations-could-haveimpact- weather-forecasts.)

Challenges like the dearth of airborne meteorological measurements or the maintenance of environmental monitoring in protected areas will gradually be resolved once previous levels of social and economic activity resume (Korten, 2020). However, actions are needed now to build reliable responses to future threats.

The COVID-19 crisis has strongly biased the production and delivery of both weather forecasting (https://news.un.org/en/story/2020/04/1060772) and climate services (i.e., climate-based information and products tailored for various end-users related to the present climate and adaptation to different scenarios) as well as the observation of oceans and remote locations (https://www.theguardian.com/sc ience/2020/apr/03/climate-monitoring-research-coronavirus-scientists#maincontent). The pandemic has dramatically lowered the quantity and quality of aircraft weather observations, thereby adversely impacting weather forecasts and modeling efforts. The European Centre for Medium-Range Weather Forecasts (ECMWF) has noted a reduction of 65% in aircraft reports received between 3 March and 23 March (Figure 8.15). On 9 April, the World Meteorological Organization (WMO) issued its concern about the impact of the crisis on the Global Observing System.[2]

However, the exceptional slowdown of societal activities that began in March 2020 has generated opportunities to capture environmental information of a novel event. For example, the "noise" associated with human activities that adversely affect seismographic records dropped sharply around the world, improving the ability to detect seismic waves and the locations of earthquake aftershocks (Gibney, 2020).

IMPACTS ON THE PRESENT CLIMATE AND CLIMATE CHANGE

Transmission of diseases by population mobility within the context of climate change received scientists' attention before the current pandemic (Amon, 2016).

The examination of the relationship between climate and coronavirus focuses on two queries: (a) how the climate can modulate the spread and persistence of the virus, and (b) the extent of the impact of the virus on economic policies taken to offset climate impacts.

The first aspect is inherently scientific and mainly involves the atmospheric and epidemiological disciplines. The second is much more complex as the economic, political, and social dynamics will affect processes that will alter our worldview.

Climatic effects on the coronavirus are currently difficult to estimate given that this pandemic is still under development. These effects, therefore, can only be speculated by comparing them to the characteristics of other coronaviruses. Reference (Araujo & Naimi, 2020) investigated the observed growth rate of coronavirus worldwide and related it to the climate, making a prediction for forthcoming seasons. They argue a specific climate exists in which the coronavirus spreads optimally. Outbreak dynamics also were investigated in terms of climate and environmental conditions (Ficetola & Rubolini, 2020) to link directly daily growth rates to the local climate. The correlation found was significant, leading them to conclude that such a link was valid, but their study also highlighted the fact that population density could be a confounding variable. These results, although very speculative, have led to initial hypotheses on the transmission conditions of SARS-CoV-2 under different combinations of atmospheric parameters (Wang et al., 2020) and to forecast conditions for the summer of 2020 (Bukhari & Jameel, 2020). An analogy with the other coronaviruses becomes fundamental to validate such hypotheses, but it is not currently possible to establish whether the virologic characteristics of the new pathogen can be assumed to be like other coronaviruses.

Analyzing the direct and indirect effects of the pandemic on the climate is more complicated as forecasts must resolve not just the contagion dynamics but also incorporate economic, social, and political aspects of the virus propagation.

Direct effects on climate change could result mainly from the global slowdown of production activities and transportation. At this stage, the overall effects are not easily determined but, for example, emissions in China—the country with the longest period of closure—have decreased by 25%, corresponding to a decrease of about 200 million tons of CO_2 in February alone (Myllyvirta, 2020a). Nevertheless, the possible decrease in CO_2 emissions is likely to be around 5% worldwide (Nash, n.d.). For the Representative Concentration Pathway (RCP) climate change scenario, Scripps Research Institute suggests a possible trend in emissions (Figure 8.16) which shows an immediate drop followed by a recovery when activities resume.

This projection leads to fundamental speculations as to what indirect effects coronavirus will have on the Earth's climate. We note that following the 2008–2009 economic crisis, CO_2 emissions exhibited rapid growth (Peters et al., 2012) and we suggest that a similar response will follow this pandemic.

Experts suggest one of two sharply divergent paths will arise from the demise of the pandemic (Allen et al., 2020). On the one hand, a feeling exists that the coronavirus will support the government, science, and business infrastructure in addressing environmental issues, including climate change (Allen et al., 2020). Although the coronavirus and climate change operate on different time scales, they represent similar phenomena in terms of the evolution and impacts of the problem. Thus, lessons from the pandemic provide lessons to be learned in environmental protection. Recovery from the pandemic, therefore, may lead the focus away from environmental concerns (Tollefson, 2020).

Surely something has already changed. COVID-19 has undermined the basic tenets of global manufacturing. Companies must now reconsider the multistep, multi-country supply chains that dominated production and derivative production. Individuals too must reconsider life choices as profound changes also await us (Myllyvirta, 2020a).

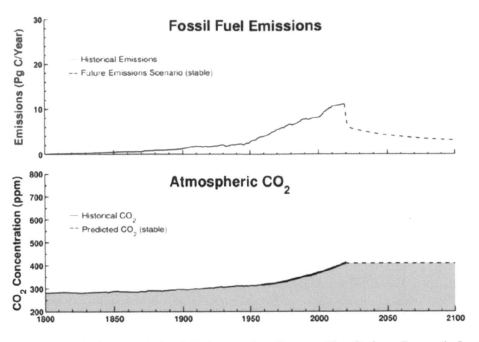

FIGURE 8.16 Emission trend for RCP6 scenario. (Source: The Scripps Research Institute, Available from https://scripps.ucsd.edu/programs/keelingcurve/.)

ARTIFICIAL INTELLIGENCE TOOLS AND TECHNIQUES TO MEASURE AND ANALYSIS THE IMPACT OF COVID-19 ON ENVIRONMENT

This section focuses on the different artificial intelligence computational approaches to demonstrate the relationship between pollution emissions and COVID-19 pandemic infection around the world.

TIME SERIES ANALYSIS

Time Series Analysis is a statistical technique that deals with time series data, or trend analysis. It is a sequence of observations collected at constant time intervals, be it daily, weekly, monthly, quarterly, or yearly, which means that data is in a series of particular time periods or intervals. The data is considered in three types:

- Time series data: A set of observations on the values that a variable takes at different times.
- Cross-sectional data: Data of one or more variables, collected at the same point in time.
- Pooled data: A combination of time series data and cross-sectional data.

Time Series Analysis involves developing models used to describe the observed time series and understand the "why" behind its dataset. This involves creating assumptions and interpretations about a given data. Time Series Forecasting makes use of the best fitting model essential to predicting the future observation based on complex processing current and previous data. Machine learning proved to be the most effective in capturing the patterns in the sequence of both structured and unstructured data and its further analysis for accurate predictions.

To understand the upshot of lockdown measures on air quality, this statistical Time Series Analysis applies to measure the impact of lockdown on National Capital Territory (NCT) Delhi, India. The objectives of applying this statistical analysis are (i) to compare the atmospheric pollutant concentrations in Delhi during the pre and during lockdown periods, (ii) to quantify the integrated air quality due to the implementation of lockdown regulation during Lockdown period, and (iii) to unveil the level of major pollutant concentration in the past few years during the same window period.

The Study Area

The present study has focused on Delhi as the administrative and second financial capital of India. NCT Delhi is the second leading megacity in the world (The World's Cities in 2018, Data Booklet, United Nations, 2018) and the largest urban agglomeration in India with 1.68 crore residents exhibiting a decadal growth rate of 21% and a density of 11,297 person/km^2 (Census, 2011; http://census2011.co.in). NCT Delhi occupies an area of about 1485 km^2 which lies between geocoordinate 28°24′17″N to 28,053′00″N and 76°50′24″E to 77°20′37″E. Geographically, the megacity is located within the Indo-Gangetic alluvial plain region with an altitude range of 198–220 m above msl and surrounded by lesser Himalaya in the north, peninsular region in the south, hilly region in the east, and Great Indian Desert in the west (Sahay, 2018; Yadav et al., 2017). NCT Delhi has a dual status of a city and a state, incorporating Kanjhawla Block, Mehrauli Block, Najafgarh Block, and Shahadra Block. The land-locked megacity is bordered with adjacent cities like Sonipat (North-West), Bahadurgarh, Jhajjar and Rohtak (West), Gurgaon and Manesar (South), Faridabad (South–East), and Noida and Ghaziabad (East) and are incorporated into the National Capital Region (NCR).

The city experiences semi-arid climate having five major seasons: Summer (Mar–May), Monsoon (Jun–Sep), short Post-monsoon (Oct–Nov), Winter (Dec–Feb), and Pre-monsoon (Mar–May). Temperature ranges between 4°C and 10°C in winter and 42°C and 48°C in summer (Kumar et al., 2017). More than 80% of the total annual precipitation occurs during the monsoon months. A momentous proportion (about 90%) of the population working in NCT Delhi residing in urban areas, which is much higher than the nationwide average of 31.16%.[3] About 6.93 million registered vehicles were on roads during 2011 in Delhi, which is the highest in the country and is further expected to increase as much as 25.6 million by 2030 (Kumar et al., 2017). NCT Delhi's existing road length is 33,198 km with about 864 km signalized road and 418 blinkers traffic intersections.[4][5]

Currently, a total of 34 air monitoring stations are in operation in NCT Delhi with a capacity to monitor and record pollutants.

Materials and Methods

Materials Used

In order to assess the air quality status in NCT Delhi during the lockdown period, data from 34 air quality monitoring stations covering different regions of the megacity has been taken into consideration. Organizations for air quality monitoring include different programs and monitoring stations: CPCB (manual ambient air quality monitoring, MAAQM); CPCB (continuous ambient air quality monitoring, CAAQM); DPCC (Delhi Pollution Control Committee) and SAFAR (System of Air Quality and Weather Forecasting and Research), IITM (Indian Institute of Tropical Meteorology), Pune. The daily or hourly concentration of seven air pollutants including particulate matters (PM2.5 and PM10), sulphur dioxide (SO_2), nitrogen dioxide (NO_2), carbon monoxide (CO), ozone (O_3), and ammonia (NH_3) have been obtained from the CPCB online portal for air quality data dissemination (https://app.cpcbccr.com/ccr/#/caaqm-dashboard-all/caaqm-landing). CPCB provides data quality assurance or quality control (QA/QC) programs by defining rigorous protocols for the sampling, analysis, and calibration.

Methodology

The AQI is usually based on pollutants criteria where the deliberation of an individual pollutant is transformed into a sole index using an appropriate aggregation method (Ott, 1978). Conventionally, calculation of the AQI was based on a maximum sub-index approach using five criteria pollutants (i.e., PM10 and PM2.5, SO_2, NO_2, and CO). In recent times, IITM, Pune has come up with a new AQI (IITM-AQI) that provides sub-index additionally for O_3 (Beig et al., 2010). IITM-AQI portrays air quality on a five-point scale with categories namely—very unhealthy, very poor, poor, moderate, and good. The revised Indian National Air Quality Standards (INAQS)[6] has taken 12 parameters [namely, Particulate Matter (PM) of N10 μm size (PM10), Particulate Matter (PM) of N2.5 μm size (PM2.5), Sulphur Dioxide (SO_2), Nitrogen Dioxide (NO_2), Carbon Monoxide (CO), Ozone (O_3), Lead (Pb), Ammonia (NH_3), Benzo(a)Pyrene (BaP), Benzene (C6H6), Arsenic (As) and Nickel (Ni)] for developing the same. Out of the 12 parameters, only four parameters have annual standards, and the rest of the first eight parameters (Table 8.2) have short-term (i.e., 1/8/24 h) and annual standards (except for O_3 and CO). In the present work, in order to investigate the possible impacts of unconventional policy intervention in form of lockdown on air pollution, seven pollutant parameters (PM10, PM2.5, SO_2, NO_2, O_3, CO, and NH_3) have been analyzed individually and as an integrated index during-lockdown period and compared with the result of the same for pre-lockdown period.

The selection of the seven parameters is primarily based on the objectives outlined earlier: period, monitoring regularity, and data accessibility. Furthermore, in the present scheme, six National Air Quality Index (NAQI) categories (CPCB, 2015) (Table 8.2) are used to assess the expected health exposure (also called—Health Breakpoints) in different quality classes as approved by the NAQS.

The sub-indices for entity pollutants at a monitoring station have been calculated based on 24-Hrs mean (8 Hrs for CO and O_3) data and health breakpoint range (CPCB, 2015). However, all the seven pollutants may possibly not monitor at all the stations simultaneously. Largely, NAQI is measured if data does exist for at least three pollutants and must include PM2.5 or PM10 within the three. Otherwise, data are regarded as inadequate for NAQI calculation. Likewise, at least 16-Hrs data is required for sub-index calculation and air quality of a pollutant is the sub-index value of that pollutant. Currently, CPCB also provides real-time NAQI rooted in a web-based system. The web-based system is programmed for the continuously monitoring stations, whereas for manual monitoring stations an NAQI calculator has been developed to obtain the NAQI values. Calculation procedure of NAQI is briefly outlined following CPCB (2015):

TABLE 8.2

National AQI Classes, Range, Health Impacts, and Health Breakpoints for the Seven Pollutants (Scale: 0–500)

AQI Class (Range)	Health Impact	PM10 24Hrs(μg/m3)	PM2.5 24Hrs(μg/m3)	SO$_2$ 24Hrs(μg/m3)	NO$_2$ 24Hrs(μg/m3)	O$_3$ 8Hrs(μg/m3)	CO 8Hrs(mg/m3)	NH$_3$ 24Hrs(μg/m3)
				Concentration Range				
Good (0–50)	Minimal impact	0–50	0–30	0–40	0–40	0–50	0–1	0–200
Satisfactory (51–100)	Minor breathing discomfort to sensitive people	51–100	31–60	41–80	41–80	51–100	1.1–2	201–400
Moderately polluted (101–200)	Breathing discomfort to the people with lung disease	101–250	61–90	81–380	81–180	101–168	2.1–10	401–800
Poor (201–300)	Breathing discomfort to people on prolonged exposure	251–350	91–120	381–800	181–280	169–208	10–17	801–1200
Very poor (301–400)	Respiratory illness to the people on prolonged exposure	351–430	121–250	801–1600	281–400	209–748*	17–34	1200–1800
Severe (401–500)	Respiratory illness to the people on prolonged exposure	N430	N250	N1600	N400	N748	N34	N1800

Principally two steps are implicated to formulate an NAQI:

1. Sub-indices: (Sub-index function symbolizes the relationship among pollutant concentration (X_i) and subsequent sub-index (I_i). This portrays ecological upshot as the concentration of a pollutant alters. It may typically take different forms like linear, non-linear, or segmented linear.

   Usually, the $I - X$ relationship is presented as below:

$$I = \alpha X + \beta$$

   where α is slope of the line, β implies intercept at $X = 0$.

   Equation for the sub-index (I_i) for a known pollutant concentration (C_p) rooted in linear segmented principle is measured as:

$$I_i = \left[\left\{(I_{HI} - I_{LO})/(B_{HI} - B_{LO}) \times (C_p - B_{LO})\right\}\right] + I_{LO}$$

   where B_{HI} refers to Breakpoint concentration $\geq$ known concentration; B_{LO} stands for Breakpoint concentration $\leq$ known concentration; I_{HI} means air quality index (AQI) value equivalent to B_{HI}; I_{LO} means AQI value equivalent to B_{LO} and C_p indicates Pollutant concentration.

2. Combination of sub-indices: After calculating sub-indices, they are combined often in a weighted additive form, non-linear aggregation form, root-mean-square form, or min or max operator form

   Weighted Additive form:

$$I = Aggregated\ Index = \sum_{i=1}^{n} w_i I_i$$

   where $\sum w_i$ equals to 1; I_i refers to sub-index for pollutant I; n is number of pollutant variables and w_i means weight of the pollutant.

   Non-Linear Aggregation Form: Root-Sum-Power Form

$$I = Aggregated\ index = \left[\sum I_i^p\right]^{\left(1/p\right)}$$

   where p is the positive real number > 1.

   Root-Mean-Square Form:

$$I = Aggregated\ Index = \left[\frac{1}{k}\left(I_1^2 + I_2^2 + I_3^2 + \ldots + I_k^2\right)\right]^{0.5}$$

   Min or Max Operator form (Ott, 1978):

$$I = \min \| max\left(I_1, I_2, I_3, \ldots, I_n\right)$$

Results

Changes in the concentrations of major pollutants were observed for the pre-lockdown and during-lockdown period. After declaration of three weeks of lockdown starting from 24th March 2020, pollution of the megacity Delhi witnessed substantial diminution of the pollutants (Figure 8.17 and Table 8.3). Especially, during the study period, PM10, PM2.5, NO_2, and CO concentrations showed significant declining trends (Figure 8.17a, b, d, e). Averaged concentrations of PM10 and PM2.5 reduced by about −51.84% and −53.11% respectively. For the traffic and industrial background stations, the magnitude of decline of PM2.5 was as high as about −62.61% and −59.74% respectively. Other pollutants that showed considerable variation between the pre- and duringlockdown period were NO_2 (−52.68%) and CO (−30.35%). However, for SO_2 (−17.97%) and NH_3 (−12.33%) the reduction was counted very low compared to the others, and no prominent definite trend was evidenced (Figure 8.17c, g). 8 Hrs average daily maximum concentration of O_3 (+0.78% overall variation) in the study period showed a negligible increase with a insignificant rising trend (Figure 8.17f). In this

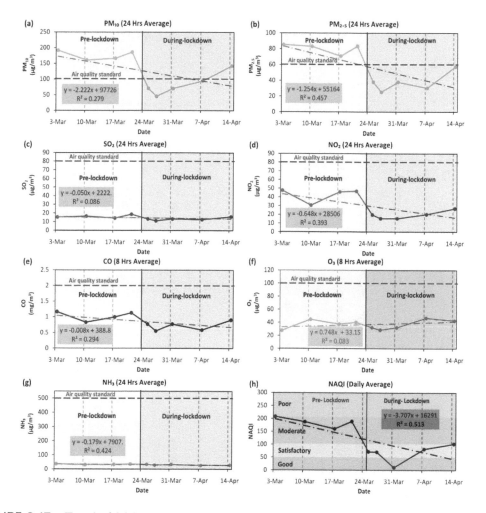

FIGURE 8.17 Trend of 24 Hrs average concentrations of (a) PM10, (b) PM2.5, (c) SO_2, (d) NO_2, (g) NH_3 & (h) NAQI and 8Hrs average daily maxima of (e) CO & (f) O_3 between 3rd March and 14th April (lockdown started on 24th March) in NCT Delhi, India.

TABLE 8.3

Mean Concentrations and Variation of Criterion Pollutants During 2nd March to 21st March (Before the Lockdown) and 25th March to 14th April (During the Lockdown) in NCT Delhi, India

| | Type of Station | | | | | | | | | |
| | Before Lockdown | | | | During Lockdown | | | | Overall Variation | |
Pollutants	NCT Delhi Avg.	Industrial Locations Avg.	Transport Locations Avg.	Residential and Other Locations Avg.	NCT Delhi Avg.	Industrial Locations Avg.	Transport Locations Avg.	Residential and Other Locations Avg.	Net	%
PM10	176.07	190.74	195.77	160.48	84.79	91.25	90.11	76.48	−91.28	−51.85
PM2.5	80.51	88.05	94.83	72.67	37.75	39.67	44.23	31.09	−42.76	−53.11
SO$_2$	16.08	15.48	14.56	14.17	13.19	14.07	12.53	11.2	−2.89	−17.97
NO$_2$	42.59	34.81	47.35	48.75	20.16	18.8	23.38	18.79	−22.44	−52.68
CO	1.03	1.33	1.13	1.01	0.72	1.04	0.71	0.64	−0.31	−30.35
O$_3$	34.05	26.37	35.07	37.36	34.32	31	38.87	37.97	0.27	0.78
NH$_3$	33.93	38.43	38.02	30.66	29.75	35.84	33.06	25.97	−4.18	−12.33
NAQI	185.99	196.38	215.29	174.78	72.64	92.45	87.29	79.8	−113.36	−60.95

TABLE 8.4

Revised Indian National Air Quality Standards (INAQS)

Pollutants	Time Weighted Average	Industrial, Residential and Other Area	Ecologically Sensitive Area (Notified by GoI)
		Concentration of Ambient Air	
PM10 ($\mu g/m3$)	24 Hrs	100	100
PM2.5 ($\mu g/m3$)	24 Hrs	60	60
SO_2 ($\mu g/m3$)	24 Hrs	80	80
NO_2 ($\mu g/m3$)	24 Hrs	80	80
O_3 ($\mu g/m3$)	8 Hrs	100	100
CO (mg/m3)	8 Hrs	2	2
	1 Hrs	4	4
NH_3 ($\mu g/m3$)	24 Hrs	400	400

Source: CPCB (2015)

case, considering that April to August in the Indian subcontinent is the usual high O_3 period (Gorai et al., 2017) due to the increase in insolation, the result is quite feasible. It is important to note that the concentration of O_3 increases especially in the industrial and transport domi-nated locations (N10% increase) (Table 8.3). The cause for this increase in the O_3 concentra-tion, especially in the industrial and transport dominated areas is the decrease of nitrogen oxide (NO) which leads to a lowering of the O_3 consumption (titration, $NO + O_3 = NO_2 + O2$) and causes an increase in the O_3 concentrations. The overall air quality reduction, as evident from NAQI value for the past lockdown and during-lockdown period (Figure 8.17h), counted about −60.95% with the net reduction counting −113.36 (Table 8.4). For the transportation and industrial location, the air quality improved up to −59.45% (net reduction in NAQI: −128.0) and −52.92 (Net reduction in NAQI: −103.93) respectively. This is a clear indication that a substantial improvement of the air quality could be expected if strict implementation of air quality control measures like lockdown is put into practice.

Spatial Pattern of National Air Quality Index (NAQI) for the Pre-Lockdown and During-Lockdown Period

Figure 8.18 depicts the pattern of variation in air quality during pre-lockdown and post-lockdown days between 3rd March and 14th April. As stated earlier, the lockdown started on 24th March and just after one day of the commencement of the lockdown (i.e., 25th March) a significant improvement in the air quality was observed (Figure 8.18e) in com-parison to that of the pre-lockdown phase. As much as about 51% reduction of NAQI was observed on the 4th day (i.e., 27th March) of the lockdown (Figure 8.18f) in comparison to the 3rd preceding day (i.e., 21st March) of the lockdown (Figure 8.18d). On an average there was about 43% decrease in NAQI during the three-week of the lockdown period (from 24th March to 14th April) in comparison to the average NAQI during the first three weeks of March (from 3rd March to 21st March). About 54%, 49%, 43%, 37%, and 31% reduc-tions in NAQI were observed in Central, Eastern, Southern, Western, and Northern regions of the NCT Delhi respectively. This diminution in NAQI was primarily associated with the alteration of prevailing pollutants, primarily PM10, PM2.5, NO_2, and CO discussed

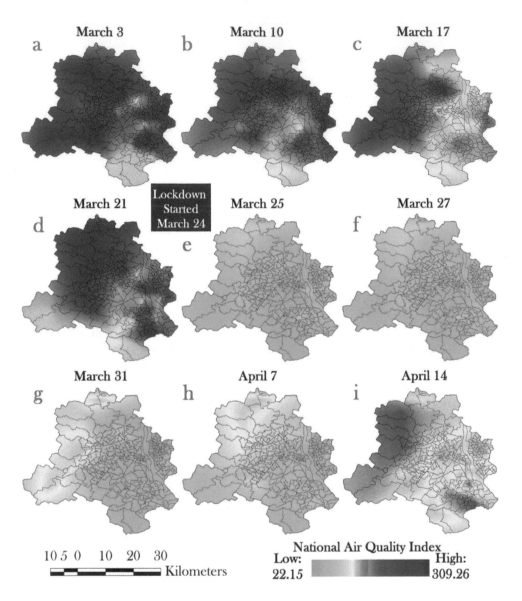

FIGURE 8.18   (a)–(i) present the changes in NAQI in the NCT Delhi during the period start from 3rd March to 14 April 2020.

afterward. However, after two weeks of lockdown, partial relaxation on necessary transportation and controlled industrial activity outside the COVID-19 infected areas resulted in a slight increase in the NAQI on the 7th April and 14th April (Figure 8.18h and i). Moreover, there was a partial restriction on power plants operating within the NCT Delhi region in particular and Northern India in general (Sharma et al., 2020) in order to procure coal-powered energy, an essential commodity during the lockdown period.

Spatial Concentration Pattern of Major Pollutants During
Lockdown and Pre-Lockdown Phase

As it could be expected, strict measures were implemented to execute the lockdown in order to minimize the movement and social contact of the people. This substantially reduced the

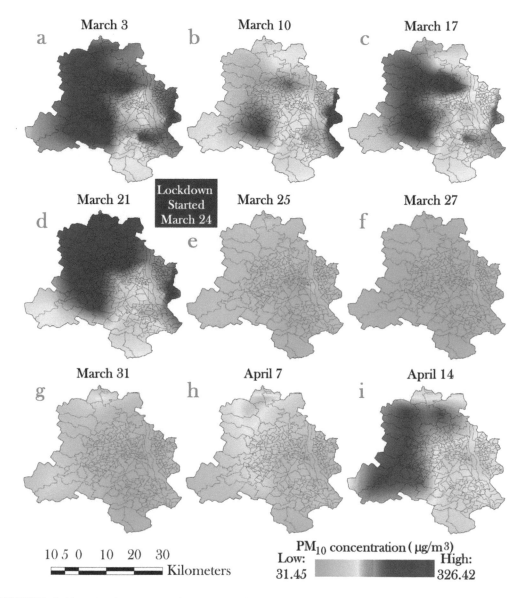

FIGURE 8.19 (a)–(i) present the status of PM10 concentration in pre-lockdown and during lockdown period over NCT Delhi.

movement of vehicles and the closing of industries, restaurants, shops, administrative centers, and many others. This caused a drastic improvement in the air quality, particularly the primary dominated ones like PM10, PM2.5, NO_2, and CO (Figures 8.19–8.22). The most momentous dissimilarity is evident for PM10 (Figure 8.19) and PM2.5 (Figure 8.20). This can be clearly seen from the spatial pattern of concentration of these two pollutants on different days of the pre-lockdown and during lockdown period. The main source of PM10 and PM2.5 in the megacity Delhi is road traffic (about 30% of the annual mean). Industrial activity, construction works, and dust re-suspension are the other sources. Notably, only within 4 days of the lockdown (from 24th March to 27th March) concentrations of the two pollutants reduced below the permissible limit. As a pertinent amount of PM10 and PM2.5 have a regional background-origin, mostly from traffic and industrial sources, slight relaxation of lockdown

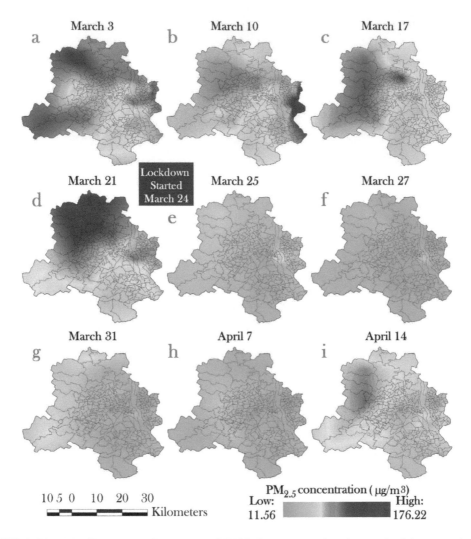

FIGURE 8.20   (a)–(i) present the status of PM2.5 concentration in pre-lockdown and during lockdown period over NCT Delhi.

measures for necessary vehicles and localized industries beyond the red zone (i.e., COVID-19 infected area) after two weeks from 7th April might influenced PM10 and PM2.5 to increase slightly on 7th April and 14th April (Figures 8.19h, i and 8.7h, i).

Important pollutants other than PM10 and PM2.5 that also showed significant reduction during the lockdown period were NO_2 and CO. In urban areas, NO_2 and CO are mainly emitted from combustion practice by and large from road traffic, particularly diesel and to a smaller degree gasoline, vehicles, manufacturing industry, and power plants. During this lockdown period, all of these sectors closed their functioning and thereby resulted in the decrease of pollutants like NO_2 and CO. In industrial locations, average concentrations of NO_2 and CO decreased by as much as −45.99% and −21.43% respectively. Whereas, in traffic-dominated locations the concentration of the two pollutants namely NO_2 and CO decreased by as much as −50.61 and −36.84% respectively.

Finally, the concentration levels of O_3 noticeably increased during the lockdown period in the megacity Delhi (Figure 8.21) as a result of three potential collective reasons. First, the

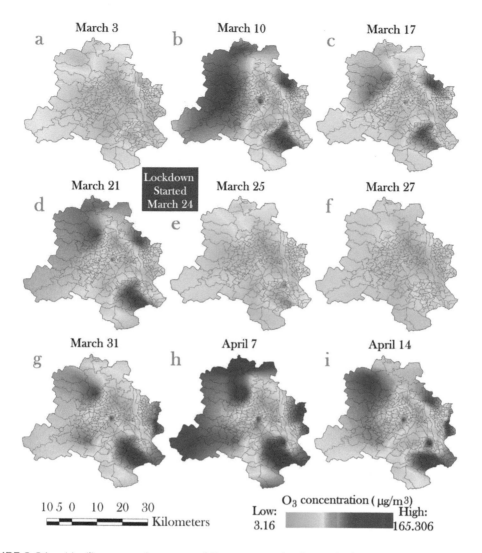

FIGURE 8.21   (a)–(i) present the status of O_3 concentration in pre-lockdown and during lockdown period over NCT Delhi.

lessening of NOx (Figure 8.22) because of the lockdown might have resulted the urban O_3 levels to bump up, in contrast to the behavior in the rural area where largely NOx concentration is limited (Monks et al., 2015). Second, the dwindling of nitrogen oxide (NO) diminished the O_3 utilization (titration, $NO + O_3 = NO_2 + O2$), and thereby caused an augmentation of the O_3 concentrations. Third, the natural increase in insolation and temperatures from March to August in the northern hemisphere as a result of the northward migration of sun leads to an increase in O_3 when the maximum O_3 is usually recorded (Gorai et al., 2017). However, the role of the climate has not been taken into consideration in this study.

NCT Delhi is a low SO_2 city (Figure 8.23) because of its interior location beyond the sea, since emissions from ship (large cargo ships, cruises, and ferries) majorly contribute to SO_2 pollution. For this reason concentration of SO_2 in NCT Delhi usually remains much below the acceptable limit (Figure 8.17c), and during this lockdown period, SO_2 concentration experienced a slight decrease in comparison to the pre-lockdown phase. On the other

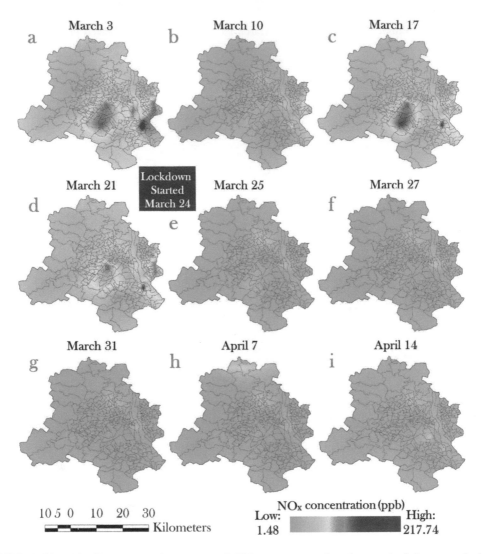

FIGURE 8.22   (a)–(i) present the status of NOx concentration in pre-lockdown and during lockdown period over NCT Delhi.

hand, it is a widely accepted fact that NH_3 originated from the non-agricultural sources is negligible (Sutton et al., 1995). Therefore, concentration of NH_3 was also much below the acceptable limit (Figure 8.17g).

However, a significant decrease in NH_3 concentration during the lockdown phase (Figure 8.24) was due to the fact that petrol engine vehicles comprise a foremost cause of urban NH_3.(Kean et al., 2000; Kirchner et al., 2002), and during lockdown transportation activity was strictly restricted.

Understanding the Pattern of PM10 and PM2.5 Concentration over the Last Four Years

In order to supplement the PM10 and PM2.5 observations as highlighted in the earlier sub-sections, we have explored the 24-Hrs pattern of concentration of the two pollutants over the last four years (from 2017 to 2020) for the same two months window (i.e., March and April)

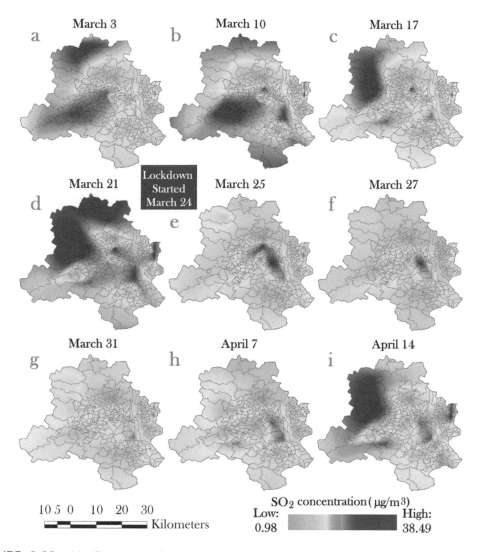

FIGURE 8.23 (a)–(i) present the status of SO_2 concentration in pre-lockdown and during lockdown period over NCT Delhi.

(Figure 8.25). Continuous observations of PM10 and PM2.5 concentrations are obtainable from the network of air quality monitoring stations maintained by the CPCB, 2016.[7] Here we have used monitoring data from Nehru Nagar located in central Delhi (Primarily residential location) as a representative station for the assessment.

Table 8.5 highlights the statistics concerning differences in the concentration of the two major pollutants during the lockdown period (i.e., from 24th March to 14th April 2020) in comparison to the previous three years (2017–2019) for the same period. It can be noticed that over the previous three years during the period from 24th March to 14th April the concentration of PM10 was substantially higher counting 24 Hrs average of about 168.32 μg/m3 (average of the year 2017, 2018, and 2019) in comparison to 2020 average counting about 73.13 μg/m3 (about –56.55% reduction). Likewise, the PM2.5 averaged concentrations for the preceding three years during the said months (2017–2019 year average 83.96 μg/m3) decreased by about –32.62% during the year 2020 for the same period (56.57 μg/m3).

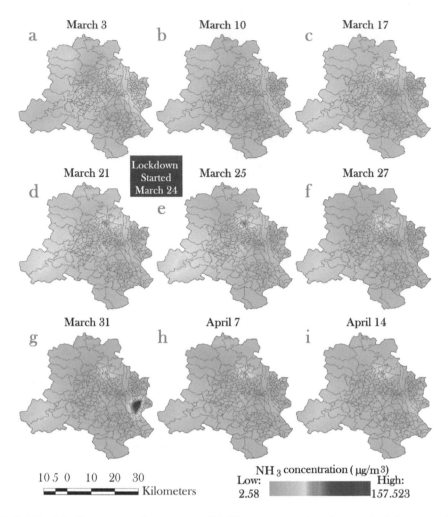

FIGURE 8.24   (a)–(i) present the status of NH_3 concentration in pre-lockdown and during lockdown period over NCT Delhi.

In comparison to the last year (i.e., 2019) during the said time period, the reduction of the two pollutants PM10 and PM2.5 was as high as about −60.46% and −38.68% respectively. The maximum concentration of PM10 was during 2017 and that of PM2.5 was during 2017 counting as high as 398.80 μg/m3 and 185.90 μg/m3 respectively. This reduced to 110 μg/m3 (−72.42% maximum reduction) and 94 μg/m3 (−49.44% maximum reduction), respectively, during 2020. The results again are a sign that implementation of lockdown led to substantial improvement of the air quality, and this could be put into practice as an alternative measure for pollution reduction.

Aside from variation of pollutant concentrations as assessed during the study period, concentrations of the pollutants may also fluctuate with the inter-seasonal disparity in the meteorological conditions. For example, during the monsoon season in the Indian subcontinent (mid-June–September) the concentrations of PM10 and PM2.5 remain much lower than that of the other seasons of a year. In late October, the pollutants are augmented primarily due to the Diwali festival in India. From November onward up to February, winter season prevails in North India with subsequent development of stagnant weather conditions

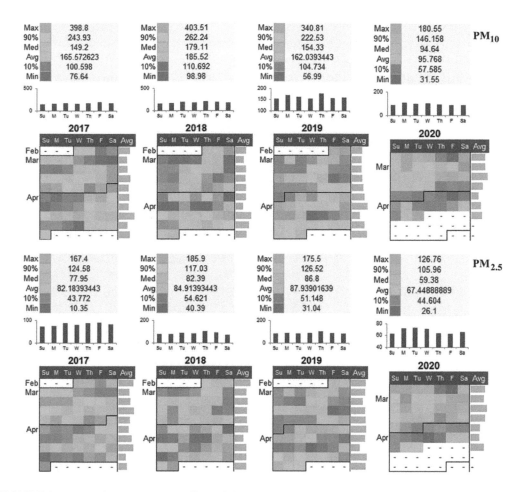

FIGURE 8.25   Daily (24 Hrs) profiles of the concentration of PM10 and PM2.5 for the month of March and April from 2017 to 2020 in Nehru Nagar, NCT Delhi.

and regular temperature inversions. This results in gathering of local and transported pollutants and augmentation of pollution level during the season. Therefore, in order to consider lockdown as an alternative policy measure once or twice a year in a long-distance race, examination of seasonal variation of pollutant concentration with respect to regional meteorological conditions is also necessary. Appendices 4, 5, and 6 may supplement this type of future research to the scientific community.

Co-Relationship between the Ambient Air Pollutants

The correlations between different air pollutant concentrations in NCT Delhi during the study period (i.e., 3rd March–14th April) are shown in Figure 8.26. The daily (24Hrs) average concentration of PM2.5 is shown to be highly correlated with the daily average concentration of SO_2 (r = 0.59), NO_2 (r = 0.35) as well as 8Hrs average concentration of CO (r = 0.45). Likewise, the daily average concentration of PM10 is also shown to be strongly correlated with the daily average concentration of SO_2 (r = 0.47), NO_2 (r = 0.46), NH_3 (r = 0.30) as well as 8Hrs average concentration of CO (r = 0.39). This visibly implies that the augmented control of regional transport activity compared to local contributions in the

TABLE 8.5

Basic Statistics Pertaining to 24 Hrs Average Concentration of PM10 and PM2.5 for the Period of 24th March–14th April During 2017–2020 in Nehru Nagar, NCT Delhi

				Periods						
							Variation (2020 and 2019)		Variation (2020 and Avg. of 2017–2019)	
		24th March–14th April								
				Avg. of						
Statistics	2017	2018	2019	2017–2019	2020	Net	%	Net	%
PM10									
Maximum	398.8	262.24	340.81	333.95	110	−230.81	−67.72	−223.95	−67.06
90%	218.08	211.43	263.99	231.17	101.67	−162.32	−61.49	−129.49	−56.02
Median	139.32	161.6	183.6	161.5	67.65	−115.95	−63.16	−93.86	−58.12
Average	157.49	162.53	184.94	168.32	73.13	−111.81	−60.46	−95.19	−56.55
10%	104.06	100.98	121.89	108.98	56.13	−65.77	−53.95	−52.85	−48.5
Minimum	86.26	98.98	96.2	93.81	31.55	−64.65	−67.2	−62.26	−66.37
PM2.5									
Maximum	167.4	185.9	175.5	176.27	94	−81.5	−46.44	−82.27	−46.67
90%	111.12	97.67	146.91	118.56	79.37	−67.53	−45.97	−39.19	−33.05
Median	73.7	80.84	83.45	79.33	52.21	−31.25	−37.44	−27.12	−34.19
Average	78.19	81.44	92.24	83.96	56.57	−35.68	−38.68	−27.39	−32.62
10%	45.42	48.37	58.8	50.86	39.47	−19.33	−32.88	−11.4	−22.4
Minimum	36.44	46.27	47.3	43.34	27.5	−19.8	−41.86	−15.84	−36.54

megacity is the key factor responsible for the reduction of pollutant concentration (Sharma et al., 2020), as during the lockdown period the regional transportation was restricted completely. Apart from these, NO_2 is significantly correlated with CO (r = 0.57) and NH_3 (r = 0.42). There is no apparent correlation between O_3 & NO_2, O_3 & CO, and O_3 & NH_3. This is also applicable in case of SO_2 & NH_3 and SO_2 & NO_2.

The reported results represent the effect of lockdown (since the third week of March 2020), imposed in order to restrict the rapid spread of COVID-19 pandemic in India, on the air quality of the National Capital City Delhi. Results were assessed based on NAQI and concentration of seven major pollutants. Delhi is internationally recognized for its extreme pollution level. Among the selected pollutants, PM10 and PM2.5 have witnessed maximum reduction followed by NO_2, CO, and NH_3. In comparison to the past three years, average concentration of PM10 and PM2.5 has decreased by about −57% and −33%, respectively. On the contrary, there is a slight increase in O_3 concentration which is expected to be primarily due to the decrease in the concentration of NO_x and particulate matter. Moreover, as anticipated, a considerable reduction in NAQI was observed during the window period of lockdown throughout the megacity. Just after one day of the commencement of lockdown (i.e., 25th March), there was about 40% improvement in the air quality. Only on the 4th day of lockdown (27th March) concentrations of PM10 and PM2.5 came within the permissible limit and there was about 51% reduction in NAQI. During the entire three weeks of lockdown, there was about 43% decrease in NAQI in comparison to the first three weeks of

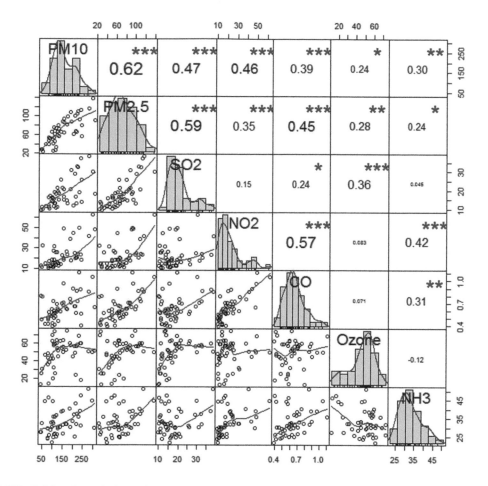

FIGURE 8.26 Co-relationships between different air pollutants. Note: The correlations are expressed as Pearson's correlation coefficient, where *, ** and *** denote significant correlations at $p < 0.1$, $p < 0.05$ and $p < 0.01$ (two-tailed) respectively.

March in 2020. About 54%, 49%, 43%, 37%, and 31% reductions in NAQI are observed in Central, Eastern, Southern, Western, and Northern regions of the NCT Delhi respectively. The region where energy footprint was high and guideline of lockdown has been obeying, the air quality improvement is found high there. Therefore, study is thought to be a useful supplement to the regulatory authorities that may lead to rethinking of the existing regulatory plans and may provide assurance toward implementing strict alternative measures like short term (2–4 day) lockdown in aim to control air quality

SUMMARY

The COVID-19 pandemic has triggered unprecedented environmental impacts in terms of spatial extent, complexity, and even uniqueness. It is the first time in history that the metabolism of all the urban agglomerations with more than one million inhabitants from Europe was virtually stopped regarding movement, traffic, and economic exchanges. The societal and economic measures adopted to contain the pandemic led to local, regional, and global impacts, both negative and positive, spanning from immediate to long-term consequences.

The full evaluation of the impacts is far from being possible with an ongoing disaster of epic proportion and tremendous complexity, and this paper pledges for several directions to be pursued by further research.

The COVID-19 pandemic provides a clear demonstration that human health and planetary health are intimately interconnected, and the role of interdisciplinary approaches in finding solutions has been clearly highlighted (Sun et al., 2020). The disaster reached the planetary scale within only two months (i.e., February through March 2020). Despite six other pandemic outbreaks having occurred during the 21st century, humankind was still not prepared to deal with a global event. Most countries adopted a strict lockdown of economies and societal activities, triggering immediate impacts on many physical and ecological systems. Longer-term consequences are also assumed, and a systemic approach is required to support the prevention, early warning, and similar impacts of environmental degradation.

The coronavirus pandemic has generated an active involvement of the research community and has garnered an early response from international, national, and local authorities. Since the events are ongoing and the end is still difficult to predict, we shall refer only to preliminary results and possible lessons to be learned. The reaction of the scientific community to the crisis was prompt and led to rapid accumulation of knowledge and operational decisions. Faced with an unprecedented interruption of data from aeronautical meteorological service providers (AMSPs) and other observational platforms, the WMO has enumerated preliminary guidelines to assist the AMSPs[8] at the beginning of April 2020. Eventually, problems associated with environmental monitoring have reinforced the need to secure backup systems to collect information, as such data are crucial for operational forecasting of ecological, weather, and hydrological conditions. Of note, relationships between weather conditions and the spread of the virus are still unclear and more research is needed to derive relevant conclusions.

The advancements of new specific techniques would be of great interest for controlling the environmental dissemination of coronaviruses (Ficetola & Rubolini, 2020), and more precise and extended monitoring would favor the collection of more relevant information. Early developments with this crisis have revealed that monitoring of socio-ecological conditions is crucial for an early intervention to limit the scale of the epidemic and the pandemic hazard. Sirkeci and Yucesahin (2020) argue that better monitoring of immigrant tracks and travel volumes could have helped countries be better prepared to contain the spread of the novel coronavirus. Data, tools, and lessons learned may provide significant improvements in preparation to fight potential pandemics in the future (Fakhruddin, 2020).

This global crisis has convincingly demonstrated that the disaster research, climate change diplomacy, and ecosystem services must reconsider their strategic and integrated development considering even the most unlikely events. Eventually, the COVID-19 pandemic will determine profound changes in the social and economic behavior at the planetary scale, and this study highlights the environmental dimension of the consequent impacts resulting from the emerging pandemic.

NOTES

1. https://www.iqair.com/us/world-air-quality
2. Impacts on the Global Observing System. Available online: https://public.wmo.int/en/resources/coronaviruscovid-19/impacts-global-observing-system (accessed on 11 May 2020).

3. SAD, 2014. Statistical Abstract of Delhi 2014. Directorate of Economics & Statistics. Government of NCT of Delhi, New Delhi.

4. NCR: National Capital Region, 2013. National Capital Region Regional Plan. Draft Revised Regional Plan 2021, National Capital Region (Approved in 33rd Meeting of the NCR Planning Board Held on 1st July 2013), July, 2013. National Capital Region Planning Board, Ministry of Urban Development, Goverment of India.

5. GoD: Government of Delhi, 2016a. Chapter 12, Transport, Economic Survey of Delhi, 2014–15. Available at:. http://delhi.gov.in/wps/wcm/connect/DoIT_Planning/planning/ economic+survey+of+dehli/economic+survey+of+delhi+2014+-+2015, Accessed date: 27 February 2016. GoD: Government of Delhi, 2016b. Statistical abstract (2016) Delhi Govt. Portal. www. delhi.gov.in.

6. CPCB, 2016b. NAQI Status of Indian Cities in 2015–16. Central Pollution Control Board (CPCB), Ministry of Environment, Forest and Climate Change, Government of India, New Delhi.

7. CPCB, 2016a. Ambient Air Quality Data at Various Locations in the Country. [WWW Document]. http://www.cpcb.gov.in/CAAQM/frmUserAvgReportCriteria.aspx, Accessed date: 10 March 2016. CPCB, 2016b. NAQI Status of Indian Cities in 2015–16. Central Pollution Control Board (CPCB), Ministry of Environment, Forest and Climate Change, Government of India, New Delhi.

8. Impacts on the Global Observing System. Available online: https://public.wmo.int/en/resources/coronaviruscovid-19/impacts-global-observing-system (accessed on 11 May 2020).

REFERENCES

Al Hajjar, S., & McIntosh, K. (2010). The first influenza pandemic of the 21st century. *Annals of Saudi Medicine*, *30*(1), 1–10.

Alexander, D. J., & Brown, I. H. (2009). History of highly pathogenic avian influenza. *Revue Scientifique et Technique (International Office of Epizootics)*, *28*(1), 19–38.

Ali, I., & Alharbi, O. M. L. (2020). COVID-19: Disease, management, treatment, and social impact. *Science of the Total Environment*, 138861.

Allen, J., Burns, N., Garrett, L., Haass, R. N., Ikenberry, G. J., Mahbubani, K., Menon, S., Niblett, R., Nye Jr, J. S., & O'Neil, S. K. (2020). How the world will look after the coronavirus pandemic. *Foreign Policy*, *20*, 2020.

Amon, J. J. (2016). The impact of climate change and population mobility on neglected tropical disease elimination. *International Journal of Infectious Diseases*, *53*, 12.

Andersen, K. G., Rambaut, A., Lipkin, W. I., Holmes, E. C., & Garry, R. F. (2020). The proximal origin of SARS-CoV-2. *Nature Medicine*, *26*(4), 450–452.

Araujo, M. B., & Naimi, B. (2020). Spread of SARS-CoV-2 Coronavirus likely to be constrained by climate. *MedRxiv*.

Ataguba, J. E. (2020). *COVID-19 pandemic, a war to be won: understanding its economic implications for Africa*. Springer.

Beig, G., Ghude, S. D., & Deshpande, A. (2010). *Scientific evaluation of air quality standards and defining air quality index for India*. Indian Institute of Tropical Meteorology.

Bloomfield, L. S. P., McIntosh, T. L., & Lambin, E. F. (2020). Habitat fragmentation, livelihood behaviors, and contact between people and nonhuman primates in Africa. *Landscape Ecology*, *35*(4), 985–1000.

Buckley, R. (2020). Conservation implications of COVID-19: Effects via tourism and extractive industries. *Biological Conservation*.

Bukhari, Q., & Jameel, Y. (2020). Will coronavirus pandemic diminish by summer? *Available at SSRN 3556998*.

Carpenter, S. R., & Turner, M. G. (2000). Hares and tortoises: interactions of fast and slow variables in ecosystems. *Ecosystems*, 495–497.

Čenčur Curk, B., Vrhovnik, P., Verbovsek, T., Dimkic, D., Marjanovic, P., Tahy, A., Simonffy, Z., Corsini, A., Nistor, M. M., & Cheval, S. (2015). Vulnerability of water resources to climate change in south-east Europe. *AQUA*.

Chatziprodromidou, I. P., Arvanitidou, M., Guitian, J., Apostolou, T., Vantarakis, G., & Vantarakis, A. (2018). Global avian influenza outbreaks 2010–2016: A systematic review of their distribution, avian species and virus subtype. *Systematic Reviews*, 7(1), 1–12.

Contini, D., & Costabile, F. (2020). *Does Air Pollution Influence COVID-19 Outbreaks?* Multidisciplinary Digital Publishing Institute.

Corlett, R. T., Primack, R. B., Devictor, V., Maas, B., Goswami, V. R., Bates, A. E., Koh, L. P., Regan, T. J., Loyola, R., & Pakeman, R. J. (2020). Impacts of the coronavirus pandemic on biodiversity conservation. *Biological Conservation*, 246, 108571.

Cornwall, W. (2020). Can you put a price on COVID-19 options? Experts weigh lives versus economics. *Science*, 10.

Cramer, W., Yohe, G., Auffhammer, M., Huggel, C., Molau, U., Dias, M. A. S., Bouwer, L., Carey, M., Coumou, D., & Hansen, G. (n.d.). Detection and attribution of observed impacts. *Cities*, 18, 1.

Cremades, R., Mitter, H., Tudose, N. C., Sanchez-Plaza, A., Graves, A., Broekman, A., Bender, S., Giupponi, C., Koundouri, P., & Bahri, M. (2019). Ten principles to integrate the water-energy-land nexus with climate services for co-producing local and regional integrated assessments. *Science of the Total Environment*, 693, 133662.

Cucinotta, D., & Vanelli, M. (2020). WHO declares COVID-19 a pandemic. *Acta Bio-Medica: Atenei Parmensis*, 91(1), 157–160.

Deliso, M. (2020). Conservationists fear african animal poaching will increase during COVID-19 pandemic. *ABC News, April*, 14.

Dong, E., Du, H., & Gardner, L. (2020). An interactive web-based dashboard to track COVID-19 in real time. *The Lancet Infectious Diseases*, 20(5), 533–534.

Dukes, J. S., & Mooney, H. A. (1999). Does global change increase the success of biological invaders? *Trends in Ecology & Evolution*, 14(4), 135–139.

El-Kafrawy, S. A., Corman, V. M., Tolah, A. M., Al Masaudi, S. B., Hassan, A. M., Müller, M. A., Bleicker, T., Harakeh, S. M., Alzahrani, A. A., & Alsaaidi, G. A. (2019). Enzootic patterns of Middle East respiratory syndrome coronavirus in imported African and local Arabian dromedary camels: A prospective genomic study. *The Lancet Planetary Health*, 3(12), e521–e528.

Evans, T. S., Shi, Z., Boots, M., Liu, W., Olival, K. J., Xiao, X., Vandewoude, S., Brown, H., Chen, J.-L., & Civitello, D. J. (2020). Synergistic China–US ecological research is essential for global emerging infectious disease preparedness. *EcoHealth*, 1–14.

Fakhruddin, B. (2020). *A data ecosystem to defeat COVID-19*.

Ferretti, L., Wymant, C., Kendall, M., Zhao, L., Nurtay, A., Abeler-Dörner, L., Parker, M., Bonsall, D., & Fraser, C. (2020). Quantifying SARS-CoV-2 transmission suggests epidemic control with digital contact tracing. *Science*, 368(6491).

Ficetola, G. F., & Rubolini, D. (2020). Climate affects global patterns of COVID-19 early outbreak dynamics. *MedRxiv*.

Field, C. B., Barros, V., Stocker, T. F., & Dahe, Q. (2012). *Managing the risks of extreme events and disasters to advance climate change adaptation: special report of the intergovernmental panel on climate change*. Cambridge University Press.

Gardner, E. G., Kelton, D., Poljak, Z., Van Kerkhove, M., Von Dobschuetz, S., & Greer, A. L. (2019). A case-crossover analysis of the impact of weather on primary cases of Middle East respiratory syndrome. *BMC Infectious Diseases*, 19(1), 1–10.

Garske, T., Cori, A., Ariyarajah, A., Blake, I. M., Dorigatti, I., Eckmanns, T., Fraser, C., Hinsley, W., Jombart, T., & Mills, H. L. (2017). Heterogeneities in the case fatality ratio in the West African Ebola outbreak 2013–2016. *Philosophical Transactions of the Royal Society B: Biological Sciences*, 372(1721), 20160308.

Gibney, E. (2020). *Coronavirus lockdowns have changed the way Earth moves. Nature, pages*.

Gorai, A. K., Tchounwou, P. B., & Mitra, G. (2017). Spatial variation of ground level ozone concentrations and its health impacts in an urban area in India. *Aerosol and Air Quality Research*, *17*(4), 951.

Grace, D., Mutua, F., Ochungo, P., Kruska, R. L., Jones, K., Brierley, L., Lapar, M., Said, M. Y., Herrero, M. T., & Phuc, P. M. (2012). *Mapping of poverty and likely zoonoses hotspots*.

Gulia, S., Nagendra, S. M. S., Khare, M., & Khanna, I. (2015). *Atmospheric pollution research*.

Gundy, P. M., Gerba, C. P., & Pepper, I. L. (2009). Survival of coronaviruses in water and wastewater. *Food and Environmental Virology*, *1*(1), 10.

Gutérres, A. (2020). The recovery from the COVID-19 crisis must lead to a different economy. *United Nations*.

Haass, R. (2020). The pandemic will accelerate history rather than reshape it. *Foreign Affairs*, *7*.

Harapan, H., Itoh, N., Yufika, A., Winardi, W., Keam, S., Te, H., Megawati, D., Hayati, Z., Wagner, A. L., & Mudatsir, M. (2020). Coronavirus disease 2019 (COVID-19): A literature review. *Journal of Infection and Public Health*.

Harrison, R. M., Masiol, M., & Vardoulakis, S. (2015). Civil aviation, air pollution and human health. *Environmental Research Letters*, *10*(4), 41001.

Hasan, S., Ahmad, S. A., Masood, R., & Saeed, S. (2019). Ebola virus: A global public health menace: A narrative review. *Journal of Family Medicine and Primary Care*, *8*(7), 2189.

Horowitz, J., Bubola, E., & Povoledo, E. (2020). Italy, pandemic's new epicenter, has lessons for the world. *New York Times*, *21*.

Insider, B. (2020). *A third of the global population is on coronavirus lockdown—here's our constantly updated list of countries and restrictions*.

Johnston, A. S. A., Boyd, R. J., Watson, J. W., Paul, A., Evans, L. C., Gardner, E. L., & Boult, V. L. (2019). Predicting population responses to environmental change from individual-level mechanisms: towards a standardized mechanistic approach. *Proceedings of the Royal Society B*, *286*(1913), 20191916.

Kean, A. J., Harley, R. A., Littlejohn, D., & Kendall, G. R. (2000). On-road measurement of ammonia and other motor vehicle exhaust emissions. *Environmental Science & Technology*, *34*(17), 3535–3539.

Kirchner, M., Braeutigam, S., Feicht, E., & Löflund, M. (2002). Ammonia emissions from vehicles and the effects on ambient air concentrations. *Fresenius Environmental Bulletin*, *11*(8), 454–458.

Kivits, R., Charles, M. B., & Ryan, N. (2010). A post-carbon aviation future: Airports and the transition to a cleaner aviation sector. *Futures*, *42*(3), 199–211.

Korten, T. (2020). With boats stuck in harbor because of COVID-19, will fish bounce back? *Smithsonian Magazine*.

Kumar, P., Gulia, S., Harrison, R. M., & Khare, M. (2017). The influence of odd–even car trial on fine and coarse particles in Delhi. *Environmental Pollution*, *225*, 20–30.

LeDuc, J. W., & Barry, M. A. (2004). SARS, the first pandemic of the 21st century. *Emerging Infectious Diseases*, *10*(11), e26.

Liu, J., Zhou, J., Yao, J., Zhang, X., Li, L., Xu, X., He, X., Wang, B., Fu, S., & Niu, T. (2020). Impact of meteorological factors on the COVID-19 transmission: A multi-city study in China. *Science of the Total Environment*, 138513.

Lo, T. Q., Marston, B. J., Dahl, B. A., & De Cock, K. M. (2017). Ebola: anatomy of an epidemic. *Annual Review of Medicine*, *68*, 359–370.

Madhav, N., Oppenheim, B., Gallivan, M., Mulembakani, P., Rubin, E., & Wolfe, N. (2017). *Pandemics: risks, impacts, and mitigation*.

Malvy, D., McElroy, A. K., de Clerck, H., Günther, S., & van Griensven, J. (2019). Ebola virus disease. *The Lancet*, *393*(10174), 936–948.

McMahon, J. (2020). *Study: coronavirus lockdown likely saved 77,000 lives in China just by reducing pollution, Forbes*.

Medema, G., Heijnen, L., Elsinga, G., Italiaander, R., & Brouwer, A. (2020). Presence of SARS-Coronavirus-2 in sewage. *MedRxiv*.

Memish, Z. A., Perlman, S., Van Kerkhove, M. D., & Zumla, A. (2020). Middle East respiratory syndrome. *The Lancet*.

Monks, P. S., Archibald, A. T., Colette, A., Cooper, O., Coyle, M., Derwent, R., Fowler, D., Granier, C., Law, K. S., & Mills, G. E. (2015). *Tropospheric ozone and its precursors from the urban to the global scale from air quality to short-lived climate forcer*.

Myllyvirta, L. (2020a). *Analysis: Coronavirus has temporarily reduced China's CO2 emissions by a quarter: CarbonBrief; 2020*.

Myllyvirta, L. (2020b). Coronavirus temporarily reduced China's CO2 emissions by a quarter. *Carbon Brief* Https://Www.Carbonbrief.Org/Analysis-Coronavirus-Has-Temporarily-Reduced-Chinas-Co2-Emissions-by-a-Quarter.

NASA. (2020). *Airborne nitrogen dioxide plummets over China*.

Nash, C. M. (n.d.). *Harvard Professor Sounds Alarm on 'Likely' Coronavirus Pandemic: 40% to 70% of World Could Be Infected This Year*.

Ott, W. R. (1978). *Environmental indices: theory and practice*.

Perry, R. W. (2018). Defining disaster: An evolving concept. In *Handbook of disaster research* (pp. 3–22). Springer.

Peters, G. P., Marland, G., Le Quéré, C., Boden, T., Canadell, J. G., & Raupach, M. R. (2012). Rapid growth in CO 2 emissions after the 2008–2009 global financial crisis. *Nature Climate Change*, 2(1), 2–4.

Plourde, A. R., & Bloch, E. M. (2016). A literature review of Zika virus. *Emerging Infectious Diseases*, 22(7), 1185.

Reiley, L. (2020). Commercial fishing industry in free fall as restaurants close, consumers hunker down and vessels tie up. *The Washington Post*.

Ripoll Gallardo, A., Pacelli, B., Alesina, M., Serrone, D., Iacutone, G., Faggiano, F., Della Corte, F., & Allara, E. (2018). Medium-and long-term health effects of earthquakes in high-income countries: a systematic review and meta-analysis. *International Journal of Epidemiology*, 47(4), 1317–1332.

Sagripanti, J., & Lytle, C. D. (2007). Inactivation of influenza virus by solar radiation. *Photochemistry and Photobiology*, 83(5), 1278–1282.

Sahay, S. (2018). Urban adaptation to climate sensitive health effect: Evaluation of coping strategies for dengue in Delhi, India. *Sustainable Cities and Society*, 37, 178–188.

Setti, L., Passarini, F., De Gennaro, G., Di Gilio, A., Palmisani, J., Buono, P., Fornari, G., Perrone, M., Pizzalunga, A., & Barbieri, P. (2020). *Position Paper Relazione circa l'effetto dell'inquinamento da particolato atmosferico e la diffusione di virus nella popolazione. SIMA-Società Italiana di Medicina Ambientale; 2020*.

Sharma, S., Zhang, M., Gao, J., Zhang, H., & Kota, S. H. (2020). Effect of restricted emissions during COVID-19 on air quality in India. *Science of the Total Environment*, 728, 138878.

Singh, A. K., Gupta, H. K., Gupta, K., Singh, P., Gupta, V. B., & Sharma, R. C. (2007). A comparative study of air pollution in Indian cities. *Bulletin of Environmental Contamination and Toxicology*, 78(5), 411–416.

Sirkeci, I., & Yucesahin, M. M. (2020). Coronavirus and Migration: Analysis of Human Mobility and the Spread of COVID-19. *Migration Letters*, 17(2), 379–398.

Sun, J., He, W.-T., Wang, L., Lai, A., Ji, X., Zhai, X., Li, G., Suchard, M. A., Tian, J., & Zhou, J. (2020). COVID-19: epidemiology, evolution, and cross-disciplinary perspectives. *Trends in Molecular Medicine*.

Sutton, M. A., Place, C. J., Eager, M., Fowler, D., & Smith, R. I. (1995). Assessment of the magnitude of ammonia emissions in the United Kingdom. *Atmospheric Environment*, 29(12), 1393–1411.

Tobías, A., Carnerero, C., Reche, C., Massagué, J., Via, M., Minguillón, M. C., Alastuey, A., & Querol, X. (2020). Changes in air quality during the lockdown in Barcelona (Spain) one month into the SARS-CoV-2 epidemic. *Science of the Total Environment*, 138540.

Tollefson, J. (2020). Climate vs coronavirus: Why massive stimulus plans could represent missed opportunities. *Nature*.

Travis, D. J., Carleton, A. M., & Lauritsen, R. G. (2002). Contrails reduce daily temperature range. *Nature*, *418*(6898), 601.

Wang, J., Tang, K., Feng, K., & Lv, W. (2020). High temperature and high humidity reduce the transmission of COVID-19. *Available at SSRN 3551767.*

Wei, Y.-M., Han, R., Wang, C., Yu, B., Liang, Q.-M., Yuan, X.-C., Chang, J., Zhao, Q., Liao, H., & Tang, B. (2020). Self-preservation strategy for approaching global warming targets in the post-Paris Agreement era. *Nature Communications*, *11*(1), 1–13.

Woolhouse, M. E. J., & Gowtage-Sequeria, S. (2005). Host range and emerging and reemerging pathogens. *Emerging Infectious Diseases*, *11*(12), 1842.

Yadav, N., Sharma, C., Peshin, S. K., & Masiwal, R. (2017). Study of intra-city urban heat island intensity and its influence on atmospheric chemistry and energy consumption in Delhi. *Sustainable Cities and Society*, *32*, 202–211.

Zhang, R., Zhang, Y., Lin, H., Feng, X., Fu, T.-M., & Wang, Y. (2020). NOx Emission Reduction and Recovery during COVID-19 in East China. *Atmosphere*, *11*(4), 433.

Zhang, Z., Xu, S., Capinha, C., Weterings, R., & Gao, T. (2019). Using species distribution model to predict the impact of climate change on the potential distribution of Japanese whiting Sillago japonica. *Ecological Indicators*, *104*, 333–340.

Zhu, Y., & Xie, J. (2020). Association between ambient temperature and COVID-19 infection in 122 cities from China. *Science of the Total Environment*, 138201.

Zibulewsky, J. (2001). Defining disaster: The emergency department perspective. *Baylor University Medical Center Proceedings*, *14*(2), 144–149.

Zumla, A., Hui, D. S., & Perlman, S. (2015). Middle East respiratory syndrome. *The Lancet*, *386*(9997), 995–1007.

9 Direct and Indirect Impacts of the COVID-19 Pandemic Crisis on Economy

KEY POINTS

- To highlight the impact of coronaviruses on various sectors of the world's top economy.
- Given the historical persistence of economic activity, the reduction in Gross Domestic Product (GDP) due to imprisonment measures is likely to drag on for several quarters.
- The overall GDP shortfall may be double, as implied by the direct initial effects of imprisonment.
- This persistence reflects two types of spillover across countries. One risk is due to repeated outbreaks of viruses worldwide due to unintentional imprisonment. A more traditional trade and financial integration is interlinks.
- Economic spillovers and spillbacks are major in major economic blocks. If only one or two areas control the epidemic, then there is no immunity from economic effects.
- Countries should adopt imprisonment, border control, and macroeconomic policies that internalize these global views.

INTRODUCTION

COVID-19 virus continues to make its way around the world since the World Health Organization (WHO) first declared COVID-19 a world health emergency in January 2020. The virus has potential health impact of the pandemic in low-income countries, particularly in African countries that already face struggling healthcare systems and a scarcity of skilled health workers, which is of grave concern. While the pathogen's epidemiological trajectory remains uncertain; various mathematical modelers have attempted to estimate the potential health impact of the disease. Their estimates range from 20% to 80% of the global population being infected.

As on 28 July 2020 there are currently no commercially available pharmaceutical interventions or vaccines to prevent infection, treat the disease, or curb the pandemic. Countries are relying on behavior change and non-pharmaceutical interventions (NPIs), including, amongst others, self-isolation of symptomatic individuals; increased hand hygiene; physical distancing; working from home where possible; and school and business closure. National and local governments have closed their borders, restricting the movement of people in an attempt to contain the spread of the disease and to flatten the peak of the epidemic, with the aim of reducing the daily demand on healthcare resources. In the United States, citizens of 40 states, along with a number of cities and counties, have been advised to stay home, while on 24th March, 1.3 billion people in India were placed under a nationwide "lockdown" for 21 days.

The economic fallout from this pandemic is likely to cripple even the most resilient of markets, threatening national and global growth. Although the pathogen has not yet completed its world tour, the global economy is already showing signs of slowing down. Service sectors, including aviation, travel, and tourism, are being hit the hardest. Business activity has ground to a halt in many sectors. Airlines have already experienced a steep fall in traffic on their highest-profit international routes. As tourism and remittances are important sources of employment and income for the poor, respectively. The pandemic is likely to have a significant economic toll. For each month that the COVID-19 crisis persists, the simulations using The International Food Policy Research Institute (IFPRI's) Social Accounting Matrix (SAM) multiplier model for Egypt suggest national Gross Domestic Product (GDP) could fall by between 0.7% and 0.8% (EGP 36–41 billion or $2.3–$2.6 billion). Household incomes are likely to fall, particularly among the poor.

Additionally, in the United States, almost 10.2 million workers filed for unemployment benefits at the end of March. Over the 18-week period from mid-March to mid-July 2020, 52.7 million Americans filed for unemployment insurance.[1,2] On a seasonally adjusted basis, the number of insured unemployed workers was 16.2 million in late-July, down from a peak of 25 million in mid-May, as indicated in Table 9.1. The total number of people claiming benefits in all programs in the week ending July 4, totaled 31.8 million, up from 1.7 million in the comparable week in 2019. The insured unemployment rate was 11.1%, also down from the peak reached in early May. On 8th May 2020, the Bureau of Labor Statistics (BLS) reported that 20 million Americans lost their jobs in April 2020, pushing the total

TABLE 9.1
Seasonally Adjusted Weekly Unemployment Insurance Claims (In Thousands)

Week Ending	Initial Claims	Change from Prior Week	Insured Unemployment	Insured Unemployment Rate	Total Claims
21-Mar-20	3,307	3,025	3,059	2.10%	3,307
28-Mar-20	6,867	3,560	7,446	5.1	10,174
4-Apr-20	6,615	−252	11,914	8.2	16,789
11-Apr-20	5,237	−1,378	15,819	10.9	22,026
18-Apr-20	4,442	−795	18,011	12.4	26,468
25-Apr-20	3,867	−575	22,377	15.4	30,335
2-May-20	3,176	−691	22,548	15.5	33,511
9-May-20	2,687	−489	24,912	17.1	36,198
16-May-20	2,446	−241	20,841	14.3	38,644
23-May-20	2,123	−323	21,268	14.6	40,767
30-May-20	1,897	−226	20,606	14.1	42,664
6-Jun-20	1,566	−331	20,544	14.1	44,230
13-Jun-20	1,540	−26	19,231	13.2	45,770
20-Jun-20	1,482	−58	19,290	13.2	47,252
27-Jun-20	1,408	−74	17,760	12.2	48,660
4-Jul-20	1,310	−98	17,304	11.8	49,970
11-Jul-20	1,307	−3	16,197	11.1	51,270
18-Jul-20	1,416	109			52,693

Source: Department of Labor, CRS calculations

number of unemployed Americans to 23 million,[3] [4] [5] out of a total civilian labor force of 158 million. The increase pushed the national unemployment rate to 14.7% (with some caveats), the highest since the Great Depression of the 1930s.[6] On June 6, BLS reported that nonfarm employment increased by 2.5 million in May, reducing the total number of unemployed Americans to 21 million[7] and pushing the unemployment rate down to 13.5%, again with some caveats.[8] On 2nd July, the BLS also released data on the employment situation in June, indicating that non-farm payroll rose by 4.8 million, lowering the unemployment rate to 11.5%.[9] More than 60% of Americans have lost hours or pay, been laid off, or closed a business in response to the pandemic, with predictions that the US jobless rate could reach as much as 30% in the second quarter of year 2020. The British Chambers of Commerce revealed that by early April, 32% of businesses in the United Kingdom will have temporarily laid-off staff. In many low-income countries, the informal sector is a substantial source of employment. In many of these workers, out-of-pocket (OOP) expenditure for healthcare already comprises a large proportion of household incomes. Increased demands on families are likely to push them further into poverty. The Organization for Economic Co-operation and Development (OECD) predicts that some countries could be dealing with the economic fallout of the COVID-19 pandemic for years to come.

Preliminary data also indicate that US GDP fell by 5.0% in the first quarter of 2020, the largest quarterly decline in GDP since the fourth quarter of 2008 during the global financial crisis.[10] In its 27th May Beige Book analysis, the Federal Reserve (Fed) reported that economic activity had fallen sharply in each of the 12 Federal Reserve districts.[11]

In Europe, governments are attempting a phased reopening of businesses, but over 30 million people in Germany, France, the United Kingdom, Spain, and Italy have applied for state support of their wages, while first-quarter 2020 data indicate the Eurozone economy contracted by 3.8% at an annual rate, the largest quarterly decline since the series began in 1995.[12] Industrial production across the Eurozone as a whole fell by 17% in April, raising the annual decline to 28%, surpassing the contraction experienced during the global financial crisis.[13] The European Commission's 8th July 2020 forecast projected that European Union (EU) economic growth in 2020 could contract by 8.3% and only partially recover in 2021.[14] After protracted talks, European leaders agreed on 21st July to a new €750 billion (about $859 billion) pandemic economic assistance package to support European economies.

On 27th May 2020, European Central Bank (ECB) President Christine Lagarde warned that the Eurozone economy could contract by 8% to 12% in 2020, a level of damage to the Eurozone economy that Lagarde characterized as being unsurpassed in peacetime.[15] Foreign investors have pulled an estimated $26 billion out of developing Asian economies not including more than $16 billion out of India, increasing concerns about a major economic recession in Asia. Some estimates indicate that 29 million people in Latin America could fall into poverty, reversing a decade of efforts to narrow income inequality. Some analysts are also concerned that Africa, after escaping the initial spread of infections, is now facing a sharp increase in rates of infection outside South Africa, Egypt, Nigeria, Algeria, and Ghana, where most of the infections have occurred to date.[16]

The true cost of COVID-19 will therefore be far greater than the direct health costs of treating cases. Indeed, the indirect costs of the disease will far outstrip the costs of testing, treating, and hospitalization of patients. The extent of these indirect costs, including the economic damage, will depend on how protracted the pandemic becomes, the steps governments take to contain it, the impact of and public adherence to behavioral measures such as physical distancing imposed by authorities, and how much economic support governments and development agencies are willing to deploy during the pandemic's immediate impact and aftermath. The availability of effective treatments and vaccines, as well as new diagnostic tests, will also determine the level of NPIs that will need to be retained. Additionally, the potential mitigating effect of heat and humidity is likely to have a bearing on the seasonality of epidemics. Some experts have warned of a second wave of the pandemic in the autumn, similar to what was observed during the 1918 Spanish flu pandemic. Indeed, Singapore has already reported an upsurge in new cases triggering a second lockdown.

Although the COVID-19 pandemic is not only the most serious global health crisis since the 1918 Great Influenza (Spanish flu), it is set to become one of the most economically costly pandemics in recent history. Although the economic impacts of the COVID-19 pandemic are globally, it is increasingly hitting low and middle-income countries and the poor. International travel restrictions and the full or partial closure of businesses and industries in Asia, Europe, and North America have led to a collapse in global travel and are expected to reduce the flows of remittances.

The readiness of healthcare systems to navigate potential recurrence will require widespread testing, real-time surveillance, rigorous contact tracing, and rapid, targeted quarantining to isolate cases and contacts (as was done in the Republic of Korea, Singapore, and Taiwan) and will influence any resulting economic shocks.

Experience with past epidemics provides some insights into the various channels through which economic costs could arise, in the short as well as longer term. At the same time, COVID-19 differs from previous episodes in several important ways. Notably, the globally synchronized lockdowns and trauma of financial markets reinforce one another into an unprecedented economic sudden stop. For these reasons, the COVID-19 global recession is unique. However, past epidemics can shed light on transmission channels to the economy, especially when stringent containment policies are not in place.

This section provides an early review of empirical studies on the economic costs of epidemics. We first review studies on past epidemics and then turn to the latest quantitative estimates of COVID-19's impact on global growth.

IMPACT ANALYSIS FROM PAST EPIDEMICS AS A STATISTICAL LESSON

Studies on past epidemics identify a number of channels through which economic costs can arise. The loss of productive workforce through mortality and illness is a key channel, particularly prominent in severe pandemics such as the 1918 influenza.[17] But the study of past epidemics provides useful insights on several of their economic consequences, including costs due to weak consumer sentiment, high exposure of the services sector, the impact of social distancing policies, and potential financial amplification. All these factors remain relevant today, albeit to different degrees. Table 9.2 summarizes the methodologies and findings of selected studies on the macroeconomic costs of past epidemics. A number of insights emerge.

First, the estimated costs of epidemics vary significantly, depending on their severity and how they were dealt with. The 1918 influenza is generally considered as the costliest epidemic in modern history.[35] Correia et al (2020)[36] estimate that this pandemic curtailed manufacturing activity by around 20%, while Barro et al (2020)[37] estimate the negative impact on GDP to be around 6–8% overall. Social distancing measures were introduced to contain the 1918 pandemic, but these varied across jurisdictions and there was no synchronized stop in economic activity. Correia et al (2020) find that the US states that introduced containment measures earlier had relatively higher medium-term growth. This suggests

TABLE 9.2

Economic Losses from Past Epidemics

Epidemic-(s)	Fatalities	Studies	Studies and Methods	Economic Losses
Influenza pandemic, 1918–19	Up to 50 million	Barro et al (2020)[18]	Cross-country panel regressions	6 ppt lower GDP growth and 8 ppt lower consumption growth overall
		Brainerd and Siegler (2003)[19]	US states data	Mortality significantly lowers growth over following decade
		Correia et al (2020)[20]	US states data	18% decline in manufacturing activity per year; prompter and more aggressive containment helped cushion the impact
SARS, 2003	774	Lee and McKibbin (2004)[21]	CGE model	0.1% loss in global GDP in 2003
		Hai et al (2004)[22]	Chinese surveys	1–2 ppt lower GDP growth in China
H5N1 avian influenza, 2003–19	455	Obayelu, A. E. (2007)[23]	Socio-economic analysis using structured interviewed scheduling process	Nigeria rural and urban communities have caused serious threat on poultry industry, food security and livelihoods. 75% poultry farms found stopped ordering and 80% households stopped purchase and consumption.
		Chang, C. C. et al. (2007)[24]	Input-Output (IO) Analysis Model and Computable General Equilibrium (CGE)	The possible damage brought by lowering domestic consumption that impact on real GDP is around −0.1%∼−0.4%, and labor demand would decrease 4.9%∼6.4%.
		Burns et al (2006)[25]	World Bank estimate	0.1% loss in annual global GDP 0.4% for Asia
Ebola, 2014–16	11,323	Huber, C. et al. (2018)[26]	Systematic review of the grey (reports produced by non-profit or nongovernmental organizations, government, or industry)	Loss of GDP, estimated economic burden of the outbreak range from $2.8 to $32.6 billion
		World Bank (2014)[27]	CGE model	2.1 ppt lower GDP growth in Guinea, 3.4 ppt in Liberia, and 3.3 ppt for Sierra Leone in the first year of the epidemic
H1N1	13	Keogh-Brown. et al. (2010)[28]	Ecomod one-country CGE model	GDP losses from the disease of approximately 0.5% of GDP for a mild pandemic to just over 2% for a severe pandemic.
		Rassy, D. et al. (2013)[29]	Single linear regressions	Mexican tourism and pork sectors losses of around $US2.8bn. Pork trade deficit of $US27m with H1N1 incidence (p=0.048, r=0.37).
MERS	780	Joo, H. et al. (2019)[30]	Interconnected sector analysis	Approx. 0.2% of GDP fall that estimated US$2.6 billion in lost revenue for the tourism.
ZIKA	3489	Macciocchi, D. et al. (2016)[31]	Linear regression mode	GDP reach 1.6% and −0.90% average return because of decreasing tourism
Hypothetical influenza pandemics		Global Preparedness Monitoring Board (2019)[32]	A 1918-type pandemic	4.8% loss in annual global GDP
		Fan et al (2016)[33][32]	A 1918-type pandemic; Includes the intrinsic cost of mortality to GDP loss	0.4–1% of GDP loss per year due to exante prospects of a pandemic, 86% of which is due to mortality and 14% to income loss. For moderate pandemics, the share of income loss is larger at 40%
		Arnold et al (2006)[34]	A 1918-type pandemic	4.25% loss in annual GDP 2.25 ppt from the supply side; 2 ppt from the demand side

that, at the time, the economic costs were due primarily to loss of lives, spread out over three years (see also Fan et al (2016))[38]. A number of studies estimate the cost of a hypothetical 1918-type influenza pandemic in the modern era. The Global Preparedness Monitoring Board (2019),[39] for example, estimates that the cost of such a pandemic could be close to 5% of global GDP. Costs associated with other milder epidemics are typically an order of magnitude lower. The estimate for the SARS epidemic in 2003, for instance, is only 0.1% of global GDP according to Lee and McKibbin (2004).[40] Those of the H1N1 "bird flu" and Ebola epidemics are similarly small, at least relative to global output.

Second, macroeconomic costs can materialize through both supply and demand effects. In response to an epidemic risk, workers may limit social interactions by reducing both labor supply and consumption. Arnold et al (2006)[41] examine the supply side channel in a 1918-like pandemic scenario, by combining an estimated loss of employee workdays with an estimated productivity per worker.[42] They conclude that, in the first year, the pandemic reduces GDP by about 2.3%. To assess the demand side, the same study draws on the SARS episode of 2003 and assumes that a pandemic's effects would be especially severe among industries whose products required customers to congregate. The overall demand side effects would reduce GDP by 2%.

Third, pandemics can have long-lasting adverse effects on the economy. On the supply side, Fan et al (2016) find that, in the case of the 1918 influenza pandemic, the most important cost was mortality and the reduction of the labor force.[43] A one-time reduction in the labor force would raise the ratio of capital to labor and lower the rate of return to capital, slowing the pace of capital accumulation and GDP growth for many years.

Pandemics may also persistently depress aggregate demand. Jordà et al (2020)[44] study the long-run effects of a sample of 12 major epidemics in Europe stretching back to the 14th century. They find that pandemics were followed by multiple decades of low natural interest rates, due to higher precautionary saving and depressed investment opportunities. Indeed, unlike wars, pandemics do not destroy physical capital, and typically give rise to a long period of excess capital per surviving worker.

Some general lessons from these studies may be relevant for the current episode. First, when an epidemic reaches a global scale with a substantial loss of lives, the economic loss can also be very high and persistent. This means that confinement measures, while costly, also have economic benefits in preserving the workforce. These are relevant for the cost-benefit assessments of alternative confinement policies, in addition to the primary objective of saving lives. The literature also makes clear that the interactions between supply and demand transmission channels are not specific to COVID-19, but a feature of epidemic shocks in general.

PANDEMIC SCENARIO

GLOBAL PANDEMIC SCENARIO

In the global pandemic scenario, we aim to capture relatively rapid recovery and limited contagion, where the shocks are implemented to the full degree in China, but other countries experience shocks amounting to only half the shocks described below:

- Underutilization of labor by 3% across all sectors in the global economy results in declining capital usage.

- Trade costs of global imports and exports increase by 25%, applied across all goods and services.
- Sharp drop in international tourism (captured via a 50% tax on inbound and outbound tourist-related services such as transport, accommodation, etc.).
- Reallocation of demand away from sectors requiring human interaction.

AMPLIFIED GLOBAL PANDEMIC SCENARIO

In the amplified global pandemic scenario, we capture a bigger reduction in annual output due to a deeper and more prolonged pandemic. The same shocks are assumed in all countries, effectively doubling the shocks for all countries and keeping the China shock unchanged.

GLOBAL ECONOMY AFFECTION AND POLICIES TO COMPETING COVID-19

GOVERNMENTS POLICY

The WHO first declared COVID-19 a world health emergency in January 2020. Since then, the emergency has evolved into a global public health and economic crisis that has affected the $90 trillion global economy beyond anything experienced in nearly a century. Governments are attempting to balance often-competing policy objectives between addressing the public health crisis and economic considerations that include, but are not limited to these:

- Confronting ballooning budget deficits weighed against increasing spending to support unemployed workers and social safety nets.
- Providing financial support for national health systems that are under pressure to develop vaccines while also funding efforts to care for and safeguard citizens.
- Implementing monetary and fiscal policies that support credit markets and sustain economic activity, while also assisting businesses under financial distress.
- Implementing fiscal policies to stimulate economic activity, while consumers in developed economies sharply increase their savings as households face limited spending opportunities, or a form of involuntary saving, and concerns over their jobs, incomes, and the course of their economies, or precautionary saving.
- Intervention by central banks and monetary authorities generally in sovereign debt and corporate bond markets to stabilize markets and ensure liquidity are raising concerns among some analysts that this activity is compromising the ability of the markets to perform their traditional functions of pricing risk and allocating capital.
- Fiscal and monetary policies that have been adopted to date to address the immediate impact of the health crisis compared with the mix of such policies between assisting households, firms, or state and local governments that may be needed going forward should the health and economic crises persist.

Policymakers and financial and commodity market participants generally expected a global economic recovery in the third quarter of 2020, assuming that there is not a second wave of transition, but much work has been done. Some forecasts, however, raise the prospects that the pandemic could negatively affect global economic growth more extensively and for a longer period of time with a slow, drawn-out recovery. Without a quick resolution of the health crisis, the economic crisis may persist longer than most forecasters have assumed and require policymakers to weigh the most effective mix of additional fiscal and monetary policies that may be required without the benefit of a relevant precedent to follow. Additional measures may have to balance the competing requirements of households, firms, and state and local governments. Various US States reversed course in late June to impose or reimpose social distancing guidelines and close down businesses that had begun opening as a result of a rise in new confirmed cases of COVID-19, raising the prospect of a delayed recovery.

In addition, a major decline in GDP among European economies was also forecast by the European Commission in July 2020, with its spring report forecasting a less vibrant recovery in 2021. Which has also been seen to a large extent. Differences in policy approaches between countries are threatening to inflict longer-term damage to the global economy by impairing international political, trade, and economic relations, particularly between countries that promote nationalism and those that argue for a coordinated international response to the pandemic. Policy differences are also straining relations between developed and developing economies and between northern and southern members of the Eurozone, challenging alliances, and conventional concepts of national security, and raising questions about the future of global leadership.

In some countries, the pandemic has elevated the importance of public health as a national security issue and as a national economic priority on a par with traditional national security concerns such as terrorism, cyber-attacks, and proliferation of weapons of mass destruction.[45] The pandemic-related economic and human costs could have long-term repercussions for economies through the tragic loss of life and job losses that derail careers and permanently shutter businesses. Fiscal and monetary measures implemented to prevent a financial crisis and sustain economic activity may also inadvertently be adding to income and wealth disparities. Within some countries, the economic fallout is widening racial and socio-economic cleavages and increasing social unrest.

Non-Government Business Policy

Recent private-sector GDP forecasts point to a substantially larger GDP short-term impact of the COVID-19 pandemic than in previous outbreak episodes, or indeed severe recessions in the past. Figure 9.1 shows selected private sector forecasts made in the last week of March all pointed to very deep contractions in the first half of 2020. For the United States, the quarterly contraction was expected to be the largest in the second quarter. It was also notable that, by the end of 2020, the level of US GDP will still be reduced to 4-10% in trend under these estimates. For the global economy, the quarterly contraction during the first two quarters ranges from 10% to 20%, as China's GDP is expected to contract by over 40% in the first quarter. But in the event the Chinese economy recovers rapidly, global GDP may recover close to trend by year-end. At the same time, there are also worse case scenarios, under which the second-quarter contraction is larger and the recovery more protracted across all major economies. It remains uncertain how fast the losses could be made up, if at all, once the global economy recovers.

The economic cost of the COVID-19 pandemic can be proxied by GDP forgone, namely the difference between current forecasts and pre-COVID-19 outlook (dashed lines in

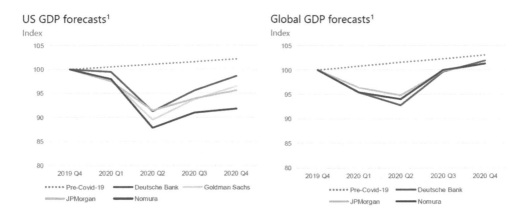

FIGURE 9.1   GDP forecasts by private sector, as of the end of March 2020. (Sources: Deutsche Bank; Goldman Sachs; JPMorgan; Nomura.) Note: [1]As of 31st March for Deutsche Bank and Goldman Sachs; as of 27th March for JPMorgan and Nomura. Pre-Covid-19 paths assume US quarterly growth of 2.1% and global growth of 3.1%.

Figure 9.1 above). Under the baseline scenario, annual output loss ranges between 5% and 9% of pre-COVID-19 estimates for the United States, and between 4% and 4.5% for the global economy. In worse scenarios, these costs could reach 11% for the United States and 8% for the global economy. The latest International Monetary Fund (IMF) (2020) forecasts released on 14th April already inch towards these scenarios, with the United States and global output losses in 2020 projected at 8% and 6% respectively. These costs are an order of magnitude higher than the estimated costs of previous epidemics, and exceed those during the Great Financial Crisis in 2008–2009—when OECD countries on average lost 3% of GDP per year.

There are also possible long-term damages from a prolonged economic shutdown, harder to quantify but potentially significant. Bankrupt firms will make no output contribution after containment is lifted, and could disrupt supply chains of surviving firms. Unemployed workers could lose skills and long-term relationships with firms which are costly and take time to re-establish. Hardship and demoralization could in turn have an impact on labor productivity. Experiences from past recessions suggest that these scars on the economic fabric can be deep and persistent (Eichengreen (2020).[46]

As now we understand that most companies have just felt a shock right now and are working on immediate stabilization. However, what might unfold in one or two months for industries like FMCG, 3PL, etc. is an unstable and unforeseen demand, shortage of suppliers for intermediate goods required to meet the market demand inventory shortages, and a broken supply chain network for distribution. Considering a likely scenario, neither optimistic nor pessimistic, that the world would recover from COVID-19 by second quarter of 2020, what they should be doing as an executive right now to face the upcoming challenges?

DIRECT AND INDIRECT COSTS

In this brief, the section outlines the direct and indirect costs of the COVID-19 pandemic which may impact the global economy. For the purposes of discussion, the indirect impacts have been broken down to supply and demand shock; however, the various sectors, agents,

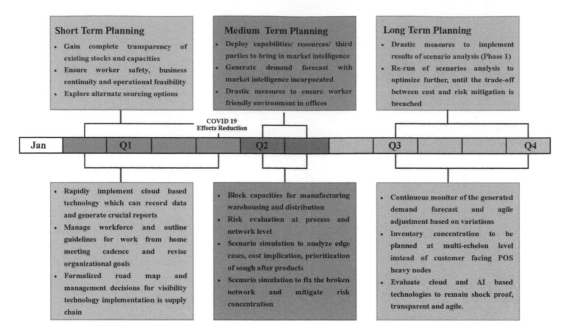

FIGURE 9.2   Non-Government Business Polices and planning in competing COVID-19 pandemic crisis.

and markets in the economy are interdependent and will have knock-on effects on one another. Short-term impacts will lead to a loss of wages and capital flows which may lead to more systemic long-term effects changes (as shown in Figure 9.2).

DIRECT COST

Direct costs include the cost of testing and contact tracing, in addition to the costs of hospitalization, intensive medical care, control interventions for managing the disease, and the salaries of healthcare workers. They will also include the cost of vaccines, treatments, rapid diagnostic tests, and antibody tests, if and when they become available. The true direct costs would also include the costs of research and development of new therapies and vaccines, although assigning a value to these may be challenging. Direct costs also include OOP expenditure. In low- and middle-income countries, this may comprise up to 50% of all health expenditure if governments do not make provisions for free testing and treatment for patients with COVID-19. OOP expenditure includes the costs of transport to/from hospitals for testing and treatment and other expenditures such as the cost of protection measures that households/businesses would not otherwise have spent money on, for example purchasing hand sanitizer and disinfectants.

INDIRECT COST

Indirect costs are all of the additional costs associated with either being ill or the economic impact of behaviors adopted to avoid becoming infected. They incorporate productivity losses arising from worker absenteeism due to morbidity and mortality, including the loss of wages as well as opportunity costs. They also include spillover effects on the economy from aversion interventions that are either government or self-imposed to avoid exposure to the virus. The outcome of these effects induces both supply and demand shocks. Supply shocks arise from the closure of businesses, hotels, restaurants, and other businesses that are deemed "non-essential." Demand shocks result from decreased consumption, travel, transport, and other unnecessary expenditures. Each of these is discussed separately below:

Supply Shocks

Manufacturing, Production and Warehousing

Production in China was substantially affected by the government-imposed shutdown in Hubei province and other areas. Hubei province plays a major role in the Chinese economy, as the largest transportation hub in central China and a significant industrial base that includes a mixture of traditional and hi-tech sectors, such as automobile manufacture, food processing, electronics equipment manufacturing, textile factories, and petrochemical industries, as well as iron and steel production. Many manufacturing firms around the world rely on imported intermediate products from China and other countries affected by the disease. For example, some car manufacturers, including Nissan and Hyundai, temporarily closed their factories outside of China because they were unable to get the parts they needed.

The slowdown in economic activity—and transportation restrictions—in affected countries will have an impact on the production and profitability of specific global companies, particularly those involved in manufacturing or in producing the raw materials used in manufacturing. Small- and medium-sized firms, especially firms that rely on intermediate goods from affected regions and which are unable to easily switch sourcing these goods, may have greater difficulty surviving the disruption. Returning businesses to operational health after such a severe shutdown will be extremely challenging, with most industries needing to reactivate their entire supply chain.

Communication channels should be established to gain complete transparency on existing assets and processes. Business leaders should be completely aware of the capacities and stock they hold in their arsenal. Armed with the right demand planning techniques, the next power play should be in securing capacities for manufacturing, production, and warehousing space. Since demand forecasting cannot be completely accurate, other edge cases like ±10% of the forecast should be simulated to understand capacity requirements and understand the cost implications associated with it.

The analysis will draw on a cross-functional team that includes marketing and sales, operations, and strategy staff, and also individuals who can tailor updated macroeconomic forecasts to the expected impact on the business. An advanced S&OP platform can better match production and supply planning with the forecasted demand in a variety of circumstances. Once capacity is blocked and the required processes are set in motion, product prioritization needs to be strategized to manufacture high-demand products that come under essentials and medical essentials for the short and medium-term requirement.

In this time of crisis, understanding current and future logistics capacity by mode and their associated trade-offs will be even more essential than usual, as well as prioritizing logistics needs in required capacity and time sensitivity of product delivery. Consequently, even as companies look to ramp up production and make up time in their value chains, they should prebook logistics capacity to minimize exposure to potential cost increases. Collaborating with partners can be an effective strategy to gain priority and increase capacity on more favorable terms. Maintaining a nimble approach to logistics management will be imperative in rapidly adapting to any situational or environmental changes.

Supply Chain Disruption

Businesses around the world are dealing with lost revenue and disrupted supply chains due to China's factory shutdowns. China has become the primary source of many crucial medical drugs, including penicillin, heparin, and medications essential for surgery. Up to 80% of the world's basic ingredients for manufacturing antibiotics are produced in China. The US pharmaceutical industry reported fears of drug shortages as India faced lockdowns on 24th March. India is the world's leading producer of high-volumes of sterile injectable drugs, supplying almost half of the generic drugs used in countries such as the United States. On 27th February, the US Food and Drug Administration (FDA) released a statement saying the United States was experiencing its first drug shortage directly related to the COVID-19 pandemic. These stock-outs can leave many people without the essential medicines they need.

At the same time, supply chains have been experiencing systemic demand shocks. The shortage of masks, gloves, and other personal protective equipment, in addition to shortages in the numbers of ventilators, has been well documented. On top of this, some individuals have been stocking up on groceries and household items in preparation for compliance with restrictions on movement, in some cases buying several months' worth of goods in a single day, particularly if they begin to see shelves with low levels of stock. A classic example of this is hygiene products, such as toilet paper, hand sanitizers, and surface disinfectants, which have seen sudden spikes in demand, leading to panic buying and stock-out situations. The shortages are compounded by the scarcity of air and ocean freight options to move products, hence lead times have doubled. An Institute for Supply Management survey revealed that more than 80% of companies believe that their organization will experience some impact because of disruption due to COVID-19. Of those, 16% of companies reported having already adjusted revenue targets downward by an average of 5.6% because of the pandemic.

The COVID-19 pandemic has shown that supply-chain disruptions could wreak greater havoc on the global economy than most governments had realized. Businesses that are nimble enough to switch suppliers and that have sufficient liquidity to survive periods of low sales and revenue will have a competitive advantage.

Education

Governments in 188 countries around the world have temporarily closed educational institutions in an attempt to contain the spread of COVID-19. These closures are impacting more than 89%, or 1.5 billion members, of the world's student population. Although necessary, school closures cause huge economic and social disruption, especially for children. In the United States, 30 million students depend on free or reduced-price meals at school for lunch, breakfast, snacks, and, in some cases, dinner. Many of these students rely on a structured support system, which they may not be receiving at home, particularly in the case of children of low-wage workers in essential businesses who cannot afford to miss work. While some schools have instituted online learning, this creates additional equity considerations, particularly when some students may not have access to a computer or a reliable internet connection at home. The long-term effects of these disruptions are difficult to estimate. While some children will catch up on missed learning, others may eventually drop out, affecting their long-term earning capacity. We will discuss this in detail in a later chapter.

Other Health Considerations

The effect of COVID-19 on the management of other diseases or illnesses cannot be ignored. In addition to the impact on the availability of medicines and medical equipment discussed above, with overburdened hotlines and healthcare systems, patients in need of medical care for other critical, non-COVID-19 related issues may fall by the wayside. Many other illnesses, such as malaria, share some of the same initial symptoms as COVID-19 and, without an expert differential diagnosis, patients may be put at risk. In March, a 28-year-old man who returned to London from Zanzibar died of malaria, after failing to get through to the National Health Service (NHS) hotline due to the volume of COVID-19-related calls. People suffering from mental health disorders, including those struggling with anxiety, depression, and substance use disorders at higher risk of becoming increasingly symptomatic as a result of uncertainty, loneliness, and isolation.

In less developed countries, the added surge in demand resulting from COVID-19 is likely to cripple struggling healthcare systems. During the 2014–2015 Ebola outbreak in West Africa, access to healthcare services was reduced by 50%, exacerbating malaria, HIV/AIDS, and tuberculosis mortality rates. The indirect impact of mortality from other diseases actually surpassed the number of deaths caused by Ebola.

Demand Shocks and Fluctuation

Inventory Crisis and Bullwhip Effect on Demand

Demand across industries are seeing an all-time dip, except for essentials and pharmaceutical products. On one side of the spectrum, we have pharmaceutical and sanitization products whose demand has splurged, and the firms are struggling to meet the demand. According to Nielson, in Malaysia, sales of sanitizers hit almost RM1 million (US$237,176) in the week ended 26th January 2020, which is more than 800% above the weekly average.[47] On the other end of the spectrum, we have industries like electronics, aviation automobiles, etc. whose demand had decreased considerably. Apple has released an investor update in which it announced that it will not be able to meet the revenue guidance it published for the March Quarter.[48] This is both because of supply and demand. Apple's production units are strained due to the high dependence on Chinese suppliers for intermediate goods. Also, demand for Apple's products in China has reduced due to the prevailing public health crisis. McKinsey predicts that the impact on demand slows down the growth of the global economy—between 1.8% and 2.2% instead of the 2.5% growth predicted at the start of the year.

Multiple industries are soon going to face a bullwhip effect in their demand forecasting. A bullwhip effect is a phenomenon of overestimating the fall in market demand which starts with the retailer on the minor scale and amplifies as it passes through the supply chain.

Thus, the actual demand forecast that the producer or manufacturer receives would be much smaller than the actual demand forecast from the retailer who sells on the ground. A rudimentary demand forecast would result in revenue loss/stocked capital due to the error from the bullwhip effect.

Leveraging technology with advanced forecasting techniques that does not stick to one algorithm, but instead use forecast errors to find the best-fit forecast, should be adopted to have a near accurate forecast of demand to balance out resource utilization, inventory management, and lost sales of demanded products. Figure 9.3 indicates the expected impact of COVID-19 on demand for various sectors relative to baseline forecast. While certain sectors like smartphones and automotive are going to see a sharp drop, there are sectors like online retail with a surge in demand. There are multiple factors like supply outages, movement restriction, etc. for the varied demand and it is evident that demand is highly uncertain in days to come.

The disrupted network will also have a significant impact on the supply lead time and this problem is yet to emerge in most parts of the world. Shipping by sea to the United States or Europe from China would take around 30 days. This indicates that the shipment from China that started from Chinese ports before the closure for the Chinese holiday in January would arrive in the United States or Europe in the last week of February. Firms usually store large inventory due to long Chinese holidays during their New Year celebrations. This might give firms some breathing space.

However, this indicates that there might be a large-scale shut down in manufacturing and production in most parts of the world for at least a month, provided China recovers completely from COVID-19 and production starts in Chinese firms before March ends. If not, the shutdown might prolong. Commercial data and analysis company Dun and Bradstreet estimate that there are around 22 million businesses (90% of all active businesses in China) within the regions impacted by COVID-19. This is likely to impact at least 56,000 companies around the world with suppliers either directly or indirectly.[49] Quarantines and lockdowns in the other parts of the world outside China are only going to increase the magnitude of this shortage in inventory of intermediate and finished goods.

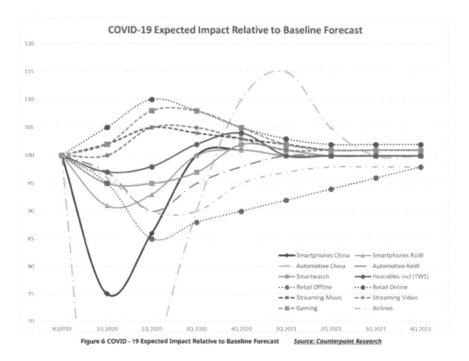

Figure 6 COVID - 19 Expected Impact Relative to Baseline Forecast   *Source: Counterpoint Research*

FIGURE 9.3   COVID-19 expected impact relative to baseline forecast

Unpredictable demand spikes and possible inventory shortages call for optimizing the inventory using advanced algorithm which can consider not only demand variability but also supply variability to generate adequate inventory levels and policies. Historically, inventory optimization techniques were largely used to avoid bullwhip effect. However, along with the bullwhip effect, the current problem would be to predict the safety stock level in the disrupted network (non-functional warehouses and factories). Leveraging technology will help enterprises to determine accurate safety stock level for current mid-term, and long-term planning and decision making.

Capital Flows and Trade in Goods and Services

Restrictions on movement and hence economic activities also have an impact on trade and investment through reduced demand for goods and services. Global declines in economic activity will reduce trade and affect imports of consumer goods from developing countries, particularly those with highly concentrated trade exposures to the EU and the United States.

Tourism and Travel Industry

The travel and tourism industry has been the hardest hit by the economic disruption from the COVID-19 pandemic, with impacts on both travel supply and demand as well as huge job losses. In 2018, the travel and tourism industry accounted for 319 million jobs worldwide. Most airlines have already cut their flying capacity by at least 75% and announced widespread staff redundancies. Flybe, a UK regional carrier, was one of the first airlines to collapse following the emergence of the pandemic. According to the International Air Transport Association (IATA), COVID-19 cost USD 252 billion as revenue in year 2020. The United Nations World Tourism Organization (UNWTO) estimated that international tourist arrivals dropped by 20 to 30% in 2020. This resulted in a loss of 300–450 billion USD in international tourism receipts. Severe acute respiratory syndrome (SARS), a previous disease outbreak caused by another newly emerged coronavirus, and which had a much narrower geographical reach and shorter impact, resulted in losses of USD 30–50 billion; this suggests that the potential losses from COVID-19 could be far higher than the estimates outlined above. The countries most likely to be negatively impacted are those that rely heavily on international tourism. For example, in the Maldives, travel and tourism contributes more than 60% of national GDP. In detail, we will discuss in later chapter.

Personal Consumption (Retail Sales, Restaurants, etc.)

The prolonged economic disruption resulting from the COVID-19 pandemic is likely to lead to lower consumer and business confidence and decreased personal spending across a broad range of categories, with spillover effects for a multitude of other sectors. For example, retailers around the world are suspending or canceling clothing orders, threatening millions of factory jobs in Asia. Businesses that were retaining employees in the hope of a temporary impact will soon begin to lay them off, meaning households will therefore have less income to spend. During the SARS epidemic in 2003, retail sales growth in China declined by almost 3%.

Some large sectors of the economy, notably food and consumer goods, are likely to suffer much less as they tend to be essential, and purchasing these goods does not involve a high risk of infection. However, other sectors, such as non-essential goods, luxury goods, and restaurants, are likely to be hit hard.

Financial Market Losses

The impact of COVID-19 is likely to spillover from the real economy to the financing and financial markets. Disruption to shipments and production may create financial problems for some firms, particularly those with heavy debt. Traders may take investment positions that are unprofitable under the current conditions, weakening trust in financial instruments and markets. This could lead to equity and corporate bond market decline and/or financial market disruption, exposing investors who have underpriced risk.

As a response to the lockdowns in Europe during March, global stock markets plunged and oil prices tumbled, losing a third of their value—the biggest daily rout since the 1991 Gulf War. The Dow Jones and the S&P 500 Index are currently trading at more than 25% below their recent record highs. Although the Dow Jones has since shown signs of bouncing back, several experts have warned that the market meltdown is far from over.

The SARS epidemic is estimated to have cost the global economy around USD 40 billion (or 0.1% of global GDP). The impact of COVID-19 is expected to be substantially higher given its extended reach. The OECD and the IMF have warned that the economic shock from the virus is already larger than the global financial crisis of 2008. While legislators across the developed world including the ECB, the UK, and the US have already begun to deliver economic relief plans to help minimize the likelihood of an economic recession, economists have estimated that the global economy will shrink to between 0.5% and 1.75% through 2020 with economic losses of USD 1–2.7 trillion. In addition, the United Nation (UN) has also projected that foreign direct investment flows could fall between 5% and 15% plunging low-income countries into further disadvantage. Although the actual economic impact of COVID-19 will be difficult to assess until the pandemic is over, bold policy measures and innovative mechanisms will be needed to protect the most vulnerable from economic ruin and to sustain economic growth and financial stability. At the same time, countries will need to prioritize a strengthening of their surveillance and response systems to safeguard against the economic impact of future threats to health security.

GDP Glimpses of Top 10 Economic Countries in the World

GDP has been standardized as an economic indicator by the national accounts of the United Nations system, which measures the total output of all final goods and services produced by a country during a given period of time (either yearly or quarterly). It is used to compare countries' economic performance, but very often comparisons are widely used to estimate and assess living standards, progress, or social welfare among countries. There are three ways to calculate GDP: the income approach, production approach, and expenditure approach. For this research purpose, we used the expenditure approach to calculate GDP as it best relates to the data used in our analysis. The expenditure method measures the total expenditure incurred by all entities on goods and services within the domestic boundaries of a country. Mathematically inclusion of GDP according to expenditure method is as follows:

$$GDP_{exp.} = C_{G\&S} + I_B + G_{P\&S} + Net\ Export$$

where, $C_{G\&S} + I_B + G_{P\&S}$ denotes the total consumer spending on goods and services, I_B denotes the total investor spending on business capital goods, $G_{P\&S}$ denotes the government spending on public goods and services and net export is the difference between export and import i.e.,

$$Net\ Export = Export - Import$$

According to the data appeared in the World Economic Outlook (WEO)[50] [51] that are compiled by the IMF considered in this research and selected top ten largest economies of the world. Besides the largest economies, these countries are the engine of the development and controlling around 66.49% economy of the world (detail in Table 9.2) according to the World Bank's update, published in July 2019.[52]

Consumer spending plays a major role in worldwide GDP growth, for example, with the US economy topping the last few years, a major reason being that almost 70% (two-third) of GDP is contributed by consumer spending, while 20% more 15% contribution is government budget and business investment respectively.[53] [54] According to IMF data, the US GDP is currently at a deficit of 5.9%.

COMPUTATIONAL MODEL FOR VISUAL ANALYSIS OF COVID-19'S IMPACT ON THE GLOBAL ECONOMY

The global economy has been interrupted so much that some are wondering if a second Great Depression is coming our way. While this is nothing more than a speculation at the moment, we can see through objective numbers that the pandemic is, indeed, impacting our economy. Below are several statistics and visualizations to give you a better understanding of where the economy stands as of now.

ENVISAGE MODEL

Environmental Impact and Sustainability Applied General Equilibrium Model (ENVISAGE) (as shown in Figure 9.4) is a computable general equilibrium (CGE) model that assesses interactions between economies and the global environment as affected by anthropogenic greenhouse gas emissions.[55] It is a recursive dynamic multi-sector, multi-region CGE model. Its emissions and climate module link economic activities directly to changes in global mean temperature. The model also links changes in temperature to impacts on economic variables such as agricultural yields or damages created by sea-level rise. Issues analyzed include the economics of climate change, impact of climate change on economy, adaptation to climate change, and distributional consequences of climate change. Here the model has been configured and used for a short-term closure with the following assumptions:

- Production elasticities have been reduced to near zero, so there is little substitution possibility across inputs in production.
- In order to capture the typically durable relationship within global value chains, trade elasticities for goods have been reduced from their standard values to represent the short-run inability to replace imported components and final goods with products from other countries. The elasticity between domestic and imported goods has been set to 0.4. The elasticity of substitution across import sources has been set to 0.8.
- Labor supply is exogenous, while wages adjust to equate demand and supply of labor. The return to capital is fixed, while supply of capital is endogenous.

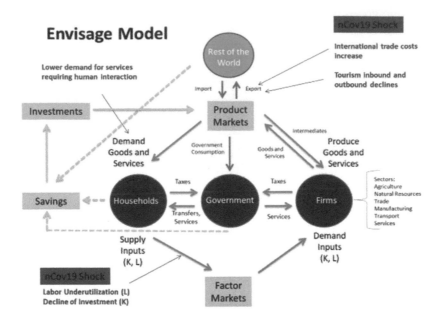

FIGURE 9.4   Implications of the COVID-19 as implemented in the ENVISAGE model.

Considering the ENVISAGE model to analysis the effect of COVID-19 on following four sets of shocks, but all are assumed to occur simultaneously, i.e., the final shock encompasses all shocks.[56] The duration of the shocks is currently unknown, though, based on prior events, it is likely to last from 8 to 12 weeks and most likely unsynchronized across countries.

World Supply Shock Capacity Reduction

The first shock is a drop in employment by 3% below the baseline. With lower availability of labor, we would expect wages, ceteris paribus, to rise, while return to capital is unchanged under our assumptions. Lower labor also means lower demand for capital, as firms need a combination of labor and capital to produce goods and services.

Underutilization of capacity takes place due to factory closures (workers stay home, leaving capital and natural resources idle) as well as social distancing forcing workers to stay at home. Due to higher rates of contagion, immediate unemployment consequences of COVID-related business closures and negative demand shock, we conservatively assume the underutilization of the labor force to be 3% on average over the whole year across all sectors of the economy.[57] There is a lot of uncertainty surrounding these assumptions, and the country-specific employment effects will depend on the duration and intensity of the pandemic and containment measures, the sectoral composition of employment, and the flexibility of the labor market.

As of global pandemic scenario assumes that the pandemic hits China the hardest, but also hurts other countries, so we use it as an example to explain the impacts on other countries. The global pandemic is expected to reduce Chinese GDP by 3.7% (all percentage changes are reported in relation to the baseline). The impact on China becomes progressively more negative as impacts of the shocks accumulate. First, the supply shock reduces GDP through reduction in employment (and capital) leading to lower production and

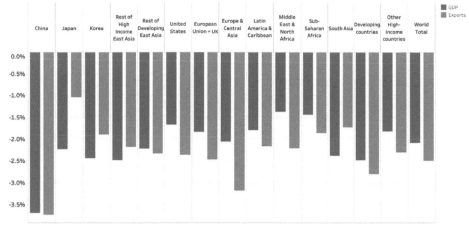

FIGURE 9.5 GDP and export implications of the global pandemic scenario (% deviation from the benchmark).

exports, as well as lower imports due to lower-income of households and shrinking production, as shown in Figure 9.5 and Figure 9.6.

Second, with higher trade costs, the price of a unit of imports and exports increases and the competitiveness of Chinese production declines due to higher costs of exporting and higher costs of inputs; final goods' prices also increase. The rising trade costs represent a productivity loss, since additional inputs are needed to bring goods to their consumers, instead of being available for consumption and investment. Further, inbound and outbound tourism decreases significantly, resulting in a further decline of Chinese GDP and exports. Finally, with the composition of expenditures changing with lower demand for sectors hit by social distancing (transport, hospitality) and relatively higher demand for goods, the composition of output tilts toward manufacturing. Loss of competitiveness and

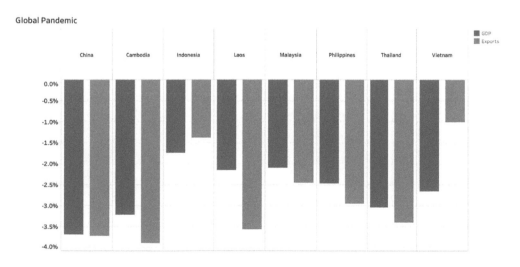

FIGURE 9.6 GDP and export implications of global pandemic scenario for EAP countries (% deviation from the benchmark).

lower-income result in a decline of total exports by 3.5%, while imports decline by 3.2%. China's exports of tourist-related activities decline by 29%, while imports of tourist-related activities decline by 37%. Real consumption by households declines by 7.2%.

Global GDP is expected to decline by 2.1% while developing countries' GDP is expected to decline by 2.5% and high-income countries by 1.9%. The biggest GDP losses under the global pandemic scenario are expected in East Asia and Pacific (EAP) countries due to their relatively deep integration through trade and direct impact on tourism, e.g., Cambodia (3.2%), Singapore (2.1%), Hong Kong SAR, China (2.3%), Thailand (3%), Vietnam (2.7%), and Malaysia (2.1%).

Exports at the global level are expected to decrease by 2.5%. China, considered to be the "world's factory," suffers a decline in production across all sectors and goods, due to an underutilization of labor and capital, and, together with an increase of its trade costs, increases the import costs for the rest of the world, which translates into a decline in global exports. China sees a contraction in exports of 3.7%. Vietnam sees a decline in its total exports by only 1% because it benefits to an extent from the gap left by the decrease in Chinese exports. Some countries in the EAP region are the most affected in terms of export declines, with Hong Kong SAR, China, suffering the biggest losses (5.2%), followed by the Lao People's Democratic Republic (3.6%), Cambodia (3.9%), and Singapore (4.4%). Selected countries see an increased demand for their tourism exports due to diversion of tourism from the EAP region, with some flows increasing by 2–3% between countries outside the EAP region, but in all countries total tourism flows decline across the board, with exports from the EAP region declining by about 30%. These small bilateral tourism export gains disappear, as the shock spreads from China and East Asia to other parts of the world.

Under amplified global pandemic scenarios, global GDP loss reaches 3.9%, while Chinese GPD declines by 4.3% (Figures 9.7 and 9.8). The biggest GDP losses are reported in the regions most integrated through trade and/or where tourism trade plays a big role in the economy. Cambodia and Thailand are expected to record GDP losses of over 6%, while Singapore; Hong Kong SAR, China; Taiwan, China; the Republic of Korea; Malaysia; and the Philippines see losses of over 4.5%, which are also of higher magnitude than in China.

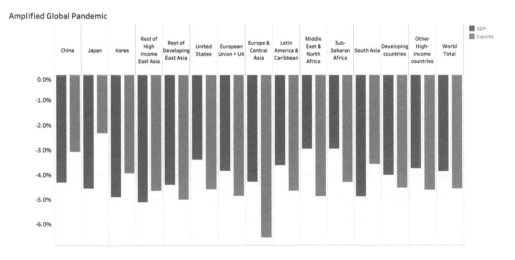

FIGURE 9.7 GDP and export implications of amplified global pandemic scenario (% deviation from the benchmark).

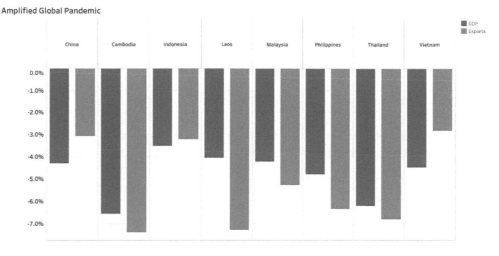

FIGURE 9.8 GDP and export implications of amplified global pandemic scenario (% deviation from the benchmark).

High-income countries could see significant losses of GDP, with the estimated loss in the EU over 3.4%, Japan—4.6%, the United States—3.4%, and Canada—3.2%. Countries in Sub-Saharan Africa (SSA) and the Middle East and North Africa (MENA) are the least affected, and under the global and amplified global pandemic scenarios, the estimated loss of GDP is estimated to be around 3%.

Under the amplified global pandemic scenario, global exports decline by 4.6%. Several countries that experience larger than global average losses of exports are in the EAP region such as Hong Kong SAR, China (9.8%), Cambodia (7.4%), Singapore (8.5%), Lao PDR (7.3%), Thailand (6.8%), but also the Russian Federation and the Philippines see losses up of 6.4%, while Canada, Europe, and the United States see declines of around 4.5%. With the amplified global spread of the virus, all countries see their total exports decline, but the least integrated regions through trade and tourism, such as MENA, SSA, and Latin America and the Caribbean, are the least affected. Some EAP countries tend to be relatively less affected in this scenario than others, but all countries' exports decline the most under the amplified global pandemic scenario, e.g., Vietnam, Japan, and The Republic of Korea.

Our estimates are broadly in line with previous studies. Annex 2 reviews several analyses by OECD, Brookings, and S&P quantifying the potential impacts of the COVID-19 outbreak. The studies use a variety of tools, with OECD relying on a macroeconomic model and Brookings applying a hybrid CGE/DSGE model with rational expectations. Most estimates on the impacts on China range from 0.5% to 2% of GDP. World GDP is expected to decline between 0.1% and 1.5%, while global trade is expected to decline between 0.2% and 3.75%. The biggest impacts are reported in the extreme scenarios by McKibbin and Fernando (2020), with Chinese GDP declining by up to 6%, with GDP declines in the United States and Japan reaching, respectively, 8% and 10%.

Trade Costs

The second shock (cumulative with the supply shock) raises the international trade costs of imports and exports by 25%. The shock is applied across all goods and services. Trade costs arise when goods cross borders.

The assumed increase in transport and transactions costs in foreign trade is driven by additional inspections, reduced hours of operation, road closures, border closures, increases in transport costs, etc. Evans et al. (2015) estimate that the outbreak of Ebola could lead to an increase in trade costs of 10%. Since COVID-19 is affecting more countries and the containment measures seem more severe due to the efforts to contain the virus, we amplified the shock increasing international trade costs of imports and exports to 25%.

The country-specific results are driven by the initial composition of output and exports by sector and destination, but also by the country's level of openness and relative changes in the competitiveness of the exporting country and its trading partners.

Under the amplified global pandemic scenario, US exports are expected to decline by almost $85 billion (2014 dollars) (Figure 9.9). The most impacted are exports of services, especially tourism and services requiring face-to-face interaction. The biggest declines are expected in exports to Europe and EAP, driven by recession and lower demand in those regions, the main destinations for US exports in services.

In the case of China, the biggest decline of exports is registered in manufacturing goods, and in Chinese exports directed to the United States, Europe, and EAP countries (Figure 9.10). There is a small increase in exports to ECA and MENA countries, where Chinese products become relatively more competitive than products of other suppliers, and where domestic producers cannot fully satisfy the domestic demand.

Finally, in the case of Thailand, the biggest impacts are on exports of manufacturing goods and services, with very little impact on agricultural goods or natural resources (Figure 9.11). Services exports to the United States and Europe register the biggest declines while manufacturing exports to China and EAP partners take the biggest hit.

International Tourism

The third shock entails a sharp drop in international tourism. This is captured via a 50% consumption tax on international tourism-related services, such as transport, accommodation, etc. This generates a typically small revenue for the relevant countries that is rebated back to households with a lump sum.[58] The export tax is applied to both outbound and inbound (tourist) services that include: accommodation, food and service activities; water, air, and other transport; and recreational and other services.

The effects of COVID-19 in the tourism, hospitality, and recreation sectors have been unprecedented. In the accommodation and lodging sectors, quarterly revenues are down 75%. Travel agents saw a slowdown in bookings of 50% in March 2020. Airlines worldwide are expected to lose $113 billion in revenues for 2020. At the peak of the outbreak, 70% of scheduled flights in China have been canceled. As of mid-March 2020, international travel has ground to a halt, with the World Travel and Tourism Council (WTTC) estimating that global travel would decline at least 25% in 2020. To capture the effects of the drop in tourism, hospitality, and recreation services, we implemented a 50% tax on the export of trade-related services, resulting in a drop in exports of tourism services at a global level of 20–32%.

Consumer Confidence and Demand Fluctuation

The fourth shock represents a Consumer Confidence and Demand Fluctuation by households who purchase fewer services requiring close human interaction, such as mass transport, domestic tourism, restaurants, and recreational activities while redirecting demand towards

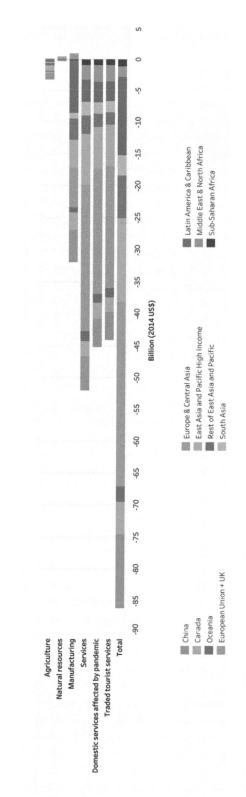

FIGURE 9.9 Impacts on US exports in the amplified global pandemic scenario (difference from the benchmark). (Note: Europe & Central Asia—Russian Federation, rest of Europe & Central Asia; East Asia and Pacific High Income—Hong Kong SAR, China; Japan; Republic of Korea; Singapore; South Asia—India, rest of South Asia; Latin America & Caribbean—Brazil, rest of Latin America & Caribbean)

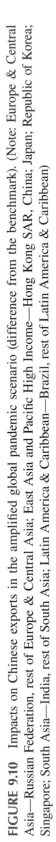

FIGURE 9.10 Impacts on Chinese exports in the amplified global pandemic scenario (difference from the benchmark). (Note: Europe & Central Asia—Russian Federation, rest of Europe & Central Asia; East Asia and Pacific High Income—Hong Kong SAR, China; Japan; Republic of Korea; Singapore; South Asia—India, rest of South Asia; Latin America & Caribbean—Brazil, rest of Latin America & Caribbean)

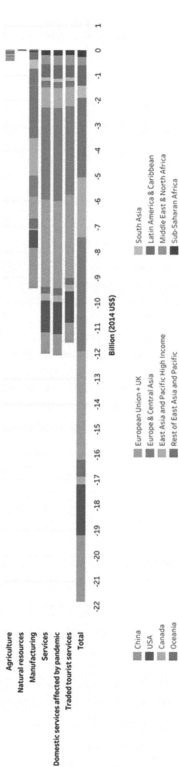

FIGURE 9.11 Impacts on Thai exports in the amplified global pandemic scenario (difference from the benchmark). (Note: Europe & Central Asia—Russian Federation, rest of Europe & Central Asia; East Asia and Pacific High Income—Hong Kong SAR, China; Japan; Republic of Korea; Singapore; South Asia—India, rest of South Asia; Latin America & Caribbean—Brazil, rest of Latin America & Caribbean)

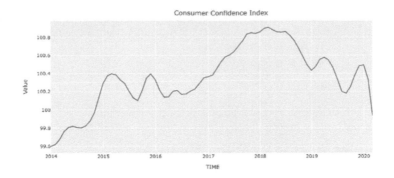

FIGURE 9.12   Consumer confidence at its lowest mode in the last five years.

consumption of goods and other services. The Consumer Confidence is falling, according to the OECD defines consumer confidence (as shown in Figure 9.12) as the following:

"This consumer confidence indicator provides an indication of future developments of households' consumption and saving, based upon answers regarding their expected financial situation, their sentiment about the general economic situation, unemployment and capability of savings. An indicator above 100 signals a boost in the consumers' confidence towards the future economic situation, as a consequence of which they are less prone to save, and more inclined to spend money on major purchases in the next 12 months. Values below 100 indicate a pessimistic attitude towards future developments in the economy, possibly resulting in a tendency to save more and consume less."

Similarly, the demand for the targeted services is assumed to drop by 15%. This results in a reallocation of household demand across sectors, while total expenditures are still driven by previous shocks and relative prices of goods in the consumption basket.

From looking at the image above, consumer confidence has dropped below 100 and on behalf of the study, it is the expectation that it will continue to drop further in the following months. What does this mean? It says that values below 100 indicate a pessimistic attitude towards future developments in the economy. This is in line with the other indicators that we looked at above.

If consumers perceive the near future to be bleak and decide to save more that means less money will circulate in the economy, which means businesses will make less money and more layoffs will occur.

It is difficult to estimate the impact of social distancing and overall decline of economic activity on those selected sectors, but anecdotal evidence suggests that it is likely to be significant. With social distancing measures and closures of nonessential businesses, the bookings through Open table network declined by 100% in the second half of March (data form the United States, the United Kingdom, and Germany). Depending on the length of the business closures, the annual impact could vary drastically. The decline of 15% at an annual level seems like a middle of the road estimate.

COVID-19 AND THE STOCK MARKET UNCERTAINTY ANALYSIS USING TIME SERIES MODEL

The analyses that are currently in place to form a measure model of the economy have proved that percentage change in GDP can help in estimating market uncertainty. The common assumption made by these current models is that the financial structure of an economic market is based on the bank or stock market. In general, this part of the research analysis makes historical changes in GDP and their impact on the stock market. These analyses can be broken down from market sectors to industry and dominate the graph of the current market to help forecast. In support of the economic analysis model, there have been studies that have proved through correlation that the stock markets are key indicators of the economy.

A study conducted by Heiberger in 2018 indicated that the S&P 500 exhibits normal growth of the economy with high correlated numbers.[59] A navy base classifier was used in this research to estimate the monetary turn of events. The model in this research effectively estimated the duration of all recessions and practically all successes during the recent 28 years. This investigation demonstrates that it is conceivable to build a model that uses monetary markets as driving pointers of economies. Research worked solely in covering specific financial states through the exam of using the Naive Bayes classifier, i.e., when the prior probability of predictor $P(X)$ is constant given the input, we can get:

$$P(C_k|X) \propto P(C_k)\prod_{i=1}^{n}P(x_i|C_k)$$

where $\propto$ means positive proportional to $P(X)$.

The Naive Bayes classification problem then becomes: for different class values of Ck, find the maximum of $P(C_k)\prod_{i=1}^{n}P(x_i|C_k)$. This can be formulated as:

$$\hat{C} = arg \min_{C_k} P(C_k)\prod_{i=1}^{n}P(x_i|C_k)$$

The prior probability of class $P(C_k)$ could be calculated as the relative frequency of class C_k in the training data.

Is used as a test of successor, growth, and recession dataset. Testing on each of the three financial states helped strengthen the model. After the end of his exam, research noticed that using all the accessible highlights, he created an overfed model. To overcome this, he extracted the most presentable highlights of the macroeconomic zone and extended the attack of his model along these lines.

The Keynesian hypothesis validly joined an examination conducted by Selmire in 2013. That examination talks about how banking guidelines can lead to retaliatory financial elements.[60] In this investigation, Selmire finds that the S&P 500 does so, according to monetary guidelines compelled by banks or government increments. The guideline emphasizes assisting with maintaining the macroeconomic situation. Like Chiarelli's discoveries, a lot of expectation models that are used depend on bank and government guidelines; among the successes, it is more enthusiastic to forecast.[61]

The S&P 500 is falling since the COVID-19 infection started as shown in Figure 9.13. In simple terms, the S&P 500 is essentially a representation of the 500 largest US public companies. Earlier this year, the S&P 500 lost over 30% of its value from its peak—the last time the S&P 500 fell this much was during the 2008 recession.

Here a question arises in everyone's mind that is "Why did the pandemic cause the stock market to drop so much in value?" Theoretically, the stock market is a reflection of how well our economy is doing and is influenced by a number of factors, like interest rates. But really the stock market is a reflection of how well we perceive the economy will be in the near future.

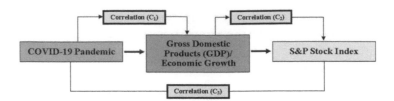

FIGURE 9.13   Working methodology of research.

And since this pandemic has spurred a lot of uncertainty about the future, investors have been selling their stocks for cash which in turn has dropped the value of the stock market.

Method and Material

Data Collection Process

Data was compiled from three different publically available sources: COVID-19 data compiled from John Hopkins COVID-19 map, GDP data compiled from WEO compiled by IMF, and stock market (e.g., S&P 500 index, etc.) from Yahoo Finance using python 3.8 *datareader* library, a data site where information is stored in one location, BEA.gov which is another website that has years of data stored and sorted, and the Bloomberg Terminal which is an up to date portal that has current changes as well as historical data. The raw monthly data was put into excel and sorted into quarterly data so that there were more meaningful data points. It was decided the data would be more useful in quarterly format because there were larger differences in those data points when compared to the monthly data.

Dataset Description

The first dataset was collected from John Hopkins COVID-19 map and compiled with two variables of confirmed cases and death counts of the world's top ten economic countries. From the beginning of COVID-19 pandemic to 22nd April 2020 total counts of variables are presented in Table 9.2. Second dataset of world's top ten economic countries' GDP over the last 5 years is presented in Table 9.3. Third dataset of S&P 500 stock index drown

TABLE 9.3

Top Ten World Economies of the World with GDP and Contribution of World GDP (%) Respectively

	Country	GDP ($ USD)	Share of World GDP (%)
1	United States	$20.49 trillion	23.89
2	China	$13.61 trillion	15.86
3	Japan	$4.97 trillion	5.79
4	Germany	$4.00 trillion	4.66
5	United Kingdom	$2.83 trillion	3.29
6	France	$2.78 trillion	3.24
7	India	$2.73 trillion	3.18
8	Italy	$2.07 trillion	2.4
9	Brazil	$1.87 trillion	2.18
10	Canada	$1.71 trillion	1.99

TABLE 9.4

Statistics of Selected Stock Indexed

	S&P 500	Crude oil	Gold	Natural Gas	Silver	Treasury Bond
Count	173	171	171	171	171	173
Mean	3016.279	49.2317	1547.608	2.153053	17.05253	145.4033
Std	242.8567	13.71511	78.52043	0.335766	1.306676	10.67145
Min	2237.4	−2.6	1452.1	1.556	11.772	133.849
25%	2919.4	49.59	1488.1	1.8405	16.858	137.9402
50%	3022.55	54.85	1519.1	2.202	17.478	141.4599
75%	3205.37	57.745	1582.8	2.4015	17.8605	147.6084
Max	3386.15	63.27	1769.4	2.862	19.391	171.29

from yahoo finance stock market management web portal from the last quarter of GDP in 2019, i.e., September 2019 to April 2020. In addition, Crude oil, Gold asset, Silver Asset, Natural gas, iShare 20+ year Treasury Bond Assets return value data collected to analysis the impact of economy on these revenue generated assets that help to clear the picture impact of economy on stock market indexes. Table 9.4 represents the summary of the stock indexed collected data.

Data Pre-Processing

Data Cleaning The extracted data has some missing values, redundant columns, unrecognized symbols of the columns, etc., which may affect the research result. So Python 3.8 - *Panda and NumPy* library help to handle the data cleaning process.

Data Normalization The purpose of data normalization is to rescaling the cleaned dataset because the COVID-19 counts are very high and somehow rapidly increasing on a daily basis, while stock index data have positive and negative uncertain values. Hence, to applying the measure the correlation between COVID-19, economic growth and stock market require a similar scale.

Model Description

The percentage change was recorded between each quarter, focusing on this research. A change in percentage in the quarter indicated that GDP (balanced for inflation) has gone down by ten quarters since 1957. According to Yahoo Finance 2017, in 2008 all three of these lobbyists were caused by the accident. His fact-finding suggests that at present most of the correlation on wage increases needs to be made as pay increases support both the same and the lower. The forecast model is expected to account for two increments and a decrease in GDP altogether. In the event that it is just ready to manufacture, it will not be a supporting model. It may be, the size of the increment can be thought about in any case and may still be helpful. Further information about how the GDP model can be used to estimate GDP growth will be additionally clarified later.

The impractical statics with Python 3.0 was used to compile the regression analysis on the percentage change from quarter to quarter between the S&P 500 and annual GDP. The graphical analysis was done with *matplotlib* library that gave a better indication of the actual relationship of information, as stock index prices were opposed on the basis that there would be no correlation between stock costs and the financial qualities used in GDP. So in order to test whether the S&P 500 stock index is a key indicator of GDP, the S&P 500 information was canceled in both quarter one and two with the goal that quarter two of the GDP was replaced by the S&P 500, would be considered the reverse of quarter three and quarter of GDP, when contrasted with the quarters of the S&P 500.

A certain interim must be set before establishing a relationship. The fixed interim was set to 95%, confidence level that the p-value should be less than 0.05 so that the invalid could be rejected. In practice, the entirety of the results met this limitation and rejected the invalid theory. This shows that there is a relationship between the two systems of information and that a large portion of the parts of the S&P 500 is driving markers of GDP. In order for this information to be factually large, everyone should consider the t-value. The t-value shows evidence of a relationship. For the results of this investigation to be voluminous, there should have been a t-value under 2 or more notables −2. Each t-value for the individual relapses found on this basis, predicts that a result is an average form. This was then run again for each individual part of the S&P 500 to find out if one is higher than the GDP compared to the other. Some parts proved to be more notable relations than others and should be used in contrast to clauses that did not appear as a relation. The exploration was then done to explain why some partitions were more prone to GDP than others.

When all the data was collected and analyzed, it had begun to focus on how this analysis could be used to support policymakers, business holders, and financial experts. Various examinations have attempted comparative investigation and have been filled as a rule or system for the GDP model. These researches cover the approach to managing abundance cash, which organizations are at a disadvantage when the economy is up/down, and why human capital enterprises are important. This data will help with various situations, for example, economy up, economy down, and up/under recruitment and how/when to fix it. The expectation is that the GDP model that was created will help producers, financial experts, and representatives step out to the plate as opposed to turning out front and back seating arrangements and being reactionary.

Results and Discussion

The data was structured and visualized with the help of a spyder (Anaconda3)-Python 3.8 environment.

Figure 9.14 represents the impact of COVID-19 on stock indexes that are highly responsible for generating tax revenue S&P500 (GPSC), crude oil (CL = F), gold (GC = F), silver (SI = F), natural gas (NG = F), iShares 20+ Year Treasury Bond (TLT). As the data of COVID-19 show, the number of people suffering from the epidemic has increased very rapidly since February 2020, the effect of which is in S&P 500 (±12.20%), crude oil (−71.80), gold (+12.90), silver ((+13.72), natural gas (−13.37), iShares 20+ Year Treasury Bond (+18.30), etc., as shown in Figure 9.15.

The stock index is experiencing high uncertainty during the COVID-19 timeline. Figure 9.15 shows the last maximum gain of the stock index that was in the month of February 2020.

Gold tends to move higher in value (Figure 9.16) when economic conditions worsen, on the other hand, crude oil price tends to the lowest, again it's a negative impression for the economic condition, and this case is no exception. For those interested, gold technically has no intrinsic value. You can't go to a grocery store and buy groceries with gold. But gold

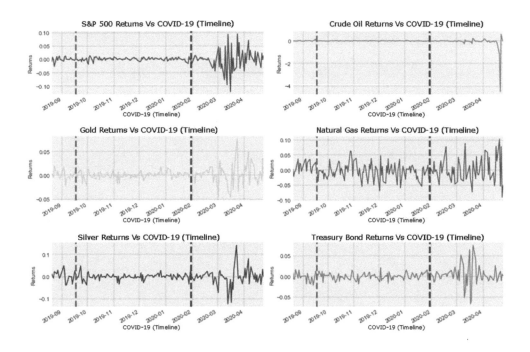

FIGURE 9.14 Impact analysis of COVID-19 on the stock index returns.

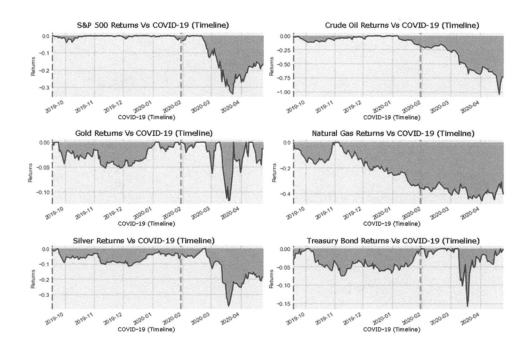

FIGURE 9.15 Stock index with highlighting maximum return during COVID-19 timeline.

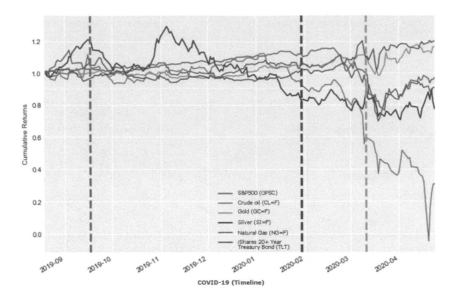

FIGURE 9.16   Cumulative returns during COVID-19 timeline.

was a currency in ancient civilization, and since then, it has been socially constructed and treated as a store of value. Thus, this may be another indicator that our economy is heading south.

According to Figure 9.17 and Figure 9.18 of course, uncertainty isn't the only factor. There are a number of other indicators, like unemployment rates and consumer confidence that indicate an economic slowdown. And that leads us to our next insight.

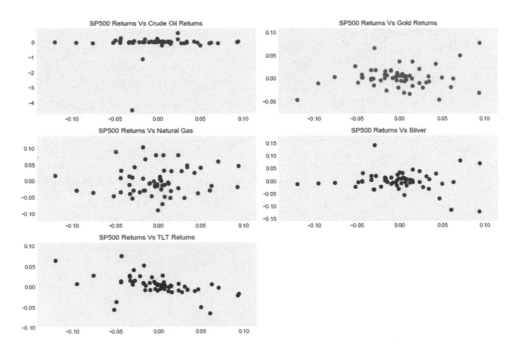

FIGURE 9.17   Impact analysis of S&P 500 stock index over five highly revenue-generating sectors.

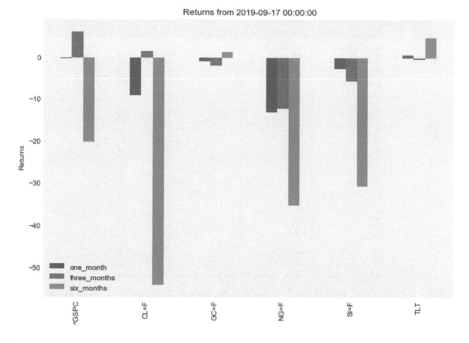

FIGURE 9.18 Stock index return analysis during COVID-19 timeline periodically (e.g., one, three, and six month).

Coronavirus and Unemployment Rates

Unemployment rates are increasing. After the 2008 recession, unemployment rates have steadily decreased from 10% all the way down to 3.5% in February 2020. However, from February to March, the unemployment rate increased by over 25% from 3.5% to 4.4%. And this might just be the start. The US Employment and Training Administration released its weekly update on initial unemployment claims (shown in Figure 9.19), giving us the first glimpse of the economic implications of the COVID-19 pandemic beyond the fluctuation we are observing in the stock market and yikes. To give some context, the peak unemployment rate during the 2008 recession was 10%. This is both scary and bad because unemployment rates affect everyone. Higher unemployment rates mean that families will have less disposable income, which means that companies' revenues will go down, resulting in more lay-offs, and the cycle continues.

For analytical purpose the data are grisly from the Federal Reserve Bank of St. Louis and Python 3.0 that illustrate a clear picture of rapid growth of unemployment (as shown in Figure 9.20) in the month of April 2020, and so forth.

Standardizing initial claims to the (growing) civilian labor force of the United States lends to some worry that estimate might be too low. Basically, the initial claims as a proportion of the civilian labor force, right now, is four times what it was at the peak of the Great Recession and the early 1980s recession. Therein, the unemployment rate was between 10% and 11%. An estimated 30% share, which is a small portion of the initial claims threshold monthly unemployment rate, is very low.

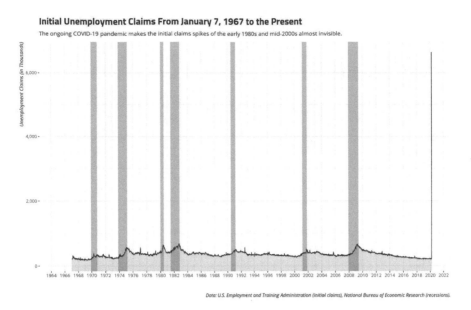

FIGURE 9.19   Initial unemployment claims from 7th January 1967 to April 2020. (Source: U.S. Employment and training administration (initial claims), National Bureau of Economic Research (recursion).)

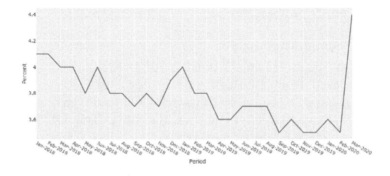

FIGURE 9.20   Clear picture of growth of initial unemployment rate from January 2018 to April 2020.

SUMMARY

The cost-benefit analysis in health policies certainly goes beyond accounting for economic gains and losses. But even from a narrow economic perspective, and the key message from the computational models presented here is that the economic spillovers and spillbacks of pandemic-type recessions are very large and the adequate course of action is far from settled. International coordination of macroeconomic policies is crucial at two levels. First, uncoordinated confinements raise the possibility that the virus will re-emerge sequentially across the globe. This would mean repeated confinements and their associated heavy toll on economic activity. Second, even a country that engineers a domestic policy package that successfully limits its domestic slowdown will not be immune from insufficient or ineffective policies put in place in other parts of the world. No one can hide from the consequences of a pandemic, and unilateral macroeconomic policies are doomed to fail. On a much more positive note, our model reflects only the "average" endogenous monetary and fiscal responses in each country as estimated from 1997 to 2019. Policy packages unveiled so far are much larger than those. Additionally, some countries have also taken crucial actions to preserve existing employment relations and avoid widespread firm-closures and bankruptcies. This should help to limit the downturn in aggregate demand and assist firms to restart production rapidly. That said, as we are in uncharted waters, it remains to be seen how spending responds when economies are still under lockdown.

NOTES

1. Unemployment Insurance Weekly Claims, Department of Labor, July 23, 2020. https://www.dol.gov/; Romm, Tony and Jeff Stein, 2.4 Million Americans Filed Jobless Claims Last Week, Bringing Nine Week Total to 38.6 Million, The Washington Post, May 21, 2020. https://www.washingtonpost.com/business/2020/05/21/unemployment-claimscoronavirus/
2. Kahn, L. B., Lange, F., & Wiczer, D. G. (2020). Labor demand in the time of COVID-19: Evidence from vacancy postings and UI claims (No. w27061). National Bureau of Economic Research.
3. This total does not include 10.9 million workers who were working part time not by choice and 9.9 million individuals who were seeking employment.
4. Bui, T. T. M., Button, P., & Picciotti, E. G. (2020). Early evidence on the impact of COVID-19 and the recession on older workers (No. w27448). National Bureau of Economic Research.
5. Li, Y., & Mutchler, J. E. (2020). Older adults and the economic impact of the COVID-19 pandemic. Journal of Aging & Social Policy, 1-11.
6. The Employment Situation-April 2020, Bureau of Labor Statistics, May 8, 2020. https://www.bls.gov/.
7. This total does not include 10.6 million workers who were working part time not by choice and 9.4 million individuals who were seeking employment.
8. The Employment Situation-May 2020, Bureau of Labor Statistics, June 5, 2020, https://www.bls.gov/. BLS indicated that some individuals were misclassified in April and May. Instead of being classified as unemployed, they were misclassified as employed, but absent from work due to coronavirus-related business closures. If such individuals had been classified as unemployed, the unemployment rate would have been five percentage points higher in April.
9. The Employment Situation-June 2020, Bureau of Labor Statistics, July 2, 2020. https://www.bls.gov/. The unemployment number does not include nine million workers who were working part time not by choice and nine million individuals seeking employment. In addition, BLS indicated that some workers had been misclassified as employed, but should have been classified as unemployed, which would have raised the rate of unemployment by one percentage point.
10. Gross Domestic Product, First Quarter 2020 (Second Estimate), Bureau of Economic Analysis, May 28, 2020. https://www.bea.gov/data/gdp/gross-domestic-product.
11. The Beige Book, Federal Reserve System, May 27, 2020. https://www.federalreserve.gov/monetarypolicy/beigebook-default.htm.
12. Stott, Michael, Coronavirus Set to Push 29m Latin Americans Into Poverty, Financial Times, April 24, 2020. https://www.ft.com/content/3bf48b80-8fba-410c-9bb8-31e33fffc3b8; Hall, Benjamin, Coronavirus Pandemic Threatens Livelihoods of 59m European Workers, Financial Times, April 19, 2020, https://www.ft.com/content/36239c82-84ae-4cc9-89bc-8e71e53d6649, Romei, Valentina and Martin Arnold, Eurozone Economy Shrinks by Fastest Rate on Record, Financial Times, April 30, 2020, https://www.ft.com/content/dd6cfafa-a56d-48f3-a9fdaa71d17d49a8.

13. Arnold, Martin, Eurozone Industrial Production Falls by Record 17.1% in April, Financial Times, June 12, 2020. https://www.ft.com/content/e3301cd6-27ce-35f0-829a-c6613849b378

14. European Economic Forecast Summer 2020, European Commission, July 8, 2020.

15. Arnold, Martin, Coronavirus Hit to Eurozone Economy Set to Dwarf Financial Crisis, Financial Times, May 27, 2020. https://www.ft.com/content/a01424e8-089d-4618-babe-72f88184ac57.

16. Pilling, David, The Pandemic is Getting Worse: Africa Prepares for Surge in Infections, Financial Times, July 20, 2020. https://www.ft.com/content/1b3274ce-de3b-411d-8544-a024e64c3542.

17. Barro et al (2020) observe how the deaths and illnesses of famous people as a result of the 1918 flu pandemic may have disproportionately affected the economy by influencing the course of history. For example, the illness of US President Woodrow Wilson may have contributed to the harsh terms of the Versailles Treaty in 1919.

18. Barro, R. J., Ursúa, J. F., & Weng, J. (2020). The coronavirus and the great influenza pandemic: Lessons from the "spanish flu" for the coronavirus's potential effects on mortality and economic activity (No. w26866). National Bureau of Economic Research.

19. Brainerd, E., & Siegler, M. V. (2003). The economic effects of the 1918 influenza epidemic.

20. Correia, S., Luck, S., & Verner, E. (1918). Pandemics depress the economy, public health interventions do not: Evidence from the 1918 flu. Public Health Interventions Do Not: Evidence from the.

21. Lee, J. W., & McKibbin, W. J. (2004, April). Estimating the global economic costs of SARS. In Learning from SARS: preparing for the next disease outbreak: workshop summary (p. 92). Washington, DC: National Academies Press.

22. Hai, W., Zhao, Z., Wang, J., & Hou, Z. G. (2004). The short-term impact of SARS on the Chinese economy. Asian Economic Papers, 3(1), 57–61.

23. Obayelu, A. E. (2007). Socio-economic analysis of the impacts of avian influenza epidemic on household's poultry consumption and poultry industry in Nigeria: empirical investigation of Kwara State. Livestock Research for Rural Development, 19(1), 4.

24. Chang, C. C., Lee, D. H., Lin, H. C., & Hsu, S. S. (2007). The potential economic impact of avian flu pandemic on Taiwan (No. 381-2016-22318).

25. Burns, A., Van der Mensbrugghe, D., & Timmer, H. (2006). Evaluating the economic consequences of avian influenza (p. 6). World Bank.

26. Huber, C., Finelli, L., & Stevens, W. (2018). The economic and social burden of the 2014 Ebola outbreak in West Africa. The Journal of infectious diseases, 218(suppl_5), S698–S704.

27. World Bank Group. (2014). The Economic Impact of the 2014 Ebola Epidemic: Short and Medium Term Estimates for West Africa.

28. Keogh-Brown, M. R., Smith, R. D., Edmunds, J. W., & Beutels, P. (2010). The macroeconomic impact of pandemic influenza: estimates from models of the United Kingdom, France, Belgium and The Netherlands. The European Journal of Health Economics, 11(6), 543–554.

29. Rassy, D., & Smith, R. D. (2013). The economic impact of H1N1 on Mexico's tourist and pork sectors. Health economics, 22(7), 824–834.

30. Joo, H., Maskery, B. A., Berro, A. D., Rotz, L. D., Lee, Y. K., & Brown, C. M. (2019). Economic Impact of the 2015 MERS Outbreak on the Republic of Korea's Tourism-Related Industries. Health security, 17(2), 100–108.

31. Macciocchi, D., Lanini, S., Vairo, F., Zumla, A., Moraes Figueiredo, L. T., Lauria, F. N., ... & Kremsner, P. (2016). Short-term economic impact of the Zika virus outbreak. New Microbiologica, 39(4), 287–289.

32. Board, G. P. M. (2019). A world at risk: annual report on global preparedness for health emergencies.

33. Fan, V. Y., Jamison, D. T., & Summers, L. H. (2016). The inclusive cost of pandemic influenza risk (No. w22137). National Bureau of Economic Research.

34. Arnold, R., De Sa, J., Gronniger, T., Percy, A., & Somers, J. (2006, July). A potential influenza pandemic: Possible macroeconomic effects and policy issues. In The Congress of the United States, Congressional Budget Office.

35. Many past epidemics resulted in extremely high fatality, due to poorer sanitary standards as well as a different social context. The bubonic plague of the 14th century claimed up to 200 million lives, while the spread of European viruses in Mexico reduced the population from an estimated 15–20 million in 1520 to less than a million in 1600.

36. Correia, S, S Luck and E Verner (2020): "Pandemics depress the economy, public health interventions do not: evidence from the 1918 flu", mimeo.

37. Barro, R, J Ursua and J Weng (2020): "The coronavirus and the Great Influenza Pandemic: lessons from the 'Spanish flu' for the coronavirus' potential effects on mortality and economic activity", NBER Working Paper, no 26866

38. Fan, V, D Jamison and L Summers (2016): "The inclusive cost of pandemic influenza risk", NBER Working Paper, no 22137.

39. Global Preparedness Monitoring Board (2019): A world at risk: annual report on global preparedness for health emergencies, September.

40. Lee, J W and W McKibbin (2004): "Estimating the global economic costs of SARS" in S Knobler, A Mahmoud, S Lemon, A Mack, L Sivitz and K Oberholtzer (eds), Learning from SARS: preparing for the next outbreak, The National Academies Press.

41. Arnold, R, J De Sa, T Gronniger, A Percy and J Somers (2006): "A potential influenza pandemic: Possible macroeconomic effects and policy issues", report to the Congressional Budget Office.

42. They assume that 30% of workers become ill, with 2.5% fatality. Those who survived would miss three weeks of work, because of either sickness, voluntary social distancing or the need to care for family members. They then compute the impact on GDP of the employment lost to the pandemic, using the average sectoral productivity per worker in 2004.

43. The concurrent World War I presented a challenge in quantifying the effect of the pandemic on mortality – see Barro et al (2020). Long-term effects on labour supply are also documented in Jordà et al (2020), who find that real wages remained elevated over more than three decades after pandemics.

44. Jordà, O, S Singh and A Taylor (2020): "Longer-run economic consequences of pandemics", unpublished manuscript, March.

45. Harris, Shane and Missy Ryan, To Prepare for the Next Pandemic, the U.S. Needs to Change its National Security Priorities, Experts Say, The Washington Post, June 16, 2020. https://www.washingtonpost.com/national-security/toprepare-for-the-next-pandemic-the-us-needs-to-change-its-national-security-priorities-experts-say/2020/06/16/b99807c0-aa9a-11ea-9063-e69bd6520940_story.html.

46. Eichengreen, B (2020): "The human-capital costs of the crisis", Project Syndicate, April.

47. https://www.nielsen.com/us/en/insights/article/2020/nielsen-investigation-pandemic-pantries-pressure-supply-chain-amidst-covid-19-fears/?utm_source=feedburner&utm_medium=feed&utm_campaign=Feed%3A+NielsenWire+%28Nielsen+Newswire%29

48. https://www.apple.com/newsroom/2020/02/investor-update-on-quarterly-guidance/

49. https://www.investindia.gov.in/team-india-blogs/impact-coronavirus-global-supply-chains

50. https://www.imf.org/en/Publications/SPROLLs/world-economic-outlook-databases#sort=%40imfdate%20descending

51. https://www.imf.org/external/datamapper/datasets

52. https://www.imf.org/external/pubs/ft/weo/2019/01/weodata/index.aspx

53. https://data.worldbank.org/indicator/NE.CON.TOTL.KD.ZG?end=2018&start=2018

54. https://apps.bea.gov/iTable/iTable.cfm?reqid=19&step=2#reqid=19&step=2&isuri=1&1921=survey

55. A full description of the ENVISAGE model is available at https://mygeohub.org/groups/gtap/File:/uploads/ENVISAGE10.01_Documentation.pdf.

56. The shocks are scaled down as compared with the shocks derived for Liberia under the Ebola epidemic, as in Evans et al. (2014).

57. This is a conservative estimate. Some estimates put potential reduction of employment at the annual level at 10%, assuming unemployment of over 30% in Q2 and returning to pre-crisis level in Q3 and Q4. https://www.stlouisfed.org/on-the-economy/2020/march/back-envelope-estimates-next-quartersunemployment-rate

58. There are a number of ways to affect demand choices by increasing the cost of purchasing the relevant good. The solution in this case has been to impose export taxes that directly affect the price of the targeted services. The revenues generated by this tax are rebated back to households.

59. Heiberger, R. H. (2018). Predicting economic growth with stock networks. Physica A: Statistical Mechanics And Its Applications, 489102-111. doi:10.1016/j.physa.2017.07.022

60. Selmier, W. (2013). Does Banking Regulation Cause Counterproductive Economic Dynamics?. National Research University Higher School of Economics.

61. Chiarella, Carl. Financial Markets and the Macroeconomy a Keynesian Perspective. New York, NY, 2009.

10 Direct and Indirect Impacts of the COVID-19 Pandemic Crisis on Food & Agriculture

KEY POINTS

- List of difficulties faced by producers and companies throughout the food supply chain.
- The collection and analysis of primary data and case studies related to specific agriculture, production, transformation, distribution, and consumption stages can provide us with valuable information about how production systems have dealt with this epidemic and how specific food supply chains can be rebuilt.
- Dynamic model approach to examine the effects of trade openness on food security for a cross-section of countries
- To analysis the impact chapter used the gross domestic product (GDP) per capita as the principle variable to measure the quantity of final goods and services on the territory of a country.

INTRODUCTION

Agriculture is the backbone of any economy. It is the primary sector that generates employment so that the entire circle of economic circulation goes on (Abdelhedi & Zouari, 2020; Kogo et al., 2020; Lopez-Ridaura et al., 2019). When we talk about the African and Asian countries' economies, the majority of the population is restricted to this sector.

The different pandemics that humanity has experienced in the past, such as the Spanish Flu, Asian Flu, Hong Kong Flu, HIV/AIDS, Severe acute respiratory syndrome (SARS), Ebola, and Swine Flu, have been shown that quarantines and panic have an impact on human activities and economic growth (Bermejo, 2004; Hanashima & Tomobe, 2012), but the effect also occurs in agricultural activities. When there is an outbreak of infectious disease, there is also an increase in hunger and malnutrition (Burgui, 2020; Sar et al., 2010).

Currently, humanity is facing another pandemic, the infection of the new coronavirus (2019-nCoV) that generates the disease known as COVID-19. As the ongoing pandemic crisis is set to have profound effects on the global economy, small-scale rural producers are to bear the brunt of it as it threatens to affect their livelihoods of all the farmers and the people who are indulging in this sector are at high risk.

At this point, it is essential to address its existing and potential impacts on the agriculture-food sector, from the perspective of both food demand and supply. Ensuring the continued functioning of global and national food supply chains will be crucial in securing food supply chain, preventing a food crisis in countries that are already experiencing food and nutrition security challenges, and reducing the overall negative impact of the pandemic on the global economy. We all need to keep supply chains functioning well is crucial to food security. It should be noted that two to three million deaths in the Bengal famine of 1943 were due to food supply disruptions—not a lack of food availability. Although it will take time to fully understand the impact of this pandemic on agriculture, adequate steps by the government involving food security and agriculture policy can help mitigate the mid and long-term effects of the crisis.

Although its share in total employment has fallen from 40.2% to 26.8% over the past two decades, agriculture provides livelihoods to more than one billion people worldwide and remains the backbone of many low-income countries, accounting for 60.4% of employment[1] and contributing up to two-thirds of gross domestic product (GDP) in some of those countries. The sector is particularly important in Africa and Asia, where its employment share is 49 and 30.5%, respectively. It is a major source of employment for women, who account for 41.9% of the agricultural workforce in the developing world (Office, 2017).

Despite its declining share in global employment, agricultural output has continued to grow (IFAD, 2016). Coupled with urbanization, increasing per capita incomes, and export opportunities, the transformation of the food system has been translating into a new pool of opportunity arises for larger agricultural-food technologies, especially digital agriculture solutions for agriculture and related non-farm sectors, such as processing, manufacturing, food marketing, logistics, transportation, and food preparation. The agriculture-food sector already employs the majority of those in self- and wage employment in developing countries. However, at present, many of these jobs are characterized by decent work deficits resulting from inter alia: weak labor market institutions, including ineffective law enforcement, labor inspection and compliance; inadequate environments for enterprise development; low productivity; climate change; prevalent informality; poor infrastructure; and limited access to social protection and other services, including education and healthcare. Additional challenges arise from farmworkers' increased exposure to various safety, health, environmental, and biological hazards, including those related to chemicals, noise, musculoskeletal injuries, heat, etc.

Agricultural workers experience the highest incidence of working poverty. A quarter of workers engaged in the sector are in extreme poverty. Despite playing an important role in national economies, providing a link with the global structures of agricultural production and trade, and feeding the world, many agricultural workers and their families suffer from poverty and food insecurity.

While agriculture-food sector jobs have been designated as essential in the context of the COVID-19 crisis in many countries, the measures adopted to slow down the pandemic may place further strain on the capacity of the sector to continue meeting demand, providing incomes and livelihoods, and ensuring safety and health for the millions of agricultural workers and producers. Urgent action to address the multiple decent work challenges faced by agricultural workers and to improve the functioning of the agriculture-food sector will be critical to effectively address crises, both present and future. Lessons need to be learned from the responses to the pandemic in agriculture with a view to "building back better." The opportunities that arise to adopt technological innovations and improve environmental sustainability should not be missed.

THE IMPACT OF COVID-19 ON AGRICULTURE-FOOD MARKET

Since the beginning of the pandemic, no significant disruptions in the supply of food have been experienced so far. However, logistical challenges within supply chains, particularly cross-border and domestic restrictions of movement e.g., quarantines and lockdown, as well as labor issues, may lead to disruptions in the functioning of agriculture and food supply system, especially if they remain in place long-term. High-value, and especially perishable commodities, such as fresh fruit and vegetables, meat, fish, milk, and flowers, are likely to be particularly affected. The health crisis has already resulted in job destruction in sub-sectors such as floriculture in a number of countries.[2] There may be a further reduction in job quality in the sector and job destruction, especially at the base of the supply chain. Women and youth are likely to feel the impact more strongly, as they are particularly exposed to socioeconomic vulnerability.

Restrictions on movement may prevent farmers from accessing markets and result in food waste. In many countries, farmers are now unable to sell their produce in local markets or to local schools, restaurants, bars, hotels, and other leisure establishments, which have been temporarily closed.

The pandemic may also have a serious impact on labor-intensive crop production and processing due to labor shortages and the temporary cessation of production. For example, Europe's agricultural sector is facing dramatic labor shortages due to border closures that prevent hundreds of thousands of seasonal workers from reaching farms that rely on their labor during the harvest period. The impact on the sector is expected to be long term. A number of major European agricultural producers, including France, Germany, Italy, Spain, and Poland, are particularly vulnerable. According to Coldiretti, the Italian organization representing farmers, over a quarter of the food produced in the country relies on approximately 370,000 regular seasonal migrant workers. Around 100,000 farmworkers may not be able to come to Italy this year, and the figure may be double that in France. In Germany, where some 286,000 seasonal migrant workers are engaged every year in fruit, vegetable, and wine production, the Government is exploring different ways of mobilizing sufficient workers for the harvest, including running direct flights for farmworkers and issuing temporary work permits for asylum seekers. On 2 April 2020, the European Commission has issued practical guidance for member States to facilitate cross-border travel for seasonal workers in critical occupations, which include food sector workers, while putting in place all necessary measures to avoid further spread of the pandemic.

The pandemic may also have a significant negative impact on the livelihoods of millions of plantation workers engaged in export-oriented, labor-intensive agricultural production in developing countries. For example, the recent temporary suspension of one of the world's largest tea auctions in Mombasa, Kenya, where tea from many eastern African countries is traded, if prolonged, could have a devastating effect on local, national, and regional economies. The immediate impact will be felt in various nodes of the chain, including factories, warehouses, and transporters, as well as farms, which may be forced to stop production and lay off pluckers, who are often among the most disadvantaged workers and highly vulnerable to economic reversal. In Kenya alone, tea provides livelihoods to some 600,000 small-scale farmers and wage workers; whereas in Malawi, the sector is the second-largest formal employer after the government, providing jobs to some 52,000 workers.

Panic-buying and food stockpiling by consumers, and national trade-related policy responses to the pandemic, especially any limitations on exports, may result in price spikes and increased price volatility, destabilizing international markets (Glauber et al., 2020). Previous crises have demonstrated that such measures are particularly damaging for low-income, food-deficit countries. The 2007–08 food crisis increased the depth of poverty among those who were already poor (Compton et al., 2010) and pushed an estimated 130–155 million people into poverty (Affairs, 2011). Casual wage workers, particularly in

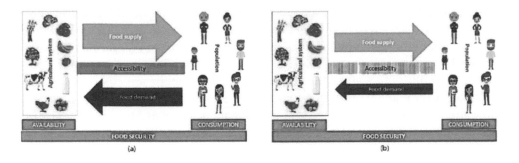

FIGURE 10.1   Food security system (a) without COVID-19 and (b) with COVID-19.

agriculture, landless farmers, small-scale traders, and commodity producers whose terms of trade declined against food grains were most affected (Compton et al., 2010). According to International Labor Organization (ILO) estimates, to maintain their standard of living and not fall into poverty, low paid workers in the worst affected countries would have had to find one additional week of employment every month (Rani & Corley-Coulibaly, 2011). Many of these countries also observed significant increases in school drop-out rates and the incidence of child labor, due to unaffordable school costs and a lack of adequate food.

The urgency of the crisis and the need for immediate action must not be used as a pretext for jettisoning the normative framework for policy solutions. Fundamental principles and rights at work and other international labor standards provide a strong basis for solutions at the national level.

Close monitoring of food prices and markets and transparent dissemination of information will strengthen governments' capacity to ensure the effective management of the food market, prevent panic buying, and guide agricultural enterprises in making rational production decisions.[3] In this context, it will be critical to ensure the free flow of international trade, while guaranteeing quality jobs in food systems.[4]

The Food and Agriculture Organization (FAO, 2020a)[5] states that COVID-19 is affecting agriculture in two significant aspects: the supply and demand for food. These two aspects are directly related to food security, so food security is also at risk. With Figure 10.1 we can simply understand the relationships between these elements, as well as the impact of COVID-19.

Food Supply

The food supply chain is a network that connects an agricultural system (the farm) with the consumer's table, including processes such as manufacturing, packaging, distribution, and storage (Chen et al., 2020).

Initially, the announcements of social isolation made people go to the supply centers and generate a shortage of some products, despite this, the food supply has stabilized because it is one of the systems that must be maintained to ensure food security. One of FAO's roles is to promote that food value chains are not interrupted and continue to operate (FAO, 2020b).[6] Thus, despite the restrictions that governments have imposed on the mobility of labor in agricultural systems, although with some problems, the supply of basic necessities is normally assured. The situation is different when it comes to goods that are imported or exported; due to the closure of borders, international trade was interrupted, although after having defined security protocols to avoid the spread of the virus, trade stabilized. This may be temporary; it depends on what countries are doing to stop the spread of the virus.

Part of the food supply system, are the social programs that some countries, mainly Latin America, have to feed millions of families and children with limited economic resources. This supply system is being served in different ways:

- Delivery of food rations of basic necessities (for example, Indonesia and Taiwan).
- Economic allocation equivalent to the cost of food rations of basic necessity (for example, Peru, Japan, and Singapore).

Interruptions to food transfers are minimal, so the food supply remains stable; although observing China's experience in this pandemic, there is a greater impact on the livestock sector due to difficulties in accessing animal feed and, on the other hand, the shortage of labor (Zhang, 2020).

Although it depends on the country and the measures that each one has adopted, globally the prices have remained stable, therefore, no spikes in the prices of basic necessities are expected, although it is more likely to occur for high-value products, especially meat and perishables. One of the indices that measure the variation of the price worldwide is the FAO Food Price Index (FFPI), a measure of the monthly variation of the international prices of a basket of food products. According to the FAO (2020c),[7] the FFPI of February 2020 had an average of 180.5 points, that is, 1.9 points (1.0%) less than in January, constituting the first month-on-month decrease after four months consecutive increases (Figure 10.2).

Both supply and demand have been affected, although a greater effect on demand, due to the pass ability restrictions that affect accessibility. Availability and consumption remain almost stable. The agricultural system includes producers, raw materials, agricultural

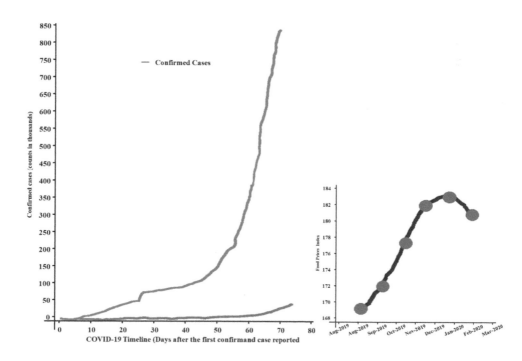

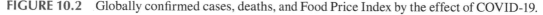

FIGURE 10.2 Globally confirmed cases, deaths, and Food Price Index by the effect of COVID-19.

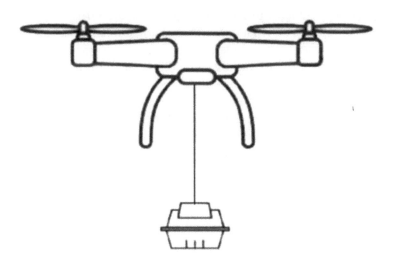

FIGURE 10.3   One way of using the latest technology (Drone-based system) for non-contact food delivery.

machinery and inputs, processing plants, and farm and industrialized food. Consumption includes people and different marketing systems.

This was due to a sharp fall in the export prices of vegetable oils and, to a lesser extent, in the prices of meat and cereals, which offset the continuing rise in the prices of dairy products and sugar.

FOOD DEMAND

Demand implies the willingness and ability of consumers to pay money for a particular good or service, during any particular period (Gottheil, 2013).

The demand for food has decreased due to uncertainty and the reduction of people's spending capacity, although this decrease is still slight; the situation could worsen if the pandemic continues for a long time, due to reduced income and job losses (FAO, 2020b).[8]

Since China represents an important market in world trade and where the COVID-19 disease started, his experience shows an increase in online demand in the food and beverage sector, due to quarantine policies (FAO, 2020a).[9] In situations like these, where a virus spreads on contact, contactless delivery services become preferred by consumers. For example, those who use drones for the product delivery (Figure 10.3).

IMMEDIATE IMPACTS

We are already witnessing the indirect effects of the pandemic on agricultural systems across the globe. Massively decreased demand for restaurant and commercial food services in combination with restrictions in labor, processing capacity, and/or storage has led to farmers discarding their output *en masse*. Quarantine measures are severely affecting labor availability for key time-critical farming from sowing vegetable crops to picking fruit. As the crisis develops, these impacts are likely to become more widely and deeply felt in agricultural sectors and national economies.

The significance and severity of the pandemic, and its likely impact on agriculture worldwide, calls for substantial reflection in both the short- and long-term. We need to understand the immediate consequences for the global network of agricultural and food systems on which we rely so heavily. We should track unexpected risks, weaknesses, and systemic shifts to understand short-term effects as well as those that may be long-lasting or permanent.

This section focused on several identified dimensions of concern with respect to COVID-19 and agricultural systems—although this list is early and limited and so is inevitably incomplete.

FOOD SECURITY

Of immediate concern of impact of COVID-19 on agriculture-food industry is the disruption to food systems and impact on food security (Torero, 2020). Food security implies that everyone has unrestricted access to food that allows them to satisfy their basic needs (Rosales & Mercado, 2020). Not taking quick action implies an imminent food crisis, with a greater effect on the most vulnerable population (Figure 10.4). Measures should focus on

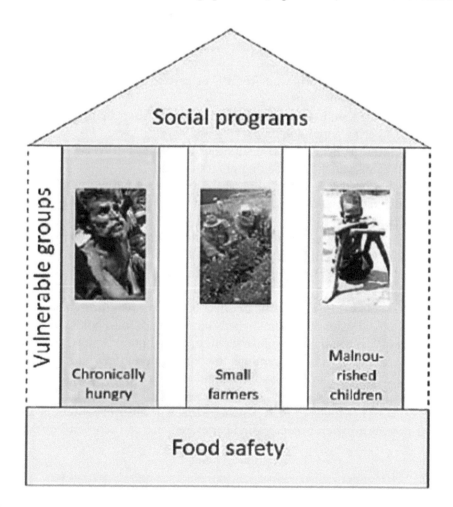

FIGURE 10.4   Groups vulnerable to a food crisis.

keeping global food supply chains active and mitigating the impacts of the pandemic across the food system. Social programs act as an umbrella that minimizes the effect of short-term crises.

The first vulnerable group: people who experience chronic hunger and do not consume enough caloric energy to live a normal life, which currently numbers about 820 million people (FAO, 2020a).[10] This group of people cannot afford any possible interruption of their livelihoods or access to food that a situation with COVID-19 could bring. If the virus spreads in countries where such people live, with health systems with limited capacity, the consequences could be serious.

A second vulnerable group: small farmers, who may be prevented from working on their land and accessing markets to sell their products or buy seeds and other essential inputs.

The third vulnerable group: children from low-income families, who are mainly nourished by food provided by social programs; the suspension of these programs due to the pandemic puts food security and nutrition at risk, and as a consequence the existence of children with limited capacity to cope with diseases (FAO, 2020d).[11] Thus, each country must direct its actions to maintain social food programs, taking the necessary precautions to avoid transmission of the virus.

Food distribution channels of almost all countries across the income spectrum have been highly disrupted, with strong negative consequences for the most vulnerable. There is widespread media coverage of sudden decreases in food security due to:

- Loss of income from workers who are fully or partially furloughed affecting their ability to purchase food;
- Stay-at-home orders and restricted physical access to food markets and/or indigenous food gathering activities;
- Closure or diminished capacity of institutions that support food social safety nets, such as food banks and school feeding programs; and
- Market disruptions such as issues with the ability of supermarkets to rapidly restock from centralized distribution systems following unprecedented demand (i.e., panic buying) for pantry staples.
- Wastage of fresh vegetables, fruits, and milk due to inability by farmers or entrepreneurs to transport them from point of production to local markets or supermarkets in nearby towns or cities.

How will these shocks ripple outwards to affect broader agricultural systems? What are the likely effects on subsistence systems where farmers and households, that are already food insecure, have less resilience against such large disruptions? How will the international, national, and local market disruptions to consumption affect larger-scale commercial farm systems, as they contend with volatile market signals and disrupted supply chains?

Will these disruptions be temporary? Or will these sudden negative shocks to food security because permanent changes in food systems? How will this impact producers, agricultural and food systems in different sectors, industries, regions, and economic circumstances?

LABOUR AVAILABILITY

A second emerging issue concerns labor availability in the agriculture-food sector. Labor has been suddenly restricted in many regions due to quarantine measures and loss of workforce from COVID-19 deaths and serious illness. There have been substantial restrictions on international labour movements and worker programs that are critical to agricultural production in some sectors or that have caused bottlenecks. Anecdotally, this seems particularly severe in horticulture, livestock production systems, and processing but also for planting and harvesting of crops that are relatively labor-intensive. The timing of labor needs is often inflexible for seasonally produced foods. Resolving these labor shortages and designing working conditions that are safe for workers and the community, is of critical importance in order to secure future growing seasons and avoid disastrous consequences for future food security and supply.

If COVID-19 is not contained, implying that free and safe movement of agriculture-food workers will not be attainable for the foreseeable future, how will our agricultural and food systems cope with this loss? Will emergency measures, such as recruiting temporary domestic volunteers or chartering special flights and paying workers during quarantines be sufficient? Can we make workers safer given that many are in dormitory-style housing and/or work on assembly lines that are incompatible with maintaining physical distancing? If workers cannot be safe, and be perceived to be so, while the virus is circulating in the community, what will the effects on food systems be? Can all regions fill their labor shortages sufficiently? What different approaches to this problem might there be? Will there be major and permanent changes in international agriculture-food labor availability and movements and, if so, how might agricultural systems adapt?

FARM SYSTEM RESILIENCE

A third clear domain of concern is farm system resilience to the COVID-19 pandemic. Which systems are resilient, and which are not? Are small farms that primarily use family labor and so are less dependent on externally hired labor, more resilient than large farms which depend on external labor? What technological measures could be adopted to reduce dependency on human labor and gain efficiency in farming? What are the short- and long-term consequences of unequal access to resilience tools and measures? How will local, regional, national, and international agricultural systems respond to large losses of agricultural production during the pandemic? Which countermeasures against the virus will have very long-term effects? How can we reorient our agricultural systems to function optimally in a post-COVID-19 world? What is the role of agricultural policy in boosting resilience of agricultural systems? Do our policies need to change going forward or are we already well equipped to safeguard our agricultural systems from similar shocks in the future? What does the COVID-19 pandemic reveal about the overall functioning of our agricultural systems?

AGRICULTURAL SYSTEM CONNECTIVITY

The COVID-19 pandemic is having an impact on international relationships far beyond the agriculture-food sector's labor force. This includes announcements of export restrictions across several countries that limit global agriculture-food trade and market access (see for example Laborde and IFPRI, 2020) (Vos et al., 2020). The agriculture-food sector is highly connected internationally. Ports that shut down or reduce activity, vastly reduced freight capacity on commercial flights for agricultural goods, and other broad global supply chain disruptions due to the COVID-19 crisis (Ivanov, 2020) have the potential to limit critical access to agricultural inputs and markets. This may negatively impact agricultural productivity for current and future seasons. The suddenness and severity of these shutdowns leave little scope for identifying suitable domestic substitutes in the short term but may spur less reliance on global agriculture-food value chains in the future. Some nations are also exploring more domestic "food sovereignty" in order to address emerging domestic food security concerns due to COVID-19. These actions have serious implications for our current globalized agriculture-food trading system and is potentially one of the most important impacts on the current food system.

OTHER IMPACTS AND QUESTIONS

Other myriad unanswered questions include understanding the impacts and consequences of:

- Wholesale shifts in market prices and the relative value of agricultural outputs on our agricultural management choices;
- New competition for critical inputs, especially water, due to increasing emphasis on public health and sanitation systems;
- Impacts of supply chain and processing disruptions on animal welfare;
- Existing economic inequality and relative resilience of agricultural systems, as well as other social network systems reliant on agricultural income generation and stability;
- The compound effects of so many human system shocks and the behavior of the natural capital systems that support agriculture overall; and
- Disruptions to research and monitoring programmers, perhaps particularly to those of PhD students and postdoctoral fellows that face time limitations.
- How will COVID-19 impact progress towards the SDGs?

COMPUTATION MODEL OF ANALYSIS

As we discussed in the previous section that the problems of food insecurity and agriculture-food supply chain are growing across the world, including economically developed countries (Long et al., 2020). In Europe, around half a million people do not have regular and sufficient access to food and about 20 million families cannot regularly afford high-quality meals (i.e., fish, meat, or their vegetarian equivalent).[12, 13] These numbers are expected to rise due to the COVID-19 pandemic. According to the FAO definition, food security is referred to as a condition in which all the people, at all times, have physical, social, and economic access to sufficient, safe, and nutritious food to meet their dietary needs and food preferences for an active and healthy life (Organization, 1996). In this section our aim to cover highly used computational methods that could be used to computing and analysis the impact of COVID-19 on various factors of agriculture-food issues:

DYNAMIC PANEL MODEL

With this model our aim is to analyze the impact of trade openness on the level of food security in European countries. According to previous studies (Dithmer & Abdulai, 2017; Headey, 2013) in this work, we adopt a dynamic model approach to examine the effects of trade openness on food security for a cross-section of countries.

In the analysis of the economic aspects, it becomes fundamental to analyze the dynamic aspect of the phenomenon, as the effects of economic policies could only be evident with the passage of time. According to previous studies, the suitable methodology for analyzing the dynamic effect of a phenomenon of time is the "dynamic panel."

One simple way of allowing dynamic effects in panel data models is including a lagged dependent variable. It is well known that the introduction of the lagged dependent variable will generally mean that standard estimators are inconsistent. Consistent estimators can be found using the GMM estimator proposed by Arellano and Bond (1991). In the following lines all the passages are described.

This particular methodology allows to capture the dynamic aspects of the commercial reforms and to face the problem of the potential endogeneity that could derive from this specification. In fact, the continuous evolution of economic processes means that the effect of economic and trade policies is completely evident only in the long run (Shen et al., 2019). Therefore, the dynamic model allows one to consider the effects of explanatory variables over time.

Impact of Pandemic on Food Safety Level

In this section we considered current food safety levels as a function of previous levels and we built the following regression models:

$$FS_{i,t} = a + \beta FS_{i,t-1} + \gamma TO_{i,t} + \delta CV_{i,t} + \mu_i + \lambda_t + \varepsilon_{i,t} \quad i = 1,2,3,\ldots,33 \text{ and } t = 1,2,3\ldots,18$$

(10.1)

where FS, which stands for food security, was our dependent variable that indicates the level of food security, in our analysis we used two different variables i.e., average protein supply and average dietary energy supply adequacy. Where protein supply average indicates national average protein expressed in grams per capita per day, while dietary energy supply adequacy is a percentage of the average dietary energy requirement in each country. We decided to use these indicators because they both offer a quantitative information on the caloric energy input of foods available for human consumption and a qualitative information on the nutritional value of foods, since the protein component represents the major macronutrient group (Dorosh et al., 2016; FAO, 2013). To, which stands for trade openness, was an independent variable that indicates the level of trade openness in each country. In this study, in order to test the robustness of the result, we chose to use three different indicators: trade openness (Heston et al., 2009), tariff (DeJong & Ripoll, 2006), and globalization (Dreher et al., 2008). CV is a set of control variables used to determine the potential level of food safety in each country. Finally, μ_i, e, and λ_t are respectively countries fixed effects and time fixed effects, while $\varepsilon_{i,t}$ is the error term.

The use of the delayed dependent variable in the model causes the phenomenon called "dynamic panel bias" (Nickell, 1981), because the lagged dependent variable is endogenous to the fixed effects in the error term, which leads to estimation problems. Normally, this estimation problem cannot be eliminated with fixed or random effects regressions, and the estimation with the ordinary least squares (OLS) method is distorted, because the lagged dependent variable is correlated with the error term $\varepsilon_{i,t}$. The common approach to dealing with non-stationary data is to apply the difference operator in order to achieve a dynamic specification in raw differences.

$$\Delta FS_{i,t} = a + \beta \Delta FS_{i,t-1} + \gamma \Delta TO_{i,t} + \delta \Delta CV_{i,t} + \mu_i + \lambda_t + \varepsilon_{i,t} \quad i = 1, 2, 3, \ldots, 33 \ and \ t$$
$$= 1, 2, 3 \ldots, 18 \tag{10.2}$$

However, this approach is capable of removing the potential distortion, as it eliminated individual effect, because it does not remove the temporal effect.

In order to solve this problem Holtz-Eakin et al. (1988) and Arellano and Bond (1991) developed an estimator for linear dynamic panel data models, called the generalized method of moments (GMM).

Despite the superiority of the difference-GMM (first-order condition and GMM) estimator over the simpler panel data estimations, if the series are very repeated the lagged levels have been demonstrated to be ineffective tools for first-differences (Bound et al., 1995). Then the performance of the difference-GMM estimator can be distorted for the small sample (Baltagi, 2008).

According to Arellano and Bond (1991) and Blundell and Bond (1998), the estimator performance can be increased by adding the original equation in levels to the system, which is known as the "system-GMM." The peculiarity of the system-GMM estimator is that it weighs the moments in inverse proportion respecting their variances and covariances, for this reason, it reduces the weight in the estimation process of the instruments highly correlated.

Data Description

We used panel data composed by the European countries over the period 2000–2017 for the dependent variable (average dietary energy supply adequacy). Regarding the dependent variable, average protein supply, we analyze the period 2000–2012 due to a lack of data for the remaining years.

The variables were selected based on the FAO (Thomas, 2006) and through the analysis of the previous empirical literature (Baltagi, 2008; Blundell & Bond, 1998; Commission, 2013). Most part of the data used in this study can be extracted from world development indicators and Food and Agriculture Organization Corporate Statistical Database (FAOSTAT). Moreover, according to Dithmer and Abdulai (2017), we considered four groups of food security determinants: the first group describes the general context of the country; the second group captures the economic and demographic development; in the third group there were control variables that measure domestic macroeconomic policies and conditions; finally in the last group we considered non-economic events such as natural disasters.

In regards the first group, we took into consideration the total amount of economic resources, the availability of resources for agricultural production, and the importance of agriculture (Fanelli, 2019).

In particular, we used the GDP per capita as the principle variable to measure the quantity of final goods and services on the territory of a country. Rural population shares the variable which indicates the importance of agriculture and refers to the share of people living in rural areas out of the total population. The availability of resources for agricultural production is measured by the arable land variable, which includes land under temporary crops, temporary meadows for mowing or for pasture, land under market or kitchen gardens, and land temporarily fallow.

With regard to the second group of food security determinants, the model included three different variables that capture the agricultural, economic, and demographic development.

In particular, in order to capture the agricultural development, we use Cereal yield (kg per hectare; FAOSTAT), as a proxy for agricultural productivity. The economic development is measured by the GDP growth rate per capita variable. Finally, the population growth variable captures the demographic development.

In regards the third group, the inflation variable, measured by the consumer price index inflation rate, expresses the domestic macroeconomic policy quality; in particular, according to Loayza et al. (2012), high inflation being associated with bad macroeconomic policies.

In the fourth group, we used natural disaster variables; this value indicates the intensity of natural disasters and it is computed through a ratio between the number of populations affected by natural disasters and the total population for each country.

Finally, regarding the last group, we selected three different variables of trade openness, in order to test the research question.

The trade openness variable, according to Heston et al. (2009) is a ratio between trade (real export and import) and GDP. The second variable was tariff (DeJong & Ripoll, 2006), which indicates ad-valorem tariff, measured as import duties. Globalization (Dreher et al., 2008) was the last variable, whereby we used the KOF (KOF is an acronym for the German word "Konjunkturforschungsstelle," meaning: "economic cycle research institute.") globalization index (0–100); The KOF index attempts to measure the degree to which a nation exchanges goods, capital, people, ideas, and information. It is a composite index that uses three dimensions: economic, social, and political, where a value close to 100 indicates a high level of globalization. Tables 10.1 and 10.2 present the variables, source of data, and their summary statistics.

TABLE 10.1
Variables and Data Sources

Variables	Unit	Data Source	Time Period
Average protein supply	(g/cap/day)	FAOSTAT	2000–2012
Average dietary energy supply adequacy	Percentage %	FAOSTAT	2000–2017
Trade openness	N°	World Development Indicators	2000–2017
Tariff	N°	World Development Indicators	2000–2017
Globalization	N°	Swiss Economic Institute	2000–2017
GDP per capita	US$	World Development Indicators	2000–2017
GDP growth	Percentage %	World Development Indicators	2000–2017
Arable land	(hectares per person)	FAOSTAT	2000–2017
Agricultural Production	(kg per hectare)	World Development Indicators	2000–2017
Rural population	Percentage %	World Development Indicators	2000–2017
Population growth	Annual Percentage %	World Development Indicators	2000–2017
Natural disaster	N°	EM-DAT	2000–2017
Inflation	Annual Percentage %	World Development Indicators	2000–2017

Note: Faostat stands for food and agriculture organization corporate statistical database; gdp stands for gross domestic product; em-dat stands for emergency events database

TABLE 10.2
Summary Statistics

Variables	Mean	Standard Deviation	Maximum	Minimum
Average protein supply	97.78	12.399	118	67
Average dietary energy supply adequacy	129.30%	11.55%	158%	101%
Trade openness	1.009	0.503	3.785	0.408
Tariff	3.2	1.777	11.9	1.22
Globalization	78.6	9.382	91.313	47.509
GDP per capita	27,028.05	23,952.97	118,823.65	354.003
GDP growth	2.73%	3.08%	25.16%	−14.758%
Arable land	8,741,911.19	21,322,651.81	124,374,000	60,000
Agricultural Production	2,227,506,805	3,535,306,006	21,419,375,209	1,010,275
Rural population	30.08%	13.05%	58.26%	2.04%
Population growth	0.23%	0.80%	2.89%	−3.847%
Natural Disaster	0.0049	0.0224	0.442	0
Inflation	4.60%	10.09%	168.62%	−4.478%

As previously mentioned, the aim of this study was to estimate the impact of the trade openness on food security through a dynamic panel model approach. According to prior studies (Dithmer & Abdulai, 2017; Thomas, 2006), we used the econometric structure described in the equation (10.1). In order to improve the robustness of the empirical results developed three regressions, with three different trade openness indicators (trade openness, tariff, and globalization).

$$FS_{i,t} = a + \beta FS_{i,t-1} + \gamma TradeOpenness_{i,t} + \delta Ln\ GDPpercapita_{i,t} + \vartheta GDPgrowth_{i,t}$$

$$+ \theta LnArableland_{i,t} + \pi lnAgriculturalproduction_{i,t} + \rho Ruralpop_{i,t}$$

$$+ \varphi LnPopgrowth_{i,t} + \tau Naturaldisaster_{i,t} + \omega LnInflationi_{i,t} + \mu_i + \lambda_t + \varepsilon_{i,t}$$

$$FS_{i,t} = a + \beta FS_{i,t-1} + \gamma Tarif\ f_{i,t} + \delta Ln\ GDPpercapita_{i,t} + \vartheta GDPgrowth_{i,t}$$

$$+ \theta LnArableland_{i,t} + \pi lnAgriculturalproduction_{i,t} + \rho Ruralpop_{i,t}$$

$$+ \varphi LnPopgrowth_{i,t} + \tau Naturaldisaster_{i,t} + \omega LnInflationi_{i,t} + \mu_i + \lambda_t + \varepsilon_{i,t}$$

$$FS_{i,t} = a + \beta FS_{i,t-1} + \gamma Globalization_{i,t} + \delta Ln\ GDPpercapita_{i,t} + \vartheta GDPgrowth_{i,t}$$

$$+ \theta LnArableland_{i,t} + \pi lnAgriculturalproduction_{i,t} + \rho Ruralpop_{i,t}$$

$$+ \varphi LnPopgrowth_{i,t} + \tau Naturaldisaster_{i,t} + \omega LnInflationi_{i,t} + \mu_i + \lambda_t + \varepsilon_{i,t}$$

Results and Discussions

In Europe, the levels of food security, assessed through the average dietary energy supply adequacy and the average protein supply variables, were lower in Eastern area (Figure 10.5).

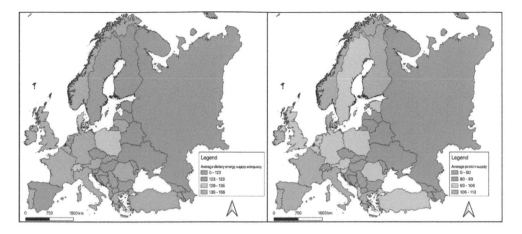

FIGURE 10.5 Geographical distribution of food security level in European countries.

In particular, from an initial exploratory analysis, it emerged that the countries characterized by greater economic development were also characterized by a certain stability in the food supply.

Considering the possibility of collinearity in the model, we computed a correlation analysis between the independent variables. The correlation results are summarized in Table 10.3 (Mason & Perreault Jr, 1991). From the results of the correlation analysis, we can affirm that there was no collinearity in the model, and for this reason, we could preserve the regression model.

Table 10.4 shows the results of the three separate dynamic panel model regressions. The values in the table are coefficients, their p-value, the standard errors (in parentheses), and summary statistics.

TABLE 10.3
Correlation Analysis

Variables	Trade Op.	Tariff	Glob	GDP Percap	GDP Growth	Arable Land	Agr. Prod.	Rur. Pop.	Pop. Growth	Nat. Dis.	Inf.
Trade openness	1										
Tariff	0.116	1									
Glob	0.167	−0.579	1								
GDPpercap	0.393	−0.276	0.708	1							
GDPgrowth	0.119	−0.248	−0.335	−0.203	1						
Arable land	−0.271	0.497	−0.226	−0.213	0.054	1					
Agr.Prod.	−0.365	0.089	0.007	−0.090	−0.067	0.612	1				
Rur.pop.	−0.139	0.166	−0.624	−0.601	0.192	−0.065	−0.123	1			
Pop.growth	0.241	−0.205	0.422	0.637	−0.073	−0.079	0.03	−0.399	1		
Nat.disaster	0.001	−0.121	−0.168	−0.080	−0.002	−0.023	−0.040	0.133	−0.061	1	
Inflation	−0.035	0.225	−0.462	−0.274	0.102	0.19	0.077	0.093	−0.111	0.21	1

Note: Trade op. stands for trade openness; Glob stands for globalization; GDPpercap stands for gross domestic product per capita; GDP growth stands for gross domestic product growth; Agr.Prod. stands for agricultural production; Rur.pop. stands for rural population; Nat.dis. stands for natural disasters; Inf. stands for inflation.

TABLE 10.4

Relationship between Dependent Variable (Average Protein Supply) and the Independent Variables

Variables	Av. Protein Supply (1)	Av. Protein Supply (2)	Av. Protein Supply (3)	Av. Dietary Energy Supply Adequacy (4)	Av. Dietary Energy Supply Adequacy (5)	Av. Dietary Energy Supply Adequacy (6)
Av. Protein supply adequacy t-1	0.06774250 *** (0.0163096)	0.0969006 *** (0.0146225)	0.0779083 *** (0.0144783)			
Av. Dietary energy supply adequacy t-1				0.944329 *** (0.0123442)	0.934857 *** (0.0126720)	0.941284 *** (0.0122497)
Trade openess	0.0754607 *** (0.0142629)			0.293482 *** (0.104098)		
Tariff		-0.0123728 *** (0.00362975)			-0.0742521 ** (0.0325249)	
Globalization			-0.000958626 (0.00143931)			0.00528695 (0.0113695)
Ln GDP per capita	0.269481 *** (0.00748153)	0.281922 *** (0.00534777)	0.298147 *** (0.0121872)	0.213976 *** (0.0657183)	0.379137 *** (0.0855967)	0.290284 ** (0.136305)
GDP growth	0.00088624 (0.00219032)	0.000487233 (0.00200030)	0.00137128 (0.00202637)	0.0104900 (0.0102529)	0.0160616 (0.0107119)	0.104712 (0.0304211)
Ln Arable land	0.113109 *** (0.00647071)	0.0888971 *** (0.00604065)	0.0952195 *** (0.00531122)	0.210299 *** (0.0701103)	0.158903 *** (0.0597781)	0.156196 *** (0.0598957)
Ln Agricultural production	-0.0204668 *** (0.00516753)	-0.0144307 ** (0.00595875)	-0.0180365 *** (0.00579867)	0.0788502 ** (0.0385403)	0.0956332 ** (0.0416021)	0.0896892 ** (0.0396425)
Rural Population	0.00766082 *** (0.000398240)	0.00742802 *** (0.000503302)	0.00766486 *** (0.000500103)	0.0131988 *** (0.00343404)	0.0137986 *** (0.00355062)	0.0138899 *** (0.00351928)
Ln Population growth	-0.00294469 (0.00394025)	-0.00180546 (0.00359173)	-0.00586717 * (0.00349110)	0.0664214 (0.0460942)	0.0626977 (0.0444805)	0.476948 (0.103866)
Natural Disaster	2.40071 (2.30896)	2.15373 (2.03266)	3.27440 (2.55524)	-6.90303 *** (2.64627)	-6.55824 *** (2.75441)	-6.48437 ** (2.74300)
Ln Inflation	0.0660458 *** (0.00784140)	0.0747960 *** (0.00900465)	0.0798373 *** (0.00939306)	-0.0112384 (0.0376728)	0.00051853 (0.0402414)	0.00852784 (0.0394147)
AR (1) errors test	-1.62376 (0.1044)	-1.60499 (0.1085)	-1.65661 (0.0976)	-3.61083 (0.0003)	-3.29418 (0.0010)	-3.59656 (0.0003)
AR (2) errors test	1.51318 (0.1302)	1.53077 (0.1258)	1.57954 (0.1142)	-0.890439 (0.3732)	-1.19194 (0.2333)	-0.890439 (0.3732)

Note: *, **, *** stands for 10%, 5%, and 1% significant level, respectively. Av. stands for average; Ln stands for natural logarithm; AR stands for autoregressive.

The first column of Table 10.4 shows the relationship between our dependent variable (average protein supply) and the independent variables. In the first model, we used Trade Openness (TO) as a variable to represent the level of commercial openness for each country. The lagged dependent variable was strongly significant, indicating that the level of food security changes only slowly over time and it depends on the past levels. This result also justifies the dynamic model specification and the employment of the system-GMM approach. From the results, we can affirm, according to previous studies (Dithmer & Abdulai, 2017; Fanelli, 2019), that when the volume of trade increases, a country's food security level has prospects for improvement. According to previous studies, the increase of food supply should generate a reduction in consumer prices, facilitating the purchase of food products, in particular for developed countries (Thomas, 2006).

In addition, our empirical results highlighted the importance of the economic aspect on food security level; the coefficient between our dependent variable (average protein supply) and the independent variable (GDP per capita) was positive and significant. Therefore, in countries with higher incomes, citizens have access to good quality food (Mary, 2019). However, this value should not be understood simply as purchasing power, but also as the ability to adopt better technologies and to improve the level of food security (Porrini et al., 2019). The impact of the primary sector on food security was confirmed by our results, in fact, the relationship between average protein supply and arable land was positive and significant, and the same result was valid for the independent variable of rural population. In particular, the coefficient of arable land captures an important aspect of domestic resource endowments, and its value indicates that the households with larger arable land having a higher level of production are more likely to be food secure (Porrini et al., 2019). However, one of the weak points of the European agricultural sector is represented by the growing impermeabilization and the constant loss of soil productivity. It has been estimated that 18% of the cultivated land undergoes a decrease in productivity every year and that urbanized areas have grown by 78% in the last 50 years, increasingly limiting areas for cultivation (Kaplan et al., 2017). The phenomenon is particularly felt in the area overlooking the Black Sea, but the Mediterranean regions are also very affected, due to intensive land use and expansion of urbanized areas. In the long run, this phenomenon could negatively affect the food security levels (Fanelli, 2020).

Finally, the value of the coefficient of the inflation variable was positive and significant, showing the importance of the macroeconomic policies in ensuring good levels of food security.

The column labeled (2) and (3) shows the results of the additional analysis to assess the robustness of our empirical results, in fact, we use alternative trade openness measures as tariff and globalization.

As shown in column (2), the ad-valorem tariff measure was significantly negatively related to average protein supply, implying that trade restrictions, on average, have detrimental effects on overall food security level. The relationship with the other independent variables was the same of the column (1).

Column (3) shows the results with the globalization variable, demonstrating that the relationship between globalization and the average protein supply variable was not significant between the European countries.

The column labeled (4) of Table 10.4 shows the analysis carried out with an alternative food security indicator, in particular, it describes the relationship between the dependent variable (average dietary energy supply adequacy) and the other selected independent variables. In column (4), we used trade openness as the variable that expresses the level of commercial openness. Also in this case, the lagged dependent variable was strongly significant. From an empirical point of view, according to previous studies (Dithmer & Abdulai, 2017; Thomas, 2006), when the volume of trade increases, in general thanks to a trade liberalization policy, food security levels also have the potential to improve. In fact, policies aimed at encouraging trade allow countries to access the global market, increasing the overall quantity of food and raw materials for agriculture (Alesandro et al., 2017). Indeed, each state can use export earnings to import at an affordable price all those goods whose domestic production is scarce or too expensive (Wacziarg & Welch, 2008). Furthermore, according to Jaffee et al. (2011), commercial opening is beneficial to food security levels because it can positively affect the employment of citizens, especially in the case of the least developed countries. The latter thanks to the trade openness, can import products made with the relatively abundant factor and with low-skilled labor, thereby creating employment opportunities and raising workers' incomes (Mary, 2019).

In addition, this alternative indicator also confirms the importance of the economic and agricultural aspects to guarantee good levels of food security. Indeed, the relationship between the dependent variable (average Energy Supply Adequacy) and the dependent variables (GDP pro capita, Arable Land, Rural Population, and Coefficient of Agricultural production) was positive and significant.

In addition, the empirical result confirms the importance of the non-economic evidence for the food security levels: the relationship between the average energy supply adequacy and the natural disaster independent variable was positive and significant, in particular, when the number of natural disaster decreases, the level of food security increases.

Moreover, from the results showed in the column labeled (5), we can confirm that the decrease in customs duties has a positive impact on improving food security levels.

Finally, as shown in the column (6), the relationship between globalization and our food security indicator was not significant in European countries.

Hence this analysis implies that commercial openness, in an economically advanced context, can have a positive impact both on security of supply, but also on the nutritional quality of the same, demonstrating the effectiveness of the commercial model proposed by the European Union, where the food sector represents a key resource from an economic, social, and cultural point of view. In addition, our analysis confirmed that the most resilient countries are those characterized by higher per capita incomes.

SPATIAL DURBIN MODEL

Infectious diseases may have spillover effects on agriculture due to their infectivity, that is, the epidemic outbreak in one province may affect the agricultural production of surrounding provinces. This article uses a spatial Durbin model to investigate the potential spillover effects of epidemics (10.4). Equation (10.3) provides the formation of a spatial Durbin model:

$$y_{i,t} = \beta_1 y_{i,t-1} + \beta_2 EP_{i,t} + \beta_3 X_{i,t} + \delta_1 \sum_{j=1}^{N} \omega_{i,j} y_{j,t} + \delta_2 \sum_{j=1}^{N} \omega_{i,j} EP_{j,t} + \delta_3 \sum_{j=1}^{N} \omega_{i,j} X_{j,t} + \lambda_i + \gamma_t + \varepsilon_{i,t}$$

$$(10.3)$$

where $y_{i,t}$ is the logarithm of the real agricultural GDP of province j in period t. $EP_{j,t}$ and $X_{j,t}$ are the vectors of epidemic variables and other control variables of province j in period t, respectively. $\omega_{i,j}$ is the element of the ith row and the jth column in the spatial weights matrix W that reflects the cross-sectional dependence between province i and j. δ_1, δ_2 and δ_3 measure the magnitude of the spillovers due to different variables, where $\delta_1 = c(\delta_{11})$, $\delta_2 = c(\delta_{21}, \delta_{22})$ and $\delta_3 = c(\delta_{31}, \delta_{32}, \ldots.)$. This article focuses on $\delta_2 = c(\delta_{21}, \delta_{22})$, which measures the spillovers on agricultural output due to the incidence rate and death rate of epidemics, respectively.

The key of the spatial Durbin model is to establish a good spatial weights matrix W, which accurately measures the cross-sectional dependence across provinces. In this article, the widely used geographical distance is applied to construct the spatial weights matrix W, in which ωij is equal to the reciprocal of the Euclidean distance between provinces i and j (Gaigné et al., 2012). Matrix W assumes that the neighboring and closer provinces have greater interaction. This article follows existing studies to standardize each row of the matrix W and assign zero to the diagonal elements.

In equation (10.3), it is assumed that epidemics in province i might not only directly affect its own agricultural production but also that of other provinces. According to LeSage and Pace (2009), the former is called direct effect, the latter is indirect effect and the sum of the two is the total effect. The direct and indirect effects of the explanatory variables in equation (10.3) are the mean sum of the diagonal and off-diagonal rows of the matrix $(I - \delta_1 W)^{-1} [I\beta_{ns} + W\beta_{ns}] \forall n, s$, respectively. It is worth noting that indirect effects measure the impacts on others, which are often regarded as spillover effects (Gong, 2018b; LeSage & Pace, 2009).

PRODUCTION FUNCTION AND GROWTH ACCOUNTING MODEL

The previous two subsections focus on the overall (direct and indirect) impact of epidemics on agricultural output (y_{it}). This article further generates a transcendental logarithmic (translog) production function model and uses the growth accounting model to analyze the impact mechanism of epidemics on agricultural output through different channels such as input factors and total factor productivity (TFP). The translog production function is in the following form:

$$y_{it} = \sum_{k=1}^{4} \rho_k Z_{i,t}^k + \sum_{k=1}^{4}\sum_{l=1}^{4} \rho_{k,l} Z_{i,t}^k Z_{i,t}^l + \theta_1 EP_{i,t} + \theta_2 X_{i,t} + \alpha + \lambda_i + \gamma_t + \varepsilon_{i,t} \qquad (10.4)$$

where $y_{i,t}$ is the logarithm of the real agricultural GDP of province i in period t. $Z_{i,t}^k$ it is the kth input in logarithm. Based on Lin (1992), epidemics and other factors that may affect agricultural productivity are introduced into the production function. The TFP in logarithm measured by the Solow residual method is

$$\widehat{TFP}_{i,t} = \widehat{\theta_1} EP_{i,t} + \widehat{\theta_2} X_{i,t} + \widehat{\alpha_i} + \widehat{\lambda_i} + \widehat{\gamma_t} + \widehat{\varepsilon_{it}} \qquad (10.5)$$

Besides the impact on agricultural TFP, epidemics may also affect the quantity and output elasticity of input factors. For example, prevention and control measures, such as a business shutdown after an epidemic outbreak, may lead to a decline in labor force. Meanwhile, the remaining labor force may have lower productivity because they suffer from panic effects due to epidemics, which may accelerate the labor-capital substitution and lead to changes in output elasticities. In order to estimate the impact of epidemics on input factors, output elasticities, and TFP, this article employs a GMM estimator of the following dynamic panel model to analyze the marginal impact through the aforementioned channels:

$$
\begin{cases}
Z_{i,t}^k = \beta_1^{1k} z_{i,t-1}^k + \beta_2^{1k} EP_{i,t} + \beta_3^{1k} X_{i,t} + \alpha + \lambda_i + \gamma_t + \varepsilon_{i,t} \quad \forall k \\
\tau_{i,t}^k = \beta_1^{2k} \tau_{i,t-1}^k + \beta_2^{2k} EP_{i,t} + \beta_3^{2k} X_{i,t} + \alpha + \lambda_i + \gamma_t + \varepsilon_{i,t} \quad \forall k \\
\widehat{TFP}_{i,t} = \beta_1^3 \widehat{TFP}_{i,t-1} + \beta_2^3 EP_{i,t} + \beta_3^3 X_{i,t} + \alpha + \lambda_i + \gamma_t + \varepsilon_{i,t}
\end{cases}
\tag{10.6}
$$

On this basis, the growth accounting model has the form:

$$
\Delta y_{i,t} \approx \underbrace{\sum_{k=1}^{4} \left(\tau_{i,t}^k z_{i,t}^k - \tau_{i,t-1}^k z_{i,t-1}^k \right)}_{Input\ Factor\ Change} + \underbrace{\Delta \widehat{TFP}_{i,t}}_{Total\ Factor\ Productivity}
\tag{10.7}
$$

where $\tau_{i,t}^k$ it is the output elasticity with respect to the kth agricultural input, which can be calculated after solving equation (10.4). Agricultural growth $(\Delta y_{i,t})$ comes from the change in input factors and TFP. The impact of epidemics on agricultural production is $\beta_2 \Delta EP_{i,t} \approx \gamma TO_{i,t}$ from equation (10.1). At the same time, the impact of epidemics on input quantity $(z_{i,t}^k)$, output elasticity $(\tau_{i,t}^k)$ and TFP $(\widehat{TFP}_{i,t})$ can be estimated from equation (10.5). We can then substitute these impacts into equation (10.6) to calculate the overall impact on agricultural production of an epidemic, which is comparable with the estimation from equation (10.1). It is worth noting that the possible spillover effects of epidemics are considered in equation (10.3) due to their infectivity. The spatial Durbin model is also introduced in equations (10.5) and (10.6) to clarify the transmission mechanism of the direct and indirect effects of epidemics on agricultural growth. As a result, we introduce a spatial dynamic panel model into the growth accounting framework.

Data and Summary Statistics

This article uses balanced panel data of 31 provinces in mainland China for 2002–2018. There are four categories of variables utilized in this article: (1) agricultural output $(y_{i,t})$—the output variable is the gross value of agricultural output, which is defined as the sum of the total value of production from farming, forestry, animal husbandry, and fisheries (in billion CNY at 1980 constant prices); (2) key explanatory variables of epidemics – the incidence rate (EP1it) and death rate (EP2it) of primary and secondary infectious diseases reported by provincial statutory reports are used to measure the infectivity and toxicity of infectious diseases, respectively; (3) other control variables—agricultural structure is measured by the output share of farming, forestry, animal husbandry, and fishery. The infrastructure condition is measured by highway density. The technological innovation is measured by the stock of patents granted per unit of GDP. The agricultural international trade is measured by the sum of agricultural imports and exports. The education level is measured by the proportion of the population that has completed high school. Irrigation refers to the irrigated land area (in million hectares). The natural disaster condition is measured by the sown area, with more than 10% less output than normal due to drought, flood, hail, frost, insect pests, and other natural disasters (in million hectares). Agricultural fiscal expenditure is the stock of fiscal expenditure on agriculture calculated by the classical perpetual inventory method (in ten billion CNY at 1980 constant prices). The degree of marketization is measured by the marketization index in Wang et al. (2017) and (4) agricultural inputs—this article follows Gong (2018a) in its input selection of China's agriculture, which includes labor, land, fertilizer, and machinery. Labor is measured as the size of the labor force (in millions) in the primary industry. Land refers to the sown area (in million hectares). Fertilizer is measured by the sum of the gross weight of nitrogen, phosphate, potash, and complex fertilizers (in millions of tons). Machinery is the total power of agricultural machinery (in millions of kilowatts).

Overall, most of the agricultural data come from China Statistical Yearbook, while some data are supplemented (e.g., the labor statistics in 2013–2015) and adjusted (e.g., the data of Chongqing and Hainan) using the China Compendium of Statistics 1949–2008 as well as provincial-level statistical yearbooks. The remaining data are collected from the databases of the National Bureau of Statistics, Ministry of Science and Technology, Ministry of Commerce and Ministry of Transport and National Health Commission. Table 10.5 reports the summary statistics of the main variables.

Results and Discussion

This empirical section applies the described models to the provincial-level panel data of 31 provinces in mainland China in order to investigate the characteristics and mechanism

TABLE 10.5
Summary Statistics

Variable	Unit/Notation	Mean	Std. Dev.	Min	Max
Agricultural output	Billion CNY at 1980 constant prices	40	30	1.6	134
Labor	Million people	9.3	7.1	0.33	33.9
Land	Million hectares	5.1	3.7	0.1	14.9
Fertilizer	Million tons	17.3	14.1	0.3	71.6
Machinery	Million kilowatts	28.1	27.3	0.9	133.5
Incidence rate	Persons per 10,000	26	10	9.1	73.8
Death rate	%	0.4	0.42	0.03	2.64
Farming share	%	54	9.4	31	81
Forestry share	%	4.7	3.4	0.7	33
Animal husbandry share	%	32.3	9.7	10.8	67.5
Fishery share	%	9	9.3	0	34
Infrastructure	Highway mileage/land area	0.47	0.348	0.033	1.951
Technological innovation	Invention patents/real GDP	2.674	4.201	0.144	44.9
Agricultural trade	Billion US dollar	4	6.5	0	42.7
Educational level	Proportion of high school completion	0.249	0.103	0.03	0.686
Irrigation area	Million hectares	2	1.5	0.1	6.1
Damage area	Million hectares	1.1	1	0	7.4
Agricultural fiscal expenditure	Billion CNY at 1980 constant prices	20	19	0	99
Marketization degree	Marketization index	6.21	2.09	0.3	11.11

TABLE 10.6

The Direct Effect of Epidemics on Agricultural Production Using Dynamic Panel Model

	(1)	(2)	(3)
Dependent Variable Agricultural Output	OLS	OLS	GMM
Incidence rate	0.014	0.014	0.002
	(0.024)	(0.023)	(0.003)
Death rate	0.040	0.037	0.035
	(0.077)	(0.073)	(0.083)
Output lagged term	0.904***	0.906***	0.906***
	(0.021)	(0.022)	(0.034)
Other control variables	Yes	Yes	Yes
Region fixed effect	Yes	Yes	Yes
Year fixed effect	No	Yes	Yes
Intercept	0.377	0.047	0.047
	(0.320)	(0.313)	(0.277)

Note(s):   Standard errors in parentheses *p < 0.1, **p < 0.05, ***p < 0.01

of epidemics on agricultural production, and then compares the estimation results under different models.

The Direct and Indirect Effects of Epidemics on Agricultural Production

In order to avoid spurious regression, this article uses an LL panel unit root test (Levin et al., 2002) and an IPS panel unit root test (Im et al., 2003) to test the stationarity of variables based on Ball et al. (2004). The test results reject the null hypothesis that there is a unit root, and thus the dynamic panel model can be applied directly.

Table 10.6 provides the estimation results of the dynamic panel model, which evaluates the direct effect of epidemics on agricultural output using the OLS and GMM models, respectively. As for the OLS results in columns (1) and (2), neither the incidence rate nor death rate has a significant effect on agricultural output. The GMM results in column (3) are basically consistent with the OLS estimates in the first two columns. The above results show that there is no significant direct effect of epidemics on agricultural output.

It is worth noting that Table 10.6 fails to take into account the potential indirect/spillover effects of epidemics. This article adopts the Breusch-Pagan LM test and the Pesaran CD test, both of which reject the null hypothesis and support the existence of cross-sectional dependence. Using the spatial weights matrix Wconstructed by geographical distance, this article estimates Moran's I index, which is statistically significant at the 1% level and confirms the existence of spatial autocorrelation geographically. As a result, it is necessary to use a spatial econometric model to capture the spillovers, and Wconstructed by geographical distance is a valid spatial weights matrix. Table 10.7 reports the estimation results of the spatial Durbin model. Column (1) shows that the infectivity and toxicity of epidemics have no significant effect on agricultural output, which is consistent with the findings in Table 10.6. The coefficient of the interaction between the spatial weight matrix W and the incidence rate of epidemics is significantly negative, whereas the coefficient of the

TABLE 10.7

The Direct and Indirect Effects of Epidemics on Agricultural Production Using Spatial Durbin Mode

Dependent Variable Agricultural Output	Estimation	Direct Effects	Indirect Effects	Total Effects
Incidence rate	−0.001 (0.005)	0.000 (0.013)	−0.016** (0.008)	−0.000144
Death rate	0.010 (0.007)	−0.002 (0.002)	0.001 (0.001)	0.001 (0.001)
W* Incidence rate	−0.031*** (0.009)	−	−	−
W* Death rate	0.019 (0.045)	−	−	−
Other control variables	Yes	−	−	−
Region fixed effect	Yes	−	−	−
Year fixed effect	Yes	−	−	−
Intercept	−1.048** (0.515)	−	−	−

interaction between the spatial weight matrix W and the death rate of epidemics is insignificant. Therefore, negative spillovers of epidemics on agricultural output exist, mainly due to the infectivity of epidemics.

Using the estimations in column (1), the direct, indirect, and total effects of epidemics on agricultural output are then captured in columns (2)–(4). The direct effect of the incidence rate of epidemics is insignificant both economically and statistically, which indicates that the rise in the incidence rate of epidemics in a province has no significant impact on its agricultural output. However, the significant negative indirect effect in column (3) indicates that when the incidence rate of epidemics in a province increases by 1%, the agricultural output in all other provinces together falls by 0.016%. As a result, the total effects of epidemics' incidence rate are negative due to the negative spillovers. In terms of the toxicity (represented by death rate) of epidemics, Table 10.7 shows that it has neither significant direct effects nor significant indirect effects on agricultural output. To summarize, there is a small negative impact of epidemics on agricultural output through spillover effects, and its magnitude depends on the infectivity (represented by incidence rate) rather than the toxicity (represented by death rate) of epidemics.

The Impact Mechanism of Epidemics on Agricultural Production

The above estimations evaluate the overall impact of epidemics on agricultural output. In order to further investigate why there exists an indirect effect rather than a direct effect, this article estimates the agricultural production function so that we can decompose its growth into two parts: the change in input portfolio and the change in TFP, which allow us to explore the impact mechanism. In other words, using the production function and growth accounting method, this article aims to identify the channels through which epidemics affect agricultural output.

Table 10.8 reports the regression results of the production function model. The first two columns provide the result of a Cobb–Douglas production function, and the second two columns provide the result of a translog production function. Theoretically, the translog functional form is more flexible than Cobb–Douglas, as it relaxes the rigid assumptions, such as the perfect substitution between inputs and the perfect competition on inputs market. Empirically, many interactions between inputs of the translog production function in

TABLE 10.8

Regression Results of Agricultural Production Function

Dependent Variable Agricultural Output	C-D Model		T-L Model	
	Coefficient	Standard Error	Coefficient	Standard Error
Labor	0.197***	−0.065	0.434*	−0.221
Land	0.239***	−0.067	0.371*	−0.213
Fertilizer	0.479***	−0.062	0.870***	−0.227
Machinery	0.153***	−0.035	0.233*	−0.13
Labor * labor	−	−	0.054	−0.048
Labor * land	−	−	0.268**	−0.118
Labor * fertilizer	−	−	0.347***	−0.106
Labor * machinery	−	−	0.003	−0.057
Land * land	−	−	0.273***	−0.093
Land * fertilizer	−	−	0.681***	−0.14
Land * machinery	−	−	0.197**	−0.078
Fertilizer * fertilizer	−	−	0.091	−0.083
Fertilizer * machinery	−	−	0.051	−0.078
Machinery * machinery	−	−	0.079***	−0.029
Other control variables	Yes	−	Yes	−
Intercept	2.000***	−0.553	1.926	−0.561
R^2	0.992	−	0.994	−
Observations	527	−	527	−

Note(s): Standard errors in parentheses *p < 0.1, **p < 0.05, ***p < 0.01

Table 10.8 have significant coefficients, and the F-test is also in favor of the translog production function. Therefore, this article adopts the translog model as the main model to predict the production function and derive TFP.

Table 10.9 presents the impact of epidemics on agricultural production through different channels. It is worth noting that this article now focuses on the incidence rate of epidemics, as the analysis above shows that the death rate of epidemics has neither a significant direct effect nor significant indirect effect on agricultural output. Column (1) of Table 10.9 reports the estimated direct impact of epidemics using a non-spatial dynamic panel model. Columns (2)–(4) provide the direct effects, indirect effects, and total effects of epidemics using a spatial Durbin model, respectively. The first row provides the estimated impacts on agricultural output. As a result, the estimation of the first column in Table 10.9 is similar to the estimation of the third column in Table 10.6, whereas the estimations of the second to the fourth columns in Table 10.9 are consistent with the estimations of those in Table 10.7. Besides the impact on agricultural output, Table 10.9 also estimates the impact of epidemics on the quantity of the four inputs, the elasticity of the four inputs and TFP.

First, the non-spatial and spatial models find consistent significantly negative direct impact of epidemics on TFP, both of which indicate an average 0.022% decrease in agricultural TFP when the incidence rate of epidemics increases by 1%. Moreover, the result of the spatial model also confirms a significantly negative indirect effect of epidemics on agricultural TFP. As a result, this article predicts that a 1% increase in epidemics will lead to a total 0.037% decrease in agricultural TFP.

TABLE 10.9

The Impact Mechanism of Epidemics on Agricultural Production

Dependent Variable	Non-spatial Direct Effects	Direct Effects	Spatial Durbin InDirect Effects	Total Effects
Agricultural output	−0.002 (0.003)	0.000 (0.013)	−0.016** (0.008)	−0.000144
Labor	0.002 (0.012)	0.001 (0.049)	−0.059 (1.439)	−0.058 (1.482)
Land	0.018* (0.011)	0.018* (0.010)	−0.010 (0.464)	0.008 (0.470)
Fertilizer	0.025***(0.009)	0.028*** (0.010)	−0.011 (0.009)	0.017 (0.011)
Machinery	0.032*** (0.012)	0.034* (0.020)	−0.012 (0.139)	0.022 (0.144)
Labor elasticity	0.006 (0.004)	0.006 (0.004)	−0.004 (0.003)	0.002 (0.004)
Land elasticity	−0.003 (0.010)	−0.004 (0.011)	−0.010 (0.211)	−0.014 (0.220)
Fertilizer elasticity	−0.008 (0.008)	−0.008 (0.010)	0.012 (0.147)	0.004 (0.154)
Machinery elasticity	0.002 (0.002)	0.003 (0.003)	0.002 (0.003)	0.005 (0.004)
TFP	−0.022** (0.010)	−0.022**(0.012)	−0.015** (0.008)	−0.037** (0.020)

Note(s):   Standard errors in parentheses *$p < 0.1$, **$p < 0.05$, ***$p < 0.01$

It is very interesting that we find both negative direct and indirect effects on TFP, but only negative indirect effects on output. The results in Table 10.9 show that the incidence rate of epidemics has a significant negative direct impact on TFP, although this can be compensated by an increasing quantity of land, fertilizer, and machinery. The self-protection measures and governmental control measures established due to epidemics will lead to resource misallocation and efficiency loss, and therefore cause TFP loss. When a province suffers from a severe epidemic, its governor is responsible for stable agricultural production and will increase agricultural inputs, including land, fertilizer, and machinery, to compensate for the expected TFP loss. The impact on labor, however, is insignificant for two reasons. On the one hand, rapid migration and urbanization make it difficult to attract additional agricultural workers. On the other hand, the infectivity characteristics of epidemics may accelerate the labor-capital substitution and lead to less labor per unit of land, as estimated.

However, the governor of a province may not foresee that its own productivity will be affected when other provinces suffer from epidemics, and may therefore fail to take actions until the productivity shocks are observed. In manufacturing, it is possible to shut down the factories during the outbreak and make up the loss by additional inputs later. In agriculture, however, inaction in one stage may not be able to be compensated later. Take SARS as an example, this disease was fully controlled in June 2003. In manufacturing, firms can buy more equipment, and workers can work overtime to make up the loss in the second half of the year. In agriculture, if the control measures prevent the farmers to get seeds during the spring sowing season or if the control measures cause poultry producers to confront shortage of feed for weeks, agriculture will suffer from irretrievable losses. In other words, the timing of the input usage is important. The results in Table 10.9 provide evidence to support this opinion, as insignificant indirect impacts of epidemics on all four inputs are found. Accordingly, the indirect loss in TFP fails to be compensated, and therefore leads to an indirect loss in agricultural output. This result highlights the importance of the timely disclosure and sharing system of epidemic information across provinces. Finally, the output elasticities with respect to the four inputs are all insignificantly affected by epidemics,

TABLE 10.10

The Accounting of Epidemics' Marginal Impact on Agricultural Production

| | Non-spatial | Spatial Durbin | | |
	Direct Effects	Direct Effects	In Direct Effects	Total Effects
A. Input quantity	0.02	0.021	0	0.021
A1. Labor	0	0	0	0
A2. Land	0.002	0.002	0	0.002
A3. Fertilizer	0.007	0.008	0	0.008
A4. Machinery	0.011	0.011	0	0.011
B. TFP	−0.022	−0.022	−0.015	−0.037
Overall impact	−0.002	−0.001	−0.015	−0.016

indicating that there is no systematic change in the agricultural production process and input-output relation caused by epidemics.

It is worth noting that Table 10.9 proves that more agricultural inputs, including land, fertilizer, and machinery, are used to mitigate TFP loss. However, whether such input expansion can fully compensate for the loss in TFP remains untested. In other words, we need to check if the aggregation of the estimated change in TFP and inputs is indeed consistent with the estimated unchanged output when epidemics collide. To tackle this problem, the estimated coefficient in Table 10.9 is then substituted into equation (10.6) to further analyze the impact of epidemics on agricultural output in the growth accounting framework. Table 10.10 uses the growth accounting method and reports the marginal impact of epidemics on agricultural production through different channels. The first column provides accounting results based on the non-spatial model, whereas the last three columns represent the accounting results based on the spatial model.

In column (1) of Table 10.10, when the incidence rate of epidemics of a province increases by 1%, its own agricultural TFP decreases by 0.022% on average. At the same time, almost all the losses in TFP are made up by increasing the quantity of different inputs. To be specific, an increase in machinery contributes the most (0.011%), followed by fertilizer (0.007%) and then land expansion (0.002%), whereas labor force remains unchanged. The advantages of machinery compared with labor are more apparent when epidemics collide, as human beings can be infected while machines cannot. Therefore, the result of a decreasing labor-capital ratio is consistent with the induced innovation theory (Gong, 2020). The overall impact of epidemics on agricultural output, through its impact on inputs and TFP, has reduced to 0.002%. The direct impacts estimated by the spatial model in column (2) are consistent with column (1), indicating the robustness of our estimations on direct effects.

In terms of the accounting for indirect effects, column (3) in Table 10.10 shows that when the incidence rate of epidemics in a province increases by 1%, the TFP of other provinces together decreases by 0.015%. However, since no significant indirect effects on inputs are found, the overall indirect impact on the agricultural output is the same as the indirect impact on TFP. Considering both the direct effects and indirect effects, agricultural TFP will decline by 0.037% when the incidence rate of epidemics in China increases by 1%. Input expansion can compensate for the direct effect on TFP, decreasing the output loss to 0.016%. It is worth noting that the overall impact estimated by growth accounting (last row in Table 10.10) is consistent with the overall impact estimated by regressing agricultural output on epidemics (first row in Table 10.9), which again confirms the robustness of our estimations.

Based on the above estimation results, as well as the current situation of agricultural production in China, we are able to summarize the impact mechanism of epidemics on agricultural production among provinces. If province experiences an epidemic outbreak, its agricultural output may not be reduced due to the increase of input use (land, fertilizer, and machinery) to make up for the loss caused by the TFP reduction. For the surrounding provinces of province i, if the outbreak of epidemics has been overlooked and the potential damage has not been considered in time, these provinces may not offset the TFP loss by increasing input factors. To sum up, although the epidemics may have a negative impact on agricultural production in province i, this negative impact is not directly reflected in the agricultural output of this province. However, the loss of production efficiency directly leads to the decline of agricultural output in these surrounding provinces, represented by the negative spillover effects captured in the above empirical results. Moreover, it is worth noting that the primary tactic to make up for the loss of TFP is to increase advanced input factors, such as fertilizer and machinery, while the contribution of labor and land input is very limited, indicating that the process of agricultural modernization may be accelerated to some extent. Finally, the mechanism analysis shows that although the overall direct impact of epidemics on agriculture is insignificant, it is at the expense of using more inputs, which is not costless. In other words, epidemics do damage the agricultural production, although we may not see a dramatic decline in output level.

The Projection of COVID-19 Impact on Agricultural Production

Finally, using the projected numbers of COVID-19 cases under different scenarios, and our estimated marginal effects, this article projects the overall impact of COVID-19 on agricultural output in China. We consider three scenarios in this estimation: conservative scenario (COS), medium scenario (MES), and worse scenario (WOS). To be specific, COS presents the most optimistic condition, where the compensation capacity of inputs to TFP loss is 100% of the level in history and no new cases of COVID-19 present after 14 April 2020. However, COVID-19 is very likely to be more severe than any other epidemics in the past two decades, and China has a growing constraint on agricultural inputs, such as labor, land and fertilizer. Therefore, the compensation capacity of inputs may be smaller than expected. As a result, MES, the medium scenario, is based on the assumption that the compensation capacity of inputs to TFP loss is 50% of the level in history and the final number of infected people is the average level (122,122) estimated by the Susceptible Exposed Infectious Recovered (SEIR) model in Yang et al. (2020). Moreover, WOS presents the most pessimistic condition, where no additional inputs can be used to make up for the TFP loss and the final number of infected people is the upper bound of the 95% confidence interval of the estimation (156,794) by the SEIR model in Yang et al. (2020).

Table 10.11 projects the impact of COVID-19 on agricultural production in China under different scenarios. Under the COS scenario, China's agricultural TFP will decrease by 1% and the input utilization will compensate for more than half of that loss (increase by 0.57%), resulting in a 0.43% loss in agricultural output. Under the MES scenario, the TFP loss due to COVID-19 will be enlarged to 1.46%, and agricultural output will decrease by 1.05%, as the limited input expansion can only recover 30% of the TFP loss. Under the WOS scenario, we are unable to increase agricultural inputs to compensate for the 1.87% TFP loss. To summarize, this article projects that COVID-19 will lower China's agricultural growth

TABLE 10.11

The Projection of COVID-19 Impact on Agricultural Production

	COVID-19 Projection		
	COS	MES	WOS
	−2	−3	−4
A. Input quantity	0.57%	0.41%	−
A1. Labor	−	−	−
A2. Land	0.05%	0.04%	−
A3. Fertilizer	0.22%	0.16%	−
A4. Machinery	0.30%	0.21%	−
B. TFP	−1.00%	−1.46%	−1.87%
Overall impact	−0.43%	−1.05%	−1.87%

rate by 0.4–2.0% in 2020. Using the same method, the estimated negative impact of SARS on agricultural growth rate in 2003 was 0.03–0.08%, which is much smaller than the projected impact of COVID-19. Furthermore, it is worth noting that the situation in China is gradually stabilizing, but the COVID-19 virus has broken out in many foreign countries, which may lead to an increase of imported cases from abroad. On this basis, if the final number of infected people exceeds 156,794, the negative impact on China's agricultural output may exceed 2%.

TIME SERIES ANALYSIS

Economic Impact on Agriculture: World

Globally, the FAO expects shifts in the supply of and demand for food. It warns of a world "food crisis" if countries do not protect vulnerable people from hunger and malnourishment, and de--clog food supply chains. Similarly, the United Nations has warned that the COVID-19 crisis could trigger "food shortages" around the world. The World Food Programme (WFP) has noted that the COVID-19 crisis is "threatening to affect millions of people already made vulnerable by food insecurity [and] malnutrition." The Ebola outbreak in Sierra Leone (2014–16) led to a major rise in hunger and malnutrition. Small and marginal farmers will also be badly affected if they are unable to continue working their land, earn remunerative product prices, and gain access to markets for purchase or sale.

World agricultural prices show signs of a rise from the third week of March 2020 (Figure 10.6). The increases are marked for rice and wheat (Figure 10.7). One reason for this rise has been the stockpiling by households of rice and wheat, and the restrictions imposed by different countries on food exports. For instance, Vietnam, the world's third-largest rice exporter, has stopped exports, which may reduce the global rice exports by 15%. If India and Thailand too ban exports, world rice prices may rise sharply soon. Russia, the world's largest wheat exporter and the largest wheat supplier to North Africa, is expected to restrict its exports. Kazakhstan, one of the world's biggest sources of wheat flour, has already banned its exports. Similar trends are noted in other crops too. Serbia, to cite an example, has stopped the export of its sunflower oil. Commentators have wondered if these

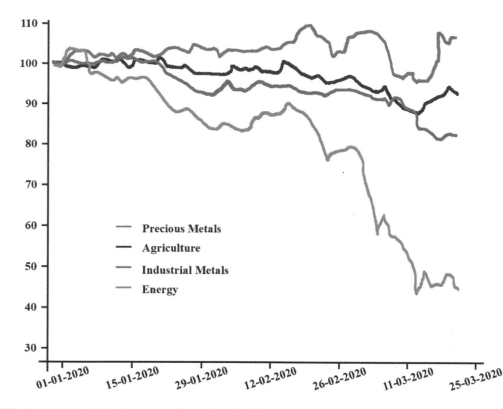

FIGURE 10.6   Global commodity price indices, January to March 2020. (Source: Capital Economics.)

policies indicate the onset of a "wave of food nationalism" that would disrupt the nature of trade flows that have existed after the 1990s.

Quite to the contrary, in some crops like corn, prices have crashed in the United States. This has been the result of low oil prices and the sharp decline in driving across the country, which together have sharply reduced the demand for ethanol. Corn is the most important input in the production of ethanol (see Figure 10.8).

At the same time, estimates also show that the world supply of rice and wheat are satisfactory. According to the U.S. Department of Agriculture (USDA) data, the total world production of rice and wheat will be a record 1.26 billion tons this year. This is more than the total combined annual consumption of rice and wheat. There is also likely to be an increase in the year--end inventories of rice and wheat to a record 469.4 million tons. These estimates, however, assume normalcy in the supply chains of these goods. USDA data also show that many countries, with variations, have inventories of rice enough to feed their populations for about one or two months (Figure 10.9). If the lockdown continues beyond two months, these countries, mainly rice importers, will be in trouble.

Let us now take the case of egg, milk, and meat prices. In the United States, there are supply shortages and a sharp rise in retail egg prices. The wholesale prices of eggs are estimated to have risen by 180% since the beginning of March 2020, as customers were purchasing 44% more eggs in the week ending 14 March 2020 than at the end of the corresponding week in 2019. Retailers are reportedly ordering six times the quantity of eggs

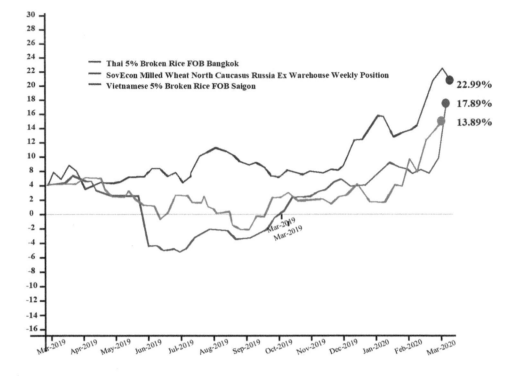

FIGURE 10.7   Year-on-year change in the export prices of rice and wheat, April 2019 to March 2020. (Source: Reuters.)

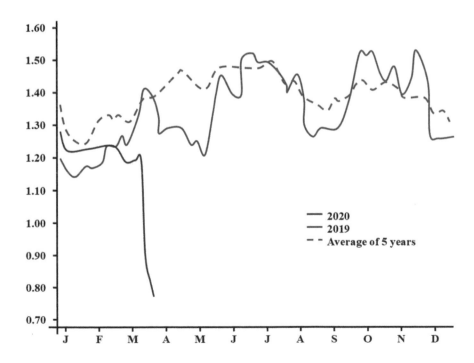

FIGURE 10.8   Prices of ethanol in Iowa, monthly, 2019 and 2020, in $ per gallon. (Source: USDA-AMS Livestock, Poultry & Grain Market News.)

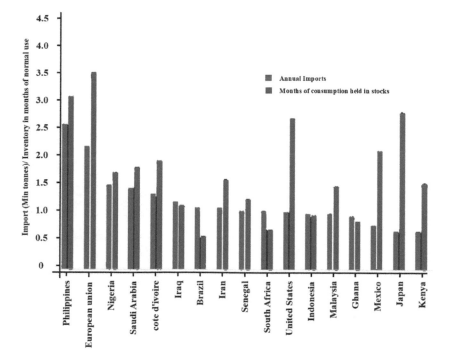

FIGURE 10.9   Number of months of rice inventories available in top rice importers, March 2020. (Source: Reuters.)

to fulfill rising demand. Figure 10.10 shows how the inventories of large eggs in the United States have been rapidly shrinking in March 2020.

In milk, China is a major importer. According to Rabobank, Chinese imports of milk are likely to fall by 19% in 2020. At the same time, the growth rate of milk production is increasing in exporting regions such as New Zealand, Australia, and the EU. COVID-19 is not expected to reduce the production of milk in the exporting countries. In the circumstances, expectations are that global milk prices will tend downwards. This had led to major worries among milk producers in these exporting countries. At the same time, local supply chain bottlenecks are likely to keep upward pressure on the retail prices of milk in most countries.

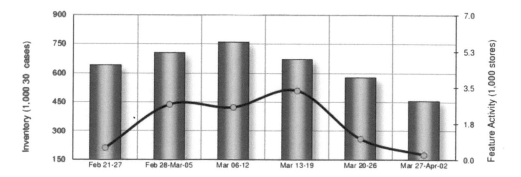

FIGURE 10.10   Inventories of large white shell eggs and retail feature activity in the United States, weekly, February 2020–March 2020, in '30 cases and 1000 stores. (Source: USDA.)

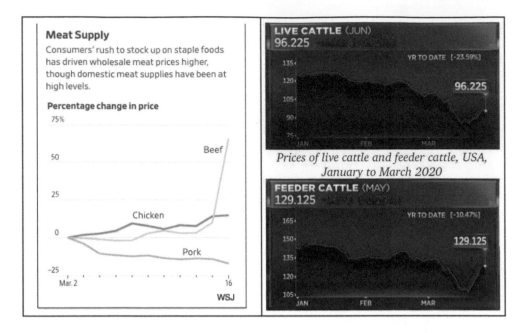

FIGURE 10.11 Different indicators of global prices of meat and cattle, March 2020. (Source: Wall Street Journal and CNBC.)

The meat sector has been in crisis for a different reason. The crisis is partly because of widespread safety fears related to meat consumption despite scientific clarifications that meat consumption is safe. Two factors at play here are China and the African Swine Fever. By the end of 2018, the African Swine Fever had hit large parts of China, killing about 50% of all pigs in the country. This led to a spike in pork prices in China, and a major shift of consumers from pork to beef consumption. Beef prices rose. The COVID-19 pandemic has led to a reduction in beef consumption in China, as well as in other major markets such as the United States.

Yet, there has been heightened retail demand and panic buying of beef in March 2020; in the week ending 15 March 2020, retail beef sales in the United States rose by 77% on a w-o-w basis. This is leading to a rise in the prices of beef and live/feeder cattle (Figure 10.11). This rise in beef prices has, however, not benefited farmers much and much of the gains have been cornered by the meat processors and packers. This is the reason why meat farmers in the United States have been asking the government to intervene even as retail beef sales and prices have been rising.

Globally, agriculture has also been hit hard by labor shortages. There are heightened fears that the absence of the seasonal migrant labor force may disrupt harvests in the United States, Europe, and Australia. France estimates that its agriculture would need 200,000 people in the next three months to compensate for the absence of migrant seasonal labor. French minister of agriculture, Didier Guillaume, is quoted as saying: "I am calling on the men and women who are not working and locked indoors to join the great army of French agriculture," and that "we need to produce to feed the French population." Germany wishes to address the labor shortage in agriculture by encouraging unemployed catering workers to shift to agricultural work. Germany faces a shortage of about 300,000 seasonal workers who annually migrate to the country to harvest fruits and vegetables. In Poland, it is the Ukrainian workers who undertake much of the agricultural labor; the unions of Polish farmers have requested their government to allow these workers to stay back in Poland. Norbert Lins, the Chair of the European Parliament's committee on agriculture, has exhorted member countries to allow safe passage of seasonal migrant workers. A report states that Lins "called on the agriculture ministers and the commission to introduce 'laissezpasser' [access passes] for seasonal workers' to ensure the right to travel to the seasonal workers using special busses or trains or even planes."

In the United Kingdom, the shortfall of seasonal workers is estimated to be 80,000. Farm unions in the United Kingdom have demanded that the government grant them a £9.3m support package in order to pay for a "land army" of workers in fruit and vegetable production. Others have demanded that the government should encourage workers thrown out of other jobs to shift to agricultural seasonal labor on farms.

In the United States, seasonal farmworkers, largely from Mexico, are employed intensively from March to April onwards. These workers come in on an H-2A visa; estimates are that the H-2A visa workers constitute about 10% of the crop farmworkers in the United States. New visa processing rules after COVID-19 may lead to a shortfall of about 60,000 H-2A workers. The current effort is to allow the existing H-2A visa holders to extend their stay in the country for work in the farms, but it is unclear whether this number would be adequate to meet the farm needs (see Figure 10.12). There is some news that the US government is currently considering liberalizing visa rules in view of the labor crisis.

Economic Impact on Agriculture: India

Let us first start with the question of prices. It is important to note that even before the COVID-19 pandemic began, Indian economy was facing a rise in food prices. Data show that food inflation had begun to rise from the middle of 2019, reaching, by January 2020, levels previously attained in 2013–14 (Figure 10.13). Data on the wholesale price indices (WPI) for selected crop groups, available only till February 2020, show that while WPI for food articles has been rising from August 2019 onwards, the rise was driven by a rise in the

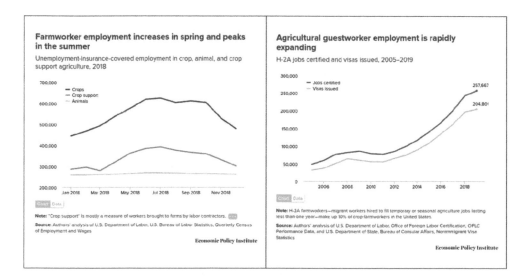

FIGURE 10.12 Importance of seasonal farmworkers in the agriculture of the United States. (Source: Economic Policy Institute.)

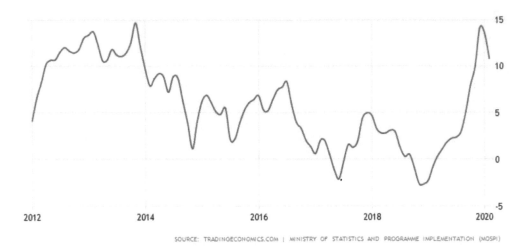

SOURCE: TRADINGECONOMICS.COM | MINISTRY OF STATISTICS AND PROGRAMME IMPLEMENTATION (MOSPI)

FIGURE 10.13 Food inflation rates in India, January 2012–February 2020. (Source: Tradingeconomics.)

prices of vegetables; within vegetables, the price of onions, followed by potato and tomato, drove the WPI up (Figure 10.14). While onion prices have come down, vegetable prices remained high even in February 2020.

According to the Reserve Bank of India's (RBI) 7th bimonthly monetary policy statement, dated 27 March 2020: "as regards inflation, the prints for January and February 2020 indicate that actual outcomes for the quarter are running 30 bps above projections, reflecting the onion price shock." However, the RBI's assessment is that food inflation pressures

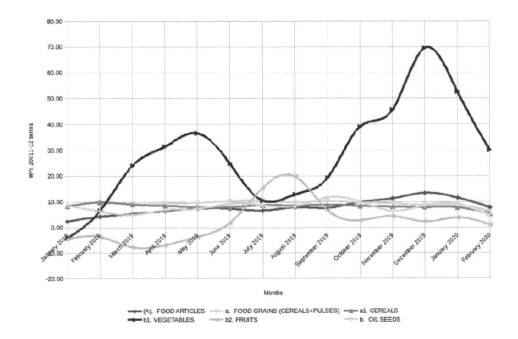

FIGURE 10.14 Percentage change in the WPI of important agricultural commodities, y-o-y. (Source: MOSPI.)

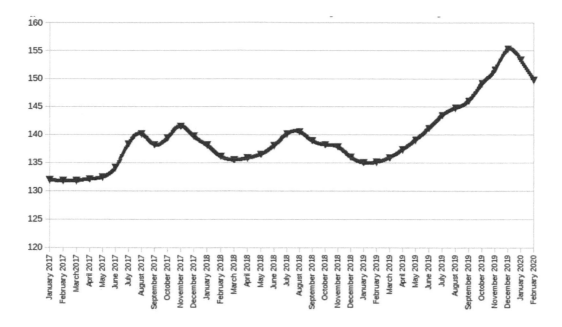

FIGURE 10.15 Consumer Food Price Index, India, January 2017–February 2020. (Source: MOSPI.)

will fall, since aggregate demand is likely to weaken because of the COVID-19 crisis. Consumer price indices (CPI) for food also indicate a similar trend of a rise after August 2019, with some weakening in January and February 2020 (Figure 10.15). The point is that if inflation rises in March 2020 and later, it will be on top of an already rising price curve.

The satisfaction of the RBI also stems from the fact that India's food grain output is projected to be at 292 million tonnes in 2019–2020, up by 2.4% from 2018 to 2019. According to reports, the stocks of wheat and rice with the Food Corporation of India (FCI), as on 1st March 2020, was 77.6 MMT. This quantity is more than three times the specified minimum operational buffer-cum-strategic stock of 21.04 MMT. With the rabi wheat harvest, which should come in by April 2020, the situation is expected to ease further. Similarly, for pulses, the National Agricultural Cooperative Marketing Federation of India (NAFED) is reported to have stocks of 2.25 MT as on 19th March 2020. Between 2014–15 and 2018–19, NAFED has made an unprecedented record procurement of 91.1 lakh MT of oilseeds and pulses (61.3 lakh MT of pulses and 30.3 lakh MT of oilseeds) under the Price Support Scheme, up by 12% from the seven lakh MT procured between 2009–10 and 2013–14. Here again, the inflow of rabi pulses into the market in April 2020 is expected to ease the situation further.

In the case of milk, AMUL has noted that its procurement from 36 lakh farmers across India is proceeding smoothly. In terms of quantity, this amounts to distributing 1.50 lakh liters of milk every day across India. As the lockdown proceeds, AMUL expects milk demand to decline. In an interview, R. S. Sodhi of AMUL stated:

In the first three-four days [of the shutdown], there was a panic sale and our sale increased by 15% or 20% as people started buying more. And after that, around Thursday, our sales declined by 30%. The reason is very simple that people had done the panic buying and the second reason for the reduction in sales is the closure of hotels, restaurants, tea shops, etc. We also started feeling the impact of migration of workers from the big cities to rural India. Our average sales will be 10–12% lower than the average.

In other words, the overall supply situation of essential food items does not appear to be too worrisome in India at this point. However, if the lockdown proceeds beyond a month, the supply situation will become tighter. Coupled with supply bottlenecks, prices may begin to rise. Here, the price curve may begin to look like a U-shaped curve, with a sharp fall in prices in the initial days of the lockdown replaced by a sharp upturn in prices in the later days.

Regardless of the apparently comfortable situation with respect to overall supply, it is important that we underline some concerns that exist at the ground level, particularly with regard to the supply chain and the smooth organization of farm operations.

First, harvesting and marketing crops at the farm level is in crisis across the country, because are (a) disruptions in the procurement of food grains by government agencies; (b) disruptions in the collection of harvests from the farms by private traders; (c) a shortage of workers to harvest the rabi crop; (d) a shortage of drivers in the transportation sector; (e) blockades in the movement of agricultural commodities across the major highways; (f) closure or limited operations of Agriculture Produce Marketing Committee (APMC) mandis; and (g) shutdowns in the retail agricultural markets. These factors have led to a crisis in a range of crops too: wheat, grapes, watermelons, bananas, muskmelon, chana, cotton, chilies, turmeric, cumin, coriander, onion, and potato.

Second, these bottlenecks have led to a fall in the farm prices of a range of commodities in agriculture. Tomato growers in Maharashtra are reported to be receiving not even Rs 2 per kg. Grape growers are reported to be facing an aggregate loss of Rs 1000 crore because of the crisis, as demand has fallen. Wheat prices in Madhya Pradesh are reported to have fallen from Rs 2200/Q to about Rs 1600/Q by 25th March 2020. For many crops, these prices are also below the Minimum Support Prices announced. In Punjab, vegetables that were sold at Rs 15/kg are reportedly being sold at a mere Rs 1/kg. In Delhi's mandis, the price of broiler chicken has fallen from Rs 55/kg in January 2020 to Rs 24/kg in March 2020. In Tamil Nadu, egg prices are reported to have fallen from Rs 4/egg to Rs 1.95/egg over the same period.

As the lockdown proceeds, these prices can be expected to rise, just as in the Western economies, the rise driven by panic buying and supply bottlenecks. Despite such price rises, farmers are unlikely to be the beneficiaries; most benefits are expected to flow to wholesale and retail traders as well as other middlemen.

Third, the return of many migrant workers to their homes has meant that harvest operations are not taking place smoothly, and many farmers are being forced to leave the crop in the field. Losses to farmers will be the highest in such cases. While mechanical harvesters can be used, lockdown regulations disrupt their free movement. Further, in some places, a shortage of drivers/operators for these harvesters has also been reported. As machine repair shops are closed and mechanics become unavailable for work, spare parts are not easily available, leading to many machines being left unused. In the rice mills of Kerala, reports indicate a shortage of migrant workers, which has led to these mills not procuring adequate supplies of paddy from farmers. Farmers have either not harvested at all, or have harvested and left the product near the fields. Labor shortages are also being experienced in most milk processing plants, cold storage units, and warehouses. According to the Chairperson of AMUL, most milk processing plants are currently operating with half of the labor force. Many workers are not reporting for work or have returned home also because of the fear of police atrocities.

Fourth, supply chains have been disrupted across the country for a range of commodities. The first official notification on lockdowns appears to have been ill-thought-out, leading to the exclusion of a number of activities from the list of essential items (this included even soap and sanitary pads till 28th March 2020). A second notification has corrected this, at least partially.

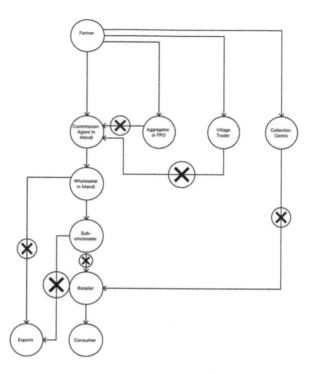

FIGURE 10.16 Representative marketing channels for vegetables in India, with potential bottle-necks. (Source: Author's estimates from news reports.)

Yet, major highways and entry points to States are seeing a pile-up of trucks unable to move forward. Lorry transport is in major shortage at many places, leading to the extremely slow movement of goods across the country. APMC mandis are not functioning every day; while some have closed down, others are operating only twice or thrice a week. In Figure 10.16, I have attempted to summarise the supply chain impacts using a generic flowchart of the marketing channels of food grains/vegetables in rural India. The bottlenecks due to the lockdown are marked as crosses at the appropriate locations. The information for this purpose has been sourced from news reports and are hence to be considered preliminary. Also, the presence or absence of bottlenecks may differ widely across states/regions.

Fifth, the shortage of livestock feed and their availability is raising the costs of production in many animal husbandry units. This is despite the fact that poultry has been declared as an essential item. This is leading to the death of many birds at the farm, or farmers undertaking panic selling at very low prices.

SUMMARY

This chapter explores several issues related to the potential impact of COVID-19 on food production and security as well. It offers casual observation with some computational analysis. Moving beyond a static, certain approach to the structure of preferences will help us understand observed behavior (e.g., stockpiling) and possibly understanding future behaviors in a COVID-19 world. Income and time constraints will matter. Tighter incomes will likely lead to substituting behaviors within and between food groups. However, people shifting food expenditures from away-from-home to in-home consumption will temper this effect. New routines forced by work-from-home requirements, school closures, and physical distancing will impact the opportunity cost of time, and may lead to new food behaviors. Muted short-run retail food price effects are evident. However, how the agricultural sector fares in light of physical distancing and possible disruptions to agricultural labor markets and production practices lends itself to the possibility of higher food prices in the long run (and possibly increased price volatility). It will be important to understand the impact on food demand arising from policy interventions related to wages and income. This understanding should take account of sociodemographic factors, and the intersection of these factors. Lastly, where and how people shop has and will continue to change as the COVID-19 pandemic evolves in Canada. Whether these changes persist will depend on the duration of the pandemic and associated economic downturn.

NOTES

1. ILOSTAT, Employment by sex and economic activity—ILO modeled estimates, November 2019.
2. Reuters, "No bed of roses: East Africa's female flower workers lose jobs as coronavirus hits exports," 11 April 2020; Martinplaut, "Tens of thousands of African jobs at risk as Europe dumps flowers during the Coronavirus crisis," 22 March 2020
3. FAO, "Agriculture-food markets and trade policy in the time of COVID-19,", 2 April 2020; Agrilinks, "Preventing Global Food Security Crisis under COVID-19," 18 March 2020.
4. Joint Statement by the Directors-General of FAO, WHO and WTO, "Mitigating impacts of COVID-19 on food trade and markets," 31 March 2020.
5. FAO—Food and Agriculture Organization. 2020a. Q&A: COVID-19 pandemic - impact on food and agriculture. Available in: http://www.fao.org/2019-ncov/q-and-a/en/
6. FAO - Food and Agriculture Organization. 2020b. FAO Director-General urges G20 to ensure that food value chains are not disrupted during COVID-19 pandemic. Available in: http://www.fao.org/news/story/en/item/1268254/icode/
7. FAO - Food and Agriculture Organization. 2020c. FAO Food Price Index. Available in: http://www.fao.org/worldfoodsituation/foodpricesindex/en/
8. FAO—Food and Agriculture Organization. 2020b. FAO Director-General urges G20 to ensure that food value chains are not disrupted during COVID-19 pandemic. Available in: http://www.fao.org/news/story/en/item/1268254/icode/
9. FAO—Food and Agriculture Organization. 2020a. Q&A: COVID-19 pandemic - impact on food and agriculture. Available in: http://www.fao.org/2019-ncov/q-and-a/en/
10. FAO—Food and Agriculture Organization. 2020a. Q&A: COVID-19 pandemic - impact on food and agriculture. Available in: http://www.fao.org/2019-ncov/q-and-a/en/
11. FAO—Food and Agriculture Organization. 2020d. FAO alerta sobre el impacto del COVID19 en la alimentación escolar de América Latina y el Caribe. Available in: http://www.fao.org/americas/noticias/ver/es/c/1267028/
12. Food Security Information Network (FSIN). In Global Report on Food Crises; World Food Program: Rome, Italy, 2020; Available online: https://www.fsinplatform.org/sites/default/files/resources/files/GRFC%20ONLINE%20FINAL%202020.pdf (accessed on 12 June 2020).
13. Eurostat. Income and Living Conditions in Europe (EU-SILC); European Union: Luxembourg, 2013.

REFERENCES

Abdelhedi, I. T., & Zouari, S. Z. (2020). Agriculture and Food Security in North Africa: a Theoretical and Empirical Approach. *Journal of the Knowledge Economy*, *11*(1), 193–210.

Affairs, U. N. D. of E. and S. (2011). *The global social crisis: Report on the world social situation 2011*. United Nations Publications.

Alesandro, O., Daniel, C., & Swinnen, J. (2017). *Trade Liberalization and Child Mortality: A Synthethic Control Method.* Working Papers Department of Economics 567787, KU Leuven, Faculty of ....

Arellano, M., & Bond, S. (1991). Some tests of specification for panel data: Monte Carlo evidence and an application to employment equations. *The Review of Economic Studies, 58*(2), 277–297.

Ball, V. E., Hallahan, C., & Nehring, R. (2004). Convergence of productivity: an analysis of the catch-up hypothesis within a panel of states. *American Journal of Agricultural Economics, 86*(5), 1315–1321.

Baltagi, B. (2008). *Econometric analysis of panel data.* John Wiley & Sons.

Bermejo, A. (2004). HIV/AIDS in Africa. *New Economy, 11*(3), 164–169.

Blundell, R., & Bond, S. (1998). Initial conditions and moment restrictions in dynamic panel data models. *Journal of Econometrics, 87*(1), 115–143.

Bound, J., Jaeger, D. A., & Baker, R. M. (1995). Problems with instrumental variables estimation when the correlation between the instruments and the endogenous explanatory variable is weak. *Journal of the American Statistical Association, 90*(430), 443–450.

Burgui, D. (2020). Coronavirus: How action against hunger is responding to the pandemic. *Available in:* Https://Www.Actionagainsthunger.Org/Story/Coronavirus-How-Action-against-Hunger-Respondingpandemic.

Chen, S., Brahma, S., Mackay, J., Cao, C., & Aliakbarian, B. (2020). The role of smart packaging system in food supply chain. *Journal of Food Science, 85*(3), 517–525.

Commission, E. (2013). Overview of CAP reform 2014–2020. *Agricultural Policy Perspectives Brief, 5.*

Compton, J., Wiggins, S., & Keats, S. (2010). Impact of the global food crisis on the poor: what is the evidence. *London, ODI, 99*, 99.

DeJong, D. N., & Ripoll, M. (2006). Tariffs and growth: an empirical exploration of contingent relationships. *The Review of Economics and Statistics, 88*(4), 625–640.

Dithmer, J., & Abdulai, A. (2017). Does trade openness contribute to food security? A dynamic panel analysis. *Food Policy, 69*, 218–230.

Dorosh, P. A., Rashid, S., & van Asselt, J. (2016). Enhancing food security in South Sudan: the role of markets and regional trade. *Agricultural Economics, 47*(6), 697–707.

Dreher, A., Gaston, N., & Martens, P. (2008). *Measuring Globalisation. Gauging Its Consequences.* Springer, New York.

Fanelli, R. M. (2019). The (un) sustainability of the land use practices and agricultural production in EU countries. *International Journal of Environmental Studies, 76*(2), 273–294.

Fanelli, R. M. (2020). The spatial and temporal variability of the effects of agricultural practices on the environment. *Environments, 7*(4), 33.

FAO, IFAD and WFP. (2013) The State of Food Insecurity in the World 2013. The multiple dimensions of food security. Rome, FAO.

FAO, U. N. F. and A. O. (2013). *The State of Food Insecurity in the World 2013.*

Gaigné, C., Le Gallo, J., Larue, S., & Schmitt, B. (2012). Does regulation of manure land application work against agglomeration economies? Theory and evidence from the French hog sector. *American Journal of Agricultural Economics, 94*(1), 116–132.

Glauber, J., Laborde, D., Martin, W., & Vos, R. (2020). COVID-19: Trade restrictions are worst possible response to safeguard food security. *Issue Post, March, 27,* 2020.

Gong, B. (2018a). Agricultural reforms and production in China: Changes in provincial production function and productivity in 1978–2015. *Journal of Development Economics, 132,* 18–31.

Gong, B. (2018b). Interstate competition in agriculture: Cheer or fear? Evidence from the United States and China. *Food Policy, 81,* 37–47.

Gong, B. (2020). New Growth Accounting. *American Journal of Agricultural Economics, 102*(2), 641–661.

Gottheil, F. M. (2013). *Principles of macroeconomics.* Nelson Education.

Hanashima, M., & Tomobe, K. (2012). Urbanization, industrialization, and mortality in modern Japan: A spatio-temporal perspective. *Annals of GIS*, *18*(1), 57–70.

Headey, D. D. (2013). Developmental drivers of nutritional change: a cross-country analysis. *World Development*, *42*, 76–88.

Heston, A., Summers, R., & Aten, B. (2009). Penn World Table. Vers. 6.3. *Center for International Comparisons, University of Pennsylvania*. Http://Pwt.Econ.Upenn.Edu.

Holtz-Eakin, D., Newey, W., & Rosen, H. S. (1988). Estimating vector autoregressions with panel data. *Econometrica: Journal of the Econometric Society*, 1371–1395.

IFAD. (2016). *Rural Development Report 2016. Fostering Inclusive Rural Transformation*. IFAD Rome.

Im, K. S., Pesaran, M. H., & Shin, Y. (2003). Testing for unit roots in heterogeneous panels. *Journal of Econometrics*, *115*(1), 53–74.

Ivanov, D. (2020). Predicting the impacts of epidemic outbreaks on global supply chains: A simulation-based analysis on the coronavirus outbreak (COVID-19/SARS-CoV-2) case. *Transportation Research Part E: Logistics and Transportation Review*, *136*, 101922.

Jaffee, S., Henson, S., & Diaz Rios, L. (2011). *Making the grade: Smallholder farmers, emerging standards, and development assistance programs in Africa-A research program synthesis*.

Kaplan, J. O., Krumhardt, K. M., Gaillard, M.-J., Sugita, S., Trondman, A.-K., Fyfe, R., Marquer, L., Mazier, F., & Nielsen, A. B. (2017). Constraining the deforestation history of Europe: evaluation of historical land use scenarios with pollen-based land cover reconstructions. *Land*, *6*(4), 91.

Kogo, B. K., Kumar, L., & Koech, R. (2020). Climate change and variability in Kenya: A review of impacts on agriculture and food security. *Environment, Development and Sustainability*, 1–21.

LeSage, J. P., & Pace, R. K. (2009). *Introduction to spatial econometrics*. Chapman & Hall/CRC.

Levin, A., Lin, C.-F., & Chu, C.-S. J. (2002). Unit root tests in panel data: asymptotic and finite-sample properties. *Journal of Econometrics*, *108*(1), 1–24.

Lin, J. Y. (1992). Rural reforms and agricultural growth in China. *The American Economic Review*, 34–51.

Loayza, N. V, Olaberria, E., Rigolini, J., & Christiaensen, L. (2012). Natural disasters and growth: Going beyond the averages. *World Development*, *40*(7), 1317–1336.

Long, M. A., Gonçalves, L., Stretesky, P. B., & Defeyter, M. A. (2020). Food Insecurity in Advanced Capitalist Nations: A Review. *Sustainability*, *12*(9), 3654.

Lopez-Ridaura, S., Barba-Escoto, L., Reyna, C., Hellin, J., Gerard, B., & van Wijk, M. (2019). Food security and agriculture in the Western Highlands of Guatemala. *Food Security*, *11*(4), 817–833.

Mary, S. (2019). Hungry for free trade? Food trade and extreme hunger in developing countries. *Food Security*, *11*(2), 461–477.

Mason, C. H., & Perreault Jr, W. D. (1991). Collinearity, power, and interpretation of multiple regression analysis. *Journal of Marketing Research*, *28*(3), 268–280.

Nickell, S. (1981). Biases in dynamic models with fixed effects. *Econometrica: Journal of the Econometric Society*, 1417–1426.

Office, I. L. (2017). *World employment and social outlook: trends for women 2017*. International Labour Office.

Organization, F. and A. (1996). *Rome Declaration on World Food Security and World Food Summit Plan of Action: World Food Summit 13-17 November 1996, Rome, Italy*. FAO.

Porrini, D., Fusco, G., & Miglietta, P. P. (2019). Post-adversities recovery and profitability: The case of Italian farmers. *International Journal of Environmental Research and Public Health*, *16*(17), 3189.

Rani, U., & Corley-Coulibaly, M. (2011). Investing in food security as a driver of better jobs. *World of Work Report*, *2011*(1), 75–96.

Rosales, G., & Mercado, W. (2020). Efecto de los cambios en el precio de los alimentos sobre el consumo de la quinua y la seguridad alimentaria rural en el Perú. *Scientia Agropecuaria*, *11*(1), 83–93.

Sar, T. T., Aernan, P. T., & Houmsou, R. S. (2010). H1N1 influenza epidemic: public health implications for Nigeria. *International Journal of Virology, 6*(1), 1–6.

Shen, J. H., Liu, X. J., & Zhang, J. (2019). Toward a unified theory of economic reform. *Structural Change and Economic Dynamics, 51*, 318–333.

Thomas, H. C. (2006). *Trade reforms and food security: country case studies and synthesis.* Food & Agriculture Org.

Torero, M. (2020). *Without food, there can be no exit from the pandemic.* Nature Publishing Group.

Vos, R., Martin, W., & Laborde, D. (2020). *How much will global poverty increase because of COVID-19.* International Food Policy Research Institute.

Wacziarg, R., & Welch, K. H. (2008). Trade liberalization and growth: New evidence. *The World Bank Economic Review, 22*(2), 187–231.

Wang, X., Fan, G., & Yu, J. (2017). Marketization index of China's provinces: NERI report 2016. *Social Sciences Academic Press: Beijing, China.*

Yang, Z., Zeng, Z., Wang, K., Wong, S.-S., Liang, W., Zanin, M., Liu, P., Cao, X., Gao, Z., & Mai, Z. (2020). Modified SEIR and AI prediction of the epidemics trend of COVID-19 in China under public health interventions. *Journal of Thoracic Disease, 12*(3), 165.

Zhang, X. (2020). Chinese livestock farms struggle under COVID-19 restrictions. *IFPRI Book Chapters*, 84–85.

11 Direct and Indirect Impacts of the COVID-19 Pandemic Crisis on Hotels, Tour and Travel Sectors

KEY POINTS

- Due to lockdown, people have engaged in panic buying and (over)-consumption of online experiences (e.g. virtual entertainment, dining, drinking, traveling).
- This experience demonstrates the people's persistence, preference, and fear of losing to their "consumerism" traditional lifestyles deemed essential for their success and happiness.
- Data characteristic analysis is helpful to tourism forecast.
- This chapter has employed the Long Short Term Memory (LSTM) approach in order to estimate the impact of the COVID-19 outbreak on tourism.

INTRODUCTION

At the beginning of 2020, the tourism industry was analyzing the trends for this new year and we sought to program a proposal based on the behavior of travelers worldwide, without even imagining that we would find, between the first and second quarter of this year, a global slowdown produced by the effect of a pandemic and the overwhelming impact of emergency measures that prevent the movement of people and, therefore, travel programs.

We thought that the world was heading toward a change of consciousness mainly based on our concern about climate change, financial and social crises, the production of more elaborate communication programs "close" to the tourist among other aspects, without considering that the impact of a global pandemic would put the tourism industry in a situation of global paralysis. The good data of the general results of the tourism industry:

1. That in 2018 there were about 4,400 million individual flights, which meant a marked growth compared to the 2,600 million made at the beginning of the decade; and
2. That the tourism industry contributed to 10.4% of the world's gross domestic product (GDP) in 2019 have become values that are no longer valid to solve the crisis in which we find ourselves.

Even though tourism attracts international attention to cities and investment and benefits to local economies, the sector has not been so badly affected by the impact of COVID-19.

Tourism and trade depend on visitors being able to travel freely from one place to another, and when a health crisis of this magnitude occurs, people stop traveling, both because of many countries' bans on the entry and exit of travelers, and because of travelers' fear of catching a disease that currently has no vaccine.

The reduction in travelers will directly affect the tourism industry, which has a direct impact on loss of income and increased unemployment. The impact of the pandemic on economies that are already slowing down has made tourism particularly vulnerable, becoming the hardest hit sector to date.

According to United Nations World Tourism Organization (UNWTO) estimates, the tourism sector, which is 80% made up of small- and medium-sized enterprises (SMEs), international tourist arrivals could fall by between 1% and 3% by 2020 globally, reducing growth from an estimated 3–4% in early January. This would translate into an estimated $30–50 billion in lost international tourism revenue for international visitor spending in the destinations.

The international movement of tourists in the world may fall this year between 20% and 30% compared to 2019, taking into account that never before have travel restrictions been introduced as those currently in place to contain the spread of the COVID-19 or coronavirus pandemic, an unprecedented decline that will mean a collapse in revenue of up to 410,000 million euros.

It is important to note that world tourism closed 2019 with nearly 1.5 billion international tourist arrivals (+4%), adding ten consecutive years of growth, while this year could see a drop to 450 million travelers. This decline would mean a drop in international tourism revenue (exports) between 273,000 and 410,000 million euros, almost a third of the 1.5 trillion reached in 2019.

Looking at the context after the 2009 crisis, international tourist arrivals fell by 4%, while the severe acute respiratory syndrome (SARS) outbreak led to a decline of only 0.4% in 2003. The impact of the SARS outbreak in 2002–2003 was mitigated by the fact that the tourism industry was not as dependent on China as it is now. After the 2008–2009 global financial crisis, increasingly wealthy Chinese consumers continued to spend when Western demand collapsed.

This time, however, there are fundamental differences. Chinese consumers are more affected by the COVID-19 than by the credit crisis; they are unlikely to come to the rescue in the same way, and there is no other emerging tourist stream to fall back on. The coronavirus "fear factor" is also greater than in previous crises, weakening financial markets. Its impact on the real economy—job losses, declining GDP, etc.—will be very significant.

Other international organizations such as the World Travel & Tourism Council (WTTC) have stated that the tourism sector is losing one million jobs worldwide every day. As an example, data from countries such as Italy are shown: the Tour Operators' Union Assoturismo of Italy, reported that the epidemic could bring tourism in that country back to the turnover it had in the mid-1960s by 2020, that is, a reduction of more than 260 million visits (−60%) compared to 2019.

CURRENT SITUATION IN THE TOURISM SECTOR

Tourism has not been free from the health, economic, and emotional impact generated by the SARS-CoV-2 coronavirus pandemic, which produces the disease known as COVID-19. All the indicators indicate that we are heading toward a change of paradigm, a new world that is yet to be discovered and we must understand it, accept it and adapt to this new context. In the social, family, and personal sphere the scale of values and perception of reality has changed. The confinement for weeks in our homes, of almost half of the world's population, surely promotes the need for freedom, to know and enjoy a leisure that in some cases has not been sufficiently attended. This is where tourism brings values and an offer of possibilities as wide as each citizen determines. In recent surveys on the needs of citizens and their relationship with tourism, several "immediate" or "direct from the heart" responses stand out:

- Sense of freedom
- Open spaces
- Security
- Health
- Normality
- Hope
- Shock and fear
- Fragility and a new vision of the World

This crisis has shown how fragile human beings are and how their planning and activities can be changed in such a short space of time that they cannot react. In a world where it seemed that the economy dominated everything, where algorithms had become the prophets of today through the knowledge of millions of data gathered in large groups of Big Data, and where even the number of travelers who would arrive at a hotel could be predicted months in advance, we are shocked and dragged along by a great tsunami caused by a virus.

Despite everything, we remain connected thanks to tools such as the Internet, which allows "mobility" between the physical and virtual worlds.

To a greater or lesser extent, this global problem that frightens us and forces us to take refuge in our homes is making us rethink the operation of the tourism sector in general and its relationship with the world.

Seeing the danger up close, not in neighboring or unknown countries, but in our own environment; observing with absolute clarity that our inaction allows the pollution of the planet to be reduced, that rivers recover their natural color, that many animals recover their natural habitat; this makes us more aware of the importance of sustainability, respect for life, social inclusion, and the health of each one of us.

All actions to recover from this crisis must maintain a balance with our planet by raising awareness of the processes related to climate change.

This crisis offers us a learning process and therefore a reorientation on the models of social, cultural, and economic development related to the tourism proposals that we present.

Tourism generates cultural, economic, and social values, and it is certain that tourism activity will recover, but it depends on the professionals in the sector acquiring the capacity to align themselves with this new conception of the world and transmit values of security, freedom, authenticity, trust, and respect for life and the planet.

COVID-19 CIRCUMSTANCES AND TOURISM

Research investigating, measuring, and predicting the COVID-19 tourism impacts is important in order to eliminate "casualties," draft, monitor, and improve response strategies (i.e., you cannot manage what you cannot measure). However, research focusing on the features and impacts of crises instead of their structural roots tends to conceal and stabilize the conditions and corollary social structures through which crises are produced (Barrios, 2017). Investigating the real roots of COVID-19 may go beyond the boundaries and scope of tourism research. Yet, the latter needs to look into and challenge the tourism "circumstances" and structures that have enabled and sometimes accelerated the global spread and impact of COVID-19. Unfortunately, the economists downplay the pandemic as a purely natural event originating and operating outside of the economic system (Nowlin, 2017). But, treating COVID-19 as an exogenous shock and phenomenon that has nothing to do with socio-economic structures and values can perpetuate and strengthen the pandemic roots during the post-COVID-era as well as constrain change and transformational processes.

COVID-19 is a crisis of the economized societies rooted in the growth-paradigm (Ötsch, 2020). COVID-19 is also a result of the intersection of broader processes of urbanization, globalization, environmental change, agribusiness, and contemporary capitalism (Allen et al., 2017). The nature of tourism (requiring traveling) and its evolution and growth paradigms are a significant contributor to such circumstances and the current socio-economic system accelerating the spread and impact of this contagious and infectious virus. Tourism is a result but also responsible for our highly interconnected and global world; pollution, waste, and climate change; global, national, and regional economic development and growth; superiority of capitalism values in people's and business decision-making but also policy and politics formulations. As climate change increases the frequency of pandemics and outbreaks, pandemics are expected to become more common in the future[1], which in turn highlights the interwoven nature and vicious circle forces between the biological, physical, and socio-economic systems.

Moreover, the economic system and mindset contributing to the COVID-19 have also been guiding and shaping the COVID-19 response and recovery strategies of governments, institutions, businesses, and people alike. This can significantly perpetuate and repeat crises as we are treating their symptoms and not their roots. For example, economic priorities for maintaining business continuity and jobs, resuming and recovering to the old "economic success growth" have been driving governments' policies and practices such as economic support (e.g., subsidies, tax reliefs) to tourism businesses and employees; debates for relaxation of restrictions for re-opening and re-starting economies at the expense of a second way and human lives. Similarly, people have engaged in panic buying and (over)-consumption of online experiences (e.g., virtual entertainment, dining, drinking, traveling) during lockdowns, that demonstrate their persistence, preference, and fear of losing to their "consumerism" traditional lifestyles deemed essential for their success and happiness. Early COVID-19 tourism research also reinforces a similar mindset, e.g., many studies trying to measure the economic impacts of COVID-19 trading them off to socio-cultural and biological impacts, studies aiming to predict and measure when tourists will start traveling again and when we can reach the old tourism targets. As governments race to minimize economic losses, and be the first to reopen borders and (tourism) businesses, and financial markets, investors, cash liquidity, and financial survival are equally pressing multinational and small tourism enterprises, they are all looking for tourism research that can "feed" and "reconfirm" their mindset and help them resume operations based on the old paradigms and business models they have founded. Debates and research are based on trading between economic benefits and losses in exchange of human rights, lives, morals, and ethics. There is no discussion on why trade-offs are the best methodology and mindset to decide, no one has re-imagined "solutions" enabling co-existence or regenerative forces between these concepts.

Overall, research, education, and our socio-economic and political system (which they shape and are shaped by each other) have all framed our mindset on how we research, measure, understand, respond, and aim to recover from the COVID-19. Consequently, we have converted COVID-19 from a biological virus contagion to a financial crisis contagion and recently, an economic race to re-build our old financial competitiveness. To avoid such perpetuations, tourism research should assume more responsibility in informing, driving, and leading sustainable futures. To that end, COVID-19 tourism research should not be solely seen, conducted, and used as a useful tool to help resume old states. Instead, COVID-19 tourism research should also challenge our growth-paradigms and assumptions that have led to the current situation and enable us to reimagine and reset tourism (Gössling et al., 2020; Hall et al., 2020; Higgins-Desbiolles, 2020; Ioannides & Gyimóthy, 2020). To achieve this, COVID-19 tourism research should criticize ontological and epistemological foundations and assumptions that underpin the current science and growth paradigms (Brodbeck, 2019). It should also deconstruct and challenge the mechanisms and systems that sustain the deleterious unsustainable tourism evolution (Higgins-Desbiolles, 2020). But to regenerate and transform tourism and its socio-economic system, tourism research should not only support new ways and perspectives of researching, knowing, and evolving. COVID-19 tourism research should also inspire, motivate, and inform all tourism stakeholders alike to adopt new ways of being, doing, and politicizing. For example, at a macro-level, COVID-19 tourism research should generate dethinking, rethinking, and unthinking of pre-assumptions and mindsets including (Higgins-Desbiolles, 2020) globalization as an unstoppable force; neoliberal capitalism as the best system and decision-making tool for organizing and allocating resources; growth as the sole way for development and success. It should also challenge the "surveillance capitalism," whose institutionalization and normalization is perceived as inevitable and unstoppable because of forces including (Zuboff, 2015) institutionalized facts (e.g., data collection, analytics, and mining); leading tech and disrupting companies being respected and treated as emissaries of a better future solving the "faults of capitalism" (e.g., sharing economy platforms "democrat icing" micro-entrepreneurship); and people seeing technologies as a necessary requirement for social and civic participation, securing employment and addressing the increasingly stressful, competitive, and stratified struggle for effective life. The COVID-19 is accelerating the institutionalization and acceptance of this algorithmic governance, management, and society, previously contested as violations of human rights, privacy and laws (Zysman, 2006), but now becoming normalized in the name of health and common good.

Technology is at the core of solutions for combating the COVID-19 and re-opening tourism and the economy (e.g., mobility tracing apps, robotised-AI touchless service delivery, digital health passports, and identity controls, social distancing and crowding control technologies, big data for fast and real-time decision-making, humanoid robots delivering materials, disinfecting and sterilizing public spaces, detecting or measuring body temperature, providing safety or security), while technology is seen as a panacea to our COVID-19 driven-needs to normalize surveillance, to ensure health and safety, to collect and analyses personal data for fast decision-making. Although COVID-19 tourism research cannot stop these technological advances, it should fight this digital Trojan horse from the inside by questioning and resetting their purposes, designs and affordances, interpretations, and application ethics. Technologies are constituted by unique affordances, whose development and expression are shaped by the institutional logics in which technologies are designed, implemented, and used (Zuboff, 2015). COVID-19 tourism research could simply investigate and advance our information and technological capabilities to collect, analyze, and use (big) data for better knowing, predicting, controlling, and modifying human behavior (e.g., tourists' and employees' behavior) as a means to produce revenue and market control (Zuboff, 2015). But such research will simply further support the making of everydayness qua data imprints an intrinsic component of organizational and institutional life and a primary target of commercialization strategies (Constantiou & Kallinikos, 2015). Technologies have always been an enabler, a catalyst of innovation and change, a disruptor of tourism, as well as a tool to build tourism resilience in crisis (Hall et al., 2017). COVID-19 has further enhanced the role of technologies in the recovery and re-imagination of tourism, while it reinforces existing paradigms in the e-tourism evolution. Developmental trends and adoption of smart destinations and tourism services, AI, robotics, and other digital advances are now accelerated to combat the COVID-19 tourism implications. COVID-19 tourism research should reimagine and re-shape the purposes, usage, and means of such technological advances that significantly form how our societies and economies are being transformed, how tourism is being practiced, managed, and how it evolves with the help and/or because of the COVID-19.

At a micro-level, COVID-19 tourism research should question and reset why tourism is viewed, practiced, and managed as a way to "escape," "relax," "socialise," "construct identities/status," "learn," and reward themselves from a routine, unpleasant, and meaningless life. Why tourism should be researched and practiced as an escape from a boring life, instead of life being rewarding and meaningful itself? Why people have to travel thousands of miles away from home to "learn" and "be happy"? Why companies have to commercialize and commoditize communities, people, and their tangible and intangible resources as tourism attractions "please" the tourists' needs and drive economic development? Tourism paradigms and mindsets like this have led and intensified crises like COVID-19 and this cannot be sustained for much longer. Consumerism and tourism should not be seen as the sole way to achieve happiness, self-expression, and (economic) development. COVID-19 tourism research should inspire tourists, businesses, and destinations alike to re-imagine and reset new mindsets, frontiers, and behaviors such as how to use and develop tourism to valorize and not consume tourism resources, to generate well-being, sustainability, and transformational learning; how to study and practice environmental/sustainable management, not as a legal necessity for lobbying and formulating policies, not as marketing tool to build brands' and people's identities, not as an expense to be minimized, but as a mindful business investment and personal lifestyle for a responsible future.

Overall, COVID-19 tourism research should not only be the mean to overcome the crisis and resume previously chartered economic growth trajectories. It should lead the refocusing, repurposing, reframing, and re-interpretation of research questions, methodologies, and outcomes, so that tourism stakeholders can in turn re-direct their actioning, conduct, and evolution. To that end, COVID-19 tourism research will be benefited by embedding, adapting, reflecting, and expanding the theoretical lenses and perspectives of a much greater plurality of disciplines and constructs to guide and implement research. Transformative (service) research, philosophy, criminology, ethics, law, anthropology, behavioral and religious studies, political science and diplomacy, governance, bioethics, rhetoric. Researching within unchartered waters, COVID-19 tourism research may also need to apply new methodological approaches and tools that are capable to combat roots and not symptoms of tourism crises and use the latter as transformational opportunity to reset research agendas and re-imagine and re-shape unthinkable tourism futures. Due to the newness of the field qualitative approaches such as (cyber)ethnography and the need for urgent, fast, and real-time research processes and outcomes, COVID-19 tourism research may also need to intensify and advance "new" methods of (big) data collection, analysis and interpretation/visualization, such as participatory sensing (i.e., using tourists as sensors for data collection).

Paradox research, as a meta-theory and/or methodology, can also be very instrumental for informing and supporting COVID-19 tourism research. Originating in philosophy and psychology (e.g., Aristotle, Confucius, Freud), paradox research (also frequently requiring multidisciplinary) has helped to inform, advance, and transform management science research (Schad et al., 2016) and organizations (Quinn & Cameron, 1988) alike. As a meta-theory, paradox research offers a powerful lens for enriching extant theories and fostering theorizing processes in management science, because it provides deeper understanding and conceptualization of constructs, relationships, and dynamics surrounding organizational tensions. By investigating contradictions between interdependent elements that are seemingly distinct and oppositional, one can better unravel how one element actually informs and defines another, tied in a web of eternal mutuality. As a methodology, the paradox lens encourages researchers to approach organizational paradoxes paradoxically (Quinn & Cameron, 1988). Incorporating paradox research into COVID-19 research may also be inevitable, as the COVID-19 circumstances, impacts, and debates have not only uncovered and intensified existing paradoxes but also generated new ones. Paradox research is also paramount to COVID-19 tourism research, if the latter is to become innovative and transformative. These are because (adapted by Schad et al. (2016)):

- Interruptions in socio-economic life can reveal structural contradictions and paradoxes, and by studying and understanding them, one can make the crisis positive and transformative.
- Paradoxes intensify, grow and intensify, as contemporary organizations and their environments become increasingly global, fastpaced, and complex; the evolution and circumstances of tourism and COVID-19 are a strong evidence of a highly interconnected, fast paced, and complex world.
- Paradox is a powerful meta-theorizing tool: opposing theoretical views may enable vital insights into persistent and interdependent contradictions, fostering richer, more creative, and more relevant theorizing.
- Paradox identifies and challenges our pre-assumptions as antinomies, theoretical paradoxes remain perplexing, even paralyzing, when researchers are confined by the past and/or assumptions.
- Paradox helps us think creatively and out-of-the-box, because contradictions provoke established certainties and tempts untapped creativity.

Paradox research is limitedly used within tourism research, but its applicability, versatility, and value are shown already in investigating macro-level tourism and destination management issues (Williams & Ponsford, 2009), business operations (Sigala et al., 2004), and tourism demand (Mawby, 2000). However, as the present and post-COVID-19 era is a fertile ground of persistent and new paradoxes in tourism, tourism researchers should seriously consider adopting a paradox lenses. For example, the circumstances of COVID-19 (e.g., stay at home lockdowns, social distancing) have necessitated and accelerated the use of technologies by both tourists (e.g., information about travel restrictions, online crisis communication, online COVID-19 alerts, and hygiene measures) and businesses (e.g., online food delivery, virtual dining, virtual wine experiences, festivals/events, virtual visits of museums, destinations). However, persistent "paradoxes" (e.g., increase use of social media and loneliness, democratization of information accessibility and information darkness, technology and (small) business empowerment/equalizing competition rules) are questioning the effectiveness of such technology solutions and have fueled debates on whether they are a "cure" or a "fertilizer" and "diffuser" of the pandemic. Not everyone has access to technology and those who have do not necessarily have the capabilities and knowledge to effectively use the technology tools and information. The persistent digital divide found in consumers and businesses (which mainly represents a socioeconomic divide of citizens and size of businesses) has converted the pandemic to an infodemic (e.g., lack or mis-information, diffusion of fake COVID-19 news and advice, emotional contagion of global depression and mental health) and a tool deepening the economic divide and competitive gap between larger and smaller tourism operators. Digital inequalities in tourists potentiated their vulnerability to COVID-19 (e.g., putting themselves and their loved ones at health risk while traveling or willing to travel during and after COVID-19), while COVID-19 vulnerability potentiates to enlarge the digital inequalities (e.g., those who have the tools and means to go through the COVID-19 impacts easily will also be the ones who can pay and access virtual tourism experiences, who will be well informed on how, where, and when to travel, and who will be able to afford to travel in the future, as increased (hygiene and technology) operating costs and transportation oligopolies may increase costs of tourism). Similarly, digital inequalities in tourism businesses potentiate COVID-19 vulnerability (as larger operators that were technology ready and "inherited" by size resilience were the first and maybe the only ones to be able to virtualize operations and experiences for maintaining business liquidity, surviving, reopening, and recovering post-COVID-19), while COVID-19 vulnerability increases digital and economic inequalities in the tourism competitive landscape (e.g., larger companies/destinations which are characterized by greater cash liquidity, know-how, technology readiness, and resilience, and so have lower COVID-19 vulnerability, will be the ones to survive and thrive post-COVID-19). Paradox research that can investigate such contrasts between the above mentioned specific and the opposition. But also interdependent elements can better define, understand, manage and address the dynamics of their concepts and the web of their eternal reciprocity.

The COVID-19 fortified and generated many other paradoxes, which are also identifiable at all tourism management levels (macro, meso, and micro) and COVID-19 tourism research can investigate for advancing and transforming research. Table 11.1 provides some ideas for applying such paradoxes in COVID-19 tourism research.

COVID-19: DISMANTLING AND RE-MANTLING TOURISM IN THREE STAGES

It is widely accepted that crisis management needs to be implemented before, during, and after a crisis. Table 11.2 provides an overview of the impacts and implications of COVID-19 on three major stakeholders (tourism demand, tourism operators, destinations, and policymakers) under three stages (representing the respond, recovery, and restart stage from the pandemic) to incorporate a transformational stage envisioned in the post-COVID-19 era. COVID-19 tourism research does not have to address issues in the last stage in order to be transformative. It can equally be transformative if it re-examines "existing" issues and relations but through new theoretical lenses and/or methodological approaches by embedding a plurality of "new" disciplines into the research designs. By doing this, one can significantly unravel unknown issues and dynamics, provide a better explanatory power and understanding of concepts and relations as well as identify and test new "remedies."

TABLE 11.1

Paradox Research: Advancing and Transforming COVID-19 Tourism Research

Paradoxes	Examples of Fields for Applying Paradox Research in COVID-19 Tourism Research
Privacy and obscurity	• Technology adoption by tourists (e.g., mobility tracking applications and other surveillance systems)
	• Design and ethics of tourism technology applications
Novelty and usefulness	• Innovating from necessity: types, processes, capabilities, facilitators and/or inhibitors of 'innovation' adopted by tourism firms to ensure business continuity and survival during COVID-19
Cooperation and competition	• Practices and strategies of destinations and policymakers to combat and re-open their economies, e.g., Intergovernmental and destinations initiatives and bilateral, multilateral (biosecurity) agreements to create 'travel bubbles' for re-opening tourism across countries (e.g., Australia-NZ, China-Taiwan-S. Korea, HK, Greece-Cyprus, Baltic States)
Global and local	• Configuration of tourism supply chains (e.g., local Vs global sourcing of food supplies, human resources, capital resources)
	• design of transportation—travel mobilities: e.g. airport and destination hubs, airline route design
	• Tourism policies and strategies, e.g., allocation of governmental interventions and subsidies between national and international firms to enable them to survive the COVID-19
Self-focus and other-focus	• Tourists' decision-making, quality evaluations and satisfaction from destinations and tourism providers under COVID-19 settings and conditions whereby self-presentation and self-safety may prevail over others' and common good
Stability and change	• Type and processes of change (of tourism firms, destinations, and tourists) supported and led by the COVID-19
	• Factors inhibiting and/or facilitating change due to COVID-19
Self-preservation and self-actualization	• motivations driving tourists'/human motivation and behavior
	• tourists' engagement with local communities and employees within a COVID-19 setting
	• employees' engagement and behavior toward tourists and organizations within a COVID-19 setting
High-tech and high-touch tourism services and experiences,	• Re-engineering of service delivery operations to make them touch-free but highly personalized and human-centered experiences
	• re-design of travelers' journeys and experiences
Profits and purpose	• aims and scope of response and recovery strategies of tourism operators and destinations within COVID-19
	• Social Corporate Responsibility of tourism operators and destinations within COVID-19 settings
	• Resetting of tourism strategies in the post-COVID-19 era
	• Tourism sustainability policies, strategies, and practices in the post-COVID-19 era

TABLE 11.2
COVID-19 and Tourism in Three Stages: Major Impacts and Some Ideas for Future Research

Stages	Respond Stage		Recovery Stage		Restart, Reform and Reset Reimagine	
	Impacts	Research Fields	Impacts	Research Fields	Impacts	Research Fields
Tourism Demand	Tourists' and/or their loved ones affected by COVID-19 and experiencing traumatic tourism experiences • Trip cancelations • Loss of money paid for travel-tourism • Trip disruptions • Loss of travel loyalty benefits and points • Quarantines and social distancing / lockdowns Travelers reading and viewing traumatic COVID-19 tourism experiences lived by others (media communication and user-generated content) Travel restrictions and travel bans Use of technology for crisis alerts and communication Panic buying and stockpiling	Experience of trauma on tourists' travel attitudes, future intentions, decision – making and experiences Impact of crisis communication on tourists' perceived risks, decisionmaking, future travel intentions and service quality evaluations Impact of fake news and misinformation on tourists' perceived risks and destination image Impact of booking restrictions and firms' cancelation policies on tourists' attitudes and behavior toward booking restrictions and booking patterns	• Social distancing • Lockdowns and stay at home • Choosing self-isolation • (excess) Use of technology (apps) for contactless services: • Shopping • Working • Information updates • Studying • Experiencing a global travel slow down resulting in reduced environmental pollution and overtourism phenomena • Multi-functional homes: remote working, home schooling, virtual social behaviors: • Virtual entertainment • Virtual social drinks • Virtual parties • Virtual events/festivals • Virtual dining • Virtual visitation of destinations and attractions	• Impact of safety and health concerns on tourists' attitudes, decision-making, and behaviors • Impact of reflecting on personal values, lifestyles and priorities on tourists' behavior (tourism segmentation strategies and criteria) • issues of social isolation and excess use of social media/ technology, on mental and psychological health, tourists' attitudes, travel intentions and behaviors • Increased priority in localism and impacts on geographies and mobilities of travel behavior and preference • Tourists' understanding of tourism's impact on climate change and overtourism problems	Experiencing a new tourism service and experience: • digital health passport and certifications • Digital identity apps • Travellers' mobility tracing apps • Crowd and social distancing technology solutions and restrictions • Contactfree travelers' journey management solutions • New hygiene standards • Social distancing redefining service etiquettes Setting new priorities determining tourists' selection, evaluation of services and consumption behavior, e.g.,: Self-care, safety, hygiene • Tourists recalibrating priorities, changing lifestyles, e.g., • Re-assessing what is essential for happiness • Deepening personal relations • Embracing a health-first mindset • New criteria for decision making	• Understanding the (new) tourists' (motivation, profile, decision-making, behavior): e.g., • Travel better not less • Travel for a purpose-meaning • Experience the other side of the common destinations • Redefinition of luxury tourism to include hygiene first, wellbeing? • Impact of COVID-19 economic recession on tourism demand • Impact of COVID-19 depression on tourism demand • Investigating the impact of the new psychology and behavior of tourists on: • Pricing strategies • Booking patterns • Segmentation and promotion strategies • Tourists' attitudes, use, adoption, and satisfaction from virtual tourism experiences • Tourists' acceptance and use of (new) technologies

(Continued)

TABLE 11.2 (Continued)

COVID-19 and Tourism in Three Stages: Major Impacts and Some Ideas for Future Research

Stages	Respond Stage		Recovery Stage		Restart, Reform and Reset Reimagine	
	Impacts	Research Fields	Impacts	Research Fields	Impacts Resetting the new business normal	Research Fields New competitors
Tourism supply—Businesses	Managing the safety and health of tourists and employees Handling customer communication and requests for: • changing travel itineraries and bookings • Cancelations of booking • Refunds and compensations	• Engagement with tourists for ensuring: individual safety, security, and stability (e.g., distress, emotional support), promoting and shifting customers to online channels and virtual experiences, building emotional bonds, trust and brand values • Employee communication and care for ensuring health, emotional stability and engagement • Ensuring cash liquidity (negative revenues: no income cash returns)	Ensure business continuity and building resilience • Repurpose of resources, e.g., staff, space, and food-cleaning supplies • Innovation from necessity, e.g.,: virtualization of experiences, remote working, innovation of business models • Acceleration of digital adoption • Customer engagement • Employee engagement • Mitigate crisis impacts • Brand communication for building brand values, e.g., messages like 'we are all together'	• Digital and economic divide within the industry • Re-skilling and up-skilling of employees • Loyalty programs: rebuilding customer trust and redesigning their value propositions and business models	• Re-opening: learnings from essential healthcare operators • New cleaning and hygiene protocols: protective equipment, masks, sanitizers, disinfecting wipes • crowd management and social distancing practices • Re-design and re-imagine the customer journey to make it contactless • Redesign of tourism experiences • Redesign of workspace and servicescape • Re-engineering business operations • Rethink of business ecosystems and partnerships • Contact-free business models • mobility tracing apps for employees and customers • Technology solutions for hygiene, health, and safety control. • Lead with purpose: association of brands with good • Update and redesign of booking forecasting, revenue management and pricing systems • Capture new demand • Accelerate digital and data analytics	• Virtual tourism experiences: a substitute or a complement of tourism experiences? (blended operating business models? • New start-ups and disruptors in the tourism value chain • Digital and economic divide • Surviving the COVID-19 recession and new operational standards, costs, and requirements • Abilities to address the sophisticated and new tourists market segments • Impact of COVID-19 economic recession on the tourism industry and structure (continued on next page)

(Continued)

TABLE 11.2 (Continued)

COVID-19 and Tourism in Three Stages: Major Impacts and Some Ideas for Future Research

Stages	Respond Stage		Recovery Stage		Restart, Reform and Reset Reimagine	
	Impacts	Research Fields	Impacts	Research Fields	Impacts	Research Fields
Destinations and policy makers	• Ensuring health and safety of tourists • Managing repatriation of citizens • Interventions to support vulnerable employees and tourism businesses • Crisis communication	• Accountability, effectiveness, and fairness of increased public expenditure • Politics – pressures and lobbying for resource allocation • Impact of crisis communication and user-generated-content on destination brand image • Securing and building the destination image	• Keeping tourists informed and interested: Promotion and visibility of destinations • Virtual visits of destinations • Engaging with destination partners and stakeholders • Provision of training and business consulting services to tourism operators e.g., Tourism Greece #GreecefromHome https://www.greecefromhome.com • Interventions to support tourism industry and jobs • Crisis communication: promote a positive and uplifting message, build and associate destination brands with good values, e.g.,#traveltomorrow by UNWTO World Travel & Tourism Council (WTTC) has launched its new #TogetherInTravel http://www.togetherintravel.com/VisitPortugal "we're-all-in-this-together" #CantSkipHope social media campaign https://www.youtube.com/watch?v=7DtcUNgd8IM&feature=emb_logo	• Impact and effectiveness of governmental interventions on building resilience and recovery abilities • impact of crisis communication on tourists' attitudes, travel intentions and destination image perceptions	• Reimagine the new types of sustainable and responsible tourism • Setting safety and health regulations and safety standards • Develop strategies for staged re-opening: relaxation of travel restrictions, creation of travel bubbles, re-opening of tourism businesses • Promotion and motivation to tourists, e.g., travel vouchers and incentives • Health passports and health identities	Re-nationalization of tourism infrastructure, superstructure and tourism operators (e.g., airlines, ferry companies, train operators) Global cooperation for addressing climate change and sustainability issues Impact of public interventions on functioning and structure of tourism industry Impact of public spending and interventions on austerity measures

TOURISM DEMAND

Tourists have experienced themselves, through their loved ones, and/or through the shared experiences of others (e.g., user-generated content) significant disruptions and health-risks in their travel and bookings plans. The tourists' experiences and/or exposure to others' experiences (that are also magnified through the emotional contagion and information diffusion of the social media) can have a significant impact on their travel attitudes, intentions, and future behaviors. Psychiatric research investigating the impact of traumatic experiences on people's lives, behaviors, and experiences of places and services (e.g., Baxter & Diehl, 1998) can provide useful theoretical lenses for understanding the travel behavior and attitudes of tourists that have been exposed to own or others' COVID-19 travel trauma. Tourism research has mainly focused on studying how tourists develop their perceived risk and the impacts of the latter on tourists' decision-making processes, future intentions, and segmentation profiles (Aliperti & Cruz, 2019; Arana & León, 2008; Dolnicar, 2005). Others have also examined the impact of the tourists' perception of crisis management preparedness certification on their travel intentions (Pennington-Gray et al., 2014). Such research is important, as risk perceptions are important for predicting future tourism demand and drafting appropriate recovery strategies (Rittichainuwat & Chakraborty, 2009). It is also relevant for COVID-19 tourism research because of the new COVID-19 standards and certification rules that companies are now required to adopt. Research has shown that perceptions of risks may differ between tourists with different origin-country, final destination, age, sex, and the typology of travel (Rittichainuwat & Chakraborty, 2009). However, the impact of crisis communication and social media on perceived risk has been totally ignored. Some research is done for examining the impact of social media use on tourists' mental health (Zheng et al., 2020) and crisis information systems and communication—social media (Sigala, 2011; Yu et al., 2020); however, given the increasing role and impact of social media on crisis communication and people's health and risks perceptions, this is an area where more research is granted. As a vaccine for COVID-19 may take long to be developed and travelers may need to live with it, tourism research might benefit from medical and health research, investigating how people behave, live, and cope with chronic and lifestyle-related diseases (e.g., AIDS).

During lockdowns, people have experienced and become familiar with virtual services and tourism experiences. Research in technology adoption would claim that increased technology familiarity and trial-ability will increase its adoption. But will this apply to the controversial technologies introduced by COVID-19? Political economy and law research explaining how people react and accept human rights "violations" (e.g., surveillance measures, freedom of speech, lockdowns) under conditions of "state of exception" like terrorism or the COVID-19 (Bozzoli & Müller, 2011; Carriere, 2019; Scheppele, 2003) can provide new lenses for studying adoption of the COVID-19 controversial technologies and restrictions Research on political ideologies could further enlighten why people's ideologies and political values may further perplex their reactions and behaviors to such interventions in their human rights.

It is claimed that while experiencing low pace, new lifestyles, and working patterns, people are reflecting and recalibrating their priorities and social values. Is that true in relation to their travel behavior? Would people require and expect greater responsibility and sustainability from tourism operators and destinations? Would they be motivated to travel more but for a meaningful purpose? Or would people go back to their previous travel behaviors and preferences? Past research (Pieters, 2013) has shown that consumers face a "material trap" in which materialism fosters social isolation and which in turn reinforces material- ism. This might explain why during lockdowns people increased their online shopping and consumption of virtual entertainment and probably they might not have reflected and reset their values. Is that true and what is its impact on tourists' behaviors? Consumer psychology and behavioral science explaining how people wish to align the time they spend with their values (congruence theory) can provide useful insights into such investigations. In addition, religion and spirituality studies can further enlighten the impact of COVID-19's living conditions on tourists' tourism sustainability preferences and attitudes as well as responses to tourism operators' and destination sustainability practices and communications. This is because religion and spirituality are found to play an important role in influencing individu- als' thoughts and behaviors (Laurin et al., 2012).

Social distancing imposed by COVID-19 includes actions such as reducing social con- tact, avoiding crowded places, or minimizing travel. Social distancing can significantly impact how people experience and evaluate leisure and travel activities like hiking, outdoor activities, and nature-based tourism or even personal services like spas, dining, and con- cierge services. Social distancing or better physical distancing may influence tourists' per- ceptions of health hazards, insecurity, and unpleasant tourism experiences. But how "far" away is enough for tourism employees and other customers to be from each other without compromising sociality, personal service, and perceptions of social distancing measures? Social distancing has not been studied before in service provision, while law and criminol- ogy research on "sexual" consent may provide a different perspective on how people define social space and the "invasion" or not of others into it.

Tourism is heavily a hedonic and sensorial experience. Servicescape design plays a major role in tourism experience by influencing customers' emotions, behaviors, attitudes, and service evaluations. However, COVID-19 operating standards require services capes to be redesigned eliminating or inhibiting sensorial elements and "changing" tourism experi- ences; e.g., smell of cleanliness instead of fragrance; social distancing and number of co- presence of clients in restaurants, festivals, and other tourism settings will influence new standards of psychological comfort and acceptable levels of perceived crowdness; raised voices may generate a wider "moist breath zone" increasing viral spread; warmer tem- peratures create relaxing environments encouraging customers to stay and spend more, but poorly ventilated or air-conditioned indoor spaces may spread COVID-19. Would tourists and tourism firms change their behavior and attitudes toward these new COVID-19 services capes? What new service etiquettes, customer expectations, behaviors, and experiences would COVID-19 determined services capes and operational procedures may generate?

These and many other fields of research have been raised due to COVID-19 conditions, and as explained a plurality of theoretical lenses can be beneficial to provide a better under- standing of these new concepts introduced in tourism research.

TOURISM SUPPLY—BUSINESSES

Tourism businesses have been racing to ensure the safety of their employees, customers, brand image, and cash liquidity. To re-start, tourism companies are re-designing experi- ences (e.g., winery experiences, museum visits, tours, sports events, in-room dining, and entertainment instead of hotel facilities) to feature smaller groups of tourists, outdoor activ- ities, and/or private experiences complying with social distancing and gathering restrictions and travelers' expectations. Tourism companies have already upgraded their cleaning procedures by adopting new standards and restraining staff. Many companies promote their hygiene certifications accredited by health expert associations. Tourism professionals are being trained to become "contact tracers" obtaining relevant certifications confirming their skills to identify cases, build rapport and community with cases, identify their contact, and stop community transmission. Restaurants, hotels, airports, public spaces are re-engineering their operations to make them contact-free or contactless. Mobile apps (for check-in, check-out, room keys, mobile payments, bookings-purchases), self-service kiosks, in-room technologies for entertainment and destination e-shopping (e.g., virtual reality for destination virtual visits to museums, attractions and destinations, movies), robots (for reception and concierge services, food delivery museum guides), artificial intelligence-enabled websites and chatbox for customer communication and services, and digital payments (e.g., digital wallets, paypal, credit cards). In addition, the new operating environment enforced by COVID-19 measures requires firms to adopt new technologies and applications to ensure management of crowds and number of people gathered in public spaces (e.g., airports, shopping malls, museums, restaurants, hotels), human disinfectors, hand sanitizer equipment, and applications identifying and managing people's health identity and profiles.

Research can conduct a reality check and benchmarking of the effectiveness of the various respond and recovery strategies adopted by tourism operators. Research can also investigate the role and the way to build resilience to fast develop and implement such strategies. However, such research is useful and important but probably not enough for investigating the resetting of the next tourism industry normal. Transformative COVID-19 research should help industry to reimagine and implement an operating environment that is human-centered and responsible for sustainability and well-being values.

DESTINATION MANAGEMENT ORGANIZATIONS AND POLICYMAKERS

Governments and destinations have been providing stimulus packages and interventions (e.g., tax reliefs, subsidies, deferrals of payments) to ensure the viability and continuity of tourism firms and jobs. Governments have intervened in mobility restrictions and closures of businesses. Because of these, COVID-19 has resulted in a greater intervention of governments in the functioning and operations of the tourism industry. The government has also become a much bigger actor in the tourism economy (e.g., re-nationalization of airlines and other tourism firms and tourism infrastructure like airports). This is very unique for COVID-19, as previous crises have generated research and institutional interest, but they did not have policy impact, specifically in tourism (Hall et al., 2020). Would such government interventions and role sustain in the future? How will this influence the structure and functioning of the industry at a national and global level? Debates have already started questioning the effectiveness of such interventions, their fairness, and equal distribution amongst tourism stakeholders (Higgins-Desbiolles, 2020), their long-term impacts in terms of austerity and cuts of public expenditures. Future research looking into these issues is highly warrantied. In their CIVID-19 reactions and responses, governments and destinations seem to have acted individually and nationalistic and recently selectively (e.g., bilateral and multilateral agreements amongst tourism bubbles). However, systems theory and crisis management would argue that crises need to be addressed collectively. What would be the impact of such governmental behaviors on the future of tourism and destinations tourism policy making and strategies? As it seems, COVID-19 has raised political, geopolitical, and governance issues that frameworks and concepts from these disciplines would need to be used to enlighten such research.

IMPACT OF THE CURRENT CRISIS ON TOURISM DESTINATIONS

The impact of the current crisis on the tourism industry is being received in a different way, be it destinations, companies, and institutions. Hence, this section's aim is to figure out which destinations countries are most visited, it's easiest to view the situation by looking at tourism on an annual basis. Otherwise, trying to figure out the countries that are most visited can be really difficult. For this purpose, we focus on two variables—tourism rates and the number of tourists that visit on an annual basis—in order to decipher which countries are the most visited nations every year.

A common theme that you will find when looking at countries with the highest rates of tourism over a given year is that they have always been popular destinations. Most of them are countries in Europe, and the majority of the most visited countries are very near to, if not directly positioned on, the coasts of different bodies of water. People want to escape their everyday life and explore places that are relaxed, low-key, and beautiful, which tend to be the areas that are beachside and provide access to gorgeous oceanic scenery.

Here are the topmost visited countries as of an analysis that was updated in 2019.

CHILE TOURISM

The Federation of Tourism Companies of Chile (Fedetur), the Hoteliers of Chile, the Chilean Association of Tourism Companies (Achet), the Chilean Association of Gastronomy (Achiga) and the Guild Association of Tourism SMEs, the president of Fedetur, Ricardo Margulis, reports that considerable losses are expected, no more than 1,900,000 foreign tourists compared to 4,500,000 in 2019, a figure that represents a drop of 56.4% compared to the previous year. This drop of nearly 2.5 million foreign visitors would imply a loss of 1.3 billion dollars.

MEXICO TOURISM

Currently the expansion of the coronavirus is taking serious scenarios in this country and the tourism sector expects losses of more than $50 billion pesos (data from the Association of Secretaries of Tourism of Mexico—Asetur), in other words, $2.4 billion dollars in a conservative situation.

In the case of the State of Baja California, one of the main tourist destinations, the impact of the coronavirus crisis would affect more than 14,000 workers, in Los Cabos after the partial or total closure of tourist establishments, mainly hotels, a significant reduction in terms of occupation has been noted.

SPAIN TOURISM

According to Exceltur, the Spanish tourist board, tourist activity in Spain has been plummeting since 1 March. Of the total number of jobs in the sector that Spain has, 2,200,000 and the ERTES (temporary suspension of the employment relationship of the company with a specific part of its workers) could reach 900,000.

In some cases, it is argued that, if the activation of the tourism sector is restarted for the month of June this year, the losses are estimated at 55,000 million euros of tourism activity, taking into account the direct and indirect activity; which represents a drop of 32.4%. The tourism lobby foresees that part of the peak summer season will be affected, if this is confirmed it would affect a fall of several points in the total Spanish GDP.

By Autonomous Communities (regions), taking into account the most touristic ones, the losses would be the following:

- Catalonia: 10,881 million euros, 34% less.
- Andalusia: 8,963 million, 32.5% less.
- Valencia: 6,730 million, 33.6% less.
- Community of Madrid: 6,383 million, down 27.9%.
- Balearic Islands: 6,076 million, 40.8% less.
- Canary Islands: 4,718 million, down 25.9%.

In the case of the Autonomous Community of Andalusia, more than 8 million tourists are expected to decrease this year due to the pandemic, with no more than 24 million tourists expected, as compared with 32.5 million in 2019.

Figure 11.1 translates into a drop in revenue generated by this activity that could reach 5,500 million euros this year, with a 13% drop in employment in the region during the period in which the activity is stopped, with more than 55,000 people out of work temporarily or permanently.

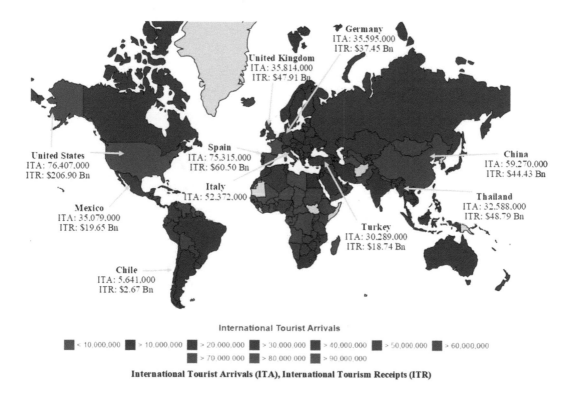

FIGURE 11.1 Most visited countries in 2020. (Source: https://worldpopulationreview.com/country-rankings/most-visited-countries)

In short, it is estimated that 2,177 million euros will be spent by tourists and hikers on tourism products and services this year (Data from Consultoría Turística).

The population of Spain is estimated to be around 46,435,537 people. With a total area calculated to be 192,588 square miles of land, the population density of Spain is about 241 people for every square mile within the country's official boundaries. Looking solely at Spain's population, data analysts have declared that Spain ranks as the 30th largest country in the world with population being the only factor in mind. Although Spain seems to have quite a high number of residents, the country's population is actually only a tiny fraction of the global population. Compared to everyone on Earth, those who live in Spain only account for 0.6% of the whole world.

CHINA TOURISM

In less than two decades, China has gone from minnows to the most powerful source market in the world, leaving the United States behind. According to the UNWTO, Chinese tourists abroad spent $277.3 billion in 2018, compared to about $10 billion in 2000, while US tourists spent collectively $144.2 billion. As their income increases year by year, Chinese nationals tend to spend more on travel, leading to a continuous increase in China's outbound tourism. As we can see in Figure 11.2, Chinese tourists in 2018 were leading the world in spending as they spent almost twice than US tourists, who came in second in this list.

China also leads global outbound tourism. With ten years of double-digit growth in spending, Chinese outbound tourism reached first place in 2012. In 2016, outbound travelers

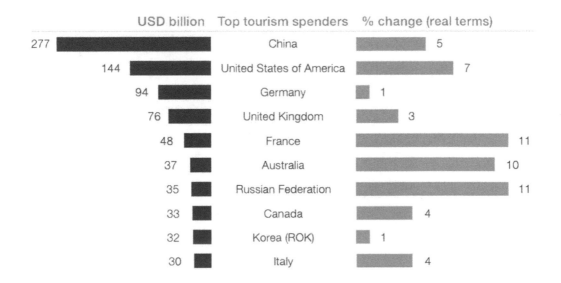

Top 10 countries by international tourism spending, 2018
Source: World Tourism Organization (UNWTO).

FIGURE 11.2 Top ten countries by international tourism spending (2018 Data). (Source: World Tourism Organization.)

from China increased by 6%, reaching 135 million, while their spending increased by 12%, to a total of $261 billion. Meanwhile, tourism spending in the United States, the second-largest source market in the world, increased by 8% in 2016 totaling $124 billion. In 2018, one-fifth of international tourism spending originated from Chinese citizens. According to recent estimates, the Chinese outbound tourism market is expected to reach $365 billion by 2025. Since traveling and experiencing other cultures have become increasingly popular among Chinese nationals, so do their expectations for better service quality and buying experiences when staying abroad. The main drivers of China outbound tourism market growth include the growth of the middle class and its affluence, the increase in the number of Chinese nationals holding a passport, an open-door policy, liberal tourism policy such as an approved destination state (ADS), others softened government agreements facilitating traveling (Jørgensen et al., 2017).

In 2018, Hong Kong, Thailand, Japan, Vietnam, and South Korea remain the top five destinations receiving travelers from mainland China, accounting altogether for more than 35% of the global share of China outbound tourism. The soaring numbers in China outbound tourism represent huge growth opportunities in terms of income and numbers of visitors for destinations and travel. They can also boost tourism-related brands and services outside China. Given the size of China's outbound tourism, countless destinations, and local businesses outside China are making great efforts to attract more Chinese travelers. In terms of the purpose of visit and spending, the top five countries benefiting large of the China outbound tourism ranging are the United States, Canada, Australia, New Zealand, and Japan (Market, 2019).

THE UNITED KINGDOM TOURISM

The United Kingdom is the home of over 66 million people. With a population size of about 66,909,462 people, the United Kingdom is a group of countries in Europe, and the United Kingdom is inclusive of Northern Ireland, Wales, England, and Scotland. The United Kingdom is an interesting place to name as one of the most visited countries, primarily because it is made up of four different countries rather than being one individual country on its own. But that is precisely why the United Kingdom attracts such a high percentage of the tourism industry every year.

People are drawn to the United Kingdom due to the fact that it is a region of multiple countries. There is more to see, do, eat, and try when you have multiple cultures in one area, so people find a lot of joy in perusing the countries of the United Kingdom and exploring the island that is home to various countries. As the 21st largest place to live in relation to population size, the United Kingdom has a density value of about 717 people for every square mile of area. Speaking of area, the total area of the United Kingdom is about 93,410 square miles. The United Kingdom is collectively the equivalent of 0.87% of everyone who lives on Earth, which is not the largest percentage to rank as given the fact that the United Kingdom is four countries in one. However, this is good news for vacationers who want to relax in an area that is not overcrowded and populated beyond belief.

TURKEY TOURISM

The population of Turkey is around 82,831,977 people since the latest headcount in 2019. As the 17th largest country in terms of population size, Turkey's population is around 1.1%

of the whole wide world's population. The country's total area amounts to about 297,156 square miles. By taking Turkey's population size and dividing the population by the nation's total area, you will end up with a value of 279. This value is known as the country's population density, which means that for every square mile of area in Turkey, there are about 297 people.

THAILAND TOURISM

The South Asian country of Thailand is a nation of 69,290,565 people. The country comprises a total area of 197,256 square miles, which amounts to a population density of around 351 people per square mile of land. As the 20th largest country in terms of the number of people who live there, Thailand is home to only 0.9% of the world's total population. While there are plenty of suburban regions in Thailand, the majority of Thai people inhabit the urban areas of the country.

GLOBAL IMPACT

According to the UNWTO[2] the international tourist arrivals will be down by 20–30% in 2020 when compared with 2019 figures, equivalent to a loss of 300–450 US$billion in international tourism receipts (exports)—almost one-third of the US$1.5 trillion generated globally. The direct contribution of the travel and tourism industry accounts today for 3.3% of the total global GDP and 4.4% in Organisation for Economic Co-operation and Development (OECD) countries (average) with picks of 14%, 13%, and 18% for countries like Spain, Italy, and Greece respectively.[3] Some countries are predicted to face more substantial blows than others due to their high reliance on the sector especially when considering an interesting comparison: of the top ten destinations by international tourists arrivals (France, Spain, United States, China, Italy, Turkey, Mexico, Germany, United Kingdom, and Thailand), eight result to be the hardest hit by COVID-19, implying that the economic shock on tourism will be further exacerbated in these countries.

According to the latest estimates, Asia will see the highest overall drop in travel and tourism revenue in 2020, with China accounting for the lion's share of lost revenue.[4] In Europe, where the tourism industry employs around 13 million people, around €1 billion in revenues per month is expected to be lost as a result of coronavirus, with Italy and Spain as countries most affected. Italy is likely to close the year with 60% less presences compared to 2019, levels equivalent to those registered in the 1960s, when the world was divided into blocks and air travel was a luxury for a few.[5] The Spanish tourism sector would experience losses of around €55 billion by 2020 with Catalonia expected to be the region most affected registering a loss in tourism turnover of almost €11 billion.[6]

Another group of countries heavily impacted are the so-called SIDS (Small Island Developing States) not only because the tourism sector accounts for almost 30% of their economy, but also because any shock of such magnitude is difficult to manage for small economies without the alternative sources of foreign exchange revenues necessary to service external debt and pay for imports. Strong shocks will also affect Sub-Saharan Africa where one out of twenty workers belongs to the tourism sector: a recent study from the African Union[7] estimates that the tourism and travel sector in Africa could lose at least $50 billion due to the pandemic outbreak and at least two million direct and indirect jobs, with devastating effects for tourism spots like Seychelles, Cape Verde, Mauritius, and The

Gambia will shrink at least 7%. Additionally, on average, the tourism sector accounts for almost 30% of the GDP of the SIDS, according to WTTC data. This share is over 50% for the Maldives, Seychelles, St. Kitts and Nevis, and Grenada. Overall, travel and tourism in the SIDS generates approximately $30 billion per year. A decline in tourism receipts by 25% will result in a $7.4 billion or 7.3% fall in GDP. The drop could be significantly greater in some of the SIDS, reaching 16% in the Maldives and Seychelles.

It is expected that for many SIDS, the COVID-19 pandemic will directly result in record amounts of revenue losses without the alternative sources of foreign exchange revenues necessary to service external debt and pay for imports.

COMPUTATIONAL MODELS FOR TOURISM DEMAND FORECASTING

This section of the chapter will focus on the computational model that can help in fore-casting the effect of the COVID-19 on tourist arrivals from different countries on the high recommended destination counties. For the purpose of forecasting the impact, we are going to use some machine learning techniques such as LSTM approach, Time Series and Regression Methods, and Support Vector Regression (SVR) model.

LSTM MODEL

This computational forecast approach is used to analyse the effect of new virus epidemic on tourist arrivals from China to the United States and Australia. The significance of this fore-cast is supported by the fact that China has become an important player in the global tour-ism market. Given the strong autoregressive patterns of tourist arrivals (Athanasopoulos & de Silva, 2012), we employ data from the SARS epidemic outbreak to train a deep learn-ing algorithm, implementing a LSTM artificial neural network. The prediction network is calibrated for the particulars of the current crisis (lockdowns, flights bans, etc.) and our forecasts are cross-validated using backtesting, a process under which the sample is split into smaller training/validations sets in order to confirm the robustness of our predictions.

The use of the LSTM approach to carry out this task is supported for two reasons. First, the errors are returned to the machine to calibrate the model during the first training phase. Also, the errors are used persistently in the machine gates of the machine. Second, LSTM networks are unresponsive to the lags between events in the time series.

This analytics in this section is threefold. First, we calculate the economic and social costs linked with the current COVID-19 outbreak. Second, we demonstrate that the use of an LSTM network can be applied to the arrivals time series, given its strong autoregressive nature, using a calibrated network with training data from a similar past event, namely the SARS epidemic. Third, we present an example of using backtesting, a technique commonly applied to financial time series, to verify the robustness of tourism forecasts.

Methodology & Data

Methodological Approach

We have employed the LSTM approach (Hochreiter & Schmidhuber, 1997) in order to estimate the impact of the COVID-19 outbreak on tourism flows of Chinese residents to the United States and Australia. LSTM modeling is a deep learning methodology, which is use-ful when attempting to model time series with high degrees autocorrelation and outperform other forecasting methods, especially when the lags are unknown (Law et al., 2019).

For tourism demand forecasting, in particular, numerous methodologies have been employed across different studies, ranging from linear, autoregressive, and other econometric models (Assaf et al., 2019; Gunter & Önder, 2016; Gounopoulos et al., 2012; Papatheodorou, 1999; Shen et al., 2011; Syriopoulos, 1995) to artificial intelligence methodologies, such as feed-forward artificial networks or support vector machines (Hassani et al., 2017; Teixeira & Fernandes, 2012). Recent trends in tourism demand suggest that machine and deep learning methods are more adaptable and can yield more accurate results (Law et al., 2019; Li & Cao, 2018). A thorough review on the evolution of forecasting techniques can be found in Song, Qiu and Park research (Song et al., 2019). Many studies, including Assaf et al. (2019) and Gounopoulos et al. (2012) confirm the autoregressive nature of the tourist arrivals time series.

LSTM networks belong to the wide category of recurrent neural networks. Their advantage is that they are capable of learning and, thus, modeling long-term dependencies (Felix et al., 2000). Their initial purpose was to overcome the errors of previous algorithms in the back-propagation of information contained in recent input events (Bengio et al., 1994). Consequently, they avoid the long-term dependency problem, since remembering recent input for long periods of time is essentially their default behavior.

The LSTM approach, similar to all recurrent neural networks, has a chain of repeating modules, but has a different structure in each module, by including four hidden network layers, which interact with each other. In our model, we implement a Stateful LSTM which means that after each iteration, cell states are preserved and are simply updated with the new information, according to the process described below.

The LSTM topology (Figure 11.3) follows the typical structure of artificial neural networks, by implementing an input and an output layer and many hidden layers in between.

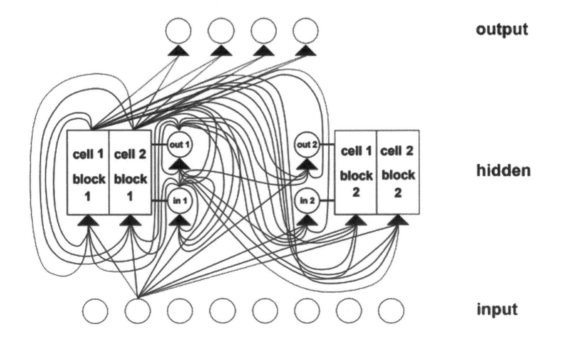

FIGURE 11.3   Example of an LSTM network.

All decisions are made in the hidden layer of the LSTM network, which, as stated earlier, includes four sub-layers.

The first decision layer in the LSTM structure is the "forget gate" layer, which decides which information should be discarded from the model memory. Note that this layer can output any values ranging from zero (completely forget) to one (use fully). The "forget" function f_t is as follows:

$$f_t = \sigma\left(W_f.(h_{t-1}, x_t) + b_f\right) \tag{11.1}$$

where σ represents a sigmoid function, W_f represents the weight vector of inputs, h_{t-1} is the forecast vector from previous periods, x_t is the new input vector and b_f is the bias of function f.

Note that the bias coefficient is a common feature of all machine learning functions and can either be set beforehand or calculated during the training phase. The bias can be used to calibrate the model, in order to help it adapt to the different circumstances of each scenario. We use it to calibrate the model to effects of the particular policies implemented in the current crisis, such as the grounding of flights and the various degrees of lockdowns in different regions. Thus, our model bases its predictions on the SARS epidemic, which holds significant similarities to the current crisis, but also encompasses the increased severity of the current pandemic, through bias calibration. We perform sensitivity analysis on the bias coefficient and generate different forecast scenarios.

The next step in the algorithm is to analyze the new information in order to determine whether it is useful. If so, it needs to be added to model memory. However, the importance of the new information needs to be scaled, in a manner similar to the "forget" function in Equation (11.1). Thus, we need to calculate the "include" function, implemented in the corresponding layer, i, as follows:

$$i_t = \sigma\left(W_i.(h_{t-1}, x_t) + b_i\right) \tag{11.2}$$

with the same notation as in equation (11.1)

In order to determine the new candidate values (vector $\tilde{C}_t$) that can be added to the neural cell's state. These are determined as follows:

$$\tilde{C}_t = tanh\left(W_c.(h_{t-1}, x_t) + b_c\right) \tag{11.3}$$

Once we have the information from equations (11.1) to (11.3), we can determine the new cell state C_t. The new state is the result of multiplying the old state, C_{t-1}, by f_t, forgetting anything that was deemed useless in the first step and then adding $i_t \times \tilde{C}_t$, which will yield the new candidate values, scaled by how much we decided to update each state value. Thus, the new cell state, calculated in the "update" layer, is:

$$C_t = f_t \times C_{t-1} + i_t \times \tilde{C}_t \tag{11.4}$$

By combining equations (11.1), (11.2), (11.3), and (11.4), we have the new cell state, C_t, as follows:

$$C_t = \sigma\left(W_f.(h_{t-1}, x_t) + b_f\right) \times C_{t-1} + \sigma\left(W_i.(h_{t-1}, x_t) + b_i\right) \times tanh\left(W_c.(h_{t-1}, x_t) + b_c\right)_t \tag{11.5}$$

The final step is to decide on the output vector and present our prediction, in a process performed in the "prediction" layer. The output function, o, is

$$o_t = \sigma\left(W_o.(h_{t-1}, x_t) + b_o\right) \tag{11.6}$$

and the prediction will then be

$$h_t = o_t \times \tanh(C_t) \tag{11.7}$$

In order to increase the robustness of our results, we will perform backtesting on the forecast data. Backtesting is a cross-validation method that involves developing different models on subsets of the data set. These models are then tested against a validation set in order to achieve the desired prediction accuracy level. In time series backtesting, both short- and long-term dependencies on previous samples must be preserved when developing our sampling plan. Our validation strategy thus splits the arrivals time series into multiple uninterrupted sequences, which are then offset at different windows in order to create robust tests for the forecasting strategies using both current and past observations.

Data

We use monthly data regarding arrivals of Chinese tourists to the United States and to Australia. This data spans the period of the SARS outbreak (2003–2004) and reaches up to October 2019, just before the outbreak of the COVID-19 pandemic. This is done to ensure that the forecasts produced are unbiased from the recent developments. The data for the United States of America was obtained from National Travel & Tourism Office (https://travel.trade.gov/), while the data for Australia was obtained from Australian Bureau of Statistics (Table 11.3) (https://www.abs.gov.au/Tourism-and-Transport).

These two countries were selected based on two premises. The first premise is the fact that they represent popular destinations for Chinese tourists, thus making China-based arrivals a significant share of the countries' tourist revenue. The second premise is data availability, since it was not possible to obtain data for other popular destinations, such as Thailand or Japan. It must be noted that the selection of the United States as a destination does not take into account the outbreak of the crisis in the country. We use it simply as a proxy to the different destinations of Chinese tourists around the world.

The arrivals data series for the United States of Americawas not deseasonalized, so the first step is to extract the underlying trend factor. The Australian data series already

TABLE 11.3

Descriptive Statistics of the Arrivals Data Series

Metric	Date	Arrivals to USA	Arrivals to Australia
Min.	1-Jan-03	15,116	17,200
1st Qu.	8-Mar-07	44,238	27,625
Median	16-May-11	90,925	44,750
Mean	17-May-11	124,178	57,916
3rd Qu.	24-Jul-15	211,059	88,275
Max.	1-Oct-19	328,423	123,600

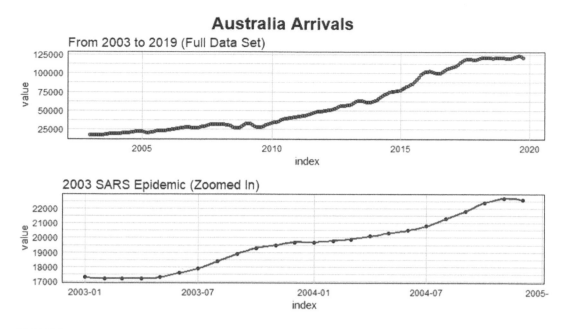

FIGURE 11.4   Arrivals of Chinese tourists to Australia.

included only the trend component. The descriptive statistics for the data for the United States and Australia arrivals are presented in Table 11.1, while the data is demonstrated graphically in Figure 11.4. We can clearly see the upward trend of Chinese arrivals to these two major economies, supporting our earlier claims about the increased importance of China as a source of tourism revenue globally.

Empirical Results and Discussion

Starting our analysis, the first step of the LSTM model is to ensure there exists a high degree of autocorrelation. This ensures the validity of LSTM as a modeling approach, since it will leverage this autocorrelation to generate a forecast for this data series (Gers et al., 2000). Our goal is to produce an 18-month forecast. Hence, we review the Autocorrelation Function (ACF), which demonstrates the correlation between a given time series and lagged versions of itself. We thus build a dataset with autocorrelations of the two data series ranging from 2 to 18 lags. We need autocorrelation to exist beyond the six-month interval, so as to be able to produce up to 18 forecasts for this data series. The ACFs for the United States of America and Australia arrivals are presented in Figures 11.5 and 11.6.

As can be expected, autocorrelation is diminishing as the lags are increasing. However, at the critical six-month lag, autocorrelation is higher than 0.5, which means that this lag is a good candidate for the optimal lag setting. This will permit us to produce the forecasts that we need using the LSTM approach. As can be expected for deseasonalized data, autocorrelation does not display any increases as the lags increase. This means that selecting six months as the optimal lag is an appropriate choice.

Our sampling plan includes three years of training data and one year of data for the validation set. It must be noted that our training set includes periods under the 2003 SARS epidemic as well as "normal" periods, which did not include any significant negative events, similar to the current crisis. In our analysis, negative events such as terrorist attacks do

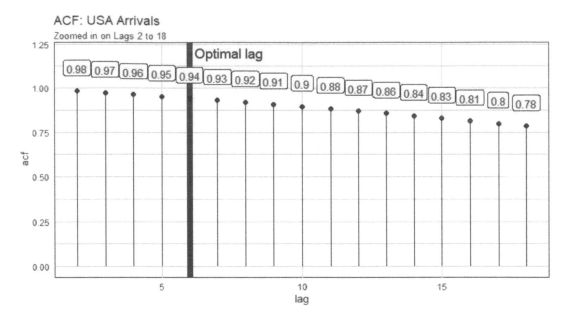

FIGURE 11.5   Autocorrelation function for arrivals to the United States of America.

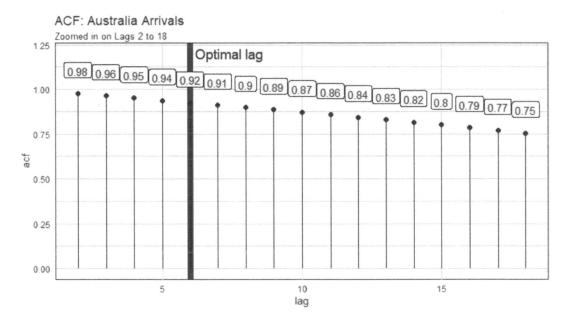

FIGURE 11.6   Autocorrelation function for arrivals to Australia.

not produce the negative impact similar to the current pandemic. Thus, as a crisis training period, we only include the period of the SARS epidemic, where the bias coefficient is used for calibration. In addition, for simplicity reasons, we develop our sampling strategy only on the US dataset.

Our backtesting strategy is presented in Figure 11.7. Using the setup above (three years for training and one year for testing), we are able to create six samples that will allow us to build our prediction model. The figure clearly demonstrates how our sampling plan

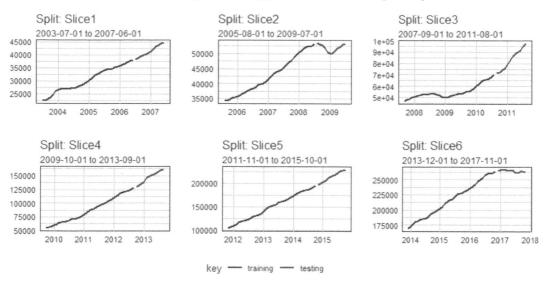

FIGURE 11.7 Rolling window backtesting strategy. (Note: This figure demonstrates the rolling window backtesting strategy.)

allows for the shift of the sampling window with each progressive data slice, using our selected training/testing splits. These samples will help us improve the accuracy of the model, despite the fact that not all of them contain a crisis period.

We first create our LSTM model approach on all the available data. This will allow us to test the validity of our model against normal conditions. Our predictions for US arrivals are presented in Figure 11.8. We can see that our predictions generally match that validation

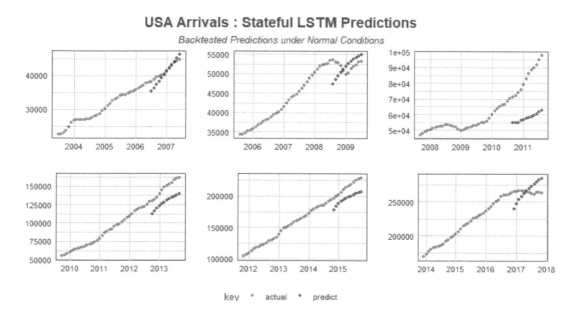

FIGURE 11.8 Stateful LSTM predictions and validation.

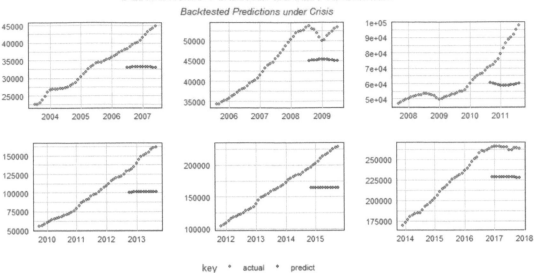

FIGURE 11.9   Stateful LSTM predictions and validation using SARS training data.

data set and thus our prediction strategy yields robust results. Note that the predictions in Figure 11.8 have been calculated using non-crisis conditions. However, our modeling approach suggests that the data from the SARS epidemic should be used to train the model. The results of implementing the SARS training data on the subsamples are presented in Figure 11.9. The discrepancy is evident but of course, these periods did not involve any major crises and thus this discrepancy can be expected.

Having completed and tested our modeling approach, we are able to present our predictions for Chinese arrivals to the United States and Australia. These predictions were generated using the LSTM network and are demonstrated in Figures 11.10 and 11.11 respectively. The figures demonstrate the pre-crisis level of October 2019 and the predicted point of commencement once travel restrictions have been lifted. Seasonality is not an issue in this forecast, since we are working with the trend component only. The t-1 time period represents the pre-crisis level, on October 2019, while the period t marks the commencement of international travel, worldwide. The next periods are the months after this date. The error bars represent the outcomes of the bias sensitivity analysis and are treated as the two extreme scenarios for recovery.

We can see that the LSTM machine predicts a significant drop in tourist arrivals after the containment of the pandemic, but that within approximately 12 months (for the United States, as shown in Figure 11.10) and six months (for Australia) tourist arrivals should return to their normal trend. It should be noted that the United States seems to be in a more difficult position according to the LSTM predictions; it will take approximately one year for tourist arrivals to return to their initial trend. However, since we do not consider our predictions to be country-specific, we assert that the two different forecast outcomes represent the range of our predictions, suggesting that it can take from 6 to 12 months to recover the losses in international tourism after the COVID-19 crisis.

It must be noted that our predictions are contingent on the resolution date for this conflict, whereby travel restrictions will have been lifted and travel for both business and leisure

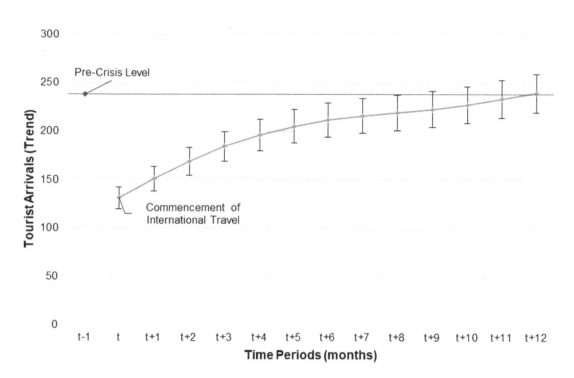

Forecast of post-crisis arrivals to USA
12 Month Horizon

FIGURE 11.10 LSTM Forecasts for Chinese Tourist Arrivals to the United States of America. This graph includes our forecast for the arrivals of Chinese tourists to the United States. The blue line represents the pre-crisis level, which will be reached in 12 months according to the LSTM forecast.

purposes will have commenced again. As the current situation continues and the drop in arrivals deepens (also see Yang et al. (2020)), the outcome of the prediction algorithm will likely be different. In addition, our model does not take into account the current problems faced by the two countries, the United States and Australia, due to the pandemic, which would of course further aggravate this crisis. These problems could be encapsulated by our model by manipulating the bias coefficient.

However, this is the power of the LSTM machine that we have implemented. Once more data becomes available, the algorithm can be called upon to generate new forecasts, using the most updated data set. Given that the training period is fixed (the 2003 SARS outbreak), the machine does not need to be retrained (unless the model bias needs to be retrained) and can thus produce results very quickly.

SUPPORT VECTOR REGRESSION (SVR)

Support vector machines (SVM) (Cortes & Vapnik, 1995; LeCun et al., 1989; Vapnik et al., 1997) are supervised learning algorithms used for classification and regression analysis. SVMs build a linear separating hyperplane, by mapping data into the feature space with the higher-dimensional, using the so-called kernel trick. The capacity of the system is controlled by parameters that do not depend on the dimensionality of feature space. One of the most important ideas in Support Vector Classification and Regression cases is that presenting the solution by means of small subset of training points gives enormous computational advantages.

Given a training data set $\{(x_1, y_1), (x_2, y_2), \ldots, (x_n, y_n)\} \subset \varkappa \times \mathbb{R}$ where $\varkappa$ denotes the space of the input patterns, the prediction for the linear model is given by:

$$f(x) = w^T x + b \tag{11.8}$$

where w is the coefficients vector, b is the bias and x is the input vector.

In the $\varepsilon - SVR$ (Vapnik, 1995) the aim is to find a function, $f(x)$, with at most $\varepsilon - deviation$ from the output y and ensure that it is as flat as possible, i.e., one seeks a small. This is formulated as a convex optimization problem to minimize

$$min \frac{1}{2}\|w\| + C \sum_{i=1}^{n} \left(\xi_i - \xi_i^* \right) \tag{11.9}$$

$$w_1 x_i - b \leq \varepsilon + \xi_i^* \qquad \forall i = 1, 2, \ldots, n \tag{11.10}$$

$$w_1 x_i + b - y_i \leq \varepsilon + \xi_i^* \qquad \forall i = 1, 2, \ldots, n \tag{11.11}$$

$$\xi_i \, \& \, \xi_i^* \geq 0 \qquad \forall i = 1, 2, \ldots, n \tag{11.12}$$

where ξ_i and ξ_i^* are slack variables that allow regression errors to exist up to the value of ξ_i and ξ_i^*, and guarantee at the same time the feasibility of the problem (11.9)–(11.12). The constant C controls the penalty imposed on observations that lie outside the ε margin and helps to prevent overfitting. This value determines the trade-off between the flatness of $f(x)$ and the amount up to which deviations larger than ε are tolerated.

The quality of estimation is measured by the loss function,

$$L = \begin{cases} 0 & if \ |y - f(x)| \leq \varepsilon \\ |y - f(x)| - \varepsilon & otherwise \end{cases} \tag{11.13}$$

It can be shown that the optimization problem (11.9)–(11.12) can be transformed into the dual problem and its solution is given by

$$f(x) = \sum_{i=1}^{n} \left(a_i - a_i^* \right) x_i^T + b \tag{11.14}$$

where a_i and a_i^* are Lagrangian multipliers. The training vectors giving non-zero Lagrange multipliers are called support vectors. Some regression problems cannot adequately be described using a linear model. In such a case, the Lagrange dual formulation allows the technique to be extended to nonlinear functions. The model can be extended to the nonlinear case through the concept of kernel $\mathcal{K}$, giving

$$f(x) = \sum_{i=1}^{n} \left(a_i - a_i^*\right) \mathcal{K}\left(x^T x\right) + b \tag{11.15}$$

Some popular kernel function used in various application of the SVR are:

The Linear Kernel: The Linear kernel is the simplest kernel function. It is given by

$$\mathcal{K}(x, y) = x^T x + c \tag{11.16}$$

where c is an optional constant.

The polynomial kernel: Polynomial kernels are well suited for problems where all the training data is normalized. It is given by:

$$\mathcal{K}(x, y) = \left(x^T x + c\right)^d \tag{11.17}$$

where d is the degree of the polynomial kernel, a is the slope, and c is a constant.

The Radial Basis Function (RBF) kernel, or Gaussian kernel:

$$\mathcal{K}(x, y) = exp\left(-\gamma \|x - y\|^2\right) \tag{11.18}$$

The γ parameter defines how far the influence of a single training example reaches.

This SVR model is now used to analyse the impact of travel anxiety on airline demand, by modeling it as a linear function of some key parameters, among which shock and fear effects are taken into account, together with other important variables representing the supply influence, the economic trend, and the demand seasonality. In the following we will explore in more details the shock and fear effects, by understanding how they can be modeled to analyze the present situation.

Let's see in more details how we can interpret these two components:

Shock

This term represents the immediate effect on bookings slow down or cancellations that are registered. This can be seen as a quantitative translation of the resistance to travel connected to the concern of having logistic or health problems due to the presence of COVID-19. In more details, this term takes into account, for example, the fear of having your travel cancelled due to a virus relapse, being blocked in a foreign country with no possibility to come back home because of frontiers closing or even worse, getting infected by the virus and bring it back to your country, being in turn the cause of a new focus. This component can be modeled as a direct function of the pandemic presence, i.e., daily contagions.

Fear

This second term is more related to the long-lasting resistance to travel that has been instilled by this unprecedented situation. This relates with travel anxiety and perceived unhealthiness of specific tourist venues as a result of the current media impact. Let's think for example to the Diamond Princess case or quarantined hotels due to the virus presence. Some travel situations naturally facilitate the creation of crowds and queues in relatively closed ambience and, in a situation where social distancing seems to be the only solution to survive and fight the virus, these situations will last in our minds as potentially risky ones for a long time. In order to quantitatively assess how much this second component is radiated yet in the traveler's minds and how the traveling products can be changed in order to survive this new reality, consumer sentiment surveys can help, together with looking ahead to countries which are slowly approaching the after-COVID-19 new normal, such as China.

Result and Discussion

Shock Effect and Willingness to Travel

As anticipated, the shock effect can be seen as a direct function of the daily contagions movements in time. In order to give a high-level interpretation of this fact, we can focus on Italy situation, by comparing Google queries for travels (viaggi in Italian) with the daily contagions trend in the last 90 days.

Even though Google trends might be also impacted by impossibility to travel due to governments travel bans, provided the generality of the keyword analyzed, we can assume that the extracted trends are mostly related to the awareness and consideration phases of the travel shopping funnel, which takes place approximately on average 45 days before the travel date. As we can see from the graph in Figure 11.11, the two compared quantities are as expected negatively correlated, meaning that the higher the number of

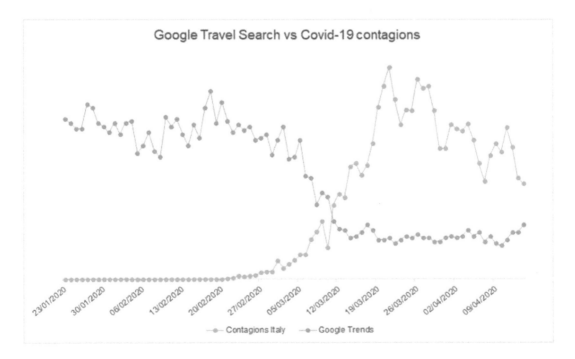

FIGURE 11.11 Google Trends for "viaggi" queries in Italy, confirmed cases data source JHU CSSE.[8]

contagions, the lower the travel searches (and willingness to travel in the short term). By understanding the interplay between these two quantities, it is possible to quantitatively measure how long the shock effect will last in the time and how intense it will be, once a forecast on future contagions has been obtained.

Fear Effect and Consumer Sentiment

The fear effect being more related to subconscious connections that our minds are now creating between COVID-19 and travel experience, it is hard to assess that quantitatively and in a stage when the shock component is still active and predominant. From an ex-post analysis on the 9/11 and SARS crises, Ito & Lee estimated in their article a negative impact out touristic demand of approximately 15% due to the fear effect. But how can we know if it is correct to assume a similar impact will occur also for the present crisis? Of course, there is no aswer yet to this question. However, various and extensive analyses on Consumer Sentiment are currently developed and periodically published by many firms and can help in having at least an idea about how travel risk perception is changing in consumers' minds (as shown in Figure 11.12). Among those, I personally suggest the weekly BCG Consumer Sentiment snapshots, for their completeness and readability. In the first two snapshots, some figures about willingness to travel are presented, which outline the increasing traveling concern due to perceived contagion risk in traveling situations.

Actually, almost 38% of the respondents see travel and taking a cruise or domestic flight as risky activities. They are also concerned about other travel-related activities, such as visiting theme parks, casinos, hotels, and taking a bus or a train. The analysis shows furthermore that respondents expect to spend on average −26% on activities that require travel and engagement in a group environment. These are first insights that tell us that for sure we will see a raising and persistent component of a fear factor which will keep slowing down

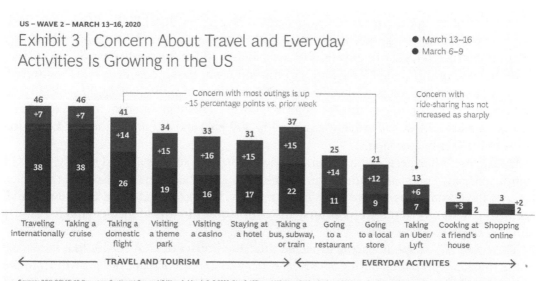

FIGURE 11.12 Weekly BCG Consumer Sentiment (Source: BCG Consumer Sentiment.)

touristic demand in the long run. However, we postpone a quantitative estimate of such a contribution to a point in time when the shock effect will be vanishing, letting us better isolating the intrinsic changes this outbrek has left in our traveling behavior.

EXPECTED IMPACTFUL SECTORS ANALYSIS

AIRLINES SECTOR

The International Air Transport Association (IATA) has published an analysis reporting that airlines may lose around 55 billion euros in bookings up to 30 June 2020, with a net quarterly loss of 35.4 billion euros. This situation is mainly due to the 38% drop in demand compared to 2019 and the drop in passenger revenue, which falls 229 billion euros.

Regarding demand, there was a decrease of about 71% in the second quarter of the year.

On the other hand, the price of fuel has also fallen substantially, although they estimate that fuel coverage will limit the benefit to a decrease of only 31%.

Fixed and semi-fixed costs amount to almost half of an airline's cost, with the latter (including crew costs) expected to fall by a third.

Another element to take into consideration is the costs to be assumed by the airlines regarding the return of cancelled tickets, which will produce very serious cash losses of 31.8 billion euros.

According to the data from the end of March this year, the number of flights in the 41 countries that make up Eurocontrol (a pan-European civil-military organization dedicated to supporting European aviation in air traffic management) was again less than 6,000, 81.3% less than the equivalent day in 2019, while passenger flights have practically disappeared from airspace, falling by 87%, i.e., 2,921 flights compared to 22,237 the previous year. Among the countries, Italy stands out with a 92% drop, Austria with 93%, and Spain with 87%.

The consequences for the airlines are being significant and translate into large economic losses. One of the most affected countries would be Spain with 11,800 million euros less, due to a reduction of 93.7 million in the number of passengers. This means that nearly 750,000 jobs and 44,842 million euros of contribution to the Spanish economy are at risk.

In the case of the United Kingdom, 113 million fewer passengers have been registered, which translates into a loss of income of 19,700 million euros, with 402,000 jobs at stake and around 29,600 million euros of contribution to the country's economy, 13.6 million are expected to be lost in Germany, risking 400,000 jobs and a contribution of 25.4 billion euros to the German economy.

In any case, all experts agree that airlines would have to survive around seven months of significantly lower demand, which tests their working capital, while pointing out that when fears of the coronavirus ease or vanish, air traffic will improve and could exceed demand, normalize it mainly in the business area and later recover it around the demand for family holidays or postponed events.

That is, a "U" shape impact is expected after the impact of COVID-19, like the shape of the impact experienced during SARS in 2002, and a return to capacity growth from the first months of early calendar 2021. Confidence in expectations is based on the recovery of passenger confidence in ensuring safety during travel, as well as the growth of the Asian middle class driving a significant increase in passenger numbers, mainly after analysis of data and experience in China.

CRUISE INDUSTRY

Despite the application of health control protocols such as thermal scanning, temperature checks, and other measures before and after boarding our ships, shipping companies suffered considerable setbacks in the stock market from published reports of contagion on some ships, coupled with recommendations from countries and organizations.

According to the Bloomberg agency, the three largest cruise operators have lost more than half of their market value in less than two months, equivalent to more than $42 billion.

In the case of ports as emblematic as Miami, considered the world capital of the cruises, the fear of the coronavirus has brought as consequence a decrease of tourists, which causes a chain of economic losses in the tourist and commercial sector difficult to evaluate for the moment in general lines. This situation may also be applicable to the main cruise ports around the world.

FAIR INDUSTRY

The Global Association of the Exhibition Industry has estimated that 134 billion euros of business was not produced by the cancellation and postponement of events until the end of the second quarter of the year worldwide. For the exhibition industry alone, the impact was 81.6 billion euros in the same period.

Broken down by region, the impact is EUR 21.8 billion and 378,000 jobs in Asia-Pacific; EUR 28.8 billion and 257,000 jobs in Europe; and EUR 29.2 billion and 320,000 jobs in North America.

TOURIST APARTMENT

According to data from the company Transparent, the global collapse of the tourist apartment business is seen with a drop in reservations in March of 23% worldwide, that is, 53% less than just one year ago.

By country, it is China that showed a greater decline in occupation in the first quarter of 2020, with a fall of 61%. It is followed by Italy (–29%), the United States (–17%), Spain (–17%), and France (–13%). With regard to cities, Rome recorded 32% of cancellations of total reservations made, followed by Venice (25%), Milan (24%), Florence (23%), Madrid (18%), and Barcelona (15%).

BUSINESS TRAVEL

In the business travel sector, the Global Business Travel Association (GBTA) with more than 1,155 companies worldwide, estimated from a survey among its members that almost half (53%) of these cancelled or suspended all non-essential travel.

In the events area, almost all GBTA member companies have cancelled (95%) or postponed (92%) meetings, conferences or events due to the coronavirus and 31% report moving meetings or events to other locations. When asked to estimate the percentage of cancelled business travel previously booked by March 2020, GBTA members estimate that approximately 89% of business travel was cancelled. This is double the estimate from the GBTA survey of March 10, 2020, when members initially estimated that 43% of business travel in March 2020 was cancelled due to the coronavirus.

Nightly Leisure

According to some tourism sectors, the International Nightlife Association estimates losses of $271 billion over the next 15 days. In Spain alone, one of the most affected countries, the total annual turnover of nightlife is close to 25,000 million euros and employs nearly 300,000 people a year. The case of New York City is especially noteworthy, where the nightlife sector has an annual turnover of 35,100 million dollars and employs nearly 300,000 people.

As a result, and due to the restrictions in all of the countries mentioned above, the International Nightlife Association has estimated that the nightlife industry worldwide will have a loss of $271.6 billion if the global health crisis is prolonged by 15 more days.

Fashion and Luxury (Shopping Tourism)

With respect to the tourism industry related to fashion and purchases of luxury products, it should be taken into consideration that the COVID-19 began in China, which represents 90% of the growth of the global luxury market during 2019, and whose impact can mean a decrease of 600 billion dollars in sales. According to data from the consulting firm BCG, it is estimated that sales of luxury goods will fall between 85 and 120 billion dollars in 2020, above its first forecast of 40 billion dollars. Although China is currently showing positive signs of recovery, domestic demand may not be matched by supply, as production of luxury goods remains blocked in Europe. It is estimated that tourism spending will continue to be affected at least until the end of the year, with major consequences for luxury brands.

Luxury brands should prepare for a drop in sales of between $85 and $120 billion by 2020, or about 29.2% of the $350 billion luxury market. The fashion and luxury category will lose between 450 and 600 billion dollars in sales.

NOTES

1. World Economic Forum (2019). Outbreak readiness and business impact protecting lives and livelihoods across the global economy. Retrieved April 24, 2020, from http://www3.weforum.org/docs/WEF HGHI_Outbreak_Readiness_Business_Impact.pdf.
2. https://www.unwto.org/impact-assessment-of-the-covid-19-outbreak-on-international-tourism
3. https://wttc.org/en-gb/
4. https://www.statista.com/forecasts/1103432/covid-19-revenue-travel-tourism-industry-country-forecast
5. http://www.assoturismo.it/assoturismo-cst-nel-2020-si-perderanno-oltre-260-milioni-di-presenze-turistiche-60-ripresa-solo-nel-2021-forse.html
6. https://elpais.com/economia/2020-04-01/exceltur-calcula-una-perdida-de-mas-del-30-del-negocio-turistico-a-causa-del-coronavirus.html
7. https://www.un.org/africarenewal/magazine/special-edition-covid-19/au-study-covid-19-could-cost-africa-500-billion-damage-tourism-and
8. https://github.com/CSSEGISandData

REFERENCES

Aliperti, G., & Cruz, A. M. (2019). Investigating tourists' risk information processing. *Annals of Tourism Research*, 79, 102803.

Allen, T., Murray, K. A., Zambrana-Torrelio, C., Morse, S. S., Rondinini, C., Di Marco, M., Breit, N., Olival, K. J., & Daszak, P. (2017). Global hotspots and correlates of emerging zoonotic diseases. *Nature Communications*, 8(1), 1–10.

Arana, J. E., & León, C. J. (2008). The impact of terrorism on tourism demand. *Annals of Tourism Research, 35*(2), 299–315.

Assaf, A. G., Li, G., Song, H., & Tsionas, M. G. (2019). Modeling and forecasting regional tourism demand using the Bayesian global vector autoregressive (BGVAR) model. *Journal of Travel Research, 58*(3), 383–397.

Athanasopoulos, G., & de Silva, A. (2012). Multivariate exponential smoothing for forecasting tourist arrivals. *Journal of Travel Research, 51*(5), 640–652.

Barrios, R. E. (2017). What does catastrophe reveal for whom? The anthropology of crises and disasters at the onset of the Anthropocene. *Annual Review of Anthropology, 46*, 151–166.

Bengio, Y., Simard, P., & Frasconi, P. (1994). Learning long-term dependencies with gradient descent is difficult. *IEEE Transactions on Neural Networks, 5*(2), 157–166.

Bozzoli, C., & Müller, C. (2011). Perceptions and attitudes following a terrorist shock: Evidence from the UK. *European Journal of Political Economy, 27*, S89–S106.

Brodbeck, K.-H. (2019). *Die Illusion der Identität und die Krise der Wissenschaften.* Working Paper Serie.

Carriere, K. R. (2019). Threats to human rights: A general review. *Journal of Social and Political Psychology, 7*(1), 8–32.

Constantiou, I. D., & Kallinikos, J. (2015). New games, new rules: big data and the changing context of strategy. *Journal of Information Technology, 30*(1), 44–57.

Cortes, C., & Vapnik, V. (1995). Support-vector networks. *Machine Learning, 20*(3), 273–297.

Dolnicar, S. (2005). Understanding barriers to leisure travel: Tourist fears as a marketing basis. *Journal of Vacation Marketing, 11*(3), 197–208.

Felix, A. G., Schmidhuber, J., & Cummins, F. (2000). Learning to forget: Continual prediction with LSTM. *Neural Computation, 12*(10), 2451–2471.

Gössling, S., Scott, D., & Hall, C. M. (2020). Pandemics, tourism and global change: A rapid assessment of COVID-19. *Journal of Sustainable Tourism*, 1–20.

Gounopoulos, D., Petmezas, D., & Santamaria, D. (2012). Forecasting tourist arrivals in Greece and the impact of macroeconomic shocks from the countries of tourists' origin. *Annals of Tourism Research, 39*(2), 641–666.

Gunter, U., & Önder, I. (2016). Forecasting city arrivals with Google Analytics. *Annals of Tourism Research, 61*, 199–212.

Hall, C. M., Prayag, G., & Amore, A. (2017). *Tourism and resilience: Individual, organisational and destination perspectives.* Channel View Publications.

Hall, C. M., Scott, D., & Gössling, S. (2020). Pandemics, transformations and tourism: be careful what you wish for. *Tourism Geographies*, 1–22.

Hassani, H., Silva, E. S., Antonakakis, N., Filis, G., & Gupta, R. (2017). Forecasting accuracy evaluation of tourist arrivals. *Annals of Tourism Research, 63*, 112–127.

Higgins-Desbiolles, F. (2020). Socialising tourism for social and ecological justice after COVID-19. *Tourism Geographies*, 1–14.

Hochreiter, S., & Schmidhuber, J. (1997). Long short-term memory. *Neural Computation, 9*(8), 1735–1780.

Ioannides, D., & Gyimóthy, S. (2020). The COVID-19 crisis as an opportunity for escaping the unsustainable global tourism path. *Tourism Geographies*, 1–9.

Jørgensen, M. T., Law, R., & King, B. E. (2017). Understanding the past, anticipating the future– a critical assessment of China outbound tourism research. *Journal of Travel & Tourism Marketing, 34*(7), 880–891.

Laurin, K., Kay, A. C., & Fitzsimons, G. M. (2012). Divergent effects of activating thoughts of God on self-regulation. *Journal of Personality and Social Psychology, 102*(1), 4.

Law, R., Li, G., Fong, D. K. C., & Han, X. (2019). Tourism demand forecasting: A deep learning approach. *Annals of Tourism Research, 75*, 410–423.

LeCun, Y., Boser, B., Denker, J. S., Henderson, D., Howard, R. E., Hubbard, W., & Jackel, L. D. (1989). Backpropagation applied to handwritten zip code recognition. *Neural Computation, 1*(4), 541–551.

Li, Y., & Cao, H. (2018). Prediction for tourism flow based on LSTM neural network. *Procedia Computer Science*, *129*, 277–283.

Mawby, R. I. (2000). Tourists' perceptions of security: The risk—fear paradox. *Tourism Economics*, *6*(2), 109–121.

Nowlin, C. (2017). Understanding and undermining the growth paradigm. *Dialogue: Canadian Philosophical Review/Revue Canadienne de Philosophie*, *56*(3), 559–593.

Ötsch, W. (2020). *What type of crisis is this? The coronavirus crisis as a crisis of the economicised society*. Working Paper Serie.

Papatheodorou, A. (1999). The demand for international tourism in the Mediterranean region. *Applied Economics*, *31*(5), 619–630.

Pennington-Gray, L., Schroeder, A., Wu, B., Donohoe, H., & Cahyanto, I. (2014). Travelers' perceptions of crisis preparedness certification in the United States. *Journal of Travel Research*, *53*(3), 353–365.

Pieters, R. (2013). Bidirectional dynamics of materialism and loneliness: Not just a vicious cycle. *Journal of Consumer Research*, *40*(4), 615–631.

Quinn, R. E., & Cameron, K. S. (1988). *Paradox and transformation: Toward a theory of change in organization and management*. Ballinger Publishing Co/Harper & Row Publishers.

Rittichainuwat, B. N., & Chakraborty, G. (2009). Perceived travel risks regarding terrorism and disease: The case of Thailand. *Tourism Management*, *30*(3), 410–418.

Schad, J., Lewis, M. W., Raisch, S., & Smith, W. K. (2016). Paradox research in management science: Looking back to move forward. *Academy of Management Annals*, *10*(1), 5–64.

Scheppele, K. L. (2003). Law in a Time of Emergency: States of Exception and the Temptations of 9/11. *The University of Pennsylvania Journal of Constitutional Law.*, *6*, 1001.

Shen, S., Li, G., & Song, H. (2011). Combination forecasts of international tourism demand. *Annals of Tourism Research*, *38*(1), 72–89.

Sigala, M. (2011). Social media and crisis management in tourism: Applications and implications for research. *Information Technology & Tourism*, *13*(4), 269–283.

Sigala, M., Airey, D., Jones, P., & Lockwood, A. (2004). ICT paradox lost? A stepwise DEA methodology to evaluate technology investments in tourism settings. *Journal of Travel Research*, *43*(2), 180–192.

Song, H., Qiu, R. T. R., & Park, J. (2019). A review of research on tourism demand forecasting: Launching the Annals of Tourism Research Curated Collection on tourism demand forecasting. *Annals of Tourism Research*, *75*, 338–362.

Syriopoulos, T. C. (1995). A dynamic model of demand for Mediterranean tourism. *International Review of Applied Economics*, *9*(3), 318–336.

Teixeira, J. P., & Fernandes, P. O. (2012). Tourism time series forecast-different ANN architectures with time index input. *Procedia Technology*, *5*, 445–454.

Vapnik, V., Golowich, S. E., & Smola, A. J. (1997). Support vector method for function approximation, regression estimation and signal processing. *Advances in Neural Information Processing Systems*, 281–287.

Vapnik, V. N. (1995). The nature of statistical learning. *Theory*.

Williams, P. W., & Ponsford, I. F. (2009). Confronting tourism's environmental paradox: Transitioning for sustainable tourism. *Futures*, *41*(6), 396–404.

Yang, Y., Zhang, H., & Chen, X. (2020). Coronavirus pandemic and tourism: Dynamic stochastic general equilibrium modeling of infectious disease outbreak. *Annals of Tourism Research*.

Yu, M., Li, Z., Yu, Z., He, J., & Zhou, J. (2020). Communication related health crisis on social media: a case of COVID-19 outbreak. *Current Issues in Tourism*, 1–7.

Zheng, Y., Goh, E., & Wen, J. (2020). The effects of misleading media reports about COVID-19 on Chinese tourists' mental health: a perspective article. *Anatolia*, *31*(2), 337–340.

Zuboff, S. (2015). Big other: surveillance capitalism and the prospects of an information civilization. *Journal of Information Technology*, *30*(1), 75–89.

Zysman, J. (2006). The algorithmic revolution—the fourth service transformation. *Communications of the ACM*, *49*(7), 48.

12 Direct and Indirect Impacts of the COVID-19 Pandemic Crisis on Human Physical and Physiological Health

KEY POINTS

- The list of challenges and concerns brought by SARS-CoV-2. Every effort should be put to understand and control the disease.
- Patients with confirmed or suspected 2019-nCoV (new coronavirus disease) may experience fear of the consequences of being infected with a potentially fatal new virus, and those in quarantine might experience boredom, loneliness, and anger.
- In the intervention with staff and patients, we found the stress-adaptation model particularly relevant.
- Use of the term "social distancing" might imply that one needs to cut off meaningful interactions. A preferable term is "physical distancing" because it allows for the fact that social connection is possible even when people are physically separated.

INTRODUCTION

To decrease the spread of the coronavirus disease (COVID-19) and to reduce the interaction between unrecognized infected and non-infected individuals, different strategies have been proposed, ranging from quarantine, local confinement, lockdown, and isolation. Although people may have sedentary behaviors and be physically active, it has been suggested that, while confined at home, individuals reduce their daily activities outside and, consequently, the level of physical activity is thought to decrease. This may have a negative impact on general heath and may contribute to sedentary behaviors (Hall et al., 2020).

The SARS-CoV-2-caused COVID-19 pandemic has resulted in a devastating threat to human society in terms of health, economy, and lifestyle. Although the virus usually first invades and infects the lungs and respiratory track tissue, in extreme cases, almost all major organs in the body are now known to be negatively impacted, often leading to severe systemic failure in some people. Unfortunately, there is currently no effective treatment for this disease. Pre-existing pathological conditions or comorbidities such as age are a major reason for premature death and increased morbidity and mortality. The immobilization due to hospitalization and bed rest and the physical inactivity due to sustained quarantine and social distancing can downregulate the ability of organs systems to resist to viral infection and increase the risk of damage to the immune, respiratory, cardiovascular, musculoskeletal systems, and the brain. The cellular mechanisms and danger of this "second wave" effect of COVID-19 to the human body, along with the effects of aging, proper nutrition, and regular physical activity, are reviewed in this chapter with three-fold goals: (1) to address the harm of physical inactivity associated with the virus outbreak to the body; (2) to highlight the COVID-19 threats and damages to the various human physiological systems; and (3) to recommend some practical strategies to mitigate the potential damage.

This chapter is organized in such a way that it will cover a brief overview on the pathology of COVID-19 and its impact on the immune system in the first section. Then, it will review the impacts of the COVID-19 outbreak and physical inactivity on the respiratory, cardiovascular, and musculoskeletal systems. Special sections will be devoted to how the virus may specifically devastate the aged population and compromise the psychological and mental well-being. Next section will provide some practical suggestions as to how good nutrition and exercise training can protect against and help recovery from the virus attack. Ultimately, the harm and suffering that the coronavirus can cause to an individual is determined by not only the endowed factors such as age, sex, race, medical conditions, but also the lifestyle of the individual during the pandemic. Finally, chapter will cover some methodological overview of essential machine learning (ML) classification methods, in the context of textual analytics, and compare their effectiveness in classifying coronavirus Tweets of varying lengths.

IMPACT OF COVID-19 AND PHYSICAL INACTIVITY ON THE IMMUNE SYSTEM

SARS-CoV-2 causes coronavirus disease (COVID-19) characterized by the major symptoms of fever, dry cough, myalgia, and fatigue. Currently, there are neither vaccines nor clinically proven effective therapeutics. Convalescent plasma and anti-viral drugs (e.g., Remdesivir) have shown some promise in treating COVID-19 patients (Scavone et al., 2020), but their widespread use awaits statistical rigor. Behavioral strategies of social distancing and hygiene are currently the best and only methods to limit the spread and reduce morbidity and mortality. As this virus strain is novel to the human immune system, we are dependent on aspects of our innate immunity to deal with the initial infection. Like most viral infections, if we survive the infection, over the course of weeks we develop antibody and cell-mediated immune responses specific to the virus. In most instances, this exposure-related "training" of our immune systems offers us long-lasting protection from re-infection or, if we are re-infected, disease symptoms are much milder. However, we currently do not know if our response to SARS-CoV-2 is sufficient to be protective and long lasting. Along with tests for the presence of viral particles and plasma antibodies, a clear need exists for research related to vaccine development and research to determine whether our immune response is adequate to protect us.

The public health recommendations (i.e., stay-at-home orders, closures of parks, gymnasiums, and fitness centers) to prevent SARS-CoV-2 spread have the potential to reduce daily physical activity (PA). These recommendations are unfortunate because daily exercise may help combat the disease by boosting our immune systems and counteracting some of the co-morbidities like obesity, diabetes, hypertension, and serious heart conditions that make us more susceptible to severe COVID-19 illness (Siordia Jr, 2020).

Exercise affects the immune system and its anti-viral defenses (Martin et al., 2009; Walsh et al., 2011). Animal experiments, administering influenza and herpes simplex viruses 1 (HSV-1) in the respiratory tract, have shown that moderate exercise, performed before (i.e., training) or after infection (for a few days before symptom onset), improves morbidity and mortality to the infection (Lowder et al., 2005; Marian L Kohut et al., 2009;

Warren et al., 2015). Conversely, preclinical studies have also shown that intense exercise leads to poorer outcomes in response to respiratory viral infections (Davis et al., 1997; Murphy et al., 2008). Follow-up studies have elucidated some understanding of the mechanisms responsible for these observations (Lowder et al., 2005; Marian L Kohut et al., 1998; M L Kohut et al., 2005; Murphy et al., 2004).

An early epidemiological study suggested that intense, prolonged exercise was associated with an increase in upper respiratory tract infections (David C Nieman et al., 1990). This work led to the concept of the inverted J theory, where moderate exercise reduces, and prolonged, high-intensity exercise increases susceptibility to infection (DAVID C Nieman, 1994). Many studies since have supported the theory with respect to individual immune parameters including those specific to viral defense. For example, salivary lactoferrin and its secretion rate increased for up to 2 hours after moderate exercise (Svendsen et al., 2016). Mucosal lactoferrin is important because it can prevent DNA and RNA viruses from infecting cells by binding and blocking host receptors. Conversely, low levels or low secretion rates of salivary immunoglobulin A, which can bind to viruses and inactivate them, have been shown to be associated with upper respiratory tract infection in some athletes undergoing intense training (Gleeson et al., 2012). In addition, because PA and exercise result in profound movement of leukocytes in blood and tissues (Rooney et al., 2018), many researchers theorize that being physically active increases immune surveillance against infectious pathogens including viruses.

Despite this, whether exercise-induced changes in the immune system affect respiratory virus susceptibility in people is unclear (Simpson et al., 2020). Indeed, controversy remains whether intense, prolonged exercise can alter immunity that leads to infectious disease risk or whether moderate exercise-induced improvements in immune response reduces it. Definitive studies where both exercise and infection are manipulated and controlled are needed and yet scarce due to ethical concerns. In one such study, moderate exercise training (40 min at 70% heart rate reserve every other day for 10 days) was initiated after nasal rhinovirus administration to determine its effects on the severity and duration of infection (Weidner et al., 1998). No differences were found in self-reported symptoms or mucus weight (collected from provided facial tissues), and it was concluded that PA and moderate exercise are safe during a rhinovirus-induced upper respiratory tract infection. Of special note is these subjects were young, healthy college students and (other than mucus weight) and no measurement of viral infection or subsequent antibody responses were completed.

At this time, we know very little about how PA or exercise might interact with the immune system to affect SARS-CoV-2 infectivity and COVID-19 disease susceptibility. As the pandemic proceeds, it will be important to perform retrospective studies to determine whether PA status had any bearing on SARS-CoV-2 infection or COVID-19 outcome; valid virus and antibody testing protocols will aid such studies. In addition, animal models determining the effect of PA and exercise on coronavirus infection and subsequent immune responses would also be informative. Current practical advice dictates that people follow social distancing and hygiene practices, and we propose exercise can be safely incorporated. Disruption of PA and exercise routines and reducing physical fitness may increase susceptibility to infection and certainly increase some comorbidities associated with poor COVID-19 outcomes if protracted. As animal studies have documented that intense training or intense, prolonged single exercise bouts can lead to reduced immune responses, it is not prudent to begin an intense training regimen or perform highly intense prolonged exercise if you are not accustomed to such activities. A good practice is to start exercising at lower intensities and durations and build up slowly. For example, walking is the most natural and practical form of exercise and beneficial to many organ systems. For those who have underlying health conditions, consultation with a primary care provider is warranted before beginning an exercise program.

COVID-19, Physical Activity, and the Respiratory System

While the clinical course of the COVID-19 pandemic continues to be investigated, many COVID-19 patients develop respiratory failure and require mechanical ventilation (MV) to maintain adequate pulmonary gas exchange. In this regard, a recent report reveals that ~54% of patients hospitalized due to COVID-19 experience respiratory failure and >30% require MV (YLiu, 2020). Although MV is often a life-saving intervention, an unwanted consequence of prolonged MV is the rapid development of respiratory muscle weakness due to diaphragm muscle atrophy and contractile dysfunction (collectively termed ventilator-induced diaphragm dysfunction, VIDD). VIDD is clinically significant because diaphragmatic weakness is a major contributor to the inability to wean patients from the ventilator (Dres & Demoule, 2018). Many COVID-19 patients often require prolonged time on the ventilator that increases the risk of weaning problems. Patients who experience difficult weaning suffer higher morbidity and mortality than patients weaned quickly on their first attempts to separate from the ventilator (Vassilakopoulos & Petrof, 2004) and unfortunately, many COVID-19 patients succumb to ICU-related complications (e.g., sepsis) (YLiu, 2020). Given that respiratory muscle weakness is a primary risk factor for failure to wean from the ventilator, developing strategies to protect the diaphragm against MV-induced weakness has become a priority in critical care medicine. Interestingly, studies into the effects of endurance exercise training on the respiratory system have led the way. Details about this story follow.

Although many organ systems adapt in response to endurance exercise training, the structural and functional properties of the lung and airways are not altered due to exercise training (McKenzie, 2012). Nonetheless, while the gas-exchange side of the respiratory system does not adapt to exercise training, "the pump" side of the respiratory system does undergo adaptive changes in response to endurance exercise. Specifically, endurance exercise training promotes numerous biochemical alterations in diaphragm muscle resulting in a phenotype that is protected against several challenges including prolonged MV (Powers et al., 2020). Indeed, as few as 10 consecutive days of endurance exercise training results in significant protection against VIDD (Morton et al., 2019; Smuder et al., 2012; Smuder et al., 2019). Therefore, it is predicted that endurance trained individuals that develop COVID-19 and require ventilator support will benefit from the exercise-induced preconditioning of the diaphragm.

Unfortunately, many patients that develop COVID-19 are not endurance trained prior to infection. Nonetheless, studies into the mechanism(s) responsible for endurance training preconditioning of the diaphragm are a powerful tool in the pursuit of pharmacological treatments to prevent VIDD and reduce weaning problems in patients exposed to long-duration ventilator support. In this regard, preclinical investigations reveal that endurance exercise training alters the abundance of ~70 cytosolic proteins and ~25 mitochondrial proteins in the diaphragm (Sollanek et al., 2017). Studies investigating which of these proteins contribute to protection of the diaphragm against VIDD reveal that exercise-induced changes in both mitochondrial proteins (e.g., superoxide dismutase 2) and cytosolic proteins (e.g., heat shock protein 72) contribute to exercise preconditioning of the diaphragm (Smuder et al., 2012; Smuder et al., 2019; Sollanek et al., 2017). This vital information has been used to develop successful pharmacological treatments to protect the diaphragm against MV-induced diaphragmatic weakness (Powers et al., 2011; Sollanek et al., 2017). Importantly, these preclinical studies provide an example of how exercise physiology research leads to improved healthcare.

IMPACT OF COVID-19 AND PHYSICAL INACTIVITY ON CARDIOVASCULAR SYSTEM

PA is critical to cardiovascular health and deemed essential during the pandemic. Part of the strategy to reduce the spread of the virus is through social isolation, but social isolation runs the risk of reduced PA with potential long-term consequences. Humans evolved as physically active animals and regular PA is in our genes (Booth et al., 2000; Lightfoot, 2011). The effects of inactivity promote genes that are detrimental to health. Inactivity for any reason reduces heart health and increases the long-term risk of coronary artery disease and sudden cardiac death. The positive impact of PA on the prevention of coronary artery disease and sudden cardiac death reduction is well known dating back to the London Bus Drivers study (Morris & Crawford, 1958; Norman, 1958). Current studies on steps per day and other measures of exercise show that regular PA promotes cardiovascular health and those who have higher levels of fitness have better exercise stress testing outcomes (Lee et al., 2019; Mandsager et al., 2018).

The muscle aches that accompany influenza and corona viral infections are a well-known symptom and a result of direct and indirect harm to the tissue. Muscle soreness is likely due to a combination of direct tissue infection and the inflammatory response of cytokines released to fight the viral invasion. Excessive cytokine release (cytokine storm) is the dark side of the immune response that is responsible for tissue damage beyond that of the direct viral infection. While both heart and peripheral muscle are infected by viruses, heart muscle infection has both short- and long-term consequences. COVID-19 is no different and may, as a novel virus, trigger more extensive tissue damage in the heart. Heart muscle infection leads to myocarditis with the potential for acute myocardial infarction, heart failure, and/or arrhythmia (Bonow et al., 2020; Inciardi et al., 2020; Yang & Jin, 2020). In the acute infection phase, the adrenergic release can trigger acute coronary syndrome or fatal arrhythmias (Sribhutorn et al., 2016). Systemic viral infections also cause an inflammatory reaction that irritates the lining of the arteries. In the coronary arteries, inflammation allows tears in the tissue holding plaques in place, leading to plaque rupture with clot formation and hence either fatal arrhythmia or local hypoxia and cardiac tissue death. Plaque rupture is a common cause of sudden cardiac arrest and death both at rest and during exercise. Muscle scarring induced by viral infection can trigger potentially fatal postinfection and exertion related arrhythmias, which can be fatal (Thompson & Dec, 2020). The cardiac effects of COVID-19 can be present in concert with or after the respiratory symptoms have abated in some patients.

During the COVID-19 pandemic, PA and exercise will play both a positive and a negative role in individual health outcomes. On the negative side, COVID-19 infection increases risk of cardiac damage and cardiac death during exercise and the increased risk may extend into the postinfection time period. PA during any systemic viral disease is not recommended because the inflammatory reaction within the muscle cells and coronary artery walls put an affected individual at risk for sudden cardiac death during and after the infection. Data from post-mortem analysis is showing this to be true for COVID-19 patients also (Inciardi et al., 2020; Yang & Jin, 2020). The accompanying myocardial scarring leaves individuals at risk for sudden cardiac death for a lifetime. Non-steroidal anti-inflammatory drugs (NSAIDs) are often used to relieve muscle discomfort but increase the risk of heart events under normal circumstances. The risk is accentuated during concurrent viral infections like COVID-19, so NSAIDs are not the choice for muscle pain control during a COVID-19 viral infection.

On the positive side, regular PA and exercise promote cardiorespiratory fitness and longevity. Our recommendation for healthy individuals during and following the COVID-19 pandemic is to remain physically active and exercise while socially distanced when you are well, stop exercise when you develop symptoms or signs of an infection, and return to PA and exercise slowly following recovery. Social distancing requires some changes in perspective while exercising. Recent models suggest the 2-m diameter "bubble" of safety changes shape with movement. The slipstream of dirty air created by running or biking requires 5–20 m of spacing for a person following directly behind an infected person to stay in clean air. The 2-m safety zone may also be broken by forced breathing that comes with vigorous exercise based on the spread of the virus among church choir members who met for practice and maintained social spacing during the rehearsal; approximately 75% of those in attendance contracted the disease.

Once completely well, it is reasonable for mildly infected individuals to gradually resume PA and exercise with a goal of returning to preinfection fitness. For people with more severe COVID-19 illness, return to PA may require testing or imaging prior to exercise. If exertion-related symptoms like palpitations, chest pain, exercise intolerance, or dyspnea occur during the return to exercise, evaluation with cardiac imaging and stress testing may be indicated to rule out COVID-19 cardiac damage before progressing to higher PA levels.

Impact of COVID-19 and Physical Inactivity on Musculoskeletal System

Staying healthy requires daily PA. Our body is constantly sensing internal environment and responding to these changes (Hawley, 2014). The increased demands from the contracting skeletal muscles during exercise represent a major challenge to the body homeostasis provoking a plethora of responses in several organs. The metabolic rate of the skeletal muscle can rise even 100-fold on activation when compared to resting conditions (Hamilton, 2018). In order to support the energy demand of the working muscle fibers, temporary acute responses occur in our organism to meet the PA and exercise challenge. As a result of the accumulation of activity sessions, the organism adapts to the metabolic demands. PA and exercise adaptations refer to the long-term changes that occur in our body as a consequence of PA and training. Heart hypertrophy and resting bradycardia are two well-known examples of these adaptations. However, the musculoskeletal system, one of the largest tissues in the body, is the main target of exercise training. Plasticity describes the ability of our muscles to adapt to variations in activity and in working demand. The adaptive event involves the whole muscle fiber structure from the sarcolemma to the mitochondria, including the myofibrils, the extracellular matrix, as well as capillaries surrounding the muscle fibers (Pette, 2001).

Exercise is one of the most frequently prescribed therapies in both health and diseases (Vina et al., 2012). However, western societal lifestyle behaviors promote physical inactivity and sedentariness (Bowden Davies et al., 2019). This situation is greatly aggravated by the containment measures imposed by the countries to control the expansion of the recent pandemic of COVID-19. A large number of people have been asked by health authorities to stay home in quarantine for an extended period of time, and this recommendation poses a significant challenge for remaining physically active. Several models have given us information on the effects of inactivity in the musculoskeletal system: bed rest and limb immobilization are extreme experimental models. Reduction of daily walking steps may indicate a more physiological model of reduced PA that reflects the risk of long-term confinement. In terms of steps walked, ~10,000 steps/day is generally considered as a high level of PA, while ~1500 steps/day is classified as a low level of PA (Bowden Davies et al., 2019).

Physical inactivity is associated with many detrimental effects, including loss of aerobic fitness (~7% reduction in VO2 peak in healthy young adults), musculoskeletal, and cognitive decline (Bowden Davies et al., 2019). It is also accompanied with metabolic effects that include alterations in insulin signaling that leads to increased peripheral insulin resistance, an increase in inflammation, as well as alterations in adipose tissue lipolysis and mitochondrial pathways (Bowden Davies et al., 2019). In skeletal muscle, physical inactivity-induced reduction in insulin sensitivity contributes to the distribution of energy substrates into other tissues, which increases central fat accumulation (Rabøl et al., 2011). The body needs regular muscular activity during the day, whereas some of the most powerful mechanisms regulating disease susceptibility such as the mitochondrial function and the lipoprotein metabolism are being downregulated during physical inactivity (Hamilton, 2018).

PA and exercise are essential in preserving muscle mass through the activation of muscle protein synthesis (Bowden Davies et al., 2019). On the contrary, the lack of muscle contractile activity during inactivity, especially in old individuals, is a leading cause of anabolic resistance and muscle atrophy (Nascimento et al., 2019). Significant muscle atrophy (1–4% losses) has been reported with only 14 days of step reduction in both young and older adults (Bowden Davies et al., 2019). Skeletal muscle adapts to a prolonged physical inactivity by decreasing not only muscle fiber size (atrophy) but also muscle function and quality (Arc-Chagnaud et al., 2020). Mechanosensor proteins, such as costameres, titin, filamin-C, and Bag3, which allow muscle fibers to sense mechanical forces, are also involved in the regulation of skeletal muscle mass. Their activation during muscle contraction regulates protein turnover through interaction with the mammalian target of rapamycin complex 1 (mTORC1) and with the main proteolytic pathways: the autophagic-lysosomal and the ubiquitin-proteasome systems (Wackerhage et al., 2019).

Mitochondrion, conventionally regarded as the "power house" of muscle energy generation, plays an important role in not only controlling the proliferation and generation of the new organelle (mitochondrial biogenesis) (Hood et al., 2016) but also regulating the elimination of dysfunctional mitochondria via mitophagy and the morphological dynamics via fusion and fission (Chan, 2006; Ji et al., 2020; Youle & Narendra, 2011). Studies in human subjects with long-term bed rest and other forms of confinements reveal that mitochondrial homeostasis is disrupted by muscle immobilization resulting in decreased protein synthesis and enhanced protein degradation (Kandarian, 2008; Schiaffino et al., 2013; Timmons et al., 2006). Research in rodents demonstrates that muscle immobilization for a period of 2–3 weeks dramatically reduces mitochondrial quantity and quality because of the downregulation of mitochondrial biogenesis, the upregulation of the ubiquitin-proteolysis, and the overexpression of mitophagic genes (Kang et al., 2015).

Research shows that deterioration of mitochondrial homeostasis due to muscle immobilization can lead to organic and systemic inflammation, an important mechanism for

COVID-19 pathogenesis. Decreased mTOR activity unleashes forkhead box O (FoxO) family transcription factor activation, which is an important reason for enhanced proteolysis and mitophagy (Ji et al., 2020; Kandarian, 2008). Increased reactive oxygen species (ROS) generation also activates nuclear factor kappa B (NFκB) signaling to produce pro-inflammatory cytokines such as TNFα, interleukin (IL)-1, and IL-6 in the muscle and exacerbates muscle atrophy and functional decline.

COVID-19 INFECTION AND THE BRAIN FUNCTION

The current coronavirus 2019 (COVID-19) pandemic not only poses a large threat to the physical health of our population, if we fail to act now, it will also have detrimental long-term consequences for mental health. This section will cover impacts of pandemic on physiological system of humans with covering various questions and answers.

Does SARS-CoV-2 Infection Threaten and Damage the Brain?

Although the main risk of COVID-19 is to cause injuries to the upper and lower respiratory track and lungs, other organs are not necessarily void of this viral infection. It is believed that the entry of SARS-CoV-2 in the human tissues is facilitated via angiotensin-converting enzyme 2 (ACE-2); however, the poor absence of ACE-2 receptors in central nervous system (CNS) does not mean that CNS is resistant against this type of viruses (Gu et al., 2005). Indeed, it has been shown that when SARS-CoV-2 types of virus was given intra-nasally to mice, the virus translocated into thalamus and brainstem and were significantly lethal, suggesting that CNS could be one of the targets of SARS-CoV-2. It is suggested that the virus can reach the CNS via neural circuits through trans-synaptic pathways (Li et al., 2013). The relatively long latency period of the virus of 5–12 days would allow the virus to significantly damage medullary neurons, and indeed, patients infected by SARS-CoV-2 reported severe neurologic symptoms manifested as acute cerebrovascular diseases, consciousness impairment, and skeletal muscle symptoms (Li et al., 2020). Therefore, these observations suggest that SARS-CoV-2s could belong to the group of neuroinvasive viruses.

One of the most common protections against viral infections is quarantine. However, social isolation often causes psychological and mental disorders including acute stress disorder, exhaustion, detachment from others, irritability, insomnia, poor concentration, indecisiveness, fear, and anxiety. Data suggest that depression, anxiety, and posttraumatic disorders have significant effects on the immune system, resulting in mast cell activation, increased generation of cytokines like IL-1, IL-37, TNFα, IL-6, and C-reactive protein (Dowlati et al., 2010). Traumatic events activate the hypothalamic–pituitary–adrenal axis (HPA) and acute inflammation via activation of NFkB and cytokine production. Apparently quarantine-associated mental and psychological disorders weaken the protective capacity of the immune system against diseases making individuals more vulnerable. Overall, it is suggested that SARS-CoV-2 virus, directly or with associated conditions like quarantine-induced mental and psychological disorders, can damage or impact the CNS negatively.

Can Physical Fitness Protect or Attenuate the Consequences of Infection?

There is currently no proven medicine to treat the viral infection; however, the progress and severity of virus-induced diseases could vary greatly. The general observation is that under the age of 60 years, mortality rates and severity of symptoms of SARS-CoV-2 infections are much less then in advanced age. To date, no data is available whether the level of physical fitness affects the progress of SARS-CoCV-2 infections. However, it is well documented that regular exercise induced adaptations enhance the effectiveness of immune system (Krüger et al., 2016), which could actually affect the severity of SARS-CoV-2 infection.

However, quarantine-associated decline in the immune system as a result of the development of depression or traumatic disorders can be prevented and/or attenuated. Indeed, the inflammatory process generated by ROS can be more effectively detoxified by antioxidant systems in various organs including the brain of well-trained individuals from adaptations to exercise training (Radak et al., 2001). In addition, exercise training can efficiently decrease depression, and is one of the power modulators of the neuroprotective and anti-depressive effects of PA, and exercise is the brain-derived neurotrophic factor (BDNF) (Kandola et al., 2019). Present data suggest depression is closely linked to structural abnormalities and dysregulation of some neuroplastic mechanisms. Many brain regions are affected by depression, but the most consistently affected area in individuals with depression is the hippocampus, which is implicated in memory, emotion processing, and stress regulation.

The exercise effect on the brain can elicit systemic influences on the entire body, as exercise-induced euphoria is associated with the release of endogenous opioids (endorphins). Endorphins are identified as three distinct peptides termed alpha-endorphins, beta-endorphins, and gamma-endorphins. Euphoria is significantly increased after running and is inversely correlated with opioid binding in prefrontal/orbitofrontal cortices, the anterior cingulate cortex, bilateral insula, parainsular cortex, and temporoparietal regions (region-specific effects in frontolimbic brain areas that are involved in the processing of affective states and mood) (Boecker et al., n.d.). Thus, regular exercise can attenuate the symptoms and consequences of quarantine-induced depression and traumatic disorders with the systemic, complex, and powerful neuroprotective effects.

RECOMMENDATION TO FIGHT AGAINST COVID-19-ASSOCIATED NEUROLOGICAL AND MENTAL DISORDERS

Since vaccination is not an available option against SARS-CoCV-2 infection at present, one alternative feasible option is to increase the effectiveness of the immune system. Research data suggest that higher level of physical fitness improves immune responses to vaccination, lowers chronic low-grade inflammation, and improves various immune markers in several disease states including cancer, acquired human immunodeficiency syndrome, cardio-vascular diseases, diabetes, cognitive impairments, and obesity (Balchin et al., 2016). The adaptive effects of exercise are dependent upon the intensity and duration of exercise sessions. Available information suggests that to boost the power of the immune system, moderate intensity exercise up to 45 min is best. On the other hand, strenuous exercise can suppress immune system function leading to upper respiratory tract infections and appearance of latent viral reactivation (Huang et al., 2020). Although a debate exists regarding possible suppressing effects of severe exercise training on immune system, moderate intensity exercise clearly upgrades the power of immune system.

Since the aged population has higher risk to suffer from SARS-CoV-2 infections and generally this group benefits the most from regular PA and exercise, moderate-intensity aerobic exercise with 2–3 sessions/week lasting not less than 30 min is suggested to as the lowest exercise dose to exert beneficial brain effects. Few studies aimed to investigate the relationship

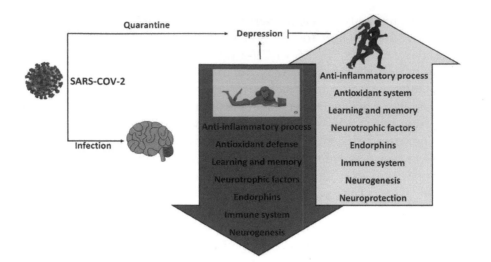

FIGURE 12.1 SARS-CoV-2 can directly attack central nervous system. The quarantine which is used to prevent the spreading of SARS-CoV-2 readily can cause depression, which has negative effects on CNS and immune system. Regular exercise with moderate intensity curbs the quarantine-associated harmful effects on the brain.

between exercise intensity and relief of depression via endorphin secretion exist. In subjects with moderate level of depression, it appears that the moderate- and high-intensity exercise can attenuate depression levels, whereas very-low intensity exercise has no effect, and the β-endorphin results are inconclusive (R. Wang et al., 2020). It appears that exercise-associated-dose response is individual and could be dependent on the type of exercise. Nevertheless, daily aerobic exercise is highly recommended for all individuals at all ages (Figure 12.1).

IMPACT OF COVID-19 ON OLDER ADULTS

COVID-19 is having a major impact on people's lives by causing hospitalizations and deaths, but also through reducing quality of life resulting from social isolation, depression, fear, and financial crisis. Older adults are experiencing the most burdensome from COVID-19. Indeed, the constellation of changes in cellular and physiological function that accompany the aging process make older people especially vulnerable to COVID-19. Hence, the identification of health-related parameters predisposing older adults to the negative outcomes associated with COVID-19 is of utmost importance. Here, we provide a brief description of the mechanisms through which SARS-CoV-2 infection might contribute to the development or progression of frailty and sarcopenia in older ages.

POSSIBLE EFFECTS OF COVID-19 ON MUSCLE ATROPHY AND PHYSICAL FUNCTION

The pathophysiological mechanisms underlying COVID-19 are under intense investigation. Evidence is accumulating that SARS-CoV-2 invades and damage multiple organs, such as the respiratory system, cardiovascular system, CNS, kidneys, and liver. Yet, no studies have investigated whether the virus directly damages skeletal muscle. However, information about the time-course of COVID-19 and related hospital outcomes allows speculating the disease may affect muscle homeostasis.

Notably, acute respiratory distress syndrome (ARDS), the most worrisome consequence of SARS-CoV-2 infection, seems to develop mainly in older adults with multimorbidity (Dowlati et al., 2010; R. Wang et al., 2020). ARDS involves bilateral pulmonary infiltration limiting hematosis and reducing oxygen supply for mitochondrial bioenergetics (Z. Wu & McGoogan, 2020). Patients with ARDS are transferred to intensive care unit (ICU) to receive adequate oxygen supplementation through non-invasive or mechanical ventilation (C. Wu et al., 2020). The combination of ARDS and ICU-related procedures may cause a major insult to muscle by increasing protein breakdown (rhabdomyolysis) and reducing protein synthesis, thereby establishing a catabolic environment leading to severe muscle atrophy (Herridge et al., 2011). Muscle wasting is experienced by 50% of ICU patients involving diaphragmatic and lower limb muscle, causing serious respiratory and physical complications that may remain for years after hospital discharge (Herridge et al., 2016). Observational studies have shown that ARDS survivors have substantially lower performance on mobility tests relative to healthy age- and sex-matched people (Herridge et al., 2011).

ARE FRAILTY AND SARCOPENIA POSSIBLE OUTCOMES OF COVID-19?

Muscle atrophy and declining physical function are key features of frailty and sarcopenia (Cruz-Jentoft & Sayer, 2019; Hoogendijk et al., 2019). Frailty is a geriatric syndrome characterized by reduced capacity to reach physiological homeostasis after a stressful event, while sarcopenia is a neurodegenerative disease that involves muscle atrophy, loss of muscle strength and power, and physical dysfunction (Hoogendijk et al., 2019). Based on the aforementioned possible complications of COVID-19, the plausibility that SARS-CoV-2 infection might promote the development of frailty and sarcopenia and accelerate their progression. Furthermore, extreme home isolation and increased physical inactivity, combined with depression and anxiety (Jawaid, 2020), could increase the susceptibility to falls or other prominent geriatric conditions (Figure 12.2). These topics are certainly areas for future investigation.

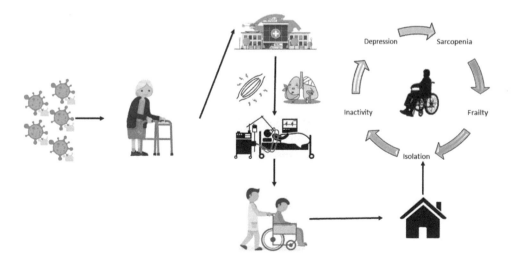

FIGURE 12.2 The detrimental effect of COVID-19 on the development of sarcopenia and frailty among people of old age. Potential influences of physical inactivity and social isolation on the pathogenesis are illustrated.

These premises have important implications during and after hospitalization, since both sarcopenia and frailty are associated with ICU complications and mortality, as well as negative outcomes after hospital discharge (Ferrante et al., 2018; Flaatten et al., 2017). Health professionals responsible for the care of older adults with COVID-19 should assess the presence of frailty and/or sarcopenia at patient admission to identify those individuals at higher risk of negative outcomes an again at discharge. Indeed, older patients who survive COVID-19 might present many conditions associated with the progression of frailty and sarcopenia, including cardiovascular, respiratory, metabolic, muscular, cognitive, psychological, and social complications. Hence, health professionals responsible for post-acute rehabilitation need to be prepared to manage weak patients with extreme fatigue when performing simple movements (e.g., sitting).

COMPUTATIONAL APPROACH TO ANALYSIS IMPACT OF COVID-19 ON HUMAN PHYSIOLOGICAL HEALTH

This section will cover four critical issues: (1) public sentiment associated with the progress of coronavirus and COVID-19, (2) the use of Twitter data, namely Tweets, for sentiment analysis, (3) descriptive textual analytics and textual data visualization, and (4) comparison of textual classification mechanisms used in artificial intelligence (AI). The rapid spread of coronavirus and COVID-19 infections have created a strong need for discovering efficient analytics methods for understanding the flow of information and the development of mass sentiment in pandemic scenarios. While there are numerous initiatives analyzing healthcare, preventative, care and recovery, economic and network data, there has been relatively little emphasis on the analysis of aggregate personal level and social media communications. McKinsey identified critical aspects for COVID-19 management and economic recovery scenarios. In their industry-oriented report, they emphasized data management, tracking, and informational dashboards as critical components of managing a wide range of COVID-19 scenarios.

There has been an exponential growth in the use of textual analytics, natural language processing (NLP), and other artificial intelligence techniques in research and in the development of applications. Despite rapid advances in NLP, issues surrounding the limitations of these methods in deciphering intrinsic meaning in text remain. Researchers at CSAIL, MIT (Computer Science and Artificial Intelligence Laboratory, Massachusetts Institute of Technology), demonstrated how even the most recent NLP mechanisms can fall short and thus remain "vulnerable to adversarial text" (Jin et al., 2019). It is, therefore, important to understand inherent limitations of text classification techniques and relevant ML algorithms. Furthermore, it is important to explore whether multiple exploratory, descriptive, and classification techniques contain complimentary synergies which will allow us to leverage the "whole is greater than the sum of its parts" principle in our pursuit for artificial-intelligence-driven insights generated from human communications. Studies in electronic markets demonstrated the effectiveness of ML in modeling human behavior under complex informational conditions, highlighting the role of the nature of information in affecting human behavior (J. Samuel, 2017). The source data for all Tweets data analysis, tables, and every figure, including the fear curve in Figure 12.3, in this research consists of publicly available Tweets data, specifically downloaded for the purposes of this research and further described in the Data acquisition and preparation discussed in coming session of this study.

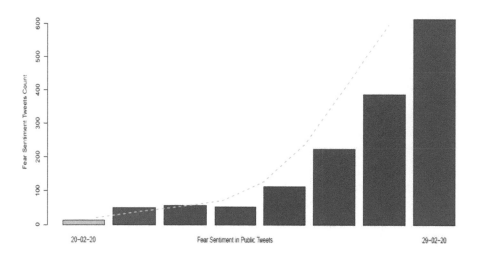

FIGURE 12.3   COVID–19's sentiment curve: the fear pandemic curve.

The rise in emphasis on AI methods for textual analytics and NLP followed the tremendous increase in public reliance on social media (e.g., Twitter, Facebook, Instagram, blogging, and LinkedIn) for information, rather than on the traditional news agencies (Heist et al., 2018; Makris et al., 2020; Shu et al., 2017). People express their opinions, moods, and activities on social media about diverse social phenomena (e.g., health, natural hazards, cultural dynamics, and social trends) due to personal connectivity, network effects, limited costs, and easy access. Many companies are using social media to promote their product and service to the end-users (He et al., 2015). Correspondingly, users share their experiences and reviews, creating a rich reservoir of information stored as text. Consequently, social media and open communication platforms are becoming important sources of information for conducting research, in the contexts of rapid development of information and communication technology (Widener & Li, 2014). Researchers and practitioners mine massive textual and unstructured datasets to generate insights about mass behavior, thoughts, and emotions on a wide variety of issues such as product reviews, political opinions and trends, motivational principles, and stock market sentiment (De Choudhury et al., 2013; Kretinin et al., 2018; Makris et al., 2020; J. Samuel, 2020; Skoric et al., 2020; Z. Wang et al., 2016). Textual data visualization is also used to identify the critical trend of change in fear-sentiment, using the "Fear Curve" in Figure 12.3, with the dotted Lowess line demonstrating the trend, and the bars indicating the day-to-day increase in fear Tweets count. Tweets were first classified using sentiment analysis, and then the progression of the fear-sentiment was studied, as it was the most dominant emotion across the entire Tweets data. This exploratory analysis revealed the significant daily increase in fear-sentiment toward the end of March 2020, as shown in Figure 12.3.

In this research article, we present textual analyses of Twitter data to identify public sentiment, specifically, tracking the progress of fear, which has been associated with the rapid spread of coronavirus and COVID-19 infections. This research outlines a methodological approach to analyzing Twitter data specifically for identification of sentiment, key words associations, and trends for crisis scenarios akin to the current COVID-19 phenomena. We initiate the discussion and search for insights with descriptive textual analytics and data visualization, such as exploratory Word Clouds and sentiment maps in Figure 12.4.

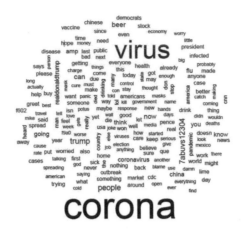

FIGURE 12.4 An instance of word cloud in Twitter data.

Early-stage exploratory analytics of Tweets revealed interesting aspects, such as the relatively higher number of coronavirus Tweets coming from iPhone users, as compared to Android users, along with a proportionally higher use of word-associations with politics (mention of Republican and Democratic party leaders), URLs, and humor, depicted by the word-association of beer with coronavirus, as summarized in Table 12.1. We observed that such references to humor and beer were overtaken by "Fear Sentiment" as COVID-19 progressed and its seriousness became evident (Figure 12.3). Tweets insights with textual analytics and NLP thus serve as a good reflector of shifts in public sentiment.

One of the key contributions of this research is our discussion, demonstration, and comparison of Naïve Bayes and Logistic methods-based textual classification mechanisms commonly used in AI applications for NLP, and specifically contextualized in this research using ML for Tweets classifications. Accuracy is measured by the ratio of correct classifications to the total number of test items. We observed that Naïve Bayes is better for small- to medium-sized tweets and can be used for classifying short coronavirus Tweets sentiments with an accuracy of 91%, as compared to logistic regression with an accuracy of 74%. For longer Tweets, Naïve Bayes provided an accuracy of 57% and logistic regression provided an accuracy of 52%, as summarized in Tables 12.6 and 12.7.

LITERATURE REVIEW

This study was informed by research articles from multiple disciplines and therefore, in this section, we cover literature review of textual analytics, sentiment analysis, Twitter

TABLE 12.1

Tweet Features Summarized by Source Category

Source	Total	Hashtags	Mentions	Urls	Pols	Corona	Flu	Beer	AbuseW
iPhone	3281	495	2305	77	218	4238	171	336	111
Android	1180	149	1397	37	125	1050	67	140	41
iPad	75	6	96	4	12	85	4	8	2
Cities	30	0	0	0	0	0	0	0	0

TABLE 12.2

Summary of Endogenous Features

Tagged	Frequency	Hashtag	Frequency
realDonaldTrump	74	coronavirus	23
CNN	21	DemDebate	16
ImtiazMadmood	16	corona	8
corona	13	CoronavirusOutbreak	8
AOC	12	CoronaVirusUpdates	7
coronaextrausa	12	coronavirususa	7
POTUS	12	Corona	6
CNN MSNBC	11	COVID19	5

and NLP, and ML methods. ML and strategic structuring of information characteristics are necessary to address evolving behavioral issues in big data (J. Samuel, 2017). Textual analytics deals with the analysis and evocation of characters, syntactic features, semantics, sentiment and visual representations of text, its characteristics, and associated endogenous and exogenous features. Endogenous features refer to aspects of the text itself, such as the length of characters in a social media post, use of keywords, use of special characters, and the presence or absence of URL links and hashtags, as illustrated for this study in Table 12.2. These tables summarize the appearances of "mentions" and "hashtags" in descending order, indicating the use of screen names and "#" symbol within the text of the Tweet, respectively.

Exogenous variables, in contrast, are those aspects which are external but related to the text, such as the source device used for making a post on social media, location of Twitter user, and source types, as illustrated for this study in Table 12.3. The table summarizes "source device" and "screen names," indicating variables representing type of device used to post the Tweet, and the screen name of the Twitter user, respectively, both external to the text of the Tweet. Such exploratory summaries describe the data succinctly, provide a better understanding of the data, and help generate insights that inform subsequent classification analysis. Past studies explored custom approaches to identifying constructs such as dominance behavior in electronic chat, indicating the tremendous potential for extending

TABLE 12.3

Summary of Exogenous Features

Source	Frequency	Screen Name	Frequency
Twitter for iPhone	3281	_CoronaCA	30
Twitter for Android	1180	MBilalY	25
Twitter for iPad	75	joanna_corona	17
Cities	30	eads_john	13
Tweetbot for i<U+039F>S	29	_jvm2222	11
CareerArc2.0	14	AlAboutNothing	11
Twitter Web Client	16	dallasreese	9
511NY-Tweets	3	CpaCarter	8

such analyses by using ML techniques to accelerate automated sentiment classification and the subsections that follow present key insights gained from literature review to support and inform the textual analytics processes used in this study (Chen et al., 2020; Reyes-Menendez et al., 2018; J. Samuel et al., 2014; Saura et al., 2019).

Textual Analytics

A diverse array of methods and tools were used for textual analytics, subject to the nature of the textual data, research objectives, size of dataset, and context. Twitter data has been used widely for textual and emotions analysis (T. Ahmad et al., 2019; Carducci et al., 2018; Rocha & Lopes Cardoso, 2018). In another instance, a study analyzing customer feedback for a French Energy Company using more than 70,000 tweets published over a year (Pépin et al., 2017) used a Latent Dirichlet Allocation algorithm to retrieve interesting insights about the energy company, hidden due to data volume, by frequency-based filtering techniques. Poisson and negative binomial models were used to explore Tweet popularity as well. The same study also evaluated the relationship between topics using seven dissimilarity measures and found that Kullback-Leibler and the Euclidean distances performed better in identifying related topics useful for user-based interactive approach. Similarly, extant research applying Time Aware Knowledge Extraction (TAKE) methodology (De Maio et al., 2016) demonstrated methods to discover valuable information from huge amounts of information posted on Facebook and Twitter. The study used topic-based summarizing of Twitter data to explore content of research interest. Similarly, they applied a framework that uses less detailed summary to produce good quality information. Past research has also investigated the usefulness of twitter data to assess personality of users, using DISC (Dominance, Influence, Compliance, and Steadiness) assessment techniques (N. Ahmad & Siddique, 2017). Similar research has been used in information systems using textual analytics to develop designs for identification of human traits, including dominance in electronic communication (J. Samuel et al., 2014). DISC assessment is useful for information retrieval, content selection, product positioning, and psychological assessment of users. So also, a combination of psychological and linguistic analysis was used in past research to extract emotions from multilingual text posted on social media (Jain et al., 2017).

Twitter Analytics

Extant research has evaluated the usefulness of social media data in revealing situational awareness during crisis scenarios, such as by analyzing wildfire-related Twitter activities in San Diego County, modeling with about 41,545 wildfire-related tweets, from May of 2014 (Z. Wang et al., 2016). Analysis of such data showed that six of the nine wildfires occurred on May 14, associated with a sudden increase of wildfire tweets on May 14. Kernel density estimation showed the largest hot spots of tweets containing "fire" and "wildfire" were in the downtown area of San Diego, despite being far away from the fire locations. This shows a geographical disassociation between fact and Tweet. Analysis of Twitter data in the current research also showed some disassociation between coronavirus Tweets sentiment and actual coronavirus hot spots, as shown in Figure 12.5. Such disassociation can be explained to some extent by the fact that people in urban areas have better access to information and communication technologies, resulting in a higher number of tweets from urban areas. The same study on San Diego wildfires also found that a large number of people tweeted "evacuation," which presented a useful cue about the impact of the wildfire. Tweets also demonstrated emphasis on wildfire damage (e.g., containment percentage and

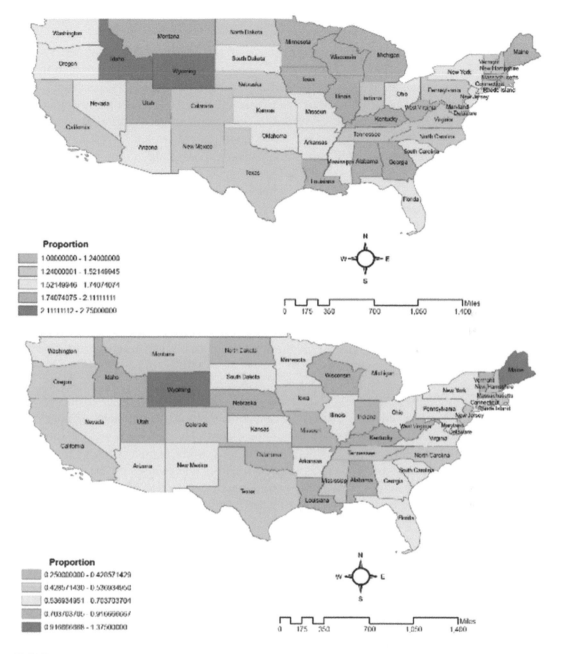

FIGURE 12.5 Sentiment map.

burnt acres) and appreciation for firefighters. Tweets, in the wildfire scenario, enhanced situational awareness and accelerated disaster response activities. Social network analysis demonstrated that elite users (e.g., local authorities, traditional media reporters) play an important role in information dissemination and dominated the wildfire retweet network.

Twitter data has also been extensively used for crisis situations analysis and tracking, including the analysis of pandemics (Fung et al., 2019; Kim et al., 2016; J. Samuel et al., 2020; Ye et al., 2016). Nagar et al. validated the temporal predictive strength of daily Twitter data for influenza-like illness for emergency department (ILI-ED) visits during the

New York City 2012–2013 influenza season (Nagar et al., 2014). Widener and Li (2014) performed sentiment analysis to understand how geographically located tweets on healthy and unhealthy food are geographically distributed across the United States (Widener & Li, 2014). The spatial distribution of the tweets analyzed showed that people living in urban and suburban areas tweet more than people living in rural areas. Similarly, per capita food tweets were higher in large urban areas than in small urban areas. Logistic regression revealed that tweets in low-income areas were associated with unhealthy food related Tweet content. Twitter data has also been used in the context of healthcare sentiment analytics. De Choudhury et al. (2013) investigated behavioral changes and moods of new mothers in the postnatal situation (De Choudhury et al., 2013). Using Twitter posts, this study evaluated postnatal changes (e.g., social engagement, emotion, social network, and linguistic style) to show that Twitter data can be very effective in identifying mothers at risk of postnatal depression. Novel analytical frameworks have also been used to analyze supply chain management (SCM) related Twitter data about, providing important insights to improve SCM practices and research (Chae, 2015). They conducted descriptive analytics, content analysis integrating text mining and sentiment analysis, and network analytics on 22,399 SCM tweets. Carvaho et al. presented an efficient platform named MISNIS (intelligent Mining of Public Social Networks' Influence in Society) to collect, store, manage, mine, and visualize Twitter and Twitter user data (Carvalho et al., 2017). This platform allows non-technical users to mine data easily and has one of the highest success rates in capturing flowing Portuguese language tweets.

Classification Methods

Extant research has used diverse textual classification methods to evaluate social media sentiment. These classifiers are grouped into numerous categories based on their similarities. The section that follows discusses details about four essential classifiers we reviewed, including linear regression and K-nearest neighbor (KNN), and focuses on the two classifiers we chose to compare, namely Naïve Bayes and logistic regression, their main concepts, strengths, and weaknesses. The focus of this research is to present a ML-based perspective on the effectiveness of the commonly used Naïve Bayes and logistic regression methods.

Linear Regression Model

Although linear regression is primarily used to predict relationships between continuous variables, linear classifiers can also be used to classify texts and documents (Vijayan et al., 2017). The most common estimation method using linear classifiers is the least squares algorithm which minimizes an objective function (i.e., squared difference between the predicted outcomes and true classes). The least squares algorithm is similar to maximum likelihood estimation when outcome variables are influenced by Gaussian noise (Zhang & Yang, 2003). Linear ridge regression classifier optimizes the objective function by adding a penalizer to it. Ridge classifier converts binary outcomes to −1, 1 and treats the problem as a regression (multi-class regression for a multi-class problem) (Pedregosa et al., 2011).

Logistic Regression

Logistics regression (LR) is one of the popular and earlier methods for classification. LR was first developed by David Cox in 1958 (Kowsari et al., 2019). In the LR model, the probabilities describing the possible outcomes of a single trial are modeled using a logistic function (Pedregosa et al., 2011). Using a logistic function, the probability of the outcomes are transformed into binary values (0 and 1). Maximum likelihood estimation methods are commonly used to minimize error in the model. A comparative study classifying product reviews reported that logistic regression multi-class classification method has the highest (min 32.43%, max 58.50%) accuracy compared to Naïve Bayes, Random Forest, Decision Tree, and Support Vector Machines classification methods (Pranckevičius & Marcinkevičius, 2017). Using multinomial logistic regression (Ramadhan et al., 2017) observed that this method can accurately predict the sentiment of Twitter users up to 74%. Past research using stepwise logistic discriminant analysis (Rubegni et al., 2002) correctly classified 96.2% cases. LR classifier is suitable for predicting categorical outcomes. However, this prediction needs each data point to be independent to each other (Kowsari et al., 2019). Moreover, the stability of the logistic regression classifier is lower than the other classifiers due to the widespread distribution of the values of average classification accuracy (Pranckevičius & Marcinkevičius, 2017). LR classifiers have a fairly expensive training phase that includes parameter modeling with optimization techniques (Vijayan et al., 2017).

Naïve Bayes Classifier

Naïve Bayes classifier (NBC) is a proven, simple, and effective method for text classification (B. Liu et al., 2013). It has been used widely for document classification since the 1950s (Kowsari et al., 2019). This classifier is theoretically based on the Bayes theorem (Pedregosa et al., 2011; Troussas et al., 2013; Vijayan et al., 2017). A discussion on the mathematical formulation of NBC from a textual analytics perspective is provided under the methods section. NBC uses maximum a posteriori estimation to find out the class (i.e., features are assigned to a class based on the highest conditional probability). There are mainly two models of NBC: Multinomial Naïve Bayes (i.e., binary representation of the features) and Bernoulli Naïve Bayes (i.e., features are represented with frequency) (Vijayan et al., 2017). Many studies have used NBCs for text, documents, and products classification. A comparative study showed that NBC has higher accuracy to classify documents than other common classifiers, such as decision trees, neural networks, and support vector machines (Ting et al., 2011). Collecting 7000 status updates (e.g., positive or negative) from 90 Facebook users, researchers found that NBC has a higher rate (77%) of accuracy to predict the sentimental status of users compared to the Rocchio Classifier (75%) (Troussas et al., 2013). Previous studies investigating different techniques of sentiment analysis (Boiy et al., 2007) found that symbolic techniques (i.e., based on the force and direction of words) have accuracy lower than 80%. In contrast, ML techniques (e.g., SVM, NBC, and maximum Entropy) have a higher level of accuracy (above 80%) in classifying sentiment. NBCs can be used with limited size training data to estimate necessary parameters and are quite efficient to implement, as compared to other sophisticated methods with comparable accuracy (Pedregosa et al., 2011). However, NBCs are based on oversimplified assumptions of conditional probability and shape of data distribution (Kowsari et al., 2019; Pedregosa et al., 2011).

K-Nearest Neighbor

KNN is a popular non-parametric text classifier which uses instance-based learning (i.e., does not construct a general internal model but just stores an instance of the data) (Kowsari et al., 2019; Pedregosa et al., 2011). The KNN method classifies texts or documents based on similarity measurement (Vijayan et al., 2017). The similarity between two data points is measured by estimating distance, proximity, or closeness function (Silva &

TABLE 12.4
Summary of Classifiers for Machine Learning

Classifier	Characteristic	Strength	Weakness
Linear regression	Minimize sum of squared differences between predicted and true values	Intuitive, useful and stable, easy to understand	Sensitive to outliers; Ineffective with non-linearity
Logistic regression	Probability of an outcome is based on a logistic function	Transparent and easy to understand; Regularized to avoid over-fitting	Expensive training phase; Assumption of linearity
Naïve Bayes classifier	Based on assumption of independence between predictor variables	Effective with real-world data; Efficient and can deal with dimensionality	Over-simplified assumptions; Limited by data scarcity
K-Nearest Neighbor	Computes classification based on weights of the nearest neighbors, instance based	KNN is easy to implement, efficient with small data, applicable for multi-class problems	Inefficient with big data; Sensitive to data quality; Noisy features degrade the performance

Eugenio Naranjo, 2020). KNN classifier computes classification based on a simple majority vote of the nearest neighbors of each data point (Buldin & Ivanov, 2020; Pedregosa et al., 2011). The number of nearest neighbors (K) is determined by specification or by estimating the number of neighbors within a fixed radius of each point. KNN classifiers are simple, easy to implement, and applicable for multi-class problems (Buldin & Ivanov, 2020; Kowsari et al., 2019; Tan, 2018).

Table 12.4 represents main features of different classifiers with their respective strengths and weaknesses. This table provides a good overview of all the classifiers mentioned in the above section. Based on a review of multiple ML methods, we decided to apply Naïve Bayes and logistic regression classification methods to train and test binary sentiment categories associated with the coronavirus Tweets data. Naïve Bayes and logistic regression classification methods were selected based on their parsimony, and their proven performance with textual classification provides for interesting comparative evaluations.

METHODS AND TEXTUAL DATA ANALYTICS

The Methods section has two broad parts, the first part deals with exploratory textual analytics, summaries by features endogenous and exogenous to the text of the Tweets, data visualizations, and describes key characteristics of the coronavirus Tweets data. It goes beyond traditional statistical summaries for quantitative and even ordinal and categorical data, because of the unique properties of textual data, and exploits the potential to fragment and synthesize textual data (such as by considering parts of the Tweets, "#" tags, assign sentiment scores, and evaluation of use of characters) into useful features which can provide valuable insights. This part of the analysis also develops textual analytics specific data visualizations to gain and present quick insights into the use of keywords associated with coronavirus and COVID-19. The second part deals with ML techniques for classification of textual data into positive and negative sentiment categories. Implicit, therefore, is that the first part of the analytics also includes sentiment analysis of the textual component of Twitter data. Tweets are assigned sentiment scores using R and R packages. The Tweets with their sentiment scores are then split into train and test data to apply ML classification methods using two prominent methods described below, and their results are discussed.

Exploratory Textual Analytics

Exploratory textual analytics deals with the generation of descriptors for textual features in data with textual variables, and the potential associations of such textual features with other non-textual variables in the data. For example, a simple feature that is often used in the analysis of Tweets is the number of characters in the Tweet, and this feature can also be substituted or augmented by measures such as the number of words per Tweet (Kretinin et al., 2018). A "Word Cloud" is a common and visually appealing early-stage textual data visualization, consisting of the size and visual emphasis of words being weighted by their frequency of occurrence in the textual corpus, and is used to portray prominent words in a textual corpus graphically (Conner et al., 2020). Early-stage Word Clouds used plain vanilla black and white graphics, such as in Figure 12.6, and current representations use

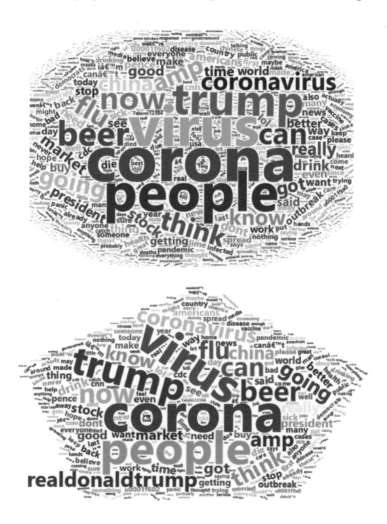

FIGURE 12.6 A couple of word cloud instances.

diverse word configurations (such as all words being set to horizontal orientation), colors, and outline shapes, such as in Figure 12.6, for increased esthetic impact. This research used R along with Wordcloud and Wordcloud2 packages, while other packages in R and Python are also available with unique Wordcloud plotting capabilities.

Data Acquisition and Preparation

The research was initiated with standard and commonly used Tweets collection, cleaning, and data preparation process, which we outline briefly below. We downloaded Tweets using a Twitter API, the rTweet package in R, which was used to gather over nine hundred thousand tweets from February to March of 2020, applying the keyword "Corona" (case ignored). This ensured a textual corpus focused on the coronavirus, COVID-19 and associated phenomena, and reflects an established process for topical data acquisition (Pépin et al., 2017; Y. Samuel et al., 2020). The raw data with ninety variables was processed and prepared for analysis using the R programming language and related packages. The data was subset to focus on Tweets tagged by country as belonging to the United States. Multiple R packages were used in the cleaning process, to create a clean dataset for further analysis. Since the intent was to use the data for academic research, we replaced all identifiable abusive words with a unique alphanumeric tag word, which contained the text "abuvs," but was mixed with numbers to avoid using a set of characters that could have preexisted in the Tweets. Deleting abusive words completely would deprive the data of potential analyses opportunities, and hence a specifically coded algorithm was used to make a customized replacement. This customized replacement was in addition to the standard use of "Stopwords" and cleaning processes (Saif et al., 2014; Svetlov & Platonov, 2019). The dataset was further evaluated to identify the most useful variables, and sixty-two variables with incomplete, blank, and irrelevant values were deleted to create a cleaned dataset with twenty-eight variables. The dataset was also further processed based on the needs of each analytical segment of analysis, using "tokenization"—which converts text to analysis relevant word tokens, "part-of-speech" tagging—which tags textual artifacts by grammatical category such as noun or verb, "parsing"—which identifies underlying structure between textual elements, "stemming"—which discards prefixes and suffixes using rules to create simple forms of base words, and "lemmatization"—which like stemming, aims to transform words to simpler forms and uses dictionaries and more complex rules and processes than in stemming.

Word and Phrase Associations

An important and distinct aspect of textual analytics involves the identification of not only the most frequently used words but also of word pairs and word chains. This aspect, known as N-grams identification in a text corpus, has been developed and studied in computational linguistics and NLP. We transformed the "Tweets" variable, containing the text of the Tweets in the data, into a text corpus and identified the most frequent words, the most frequent Bigrams (two-word sequences), the most frequent Trigrams (three-word sequences), and the most frequent "Quadgrams" (four-word sequences, also called Four-grams). Our research also explored longer sequences, but the text corpus did not contain longer sequences with sufficient frequency threshold and relevance. While identification of N-grams is a straightforward process with the availability of numerous packages in R and Python, and other NLP tools, it is more nuanced to identify the most useful N-grams in a text corpus, and interpret the implications. In reference to Figure 12.7, it is seen that in some scenarios, such as with the popular use of words "beer," "Trump," and "abuvs" (the tag used to replace identifiable abusive words),

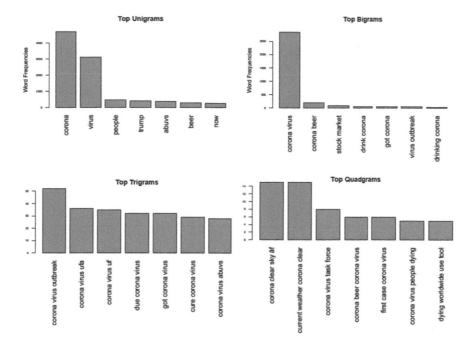

FIGURE 12.7   N-grams.

and Bigrams and Trigrams such as "corona beer," "stock market," "drink corona," "corona virus outbreak," and "confirmed cases (of) corona virus" (a Quadgram) indicate a mixed mass response to the coronavirus in its early stages. Humor, politics, and concerns about the stock market and health risks words were all mixed in early Tweets based public discussions on coronavirus. Additional keyword and sentiment analysis factoring the timeline, showed an increase in seriousness, and fear in particular, as shown in Figure 12.6, indicating that public sentiment changed as the consequences of the rapid spread of coronavirus, and the damaging impact upon COVID-19 patients became more evident.

Geo-Tagged Analytics

Data often contain information about geographic locations, such as city-, county-, state-, and country-level data or by holding zip code and longitude and latitude coordinates, or geographical metadata. Such data are said to be "Geo-tagged," and "Geo-tagged Analytics" represents the analysis of data inclusive of geographical location variables or metadata. Twitter data contains two distinct location data types for each tweet: one is a location for the tweet, indicating where the Tweet was posted from, and the other is the general location of the user, and may refer to the place of stay for the user when the Twitter account was created, as shown in Table 12.5. For the coronavirus Tweets, we examined both fear-sentiment and negative sentiment and found some counter-intuitive insights, showing relatively lower levels of fear in states which were significantly affected by a high number of COVID-19 cases, as demonstrated in Figure 12.5.

Association with Non-Textual Variables

This research also analyzed coronavirus Tweets texts for potential association with other variables, in addition to endogenous analytics, and the time and dates variable. Using a

TABLE 12.5

Location Variables (Tagged and Stated Locations)

Tagged	Frequency	Stated	Frequency
Los Angeles, CA	183	Los Angeles, CA	78
Manhattan, NY	130	United States	75
Florida, USA	84	Washington, DC	60
Chicago, IL	71	New York, NY	54
Houston, TX	65	California, USA	49
Texas, USA	57	Chicago, IL	40
Brooklyn, NY	51	Houston, TX	39
San Antonio, TX	51	Corona, CA	33

market segmentation logic, we grouped Tweets by the top three source devices in the data, namely: iPhone, Android, and iPad, as shown in Figure 12.8, which is normalized to each device count. This means that Figure 12.8 reflects comparison of the relative ratio of device property count to total device count for each source category, and is not a direct device-totals comparison. Our research analyzed direct totals comparison as well, and the reason for presenting the source device comparison by relative ratio is because the comparison by totals simply follows the distribution of source device totals provided in Table 12.1. We observed that, higher ratio of: iPhone users made the most use of hashtags and mentions of "Corona," iPad users made the most mention of URLs and "Trump," and Android users made the most mention of "Flu" and "Beer" words. Both iPhone and Android users have similar ratios for usage of abusive words.

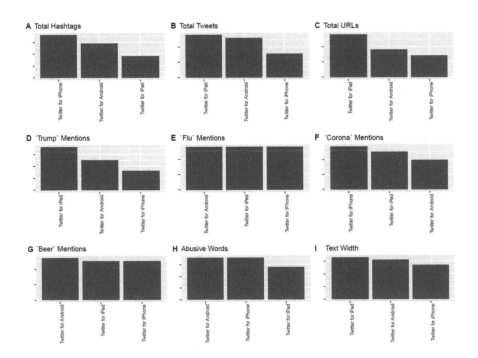

FIGURE 12.8   Source device comparison by relative ratio.

SENTIMENT ANALYTICS

One of the key insights that can be gained from textual analytics is the identification of sentiment associated with the text being analyzed. Extant research has used custom methods to identify temporal sentiment as well as sentiment expressions of character traits such as dominance (J. Samuel et al., 2014), and standardized methods to assign positive and negative sentiment scores (He et al., 2015; Ravi & Ravi, 2015). Sentiment analysis is broadly described as the assignment of sentiment scores and categories, based on keyword and phrase match with sentiment score dictionaries, and customized lexicons. Prominent analytics software including R, and open-source option, have standardized sentiment scoring mechanisms. We used two R packages, Syuzhet and sentimentr, to classify and score the Tweets for sentiment classes such as fear, sadness, and anger, and sentiment scores ranging from negative (around −1) to positive (around 1) with sentiR.[1,2] We used two methods to assign sentiment scores and classifications: the first method assigned a positive to negative score as continuous value between 1 (maximum positive) and −1 (minimum positive).

MACHINE LEARNING WITH CLASSIFICATION METHODS

Extant research has examined linguistic challenges and has demonstrated the effectiveness of ML methods such as SVM (Support Vector Machine) in identifying extreme sentiment (Almatarneh & Gamallo, 2019). The focus of this study is on demonstrating how commonly used ML methods can be applied, and used to contribute to classification of sentiment by varying Tweets characteristics, and not the development of contributions to new ML theory or algorithms. Unlike linear regression, which is mainly used for estimating the probability of quantitative parameters, classification can be effectively used for estimating the probability of qualitative parameters for binary or multi-class variables—that is when the prediction variable of interest is binary, categorical, or ordinal in nature. There are many classification methods (classifiers) for qualitative data; among the most well-known are Naïve Bayes, logistic regression, linear, and KNN. The first two are elaborated upon below in the context of textual analytics. The most general form of classifiers is as follows:

How can we predict responses Y given a set of predictors $\{X\}$? For general linear regression, the mathematical model is

$$Y = \beta_0 + \beta_1 x_1 + \beta_2 x_2 + \cdots + \beta_n x_n \tag{12.1}$$

The aim is to find an estimated $\widehat{Y}$ for Y by modeling values of $\hat{\beta}_0, \hat{\beta}_1, \ldots, \hat{\beta}_n$ for $\beta_0, \beta_1, \beta_2, \ldots \beta_n$. These estimates are determined from training datasets. If either the predictors and/or responses are not continuous quantitative variables, then the structure of this model is inappropriate and needs modifications. X and Y become proxy variables and their meaning depends on the context in which they are used; in the context of the present study, X represents a document or features of a document and Y is the class to be evaluated, for which the model is being trained.

Below is a brief mathematical-statistical formulation of two of the most important classifiers for textual analytics, and sentiment classification in particular: Naïve Bayes which is considered to be a generative classifier, and Logistic Regression which is considered to be a discriminative classifier. Extant research has demonstrated the viability of the using Naïve Bayes and Logistic Regression for generative and discriminative classification, respectively (Jurafsky & Martin, 2018).

Naïve Bayes Classifier

Naïve Bayes Classifier is based on Bayes conditional probability rule (Bayes, 1991). According to Bayes theorem, the conditional probability of $P(x|y)$ is,

$$P(x|y) = \frac{P(y|x)P(x)}{P(y)} \tag{12.2}$$

The Naïve Bayes classifier identifies the estimated class $\hat{c}$ among all the classes $c \in C$ for a given document d. Hence the estimated class is,

$$\hat{c} = \arg\max_{c \in C} P(c|d) = \arg\max_{c \in C} \frac{P(d|c)P(c)}{P(d)} \tag{12.3}$$

Simplifying (12.3) (as $P(d)$ is the same for all classes, we can drop $P(d)$ from the denominator) and using the likelihood of $P(d|c)$, we get,

$$\hat{y} = \arg\max_{c \in C} P(y_1, y_2, \ldots, y_n|c) P(c) \tag{12.4}$$

where, $y_1, y_2, \ldots, y_n$ are the representative features of document d.

However, (12.4) is difficult to evaluate and needs more simplification. We assume that word position does not have any effect on the classification and the probabilities $P(y_1|c)$ are independent given a class c, hence we can write,

$$P(y_1, y_2, \ldots, y_n|c) = P(y_1|c) \times P(y_2|c) \times \ldots \times P(y_n|c) \tag{12.5}$$

Hence, from (12.4) and (12.5) we get the final equation of the Näive Bayes classifier as

$$C_{NB} = \arg\max_{c \in C} P(c) \prod_{y_1 \in Y} P(y_i|c) \tag{12.6}$$

To apply the classifier in the textual analytics, we consider the index position of words (w_i) in the documents, namely replace y_i by w_i. Now considering features in log space, (12.6) becomes,

$$C_{NB} = \arg\max_{c \in C} \log P(c) + \sum_{i \,\epsilon\, \text{positions}} \log P(w_i|c) \tag{12.7}$$

Classifier Training

In (12.7), we need to find the values of $P(c)$ and $P(w_i|c)$. Assume N_c and N_{doc} denote the number of documents in the training data belong in class c and the total number of documents, respectively. Then,

$$\hat{P}(c) = \frac{N_c}{N_{doc}} \tag{12.8}$$

The probability of word w_i in class c is,

$$\hat{P}(w_i|c) = \frac{count(w_i,c)}{\sum_{w \in V} count(w,c)} \tag{12.9}$$

where $count(w_i,c)$ is the number of occurrences of w_i in class c, and V is the entire word vocabulary.

Now, since Naïve Bayes multiplies all the features likelihood together (refer to (12.6)), the zero probabilities in the likelihood term for any class will turn the whole probability to zero, to avoid such situation, we use the Laplace add-one smoothing method, hence (12.9) becomes,

$$\hat{P}(w_i|c) = \frac{count(w_i,c)+1}{\sum_{w \in V}(count(w,c)+1)} = \frac{count(w_i,c)+1}{\sum_{w \in V}(count(w,c)+|V|)} \tag{12.10}$$

From an applied perspective, the text needs to be cleaned and prepared to contain clear, distinct, and legitimate words (w_i) for effective classification. Custom abbreviations, spelling errors, emoticons, extensive use of punctuation, and such other stylistic issues in the text can impact the accuracy of classification in both the Naïve Bayes and logistic classification methods, as text cleaning processes may not be 100% successful.

Application of Naïve Bayes for Coronavirus Tweet Classification

This research aims to explore the viability of applying exploratory sentiment classification in the context of coronavirus Tweets. The goal, therefore, was directional and set to classifying positive sentiment and negative sentiment in coronavirus Tweets. Tweets with positive sentiment were assigned a value of 1, and Tweets with a negative sentiment were assigned a value of 0. We created subsets of data based on the length of Tweets to examine classification accuracy based on length of Tweets, where the lengths of Tweets were calculated by a simple character count for each Tweet. We created two groups, where the first group consisted of coronavirus Tweets which were less than 77 characters in length, consisting of about a quarter of all Tweets data, and the group consisted of coronavirus Tweets which were less than 120 characters in length, consisting of about half of all Tweets data. These groups of data were further subset to ensure that the number of positive Tweets and Negative Tweets were balanced when being classified. We used R and associated packages to run the analysis, train using a subset of the data, and test the accuracy of the classification method using about 70 randomized test values. The results of using Naïve Bayes for coronavirus Tweet Classification are presented in Table 12.6.

TABLE 12.6
Naïve Bayes Classification by Varying Tweet Lengths

	Tweets (nchar < 77)		Tweets (nchar < 120)	
	Negative	Positive	Negative	Positive
Negative	34	1	34	1
Positive	5	30	29	6
	Accuracy:	0.9143	Accuracy:	0.5714

Interestingly, we found strong classification accuracy for short tweets, with nine out of every ten tweets correctly classified, giving us an accuracy of around 91.43%. We observed an inverse relationship between the length of Tweets and classification accuracy, as the classification accuracy decreased to 57% with an increase in the length of Tweets to below 120 characters. We calculated the Sensitivity of the classification test, which is given by the ratio of the number of correct positive predictions (30) in the output, to the total number of positives (35), to be 0.86 for the short Tweets and 0.17 for the longer Tweets. We calculated the Specificity of the classification test, which is given by the ratio of the number of correct negative predictions (34) in the output, to the total number of negatives (35), to be 0.97 for both the short and long Tweets classification. Naïve Bayes thus had better performance with classifying negative Tweets.

Logistic Regression

Logistic regression is a probabilistic classification method that can be used for supervised ML. For classification, a ML model usually consists of the following components (Jurafsky & Martin, 2018):

1. A feature representation of the input: For each input observation $\left(x^{(i)}\right)$, this will be represented by a vector of features, $[x_1, x_2, ..., x_n]$.
2. A classification function: It computes the estimated class $\hat{y}$. The sigmoid function is used in classification.
3. An objective function: The job of objective function is to minimize the error of training examples. The cross-entropy loss function is often used for this purpose.
4. An optimizing algorithm: This algorithm will be used for optimizing the objective function. The stochastic gradient descent algorithm is popularly used for this task.

The Classification Function

Here we use logistic regression and sigmoid function to build a binary classifier. Consider an input observation x which is denoted by a vector of features $[x_1, x_2, ..., x_n]$. The output of classifier will be either $y = 1$ or $y = 0$. The objective of the classifier is to know $P(y = 1 \mid x)$, which denotes the probability of positive sentiment in this classification of coronavirus Tweets, and $P(y = 0 \mid x)$, which correspondingly denotes the probability of negative sentiment. w_i denotes the weight of input feature x_i from a training set and b denotes the bias term (intercept), we get the resulting weighted sum for a class,

$$z = \sum_{i=0}^{n} w_i x_i + b \qquad (12.11)$$

representing $w \times x$ as the element-wise dot product of vectors of w and x, we can simplify (12.11) as

$$z = w \times x + b$$

We use the following sigmoid function to map the real-valued number into the range [0, 1],

$$y = \sigma(z) = \frac{1}{1 + e^{-z}} \qquad (12.12)$$

After applying sigmoid function in (12.12) and making sure that

$$P(y = 1|x) + P(y = 0|x) = 1,$$ (12.13)

we get the following two probabilities,

$$P(y = 1|x) = \sigma(w \times x + b) = \frac{1}{1 + e^{-(w \times x + b)}}$$ (12.14)

$$P(y = 0|x) = 1 - P(y = 1|x) = \frac{e^{-(w \times x + b)}}{1 + e^{-(w \times x + b)}}$$ (12.15)

considering 0.5 as the decision boundary, the estimated class $y\hat{}$ will be

$$y = \begin{cases} 1 & if \ P(y = 1|x) > 0.5 \\ 0 & otherwise \end{cases}$$ (12.16)

Objective Function

For an observation x, the loss function computes how close the estimated output $\hat{y}$ is from the actual output y, which is represented by $L(\hat{y}, y)$. Since there are only two discrete outcomes $(y = 1 \ or \ y = 0)$, using Bernoulli distribution, $P(y|x)$ can be expressed as,

$$P(y|x) = \hat{y}^y (1 - \hat{y})^{1-y}$$ (12.17)

taking log both sides in (12.17),

$$log \ P(y|x) = log\left[\hat{y}^y (1 - y)^{1-y}\right] = y \log \hat{y} + (1 - y)\log(1 - y)$$ (12.18)

To turn (12.18) into a minimizing function (loss function), we take the negation of (12.18), which yields,

$$L(\hat{y}, y) = -\left[y \log \hat{y} + (1 - y)\log(1 - \hat{y})\right]$$ (12.19)

substituting $\hat{y} = \sigma(w \times x + b)$, from (12.19), we get,

$$L(\hat{y}, y) = -\left[y \log \sigma(w \times x + b) + (1 - y)\log(1 - \sigma(w \times x + b))\right]$$

$$= -\left[y \log \frac{1}{1 + e^{-(w \times x + b)}} + (1 - y)\log\left(\frac{e^{-(w \times x + b)}}{1 + e^{-(w \times x + b)}}\right)\right]$$ (12.20)

Optimization Algorithm

To minimize the loss function stated in (12.20), we use the gradient descent method. The objective is to find the minimum weight of the loss function. Using gradient descent, the weight of the next iteration can be stated as

$$w^{(k+1)} = w^k - \eta \frac{d}{dw} f(x; w)$$ (12.21)

where $\frac{d}{dw} f(x; w)$ is the slop and η is the learning rate.

Considering θ as vector of weights and $f(x; \theta)$ representing $\hat{y}$, the updating equation using gradient descent is,

$$\theta^{(k+1)} = \theta^k - \eta \nabla_\theta L\big(f(x;\theta), y\big) \tag{12.22}$$

where

$$L\big(f(x;\theta), y\big) = L(w, b)$$

$$= L(\hat{y}, y) = -\Big[y \log \sigma(w \times x + b) + (1 - y) \log(1 - \sigma(w \times x + b)) \Big] \tag{12.23}$$

and the partial derivative $\left(\frac{\partial}{\partial w_i}\right)$ for this function for one observation vector x is,

$$\frac{\partial L(w, b)}{\partial w_i} = \Big[\sigma(w \times x + b) - y \Big] x_j \tag{12.24}$$

where the gradient in (12.24) represents the difference between $\hat{y}$ and y multiplied by the corresponding input x_j. Please note that in (12.22), we need to do the partial derivatives for all the values of x_j where $1 \leq j \leq n$.

Application of Logistic Regression for Coronavirus Tweet Classification

The purpose is to demonstrate application of exploratory sentiment classification, to compare the effectiveness of Naïve Bayes and logistic regression, and to examine accuracy under varying lengths of coronavirus Tweets. As with classification of Tweets using Naïve Bayes, positive sentiment Tweets were assigned a value of 1, and negative sentiment Tweets were denoted by 0, allowing for a simple binary classification using logistic regression methodology. Subsets of data were created, based on the length of Tweets, in a similar process as for Naïve Bayes classification and the same two groups of data containing Tweets with less than 77 characters (approximately 25% of the Tweets), and Tweets with less than 125 characters (approximately 50% of the data) respectively, were used. We used R and associated packages for logistic regression modeling, and to train and test the data. The results of using logistic regression for coronavirus Tweet Classification are presented in Table 12.7.

We observed on the test data with 70 items that, akin to the Naïve Bayes classification accuracy, shorter Tweets were classified using logistic regression with a greater degree of accuracy of just above 74%, and the classification accuracy decreased to 52% with longer

TABLE 12.7

Logistic Classification by Varying Tweet Lengths

	Tweets (nchar < 77)		Tweets (nchar < 120)	
	Negative	Positive	Negative	Positive
Negative	30	5	21	14
Positive	13	22	19	16
	Accuracy:	0.7429	Accuracy:	0.52

Tweets. We calculated the Sensitivity of the classification test, which is given by the ratio of the number of correct positive predictions (22) in the output, to the total number of positives (35), to be 0.63 for the short Tweets, and 0.46 for the longer Tweets. We calculated the Specificity of the classification test, which is given by the ratio of the number of correct negative predictions (30) in the output, to the total number of negatives (35), to be 0.86 for the short Tweets, and 0.60 for the longer Tweets classification. Logistic regression thus had better performance with a balanced classification of Tweets.

The classification results obtained in this study are interesting and indicate a need for additional validation and empirical model development with more coronavirus data, and additional methods. Models thus developed with additional data and methods, and using Naïve Bayes and logistic regression Tweet Classification methods can then be used as independent mechanisms for automated classification of coronavirus sentiment. The model and the findings can also be further extended to similar local and global pandemic insights generation in the future. Textual analytics has gained significant attention over the past few years with the advent of big data analytics, unstructured data analysis and increased computational capabilities at decreasing costs, which enables the analysis of large textual datasets. Our research demonstrates the use of the NRC sentiment lexicon, using the Syuzhet and sentimentr packages in R, and it will be a useful exercise to evaluate comparatively with other sentiment lexicons such as Bing and Afinn lexicons. Furthermore, each type of text corpus will have its own features and peculiarities, such as Twitter data will tend to be different from LinkedIn data in syntactic features and semantics. Past research has also indicated the usefulness of applying multiple lexicons, to generate either a manually weighted model or a statistically derived model based on a combination of multiple sentiment scores applied to the same text, and hybrid approaches (Sharma & Jain, 2020), and a need to apply strategic modeling to address big data challenges. We have demonstrated a structured approach which is necessary for successful generation of insights from textual data. When analyzing crisis situations, it is important to map sentiment against time, such as in the fear curve plot (Figure 12.3), and where relevant geographically, such as in Figure 12.5 a,b. Associating text and textual features with carefully selected and relevant non-textual features is another critical aspect of insights generation through textual analytics as has been demonstrated through Tables 12.1–12.7.

A DIGITAL MENTAL HEALTH REVOLUTION

We argue that what we need during a public health crisis like this is a digital mental health revolution: scaling up the delivery of confidential mental health services to patients across a wide range of platforms, from telemental health to mobile interventions such as apps and text messaging. Here, we provide an overview of technological tools which could help to decrease the mental health burden of COVID-19, provide recommendations on how they could be used and scaled-up, and discuss considerations and limitations of mental health technology applications.

TELEHEALTH

There is a crucial role for the use of teleconferencing software for therapy sessions during the COVID-19 pandemic. Most studies of teleconferencing services showed that effectiveness is comparable to in-person services across disorders including depression, posttraumatic stress disorder, and anxiety disorders (Ralston et al., 2019). China has had some success with this approach. Researchers recently wrote in a Lancet Commentary that during the worst of the outbreak in January, China successfully provided online psychological counseling, and self-help was widely rolled out by mental health professionals in medical institutions, universities, and academic societies (S. Liu et al., 2020).

In the United States, the pandemic has also catalyzed a rapid adoption of telehealth (Wosik et al., 2020). Medicare now allows for billing for telehealth. Further, the Health Insurance Portability and Accountability Act (HIPAA) has been revisited to permit more medical providers to use HIPAA-compliant platforms to communicate with patients. This removes a major barrier to wider adoption of telemedicine and could also provide an outstanding opportunity for patients who previously did not feel comfortable seeking mental healthcare to now approach these services.

However, it is important to attend to disparities in technology access and digital literacy. Before the pandemic, only one in ten patients in the United States used telehealth, and 75% said that they were unaware of telehealth options or how to access it (Power, 2019). Recent data from primary care clinics showed that, though video care consults went up by 80% in late March and early April, minority groups represented a smaller portions of these visits (Nouri et al., 2020). This is partly explained because of a lack of Internet availability, which varies due to limited data plans and lack of Wi-Fi, and inability to use smartphone features such as downloading apps (Anderson et al., 2016). At the moment, some US telecom providers are offering free Internet services (Horowitz et al., 2020). However, longer-term strategies need to be developed to prevent further widening of the digital divide (Yoon et al., 2020), including providing affordable, high-speed Internet access, improving usability of telehealth programs, and providing appropriate guidance/training for patients using these services.

MENTAL HEALTH SMARTPHONE APPLICATIONS

Importantly, the use of personal mobile phones presents an opportunity for broad scaling of interventions. Over 90% of Americans have some type of mobile phone and over 80% have smartphones (Sheet, 2018). Even among low-income Americans (71%) and older adults (53%) smartphone ownership is high. Mental health apps have shown effectiveness in decreasing symptoms of depression (Firth, Torous, Nicholas, Carney, Pratap, et al., 2017) and anxiety (Firth, Torous, Nicholas, Carney, Rosenbaum, et al., 2017). Because of COVID-19, multiple meditation and wellness apps designed by the private sector have now temporarily opened up free memberships to aid in easing anxiety, the majority of these being mindfulness apps (TechCrunch, 2020).

However, there are over 10,000 consumer-available mental health apps in app stores and many of these are not evidence based (Larsen et al., 2019). Further, though many people download mental health apps, research shows low rates of continued use over longer periods of time (Baumel et al., 2019). It is crucial that mental health providers recommend apps that are backed up by evidence. One helpful resource is Psyberguide (www.psyberguide. org), a non-profit that rates apps based on the strength of the scientific research that supports it, ease of use, and its privacy policies (Lipczynska, 2019). Lastly, in order to improve engagement, providers should follow up with patients on their usage of these apps and integrate the app content into their treatment.

Texting Applications

In addition to apps, text-messaging platforms could be leveraged to help people cope with mental health challenges evoked by COVID-19. Because texts are also delivered via individuals' devices, they are easy to provide to many at once using automated text-messaging platforms. Text-messaging interventions have demonstrated effectiveness in behavioral health promotion and disease management (Berrouiguet et al., 2016). Importantly, text-messaging is an appropriate tool for low digital literacy populations and underserved groups (Around, 2019). For instance, our own HIPAA approved texting platform, HealthySMS, was developed with and for low-income populations (mostly Spanish speakers) and shows high acceptability in underserved populations (Aguilera & Berridge, 2014). We recently rolled out a text-messaging study to provide wide-scale support to interested individuals in the United States via daily automated text-messages, containing tips on coping with social distancing and COVID-19 anxiety.

For crisis situations, Crisis Text Line provides free confidential help via text-message. This platform has seen the mention of "coronavirus" in 24% of conversations from March 30th to April 6th. Furthermore, Caremessage, a non-profit organization, has temporarily provided free access to their messaging platform and COVID-19 template text-messaging library with health information. In addition, reliable information can also be delivered by health and government organizations automated via text messages. Scaling of information delivery to patients and the public could also relieve health professionals and public health departments, who are already understaffed, underfunded, and overburdened (Horowitz et al., 2020).

Social Media

Social media plays a complicated role in the management of mental health. On the one hand, it can provide positive and supportive connections during a time of physical isolation. Earlier work shows that many people with mental illness are increasingly turning to social media to share their experiences and seek mental health information and advice (Naslund et al., 2019). On the other hand, it can also serve to increase depression and anxiety symptoms based on negative social comparisons and the spread of distressing information (Primack et al., 2017). For instance, in a recent cross-sectional survey of almost 5,000 participants in China, increased social media exposure on COVID-19 was associated with increases in anxiety and depression symptoms (Gao et al., 2020).

Social media has played a large role in the spread of information since the start of the COVID-19 outbreaks, including misinformation and "fake news." Large social media platforms are now reportedly taking steps to remove false content or conspiracy theories about the pandemic, using artificial intelligence (AI); and distribute reliable information, such as developed by the World Health Organization (Cahane, 2020).

In China, the government provided online mental health education through popular social media platforms, such as WeChat, Weibo, and TikTok during the height of the outbreak in January. In the United Kingdom, the National Health Service (NHS) is working with Google, Twitter, Instagram, and Facebook to provide the public with accurate information about COVID-19.

Social media also provides a unique opportunity for health professionals to distribute accurate information to their patients and the public, or to highlight available mental health resources. In Wuhan, China, mental health professionals uploaded videos of mental health education for the general public through WeChat and other Internet platforms at the early stage of the outbreak (S. Liu et al., 2020). In the United States and Europe, many physicians have turned to Twitter to share medical information. The social media site has now implemented a mechanism to verify physicians and other scientific experts in an effort to counteract coronavirus misinformation.

However, because of the overload of information on social media, misinformation might still spread too fast to be intercepted by AI algorithms (Vosoughi et al., 2018). A recent report of responses from more than 8,000 people from six countries showed that one-third reported seeing a significant amount of false or misleading COVID-19 information on social media or messaging platforms (Nielsen et al., 2020).

Further, posting information on social media raises the question of how health professionals should respond to the information posted by patients, and how that can impact the therapeutic relationship. Currently, there are no clear guidelines for health professionals, to determine how to act on social media. This calls for a push in quickly establishing such a consensus.

NOTES

1. Jockers, M. L. Syuzhet: Extract Sentiment and Plot Arcs from Text, R Package Version 1.0.4; CRAN, 2017. Available online: https://cran.r-project.org/web/packages/syuzhet/syuzhet.pdf (accessed on 11 June 2020).
2. Rinker, T. W. sentimentr: Calculate Text Polarity Sentiment; Version 2.7.1; Buffalo: New York, NY, USA, 2019.

REFERENCES

Aguilera, A., & Berridge, C. (2014). Qualitative feedback from a text messaging intervention for depression: benefits, drawbacks, and cultural differences. *JMIR MHealth and UHealth*, 2(4), e46.

Ahmad, N., & Siddique, J. (2017). Personality assessment using Twitter tweets. *Procedia Computer Science*, *112*, 1964–1973.

Ahmad, T., Ramsay, A., & Ahmed, H. (2019). Detecting emotions in English and Arabic tweets. *Information*, *10*(3), 98.

Almatarneh, S., & Gamallo, P. (2019). Comparing supervised machine learning strategies and linguistic features to search for very negative opinions. *Information*, *10*(1), 16.

Anderson, M., Perrin, A., Jiang, J., & Kumar, M. (2016). 13% of Americans don't use the internet. Who are they. *Pew Research Center*, 7.

Arc-Chagnaud, C., Py, G., Fovet, T., Roumanille, R., Demangel, R., Pagano, A. F., Delobel, P., Blanc, S., Jasmin, B. J., & Blottner, D. (2020). Evaluation of an antioxidant and anti-inflammatory cocktail against human hypoactivity-induced skeletal muscle deconditioning. *Frontiers in Physiology*, *11*.

Around, S. O. I. G. R. (2019). The world, but not always equally. *Pew Research Center's Global Attitudes Project*.

Balchin, R., Linde, J., Blackhurst, D., Rauch, H. G. L., & Schönbächler, G. (2016). Sweating away depression? The impact of intensive exercise on depression. *Journal of Affective Disorders*, *200*, 218–221.

Baumel, A., Muench, F., Edan, S., & Kane, J. M. (2019). Objective user engagement with mental health apps: systematic search and panel-based usage analysis. *Journal of Medical Internet Research*, *21*(9), e14567.

Bayes, T. (1991). An essay towards solving a problem in the doctrine of chances. 1763. *MD Computing: Computers in Medical Practice*, *8*(3), 157.

Berrouiguet, S., Baca-García, E., Brandt, S., Walter, M., & Courtet, P. (2016). Fundamentals for future mobile-health (mHealth): a systematic review of mobile phone and web-based text messaging in mental health. *Journal of Medical Internet Research*, *18*(6), e135.

Boecker, H., Sprenger, T., & Spilker, M. E. (n.d.). ea (2008). The runner's high: opioidergic mechanisms in the human brain. *Cerebral Cortex*, *18*, 2523–2531.

Boiy, E., Hens, P., Deschacht, K., & Moens, M.-F. (2007). Automatic sentiment analysis in on-line text. *ELPUB*, 349–360.

Bonow, R. O., Fonarow, G. C., O'Gara, P. T., & Yancy, C. W. (2020). Association of Coronavirus Disease 2019 (COVID-19) with myocardial injury and mortality JAMA cardiol. *Published Online March*, *27*.

Booth, F. W., Gordon, S. E., Carlson, C. J., & Hamilton, M. T. (2000). Waging war on modern chronic diseases: primary prevention through exercise biology. *Journal of Applied Physiology*, *88*(2), 774–787.

Bowden Davies, K. A., Pickles, S., Sprung, V. S., Kemp, G. J., Alam, U., Moore, D. R., Tahrani, A. A., & Cuthbertson, D. J. (2019). Reduced physical activity in young and older adults: metabolic and musculoskeletal implications. *Therapeutic Advances in Endocrinology and Metabolism*, *10*, 2042018819888824.

Buldin, I. D., & Ivanov, N. S. (2020). *Text classification of illegal activities on onion sites*. 2020 IEEE Conference of Russian Young Researchers in Electrical and Electronic Engineering (EIConRus), 245–247.

Cahane, A. (2020). *The Israeli emergency regulations for location tracking of Coronavirus carriers. Lawfare, March 21.*

Carducci, G., Rizzo, G., Monti, D., Palumbo, E., & Morisio, M. (2018). Twitpersonality: computing personality traits from tweets using word embeddings and supervised learning. *Information*, *9*(5), 127.

Carvalho, J. P., Rosa, H., Brogueira, G., & Batista, F. (2017). MISNIS: an intelligent platform for twitter topic mining. *Expert Systems with Applications*, *89*, 374–388.

Chae, B. K. (2015). Insights from hashtag# supplychain and Twitter Analytics: considering Twitter and Twitter data for supply chain practice and research. *International Journal of Production Economics*, *165*, 247–259.

Chan, D. C. (2006). Mitochondrial fusion and fission in mammals. *Annual Review of Cell and Developmental Biology*, *22*, 79–99.

Chen, X., Xie, H., Cheng, G., Poon, L. K. M., Leng, M., & Wang, F. L. (2020). Trends and features of the applications of natural language processing techniques for clinical trials text analysis. *Applied Sciences*, *10*(6), 2157.

Conner, C., Samuel, J., Kretinin, A., Samuel, Y., & Nadeau, L. (2020). A picture for the words! textual visualization in big data analytics. *ArXiv Preprint ArXiv:2005.07849.*

Cruz-Jentoft, A. J., & Sayer, A. A. (2019). Sarcopenia. *The Lancet*, *393*(10191), 2636–2646.

Davis, J. M., Kohut, M. L., Colbert, L. H., Jackson, D. A., Ghaffar, A., & Mayer, E. P. (1997). Exercise, alveolar macrophage function, and susceptibility to respiratory infection. *Journal of Applied Physiology*, *83*(5), 1461–1466.

De Choudhury, M., Counts, S., & Horvitz, E. (2013). *Predicting postpartum changes in emotion and behavior via social media.* Proceedings of the SIGCHI Conference on Human Factors in Computing Systems, 3267–3276.

De Maio, C., Fenza, G., Loia, V., & Parente, M. (2016). Time aware knowledge extraction for microblog summarization on twitter. *Information Fusion*, *28*, 60–74.

Dowlati, Y., Herrmann, N., Swardfager, W., Liu, H., Sham, L., Reim, E. K., & Lanctôt, K. L. (2010). A meta-analysis of cytokines in major depression. *Biological Psychiatry*, *67*(5), 446–457.

Dres, M., & Demoule, A. (2018). Diaphragm dysfunction during weaning from mechanical ventilation: an underestimated phenomenon with clinical implications. *Critical Care*, *22*(1), 73.

Ferrante, L. E., Pisani, M. A., Murphy, T. E., Gahbauer, E. A., Leo-Summers, L. S., & Gill, T. M. (2018). The association of frailty with post-ICU disability, nursing home admission, and mortality: a longitudinal study. *Chest*, *153*(6), 1378–1386.

Firth, J., Torous, J., Nicholas, J., Carney, R., Pratap, A., Rosenbaum, S., & Sarris, J. (2017). The efficacy of smartphone-based mental health interventions for depressive symptoms: a meta-analysis of randomized controlled trials. *World Psychiatry, 16*(3), 287–298.

Firth, J., Torous, J., Nicholas, J., Carney, R., Rosenbaum, S., & Sarris, J. (2017). Can smartphone mental health interventions reduce symptoms of anxiety? A meta-analysis of randomized controlled trials. *Journal of Affective Disorders, 218*, 15–22.

Flaatten, H., De Lange, D. W., Morandi, A., Andersen, F. H., Artigas, A., Bertolini, G., Boumendil, A., Cecconi, M., Christensen, S., & Faraldi, L. (2017). The impact of frailty on ICU and 30-day mortality and the level of care in very elderly patients (≥ 80 years). *Intensive Care Medicine, 43*(12), 1820–1828.

Fung, I. C.-H., Yin, J., Pressley, K. D., Duke, C. H., Mo, C., Liang, H., Fu, K.-W., Tse, Z. T. H., & Hou, S.-I. (2019). Pedagogical demonstration of Twitter data analysis: a case study of World AIDS Day, 2014. *Data, 4*(2), 84.

Gao, J., Zheng, P., Jia, Y., Chen, H., Mao, Y., Chen, S., Wang, Y., Fu, H., & Dai, J. (2020). Mental health problems and social media exposure during COVID-19 outbreak. *Plos One, 15*(4), e0231924.

Gleeson, M., Bishop, N., Oliveira, M., McCauley, T., Tauler, P., & Muhamad, A. S. (2012). Respiratory infection risk in athletes: association with antigen-stimulated IL-10 production and salivary IgA secretion. *Scandinavian Journal of Medicine & Science in Sports, 22*(3), 410–417.

Gu, J., Gong, E., Zhang, B., Zheng, J., Gao, Z., Zhong, Y., Zou, W., Zhan, J., Wang, S., & Xie, Z. (2005). Multiple organ infection and the pathogenesis of SARS. *Journal of Experimental Medicine, 202*(3), 415–424.

Hall, G., Laddu, D. R., Phillips, S. A., Lavie, C. J., & Arena, R. (2020). A tale of two pandemics: how will COVID-19 and global trends in physical inactivity and sedentary behavior affect one another? *Progress in Cardiovascular Diseases.*

Hamilton, M. T. (2018). The role of skeletal muscle contractile duration throughout the whole day: reducing sedentary time and promoting universal physical activity in all people. *The Journal of Physiology, 596*(8), 1331–1340.

Hawley, J. (2014). a., Hargreaves M, Joyner MJ, Zierath JR. *Integrative Biology of Exercise. Cell [Internet]. Elsevier Inc, 159*, 738–749.

He, W., Wu, H., Yan, G., Akula, V., & Shen, J. (2015). A novel social media competitive analytics framework with sentiment benchmarks. *Information & Management, 52*(7), 801–812.

Heist, N., Hertling, S., & Paulheim, H. (2018). Language-agnostic relation extraction from abstracts in Wikis. *Information, 9*(4), 75.

Herridge, M. S., Moss, M., Hough, C. L., Hopkins, R. O., Rice, T. W., Bienvenu, O. J., & Azoulay, E. (2016). Recovery and outcomes after the acute respiratory distress syndrome (ARDS) in patients and their family caregivers. *Intensive Care Medicine, 42*(5), 725–738.

Herridge, M. S., Tansey, C. M., Matté, A., Tomlinson, G., Diaz-Granados, N., Cooper, A., Guest, C. B., Mazer, C. D., Mehta, S., & Stewart, T. E. (2011). Functional disability 5 years after acute respiratory distress syndrome. *New England Journal of Medicine, 364*(14), 1293–1304.

Hood, D. A., Tryon, L. D., Carter, H. N., Kim, Y., & Chen, C. C. W. (2016). Unravelling the mechanisms regulating muscle mitochondrial biogenesis. *Biochemical Journal, 473*(15), 2295–2314.

Hoogendijk, E. O., Afilalo, J., Ensrud, K. E., Kowal, P., Onder, G., & Fried, L. P. (2019). Frailty: implications for clinical practice and public health. *The Lancet, 394*(10206), 1365–1375.

Horowitz, J., Bubola, E., & Povoledo, E. (2020). Italy, pandemic's new epicenter, has lessons for the world. *New York Times, 21.*

Huang, T., Yq, W., Liang, Y., & Tb, H. (2020). Novel Coronavirus patients' clinical characteristics, discharge rate and fatality rate of meta-analysis. *Journal of Medical Virology.*

Inciardi, R. M., Lupi, L., Zaccone, G., Italia, L., Raffo, M., Tomasoni, D., Cani, D. S., Cerini, M., Farina, D., & Gavazzi, E. (2020). Cardiac involvement in a patient with coronavirus disease 2019 (COVID-19). *JAMA Cardiology.*

Jain, V. K., Kumar, S., & Fernandes, S. L. (2017). Extraction of emotions from multilingual text using intelligent text processing and computational linguistics. *Journal of Computational Science, 21*, 316–326.

Jawaid, A. (2020). Protecting older adults during social distancing. *Science*, *368*(6487), 145.

Ji, L. L., Yeo, D., & Kang, C. (2020). Muscle disuse atrophy caused by discord of intracellular signaling. *Antioxidants & Redox Signaling.*

Jin, D., Jin, Z., Zhou, J. T., & Szolovits, P. (2019). Is bert really robust? Natural language attack on text classification and entailment. *ArXiv Preprint ArXiv:1907.11932.*

Jurafsky, D., & Martin, J. H. (2018). Speech and language processing (draft). *Chapter A: Hidden Markov Models (Draft of September 11, 2018). Retrieved March, 19,* 2019.

Kandarian, S. (2008). The molecular basis of skeletal muscle atrophy–parallels with osteoporotic signaling. *J Musculoskelet Neuronal Interact*, *8*(4), 340–341.

Kandola, A., Ashdown-Franks, G., Hendrikse, J., Sabiston, C. M., & Stubbs, B. (2019). Physical activity and depression: towards understanding the antidepressant mechanisms of physical activity. *Neuroscience & Biobehavioral Reviews*, *107*, 525–539.

Kang, C., Goodman, C. A., Hornberger, T. A., & Ji, L. L. (2015). PGC-1α overexpression by in vivo transfection attenuates mitochondrial deterioration of skeletal muscle caused by immobilization. *The FASEB Journal*, *29*(10), 4092–4106.

Kim, E. H.-J., Jeong, Y. K., Kim, Y., Kang, K. Y., & Song, M. (2016). Topic-based content and sentiment analysis of Ebola virus on Twitter and in the news. *Journal of Information Science*, *42*(6), 763–781.

Kohut, M. L., Martin, A. E., Senchina, D. S., & Lee, W. (2005). Glucocorticoids produced during exercise may be necessary for optimal virus-induced IL-2 and cell proliferation whereas both catecholamines and glucocorticoids may be required for adequate immune defense to viral infection. *Brain, Behavior, and Immunity*, *19*(5), 423–435.

Kohut, Marian L., Davis, J. M., Jackson, D. A., Colbert, L. H., Strasner, A., Essig, D. A., Pate, R. R., Ghaffar, A., & Mayer, E. P. (1998). The role of stress hormones in exercise-induced suppression of alveolar macrophage antiviral function. *Journal of Neuroimmunology*, *81*(1–2), 193–200.

Kohut, Marian L., Sim, Y.-J., Yu, S., Yoon, K. J., & Loiacono, C. M. (2009). Chronic exercise reduces illness severity, decreases viral load, and results in greater anti-inflammatory effects than acute exercise during influenza infection. *The Journal of Infectious Diseases*, *200*(9), 1434–1442.

Kowsari, K., Jafari Meimandi, K., Heidarysafa, M., Mendu, S., Barnes, L., & Brown, D. (2019). Text classification algorithms: a survey. *Information*, *10*(4), 150.

Kretinin, A., Samuel, J., & Kashyap, R. (2018). When the going gets tough, the tweets get going! an exploratory analysis of tweets sentiments in the stock market. *American Journal of Management*, *18*(5).

Krüger, K., Mooren, F.-C., & Pilat, C. (2016). The immunomodulatory effects of physical activity. *Current Pharmaceutical Design*, *22*(24), 3730–3748.

Larsen, M. E., Huckvale, K., Nicholas, J., Torous, J., Birrell, L., Li, E., & Reda, B. (2019). Using science to sell apps: evaluation of mental health app store quality claims. *NPJ Digital Medicine*, *2*(1), 1–6.

Lee, I.-M., Shiroma, E. J., Kamada, M., Bassett, D. R., Matthews, C. E., & Buring, J. E. (2019). Association of step volume and intensity with all-cause mortality in older women. *JAMA Internal Medicine*, *179*(8), 1105–1112.

Li, Y., Bai, W., & Hashikawa, T. (2020). The neuroinvasive potential of SARS-CoV2 may play a role in the respiratory failure of COVID-19 patients. *Journal of Medical Virology*, *92*(6), 552–555.

Li, Y., Bai, W., Hirano, N., Hayashida, T., Taniguchi, T., Sugita, Y., Tohyama, K., & Hashikawa, T. (2013). Neurotropic virus tracing suggests a membranous-coating-mediated mechanism for transsynaptic communication. *Journal of Comparative Neurology*, *521*(1), 203–212.

Lightfoot, J. T. (2011). Current understanding of the genetic basis for physical activity. *The Journal of Nutrition*, *141*(3), 526–530.

Lipczynska, S. (2019). Psyberguide: a path through the app jungle. *Journal of Mental Health*, *28*(1), 104.

Liu, B., Blasch, E., Chen, Y., Shen, D., & Chen, G. (2013). Scalable sentiment classification for big data analysis using naive bayes classifier. *2013 IEEE International Conference on Big Data*, 99–104.

Liu, S., Yang, L., Zhang, C., Xiang, Y.-T., Liu, Z., Hu, S., & Zhang, B. (2020). Online mental health services in China during the COVID-19 outbreak. *The Lancet Psychiatry*, 7(4), e17–e18.

Lowder, T., Padgett, D. A., & Woods, J. A. (2005). Moderate exercise protects mice from death due to influenza virus. *Brain, Behavior, and Immunity*, 19(5), 377–380.

Makris, C., Pispirigos, G., & Rizos, I. O. (2020). A distributed bagging ensemble methodology for community prediction in social networks. *Information*, 11(4), 199.

Mandsager, K., Harb, S., Cremer, P., Phelan, D., Nissen, S. E., & Jaber, W. (2018). Association of cardiorespiratory fitness with long-term mortality among adults undergoing exercise treadmill testing. *JAMA Network Open*, 1(6), e183605–e183605.

Martin, S. A., Pence, B. D., & Woods, J. A. (2009). Exercise and respiratory tract viral infections. *Exercise and Sport Sciences Reviews*, 37(4), 157.

McKenzie, D. C. (2012). Respiratory physiology: adaptations to high-level exercise. *British Journal of Sports Medicine*, 46(6), 381–384.

Morris, J. N., & Crawford, M. D. (1958). Coronary heart disease and physical activity of work. *British Medical Journal*, 2(5111), 1485.

Morton, A. B., Smuder, A. J., Wiggs, M. P., Hall, S. E., Ahn, B., Hinkley, J. M., Ichinoseki-Sekine, N., Huertas, A. M., Ozdemir, M., & Yoshihara, T. (2019). Increased SOD2 in the diaphragm contributes to exercise-induced protection against ventilator-induced diaphragm dysfunction. *Redox Biology*, 20, 402–413.

Murphy, E. A., Davis, J. M., Brown, A. S., Carmichael, M. D., Van Rooijen, N., Ghaffar, A., & Mayer, E. P. (2004). Role of lung macrophages on susceptibility to respiratory infection following short-term moderate exercise training. *American Journal of Physiology-Regulatory, Integrative and Comparative Physiology*, 287(6), R1354–R1358.

Murphy, E. A., Davis, J. M., Carmichael, M. D., Gangemi, J. D., Ghaffar, A., & Mayer, E. P. (2008). Exercise stress increases susceptibility to influenza infection. *Brain, Behavior, and Immunity*, 22(8), 1152–1155.

Nagar, R., Yuan, Q., Freifeld, C. C., Santillana, M., Nojima, A., Chunara, R., & Brownstein, J. S. (2014). A case study of the New York City 2012-2013 influenza season with daily geocoded Twitter data from temporal and spatiotemporal perspectives. *Journal of Medical Internet Research*, 16(10), e236.

Nascimento, C. M., Ingles, M., Salvador-Pascual, A., Cominetti, M. R., Gomez-Cabrera, M. C., & Viña, J. (2019). Sarcopenia, frailty and their prevention by exercise. *Free Radical Biology and Medicine*, 132, 42–49.

Naslund, J. A., Aschbrenner, K. A., McHugo, G. J., Unützer, J., Marsch, L. A., & Bartels, S. J. (2019). Exploring opportunities to support mental health care using social media: a survey of social media users with mental illness. *Early Intervention in Psychiatry*, 13(3), 405–413.

Nielsen, R. K., Fletcher, R., Newman, N., Brennen, S. J., & Howard, P. N. (2020). *Navigating the 'infodemic': how people in six countries access and rate news and information about coronavirus*. Reuters Institute.

Nieman, D. C. (1994). Exercise, upper respiratory tract infection, and the immune system. *Medicine and Science in Sports and Exercise*, 26(2), 128–139.

Nieman, D. C., Johanssen, L. M., Lee, J. W., & Arabatzis, K. (1990). Infectious episodes in runners before and after the Los Angeles Marathon. *J Sports Med Phys Fitness*, 30(3), 316–328.

Norman, L. G. (1958). The health of bus drivers. A study in London Transport. *Lancet*, 807–812.

Nouri, S., Khoong, E. C., Lyles, C. R., & Karliner, L. (2020). Addressing equity in telemedicine for chronic disease management during the Covid-19 pandemic. *NEJM Catalyst Innovations in Care Delivery*, 1(3).

Pedregosa, F., Varoquaux, G., Gramfort, A., Michel, V., Thirion, B., Grisel, O., Blondel, M., Prettenhofer, P., Weiss, R., & Dubourg, V. (2011). Scikit-learn: machine learning in Python. *The Journal of Machine Learning Research*, 12, 2825–2830.

Pépin, L., Kuntz, P., Blanchard, J., Guillet, F., & Suignard, P. (2017). Visual analytics for exploring topic long-term evolution and detecting weak signals in company targeted tweets. *Computers & Industrial Engineering, 112*, 450–458.

Pette, D. (2001). Historical perspectives: plasticity of mammalian skeletal muscle. *Journal of Applied Physiology, 90*(3), 1119–1124.

Power, J. D. (2019). US telehealth satisfaction study. *SM, JD Power.*

Powers, S. K., Bomkamp, M., Ozdemir, M., & Hyatt, H. (2020). Mechanisms of exercise-induced preconditioning in skeletal muscles. *Redox Biology, 35*, 101462.

Powers, S. K., Hudson, M. B., Nelson, W. B., Talbert, E. E., Min, K., Szeto, H. H., Kavazis, A. N., & Smuder, A. J. (2011). Mitochondrial-targeted antioxidants protect against mechanical ventilation-induced diaphragm weakness. *Critical Care Medicine, 39*(7), 1749.

Pranckevičius, T., & Marcinkevičius, V. (2017). Comparison of naive bayes, random forest, decision tree, support vector machines, and logistic regression classifiers for text reviews classification. *Baltic Journal of Modern Computing, 5*(2), 221.

Primack, B. A., Shensa, A., Escobar-Viera, C. G., Barrett, E. L., Sidani, J. E., Colditz, J. B., & James, A. E. (2017). Use of multiple social media platforms and symptoms of depression and anxiety: a nationally-representative study among US young adults. *Computers in Human Behavior, 69*, 1–9.

Rabøl, R., Petersen, K. F., Dufour, S., Flannery, C., & Shulman, G. I. (2011). Reversal of muscle insulin resistance with exercise reduces postprandial hepatic de novo lipogenesis in insulin resistant individuals. *Proceedings of the National Academy of Sciences, 108*(33), 13705–13709.

Radak, Z., Taylor, A. W., Ohno, H., & Goto, S. (2001). Adaptation to exercise-induced oxidative stress: from muscle to brain. *Exercise Immunology Review, 7*, 90–107.

Ralston, A. L., Andrews III, A. R., & Hope, D. A. (2019). Fulfilling the promise of mental health technology to reduce public health disparities: review and research agenda. *Clinical Psychology: Science and Practice, 26*(1), e12277.

Ramadhan, W. P., Novianty, S. A., & Setianingsih, S. C. (2017). *Sentiment analysis using multinomial logistic regression.* 2017 International Conference on Control, Electronics, Renewable Energy and Communications (ICCREC), 46–49.

Ravi, K., & Ravi, V. (2015). A survey on opinion mining and sentiment analysis: tasks, approaches and applications. *Knowledge-Based Systems, 89*, 14–46.

Reyes-Menendez, A., Saura, J. R., & Alvarez-Alonso, C. (2018). Understanding# WorldEnvironmentDay user opinions in Twitter: a topic-based sentiment analysis approach. *International Journal of Environmental Research and Public Health, 15*(11), 2537.

Rocha, G., & Lopes Cardoso, H. (2018). Recognizing textual entailment: challenges in the Portuguese language. *Information, 9*(4), 76.

Rooney, B. V, Bigley, A. B., LaVoy, E. C., Laughlin, M., Pedlar, C., & Simpson, R. J. (2018). Lymphocytes and monocytes egress peripheral blood within minutes after cessation of steady state exercise: a detailed temporal analysis of leukocyte extravasation. *Physiology & Behavior, 194*, 260–267.

Rubegni, P., Cevenini, G., Burroni, M., Dell'Eva, G., Sbano, P., Cuccia, A., & Andreassi, L. (2002). Digital dermoscopy analysis of atypical pigmented skin lesions: a stepwise logistic discriminant analysis approach. *Skin Research and Technology, 8*(4), 276–281.

Saif, H., Fernández, M., He, Y., & Alani, H. (2014). *On stopwords, filtering and data sparsity for sentiment analysis of twitter.*

Samuel, J. (2017). Information token driven machine learning for electronic markets: performance effects in behavioral financial big data analytics. *JISTEM-Journal of Information Systems and Technology Management, 14*(3), 371–383.

Samuel, J. (2020). Eagles & lions winning against coronavirus! 8 principles from Winston Churchill for overcoming Covid-19 & fear. *Preprint Category: Motivational Article Citation (APA): Samuel, J., Eagles & Lions Winning Against Coronavirus, 8.*

Samuel, J., Holowczak, R., Benbunan-Fich, R., & Levine, I. (2014). *Automating discovery of dominance in synchronous computer-mediated communication.* 2014 47th Hawaii International Conference on System Sciences, 1804–1812.

Samuel, J., Rahman, M., Ali, G. G., Samuel, Y., & Pelaez, A. (2020). Feeling like it is time to reopen now? COVID-19 new normal scenarios based on reopening sentiment analytics. *Nawaz and Samuel, Yana and Pelaez, Alexander, Feeling Like It Is Time to Reopen Now.*

Samuel, Y., George, J., & Samuel, J. (2020). Beyond stem, how can women engage big data, analytics, robotics and artificial intelligence? An exploratory analysis of confidence and educational factors in the emerging technology waves influencing the role of, and impact upon, women. *ArXiv Preprint ArXiv:2003.11746.*

Saura, J. R., Palos-Sanchez, P., & Grilo, A. (2019). Detecting indicators for startup business success: sentiment analysis using text data mining. *Sustainability, 11*(3), 917.

Scavone, C., Brusco, S., Bertini, M., Sportiello, L., Rafaniello, C., Zoccoli, A., Berrino, L., Racagni, G., Rossi, F., & Capuano, A. (2020). Current pharmacological treatments for COVID-19: What's next? *British Journal of Pharmacology.*

Schiaffino, S., Dyar, K. A., Ciciliot, S., Blaauw, B., & Sandri, M. (2013). Mechanisms regulating skeletal muscle growth and atrophy. *The FEBS Journal, 280*(17), 4294–4314.

Sharma, S., & Jain, A. (2020). Hybrid ensemble learning with feature selection for sentiment classification in social media. *International Journal of Information Retrieval Research (IJIRR), 10*(2), 40–58.

Sheet, M. F. (2018). Pew Research Center: internet. *Science & Tech, 5.*

Shu, K., Sliva, A., Wang, S., Tang, J., & Liu, H. (2017). Fake news detection on social media: a data mining perspective. *ACM SIGKDD Explorations Newsletter, 19*(1), 22–36.

Silva, I., & Eugenio Naranjo, J. (2020). A systematic methodology to evaluate prediction models for driving style classification. *Sensors, 20*(6), 1692.

Simpson, R. J., Campbell, J. P., Gleeson, M., Krüger, K., Nieman, D. C., Pyne, D. B., Turner, J. E., & Walsh, N. P. (2020). Can exercise affect immune function to increase susceptibility to infection? *Exercise Immunology Review, 26*, 8–22.

Siordia Jr, J. A. (2020). Epidemiology and clinical features of COVID-19: a review of current literature. *Journal of Clinical Virology*, 104357.

Skoric, M. M., Liu, J., & Jaidka, K. (2020). Electoral and public opinion forecasts with social media data: a meta-analysis. *Information, 11*(4), 187.

Smuder, A. J., Min, K., Hudson, M. B., Kavazis, A. N., Kwon, O.-S., Nelson, W. B., & Powers, S. K. (2012). Endurance exercise attenuates ventilator-induced diaphragm dysfunction. *Journal of Applied Physiology, 112*(3), 501–510.

Smuder, A. J., Morton, A. B., Hall, S. E., Wiggs, M. P., Ahn, B., Wawrzyniak, N. R., Sollanek, K. J., Min, K., Kwon, O. S., & Nelson, W. B. (2019). Effects of exercise preconditioning and HSP72 on diaphragm muscle function during mechanical ventilation. *Journal of Cachexia, Sarcopenia and Muscle, 10*(4), 767–781.

Sollanek, K. J., Burniston, J. G., Kavazis, A. N., Morton, A. B., Wiggs, M. P., Ahn, B., Smuder, A. J., & Powers, S. K. (2017). Global proteome changes in the rat diaphragm induced by endurance exercise training. *PLoS One, 12*(1), e0171007.

Sribhutorn, A., Phrommintikul, A., Wongcharoen, W., Eakanunkul, S., & Sukonthasarn, A. (2016). The modification effect of influenza vaccine on prognostic indicators for cardiovascular events after acute coronary syndrome: observations from an influenza vaccination trial. *Cardiology Research and Practice, 2016.*

Svendsen, I. S., Hem, E., & Gleeson, M. (2016). Effect of acute exercise and hypoxia on markers of systemic and mucosal immunity. *European Journal of Applied Physiology, 116*(6), 1219–1229.

Svetlov, K., & Platonov, K. (2019). *Sentiment analysis of posts and comments in the accounts of Russian politicians on the social network.* 2019 25th Conference of Open Innovations Association (FRUCT), 299–305.

Tan, Y. (2018). An improved KNN text classification algorithm based on K-medoids and rough set. *2018 10th International Conference on Intelligent Human-Machine Systems and Cybernetics (IHMSC), 1*, 109–113.

TechCrunch, C. E. (2020). Apr 04. *Why Telehealth Can't Significantly Flatten the Coronavirus Curve-yet URL:* Https://Techcrunch.Com/2020/04/04/Why-Telehealth-Cant-Significantly-Flatten-the-Coronavirus-Curve-yet/*[Accessed 2020-05-25]*.

Thompson, P. D., & Dec, G. W. (2020). *We need better data on how to manage myocarditis in athletes.* SAGE Publications Sage UK: London, England.

Timmons, J. A., Norrbom, J., Schéele, C., Thonberg, H., Wahlestedt, C., & Tesch, P. (2006). Expression profiling following local muscle inactivity in humans provides new perspective on diabetes-related genes. *Genomics, 87*(1), 165–172.

Ting, S. L., Ip, W. H., & Tsang, A. H. C. (2011). Is Naive Bayes a good classifier for document classification. *International Journal of Software Engineering and Its Applications, 5*(3), 37–46.

Troussas, C., Virvou, M., Espinosa, K. J., Llaguno, K., & Caro, J. (2013). Sentiment analysis of Facebook statuses using Naive Bayes classifier for language learning. *IISA 2013*, 1–6.

Vassilakopoulos, T., & Petrof, B. J. (2004). Ventilator-induced diaphragmatic dysfunction. *American Journal of Respiratory and Critical Care Medicine, 169*(3), 336–341.

Vijayan, V. K., Bindu, K. R., & Parameswaran, L. (2017). *A comprehensive study of text classification algorithms.* 2017 International Conference on Advances in Computing, Communications and Informatics (ICACCI), 1109–1113.

Vina, J., Sanchis-Gomar, F., Martinez-Bello, V., & Gomez-Cabrera, M. C. (2012). Exercise acts as a drug: the pharmacological benefits of exercise. *British Journal of Pharmacology, 167*(1), 1–12.

Vosoughi, S., Roy, D., & Aral, S. (2018). The spread of true and false news online. *Science, 359*(6380), 1146–1151.

Wackerhage, H., Schoenfeld, B. J., Hamilton, D. L., Lehti, M., & Hulmi, J. J. (2019). Stimuli and sensors that initiate skeletal muscle hypertrophy following resistance exercise. *Journal of Applied Physiology, 126*(1), 30–43.

Walsh, N. P., Gleeson, M., Shephard, R. J., Gleeson, M., Woods, J. A., Bishop, N., Fleshner, M., Green, C., Pedersen, B. K., & Hoffman-Goete, L. (2011). *Position statement part one: immune function and exercise.*

Wang, R., Pan, M., Zhang, X., Fan, X., Han, M., Zhao, F., Miao, M., Xu, J., Guan, M., & Deng, X. (2020). Epidemiological and clinical features of 125 Hospitalized Patients with COVID-19 in Fuyang, Anhui, China. *International Journal of Infectious Diseases.*

Wang, Z., Ye, X., & Tsou, M.-H. (2016). Spatial, temporal, and content analysis of Twitter for wildfire hazards. *Natural Hazards, 83*(1), 523–540.

Warren, K. J., Olson, M. M., Thompson, N. J., Cahill, M. L., Wyatt, T. A., Yoon, K. J., Loiacono, C. M., & Kohut, M. L. (2015). Exercise improves host response to influenza viral infection in obese and non-obese mice through different mechanisms. *PloS One, 10*(6), e0129713.

Weidner, T. G., Cranston, T., Schurr, T., & Kaminsky, L. A. (1998). The effect of exercise training on the severity and duration of a viral upper respiratory illness. *Medicine and Science in Sports and Exercise, 30*(11), 1578.

Widener, M. J., & Li, W. (2014). Using geolocated Twitter data to monitor the prevalence of healthy and unhealthy food references across the US. *Applied Geography, 54*, 189–197.

Wosik, J., Fudim, M., Cameron, B., Gellad, Z. F., Cho, A., Phinney, D., Curtis, S., Roman, M., Poon, E. G., & Ferranti, J. (2020). Telehealth transformation: COVID-19 and the rise of virtual care. *Journal of the American Medical Informatics Association, 27*(6), 957–962.

Wu, C., Chen, X., Cai, Y., Xia, J., Zhou, X., Xu, S., Huang, H., Zhang, L., Zhou, X., & Du, C. (2020). Risk Factors Associated With Acute Respiratory Distress Syndrome and Death in Patients With Coronavirus Disease 2019 Pneumonia in Wuhan, China. JAMA Intern Med [Internet]; 2020 [cited 2020 Mar 21]. *Online Ahead of Print.*

Wu, Z., & McGoogan, J. M. (2020). Characteristics of and important lessons from the coronavirus disease 2019 (COVID-19) outbreak in China: summary of a report of 72 314 cases from the Chinese Center for Disease Control and Prevention. *JAMA, 323*(13), 1239–1242.

Yang, C., & Jin, Z. (2020). An acute respiratory infection runs into the most common noncommunicable epidemic—COVID-19 and cardiovascular diseases. *JAMA Cardiology.*

Ye, X., Li, S., Yang, X., & Qin, C. (2016). Use of social media for the detection and analysis of infectious diseases in China. *ISPRS International Journal of Geo-Information, 5*(9), 156.

YLiu, Z. (2020). ZXiang JWang YSong BGu X et al. Clinical course and risk factors for mortality of adult inpatients with COVID-19 in Wuhan, China: a retrospective cohort study. *Lancet, 395*, 1054–1062.

Yoon, H., Jang, Y., Vaughan, P. W., & Garcia, M. (2020). Older adults' Internet use for health information: digital divide by race/ethnicity and socioeconomic status. *Journal of Applied Gerontology, 39*(1), 105–110.

Youle, R. J., & Narendra, D. P. (2011). Mechanisms of mitophagy. *Nature Reviews Molecular Cell Biology, 12*(1), 9–14.

Zhang, J., & Yang, Y. (2003). *Robustness of regularized linear classification methods in text categorization.* Proceedings of the 26th Annual International ACM SIGIR Conference on Research and Development in Information Retrieval, 190–197.

Index